GAMES NATIONS PLAY

EIGHTH EDITION

GAMES NATIONS PLAY

EIGHTH EDITION

John W. Spanier

University of Florida

PRESS

A Division of Congressional Quarterly Inc.
Washington, D.C.

Illustration acknowledgments: Figure 2-2, reprinted with permission of *The Encyclope-dia Americana*, ©1986 by Grolier Inc.; Figure 8-2, copyright ©1991 by the New York Times Company, reprinted by permission.

Printed in the United States of America

Library of Congress Cataloging-in-Publication Data

Spanier, John W.
    Games nations play / John Spanier.— 8th ed.
        p.   cm.
    Includes bibliographical references and index.
    ISBN   0-87187-721-X
    1. International relations.   I. Title.
JX1391.S7   1992
    327.1—dc20

                                                          92-21010
                                                              CIP

To Suzy for her support, patience,
and tolerance through eight editions

Contents

Part Two

THE FIRST LEVEL OF ANALYSIS: THE STATE SYSTEM

CHAPTER 7

The Ability to Play: Calculating Power 159

CHAPTER 8

The Changing State System: A Conclusion 185

Part Three

THE SECOND AND THIRD LEVELS: FOREIGN POLICY

CHAPTER 9

National and Elite Styles in Foreign Policy: American and Soviet Perceptions and Behavior during the Cold War 215

CHAPTER 10

The Developing Countries: The Primacy of Domestic Concerns 261

CHAPTER 11

The Games Policy Makers Play   306

CHAPTER 12

Foreign Policy: A Conclusion   350

Part Four

HOW TO PLAY—POLITICALLY, MILITARILY, ECONOMICALLY

CHAPTER 13

The Balance of Terror   371

Part Five

FROM STATE SYSTEM TO GLOBAL SYSTEM

TABLES

FIGURES

Preface

The first edition of this book was published in 1972. Publication of this eighth edition, appearing twenty years later, owes much to Saddam Hussein, Iraq's ruthless dictator.

The academic year 1990-1991 was a sabbatical one for me. I had been awarded a Fulbright scholarship to teach in Israel from January to June 1991, but in the summer of 1990, before going overseas, I also had to decide whether to undertake another edition of *Games Nations Play*. By that time, the cold war was over, and, not unexpectedly, most of the world was euphoric. Soviet communism had collapsed, and the Soviet Union's former satellites in Eastern Europe had thrown off their Soviet shackles. East Germany had vanished to become part of a new, reunified Germany. Democracy appeared to be the wave of the future, which meant that the zone of peace was expanding. And because nuclear weapons had rendered total war suicidal and limited wars had become too long and expensive to fight, war was becoming obsolete—at least among the industrial great powers, formerly the principal contestants.

Then Saddam Hussein annexed Kuwait in his bid to become the dominant power in the Persian Gulf with his hand on the world's oil spigot. He also had his sights on the leadership of the Arab world. After eliminating the moderate, pro-Western states, he would direct all Arabs in an anti-American, anti-Israeli crusade. This instance of aggression was particularly notable not only because it occurred so soon after the end of the cold war and in the midst of the accompanying optimism but also because the end of that conflict provided opportunities for regionally ambitious powers to seek local hegemony. In Iraq's case, it was also thought to be seeking nuclear (as well as chemical and biological) weapons. Thus, if not reversed, its invasion of Kuwait and its threat to Saudi Arabia might set a dangerous precedent.

It was Iraq's invasion of Kuwait and the war that followed, more than the end of the cold war itself, that inspired this new edition of *Games*, for that conflict suggested that the post-cold war world was less a "new international order" than a continuation of the old order in a new context. The Gulf war gave me the time needed to write; the visit to Israel was postponed. It also may have saved my life. The canceled trip resulted in early diagnosis of a medical condition serious enough to require immediate major surgery. Thus, I may be the only person in the world who owes his life to Saddam Hussein!

Thus, this eighth edition focuses on three topics. The first is the end of the cold war, Soviet domestic problems, and the internal struggle for the redefinition of the Soviet national interest. In seeking to lead his country to transform itself while trying to survive resistance from the right and the threat of internal dissolution from the fifteen republics, Gorbachev zigzagged from reform to repression to reform again. And there were dramatic changes in the Soviet Union—including abandonment of the Communist party's constitutional monopoly of power and, with it, Marxism-Leninism as the official ideology, as well as a declared commitment to transforming the Soviet Union into the image of its former, free-market enemies. But the end result was the collapse of the Soviet Union after those who opposed Gorbachev's reforms— the military, secret police, government bureaucracy, and party functionaries—attempted a coup in August 1991. When the coup fizzled quickly it removed the Communist party as the last major obstacle to radical reform. It also led to the disintegration of the Soviet state as its fifteen republics sought independence.

The second topic highlighted in this edition is the 1990-1991 Persian Gulf conflict. Events in the Gulf reinforced the new post-cold war emphasis on regionalism, already evident in Europe with the rise once more of a united Germany and the retraction of Soviet power from Eastern Europe. Operations Desert Shield and Desert Storm also suggested other themes that would benefit from analysis: presidential leadership in the decision-making process; the ability of U.S. democracy to wage war in this new era, as well as what kinds of war; whether the conduct of hostilities reverses the post-World War II trend of small powers beating big powers in prolonged hostilities; the correctness or incorrectness of the thesis that war is becoming obsolete; and what this conflict suggests about dealing with the growing danger of the diffusion of sophisticated conventional arms to regional states and, even worse, the proliferation of weapons of mass destruction to despotic, ambitious regimes.

The third new topic is the realignments and redistribution of power in the international system following U.S. emergence from the cold war and the Gulf war as the only remaining superpower. Still, the United States is faced with limits on what it can achieve with its power. Not only is its military power no longer matched by its economic and financial strength, but Washington also must confront the growing power, especially economic, of such countries as Germany and Japan and, potentially, the more united European Community that will emerge after 1992, as well as the widespread diffusion of power to smaller actors who refuse to submit to the dictates of the great powers. Chapter 6, as before, focuses on the issue of polarity in the state system and then uses it to explain the four decades of the cold war. But additional material deals at some length with the changing power relations in Europe and the reemergence of the "German problem," stemming from the collapse of Soviet power. This chapter also analyzes the trend toward regionalism outside Europe and illustrates this with the recent events in the Persian Gulf. Chapter 8, much of which is also new, concentrates on the changing power relations among the United States, the former Soviet Union, Japan, Germany, and, more broadly, the European Community, resulting from their economic and technological growth or decline. It then examines the new post-cold war "unipolycentric" international system and the ambiguities and complexities involved in accurately describing and explaining contemporary international politics.

In spite of all these changes in the new world order, some things remain the same. This edition continues the focus on the "games nations play"—that is, the strategies and tactics states devise to achieve their security and other objectives. Although there are many ways to understand this subject, I employ three levels of analysis. The first focuses on the state system and emphasizes the balance of power among nations. The second concentrates on nation-states themselves, emphasizing their domestic character. And the third level deals with decision making: policy makers' perceptions of reality and the institutions that formulate and execute policy. This three-dimensional approach, which is a modification of Kenneth Waltz's "three images" and David Singer's "levels of analysis," allows students to view a single policy or set of policies from three different—and often conflicting—perspectives.

This threefold scheme reflects my view that international events must be analyzed in the context of the state system, the environment in which they occur. This is basic. But the analyst also must pay attention to the goals of nations and their general behavior patterns, as these patterns are shaped by their societies and specific policy makers. The state-system environment has a powerful effect on states—for example, on their objectives and their degrees of choice among alternative policies—but their internal character and politics also exert major influences. To borrow Carl von Clausewitz's observation that war is the continuation of politics by other means, one could also say that foreign policy often is the conduct of domestic politics by other means.

Nothing illustrates the significance of the second and third levels more than the recent changes in the Soviet Union and Eastern Europe. The Communist totalitarian system and Marxist-Leninist ideology—which, together with the bipolar division of power after World War II, had precipitated the cold war—are being replaced by political pluralism and elements of free-market economics. Above all else, the coming into power of Mikhail Gorbachev, who in response to the ailing Soviet economy was willing to risk structural reforms, makes it now possible to talk of a post-cold war era.

The state system has endured, and states have been the primary international actors for more than 300 years. My emphasis on the nation-state, however, does not imply a neglect of nonstate actors, transnational forces, or analysis of "world order" politics. The economic, technological, and other forces of change in the contemporary world are discussed at length. Nevertheless, I contend that the state-centered system not only has survived but also in some respects is stronger than ever. One need but note the ethnic nationalism throughout Eastern Europe, often tinged with antisemitism, which led to civil war in Yugoslavia and threatens to tear apart several other nations in the area, including those belonging to the newly formed Commonwealth of Independent States, the loose confederation that replaced the Soviet Union after its collapse in late 1991.

Finally, this edition sharpens the reorganization of this book that was evident in the seventh edition. Part One provides the framework for study, and Part Two presents the first level of analysis, which is the state system. Part Three addresses the second and third levels of analysis—the domestic character of nation-states and decision making, respectively. The military and economic instruments of power constitute Part Four. This arrangement allows a balanced, logical treatment of the three levels and an uninterrupted analysis of state behavior before proceeding to the means that states use to achieve their objectives. In this edition, concluding chapters (8 and 17) have been added to Parts Two and Four to give meaning and draw conclusions, however tentative, to the analyses in those parts. Chapter 17 focuses on states' use of their military and economic instruments to achieve their objectives in a changing international system. Part Five (From State System to Global System) does not have a summary chapter as such. But Chapter 20, which analyzes some of the principal features of the new post-cold war strategic environment, especially the diffusion of mass-destruction weapons to smaller states, serves that purpose. Indeed, by doing so and clarifying that the new system is not so much the much discussed new international order but the old international system in a new context, this chapter summarizes the basic approach and themes of *Games Nations Play*.

An author is indebted to many people. I am grateful to the undergraduates at the University of Florida, who over the years have taken my introductory international politics course, who have been exposed to different ways of organizing this material, and who have been kind and gentle in suggesting helpful improvements. Special thanks is also due to Timothy Lomperis of Duke University, whose detailed criticisms of the drafts of this as well as the last two editions were very insightful and helpful; to Joseph Nogee of the University of Houston, who has never failed to let me know what improvements I should make; to Sabra Bissette Ledent, who meticulously and with good humor (and, no doubt, sometimes despair) edited this, as well as the last, edition; and to my surgeon, Bill Mayfield, without whose skill this eighth edition would not have appeared.

J.S.

Part One

THE STUDY AND ANALYSIS OF INTERNATIONAL POLITICS

CHAPTER 1

War and Thinking About International Politics

The years 1989 and 1990 were truly revolutionary ones. In 1989, the Soviet Union relinquished its control of Eastern Europe—the scene of the thrust of Soviet power at the end of World War II that precipitated the cold war. But in the late 1980s, Moscow stood by as hard-line pro-Soviet Communist governments were swept aside first in Poland, then in Hungary and Czechoslovakia, later in East Germany, and finally in Romania and Bulgaria. Eventually, in all these countries—except Romania and Bulgaria, where the Communists managed to get reelected under other names—non-Communist governments came into power. The most dramatic event, however, occurred in East Germany, where the Berlin Wall, built in 1961 to prevent East Berliners from fleeing to West Germany, was opened in November 1989. Long the symbol of what the cold war was all about—tyranny versus freedom—this opening, like no other event, appeared to mean that the long cold war was, after forty-five years, finally over. This was followed within a year, initially against Soviet opposition, by the even more dramatic disappearance of East Germany, as the two parts of the previously divided Germany were reunited in early October 1990.

If 1989 was the Year of the Collapsing Satellite Regimes in Eastern Europe, then 1990 was the first Year of the Disintegration of the Communist System in the Soviet Union. Mikhail Gorbachev, the Soviet leader who had come to power in 1985, had since 1987 been transforming his country's totalitarian system. He had allowed greater freedom of political debate than ever before; genuine opposition, including the organization of groups beyond Communist party control; and growing competition in elections. Moreover, he encouraged the formerly supine Supreme Soviet, the Soviet legislature, to assert its powers, and, most startling of all, in 1990 he officially abandoned the Communist party's seventy-three-year monopoly of power. These changes, if they

3

continued, suggested radical changes in the Soviet system. In his public declarations, Gorbachev even appeared to be moving away from the failing, highly centralized and bureaucratized Soviet command economy to a market economy (although in reality he remained reluctant to dismantle Moscow's power). The repudiation of Marxism-Leninism appeared complete. Communism as an ideology had shown itself to be a "grand failure." [1]

Indeed, 1991 witnessed two revolutionary, climactic events that matched, if not surpassed, the drama and consequences of the 1917 Bolshevik Revolution: the end of communism and of the Soviet Union. As their power slipped, the hard-line Communists who had resisted Gorbachev's reforms staged a coup. But they failed. Discredited and disgraced, they were swept aside by the fury of the Soviet people, speeding up the transformation of the Soviet Union to a politically pluralistic society and market economy. But in the process, the nation, composed of fifteen republics, fell apart. On December 25, 1991, the Soviet Union expired, replaced by a loose association called the Commonwealth of Independent States. Its future cohesion remained unknown. But, in a real sense, Russia, spanning the Eurasian continent and eleven time zones, was the Soviet Union's successor state. As startling as all the recent changes had been, who would have predicted that 1991 would be the year that the "evil empire," as President Ronald Reagan had called it, would end up on "the ash heap of history," as he had predicted in 1982?

Because of increasing preoccupation with domestic matters in the late 1980s, the Soviets had shifted their priorities from foreign to domestic policy. Deluged with economic and ethnic problems at home, the cold war had to be ended. Large numbers of Soviet troops were withdrawn from Eastern Europe; the rest were scheduled to be withdrawn before the end of 1991, except from the former East Germany, where they were to be pulled out in 1994. Regional confrontations in Africa, Asia, and Latin America, previously pursued by force, were now settled diplomatically. An arms control agreement signed in 1987 eliminating all U.S. and Soviet medium-range missiles was followed in 1990 by a major agreement substantially lowering the manpower and weapons levels of the two superpowers' respective alliances, the Warsaw Treaty Organization and the North Atlantic Treaty Organization. A radical reduction in strategic nuclear weapons, with a 50 percent reduction in key missile systems and warheads, was signed in 1991.

The ending of the cold war gave rise to a sense of euphoria in the West. The world seemed to stand on the verge of a new era. This hope, to be sure, was partly based on the Soviet Union's termination of its expansionist and confrontational policies and the expectation of future superpower cooperation in maintaining the peace. But it also was based on more fundamental forces that were said to be changing the very nature of international politics. One was the spread of democracy to Eastern Europe, including the Soviet Union, and to areas of Asia and Latin America. Democracy, especially in the democratic West, was believed to be associated with peaceful international behavior.[2] Thus, the "zone of peace" was spreading throughout the world. Increasingly, too, it was claimed that war had become obsolete. Not only had nuclear weapons made war too suicidal to fight, but as nations had grown more civilized, war had become ever more repugnant as an instrument of state policy, just as slavery and dueling, once widely accepted practices domestically, had become unthinkable in modern societies. Thus, war among great powers was viewed as a thing of the past, and, given the high cost of even conventional or nonnuclear warfare, it might become obsolete among the developing nations as well.[3] Finally, the industrialized societies of the West, as well as a growing number of resource-rich and rapidly industrializing countries in the underdeveloped areas of the world, were increasingly joining together as transnational economic and financial forces wove a widening and deepening web of interdependence. Thus, all the great Western industrial powers, once so prone to fight one another, had after World War II become not only democratic and capable of peaceful coexistence, but also willing to cooperate with one another in advancing their common prosperity. Peace and prosperity, therefore, seemed assured. Economics and nations' common welfare would supersede conflict between individual nations and the use of force. Economics, which tied nations together in their search for greater wealth and a higher standard of living, was the wave of the future. Conflict, which separated them into antagonists, too often escalating into warfare, was the way of the past. One optimistic commentator even talked of the "end of history."

> What we may be witnessing is not just the end of the cold war, or the passing of a particular period of postwar history, but the end of history as such: that is, the end point of mankind's ideological evolution and the universalization of Western liberal democracy as the final form of human government.... [The implications are] the growing "Common Marketization" of international relations, and the diminution of the likelihood of large-scale conflict among states.[4]

Just as all these expressions of hope for the future were being voiced, the world was rudely awakened on August 2, 1990, by Iraqi leader Saddam Hussein's invasion and seizure of the tiny oil kingdom of Kuwait on the Persian Gulf, and the threat this action posed to Saudi Arabia. President George Bush organized an international coalition to oppose Iraq and compel its withdrawal from Kuwait. When economic sanctions did not appear enough to achieve this purpose, coalition forces launched their attack on Iraq just after the United Nations' deadline of January 15, 1991, passed without a pullout of Iraqi forces from Kuwait. Iraq reportedly had the fourth largest army in the world, and it was well equipped, with matériel such as chemical weapons and missiles. But poor leadership, bad morale, a defensive strategy, and several weeks of intense, round-the-clock allied bombing of Iraq's economic and military infrastructure and of Iraqi forces in Kuwait and southern Iraq, led to that army's quick defeat once the ground war began.

In the midst of all the euphoria over the ending of the cold war—in particular, the expectations that international conflicts and wars would in this dawning new age become relics of the past—was this case of old-fashioned aggression by one country against a small neighbor an aberration? Was the ensuing war—which at least was not a superpower war fought with nuclear weapons—the tragic end of the old era? Or did it mean that the nature of international politics had not fundamentally changed and that the hostilities with Iraq were merely a continuation of the historic pattern of state behavior? In short, was this the beginning of what President Bush called a "new world order," or was it just the old world disorder in a new configuration? Indeed, in a system of nation-states, each dependent on itself for its own security and prosperity, could the basically conflictual character of international rivalry be transformed and, if so, how and to what degree? [5] Or did the end of the cold war and the regional hostilities that erupted in the Middle East-Persian Gulf area suggest, more accurately, that while old conflicts disappear, they may reappear or new ones supersede them?

This question was rudely—even if only briefly—underlined in August 1991 when the movement toward the political decentralization and economic restructuring of the Soviet Union was interrupted by a coup to overthrow President Gorbachev, staged by antireform forces in the military, the secret police, and the Communist party. Had the coup not fizzled so surprisingly quickly, would the hard-liners have rekindled the U.S.-Soviet conflict? And even if such a move did not bring back the cold war, would it not have been detrimental to the cooperation that Gorbachev had established with Presidents Reagan and Bush? The fundamental question suggested by all these rapid turns of events, including the near possibility of a revival of the American-Soviet conflict, was which was the most striking feature of international politics: the extent and rapidity of changes or the amazing persistence of tradition so aptly summed up by the French expression *plus ça change, plus c'est la même chose* (the more things change, the more they stay the same)? [6]

The twentieth century, with its two world wars (1914-1918 and 1939-1945) and numerous smaller wars, certainly signals restraint about expecting radical changes in the nature of international politics. Conflict and war historically have been its chief characteristics. Judging by the recent war with Iraq, which followed its eight-year-long war with Iran, the central issue among states, still the primary actors on the world stage, remains the issue of war and peace, even though a war between the United States and Russia, which has inherited the bulk of the former Soviet Union's nuclear arsenal, is unlikely in the foreseeable future. But wars launched by ambitious regional powers, which may increasingly be armed with weapons of mass destruction, continue to threaten the survival of the international system itself. After World War I ended, Winston Churchill, who became Great Britain's prime minister during World War II, wrote,

> Mankind has got into its hands for the first time the tools by which it can unfailingly accomplish its own extermination. . . . Death stands at attention, obedient, expectant, . . . ready, if called on, to pulverise, without hope of repair, what

is left of civilisation. He awaits only the word of command. He awaits it from a frail, bewildered being, long his victim, now—for one occasion only—his Master.[7]

Although war, not surprisingly, is often regarded as somehow abnormal—at best an awful error, at worst a criminal undertaking—the fact is that the history of war is as old as human history. In this century, the brutality of war has greatly influenced thinking about international politics. This is why this chapter will look first at the impact of war in this century and then at some of the principal schools of thought about international conflict and the wars it has produced. That examination will place the discipline, as well as the approaches used in this book, in perspective. Later chapters (especially in Parts Four and Five), will examine and analyze the degree to which democracy, industrialization, and war itself are transforming the nature of international politics.

SHOCK OF WORLD WAR I

World War I was a cataclysmic experience for Europe. With the exception of the French Revolution, World War I was the first total war Europe had experienced since the Treaty of Westphalia (1648) ended the slaughter of the Thirty Years' War. To be sure, Europe had witnessed a number of wars during the nineteenth century, but they had been minor and of brief duration. World War I also was expected to last only a few months, and casualties were expected to be no heavier than in past wars. But, after the almost 100 years of relative peace that followed the Congress of Vienna in 1815, which brought the war with Napoleon to a close, Europe suffered the shock of a four-year total war and a terrible bloodletting. Once Germany's initial offensive into France was halted, the war on the western front bogged down in the trenches. First one side, then the other tried to break through the opponent's lines, but neither could do so. Successive lines of barbed wire protected each side's trenches. The murderous machine-gun and rapid rifle fire mowed down row after row of advancing infantry. Breakthroughs became impossible.

Yet the offensives continued. The generals had learned, after all, that the only defense was offense. Thus, headquarters continued to hurl their armies into battles. The artillery first laid down a barrage, sometimes lasting a week or longer, on the opponent's trenches. This tactic was supposed to pulverize the enemy's position and shatter the morale of its troops. It was a simple idea that should have worked but never did. Killing became the objective. If enemy lines could not be ruptured, at least the enemy could be worn down by the various offensives. Sooner or later, these constant blows would wear down troop reserves, and morale would collapse. World War I was not a war of mobility and maneuver but a war of attrition—an organized, four-year-long attempt by both sides to gain victory simply by bleeding each other to death. It was an unsophisticated strategy.

The French lost 955,000 men in five months of 1914; in 1915, 1,430,000 men; and in 1916, 900,000 men. The losses for single battles were staggering. The 1916 German attempt to bleed the French at Verdun led to a ten-month battle that cost France 535,000 casualties and Germany 427,000—almost a million men altogether. A British attempt to pierce German lines in the same year resulted in the five-month Battle of the Somme. Although they pounded the German lines with artillery for eight days before sending troops into battle, the British gained only 120 square miles, at the cost of 420,000 men, or 3,500 per square mile. The Germans lost 445,000 men. Some estimates place the total Somme casualties at 1.2 million, the highest of any battle in history. At Ypres in 1917, the British bombardment lasted nineteen days; 321 train-loads of shells were fired, the equivalent of a year's production by 55,000 war workers. This time the English forces captured forty-five square miles, at the cost of 370,000 men, or 8,222 per square mile. By comparison, total British Empire casualties during the six years of World War II were almost 1.25 million, including 350,000 dead and 91,000 missing. Approximately 8.5 million men in uniform were killed during the four years of the Great War, as World War I was called, and the number of dead civilians totaled an additional 1.5 million.[8]

But the impact of war cannot be measured merely by citing statistics of the dead. The real impact also must be understood psychologically. Losses are not just quantitative; they are qualitative as well. A nation can ill afford to lose millions of men, nor can it afford to lose almost an entire generation. Is it any wonder that the nations of Europe, which lost so many of their young men who would have fathered children, also lost their self-confidence and their hope for the future? Those who would have supplied this vigor and optimism, had they grown up and become the leaders of government, business, labor, and science, lay dead in Flanders Field.

For Europe, then, the Great War was the Great Divide. The nineteenth century had been one of confidence. Democracy was spreading in Europe and was expected to spread to all other continents too, as soon as colonialism had prepared the natives of Asia and Africa for self-government. The future would belong to the common people; their rights and freedom would supplant the traditional privileges of the few. For the first time in history, people would join together across national boundaries in a new world of mutual understanding and good will. Peace would be both inevitable and permanent. Science and technology would improve everyone's standard of living; the age-old economics of scarcity would be transformed into an economics of abundance and affluence. Poverty and misery would be ended forever. This optimism and faith in progress were aptly voiced by an American, Andrew Carnegie, in his instructions to the trustees of the Carnegie Endowment for International Peace: "When ... war is discarded as disgraceful to civilized man, the trustees will please then consider what is the next most degrading evil or evils whose banishment ... would most advance the progress, elevation and happiness of man." [9] It was just a matter of time then until war would be eliminated. It would have been contrary to the spirit of the age to ask whether this abolition of war could indeed be achieved.

The Great War changed this optimism to pessimism, this confidence to doubt and fear. The West's utter certainty about its own greatness and future lay shattered on the battlefields among the decaying corpses. For the first time, Western scholars talked about the "decline of the West." Europe's imperial control was weakened abroad, and at home the expected trend toward democracy was halted, if not reversed. Fascism took over in Italy, nazism gained power in Germany, and Benito Mussolini and Adolf Hitler together helped Francisco Franco seize control of Spain. In eastern Europe, only Czechoslovakia could be considered a democratic country. The nineteenth century had believed in the supremacy of reason and its ability to make the world a safer and better place in which to live. In the interwar period, demagoguery and the manipulation of hysterical crowds, totalitarianism and its warlike spirit, seemed the wave of the future.

As the structure and hopes of the previous 100 years began to crash all around them, the leaders of France and England became concerned above all with avoiding another war. "No more war, no more war" became their cry. And who could blame them? These leaders were concerned not merely with their personal survival. They were men of honorable intentions and decent motives, greatly concerned about the welfare of their citizens and repelled by the horror and senselessness of modern war. It is easy today to sneer at the appeasement of Hitler, but to the survivors of World War I another war could only mean the slaughter and seemingly wasteful sacrifices of Verdun and the Somme. They still heard the "soldiers marching, all to die." And they remembered that the strain of that war had collapsed four of Europe's great empires: Austria-Hungary, Ottoman Turkey, Imperial Russia, and Imperial Germany. They also recalled that, despite Germany's grievous losses, its European opponents had suffered twice as many losses—and their populations were smaller than Germany's. If fighting another war involved another such blood bath, surely they would be signing their nations' death warrants. Their social structures and morale could not absorb such losses for the second time in two generations. To most people who had lived through the tragic war years, peace became a supreme value. The appeasement of Hitler during the 1930s was to them not just the only policy—it was an absolute necessity. Surely it was saner to resolve differences with reason than with guns. Would it not be better to understand each other's legitimate grievances and settle differences in a spirit of good will rather than by war? Was it not preferable to make mutual concessions, thereby diminishing distrust and fear, and build the mutual confidence that could be the only basis of a firm peace? To ask these questions was to answer them for most of the survivors of World War I. Between the alternatives of appeasement and war, no one of good will and humanity had a choice.

Thus, war had become so costly that questions about its usability were widespread. Instead of the short and not very costly conflict that the diplomats, soldiers, and others had expected, the long and extremely costly Great War was the first modern war to raise the issue of the legitimacy and rationality of warfare as an instrument for advancing a nation's purposes. After 1945 and six years of fighting in which the loss of life, military (17 million) and civilian (34 million), exceeded that of the First World War fivefold, the futility of another total war became obvious to all. World War II had ended with the dropping of two atomic bombs, each of which had caused heavy loss of life and widespread destruction. The atomic bomb was quickly called the "absolute weapon." What was the point of defending one's way of life if, in the process, that way of life was utterly destroyed? In the nuclear age total war had become irrational; the costs of such a war completely exceeded any conceivable gains. One knew that without even having to fight. Had the leaders of Europe who went to war in 1914 been able to look into a crystal ball and foresee what the costs would be, they might have chosen a different course. Today, we have that crystal ball.[10]

GAMES NATIONS PLAY

The problem is that war cannot be isolated from international conflict in general. More specifically, states have long used war to transact their business. Despite the growing costs of war in the twentieth century, the "games nations play" continue. The games analogy is used because the principal players—states—reject any higher authority.[11] Each state, like any player in a competitive game, seeks to advance its own interests in conflict with those of other states. In this pursuit of its national interests, a state will resort to the use of force if it cannot achieve or defend its goals in any other way. States play this game, of course, with different capabilities; the main players historically have been the most powerful states. The stakes or payoffs are critical: survival, a degree of security, influence, and status, as well as wealth, are some of the principal ones.

Because each state looks at the world from its particular perspective and must plan its moves—its strategy—to enhance its security and other objectives, the games analogy is an apt one. Each state is a player, and each plays to win in a game in which it competes with almost 170 other nations. And although the great powers have in the past been the chief players, today many other less influential nations are active participants in the game. Each must therefore concern itself with competing effectively, especially with those states that are its immediate rivals. In this context, the term *strategy* is not defined in its usual narrow military sense, referring to winning a war. Instead, it is defined as a set of calculated moves, a set of decisions, in a competitive and conflictual situation in which the outcome is not governed by pure chance.[12] In other words, the idea of strategy is used as it would be when speaking of chess or football, games that are governed by known formal rules, or politics or dating, activities governed mainly by informal rules. In international politics, as political scientist John Lovell has said, each state seeks to advance its "national interests" in conflict with those of other states in a game whose rules are largely informal and unwritten, evolving mainly through the behavior of the strongest players.[13] A state may advance its interests offensively or defensively, but in either case the players must weigh carefully the alternative means of achieving their objectives and then choose the option that will maximize their gains and minimize their losses, as well as their risks and costs.

Thus, there are lots of games going on, such as *adversary games*, in which two or more states are engaged in conflict, and *alignment games*, in which states seek help from other states or seek to attract allies away from their adversaries either in a straight de-alignment or a realignment toward themselves. Just as the alignment game is subsidiary to the adversary game, so too is the arms competition or *preparedness (arms race) game*, in which adversaries seek at a minimum to stay even with their opponents' strengths or at maximum to gain superiority.[14] Another is the *economic game*, played because to maintain its well-being, a state usually must import goods and materials, as well as export the same, and ideally maintain a balance between the two. The basic game, however, which historically has constituted the essence of international politics, is the great-power adversary *political-military game*. In a decentralized system of sovereign states, the lack of a superior and legitimate world government—to allocate political, military, and economic goods peacefully and manage the political and economic relations among states peacefully—ensures the survival of the state system, "the womb in which war develops." [15] Thus, international politics focuses on the relations or interactions among states, although states are not the only players. The "games nations play" is therefore basically about *who gets what, when, how* (see Chapter 5).[16]

Now that the essence of international politics has been defined, how can one better understand it? The answer depends on how it is studied. What follows is a brief examination of some of the principal ways this has been done.

THEORIZING ABOUT INTERSTATE RELATIONS

Historical Approach

Before the outbreak of World War I, not much attention was given to a theory of international politics. Indeed, international politics was never a preoccupation of Western political thought, which focused primarily on domestic issues. Thinking about conflict among states was largely intermittent and fragmentary. By contrast, Western thinking about order, justice, and liberty within Western states has been ongoing and well developed; these subjects are found in the works of Plato and Aristotle. Before the twentieth century, however, only a handful of writers produced works on interstate politics that have become classics: Thucydides, who wrote about the war between Athens and Sparta in ancient Greece; Niccolò Machiavelli, who sought to advise a prince on how to unify Italy; and Thomas Hobbes, an English philosopher who speculated about the life of man in a state of nature. One could even add a few names like Polybius, who wrote about the war between Rome and Carthage; David Hume, who wrote on the balance of power; and Hugo Grotius, who wrote extensively about international law.

If there was a focus at all, it was diplomatic history. In a sense, this was international politics because it recounted what had transpired between nations in the past. But in another sense, diplomatic history cannot be equated with a theory of international politics. Discovering what happened in the years immediately before 1914 can yield an enormous amount of information on specific political and military leaders, the political climate and social and economic conditions within specific countries, their planned military strategies and armaments, and how all these interacted to produce World War I. But this is not to say that some of the issues, such as why the war occurred or who was most responsible for it, will ever be settled; historians in each generation tend to reinterpret earlier events. Nevertheless, diplomatic history can tell us much about such events.

Indeed, that is precisely its shortcoming. Historians focus on descriptions of specific events, which are unique to those times and places. While they can tell us how and why a specific war happened, they do not tell us why wars occur more generally. A *theory* of international politics would attempt to answer this question. Such a theory would not look at each war as unique but would analyze many wars. It would then specify from the data exactly which conditions seem repeatedly to result in war. For example, if the study of a half dozen wars showed that the victors fell out with each other four times out of six, leading to a new struggle and possibly war, one could generalize and state: if, at the end of hostilities, the victors cannot agree on peace terms—or, more crudely, a division of the spoils—a new war may result. Of course, war may not break out each time this situation occurs, but, if it happened often enough in the past, it is likely to occur in the future.

Other conditions that have led to war also can be identified. It took the trauma of World War I, however, to bring about a more sustained search for a theory of international politics. As a discipline, international politics is a product of the twentieth century and, to a large extent, a product of American scholarship.

Utopianism

World War I was a shock for Europe, the worse for not having been expected. Why did it occur? How could such senseless slaughter have gone on? Alliances, arms races, and secret diplomacy frequently were cited as the causes. Power politics was blamed; it was alleged that all the great powers had recklessly pursued their national interests. Not surprisingly then, the beginning of thinking about international politics started with utopian aspirations: there must be no recurrence of world war. Thus, the motive spurring on the initial theorizing was the passionate desire to avoid another war.[17] War was a disease infecting the body politic; it had to be cut out. But wishing prevailed over careful analysis, and the focus was on the end to be achieved. President Woodrow Wilson typified this mood. On his way to Paris to attend the postwar peace conference, Wilson was asked whether his plan for a League of Nations to keep the peace would work. He replied, "If it won't work, it must be made to work." [18]

The resulting study of international politics concentrated on three different approaches. First, there was the emphasis on the League of Nations, in which the nations of the world would be represented. In this forum negotiations and debates could be observed by the publics of all countries, making it impossible for secret diplomacy to produce another war. The assumption was that national leaders, unrestrained by public opinion, might intrigue again in the future. Ordinary people, who did the fighting and dying, were believed to be peaceful and thus would watch for and prevent agreements secretly made; agreements or covenants were to be arrived at openly. It was expected therefore that nations would cooperate within the league's framework, de-emphasizing their nations' egotisms and selfish interests. Second, there were disarmament conferences that aimed to reduce, if not eliminate, the number of arms possessed by the great powers. Examples include German disarmament in the Treaty of Versailles (1919) and the Washington Naval Conference (1921-1922), limiting naval rivalry in the Pacific. Third, there were legal efforts to decrease the likelihood of war. A specific American contribution was the Kellogg-Briand Pact (1928), which for the first time outlawed war as an instrument of state policy—except, of course, wars conducted in "self-defense." Collectively, the twenty years between the two world wars were a time when thinking about international politics, both academically and popularly, in the English-speaking world was characterized by the almost complete neglect of the reality of power. The fundamental assumption of the utopian or idealistic approach was a natural harmony of interest among nations. All shared a common interest in peace. Any nation that disturbed the peace was both irrational and immoral. It also was undemocratic; since the people were peaceful and members of a free society, their opinion would prevail.[19]

The search for an end to war was accompanied by a political shift in the domestic policies of the Western democracies, especially Britain and France, which, until World War I, often had been belligerents. This political change was to have a profound impact on the conduct of foreign policy. Before 1914, the conduct of foreign policy had been left basically to the diplomats and soldiers. Foreign policy was usually regarded not as a matter for popular opinion and party politics but as a matter for experts. This was as true for the democracies as for the more autocratic states such as Germany and czarist Russia. But after the slaughter of World War I, the people of the Western democracies, who had suffered so much, wanted control over foreign policy as they had over domestic policy. Georges Clemenceau, France's premier, uttered a line that was to become famous: "War is much too serious a matter to be entrusted to the military," and foreign policy, he implied, to the diplomats. In short, foreign policy was now, like domestic politics, to be subjected to popular accountability. The result was twofold. First, a vengeful public opinion in Britain and France was a major reason for the punitive peace treaty imposed on Germany in 1919. And, second, during the 1930s a fearful public opinion was the reason for the appeasement of Hitler; it made a policy of opposition to Germany—as well as to Italy and Japan—impossible. Ironically, the public yearning for peace produced the same result that the soldiers and diplomats had produced earlier.

Realism

Just as World War I was blamed on power politics, it was widely believed that World War II stemmed from the neglect of power politics. If an arms race and close alliances were thought to be responsible for the hostilities of 1914-1918, the failure of the British and French to match German arms and to stand together against Hitler precipitated what Churchill was to call the "unnecessary war." [20] Realism was the reaction to interwar idealism. If war was to be prevented, more than wishful thinking was needed. The reality was that there were ambitious and warlike states that were unappeasable and had to be opposed, and that this required, among other things, a willingness to risk war and strong military forces to support a policy of deterrence. To fear risking war left the states that most desired peace at the mercy of the more ruthless states. Not to build the required strength to avoid provoking a potential aggressor left a state with no choice but to submit to an aggressor's demands and to become a victim.

Realism was to become the dominant school of thinking in postwar America, now the West's chief defender against the Soviet Union. Realism resurrected traditional ideas: that states were the primary actors in international politics; that the environment or state system in which states lived was essentially anarchical; that conflict in this system could be managed at best to reduce the likelihood of war, but war could not be abolished. The central point was that there was no final solution to the problem of war. Appeals to humanity's common interest in survival, appeals to replace the state system with some form of world government, were all in vain. Management of the system had to be rooted in every state's "national interest," and the best way of preserving peace was to maintain the balance of power. The key to the conduct of foreign policy was prudence: states needed to be cautious, not launch crusades against one another. They also had to be flexible and accommodating in their diplomacy. The key figures in the realist revolution were Hans Morgenthau, a

German refugee scholar; George Kennan, a U.S. diplomat and historian of Russia; and Reinhold Niebuhr, a Protestant minister.

Realism, however, soon came under attack. For one thing, it became identified with Morgenthau, whose book *Politics among Nations* had a profound influence on American academia.[21] The works of more sophisticated analysts—such as Arnold Wolfers, John Herz, Kennan, and Niebuhr—were largely overlooked at first.[22] One frequent criticism of Morgenthau, and therefore of realism in general, was that, although it claimed to describe international politics as it was and not in utopian terms, its frequent advice to policy makers on the conduct of foreign policy suggested that states did not in fact behave as the realists described. A second criticism was that, despite their common outlook, realists often disagreed with one another. For example, Morgenthau surprisingly came out early against U.S. intervention in Vietnam, but other realists supported that policy. Such disagreements raised questions about the value of realism as a guide to making the "correct" foreign policy. A third criticism was that if governments continued to cling to realism in their conduct of foreign policy, nuclear war would be inevitable, an unacceptable result. Most of all, perhaps, the realism was alien to the American outlook. The emphasis on power and the acceptance of conflict and war as natural rather than abnormal and transitory were "un-American" (see Chapter 9). Realism was especially offensive because it appeared at best amoral, if not downright immoral, in a country that prides itself on being a morally superior nation and that often feels guilty when its foreign policy is not—or does not appear to be—moral.[23]

Behaviorism

Both idealism and realism supplied a unifying focus. What followed in the 1960s and 1970s had no such focus. Instead, what displaced realism—or attempted to do so—was a host of different approaches, some of which were called theories and others, more cautiously, pretheories. Most were characterized by their way of investigating international politics. The word *investigating* is a clue to this new approach. Utopianism had posited a purpose that had to be achieved. "The wish is father to the thought" was its origin, and its aim was to cure a "sick" international body politic. The actual behavior of states was not a matter for investigation; that behavior was all too clear and it had to be changed! Realism, by contrast, asserted that the twenty years from 1919 to 1939 demonstrated conclusively that the Western democracies' neglect of the reality of power led to the very result their behavior sought to avoid; that those states willing to resort to power—all antidemocratic states—threatened to become dominant; and that those states that believed in reason, mutual good will, and accommodation, but that were not backed by sufficient power, had to retreat and, in the final analysis, had to go to war anyway to save themselves. But the fact that realists had to advise states about how they should behave to better protect themselves suggested realism's weakness— states often acted in ways seemingly contradictory to their best interests.

This is where behaviorism entered. Rejecting both an end to be achieved and *a priori* assumptions about how states behave, its advocates stated that their purpose was to investigate international politics without any reformist desires or biased preconceptions.[24] Their analyses would be *value free* or *empirical*. They intended to observe the many forms of state behavior, collect the necessary data, and carefully draw conclusions from their studies. In opposition to earlier researchers, who were then almost scornfully called *traditionalists* for their reliance on the study of history, diplomatic memories, and experiences, the behaviorists claimed to be political *scientists*. Obviously, political scientists interested in international politics were part of a larger group of analysts looking at other fields, such as American and comparative politics, as well as novel areas, such as political methodology. Methodology was in fact the heart of the behavioral approach: how to study a particular type of human activity. And the change in the technique for studying political science was only part of a far larger movement spreading across all American social sciences.

The scientific method claimed not only an unbiased approach to research—that investigators could separate their own values from "the facts" and the manner in which they organized these facts—but also, as already suggested, an ability to generalize about the behavior of states and other political actors in the international arena. Political scientists looked for patterns of behavior such as the one mentioned earlier: when one of the victors of a war perceives that its interests are not satisfied at the postwar peace conference—or, at least, that its gains are not as great as those of some of its fellow victors—conflict results and war may occur. Or, if the defeated state harbors grievances against the victors because of the harshness of the settlement they imposed on it, the loser may seek to remedy this matter militarily, as well as to avenge its previous humiliation. These generalizations about the conditions under which past wars have erupted allow theorists to hypothesize that *if* the above conditions exist, *then* war results.

What especially characterized much of the behavioral inquiry during the 1950s, 1960s, and 1970s was its use of aggregate data, quantitative techniques, computers, formal models, and the general "laws" of behavior, as well as its rather arrogant attitude toward earlier methods of research.[25] Often implicit in behaviorists' attitudes was the claim that if it could not be quantified, it was not worth saying. Earlier analyses of international politics tended to be dismissed as not only traditional but also impressionistic, if not poetic. Only quantitative methods, it was asserted, could be free from bias and produce accurate and verifiable empirical studies of the behavior of international actors. Despite this strong, and occasionally dogmatic, point of view, it is fair to say that even nonquantitative scholars were deeply influenced by the behavioral approach. For whatever its claims to being scientific, let alone holding the only correct approach to the truth, its essence was an emphasis on careful scholarship and analytical precision. Its goals, as two of its proponents have suggested, were to substitute verifiable knowledge for subjective belief, testable evidence for intuitive explanations, and data for appeals to "expert" or "authoritative" opinion.[26] Traditional scholars, probably feeling defensive, and also wishing to avoid being considered outside the mainstream of American political science, reacted by demonstrating greater care in their research activities.

The intensity of the battle between the traditional and scientific or empirical approaches therefore diminished over time. Traditional scholars showed more precision in their analyses, and at least some of the behaviorists interested in international politics were ready to admit that several charges leveled by the traditionalists were not totally unjustified. These charges included a preoccupation with what sometimes appeared to be methodology for the sake of methodology; a focus on issues to which their methods could be applied, frequently issues of secondary or even lesser significance, if not irrelevant; and a disregard of a world of nuclear weapons, widespread poverty, and injustice.

But even more basic, every study, no matter how carefully carried out, begins with some assumptions. They may be implicit and the investigators unaware of their influence. Nevertheless, researchers' selection of facts and how the facts are organized and interpreted are hardly value free. Every social scientist starts with a purpose, perhaps to eliminate war or make a better world. "It is the purpose of promoting health which creates medical science. . . . Desire to cure the sickness of the body politic has given its impulse and its inspiration to political science. . . . Purpose and analysis became part and parcel of a single process." [27]

Contemporary Approaches and Visions

All this being said, do any of these approaches to the analysis of international politics help explain what kind of world is emerging in this post-cold war era? As a matter of fact, they do. The utopian school's assumption of a harmony of interest among nations, noted earlier, derived from the *laissez-faire* school of economics of Adam Smith. That free-market philosophy, when applied to the relations among states rather than individuals acting as producers and consumers in the domestic market, translated into the classical liberal tradition of free trade. Economically, its principal benefit was a higher standard of living for those states exchanging goods; politically, it created a common interest in peace. Because war would disrupt free trade, it was counterproductive.

Its modernized, twentieth-century form, interdependence—the close linking of states to one another—also focused on the formation of transnational economic, social, and technological bonds. Functionalism, a form of this thesis popular during the 1950s, emphasized the almost automatic nature of growing ties between nations, a process that was supposed to lead to the United States of Europe.[28] In its 1970s and 1980s version, the emphasis shifted from regional interdependence to global interdependence.[29] The claim remained the same: the growing ties between countries will increasingly shift state

behavior from that marked by conflict and the use of force to that characterized by cooperation based on common interests. A principal indicator of this
shift from realism to interdependence will be the *regimes* that states establish,
incorporating the rules governing their cooperation or decision-making procedures. These rules will be used to resolve disputes over various issues,
whether military or economic.[30] This vision of an emerging global post-cold
war world is thus both liberal and optimistic, for it suggests that if the
expansion of democracy and free trade beyond North America (the United
States and Canada), Western Europe, and the newly industrializing countries
in Asia to the rest of the world is successful, world peace will be assured.
While nations will remain nations, their importance will decline as they are
embraced by a global shopping mall that will produce greater prosperity for
all peoples. Multilateral institutions and approaches are emphasized for resolving such international problems as the environment, which affects everyone.

An alternative vision of the post-cold war period, deriving from the realist
approach, is more conservative and pessimistic. The collapse of the Soviet
state does not necessarily mean the end of the historic conflict among states.
Specific rivalries may disappear, but new ones are likely to take their place.
They may be of a different nature, scope, or intensity, but they will be
worrisome. One such set of conflicts will be economic, and it will occur
among the nations that until recently were allied against the Soviet Union.
National concerns about jobs, employment, and prosperity will lead the
principal industrial powers, all of them Western and democratic, to engage
increasingly in trade wars, as free trade gives way to economic rivalry among
states who no longer need one another for their greater collective security
against an external threat. Indeed, not only do these exponents of free trade
not practice fully what they preach, but their rivalry will lead increasingly to
the formation of larger trading blocs in Western Europe, North America, and
East Asia, another indication of the decline of liberal economic values.

A second set of conflicts will spring from the new competition and rivalry
among states in the major regions of the world. With the end of the American-Soviet conflict—which, on the one hand, involved them in regional
quarrels but which, on the other hand, also restrained such quarrels from
escalating and involving the superpowers in war—regionally ambitious states
seeking to establish local dominance are free to pursue their goals. Iraq was
the first example but is unlikely to be the last, for the future will see the
extensive proliferation of nuclear, chemical, and biological weapons to smaller countries. Ruthless leaders such as Iraq's Saddam Hussein, controlling
instruments of mass destruction, are not a prescription for a harmonious and
peaceful world in which the use of force has become obsolete.

Another Approach: Three Levels of Analysis

Theories of international politics, then, are intended to help those seeking to
organize, interpret, and even predict "reality." To make any sense at all of

international politics, one must start by learning how to cope with enormous amounts of fragmented information. Each person perceives reality by abstracting from the totality of experience those parts that he or she considers relevant. And such perceptions are selective. They are bound to be, for obviously no one sees every aspect of reality; the world is so complex and perplexing that simplification is necessary even to begin to understand it. These perceptions of reality are called *theories*. Other words, often used interchangeably with theory, are *approach, paradigm*, or *analytical framework*. Whatever the words, they are a way of looking at a subject from a particular perspective—such as those described earlier. One looks to them for help in organizing much of that random information, selecting the relevant facts or data, arranging them in some intelligible order, and thereby interpreting and understanding reality or "what's going on" a bit better. If the perspective adopted is that of the state system, with a focus on the relationships between states and the balance of power, the world will be seen quite differently than it would be from a Marxist perspective, with its emphasis on class struggle, international capitalism, economic dominance, and dependency among states.

Each theory or approach organizes the facts differently; indeed, each is likely to pick out quite different facts. Inherent in each are certain assumptions about what features are important and what events and other factors need to be described and analyzed. Such theories may be informed and sophisticated, producing carefully formulated hypotheses as a result of precise and dispassionate observation and analysis, or they may be simple and intuitive, realizing rather crude generalizations. Indeed, some of these theories are based on *a priori* assumptions that the researcher makes, never proves, yet illustrates with many examples. Marxism is one such approach with its doctrinaire insistence that war is the result of economic conditions—specifically, the result of capitalists searching for foreign markets.

Whatever it is, a theory helps one organize and interpret the reality called international politics. Those theorizing, as already noted, must first simplify this reality because they cannot possibly describe all aspects of international politics; they must be selective. They isolate and emphasize certain aspects of this reality and throw those aspects into bold relief, enabling them to make a "conceptual blueprint" of the political life among states. In a sense, they act as an artist would when viewing a panorama. Artists cannot include every detail in their paintings; instead, they select and highlight certain parts of the view, relegate others to the background, and omit still others. The finished painting will be the landscape as seen by the artist's eyes, from a particular physical position and mental perspective. The painting is, in this respect, a partial representation of actuality, emphasizing those features that the artist most wanted to communicate.

Theorists too paint a picture; indeed, to get as complete a picture of the international political landscape as possible, they view that landscape from different perspectives, or "levels of analysis." The problem is one of scope and emphasis. The view is three-dimensional, including the state system, the nation-state, and decision making.[31] At the first level, one considers the behavior of states as shaped by the international system and the rules they must respect if they are to survive and be secure. The focus is on the environment in which states live, where their concern is with the balance of power or equilibrium. The system, it is assumed, imposes its own logic on each member state. Neglect of the balance threatens the security of states and upsets the system's equilibrium. States therefore ought to act to preserve the balance.

At the second level, state behavior is explained not as the outcome of the external environment, but as a reflection of the state's nature (whether capitalist or socialist, democratic or totalitarian, developed or undeveloped). The focus here is on the individual member states rather than the overall system in which they live. The concern is with the kind of economic or political system a state possesses, its degree of development, as well as such factors as its class structures, the character of its elites, and "national style." The assumption is that there is a relationship between a state's domestic character and its foreign policy.

At the third level, foreign policy is explained as a product of the domestic system, but the focus is not on social, economic, political, and cultural characteristics. Instead, it is on the people involved in making and executing foreign policy decisions. Similar states—for example, two capitalist countries or two Communist countries—often pursue quite different policies. Therefore, it is necessary to look at the people making foreign policy, the institutions involved, and the processes of decision making to understand why specific states do what they do.

Together, these three levels of analysis give a comprehensive picture of the "games nations play"—particularly, why and how and for what purposes they play these games. No one level by itself presents the complete picture. The focus on individual states parallels the psychologist's concentration on the individual's personality and character. But, obviously, an individual's behavior can be understood properly only if it is related to the social environment—family, peer groups, and society in general—of that individual. Rather than continue in this abstract fashion, the next chapter takes a preliminary look at case studies at each level of analysis before each level is studied later in greater detail.

For Review

1. Why did the end of the cold war create such optimistic expectations about a peaceful future?
2. What kinds of games are played by nations?
3. How has war in this century, particularly World War I, influenced the study of international politics?

4. What were some of the "isms" influencing the past study of international politics?
5. What are the two schools of thought currently receiving much attention?

Notes

1. Zbigniew Brzezinski, *The Grand Failure* (New York: Scribner's, 1989).
2. Michael W. Doyle, "Liberalism and World Politics," *American Political Science Review* (December 1986): 1151-1169, "Kant, Liberal Legacies and Foreign Affairs," *Philosophy and Public Affairs* (Summer and Fall 1983): 205-235 and 323-353 respectively.
3. John Mueller, *Retreat from Doomsday* (New York: Basic Books, 1989).
4. Francis Fukuyama, "The End of History?" *National Interest* (Summer 1989). Also see by Fukuyama, *The End of History and the Last Man* (New York: Free Press, 1992).
5. Robert Jervis, "The Future of World Politics: Will It Resemble the Past?" *International Security* (Winter 1991/92): 39-73. Also see Richard Nixon, *Seize the Moment* (New York: Simon & Schuster, 1992).
6. Arnold Wolfers, *Discord and Collaboration* (Baltimore: Johns Hopkins University Press, 1962), xvii.
7. Winston S. Churchill, *The Gathering Storm*, vol. 1 of *The Second World War* (Boston: Houghton Mifflin, 1948), 40.
8. On the slaughter of World War I, see Theodore Ropp, *War in the Modern World*, rev. ed. (New York: Collier, 1962); Hanson W. Baldwin, *World War I: An Outline History* (New York: Harper & Row, 1962); Leon Wolff, *In Flanders Field* (New York: Viking, 1958); and, particularly, Alistair Horne, *The Price of Glory: Verdun 1916* (New York: St. Martin's Press, 1962).
9. Quoted in *Political Realism and the Crisis of World Politics* by Kenneth W. Thompson (Princeton, N.J.: Princeton University Press, 1960), 18.
10. Harvard Nuclear Study Group, *Living with Nuclear Weapons* (New York: Bantam Books, 1983), 43-44.
11. On games and the strategies employed, whether formal ones as in football or baseball, or informal ones as in courting, see Eric Berne, *Games People Play* (New York: Grove Press, 1964). The title of this book obviously was influenced by Berne's. Also see John P. Lovell, *Foreign Policy in Perspective* (New York: Holt, Rinehart & Winston, 1970), part 2.
12. Lovell, *Foreign Policy in Perspective*, 65.
13. Ibid.
14. Glenn H. Snyder and Paul Diesing, *Conflict among Nations* (Princeton, N.J.: Princeton University Press, 1977), 429.
15. Carl von Clausewitz, *On War*, ed. and trans. Michael Howard and Peter Paret (Princeton, N.J.: Princeton University Press, 1976).
16. Harold D. Lasswell, *Politics: Who Gets What, When, How* (New York: Meridian Books, 1958).
17. Edward H. Carr, *The Twenty Years' Crisis, 1919-1939* (London: Macmillan, 1951), 8.
18. Ibid.
19. Ibid., 43-46, 50-53.

20. Churchill, *Gathering Storm*, iv.

21. Hans J. Morgenthau, *Politics among Nations* (New York: Knopf, 1950).

22. Wolfers, *Discord and Collaboration;* John H. Herz, *Political Realism and Political Idealism* (Chicago: University of Chicago Press, 1951); George F. Kennan, *American Diplomacy 1900-1950* (Chicago: University of Chicago Press, 1951); and Reinhold Niebuhr, *Moral Man and Immoral Society* (New York: Scribner's, 1952). Henry Kissinger was one of the younger realists. For his memoirs as the president's national security assistant and secretary of state during the years 1969-1976, see *White House Years* and *Years of Upheaval* (Boston: Little, Brown, 1979 and 1982, respectively). For a thoughtful critique, see Michael Joseph Smith, *Realist Thought from Weber to Kissinger* (Baton Rouge: Louisiana State University Press, 1987).

23. Joel H. Rosenthal, *Righteous Realists* (Baton Rouge: Louisiana State University Press, 1991). Rosenthal argues that moral principles have played as great a role in U.S. foreign policy since 1945 as power politics.

24. Klaus Knorr and James N. Rosenau, eds., *Contending Approaches to International Politics* (Princeton, N.J.: Princeton University Press, 1969); Morton Kaplan, *Systems and Process in International Politics* (New York: Wiley, 1957); James N. Rosenau, ed., *International Politics and Foreign Policy*, 2d ed. (New York: Free Press, 1969); and Rosenau, *The Scientific Study of Foreign Policy*, 2d ed. (New York: Nichols, 1980).

25. Rosenau, *International Politics and Foreign Policy;* J. David Singer, ed., *Quantitative International Politics* (New York: Free Press, 1968); Dina A. Zinnes, *Contemporary Research in International Relations* (New York: Free Press, 1976); and Herbert C. Kelman, ed., *International Behavior* (New York: Holt, Rinehart & Winston, 1965).

26. Charles W. Kegley, Jr., and Eugene R. Wittkopf, *World Politics*, 2d ed. (New York: St. Martin's Press, 1985), 21.

27. Carr, *Twenty Years' Crisis*, 3. Also see Yale H. Ferguson and Richard W. Mansbac, *The Elusive Guest* (Columbia: University of South Carolina Press, 1988), 32-34.

28. Ernst B. Haas, *The Uniting of Europe* (Stanford, Calif.: Stanford University Press, 1958).

29. Seyom Brown, *New Forces in World Politics* (Washington, D.C.: Brookings, 1974); and Robert O. Keohane and Joseph S. Nye, *Power and Interdependence* (Boston: Little, Brown, 1977).

30. Stephen D. Krasner, "Structural Causes and Regime Consequences," *International Organization* (Spring 1982): 185-206. The entire issue is devoted to regimes.

31. The basic organization of this book was suggested by Kenneth N. Waltz's notion of "three images," introduced in *Man, the State and War* (New York: Columbia University Press, 1959). Also see J. David Singer, "The Level-of-Analysis Problem in International Relations," *World Politics* (October 1961): 78-80. Only two changes have been introduced here: the order of the three images or levels of analysis has been reversed, and Waltz's first image (the third level here), based on the traditional and behavioral analysis of man, has been replaced by emphasis on official policy makers and decision making.

C H A P T E R 2

The Three Levels of Analysis: A Framework for the Study of International Politics

STATE-SYSTEM LEVEL

International politics can be analyzed on three levels: the state-system level, the nation-state level, and the decision-making level. The term *state system* refers to the international system that comprises all existing political units that interact with one another according to some regular and observable pattern of relations. The term *system* is used for two reasons. First, it encompasses all the sovereign states and therefore possesses the virtue of being *comprehensive*. Second, it helps place the focus on the relations or *interactions* among the component units. The behavior of each state depends on the behavior of other states. In gamesmanship, each player's move or "strategy"— the set of moves he or she makes in the expectation of winning—is influenced by the moves of every other player.

A system then is simply an abstract but convenient way of defining some part of reality for purposes of analysis. One speaks, for example, of a human being's circulatory system, the parts of which—veins, arteries, organs, and cells—must all work properly if the larger system is to give peak performance or to run at all. Similarly, a car has a cooling system, ignition system, electrical system, and exhaust system. Each system, in turn, has subsystems—for example, the electrical system includes a battery, alternator, and spark plugs. Each system also may be considered a subsystem of the larger system, the car. All the subsystems must work together if the car is to run properly; the failure of one affects all the others.

In international politics, each state is part of the system, and each is the guardian of its own security and independence. Each regards other states as potential enemies that may threaten fundamental interests. Consequently, states generally feel insecure and regard one another with apprehension and distrust. All become very concerned about their strength, or power. To prevent an attack, a state must be as powerful as potential aggressors; a disproportion of power may tempt another state. A "balance of power," or equilibrium, is desirable to deter an assault. "Equilibrium is balanced power, and balanced power is neutralized power." [1] A balance of power is thus a prerequisite for each nation's security, if not for its survival, as well as for the preservation of the system itself. Any attempt by any nation to expand its power and attain dominance or hegemony, which would allow it to impose its will on the other states, will be resisted. When the balance is disturbed, the tendency is to take responsive action to return to a position of equilibrium. If states disregard this operational rule that power must be counterbalanced, they place their own security in jeopardy. *"Balance of power" is therefore an empirical description of how states act (or, more accurately, how most of them, especially the great powers, act most of the time). It is also a recommendation for the way states should act.* In political scientist Inis Claude's words: "When any state or bloc becomes powerful, or threatens to become inordinately powerful, other states *should* recognize this as a threat to their security and respond by taking equivalent measures, individually or jointly, to enhance their power." [2] In short, the foreign policy of a state reflects the distribution of power within the state system; as that distribution changes, so does that state's foreign policy.

Balance of Power and U.S. Intervention in Two World Wars

The impact of a shift in the distribution of power is well demonstrated by the involvement of the United States in the two world wars of this century. The country's isolation from European "power politics" during most of the nineteenth century and the early twentieth century was the product of a balance of power on the European continent. A threat to this isolationism arose from the possibility that one state or a coalition of states might conquer most of Europe, organize its vast human and industrial resources, and use those resources to menace the United States. Britain, to protect its own security, had long opposed any state's hegemony and thereby had made it possible for the United States to maintain its isolationism. But in 1871, during its war with France, Prussia finally succeeded in uniting the German confederation, and the new Germany became the country with the largest population in Europe, except for Russia. Germany then launched a massive program of industrialization, and it was only a matter of time until its power overtook Britain's. Unlike previous occasions, British power, even when added to that of France and Russia, was not sufficiently great to defeat Germany in World War I. When czarist Russia collapsed in 1917, the transfer of German soldiers from the eastern front to the western front raised the distinct possibility of a German victory. It was at that point that Germany's unrestricted submarine warfare, which included attacks on U.S. shipping, precipitated American intervention. This intervention made it possible to contain the German spring offensive of 1918 and to bring about Germany's defeat. [3]

A little more than two decades later, the United States, which had retreated into isolationism again, was compelled once more to concern itself with the European balance of power. Germany's defeat of France in 1940 brought the United States once again face to face with the specter of an invasion and the defeat of Britain, despite the latter's large navy. President Franklin Roosevelt thus set out to strengthen Britain to withstand any Nazi assault.[4] He sent fifty old destroyers to help defend the English Channel and set up the Lend-Lease program to supply Britain with arms and ammunition. By the time of the Japanese attack on Pearl Harbor in December 1941, the United States was already engaged in an undeclared naval war with Germany in the Atlantic. American warships escorted British merchant ships filled with war supplies as far as Iceland, where the British navy took over escort duty. American merchant ships were later permitted to sail to British harbors. The American navy even reported the positions of German submarines to British warships and shot at the submarines when they allegedly shot first. The balance of power had made this larger U.S. commitment to Britain necessary, even though such actions increased the risk of war with Germany. In fact, war with Germany was merely a matter of time; German submarines sooner or later would start sinking American ships to force Britain to surrender. The German invasion of the Soviet Union in 1941 briefly postponed the Battle for the Atlantic, and when the battle did take place, the United States was already at war. But had Adolf Hitler, before Pearl Harbor, given the order to sink all ships bound for Britain, Roosevelt, like President Woodrow Wilson before him, would have had to ask Congress for a declaration of war.

Beginning of the U.S.-Soviet Cold War

Nowhere are the continuity of a policy and the degree to which the distribution of power narrows a nation's range of choices in its foreign policy revealed more clearly than in the eruption of the cold war. During World War II, the United States, allied with the Soviet Union, believed it had established the basis for a postwar era of harmony and peace.[5] American policy makers recognized that the Soviet rulers had reasons for being suspicious of the West: for example, Western intervention in the civil war that broke out in that country when the Communists seized power, and the Western appeasement of Hitler, especially in the Munich agreement, which gave the Nazi dictator the Sudetenland in Czechoslovakia—and eventually the rest of the country—and which the Kremlin might well have viewed as a Western attempt to "open the gates to the East." But Roosevelt believed that four years of wartime cooperation with the United States and Britain had dissolved Soviet suspicion of Western intentions and had replaced it with sufficient mutual respect and confidence to ensure that possible conflicts between the Soviets and the Western nations could be resolved amicably.

American policy makers apparently were unable to conceive that the Soviet Union, which they acknowledged would emerge as the new dominant power in Europe, would replace Germany as the gravest threat to the European and global balance of power.[6] During the war, the American government there-fore did not aim at reestablishing a European balance of power to safeguard the United States. It expected such security to result from a new era of Soviet-American cooperation. Indeed, in the words of American secretary of state Cordell Hull, "There will no longer be need for spheres of influence, for alliances, balance of power, or any other of the special arrangements through which, in the unhappy past, the nations strove to safeguard their security or promote their interests." [7]

Unlike the United States, with its isolationist tradition, the Soviet Union had been a longtime player of power politics. It was therefore bound to feel fearful. Russia had, after all, capitulated to Germany during World War I and had come close to defeat during World War II. And more than a century earlier, Napoleon had invaded and almost defeated it. In fact, Russia had a long history of invasions and frequent defeat. As World War II was ending, then, the Soviet Union could foresee the possibility of conflict with another Western power, whose population was almost as large as its own, whose industrial strength was far greater, and whose enormous military power had been further increased in the closing days of the war by the atomic bomb.

Thus, as the Red Army was driving back the German armies, Soviet actions were typical of a great power, regardless of its ideology, trying to provide for its security. It imposed Soviet control over all of Eastern Europe—Poland, Hungary, Bulgaria, Romania, and, after Germany's defeat, then-East Germany—and it turned the states there into satellites. Yugoslavia was already under the control of Marshal Tito, a Stalin favorite. Czechoslovakia, although under the Red Army's shadow, was not transformed into a Soviet satellite until 1948, several years later. Soviet power thus stood in the center of Europe. But this expansion also led Stalin to try to dominate Iran and to turn Turkey into another satellite in an effort to gain control of the Dardanelles and, thereby, gain access to the Mediterranean. And he backed Tito's support of the Communists in the civil war in Greece (see Figure 2-1).

These actions led to the U.S. policy of containment. As weary and devas-tated as the Soviet Union was because of the war, it emerged as a major power in the Eurasian land mass. Its armed forces were reduced—according to Nikita Khrushchev's report in 1960—from 12 million to 3 million; Western estimates in the late 1940s were 1-2 million higher, exclusive of approximately half a million security troops.[8] Still, all the other former major powers in Europe had collapsed. Germany was in ruins; France had not recovered from its defeat and occupation; and Britain foundered soon after victory. Nowhere in Europe was there any countervailing power; the only such power lay outside of Europe. Thus, the distribution of power in the state system left the United States no choice. It was not what the government wished to do that was to matter; it was what it *had* to do. A new balance had to be established. As political scientist Paul Seabury has noted, bipolarity was "a contradiction in which two powers—America and Russia—were by historical circumstances

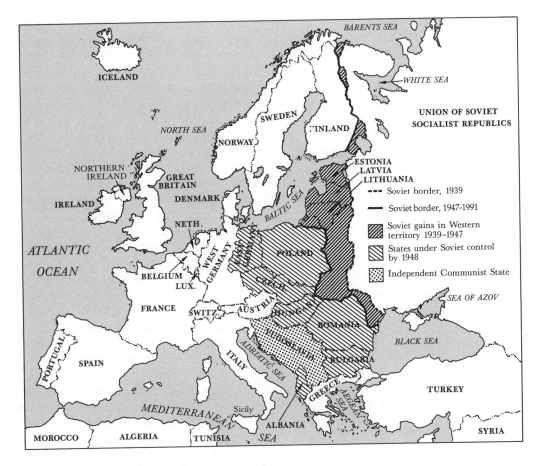

Figure 2-1 Soviet Expansion in Europe, 1939-1991

thrown into a posture of confrontation which neither had actually 'willed,' yet one from which extrication was difficult." [9] Or, as historian Louis Halle has pointed out, the historical circumstances of 1945 "had an ineluctable quality that left the Russians little choice but to move as they did. Moving as they did, they compelled the United States and its allies to move in response. And so the Cold War was joined." [10]

The United States after the Cold War

Why, now that the forty-five-year American-Soviet rivalry is over, is there still concern over the balance of power? Soviet power has retracted from its position in the center of Europe: East Germany no longer exists, having become part of a reunified, democratic Germany; Soviet troops have been withdrawn from Hungary and Czechoslovakia; and Moscow is preoccupied at home. Thus, a main cause of the cold war—the forward thrust of Soviet power—has vanished. But in a state system in which each member state is responsible for its own safety because there is no world state that can resolve conflicts among them or enforce the peace, great conflicts like the cold war may lose their intensity and possibly disappear, but they do not alter the basic character of the system or behavior of states. States still have to worry about their security and status in the system.

Old conflicts, therefore, may revive or new ones take their place. Communism is dead, and the Soviet state has given way to the Commonwealth of Independent States. But Russia, the successor state to the now disintegrated Soviet Union, is still the largest state in Europe in population and resources. And while the Russian economy after seventy-four years of communism will not be cured quickly, Russia remains a potentially formidable state with sizable conventional military forces and a nuclear arsenal rivaling that of the United States. Indeed, Communist ideology may vanish, but Russian power will not. Even if Communist ideology intensified the cold war conflict, the basic cause of conflict was Soviet power and its extension into the center of Europe.

So, although the cold war may be over, the geopolitics goes on.[11] Despite the current Russian emphasis on "partnership and friendship" with the United States, security, territorial, and economic imperatives will continue to affect both the Russian and American competition for influence; intentions can change, especially when a great power, weak at the moment, regains its strength and reasserts itself. In addition, Russia will remain the only nation that can destroy the United States. The ability of the two nuclear powers to mutually destroy one another is an existential fact with consequences. One is that each will keep a cautious eye on the other to make sure that the other does not gain some perceived advantage that might, under changing circumstances, be turned to its own disadvantage.

> [E]ach must still keep a wary eye on the other, and each must take care that his competitor-partner does not accumulate too many assets that might be turned to malign uses. And so American policy must still harken the commands of the self-help system, cooperating where it can and competing where it must.[12]

A Defense Department study of U.S. strategy in the post-cold war world specifically warned against the possible failure of democracy to take root in Russia and Ukraine and the reemergence of an authoritarian regime "bent on regenerating aggressive military power." Thus, despite the welcome improvement of relations with Russia especially, the fact that it remained the only country that could destroy the United States required the United States "to target vital aspects of the former Soviet military establishment."[13] Former president Richard Nixon too has warned of the dire consequences of a failure of Russia's transformation to democracy. It could lead to a rebirth of despotism and a new assertive foreign policy.[14]

Moreover, with the U.S.-Soviet rivalry that so long dominated the international system no longer prominent, other conflicts—even if they do not have the scope and intensity of the former superpower conflict—will take its place. The Iraqi aggression against Kuwait in August 1990 proves the point. The invasion and seizure of the tiny oil state resulted from the breakdown of the regional balance between Iran and Iraq in the Persian Gulf. During the 1970s, while still governed by the shah, Iran, then strongly pro-American, was in effect the ruler of the Gulf. But after the Shiite Muslim clerics gained power in 1979, eliminated their enemies, and consolidated their power, Iraq thought it could exploit Iran's weakness by attacking it and winning a quick victory. The resulting eight-year-long war, during which the two combatants basically neutralized one another, benefited the weaker oil kingdoms on the Gulf. When late in that war it appeared that the Iranians might finally be gaining the upper hand, the United States intervened in the Gulf, essentially helping Iraq.

But after the war ended in 1988 with Iran defeated, there no longer existed any countervailing power to Iraq's formidable forces. When its ruler, Saddam Hussein, exploited this situation in 1990, sparsely populated Saudi Arabia, feeling threatened after Iraq's invasion of its neighbor, called on the United States to defend it and free Kuwait. The United States then did so, resorting to war when diplomacy and economic sanctions failed to persuade Iraq to withdraw. But even while fighting Iraq, the United States had to keep in mind the need for a postwar balance of power. This meant that while destroying Iraq's offensive military capability to threaten other states in the region, it did not want to destroy Iraq totally, thereby enticing Syria or Iran again to seek hegemony. This would create an unstable situation.

After Iraq's downfall, civil war broke out in that country, involving the Kurds in northern Iraq (who make up 20 percent of the population) and the Shiites in southern Iraq (who constitute 55 percent of Iraq's population and share the religious faith of the Shiites in neighboring Iran, who assisted their revolt against Saddam Hussein)—the remaining 25 percent being Sunni Arabs living in central Iraq. But, for the reason just noted, the United States refused to intervene in that civil war and instead provided mainly humanitarian assistance to the hundreds of thousands of refugees fleeing Saddam's wrath and vengeance. It preferred to continue living with Saddam Hussein (at least before he played nuclear hide-and-seek in his continuing quest for nuclear weapons), to Iraq's possible dismemberment as it became a killing field like Lebanon, or external intervention as outside powers sought to feast on the nation's dying carcass. As noted, Syria and especially Iran were the most likely beneficiaries. If Iraq were to disintegrate, Iran would presumably seek to impose a fundamentalist Islamic regime on southern Iraq, perhaps even aiming to convert all of Iraq to Shiism. In any case, Iran would be the most likely to emerge as the regionally dominant power.

Whatever happens, it is in the interest not only of the United States but also of Saudi Arabia, Egypt, and Israel, that no powerful anti-Western state dominate this oil-rich area. Iraq must remain therefore an important component of a future regional balance. And so, of course, must the United States, which has become the extraregional or external balancer because the leading Arab states were unable to maintain a military balance among one another. As this early demonstration of the continuing nature of the game of "power politics" shows, American interests in the post-cold war world cannot be scaled back easily as the Soviet threat declines. Given its size, position, and weight in the balance, the United States cannot just get out of harm's way; its interests will continue to be affected by events outside its borders, such as Iraq's continuing postwar quest for nuclear weapons.

Price of Ignoring the Balance

Britain in the 1930s.   The price of failure to heed the operational rule of balancing the power of a potential opponent is loss of security and probably war. World War II, which fathered the cold war, could have been prevented if Britain and France had remobilized sufficient forces to contain Germany's various moves over a six-year period to upset the European balance.[15] Not until after Hitler had rearmed, reoccupied the Rhineland, and gobbled up Austria, the Sudetenland part of Czechoslovakia, and the rest of that country a few months later, did Britain's leaders decide that he could not be allowed to go any farther (see Figure 2-2). Hitler, however, believing that Britain's announced support of Poland was meaningless and that his latest challenge would go unmet as before, attacked Poland. Britain then declared war on Germany, as did France. World War II thus began under the worst of all possible circumstances for the Western powers because Germany was no longer the weak power it had been at the time of Hitler's first expansionist moves in the mid-1930s.

The outbreak of World War II, therefore, stands as a monument to a single lesson: decent personal motives, like those of Prime Minister Neville Chamberlain, who wanted nothing more than to spare Britain the horror of another war, do not necessarily produce successful policies. At the very least, they require an understanding of the nature of the state system, its demands on national leaders, and the rules of its operation. The American conduct of World War II was to underscore the importance of such understanding. U.S. leaders did not expect the Western coalition with the Soviet Union to collapse after Germany's defeat. They did not understand that once the common purpose had been achieved, the partners would have to concern themselves with securing their own protection in a new balance of power. They did not recognize that, even during the war, each alliance member had to take precautionary steps, in anticipation of possible future conflict and perhaps even war, to ensure itself a strong postwar position.

United States and China in the 1950s and 1960s.   The most obvious case of postwar neglect followed the 1949 collapse of Nationalist China and the

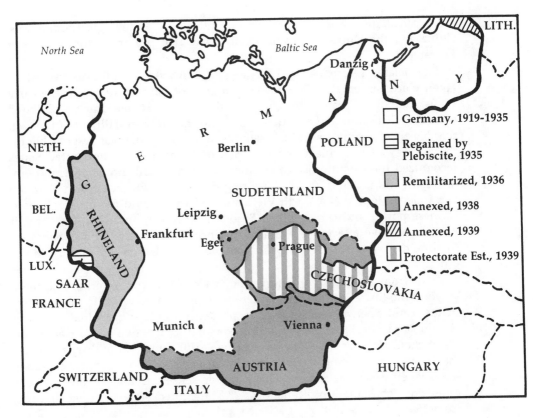

Figure 2-2 German Expansion, 1935–1939

control of mainland China by a Communist government. The new Chinese People's Republic quickly formed an alliance with the Soviet Union, which in the United States was immediately referred to as the "Sino (Chinese)-Soviet bloc," as if it were a single actor, although historically China and Russia had been antagonists. Even Stalin's Soviet Union was hardly considered a friend of the Chinese Communists in their civil war with the Nationalist government. What is amazing is that the United States did not attempt to play a "divide and rule" game. As late as the early 1960s, when President John Kennedy initially intervened in Vietnam, American policy makers continued to talk of the "Sino-Soviet bloc," even though differences between the Soviet Union and China had increased since 1956. But it was not until 1972 that an American president, Richard Nixon, exploited this growing split between the two Communist giants. During the 1960s and early 1970s, Soviet military power had grown enormously; in 1969 came the first of a number of border clashes. Fearing for their security, the Chinese Communists were looking for a way to deter a possible Soviet attack. Simultaneously, the United States, weary of international involvement after the Vietnam War, was looking for help in containing the increasingly powerful Soviet Union. The Sino-American reconciliation was a natural result. Putting aside ideological differences, China and the United States acted in a way that preserved the balance of power.

This belated reconciliation had one cost, however. Had the reconciliation taken place earlier, the Vietnam War might not have occurred. In the early 1960s, the United States thought not only that the Soviet Union and China were still close allies but also that China was the far more militant of the two, that North Vietnam was China's satellite, and that China was responsible for the strategy of guerrilla warfare in South Vietnam. Had the United States recognized the Communist government early and had diplomatic representatives in China, the United States might have known that North Vietnam was independent, that a North Vietnamese victory would not have enhanced Chinese power and certainly not Sino-Soviet power, and, therefore, that it would not have affected the central balance between the United States on the one hand and the Soviet Union, or the Soviet Union and China, on the other.

Aside from avoiding U.S. intervention in Vietnam, the American failure to exploit Sino-Soviet differences represented an even more profound mistake. In any conflict between major powers, prudence would suggest that no power should face more opponents than it needs to; if it faces two or more adversaries, it should concentrate on the most powerful opponent and try to isolate that power by drawing the others away from it. Why confront two strong states when it is unnecessary? This common-sense and logical rule has been called the "conservation of enemies." [16] The United States ignored that rule from 1949 to 1972—and paid a heavy price.

Why did Britain in the 1930s and the United States during the cold war years follow the wrong course of action? The second and third levels of analysis will give the answer.

NATION-STATE LEVEL

While the state-system level of analysis emphasizes the *external* determinants of state behavior, the nation-state level attributes such behavior to *internal* characteristics: political system, historical experience, nature of the economy, or social structure. The emphasis is not on the likeness of states, the similarity of their motives, or the insignificant impact of domestic attributes. Rather, it is on the differences among states in motivations, attitudes, and internal composition or domestic structure. States are therefore categorized as democratic, revolutionary, capitalist, developing, and so forth—the democratic and revolutionary states are described below. Political scientists and diplomatic historians frequently have attributed certain characteristic patterns of behavior to such categories.

Democratic States

Allegedly, democratic states behave differently than nondemocratic states. For example, it has been hypothesized that democracies are basically peaceful. One reason for this hypothesis is the accountability of the rulers of democratic states to those they govern. Thus, given regular elections, it is not surprising that successive British governments were sensitive to public opinion and a mood that throughout the period between the two world wars was overwhelmingly influenced by memories of World War I. Democratic leaders, not unnaturally, also believe in compromise and the peaceful resolution of conflicting interests. In Britain, there was a widespread popular demand that another bloodletting be avoided if at all possible. British leaders thought they had no choice; the antiwar mood was far too pervasive. In 1933, the students of the Oxford Union passed a resolution refusing "to fight for King and country." In 1935, there was a general election in which Prime Minister Chamberlain, knowing that Britain should rearm, pledged not to do so because he felt certain that favoring rearmament would lose the election for the Conservatives. Germany, it was widely believed, had some legitimate grievances outstanding from the harsh peace imposed on it at the end of World War I. If these grievances could be satisfied by a conciliatory policy and a willingness to compromise, war could be avoided. In 1938, cheering British crowds welcomed Chamberlain back from Munich, assured that he had brought them "peace in our time." [17]

A second and more fundamental reason for democracies' alleged peaceful behavior is the increasing mass participation in voting and political decision making. As a result, these countries are primarily oriented inward, concerned with social programs to improve the electorate's lives and standard of living. Democracies have become welfare states. In the absence of clearly visible and recognizable threats to their security, they do not spend much money on arms. Popular interest in foreign affairs is at best sporadic, responding to specific crises; only then will money be allocated for arms.[18] Modern democratic societies, moreover, emphasize values—such as health, education, and welfare—that are in conflict with the conduct of foreign policies that emphasize force and killing.

These generalizations help explain Britain's policies during the 1930s. The British propensity to look inward was enforced by the need to do something about the economy, which even before the Great Depression was suffering large-scale unemployment. Foreign policy became a secondary matter. Memories of the war of 1914-1918 reinforced this ordering of priorities. It was not until Hitler's immense threat to Britain's security became *unambiguously clear* to both the public and its leaders that foreign policy became more important than domestic policy. Then Britain took a firm stand opposing further German expansion, and the result was World War II.

The war that broke out in September 1939 was the second in twenty years to have been precipitated by Germany. It was also the twentieth century's second total war—a war fought for the total destruction and unconditional surrender of the enemy. Again, the democratic typology can be used to analyze what happened. George Kennan, American diplomat and scholar, has noted that, when democracies turn from their inward, peaceful preoccupations toward the external arena and are compelled to fight, they become ferocious:

> A democracy is peace-loving. It does not like to go to war. It is slow to rise to provocation. When it has once been provoked to the point where it must grasp the sword, it does not easily forgive its adversary for having produced this situation. The fact of the provocation then becomes itself the issue. Democracy fights in anger—it fights for the very reason that it was forced to go to war. It fights to punish the power that was rash enough and hostile enough to provoke it—to teach that power a lesson it will not forget, to prevent the thing from happening again. Such a war must be carried to the bitter end.[19]

Various reasons have been adduced to support this hypothesis about the warlike nature of democracy once it is engaged in military conflict. If war and violence are considered evil—the very denial of democracy's humanitarian ideals—their use demands a moral stance; when it becomes necessary to resort to force, it must be for defensive and noble reasons. The complete destruction of the aggressor regime—particularly if its way of life is authoritarian (as was that of Germany) and therefore by democratic standards inferior, immoral, and warlike—becomes a spiritually uplifting cause. Once destroyed, the vanquished nation can be sent to democratic reform school and transformed into a peaceful state. But beyond this general need for moral justification lies the reality of war. War disturbs the scale of social priorities in an individualistic and materialistic culture. It separates families, it kills and wounds, it demands economic sacrifice, and it imposes regimentation and discipline. If a society that emphasizes personal dignity and the development of individual, family, and social welfare must go to war, the sacrifices demanded must be commensurate with some wholesome, ennobling, and morally transcending goal. Total victory, in this context, becomes the minimum aim.

Yet, if the above thesis about democratic behavior in peacetime is correct, then an optimistic conclusion can be drawn about the post-cold war era. Regardless of Britain's reaction to Nazi Germany and the democracies' crusading style in hot and cold wars against undemocratic and antidemocratic nations, democracies can be expected to behave peacefully toward one another.[20] The absence in modern times of wars among democracies may stem perhaps from the fact that until recently there were only a relatively small number of such states and they were not always neighbors. Nevertheless, this record contrasts starkly with the number of wars among undemocratic states and between democratic and undemocratic states. Since democracy, after all, is a system based on elections, voting, compromise, and the peaceful settlement of conflicting interests, democratic leaders may therefore presume that similar disputes among like-minded states also should be settled by conciliation rather than force. Moreover, democracies can hardly claim the right to rule other democratic states because they believe in each democracy's claim to self-determination. Thus, democratic leaders cannot justify a war against a fellow democracy. It is one thing to crusade against a tyranny to free its people, but quite another to free people already free.[21]

The recent spreading of democracy to Eastern Europe and to countries in Asia and Latin America, despite at times painful progress and even setbacks and some reversals, is thus a most hopeful sign that war will become a less-frequent occurrence than in the past. At least among the advanced industrial countries, who fought two world wars in this century, war is unlikely to recur now that they are all democratic. Germany and France, after fighting three wars since 1870, are today allies and partners in the formation of a united Europe. If there is one reason that, despite bad memories about German aggression in the past, its former enemies in Europe, west and east, do not expect a repeat performance, it is the internal transformation of Germany from an authoritarian state under the kaiser and a totalitarian state under Hitler to a democratic one since its defeat and occupation by the Western democracies: the United States, Britain, and France.[22]

In officially declaring the end of the cold war on November 20, 1990, and signing the Charter of Paris, the thirty-five member states of the Conference on Security and Cooperation in Europe (CSCE)—which includes the United States, Canada, and all European states, North Atlantic Treaty Organization (NATO) and former Warsaw Pact members, as well as neutral states—declared democracy to be the basis of the new European order. Later, in 1991, after they gained independence from the Soviet Union, the three Baltic republics became members of the CSCE. At that time, Mikhail Gorbachev suggested to a CSCE human rights conference meeting in Moscow that the "human dimension" should become the foundation of what he called the "common European house."[23] After Gorbachev's disappearance from power after the Soviet Union's collapse, the CSCE in early 1992 admitted ten more former Soviet republics, signaling their formal acceptance as independent states in the European society of nations.

Revolutionary States

Whether democratic France in aristocratic Europe in the late eighteenth and early nineteenth centuries or the Soviet Union in the twentieth century, the *revolutionary state* (a term coined by Henry Kissinger) presents a total challenge to the international order.[24] Unlike traditional states that recognize one another's right to live and accept the principle of live and let live, the revolutionary state repudiates the existing order by not accepting the legitimacy of the other states in the system because of their different socioeconomic systems; it rejects their domestic structures. The revolutionary state's leaders pose two questions: Why do the masses live in poverty, ill health, and ignorance? Why is the human race constantly cursed by war? The revolutionaries point accusingly at the *ancien régime*. The majority of people are destitute because they are exploited by a privileged minority. Wars are fought because they pay dividends in the form of enhanced prestige, territorial acquisition, and economic gains. Although the few profit, it is the masses who are compelled to do most of the fighting and dying. People can be freed from economic exploitation, political subjugation, and international violence only by the destruction of the existing system and the overthrow of the ruling classes. In short, the revolutionary state condemns the existing order as unjust and assumes the duty of bringing *justice* to humanity.

By the very nature of its belief, the revolutionary state is thus committed to universal goals—that is, to transforming the prevailing political, economic, and cultural system that has condemned humanity to eternal slavery and to creating a "new order" in which, for the first time in history, people will be truly free from oppression and need. The proclamation issued by the National Convention of the Republic after the French Revolution is characteristic of the revolutionary state as a missionary power engaged in a "just war" to establish eternal domestic social justice and international peace:

> The French Nation declares that it will treat as enemies every people who, refusing liberty and equality or renouncing them, may wish to maintain, recall, or treat with the prince and the privileged classes; on the other hand, it engages not to subscribe to any treaty and not to lay down its arms until the sovereignty and independence of the people whose territory the troops of the Republic shall have entered shall be established, and until the people shall have adopted the principles of equality and founded a free and democratic government.[25]

Revolutionary states, in short, are likely to attack nonrevolutionary countries. Indeed, on occasion the nations who may be potential victims may launch a preventive war.

If this typology of revolutionary states is valid, in the years immediately after World War II Stalin's Soviet Union viewed the United States not as just another state trapped by the same security problems but as a capitalist state that was its enemy. And no words to the contrary, professing peaceful intentions, could persuade it otherwise.[26] Thus, the Soviet leader rejected the notion that national insecurity and international conflict were the result primarily of the state system. He believed that international antagonism and hostility, as well as domestic poverty, unemployment, ill health, and ignorance, were caused by the internal nature of the leading states in the system. Capitalism was viewed as the cause of all social evil. Only in a political system in which the Communist party, representing the exploited majority (the proletariat), had control and in which all the forces of production were removed from private ownership so that they could be used for the benefit of all people, instead of for the profit of the privileged few, could human beings finally live free from social injustice, deprivation, and war. As a total critique of capitalist society and a promise to deliver the masses from evil and bring them domestic justice and external peace, communism in fact constituted a secular religion of damnation and salvation. It conferred upon the Soviet

Union the messianic duty of converting all people to the "true faith" (see Chapter 9).

Consequently, according to this interpretation of the foreign policy behavior of a revolutionary state, the Soviet Union was engaged in an irreconcilable struggle with non-Communist states, seeking hegemony in the state system. Soviet hostility toward the West predated 1945 because it was to a large degree ideological and preconceived.[27] V. I. Lenin and Stalin had felt it even before they seized power and before Western governments had adopted anti-Soviet policies. It was an enmity deduced from principles and based not on what Western governments did but on what they were alleged to be; Western actions were almost irrelevant. Once non-Communist states were declared hostile and official declarations and policies were formulated on that assumption, it was hardly astounding that the West became less friendly and that Soviet leaders reaped the fruits of the policies that they had sown. Communist ideology, in short, raised the level of mutual fear and suspicion resulting from the state system and caused Stalin's Soviet Union to undertake both "defensive expansionism" (because of its enhanced apprehension of capitalist attack) and "offensive expansionism" (because of its determination to expand the socialist world).

Any modus vivendi like the one finally worked out between czarist Russia and the monarchies of Britain, France, and Austria-Hungary in 1815 after Napoleon's defeat was, in the circumstances of 1945, therefore excluded. According to the second level of analysis, the cold war would have erupted regardless of the emergence of bipolarity because Russia had become the *Soviet Union,* and its aims and objectives extended far beyond those historically entertained by the czars.

It is not only that the revolutionary state cannot envision long-term coexistence with traditional states; it has difficulty accepting other revolutionary states as equals as well. Because its leaders believe that their ideology gives them special insight into the historical processes, legitimates their power and right to govern, and instills in them a monopoly on the knowledge of how to create the truly just society here on earth—not in the life hereafter—they claim total power domestically. They do not tolerate domestic criticism and opposition, and there is no such thing as a loyal opposition. Opposition is considered counterrevolutionary and is to be squashed. Therefore, even when several revolutionary states share the same ideological outlook, they cannot coexist as equals. Each state claims that its reading of the ideology is the correct one and dismisses contrary views as heretical. As for its leaders, not having been raised with the democratic spirit of tolerance and compromise—but rather ideological conformity and rooting out of dissent—the relationship can only be an unequal one. Smaller states become satellites, and because the larger and stronger states are unwilling to accept this status, a schism among them tends to occur. A cooperative and peaceful world, as among democratic states, is unlikely among revolutionary states.

DECISION-MAKING LEVEL

Who actually makes foreign policy decisions? Common sense says that "the United States" does not make these decisions; the people who occupy the official political positions responsible for foreign policy do. It is this decision-making level of analysis that is probably the most familiar to many people. At election time, Americans debate the virtues of the leading candidates, their expressed and implied views, their alleged values, and groups to which they may be beholden. Citizens watch how candidates handle themselves on television—whether or not they have "substance," are sincere, and remain cool under pressure. Apparently, who is president matters. It affects the priorities between domestic and foreign policies, the kinds of foreign policies that will be adopted, the extensiveness of foreign commitments, and the weapons to be produced.

Three aspects of decision making are emphasized here: the policy maker's perceptions of the world, the different kinds of decisions made, and the corresponding decision-making processes. The central point of the decision-making approach is that it allows an observer to understand and analyze individual decisions in some detail. This approach is particularly revealing when a state's actions do not seem consistent with first- or second-level expectations. How does one explain a state's policy that appears to ignore the balance of power? If a certain category of state—for example, revolutionary—is supposed to produce a particular type of behavior, but two states of that type act quite differently, how does one account for that? A look at the leaders who made the decisions, their responsibilities and perspectives, and the way their decisions were arrived at is likely to reveal the answers.

Policy Makers and Their Perceptions

The first aspect of decision making—policy makers' perceptions of the world—is very important for the obvious reason that it is the link between the external environment and policy decisions: the real world is the world perceived, whether correctly or not. The emergence of World War II provides a good illustration.

In the 1930s, British prime minister Chamberlain not only shared his fellow citizens' desire to avoid another total war but also thought his policy of appeasing Hitler's demands would achieve that end. He thought this because he saw Hitler as one of his own kind, a statesman who had been born and bred in a system founded on nationalism. He could even cite a supporting precedent, for Otto von Bismarck, after Germany's unification in 1871, had declared that Germany was satisfied and would thereafter support the new European status quo. Hitler talked in terms of national self-determination, and why should Chamberlain not believe that the new German leader was merely a cruder version of the Prussian aristocrat and German chancellor; that he, too, would be sated once he had achieved his apparently nationalistic aims. If Nazi Germany had, in fact, been merely a nationalist state, the differences between it and France and Britain could probably have been resolved without precipitating a war. But Hitler harbored aims beyond restoring Germany's 1914 frontiers.

Winston Churchill, from his understanding of British history, knew that Britain's foreign policy had long been one of opposition to any power seeking to dominate Europe, whether Philip II of Spain, Louis XIV or Napoleon of France, or the German kaiser. He perceived each of Hitler's limited demands and moves as part of a larger pattern that would lead to Germany's destruction of the European equilibrium. For this reason, he counseled opposition, condemned the Munich agreement, and ridiculed Chamberlain's claim that he had brought back "peace in our time." Instead, Churchill said bluntly, "We have sustained a total and unmitigated defeat." [28] As Churchill himself intimated, had he been prime minister in the late 1930s, World War II might have been avoided. Churchill's perception of Hitler and Nazi objectives was correct, Chamberlain's perception mistaken. Possibly Churchill could have convinced the British public of the true nature of the Nazi regime, placed the German dictator's repeated demands in their proper perspective, and led Britain to oppose *his* moves and speed up rearmament.

Vietnam illustrates the issue of perception even more poignantly. American participation in the Vietnam War, which ranks as one of the most unpopular wars in American history, often has been cited as an instance of misperception by the administrations of John Kennedy and Lyndon Johnson. Kennedy's inaugural address, it is said, was permeated with a sense of the bipolar conflict and confrontation of the 1940s and 1950s.[29] He pledged that the United States would be

> unwilling to witness or permit the slow undoing of those human rights to which this nation has always been committed, and to which we are committed today at home and around the world. . . . We shall pay any price, bear any burden, meet any hardship, support any friend, oppose any foe, in order to assure the survival and the success of liberty.

His conviction that the nation confronted a united and aggressive Communist bloc was reinforced by the Soviet Union's announcement that it would support wars of national liberation. Not surprisingly, therefore, when such a war broke out in South Vietnam, the administration thought that the Soviets or Chinese had instigated it and, starting in 1961, sent in more than 16,000 military "advisers." [30] A few weeks before his death, Kennedy declared that, if South Vietnam fell, it would "give the impression that the wave of the future in Southeast Asia was China and the Communists." [31] Johnson, who relied principally on his predecessor's counselors for his policy advice, certainly saw the issue that way and in 1965 began massive U.S. intervention.

Critics of the war claim that the commitment of military advisers by Kennedy and of half a million troops by Johnson was based on the "old myths" of the cold war instead of the "new realities" that had begun to emerge in the mid-1960s.[32] One of these new realities was that the Communist bloc was badly fragmented along nationalistic lines. An extension of Hanoi's control to South Vietnam, therefore, did not mean parallel extension of Soviet or Chinese power. Indeed, it was argued, a nationalistic Communist Vietnam would be a barrier to an extension of Chinese power. Nor would the loss of Saigon mean the collapse of neighboring nations; whether successful guerrilla wars occurred in those countries would depend on their indigenous conditions. In short, had the perceptions of the policy makers during the Kennedy-Johnson period more accurately reflected the changing nature of the international system, the United States could have avoided becoming involved in South Vietnam.

Different Policies, Different Policy Processes

Policy makers make, of course, different kinds of decisions, the second aspect of decision making, and they arrive at them by different means, the third aspect of decision making. Three kinds of decisions and policies—crisis, security, and domestic—are described here. (The distinctions among them, although discussed here specifically in the context of American foreign policy, are broadly applicable to other democracies, if not most states.)

In the past, the first, crisis policy, has been related primarily to great-power confrontations, especially direct U.S.-Soviet confrontations. They were considered crises because of the possibility of escalation to nuclear war. The frequent cold war crises over Berlin always posed this danger, although the most serious remains the Cuban missile confrontation in 1962. In crises, decision making "rises to the top." [33] Relatively few policy makers participate: the president, the principal presidential foreign policy advisers, and other selected officials and advisers. The bureaucracy is largely bypassed in the making of a crisis policy, but it plays the primary role in carrying it out. Congress plays virtually no role as well. Time is too short for major opposition to be heard and have an impact; in a crisis Congress essentially rallies around the flag.

Security policy refers to the more normal noncrisis foreign and defense policies. Such policies range from foreign-aid bills and defense budgets to arms control policies, arms transfers to allies and other friendly nations, organization and operation of the government's intelligence apparatus, and, not least, conduct of limited wars. In contrast to crisis policy, these policies involve a far larger number of policy makers and much more time is needed to arrive at decisions. The executive branch continues to act as initiator of the policy and, usually, to play the central role. In addition to the president and White House staff concerned with national security affairs, all the bureaucracies officially responsible for the conduct of foreign policy, such as the State Department and Defense Department, are involved. Other actors might be the Congress, interest groups, and the public. Before the Vietnam War, these latter usually had supported presidential policy; since Vietnam, they often have been more critical and opposed. Nevertheless, the initiative and responsibility for foreign policy remain primarily with the executive branch.

Domestic policy and intermestic policy (stemming from the telescoping of the words *international* and *domestic,* and denoting erosion of the traditional distinction between foreign and domestic policies) revolve largely, although not exclusively, around the objective of welfare or prosperity. In most nations of the world, especially democratic ones, people have increasingly expected governments to provide economic growth, rising incomes, and many social programs. For most citizens, these pocketbook issues are more important than most foreign policies. In recent years, however, many domestic issues have become entangled with foreign policy as the economic health of nations has grown more and more dependent on importing raw materials or exporting manufactured goods or food items. In the United States, these domestic/intermestic issues involve by far the largest number of actors. The jurisdictions of most executive departments are domestic, even if they have an increasing interest in foreign policy and economic issues. Congress, which considers its expertise in domestic affairs far greater than its skill in foreign ones, therefore plays a much larger role in domestic/intermestic policy and often takes the initiative. Interest groups and the various "publics" concerned with domestic/intermestic issues also are active and assertive.

Presidential leadership is the most dramatically visible in crisis policy, the least in domestic and intermestic policies. The more bureaucrats, legislators, and interest groups involved in the policy process, and the more time available to reach decisions, the more constrained the presidential leadership will be (see Figure 2-3).

COMBINING THE THREE LEVELS

One question remains: Which level of analysis should be used in understanding international politics? In this book all three are used. Although the state-system level is fundamental, it cannot by itself explain the world politics of the post-cold war era. One final look at two of the different and previously mentioned historical experiences that have molded the present-day world may help one understand why.

British Policy before World War II

As stressed in the earlier discussion of British policy toward Germany in the late 1930s, the first-level or state-system analysis will reveal that Britain did not adopt the policies it should have leading up to World War II, largely because of the pacifist mood of the British public and Prime Minister Chamberlain's misperception of Hitler's intentions. The second-level (nation-state) and third-level (decision-making) analyses explain why Chamberlain pursued the policies he did. If Churchill had been prime minister, war might have been avoided, for he perceived Hitler's aims correctly. Indeed, had a British leader been able to explain to the public the dire threat to the nation's security

Increasing degree of presidential leadership

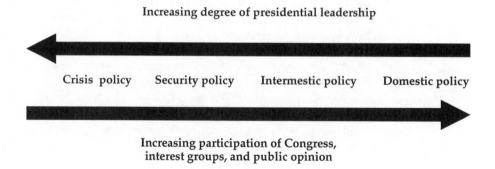

Crisis policy   Security policy   Intermestic policy   Domestic policy

Increasing participation of Congress,
interest groups, and public opinion

Figure 2-3 Different Policies, Different Actor Participation

with Churchill's eloquence and persuasiveness, Britain might have stood up to Hitler.

But is this analysis of what would have happened an accurate one? It is doubtful. Memories of World War I were too vivid, the desire to avoid its repetition too strong. Chamberlain's policy of appeasement was quite representative of British opinion. How horrible, he had said in a radio address when war with Germany over Czechoslovakia loomed, that the British should be digging trenches and trying on gas masks because of a quarrel in a faraway country between people of whom they knew nothing.[34] When Hitler's message that he would see Chamberlain at Munich arrived, the prime minister was addressing the House of Commons. Interrupting his speech with the news, he was cheered by the Commons. "At once pandemonium broke forth. Everyone was on his feet, cheering, tossing his order papers in the air, some members in tears. It was an unprecedented and most unparliamentary outburst of mass hysteria and relief, in which a few did not join." [35] Upon his return from Germany, Chamberlain was met by a jubilant crowd.

Perhaps the most significant and symbolic aspect of Churchill's career during the late 1930s was precisely that he was not a member of the government. Like Cassandra, he stood with a small group warning of "the gathering storm" over Europe. But Britain did not want to hear him. Churchill was widely condemned as a warmonger in the 1930s. Even when war erupted, Churchill did not take over the prime ministry from the man whose policies had failed so dismally. Chamberlain did not fall until after Germany's unexpected takeover of Denmark and the defeat of British forces in Norway in the spring of 1940. It took both the outbreak of war and a disaster to make Churchill prime minister.

Although the state-system level of analysis can suggest what Britain should have done, the nation-state and decision-making levels best explain what actually happened. The state-system level correctly predicted that failure to play by the rules of the game would mean loss of security and the necessity to fight a war to recover it. But the climate of British public opinion ruled out doing what should have been done. As this example shows, one must be careful not to exaggerate the importance of a nation's leader. Foreign policy is not simply a reflection of his or her preferences and perceptions. The leader makes policy within the confines of a state system, a national political system, and a specific policy process.

U.S. Policy after World War II

The immediate postwar policy in the United States is a striking example of the mutually reinforcing nature of all three levels of analysis. "Rarely has freedom been more clearly the recognition of necessity," observed Harvard political scientist, Stanley Hoffmann, "and statesmanship the imaginative exploitation of necessity. America rushed to those gates at which Soviet power was knocking." [36] At the nation-state and decision-making levels, policy makers ended up doing what they had to do. After the surrender of Japan, eighteen months passed before the official declaration of the containment policy. The American desire for peace, symbolized by a massive postwar demobilization, was intense. Hostile Soviet acts were necessary to erode the widespread admiration for the Soviet Union, the result of the latter's heroic wartime resistance. Not until Britain's support for Greece and Turkey was withdrawn in early 1947 did the United States face the fact that only it possessed the power to establish a new balance of power that would secure both Europe and America while preserving the peace. [37]

President Harry Truman was keenly aware of the strategic significance of the eastern Mediterranean and went before a joint session of Congress to explain to the whole country the new situation facing the United States. American expectations for postwar cooperation with Moscow had by then vanished. Truman was therefore able to mobilize both congressional and popular support for an anti-Soviet policy. [38] Thus, in this example, the state-system level is of primary importance in explaining U.S. policy. The nation-state and decision-making levels reveal how accurately the policy makers perceived "reality" and how they were able in a democratic society to mobilize popular support for the new containment policy.

The Post-Cold War Era

If the British example suggests that a country's policy may be contrary to the one that, according to the first level of analysis, it should have adopted, and that the other two levels can explain the reasons for that country not doing what it should have done, and if the post–World War II example of U.S. foreign policy demonstrates how all three levels can reinforce one another in explaining American policy as it shifted from one of ally of the Soviet Union to its adversary, then the post–cold war period is an apt instance of divergent analyses. At the first level, as long as there are states, the political-military game will continue. The Soviet Union may disappear as a great power, but Russia (or perhaps a new, reconstituted union if the Commonwealth of Independent States fails) will some day become a principal actor again. Even if Russia does not renew czarist and Soviet Russia's historic expansion, other states and challengers may do so. It could be a large state, a China or India, only potential superpowers today, or a smaller state, such as Iraq, armed with modern weapons of mass destruction.[39] The "games nations play" did not end with the conclusion of the Napoleonic wars or of World Wars I and II. And there is little reason to believe that the end of the cold war will be any different. Among competing states, clashing interests and conflicts are unavoidable.

The second level of analysis, however, would come to the opposite conclusion. If democracy is associated with peaceful behavior in the international arena, then the spread of democracy to Eastern Europe and the former Soviet Union, if it takes root, as well as its recent growth in Latin America and parts of Asia, however fragile, cannot but benefit peace. While democracies have fought many wars, they have not attacked each other. Logically, therefore, a largely or wholly democratic world will be a peaceful world. Democratic leaders, responsible to their publics and held accountable by elections, will tend to settle differences with other democratic states by compromise, as they do in domestic politics.

In the remainder of this book, the three levels of analysis are discussed in three sections. Part Two focuses on the state system; Part Three concentrates on the second and third levels; and Part Four analyzes the means that states use to achieve their aims. Part Five then deals with the possible transformation of the state system to a global system. But, in fact, the division is not quite that neat. An analysis of the state system cannot be separated, for example, from the policy makers' perceptions of the system or from crisis decision making. And, in analyzing the second and third levels, it is not always possible to keep the specific political system separate from decision-making institutions and processes. Nevertheless, the broad distinction between the external environment in which states exist and the internal characteristics of the specific actors remains paramount.

For Review

1. At the first level of analysis, what special insights into how states behave are gained by focusing on how states interact?
2. What role does "balance of power" play in international politics?
3. How do the first-level explanations of international politics differ from those at the second level of analysis?
4. At the second level, what are the alleged relationships between the different types of states and their foreign policies?
5. How does the third-level focus on policy makers and governmental decision-making institutions help explain state behavior?

Notes

1. Nicholas J. Spykman, *America's Strategy in World Politics* (New York: Harcourt, 1942), 21. Also see Raymond Aron, *Peace and War* (Garden City, N.Y.: Doubleday, 1966); and Stanley Hoffmann, *The State of War* (New York: Holt, Rinehart & Winston, 1965). For a more extensive discussion of the various ways in which analysts use the term *balance of power*, see Ernst B. Haas, "The Balance of Power: Prescription, Concept, or Propaganda," *World Politics* (July 1953): 442-477; and Inis L. Claude, Jr., *Power and International Relations* (New York: Random House, 1962), 11-39.

2. Claude, *Power and International Relations*, 43 (emphasis added).

3. Edward H. Buehrig, *Woodrow Wilson and the Balance of Power* (Bloomington: Indiana University Press, 1955); and Arthur S. Link, *Wilson the Diplomatist* (Baltimore: Johns Hopkins University Press, 1957), passim, esp. 61-90.

4. For the period 1937-1941, the most detailed analysis is found in *The Challenge to Isolation* by William L. Langer and S. Everett Gleason (New York: Harper & Row, 1952); and Langer and Gleason, *The Undeclared War* (New York: Harper & Row, 1953). A briefer study is *The Reluctant Belligerent* by Robert A. Divine (New York: Wiley, 1965).

5. William H. McNeill, *America, Britain and Russia—Their Cooperation and Conflict, 1941-1946* (London: Oxford University Press, 1953), written for the Royal Institute of International Affairs; and Herbert Feis, *Churchill-Roosevelt-Stalin: The War They Waged and the Peace They Sought* (Princeton, N.J.: Princeton University Press, 1957). A shorter study is *American Diplomacy during the Second World War, 1941-1945* by Gaddis Smith (New York: Wiley, 1966). A recent study that tells the story by focusing on the leaders is Robin Edmonds, *The Big Three* (New York: Norton, 1991).

6. Robert E. Sherwood, *Roosevelt and Hopkins: An Intimate History* (New York: Harper & Row, 1948), 748.

7. Cordell Hull, *The Memoirs of Cordell Hull* (New York: Macmillan, 1948), 2: 1314-1315. Also see Sherwood, *Roosevelt and Hopkins*, 70, for the post-Yalta view of the president's closest adviser. An overall evaluation of Roosevelt as a wartime leader may be found in Warren F. Kimball, *The Juggler* (Princeton, N.J.: Princeton University Press, 1991).

8. Thomas W. Wolfe, *Soviet Power and Europe, 1945-1970* (Baltimore: Johns Hopkins University Press, 1970), 10.

9. Paul E. Seabury, *The Rise and Decline of the Cold War* (New York: Basic Books, 1967), 59.

10. Louis J. Halle, *The Cold War as History* (New York: Harper & Row, 1967), xiii.

11. Bruce Porter, "The Coming Resurgence of Russia," *National Interest* (Spring 1991): 14-23.

12. Josef Joffe, "Entangled Forever," *National Interest* (Fall 1990): 37-38.

13. Patrick E. Tyler, "U.S. Strategy Plan Calls for Insuring Rivals Develop," and "Excerpts from Pentagon's Plan: 'Preventing the Re-emergence of a New Rival,'" *New York Times*, March 8, 1992.

14. Richard Nixon, "The Challenge We Face in Russia," *Wall Street Journal*, March 11, 1992.

15. William J. Newman, *The Balance of Power in the Interwar Years, 1919-1939* (New York: Random House, 1968); Arnold Wolfers, *Britain and France between Two Wars* (New York: Norton, 1966); Winston S. Churchill, *The Gathering Storm*, vol. 1 of *The*

Second World War (Boston: Houghton Mifflin, 1948), 90; and Donald Cameron Watt, *How War Came* (New York: Pantheon Books, 1989).

16. Frederick H. Hartmann, *The Relations of Nations*, 6th ed. (New York: Macmillan, 1983), 18.

17. Among other sources on this period, see Churchill, *Gathering Storm;* Charles L. Mowat, *Britain between the Wars, 1918-1940* (Chicago: University of Chicago Press, 1955); and A. J. P. Taylor, *English History, 1914-1945* (New York: Oxford University Press, 1965).

18. Walter Lippmann has defined the role of democratic public opinion negatively. Precisely because of its emphasis on wealth and welfare, Lippmann argues, democratic opinion makes it difficult to take the necessary preparations to avoid war:

    The rule to which there are few exceptions . . . is that at the critical junctures, when the stakes are high, the prevailing mass opinion will impose what amounts to a veto upon changing the course on which the government is at the time proceeding. Prepare for war in time of peace? No. It is bad to raise taxes, to unbalance the budget, to take men away from their schools or their jobs, to provoke the enemy.

    Walter Lippmann, *The Public Philosophy* (Boston: Little, Brown, 1955), 19-20.

19. George F. Kennan, *American Diplomacy 1900-1950* (Chicago: University of Chicago Press, 1951), 65-66.

20. R. J. Rummel, "Libertarianism and International Violence," *Journal of Conflict Resolution* (March 1983): 27-71. A more skeptical analysis may be found in Maoz Zeev and Abdolali Nasrin, "Regime Types and International Conflict, 1816-1976," *Journal of Conflict Resolution* (March 1989): 3-35. Also see Robert L. Rothstein, "Democracy, Conflict, and Development in the Third World," *Washington Quarterly* (Spring 1991): 43-63.

21. Michael Doyle, "Liberalism and World Politics," *American Political Science Review* (December 1986): 1151-1169. Also see Randolph L. Schweller, "Domestic Structure and Preventive War: Are Democracies More Pacific?" *World Politics* (January 1992): 235-269. For an empirical and opposing view, see Steve Chan, "Mirror on the Wall . . . Are the Freer Countries More Pacific?" *Journal of Conflict Resolution* (December 1984): 617-648.

22. Stephen Van Evera, "Primed for Peace: Europe after the Cold War," *International Security* (Winter 1990/1991): 7-57.

23. Excerpts from the Charter of Paris may be found in R. W. Apple, "35 Lands Proclaim a United Europe in Paris Charter," *New York Times,* November 22, 1990. Also see Craig R. Whitney, "Moscow Rights Conference Sees Danger in Nationalism," *New York Times,* September 11, 1991.

24. Henry A. Kissinger, *Nuclear Weapons and Foreign Policy* (New York: Harper & Row, 1957), 326; and Kissinger, *A World Restored* (New York: Grosset & Dunlap, 1964). Also see Stephen M. Walt, "Revolution and War," *World Politics* (April 1992): 321-368.

25. Quoted from Carlton J. H. Hayes, *The Historical Evolution of Modern Nationalism* (New York: Macmillan, 1950), 40.

26. Among the many works on the beginning of the cold war, see John Lewis Gaddis, "The Emerging Post-Revisionist Synthesis on the Origins of the Cold War," *Diplomatic History* (Summer 1983): 171-204; Vojtech Mastny, *Russia's Road to the Cold War* (New York: Columbia University Press, 1979); William Taubman, *Stalin's*

American Policy (New York: Norton, 1982); and Randall B. Woods, *Dawning of the Cold War* (Athens: University of Georgia Press, 1991).

27. George F. Kennan, *Russia and the West under Lenin and Stalin* (Boston: Little, Brown, 1961), 181.
28. The drama of Munich is captured by John Wheeler-Bennett in *Munich: Prologue to Tragedy* (London: Macmillan, 1948).
29. Townsend Hoopes, *The Limits of Intervention* (New York: McKay, 1969), 7-13.
30. Ibid., 13-16.
31. Tom Wicker, *JFK and LBJ: The Influence of Personality upon Politics* (Baltimore: Penguin, 1969), 192.
32. See J. William Fulbright, *The Arrogance of Power* (New York: Vintage, 1967), pt. 2; Arthur M. Schlesinger, Jr., *The Bitter Heritage* (New York: Fawcett, 1967); and Theodore Draper, *Abuse of Power* (New York: Viking, 1966).
33. Ole Holsti, "The 1914 Case," *American Political Science Review* (June 1965): 365-378; and Glen D. Paige, *The Korean Decision* (New York: Free Press, 1968), 273ff.
34. *Times* (London), September 28, 1938; and Wheeler-Bennett, *Munich*, 157-158.
35. Mowat, *Britain between the Wars*, 617.
36. Hoffmann, *State of War*, 163.
37. Joseph M. Jones, *The Fifteen Weeks* (New York: Viking, 1955).
38. Ibid., 63-64.
39. Nicholas D. Kristof, "As China Looks at World Order, It Detects New Struggles Emerging," *New York Times*, April 21, 1992.

Part Two

THE FIRST LEVEL OF ANALYSIS: THE STATE SYSTEM

CHAPTER 3

The Players:
States and
Other Actors

CHARACTERISTICS OF STATES

Since the Peace of Westphalia in 1648, the primary political actor in the state system has been the sovereign *state*. The number of states has more than tripled since 1945, when there were fifty-one members of the United Nations—nineteen from Europe and related areas, twenty from Latin America, and only twelve from Asia and Africa. Forty-seven years later, the developing countries of Asia and Africa alone constituted more than half of the 161 UN members. If the developing countries of Latin America are included, these states constitute a sizable majority. Altogether there are over 170 states today, including some, such as most of the former Soviet republics, that are not yet members of the United Nations. Some forecasters predict 200 states by the year 2000. As different as these states are in size, human and natural resources, and political and economic systems, they share certain characteristics: sovereignty, territory, population and nationalism, and recognition by other states.

Sovereignty

Each state is considered sovereign. Sovereignty refers to a state's government—not that of any other state—deciding how it will manage its own affairs. This may mean, as in the words of the U.S. Constitution, that the state's government will "insure domestic Tranquility, provide for the common defence, promote the general Welfare. . . ." All governments are concerned with maintaining domestic peace and national defense, but how capable they are of doing so varies. In Lebanon, where armed factions, representing the Christian, Sunni and Shiite Muslim, and Druse populations, were engaged in a civil war from 1975 to 1991, governmental authority just disappeared. With additional external interventions by the Palestine Liberation Organization (PLO), the Israelis (who invaded in 1982), and the Syrians (who with their troops sought to incorporate Lebanon into a Greater Syria)—all supporting different domestic factions and adding to the bloodshed—the capital city of Beirut, once considered the Paris of the Middle East, was destroyed. One Druse leader reportedly said that things were so bad in Beirut that not even the laws of the jungle were respected any longer! It was amid this anarchy that American and other Western hostages were seized and held by pro-Iranian terrorists.

If anyone exercised authority in Lebanon at that time, it was Syria, which intervened in 1975 to save the Christians from defeat by an alliance of Lebanese Muslims and the PLO. Later, it switched sides and, together with other Arab diplomats, fashioned in 1989 a new constitution reflecting the emergence of a Muslim majority. The Christians, who had long dominated Lebanese politics, resisted the Syrian-supported government until late 1990, when Syrian troops in Beirut finally crushed the Christian militia (whose arms before the 1990 arms embargo against Iraq had been supplied by Saddam Hussein, the Syrian leader's principal rival for leadership of the Arab world). Thus, Syrian intervention made peace a possibility again as all the militias were moved out of Beirut and Lebanon became a Syrian satellite, nominally sovereign but in fact under Syrian control exercised by 40,000 troops.[1]

Governments also are concerned with providing their citizens with general welfare. But again, their concern varies. In democracies, elections not only have provided an extension of freedom but also have created broadly based welfare states. In the case of undemocratic states, however, sovereignty can mean the brutal treatment of their own populations. In Cambodia, for example, from 1975 to 1979 the Pol Pot regime killed an estimated 1 million of its 8 million people, and 600,000 fled into exile. After it had unified Vietnam in 1975, the victorious North treated the southern population, especially the ethnic Chinese, so harshly that 900,000 fled in rickety boats, and many drowned in the process. At least 10,000 Vietnamese were imprisoned because they worked for the Americans. Adolf Hitler slaughtered the German Jews during World War II. And Stalin killed an estimated 12-15 million people in the forced collectivization of the peasantry and the elimination of the class of small landholders during the 1920s, allowed 5 million to die during the 1933 famine while he increased grain exports, and killed several million more during the Great Purges in the later 1930s.

All governments, regardless of how they treat their citizens, however, reject foreign interference in their domestic affairs. The Soviets for many years repeatedly dismissed Western human rights campaigns in behalf of Soviet dissidents. But this did not stop Westerners from continuing to champion human rights. President Ronald Reagan, during the 1988 Moscow summit, made them the centerpiece of a public speech, much to the annoyance of his host. But President George Bush went the furthest in interfering in Soviet domestic affairs when, during the abortive coup against Soviet president Mikhail Gorbachev in August 1991, he declared that the coup leaders, having seized power by extraconstitutional means, were illegitimate and that the United States would refuse to deal with them. It was a daring position to take before the coup's failure was known. Had the coup succeeded, the new government would certainly have been more anti-American than it would have been anyway because of its hard-line Communist membership, and Bush would have had to negotiate with it because it had established control.

When in 1988 the United States tried to remove Panama's ruler, Gen. Manuel Noriega, a drug runner indicted by two U.S. grand juries, no Latin American country was willing to recognize America's right to intervene in the domestic affairs of the region—even if, as in this case, it was reportedly to restore democracy in Panama.[2] This reaction was not out of sympathy for Noriega but from long memories and the recent examples of Grenada and Nicaragua. By defending the principle of sovereignty, the Latin American countries were defending themselves and denying the right of an outside power to decide which country's government it wished to remove. More specifically, for these mostly weak countries the claim of sovereignty was a principal means of fending off the United States' claim to being the regional policeman.

Nevertheless, the sovereignty of smaller states historically has been constrained by their dependence on the good will and tolerance of the great powers, both neighboring and far off, on whom they depend for their security or markets in which to sell their goods. For example, before 1989 the states of Eastern Europe were Moscow's satellites, but the Soviets had to intervene directly in 1953, 1956, and 1968, and indirectly (via the Polish army in Poland) in 1981, to ensure these nations' loyalty to the Soviet Union, the Soviet bloc, and the military alliance known as the Warsaw Treaty Organization. Even today after such countries as Poland and Hungary have repudiated communism, they remain sensitive to the security concerns of Russia and the other republics of the former Soviet Union.

Usually, only a defeat in war will allow a foreign state to take over sovereign control and make and enforce the rules for the vanquished state's people, as the United States did in post-World War II Japan. An interesting variation on this occurred in Iraq after its defeat in 1991 when civil war broke out as Shiite Muslims in the south and Kurds in the north revolted unsuccessfully against Saddam Hussein's tyrannical rule and mistreatment of them. As millions of Kurds fled for fear of retribution from Saddam—he had, after all, gassed them a few years earlier—and the lives of thousands of people were threatened by the wintry weather in the mountains bordering Turkey, vivid television coverage of these events compelled action. It forced President Bush, who was being criticized increasingly for his determination to stay out of the Iraqi civil war, to act. He then announced the establishment of informal "safe havens" in northern Iraq where America and its European allies in the recent war would use their military forces to provide aid and set up camps for the waves of fleeing Kurds. Avoiding the issue of Iraqi sovereignty, the administration warned Saddam Hussein not to interfere militarily with the aid effort above the thirty-sixth parallel and not to pursue or attack the Kurds in this area.

Eventually, allied forces were replaced by UN personnel and workers from international relief agencies. Everyone assumed that Saddam Hussein would not dare launch an attack and risk another clash with the United States. Thus the relief personnel would be able to carry out their duties without Iraqi interference in that part of Iraq. In fact, northern Iraq above the thirty-sixth parallel was transformed into a sanctuary for the Kurds* against their own government—certainly a constraint on the latter's sovereignty. When allied forces withdrew after five months, the United States warned Saddam Hussein that he was not to send Iraqi forces or police above the parallel and that any aircraft and helicopters would be shot down. He also was warned that some allied forces would be left in Turkey to reintervene if he took advantage of the allied pullout to take his revenge on those hapless people. Nevertheless, when the UN agencies and allied military observers leave in 1992, the almost 4 million Iraqi Kurds will once more face Baghdad alone.[3] The question is whether, based on the earlier intervention and precedent, the world will be ready to recognize once again the right to intervene in another sovereign nation's affairs—Iraq's or any other nation's—on humanitarian grounds.

As these examples demonstrate, although the principle of sovereignty acknowledges each government's exclusive jurisdiction over its nation's territory and people, in practice that concept is not always fully exercised. This is even true for more powerful countries. How sovereign during the cold war were Italy or West Germany, whose independence depended on the U.S. nuclear deterrent? How sovereign is the United States today as it becomes increasingly dependent on Japan for vital technologies for its industries and critical electronics for its military hardware? How much control over its economy does the United States, the world's largest debtor nation after eight years of the Reagan administration and four years of the Bush administration, have as foreigners buy up American businesses and real estate? Whether an individual, corporation, or nation, being in debt means loss of control over one's affairs. World power and influence historically have been associated with creditor nations. America emerged as a world power as a creditor supplying investment capital to the rest of the world. Now as a debtor, America's post-cold war and post-Desert Storm role in the world will have to be reexamined. Sovereignty is never absolute. The 1970s demonstrated painfully that the Western industrial countries were unable to fully control their

---

* In fact, the focus on the some 700,000 Kurds amassed on Turkey's frontier overlooked the Shiites who had fled to Iran from southern Iraq, as well as the over 1 million Kurds who were allowed into Iran. Although Iran could not support all these refugees, it received little international help.

own economies as world oil prices escalated and Western inflation and unemployment followed. And the events of 1990-1991 demonstrated vividly once again how dependent the Western economies are on Middle Eastern oil. In an age of increasing interdependence in which goods and capital flow freely across borders and of the economic integration of nations, as in Western Europe, sovereignty is relative. Economies are becoming so intertwined that governments no longer fully control them. Among the Western industrial states, where interdependence is the most advanced, annual summit conferences of the political and economic leaders seeking greater coordination of economic policies have become more and more critical.

Territory

Another characteristic of a state is its territory. Frontiers separate one state from another. When crossing a border or flying from one country to another, travelers normally have to show immigration officials some sort of identification and proof of their citizenship and have their luggage searched, if customs officials deem it necessary. Sometimes crossing a border can be a grim business, as it used to be going through the Berlin Wall. The frontier dividing East Germany from West Germany was marked by barbed wire, watchtowers, and armed guards. One may, of course, be forbidden entry into some countries, and sometimes citizens can leave their countries only by escape. But most frontiers are not like that. Nor does the existence of borders mean that they are not, on occasion, contested.

In any event, all states possess territory; without territory there would be no state. When a state relinquishes control of a piece of territory, as the colonial countries of Europe did after World War II, another state is established, and it exercises authority over the territory. In this way, the British gave up their colony in India and transferred its control to a sovereign native government. India defined her frontiers as those established by the British and defended them against Chinese territorial claims. When Austria-Hungary completely disintegrated after World War I, the separate states of Austria, Hungary, Yugoslavia, and Czechoslovakia governed the areas each inherited. It is this association of a state with land that is central to a state's conception of itself, and it is for the preservation of this territorial integrity that states go to war.

As the Soviet Union disintegrated in the latter half of 1991, the fifteen republics that had constituted it divided into separate sovereign republics, claiming control over their territories, people, and resources, as well as the conduct of their foreign policies. Indeed, the three Baltic republics officially seceded even before the Soviet Union's collapse and were recognized internationally as new states. The republics constituting the new Commonwealth of Independent States have been gaining recognition as independent states since late December 1991.

Population and Nationalism

States possess more than land; they have populations, ranging from the more than 1 billion people in the People's Republic of China to the fewer than

100,000 people in the Caribbean island of Dominica. The fact that the terms *state* and *nation-state* are often used interchangeably suggests one additional characteristic of modern states: the national loyalty that populations feel to their countries. Before 1789 and the French Revolution, most states were ruled by kings, and most people living within the territorial confines of such dynastic states did not really identify with them. At times, kings even traded people and lands. But the nationalism born in France and then stirred up in the rest of Europe in reaction to French conquest led people increasingly to identify with their nations.

It is difficult to define a nation exactly, but it can be said that it is a collective identity shared by people living within certain frontiers as a result of their common history (plus a good deal of mythology dramatizing the past), expectations of remaining together in the future, and usually a common language that allows them to communicate more easily with one another than with the inhabitants of neighboring nations who speak different languages. Ernest Renan, a Frenchman, characterized a nation as "a daily plebiscite," a continual emotional commitment to a group of people distinct from every other segment of humanity, celebrating their "nationhood" with anthems, poetry, statues of heroes who have defended it, and other symbols.

But nationality and geographical boundaries do not always coincide in real life. The Soviet Union was a multinational state of 288 million people composed of 104 nationalities, of which the Great Russians, who historically have controlled Russia, were the most numerous. They lost their majority status because "the battle of the bedroom" had been won by the other nationalities, especially the Muslims of Central Asia, who now constitute 14 percent of the total population of the former Soviet Union. Often hated by the many other nationalities that comprised the contemporary Soviet Union, the Great Russians, even before Gorbachev, had to be concerned about their future control and dominance of a nation that sprawled over one-sixth of the world's land surface. Textbooks there were published in fifty-two languages, and the state radio broadcast in sixty-seven languages.[4]

But after Gorbachev's reforms began, tensions broadened to include conflicts not only between the Russians and non-Russian nationalities, but also among the various non-Russian nationalities. Neither he nor the other Soviet leaders anticipated the strength of the resurgence of national identity of the fifteen Soviet republics. Gorbachev believed that his program of economic reconstruction required liberalization of the political system. But by eliminating or loosening central controls, he set off forces that threatened to disintegrate the Soviet Union itself. Indeed, there appeared to be a contradiction between what was needed to stimulate the Soviet economy and the coercive means needed to maintain national cohesion and stabilize a multinational state. The introduction of democracy and a market economy may be what the Soviet Union needed, but *glasnost* and *perestroika* risked disintegrating the nation they were supposed to preserve as they sought to transform its political and economic system.

In the three Baltic republics (Latvia, Lithuania, and Estonia) annexed by Stalin in 1940, anti-Soviet feelings have always run high. Indeed, Gorbachev's reforms encouraged them to seek to regain their independence from the Soviet Union, as did Moldavia (now called Moldova), Armenia, and Georgia, Stalin's birthplace. All six are small republics. But even more important, the three Slavic states—Russia, Ukraine, and Byelorussia (now known as Belarus)—the first two being the largest Soviet republics, all declared it their sovereign right to decide their own economic policies and defied orders from the center. They even claimed the right to pursue their own foreign policies. (Theoretically, they had that right under the Soviet constitution. Ukraine and Belarus were represented in the United Nations, but in reality Moscow decided foreign policy issues for all the republics. Now both states claimed that they wished to pursue independent, neutral, and nonnuclear policies!) At best, the Soviet Union was being transformed into a new, more decentralized federation; at worst, it was disintegrating, like the Austro-Hungarian empire on the eve of World War I. The last of Europe's colonial empires (although not often thought of as such because Russia ruled a geographically contiguous empire instead of overseas colonies), the Soviet Union was unraveling as the same nationalist forces that earlier had ended the Dutch, French, British, and other empires threatened its integrity. Clearly, the republics rejected the sense of common destiny that is necessary for national cohesion.

It was this fear of disintegration, as well as the loss of their privileges if they lost power, that drove the largely Russian reactionaries—members of the old Soviet elite (military, secret police, and party functionaries)—to launch their coup against Gorbachev in August 1991. But when the coup fizzled, the decentralization it was intended to prevent accelerated. The three days of the coup marked a turning point in the country's history. After a thousand years of first czarist and then Communist autocracy, the Soviet Union, historically a highly centralized state, tumbled into "uncontrolled disintegration" as republic after republic declared its independence from Moscow and several established themselves as new nations. Initially, they declared that they would negotiate a new union treaty and a permanent successor to the Soviet Union. The key reason was their economic interdependence; without cooperation they would be unable to reverse the nation's economic plunge. The proposed confederation would represent the collective interests of the member republics internationally and maintain control over the armed forces and 27,000 strategic and tactical nuclear weapons, while permitting the republics to determine the limits of the central government's power and guard against revival of a dictatorial center.

Yet, at the moment of decision, the seven republics that had endorsed the new union would not commit themselves, leaving its fate in the hands of their nationalistic parliaments. When the Ukraine, a key republic with a fifth of the Soviet population and a fifth of its industrial and agricultural output, voted overwhelmingly for independence on December 1, 1991, thus becoming Europe's fourth largest nation, it became clear that endless negotiations during a worsening economic situation could not stop the rapid rate of Soviet disintegration. Without Ukraine (Ukrainians dropped the article "the" when referring to their country), Russia was left as the dominant republic among the remaining Soviet republics. Indeed, Russia's status as the successor state became overwhelmingly clear during this period. When the central government declared bankruptcy in November 1991, Russia assumed its debts and promised to fund what remained of the central government's ministries. In capitalist language, this act constituted a buyout of the former Soviet Union as Russia took control of what was left. Symbolically, Russia claimed the Soviet Union's permanent seat as one of the five great powers on the United Nations Security Council.

The Soviet Union was formally buried on December 8, 1991, when in an act of desperation to stem the complete disintegration of the former USSR, the presidents of the three Slavic republics—Russia, Ukraine, and Belarus—representing 73 percent of the population and 80 percent of the territory of the Soviet Union, decided to establish a commonwealth of fully independent countries and invited other republics to join, not negotiate, the new association. The three presidents declared, "The U.S.S.R., as a subject of international law and geopolitical reality, is ceasing its existence." The new Commonwealth of Independent States (CIS) assumed all international obligations of the Soviet Union, including control over its nuclear arsenal. Coordinating bodies would be established to decide on cooperative policies in foreign affairs, defense, and economics. Subsequently, the commonwealth agreement was signed by eleven of the remaining twelve Soviet republics after the defections of the three Baltic states; only Georgia did not join (see Table 3-1). Gorbachev, then, had become an historical relic, president of a country that no longer existed. On December 25, 1991, seventy-four years after the Bolshevik Revolution, the red hammer-and-sickle flag that had flown over the Kremlin was lowered.[5]

But there was one problem. What would be recognized as the Soviet Union's successor state? Since only states can be represented in the United Nations, the commonwealth could not take the Soviet Union's seats in the Security Council and General Assembly. A state, as noted, must have a government able to exercise executive and legislative authority over a population and able to conduct an independent foreign policy. Without such powers, it cannot carry out UN decisions. But because the commonwealth's purpose was only to coordinate the foreign and domestic policies of the member republics, it was in fact an international organization. Thus, Russia was given the former USSR's seats.[6] Belarus and Ukraine had had seats in the General Assembly since World War II; the other republics too would seek membership.

The Soviet Union was not the only country wrenched apart by nationalism—a nationalism that seemed all the stronger because it had been so long suppressed. In Czechoslovakia, the Slovaks wanted to hyphenate Czecho-Slovakia. To appease the Slovaks' reassertive nationalism, the country was

Table 3-1 Members of the Former USSR

Present-day Status and Republic	Population (to nearest 100,000)
Commonwealth of Independent States	
Armenia	3,300,000
Azerbaijan	7,100,000
Belarus (formerly Byelorussia)	10,200,000
Kazakhstan	16,500,000
Kyrgyzstan (formerly Kirghizstan	4,400,000
Moldova (formerly Moldavia)	4,300,000
Russia	147,400,000
Tajikistan (formerly Tadzhikistan)	5,100,000
Turkmenistan	3,600,000
Ukraine	52,000,000
Uzbekistan	19,900,000
Other Independent States	
Estonia	1,500,000
Latvia	2,700,000
Lithuania	3,700,000
Georgia	5,500,000

officially renamed the Czech and Slovak Federative Republic, but the government has barely been able to keep the ethnically split nation together. In Yugoslavia, also deeply split ethnically, the conflict came to blows (see Figure 3-1). During World War II, fighting between Croats and Serbs killed over a million people, twice the number killed by the occupying Germans. After Slovenia and Croatia elected non-Communist governments in 1991 (although their leaders were former Communists), they voted for independence. That stirred the opposition of Serbia since it would weaken the Serbs who dominated Yugoslavia's bureaucracy and army and who wanted to maintain firm central power and even to realize their old dream of a Greater Serbia at the expense of their ethnic rivals. A civil war ensued as the army sought to prevent the defections of the two republics. After fourteen cease-fires, all arranged by the European Community (EC) and all of which failed to stop the Serbian-controlled Yugoslav army, the United Nations tried its hand in 1992 by deploying 14,000 UN peace-keeping troops to separate the combatants and end the bloody civil war. By then, the EC had recognized Croatia and Slovenia as independent republics. But when Bosnia and Herzegovina, as well as Macedonia also declared their independence, the civil war erupted anew. Yugoslavia was reduced to Serbia and Montenegro. Freed from the constraints of communism and the cold war, the various minorities in Eastern Europe filled the vacuum left by communism by reasserting their nationalism and rekindling old feuds.[7]

Figure 3-1 The Breakup of Yugoslavia, 1992

Democratization of these ethnically divided societies is not likely to proceed until they solve their problems of national identity. Indeed, by permitting open expression of ethnic grievances and aspirations, democratization may initially accentuate ethnic conflicts, especially because the dividing lines between the various nationalities have been blurred by centuries of migration and colonization. For example, a third of Estonia's and Latvia's populations are Russian, and 10 million other Russians live in Ukraine. In Kazakhstan, the Russian "minority" is as large as the native Kazakh population; in Armenia,

Christian Armenians are surrounded by mainly Muslim Azerbaijanis. And Serbs live in Croatia, Slovenia, and Bosnia. This ethnic checkerboard defies the nationalists' visions of a homogeneous, cohesive state, yet the search for such a state ignited savage fighting in Yugoslavia and raised the potential for conflict among the Soviet republics.

Israel is another example of a society deeply divided by nationalism. Within the 1948 boundaries established at its birth and the resulting war of independence, the Jewish state established a strong sense of identity and unity. But since Israel's conquest of the Arab West Bank and Gaza Strip in 1967 after the war with Egypt, Syria, and Jordan, and because of the unwillingness of any Arab leader to negotiate a "peace-for-land" deal, these territories have become virtually part of Israel. Israel's right-wing Likud party, claiming biblical inheritance, has said that the West Bank, especially, is part of Israel. The party calls this territory by its Hebrew names of Judea and Samaria and appears unwilling to trade peace for territory. Yet in 1990, Israel had 3.8 million Jews and 800,000 Israeli Arabs; the West Bank, however, was home to over 800,000 Arabs and the Gaza Strip to over 500,000. These over 2 million Arabs had a birth rate more than double that of Israeli Jews. In short, in the "demographic war" the Arab population already constituted over half the population, and one day it would have been the majority—except for massive post-cold war Soviet immigration, estimated to reach 2 million Jews by 1996. The longer Israel holds the land and tries to consolidate its hold by allowing Jews to settle on it, the more frustrated and nationalistic the Palestinians in the West Bank and Gaza will become—unless they are expelled and forced into Jordan. Israel therefore faces a growing internal security problem, an example of which was visible globally on television in 1988 as Arab youth, in what became known as the *Intifada* or "Uprising," stoned Israeli soldiers, who often tried to suppress their attackers with brutal beatings.[8] The Jewish and Arab populations, including Israeli Arabs, thus became even more divided. As an increasingly binational rather than Jewish state, Israel faced a fundamental question: Can Israel exist with any degree of harmony and coherence if it exercises permanent rule over a foreign population that is not linked to it by language, faith, historical experience, nationalistic feelings, or common loyalty?[9] By incorporating a hostile and disenfranchised population, will Israel create for itself a permanently unsolvable conflict?

As the *Intifada* continued and as, after Iraq's invasion of Kuwait, the Palestine Liberation Organization (PLO) embraced Iraqi strongman Saddam Hussein as the potential liberator of the Palestinians, the Palestinian-Israeli conflict was reduced to fundamental feelings of hatred and anger. Palestinians had become increasingly radicalized and Israeli attitudes had hardened even before the war. The Likud party was determined to hang onto what it called the "liberated territories," but even moderates who had favored talking to the Palestinians and some settlement of their claim to self-determination found that there was nothing left to talk about after the Palestinians favored Saddam Hussein and cheered the dropping of Iraqi SCUD missiles on Tel Aviv.

Most nations' security problems are external; Israel's is external as well as internal.

Before Eastern Europe's "decommunization," such potentially divisive nationalism, leading ultimately to disintegration and possible civil war, occurred more frequently in developing countries. Maintaining national unity remains a primary problem for many of these new states because they are composed of various ethnic or tribal groups, often with different religious beliefs, different languages, and little else in common except the shared experience of colonial rule. For example, some states, such as Nigeria, Zaire, and India, experienced civil wars upon becoming independent; others, such as Pakistan, which emerged out of India, broke into even smaller sovereign states. (See Chapter 10 for a fuller analysis.)

Clearly, nationalism remains the principal force in the world today, for the nation is the largest political organization with which most people can identify. They may give their loyalty to their family, tribe, religion, or region, but it is generally their nation that commands their ultimate loyalty and for which most have in the past been willing to sacrifice their lives if necessary. This is less a matter of blind patriotism than a recognition that the nation is the largest secular community in which a meaningful life can be lived. And as yet there is no viable substitute for it. It is thus ironic that the recent widespread demand for national self-determination by so many nationality groups is threatening to disintegrate current nations. After all, if Croatia, Lithuania, Moldova, and Kazakhstan can gain independence, why not Spain's Basques, Canada's Québecois, Czechoslovakia's Slovaks, or Great Britain's Scots?

Recognition by Other States

Generally, a state is officially recognized by other states when it is perceived as having established control over the people within its boundaries. At that point it is customary to exchange ambassadors and undertake agreements. In reality, however, matters are not always so straightforward. For example, the state of Israel has existed since 1948, but, of the Arab states, only Egypt has recognized it, taking thirty years to do so; the others still refuse, even though they have lost four wars with Israel. Recognition means acceptance of a state as a legitimate political entity. Even without recognition, however, diplomatic relations can exist. The United States did not recognize mainland China until 1979, but, just as the Arab states have negotiated cease-fires and prisoner exchanges with Israel, the United States negotiated with China to end the Korean War, attended the great-power conference ending the first Indochina war in 1954, and occasionally met with Chinese officials to explore certain issues. Similarly, North Vietnam and the United States negotiated an end to that war, even though neither recognized the other officially. The disadvantage of such relations is that they are intermittent and do not easily permit mutual and accurate assessment of intentions and capabilities.

The basic practice is to extend *de facto* recognition when a new state is born; the fact of its existence is the key. But some states will extend recognition only *de jure*—that is, when they approve of the new government. The United States was slow to officially recognize both the Soviet and the Communist Chinese governments, taking sixteen and thirty years, respectively, to do so. Sometimes the situation becomes an awkward one. The United States recognized the Sandinista government in Nicaragua, but President Ronald Reagan's administration was committed to its overthrow. Or different states recognize rival governments of another state. During the cold war, Moscow and Washington at times recognized rival governments in North and South Korea, North and South Vietnam, Communist and Nationalist China, and East and West Germany (and, after unification, the new state). Vietnam no longer exists, but the United States has not recognized the new, unified Communist People's Republic of Vietnam. Washington has withdrawn recognition of the Nationalists on Taiwan and opened official diplomatic relations with Communist China. It continues, however, to supply arms to Taiwan. Because both the Communists and Nationalists agree that there is only one China, the United States is in effect supplying weapons to a province that is in rebellion against the government that Washington recognizes as the legitimate ruler of China!

Even more bizarre is the situation of Hong Kong, a British colony leased from China for ninety-nine years until 1997. Adjoining the Chinese mainland, Hong Kong is a thriving capitalist society whose inhabitants enjoy Western-style freedoms. In 1984, China and Britain agreed to resolve Hong Kong's future status by a solution known as "one country, two systems." The Chinese Communist flag will wave over Hong Kong as it again becomes part of (Communist) China, but for fifty more years Hong Kong will be an autonomous administrative region of China with its own capitalist social and economic system and a Western way of life. Why does Beijing not just demand the Crown Colony's return or take it, as it could easily do? The reasons are twofold: first, Hong Kong's position as a trading and international financial center is economically beneficial to mainland China, and, second, Beijing would like to tempt the Nationalist Chinese on Taiwan to make the same kind of agreement. China could thus be reunited as a single country, while Taiwan, like Hong Kong, enjoyed self-government, its higher standard of living, its different economic and political systems, and its own army (supplied with weapons by the United States). Whether, of course, Beijing will tolerate free trade and free speech in Hong Kong when the British lease expires and whether an arrangement similar to Hong Kong's will be acceptable to Taiwan are widely questioned after the brutal suppression of the pro-democracy movement in Beijing in 1989. Indeed, many of Hong Kong's residents have already left or are planning to leave.

But perhaps the most bizarre situation occurred in late 1988. Before that date the Palestine Liberation Organization, the self-proclaimed representative of the Palestinian people, had been committed to the destruction of Israel (using terrorism) in its pursuit of a Palestinian state encompassing the former British mandate of Palestine. Then, in 1988, the PLO declared the establishment of an independent Palestinian state limited to the West Bank and the

Gaza Strip (with PLO leader Yasir Arafat serving as president). Yet these territories, captured by Israel in the 1967 war, were still controlled by it. Implicit in this act was recognition of Israel's right to exist, a precondition for any negotiations, but the PLO still refused to make that recognition explicit. Despite the fact that the Palestinian state was unborn, within two weeks over sixty states, especially Arab ones, had extended recognition to the nonexisting state, which all Israeli political parties opposed as a mortal threat to Israel's survival. This opposition was reinforced after Yasir Arafat hailed Saddam Hussein as a potential liberator of Palestine in 1990.

If these two instances seem bizarre, the practical problem of whom to deal with was already pressing in the case of Gorbachev's Soviet Union, as the central government's authority declined. With Gorbachev facing ever greater resistance from the republics, all of whom claimed their laws were superior to those of the Soviet Union, with whom should other states deal? Could the United States and its NATO allies conclude a series of arms control agreements with Gorbachev and expect the Soviet government to implement them? Even before August 1991, the question had been how long that government might remain in charge and whether Gorbachev could in fact commit the Soviet Union to any long-term commitments. If the U.S. Senate ratified the 1991 START strategic nuclear arms agreements, with whom was the United States dealing—the Soviet Union or Russia, Ukraine, Belarus, and Kazakhstan (the four republics in whose soil the strategic nuclear weapons were based), or all of them?

Even more to the point as the Soviet Union unraveled was the question of who would control its huge nuclear arsenal. While Russia with the largest territory is the base of most of the USSR's nuclear arsenal, the other three republics had announced that they did not want any nuclear weapons on their territory. Yet would they demand the right to participate in strategic decisions (just as if, for example, the governors of American states demanded to have their voices heard before the federal government made its military decisions)? Moscow, like Washington, in the past exercised stringent controls over its nuclear arms to prevent unauthorized firing. Would this tight control survive the erosion of Moscow's authority? Would Soviet republics with nuclear arms be tempted to use those arms on each other? [10] The big question for the United States and its allies before the summer of 1991 was whether they should not hedge their bets on Gorbachev by making increasing contacts with the republics. It was striking that when Gorbachev visited Japan in 1991, he took along the *Russian* foreign minister. Immediately afterward, the Russian prime minister and foreign minister visited Washington. And when President Bush attended the 1991 summit conference in Moscow, he met there with Boris Yeltsin and visited Kiev, Ukraine's capital, to address its legislature.

The abortive coup right after the summit, speeding up the dissolution of the Soviet Union, and the flow of power from the center in Moscow to the governments of the republics, meant that Washington could no longer deal solely or even mainly with the Soviet central government. Apart from now dealing with the three Baltic republics (and Georgia and Moldova), whose independence was recognized by over thirty states before Moscow let them go officially, the United States had to deal with what was left of the central government, as well as the governments of the remaining republics which, as independent entities, all claimed the right to determine their own foreign policies. But this was not the case for long as Russia emerged as the successor state to the Soviet Union and Ukraine declared its independence. Together with Belarus, they proclaimed the CIS to be the replacement for the Soviet Union.

This left the START treaty in limbo. If one of the republics refused to accept the arms control agreement signed by the United States and the former Soviet Union, the president would have to consult with the Senate to decide whether to amend or withdraw from the treaty. Before extending recognition to Ukraine, Belarus, and Kazakhstan, therefore, the United States sought reassurances that they remained committed to the goal of eliminating their nuclear weapons. There was great concern about who would control the former Soviet nuclear arsenal. When the CIS formally replaced the Soviet Union, it reassured the West that it would maintain a common defense with a single unified command over nuclear weapons; all nuclear weapons in the three republics were to be destroyed or transferred to Russia. In 1992, the four former Soviet republics with nuclear weapons all agreed to adhere to the START treaty. The United States, which had previously recognized Russia, also announced that recognition for the remaining republics would depend on their observance of human rights and democracy.

CLASSIFICATION OF STATES

Great Powers and Small Powers

The most widespread and traditional means of distinguishing among states is in terms of the power they possess. The components of power include geographic location, size, population, industry, and wealth (see Chapter 7). Most observers have long distinguished between "great powers" and "small powers." Almost by definition, the great powers, with their significant military capacity, have been considered the primary actors in the state system because they play the leading role in security issues in international politics. Indeed, according to one student of war, Jack Levy, from 1480 to 1940 there were about 2,600 important battles involving European states.[11] During those 460 years, France participated in 47 percent of the battles, Austria-Hungary in 34 percent, Prussia (Germany) in 25 percent, and Britain

Table 3-2 The Great Powers

	World War I	World War II	Cold War and Détente	Post-Cold War
Austria-Hungary	x	—	—	—
Britain	x	x	x	x
France	x	x	x	x
Italy	x	x	x	x
Japan	x	x	x	x
Germany	x	x	x	x
Russia/Soviet Union/Russia	x	x	x	x
United States	x	x	x	x

and Russia in approximately 22 percent. At least one great power participated in about two-thirds of the wars during these almost five centuries,
leading Levy to denote them "the most frequent fighters." [12] Also according
to Levy,

> The Great Powers constitute an interdependent system of power and security
> relations. . . . This is an open rather than a closed system, for it is affected
> to some extent by the larger world system of which it is a part. The primary
> influences on the Great Powers, however, derive from within the Great Power
> system, and their patterns of interaction can be explained largely by the internal
> dynamics of that system. . . . The Great Power system may be a subsystem of the
> larger international system, but in fundamental respects it is a dominant sub-
> system. [13]

Primacy of Great Powers.   Particularly striking is the remarkable stability in
the ranking of great powers, despite vast geographic, industrial, and social
changes in Europe during the nineteenth century. This is revealed in a list of
the great powers since World War I (see Table 3-2).

Stability in these rankings does not mean that changes in individual
positions have not occurred. Prussia, which made its mark against Napoleon,
became part of an enlarged and united Germany in 1871 after the defeat of
France. Germany then replaced France as the Continent's preeminent power
and became a rival to Britain, at that time the leading power in the world.
Austria-Hungary, by contrast, declined after the Napoleonic Wars, lost its
place as the primary power in central Europe to Prussia in 1866, and
collapsed in World War I, which also exhausted France and Britain. It was
American power that was critical in defeating Germany in World War I, and
U.S. and Soviet power that accomplished this end in World War II. As
continental powers with populations and resources to match, dwarfing the
great powers of the past, the United States and Soviet Union emerged as
superpowers after 1945. And Russia, the Soviet Union's successor state, has the
potential to reemerge as a superpower. Indeed, perhaps the members of the

CIS, after a number of years spent relishing some of their long-denied nationalism, will want to establish a stronger union that can deal more successfully with their foreign and domestic problems than they can separately.

The international system has, in any case, always granted a special place to the great powers. During the nineteenth century, the Concert of Europe was composed exclusively of the great powers. They were the self-appointed board of directors of the European "corporation," meeting from time to time to deal with significant political problems that affected the peace of Europe. This special great-power status and responsibility were reflected in the 1920 League of Nations Covenant, which gave such powers permanent membership on the league's Council; the Assembly, composed of the smaller nations, was expected to meet only every four or five years. In those days, "the world seemed to be the oyster of the great powers." [14] After Germany's second defeat, the great powers' privileged status and obligations were again recognized in the United Nations Charter provision that conferred upon the United States, the Soviet Union, Britain, France, and China (which at the time was still controlled by the Nationalists) permanent membership in the UN Security Council. The General Assembly was not expected to play a major role in preserving the peace. Interestingly enough, these same five states were, by 1971, when Communist China was admitted to the United Nations, also the only countries to have nuclear weapons. Great powers, in short, not only possess great military power, and are recognized as great powers by other states, but also are accorded formal recognition of their status by their participation in concerts and congresses and by their permanent membership in the UN Security Council.

But beyond recognition of their special status as the chief game players, great powers are distinguished by the scope of their interest in and capacity for intervening in affairs beyond their own frontiers. It may be true that power "makes ambitious projects feasible and increases ... their chances of success; [and] weakness constrains, restrains and limits choice and independence," [15] but this emphasis on power puts the cart before the horse. A great power mobilizes its resources to project its power because, by definition, it has interests beyond the security of its frontiers. For a superpower like the United States, national security is virtually a given if security means only the security of American territory.

Admittedly, the Soviet Union threatened this territory with its intercontinental-range missiles. But if the security of the United States was the sole objective of American foreign policy, it needed only a nuclear capability to deter such an attack; it would not have had to intervene in Europe and other areas and pursue a global policy. It did so because a great power's interests extend beyond the defense of its territory. Indeed, a great power that would limit its interests to merely defending its territory would be renouncing its status. A small power's interest is survival; it often does not have the luxury of pursuing other interests. But for a great power beyond physical security, national interest dictates nothing. A superpower *claims* an interest. It is not given. Once a great power defines national interest beyond the terms of its own safety, it necessarily enters the realm of values. There are no objective criteria for decoding whether the Persian Gulf, Southeast Asia, Grenada, or even Europe are vital American interests. It depends on what you think we are to do in the world. *To have any interest beyond one's frontiers and one's immediate security is, in other words, to talk about thoughts.*[16]

This definition of a great power is not irrelevant to a rethinking of the U.S. role in a world in which the Soviet threat has largely disappeared. Should the nation essentially withdraw to the Western hemisphere? Does it continue to maintain an interest in Western Europe even though it no longer needs to defend its allies there? Can the Third World—with the exception of the Persian Gulf area—now be largely written off because Washington no longer needs to compete with Moscow for friends and allies? How does the United States define its role and interests in the post-cold war world?

Small Powers as Victims.   In contrast to great powers, small powers have often acted less than been acted on. A critical difference between them is that a great power can occasionally make major mistakes without suffering a fatal blow because it can, once it has recognized its error, exercise its great capability to correct its earlier blunder. A small power cannot. A great power can even wait to see if another state will attack it; its margin of safety being greater, it is less likely to attack its adversary preemptively. Again, a small power usually does not have that luxury; it can disappear at any moment, and it knows that only too well. Czechoslovakia was sacrificed by Britain and France in the appeasement of 1938, and later, after World War II, it was trapped behind the Iron Curtain and its government was subverted by a Soviet-inspired coup d'état. Its independence—like that of Poland, Hungary, Bulgaria, and Romania—was extinguished as the Soviets transformed the country into a satellite; all later efforts to assert independence were squashed. Lithuania, Estonia, and Latvia, now once more independent, were annexed in 1940 by a Moscow seeking to expand outward in anticipation of a possible German attack.

Small countries, to repeat, often have no option but to submit to a great power's interests and demands, something the Latin Americans learned in the nineteenth century. Under the Monroe Doctrine, the United States has intervened frequently in Latin America. Especially since the failure of the 1961 U.S.-sponsored invasion of Cuba, the United States has intervened either overtly or covertly on several occasions to prevent "another Cuba" and to contain Cuban and Soviet influence in the Western Hemisphere: in the Dominican Republic during the Johnson presidency, in Chile during the Nixon presidency, and in Grenada and Nicaragua during the Reagan presidency.

Thus, the general proposition remains true: a small country, if it lies close to a great power, must be very careful. It had better not give offense, and it must be especially aware of and sensitive to the great power's interests. Panama's former ruler Gen. Omar Torrijos Herara summed up coldbloodedly how great powers historically have treated smaller countries. Commenting on the fall from power of the shah of Iran and the refusal initially of Britain and the United States to give the shah asylum, Torrijos said, "This is what happens to a man squeezed by the great nations. After all the juice is gone, they throw him away." [17] Cuban leader Fidel Castro would have agreed with that apt description in 1991 when Moscow unexpectedly announced that Soviet troops would be withdrawn and the subsidies that had kept the Cuban economy afloat for thirty years would be ended. Castro had been neither forewarned nor consulted.

While these states were all victims of either the great powers' dealings or geographic positions, Israel managed to survive the efforts of the surrounding Arab states to crush it at birth. But, surrounded by states that, having failed to eliminate it, refused to accept its existence, Israel—a country about the size of Rhode Island—twice struck preemptively at Egypt and its allies as they appeared to be getting ready to attack in 1956 and 1967. This tactic was for political reasons not employed in 1973, and, as a result, the fighting cost Israel heavy casualties and loss of prestige which, in turn, affected its leverage in later diplomatic efforts to arrange a more lasting peace with Egypt. In those negotiations, Israel was always very conscious of its dependence on the United States for weapons and money. It also was constantly afraid of being betrayed by Washington, and of being forced to make concessions it did not want to make to ensure oil for the United States. These Israeli suspicions, occasionally bordering on paranoia, were excessive, considering the long history of U.S. support and commitment to Israel's existence, but they continue. This situation reflected in good part the power difference between the two countries. The United States, as a relatively secure superpower, could suggest concessions it felt sure would lead to a comprehensive peace. Israel, as a small state, was very insecure despite repeated military victories over its neighbors, and it remained apprehensive lest concessions would weaken it.

The Hierarchy of States.   Actually, the division of countries into great and small powers, although useful, is rather unsophisticated. It is useful because it simplifies the analysis and conduct of international politics by allowing the scholar and diplomat to focus on the demands of the great powers and the interaction among them. And it does tell the essential story. The needs of the weak have in the past either been ignored or received negligible attention. While oversimplified, the old axiom that the strong do as they please and the weak suffer as they must expresses a truth about the relations among nations. But the international hierarchy of states is in reality far more complex than the simple hierarchy of great and small powers.

At the top of the hierarchy after World War II were the United States and the Soviet Union. As *superpowers* they were in a category all by themselves. Usually their status was equated with their vast nuclear forces; the small forces of other nuclear nations were not comparable. But, even if nuclear arms had never been invented, these two countries would still have been super-powers. As countries with populations of more than 200 million people and sizable industries, they were able to afford large conventional and nuclear forces and to use their wealth and technology to advance their aims. One of the paradoxes of the post-World War II state system has been that it has witnessed simultaneously a massive expansion of states but a significant contraction of primary actors, such as the superpowers, in the system.

After these two powers were the second-rank powers: Britain, France, Germany, Japan, and China. Three of them (Britain, France, and China) were small nuclear powers; two (Germany and Japan) were economic and financial juggernauts. Although the three European states had been pre-World War II members of the great-power club, they collapsed after the war. They all have since recovered, however. Even before its reunification in 1990, Germany had again become the strongest state in Europe west of the Soviet Union. But all these once-great powers had become essentially regional powers, limiting their roles basically to Europe after they lost their empires. One symptom of this decline was their lack of power projection capability. Britain's last major foreign intervention was against Egypt during the 1956 war over the Suez Canal, but it was a dismal failure, ending in the collapse of the British government. It was 1982 before Britain again acted far outside Europe. When Argentina seized the Falkland Islands located off its coast, Britain sent a large naval unit to restore British control and sovereignty. But this expedition's success depended in large measure on U.S. assistance.

The preoccupation of the European states also stemmed from their realiza-tion during the cold war that if they were ever again to play a leading role in a superpower world, they must pool their resources and conduct united foreign and defense policies in a united Europe. Otherwise, even as economi-cally prosperous states, they would remain dependent on the United States for their defense. In 1990, as they moved closer to the final push toward European integration, it was symptomatic of their status that after the Iraqi invasion of Kuwait, the European states waited to see what the United States would do and only then did they act by rallying behind it. For the first time in years, Britain and France sent sizable military contingents to Saudi Arabia (35,000 and 10,000, respectively). But Japan, whose post-war role had been limited mainly to trade, and which, like Germany, had built a world-class economy and gained great financial clout, refused to commit itself politically beyond North Asia. Like Germany, it limited its contribution to money for Gulf operations, even though it imported a greater portion of its oil from the area than did the United States.

China, a nuclear power but still backward economically despite rapid economic growth during the 1980s, also was not active politically in Asia. It was grappling domestically with a succession struggle among the political leadership, the tension between preserving Communist ideological orthodoxy and the desire of many Chinese, especially the young and educated, to live a freer life, and the paradox of combining central controls and socialist economics with free-market incentives to encourage agricultural and industrial productivity and attract foreign investments.

The remaining nations can be divided into middle-rank powers such as Italy and Spain in Europe, India in Asia, and Brazil in Latin America (the latter two potential superpowers), and minor powers such as Colombia, Hungary, Norway, and South Korea. Middle-rank and minor powers have little capacity to act beyond their regions or even their frontiers. Many of the smaller states have virtually no individual influence. Finally, most of the microstates such as Brunei (population 316,000), Cape Verde (354,000), Djibouti (320,000), Grenada (84,000), the Seychelles (68,000), and the newest members of the United Nations, Micronesia (108,000) and the Marshall Islands (40,000), are not economically viable and are dependent on other states: their sovereignty is in name only.

The ranking of states is, however, frequently misleading. Even if it were this easy to calculate power and predict who will influence whom and, in war, who will beat whom, it would have been difficult—if not impossible—to predict in the 1960s North Vietnam's victory over the United States; or in the 1970s the quaking of the West European industrial countries before their former colonies in OPEC (Organization of Petroleum Exporting Countries), most of whose member countries have tiny populations, no industry, and no military muscle; or in the 1980s the defeat of the Soviet Union by the Afghan resistance. Equally difficult to foresee was Israel's persistent defiance since the 1970s of American pressures for more conciliatory behavior, despite its almost complete dependence politically, economically, and militarily on the United States, or the substantial sums of economic and military aid that had to be paid by the United States to small countries for establishing military bases (for example, the Philippines). Indeed, if power calculations alone could accurately forecast how events would turn out, why have a contest of power, especially a war?

A ranking of states by power may give an initial quick impression of which states are likely to achieve their aims and which are not, but even if such a ranking is useful, even necessary, it is clearly not sufficient. States may be classified according to amounts of power, but power relations among states may be quite complex. The components of power, as will be repeatedly emphasized, are not automatically translated into equivalent influence or ability to achieve desired goals. Rankings are not necessarily very accurate guides in a world in which arms may not confer more political leverage, economically advanced countries appear politically vulnerable and weak, and states with relatively less military and economic strength often appear to dictate events to more powerful states.

Status Quo States versus Revisionist States

States also can be classified according to their aims in the state system: Are they generally willing to accept things as they are, or do they seek to change them? If they are largely willing to accept the existing situations, they are so-called status quo powers. The status quo can therefore be identified with such words as *satisfied, defense,* and *preserve.* Revisionist powers are not content with things as they are, and revisionism is associated with such words as *expansion, offense,* and *change.* The terms *status quo* and *revisionist* were particularly useful in the past when they were associated with peace treaties concluded at the ends of wars. As territorial settlements were usually involved, the victors sought to preserve the status quo, which generally benefited them; the vanquished states wished to arrange changes to alleviate some of the grievances outstanding from the war.

Designation of a state as status quo or revisionist looks straightforward, but it often is not. During World War II, the United States thought the Soviet Union was basically a status quo power. After the war, the Soviet Union was redefined as revisionist. Even in the first years after Gorbachev came to power, the central question in the West remained whether the Soviet Union was still a revisionist state or had become a status quo power. Did Moscow still seek to fulfill the ideological objective of world revolution? Or had it become conservative as the revolutionary fervor of an earlier day had evaporated, and as the Soviet Union—over seventy years after the revolution—had become a highly bureaucratic and industrialized nation with much to lose in a nuclear war? Was its emphasis on domestic reform an indicator of its shift from a revisionist to a status quo power, or did it represent only a tactical change until the Soviet Union recovered its economic strength? The answers to these questions obviously held enormous policy implications for the West, particularly in view of repeated Soviet efforts in the past to divide and weaken it by appearing to pursue moderate policies and shed its revolutionary goals—only to launch a new expansionist phase after having aroused the West's hopes for a change in Soviet behavior.

In short, the questions of how revisionist a state is and on what issues, and to what extent it has become *in practice* a status quo nation even though it may still articulate revisionist purposes and slogans, are not easy to answer and become matters of controversy, if not confusion. What are the criteria of judgment—declaratory statements or acts? If so, what kind? How especially does the observer decide when a status quo power has become revisionist or the reverse? Despite all of the ambiguities and difficulties involved in classifying states in this manner, such a classification can be useful in analysis if applied with care and with awareness of the complexities involved.

North-South States (Rich Nations and Poor Nations)

Another way of looking at the world is to divide it into North and South or rich and poor. These terms are handy tags, even though also oversimplified. *North* refers to all the industrialized, higher-income states, both West (the United States, its European allies, and Japan) and East (the former Soviet

Union). *South* includes the former colonial countries that had been governed from London, Paris, Brussels, and other Western capitals. During the cold war, these poorer or basically agrarian, low-income, low-productivity nations used their status between the West and East to enhance their bargaining strength and attract economic assistance from both for their own development; in other words, they learned to play both ends against the middle. But during the détente of the 1970s as their leverage declined, these less-developed—or, more politely, developing countries—increasingly focused their attention on the richer Western states, which supposedly dominated the international economy and exploited them. The developing countries demanded a new international economic order.

Since 1973 and OPEC's quadrupling of oil prices and the oil embargo against the United States, the conflict between rich and poor has shared center stage in the world arena with the older adversary relationship between East and West—and that rich-poor conflict has survived the end of the great-power conflict. The problems of overpopulation, hunger, and poverty faced by the nations of the South remain very much part of the international agenda, and they are voiced especially in the United Nations Conference on Trade and Development (UNCTAD), which has been called a "trade union of the poor." [18]

A Vanishing Category: West, East, and Nonaligned States (First, Second, and Third Worlds)

The tripartite classification of states much in vogue during the cold war years has lost its relevance except for one term. It was not based on power or goals but on states' relations with the superpowers—alignment with the United States (the West), with the Soviet Union (the East), or with neither (states termed *nonaligned*). The three divisions also were known as the First, Second, and Third Worlds. This categorization was especially useful during the many years that the Western alliance (the North Atlantic Treaty Organization, or NATO) confronted the Soviet Union and its allies in Eastern Europe, as well as China, in two solid blocs, often called in the West the Free World and the Communist World. The third bloc or *Third World*, a term still in vogue, incorporated the new nations. What united them was their former colonial history, their economically underdeveloped state or poverty, their sharing of the "revolution of rising expectations," and a foreign policy of nonalignment. But, composed as it was of more than 100 nations of varying sizes, histories, ideologies, and political and economic systems, it can no longer be considered a bloc. Rather, the Third World could be split into the oil-exporting countries; the newly industrialized countries (NICs), sometimes referred to as "export platforms" (Hong Kong, Singapore, South Korea, Taiwan); and the many developing countries with an average per capita income of $500 or less. The principal reason for still listing this category at all is to demonstrate that classifications must be revised as international conditions change. No classification lasts forever. The Second World has disappeared entirely.

NONSTATE ACTORS

Individual nation-states are complemented by other actors. Some are groups of states—intergovernmental organizations (IGOs), or, as they were more commonly called in the past, international organizations. Others are nongovernmental organizations (NGOs).

Intergovernmental Actors

Intergovernmental organizations are voluntary associations of sovereign states, organized to pursue the many different purposes for which states wish to cooperate through some sort of formal and often long-term structure. Decisions made by such IGOs are the product of negotiations among the governmental representatives assigned to them, including foreign and defense ministers, who attend specified meetings. The day-to-day business of each IGO is carried out by its bureaucracy, and its institutional machinery may be relatively small or large and complex, as in the European Community (EC).

During the nineteenth century, in the wake of the twenty-five years of war that followed the French Revolution, the great powers met repeatedly in the Concert of Europe, a series of multilateral summit conferences designed to deal collectively with potentially troublesome issues ranging from the division of Africa to the regulation of international traffic on Europe's rivers to the admission of new states to the European system.[19] Indeed, in 1899 the states, mainly European, convened in The Hague in the Netherlands to discuss the causes, control, and prevention of war itself, producing, among other things, institutions for the peaceful settlement of disputes. Just as significant, if not more so, than these intermittent, ad hoc, high-level meetings of Europe's political leaders were the public international unions that dealt with the increasing number of transnational nonpolitical issues resulting from the proliferating technological, socioeconomic, and cultural "interdependence." In response to the

> unprecedented international flow of commerce in goods, services, people, ideas, germs, and social evils . . . [the] process of international organization . . . quickly resulted in the establishment of a profusion of agencies whose terms of reference touched upon such diverse fields as health, agriculture, tariffs, railroads, standards of weight and measurement, patents and copyrights, narcotic drugs, and prison conditions.[20]

The first of these agencies was the International Telegraphic Union and the Universal Postal Union. The evolution of these types of IGOs testified to the existence of "an area of international affairs within which sovereign states have a common interest in cooperative endeavor." [21] Moreover, such cooperation was the result of need, not idealism.

It is this need that has resulted in the rapid growth of IGOs, from fewer than 200 in the first decade of this century to well over 4,000 by the beginning of the 1990s. IGOs may be classified by scope and function. As for scope, an organization may be global or regional. The United Nations includes most existing states and strives for universal membership. The International Bank for Reconstruction and Development (or World Bank), International Monetary Fund, and General Agreement on Tariffs and Trade (GATT) have broad memberships, although not universal; Western states, especially the United States, are the most prominent members. The developing countries, believing that GATT's promotion of free trade was counter to their interests, started UNCTAD, in which they organized the Group of 77 (now over 100 members) to enhance their bargaining power. By contrast, organizations like the Commonwealth (no longer preceded by *British* because all of its members are regarded as equals) comprise states in almost every area of the world; far short of universal membership, the Commonwealth is nevertheless a global organization. Similarly, OPEC, the nucleus of which is Arab (Saudi Arabia, Algeria, Qatar, Kuwait, Libya, Iraq, and the United Arab Emirates), has other members in the Middle East (Iran), Africa (Nigeria and Gabon), Southeast Asia (Indonesia), and Latin America (Venezuela and Ecuador). Mexico accepted "observer" status in OPEC in 1982. Other producer cartels also have multiregional or global membership.

Most IGOs, however, are regional. Many areas have organizations through which member states may promote regional cooperation or resolve common political problems or internal quarrels. The Organization of American States (OAS), the Organization for African Unity (OAU), the Arab League, and the current post-cold war forty-eight-nation Conference on Security and Cooperation in Europe (CSCE), are four examples. There are also military alliances such as NATO, which has survived the end of the cold war, as well as the (Persian) Gulf Cooperation Council (composed of Saudi Arabia, Kuwait, Bahrain, Oman, Qatar, and the United Arab Emirates), a regional IGO whose purpose was to defend its members against Iran (it was less successful against Iraq). As with global organizations, regional organizations are not always completely regional. NATO, for example, has members from North America (Canada and the United States) and the eastern Mediterranean (Greece and Turkey), but the bulk of its membership is European.

A second method of classification is by function: political, military, economic, or social. The United Nations and the OAU are basically political organizations, but they may carry out other tasks as well. NATO obviously had a primarily military purpose during the cold war. The European Coal and Steel Community (ECSC) was proposed by France's foreign minister Robert Schuman in 1950 to integrate these two sectors of the economies of West Germany, France, Italy, and the Benelux countries (Belgium, the Netherlands, and Luxembourg). The ECSC's success led to the formation in 1958 of the European Economic Community (EEC), whose purpose was to integrate the economies of the six different countries into one single economy by eliminating trade barriers and other obstacles to the economic foundation of a United States of Europe (by 1986 the EEC had doubled its membership). Organiza-

Table 3-3 A Select Group of Intergovernmental Organizations

Purpose	Global	Regional
Political	United Nations Commonwealth	Organization of American States (OAS) Organization of African Unity (OAU) Arab League Organization of the Islamic Conference Conference on Security and Cooperation in Europe (CSCE)
Military		North Atlantic Treaty Organization (NATO)
Economic	Organization of Petroleum Exporting Countries (OPEC) International Labor Organization (ILO)	Organization of Arab Petroleum Exporting Countries (OAPEC) European Economic Community (EEC) (includes European Coal and Steel Community, or ECSC) Association of Southeast Asian Nations (ASEAN) African Development Bank
Social/scientific	World Health Organization (WHO) United Nations Educational, Scientific and Cultural Organization (UNESCO)	European Space Agency

tions dealing with health, education, communications, and food, such as the World Health Organization (WHO) and the United Nations Educational, Scientific and Cultural Organization (UNESCO), focus on social purposes. It should be noted that few regional IGOs are concerned with issues of peace and security; most have economic or social functions (see Table 3-3).

From IGO to Subregional Groupings

In recent years, some regional organizations have become more and more divided and unable to act with a united front. For example, in 1982, when Argentina forcibly seized the British-owned Falkland Islands, most of Spanish- and Portuguese-speaking Latin America, from democratic Venezuela to Communist Cuba, supported Argentina. Although the depth of this support for Argentina's aggression was questionable, there was a surface solidarity constituting a majority. The United States supported Britain and helped its military efforts to retake the islands. Because its English-speaking members, mainly Caribbean, refused to support Argentina, the Organization of American States splintered into eighteen Latin and thirteen English-speaking countries. Indeed, the initial diplomatic efforts to resolve the conflict focused on the United Nations. The OAS also was not involved in efforts to resolve differences between the United States and Nicaragua resulting from the 1979 Sandinista revolution. Rather, this endeavor fell to the Contadora countries, composed of Mexico, Venezuela, Colombia, and Panama. When these efforts failed, the Central American presidents, organized by Costa Rica's president Oscar Arias Sanchez, took the initiative in devising a peace plan, which ended the contra war and provided for a free election in which the Sandinistas were defeated. In 1962, the OAS supported the United States during the Cuban missile crisis. But in 1983, the OAS did not approve U.S. intervention on the island of Grenada; Washington therefore sought legitimation for its action from a previously little-known alliance of small Caribbean islands, the Association of East Caribbean States. In 1987, the presidents of six Latin American states (Colombia, Mexico, Panama, Peru, Uruguay, and Venezuela) met for the first time ever without the United States and agreed that Cuba should be invited to rejoin all regional organizations. And not only did Latin America oppose U.S. intervention against Panama's Gen. Manuel Noriega, but the OAS also refused to take a collective strong stand, as desired by the United States, after Noriega stole the election from opposition parties in 1989. Washington had wanted the OAS to help negotiate a transition from Noriega to a more democratic Panama.

Other IGOs have similarly broken down into smaller, more workable groups. Leading examples are, in the Middle East, the Gulf Cooperation Council (GCC), the Arab Cooperation Council (Egypt, Iraq, Jordan, and Yemen), and the Maghreb Union (Algeria, Libya, Mauritania, Morocco, and Tunisia);[22] in Africa, the Organization of Front-Line States (Angola, Botswana, Mozambique, Tanzania, and, since 1980, Zimbabwe), initially formed to help Zimbabwe become independent and more recently involved with South Africa's racial turmoil and independence for Namibia; and in Asia, ASEAN, the Association of Southeast Asian Nations (Indonesia, Malaysia, the Philippines, Singapore, Thailand, and, since 1984, Brunei), which deals mainly with members' common economic issues, although the association also has become concerned with security issues.

But even some of these groups have proven ineffective. The GCC, whose members had backed Iraq during its war against Iran, found itself helpless against Saddam Hussein in 1990 when he seized Kuwait and incorporated it as a province of Iraq. For one thing, GCC members have a history of quarreling with one another, and, despite having a combined population equal to that of Iraq and having spent billions of dollars buying high-tech Western weapons, they have never mobilized their populations. As endangered as these countries were, they had no military draft; in terms of sheer numbers of men, their contribution in proportion to that of the multinational force was minimal. Thus, they were in effect dependent on external support: the United States and the coalition it organized against Iraq and, possibly, Iran as a counterbalance against Iraq once the Kuwaiti problem had been resolved and the foreign forces had been withdrawn. It was doubtful that the United States, the friend of Israel, would long station ground forces in Saudi Arabia since this might, among other things, undermine the traditional culture and the legitimacy of its ruling family.

Supranational Actors

There is one significant exception to the rule that in intergovernmental organizations the participating members maintain their autonomy. Since 1950 in Western Europe, there has been a revolutionary attempt to move beyond the nation-state toward a supranational actor. The six members of the European Coal and Steel Community had joined in an IGO to transfer the authority of their governments in specified economic sectors to a new federal authority, which was to be established above them. Decisions were to be made by this higher authority; they would no longer be arrived at by negotiations among the member governments. Thus by 1958, the ECSC had been succeeded by the European Economic Community. This six-member organization was joined later by Britain, Denmark, Ireland, Greece, Spain, and Portugal. The EEC, together with the ECSC and the European Atomic Energy Community (Euratom), formed in 1958, constitute the European Community (EC). Although the EC has not made the progress originally expected in moving toward political union, the twelve member states will take a major step forward when on January 1, 1993, they remove the last barriers to economic union in the expectation of making European corporations more competitive in the global economy and turning Europe into an economic superpower. The EC also is planning to move toward a single European currency to help this process along.

Nongovernmental or Transnational Actors

Increasingly visible since World War II has been the transnational actor, the nongovernmental organization. It is characterized by a headquarters in one country and centrally directed operations in two or more countries. The term *transnational* is appropriate because the NGO performs its functions not only across national frontiers but also often in disregard of them. The increase in the number, size, scope, and variety of NGOs since World War II has led observers to speak of a transnational organizational revolution in world politics.[23] NGOs differ from IGOs in a number of significant ways. IGOs are composed of nation-states, and their actions depend on their members' common interests. Conflicting interests must first be reconciled through negotiations, which may not always be successful or rapid. The transnational organization represents its own interests and pursues them in many nations.

> The international organization requires *accord* among nations; the transnational organization requires *access* to nations.... The restraints on an international organization are largely internal, stemming from the need to produce consensus among its members. The restraints on a transnational organization are largely external, stemming from its need to gain operating authority in different sovereign states. International organizations embody the principle of nationality; transnational organizations try to ignore it.[24]

Multinational Corporations. The most prominent contemporary NGO is the multinational corporation (MNC), the usually huge firm that owns and controls plants and offices in many countries and sells its goods and services around the world. MNCs may be classified according to the kinds of business activities they pursue:[25]

Extractive (resources)
  oil (Mobil)
  copper (Kennecott)
Agriculture (Standard Brands)
Industrial
  capital equipment (Navistar International)
  automobiles (General Motors)
  consumer goods (Colgate-Palmolive)

Service
  tourism (Hilton Hotels, Holiday Inns)
  retail (Sears)
  transportation (Hertz)
  public utilities (General Telephone and Electronics)
Banking (Chase Manhattan)
Conglomerates (International Telephone and Telegraph)

The sheer size of these MNCs is one of the reasons they are now often listed as actors of increasing importance internationally. Lester Brown, a self-styled world watcher, who has ranked nations and MNCs according to gross national product (GNP, the total worth of goods and services produced) and gross annual sales, found that in the early 1970s the first twenty-two entries were the twenty-two largest nations, ranging from the United States to Argentina.[26] The twenty-third was General Motors, followed by Switzerland and Pakistan; Standard Oil of New Jersey and Ford ranked twenty-seventh and twenty-ninth, respectively; Royal Dutch Shell was thirty-sixth, ahead of Iran and Venezuela; and General Electric and International Business Machines were forty-third and forty-fifth, respectively, ahead of Egypt, Nigeria, and Israel. Of the top fifty, forty-one were nations, and nine were MNCs; of the second fifty, eighteen were nations, and thirty-two were MNCs. Clearly, many MNCs have resources much greater than those of most members of the United Nations, and many operate on a geographical scale exceeding that of the great empires of the past. Oil has enhanced these trends. After the 1973 oil crisis, Exxon overtook General Motors as the world's largest corporation. The oil companies all profited enormously; so, of course, did the oil-producing states, raising them in the ranking. After the collapse of oil prices in the early 1980s, General Motors again became the largest MNC. But Exxon, Mobil, Texaco, Royal Dutch Shell, and British Petroleum remain among the leading MNCs. By the late 1980s, more than half the world's nations had smaller GNPs than the annual sales of any of the leading forty MNCs listed in a ranking of the top 100 nations and MNCs.

Regardless of the actual rankings, the implications are obvious. One is the strength of MNCs compared to that of the weaker countries and the influence they can presumably exert within nations. An early fear was that these "new sovereigns" might become more powerful than the governments of many countries, gain control of their economies, and thus dictate their futures. Another fear, of even greater significance, was their possible effects on the state system itself. Because of the MNCs' multinational production, distribution, and service, some observers have argued that the MNCs will make the nation-state obsolete. The MNCs have already ushered in a global economy, increasingly tying the industrial nations together in an interdependent relationship (see Chapter 16). Their role in helping the developing countries advance also has gained importance. Since many of the government-run economies of developing countries have been unable to induce sufficient economic growth and make their industries profitable, a number of these countries reassessed the potential threat the large MNCs posed to their independence and since the 1980s, have welcomed American, European, and Asian MNCs to invest in their countries.

Religious, Humanitarian, and Professional Actors.   One of the oldest and most visible NGOs is the Roman Catholic church, with its membership of almost a billion people. To do its work, the church has learned over the centuries to coexist with all manner of governments, including fascist ones. The political influence of the church can hardly be doubted. Even the former Communist governments in Eastern Europe treated the church with caution. In 1989, a first-ever meeting took place between an atheist Soviet leader and the pope.

The church's influence is worldwide. In 1985 at a Synod of Bishops in Rome, the church welcomed representatives from thirty-four African countries, seventeen Asian countries, and twenty-two Latin American and Caribbean countries. "Their voices were varied, but their message was clear: This is the new Catholic church, the church of the third world, and it is the church of the future." [27] Almost 50 percent of the world's Catholics live in the Third World. The most significant fact about the church, however, is its changed political orientation since the 1970s. Earlier, the church tended to be associated with authoritarian regimes; democracy was generally linked to protestantism. But since the seventies, starting in Portugal and Spain in the mid-1970s, followed by Catholic South and Central America, then Asia's one Catholic country, the Philippines, and finally in the mid-1980s Poland and Hungary, the two Catholic countries the most active in the struggle for democracy in the area, the power of the church has been arrayed against dictatorial regimes. This has deprived those regimes of whatever legitimacy they had gained from the church and brought its vast resources—its organization (national and transnational), wealth, and prestige—to the assistance and protection of pro-democratic opposition movements. Through its courageous bishops worldwide and, above all, the leadership of Pope John Paul II, a Pole whose papal visits to many countries have coincided with critical moments in the democratization process, the church has played a key role in denouncing violations of human rights and declaring itself to be a guardian of freedom.[28]

Other well-known NGOs are the International Red Cross, whose concern in wartime is with prisoners of war and in peacetime with natural and manmade disasters; Amnesty International, an organization that has gained prominence because of its monitoring of human rights abuses in many countries; and the French organization, Doctors without Borders, which has sent physicians all over the world to assist victims of oppression and war, even in Afghanistan, where its personnel often worked in great danger of being captured and possibly executed by the Soviets. Other examples of professional and social NGOs are the International Political Science Organization; the International Studies Association (which includes many of the "famous" textbook writers students so enjoy reading!); the International Skeletal Society, whose members are radiologists, orthopedists, and pathologists; and the better-known Rotary Club. Their main function is to link human beings in different countries. Most have little influence on the conduct of their nations' foreign policies, but they do foster many international friendships as well as advance professional knowledge. Some, though nonpolitical, have become politicized. The Olympic Games, for example, organized by the International Olympic Committee, overlap with the East-West competition, notwithstanding national protestations to the contrary.

'National Liberation' Groups.   An actor of great post-1945 importance in the state system is the self-styled "national liberation" organization. Perhaps the best known of these since the 1960s has been the Palestine Liberation Organization. Even before it declared the existence of a Palestinian state, it had been recognized as the legitimate representative of the Palestinians by the Arab states, granted observer status at the United Nations, and represented at meetings of the nonaligned countries as a full-fledged member. PLO leader Yasir Arafat had been received by the political leaders of Europe and Japan, usually with the honors reserved for a visiting head of state. Even the pope received him in 1982. Despite subsequent attempts by President Hafez al-Assad of Syria to wrest control of the PLO from Arafat, the PLO has gained full diplomatic status in fifty-five countries and has established nearly 100 foreign missions—more than Israel![29] In 1988, Arafat even declared the existence of a Palestinian state with himself as president, although the West Bank and Gaza Strip were still occupied by Israel and considered "liberated territories" by the right-wing Israeli government, whose declared position has been that it will not trade land for peace. Later the same year, Arafat publicly denounced terrorism and acknowledged Israel's right to exist. But subsequently he refused to denounce a major terrorist attempt by one of the organizations within the PLO, and in 1990 he embraced Saddam Hussein, thereby strengthening the Israeli suspicion that Arafat was merely posturing when he said he rejected terrorism. In any case, the upshot was reinforcement of Israel's unwillingness to negotiate with him.

There was something deliciously ironic and certainly paradoxical about Arafat's endorsement of the Iraqi conqueror of Kuwait as a potential liberator of territory when the PLO leader had always asserted that Israel had to give up the land it had conquered in an act of aggression (but in fact had captured after the war with Egypt, Syria, and Jordan in 1967)! Arafat's alignment of the PLO with Saddam Hussein, therefore, undermined the legal and moral basis of his claim that the seizure and occupation of territory were unacceptable and destroyed his credibility as a man who wanted a peaceful solution to the Palestinian problem. This was reinforced by Arafat's later condemnation of "American aggression" when the war started. This failure to denounce the aggression against Kuwait and to support the UN resolutions demanding Iraq's withdrawal not only reinforced the determination of the Israeli government never to negotiate with him but also alienated the Arab sheiks who had long bankrolled the PLO. In short, Arafat may have irreparably damaged the PLO's future influence; his endorsement of Iraq discredited and "defunded" him. The 1991 disarmament of the PLO in southern Lebanon by the Lebanese army further weakened the organization. During the subsequent Middle East peace process, the willingness of the Palestinians on the West Bank to negotiate with Israel on the limited issue of their autonomy, despite past PLO opposition to negotiations with Israel on any issue but the establishment of a Palestinian state, reflected that weakness.

Other well-known post-World War II national liberation organizations include the Patriotic Front, which fought a guerrilla war against the white-dominated government of Rhodesia, claiming that it represented the interests of the majority of black Rhodesians (it later won power in a free election and now controls the new state of Zimbabwe); the Southwest African People's Organization (SWAPO), which gained power in Namibia, a former German colony that was administered by South Africa from the end of World War I to 1989, when it became independent; the Mau Mau in Kenya, which brought British colonialism to an end and brought self-government to that country; the Polisario, which is fighting Morocco for control of the Western Sahara; and the Farabundo Marti Liberation Front, which until 1992, when it signed a cease-fire agreement, had sought to capture power in El Salvador.

Obviously, the PLO and some of these national liberation movements have exerted considerable leverage in international politics—more than many states—in their efforts to found states of their own. They may well be called "states-in-waiting." A key means of achieving this goal has been the waging of guerrilla warfare against the government in power. Communist national liberation groups have been particularly successful in this regard: the liberation of Yugoslavia from German occupation in World War II; the long Chinese Communist civil war against the Nationalist Chinese government, which ended with China becoming a Communist nation; Fidel Castro's campaign against the Batista regime in Cuba, which turned Cuba into a Communist nation; the Viet Cong's battle against the pro-American government in South Vietnam, which led to American military intervention; and the Sandinista campaign against the Somoza dictatorship in Nicaragua.

Note the names of some of these movements' leaders: Tito, Mao Zedong, Castro, and Ho Chi Minh. All were charismatic leaders who became famous during their military struggles, which they won. These feats testify not only to their skill as military leaders but also to their ability to organize political discontent in their nations. They were, above all, astute and ruthless politicians and "nation-builders," who, after acquiring power, governed their nations. By contrast, no terrorist leader has successfully overthrown an established government and become a successful "father of his country."

Terrorists

Although national liberation movements do resort to terror, the features that distinguish them from terrorist groups are several (also see Chapter 20). While national liberation groups organize the masses (for example, peasants who do not own their own land), terrorists tend to be narrowly based. National liberation groups tend to originate in rural areas; terrorists in cities. The former are usually led by renowned individuals who have great appeal, but the latter are normally anonymous. One tends to carve out rural areas as "liberated territory"; the other hides among the multitudes in an urban environment. One wages a protracted conflict or guerrilla war; the other engages in sporadic violence. Both claim to be motivated by a good cause, and both start out from positions of weakness. The national liberation group, however, hopes to isolate the government by neutralizing public opinion while defeating government forces; the terrorist group expects to frighten its enemies into making concessions or surrendering.

A national liberation movement is a serious threat because it may defeat the government, but terrorism constitutes essentially a set of irritating pinpricks not likely to succeed. Nevertheless, given the multiplicity of causes, terrorism is increasingly the means used by desperate or angry individuals and groups anxious to publicize their grievances and aspirations, whether the Party of God (the Iranian-sponsored Islamic fundamentalists whose favorite targets are Americans) or the Red Brigade in Italy. Hijackings, assassinations, kidnappings, attacks on embassies, and other acts of terror have drawn the world's attention to the demands of these groups and have compelled governments to take notice and in some instances even to negotiate with them.

Drug Trafflckers

A group that probably deserves separate mention is drug traffickers, who are engaged in a profitable transnational business. Of these, the most prominent is the Medellin (Colombia) cartel, the world's biggest cocaine organization which is also a terrorist group—hence the term *narco-terrorists*. It has murdered presidential candidates, a justice minister, an attorney general, police officers, newspaper editors, drug informants, and hundreds of civilians unlucky enough to be near explosions or assassination attempts. The government of Colombia generally has been helpless in the struggle against the cocaine drug lords, whose income from exports is greater than that from the country's best-known legal export, coffee. Moreover, Colombia no longer holds a monopoly in cocaine manufacturing; refineries have spread to Bolivia and Peru as sales to Europe, Japan, and Australia have risen sharply.

The Principal Actor

Clearly, then, states are not the only actors on the world scene. Indeed, the proliferation of nonstate actors has led some observers to conclude that states are of declining importance and that nonstate actors are gaining in status and influence. Note, for example, what two writers have said about the multinational corporation: "The rise of the planetary multinational enterprise is producing an organizational revolution as profound in its implications for modern man as the Industrial Revolution and the rise of the nation-state itself." The MNC or planetary corporation is ushering in a world economy, and the corporation itself is "the first institution in human history dedicated to centralized planning on a world scale." Whereas men like Napoleon and Hitler failed in their conquest of much of the world, the managers of the corporate giants "proclaim their faith that where conquest has failed, business can succeed." [30] Even now, these managers make daily business decisions that have more impact on our daily lives in terms of what we wear, eat, and drink, what work we do, and where we live than do governments.

More broadly, the rise of MNCs and the vast growth of so many other kinds of nonstate actors are said to challenge and weaken, if not actually undermine, the "state-centric" concept of international politics and replace it with a "transnational" world in which relationships are considerably more numerous and complex than just traditional state-to-state ones. There are in fact three sets of relationships. In the first, states deal with one another directly or as members of IGOs (for example, when the United States and Russia negotiate an arms control agreement, the Indian prime minister visits England, or a Brazilian official talks to the World Bank about a loan). States also deal increasingly with NGOs (for example, when the United States negotiates with Shiite Amal militia in Lebanon for the release of hostages seized on a TWA plane, or a U.S. environmental group, the Natural Resources Defense Council, negotiates with the Russian government about verifying a low-threshold Russian nuclear test, or a developing country negotiates with an MNC to set up a factory within its borders). Finally, NGOs deal with one another (for example, when Shiite, Druse, and Christian militia fight one another in Lebanon, when Ford and Mazda produce cars for the U.S. market, or, in a more pleasurable way, when the Montreal Expos play the Houston Astros).

Despite the proliferation of nongovernmental organizations, the state remains—as it has remained for 300 years—the primary actor in the state system. The birthrate of new states has been high; it has increased fourfold since World War II. Nationalism seems especially rife in Eastern Europe and the developing countries. People can, of course, be loyal to more than one organization, but the nation-state remains for most people the object of their most intense loyalty. For the millions who have finally achieved the much desired and long sought-after national statehood, it is a new and exhilarating experience. Even transnational loyalties such as communism until its collapse,

Zionism, or. Islamic fundamentalism have become identified with specific nation-states such as the former Soviet Union, Israel, and Iran, respectively.

States also remain unique because of their control of territory. The MNCs need access to territory to make profits; the Roman Catholic church needs access to territory to reach people and save souls; terrorists and national liberation groups need access to bases from which to pursue their campaigns. During the 1970s and early 1980s, the PLO operated from its base in Lebanon; the former Patriotic Front conducted its war from the countries surrounding Zimbabwe. Such liberation groups cannot survive without at least the acquiescence of the states in which they are based and without the active support of other states, such as Libya, who supply them with weapons, training, and money. Finally, the state remains the principal user of *legitimate* force. It can enforce decisions at home and decide whether to go to war and when.

The state has survived since the Peace of Westphalia in 1648, but throughout this period it has never been the sole actor in the system. There always have been significant nongovernmental organizations such as the Catholic church; the large European trading companies such as the British East India Company, which had its own armed forces and controlled territory, something no modern MNC does; antislavery societies; and great financial houses such as the Rothschilds'.[31] Moreover, these organizations have deeply affected domestic and foreign policies. But the state remains the principal actor and the system has long been defined by its principal actor, not by all the types of actors within it.[32] Despite the rapid rise of trans- and supranational forces in this century, the state remains alive and well.

But this does not mean that nonstate actors and transnational activities are unimportant. It only means that they have not yet rendered the state system obsolete. As long as states remain the major actors, the structure of international politics remains state-centric. States continue to dictate the terms of coexistence for themselves and other actors in the system. Kenneth Waltz, a political scientist, has remarked that a theory of international politics that denies the central role of states will be needed only if nongovernmental actors rival or surpass the influence of the great powers, not just a few of the lesser ones, on issues of war and peace. This is most unlikely. Despite the profusion of nonstate actors, the structure and processes of international politics remain basically the same; a new kind of international politics is not yet evident.[33] Moreover, states have a strong record of survival; few ever die. But business organizations do go out of existence. Who is more likely to be around in a hundred years, the United States or IBM? Given the longevity of the state as the principal actor, any analysis of international politics must start with the state and its motivations, objectives, and interaction with other states. Only then can one also understand the role and impact of other actors.

For Review

1. What is a *sovereign state,* and what are some of its chief characteristics?
2. Is there a difference between *nationality* and *nationalism*?
3. What are the various classifications used for states?
4. Of the nonstate actors in international politics, what is an *intergovernmental organization* (IGO)? A *supranational organization*?
5. What is a *nongovernmental organization* (NGO), and how does it differ from an IGO?

Notes

1. The depressing story of Lebanon is told by British journalist Robert Fisk in *Pity the Nation* (New York: Atheneum, 1990).
2. Alan Riding, "In Latin America, Noriega Is a Principle," *New York Times,* April 24, 1988.
3. Chris Hedges, "Kurds Find Hope of Freedom Slipping Out of Their Grasp," and "Iraqi Army Shells Kurdish Foes in Apparent Violation of Truce," *New York Times,* February 6 and March 31, 1992.
4. Bill Keller, "Demographics Puts Strain on Soviet Ethnic Seams," *New York Times,* December 28, 1987; and Philip Taubman, "Estonia Asserts a Right of Veto on Soviet Laws," *New York Times,* November 17, 1988.
5. From the *New York Times,* see Bill Keller, "After the Breakup: E Pluribus . . . What?" August 30, 1991; Andrew Rosenthal, "Farewell, Red Menace," August 30, 1991; Francis X. Clines, "A Gamble With Chaos," September 1, 1991; "Republics Rebuff Gorbachev on a New Union Accord," September 3, 1991; Serge Schmemann, "The Soviet Shell," November 26, 1991; "Declaring Death of Soviet Union, Russia and Two Republics Form a New Commonwealth," December 2, 1991; and Celestine Bohlen, "The Union Is Buried. What's Being Born?" December 9, 1991.
6. Richard N. Gardner and Toby Trister Gati, "Russia Deserves the Soviet Seat," *New York Times,* December 19, 1991.
7. See, for example, F. Stephen Larrabee's aptly titled article "Long Memories and Short Fuses," *International Security* (Winter 1990/91): 58-91. Also see Henry Kamm, "As Slovak Separation Gains, Havel Faces the Unthinkable," *New York Times,* November 20, 1991; V. P. Gagnon, Jr., "Yugoslavia; Prospects for Stability," *Foreign Affairs* (Summer 1991): 17-35; James Gow, "Deconstructing Yugoslavia," *Survival* (July/August 1991): 291-311; and for a historic perspective, Aleksa Djilas, *The Contested Country* (Cambridge, Mass.: Harvard University Press, 1991).
8. Ann Mosley Lesch and Mark Tessler, *Israel, Egypt and the Palestinians* (Bloomington: Indiana University Press, 1989); Don Peretz, *Intifada* (Boulder, Colo.: Westview Press, 1990); and Robert O. Freedman, ed., *The Intifada* (Gainesville: University of Florida Press, 1991).
9. Deborah J. Gerner, *One Land, Two Peoples* (Boulder, Colo.: Westview Press, 1990). Also see Ehud Sprinzak, "With Friends Like These," *New York Times,* August 15, 1991.

10. William J. Broad, "Guarding the Bomb: A Perfect Record, But Can It Last?" *New York Times,* January 29, 1991; Gabriel Schoefield, "Loose Cannon," *New Republic,* March 11, 1991, 16-18; and John J. Fialka, "The Risk Now Posed by the Soviet 'Nukes' Is One of Management," *Wall Street Journal,* November 20, 1991.

11. Jack S. Levy, *War in the Modern Great Power System, 1495-1975* (Lexington: University Press of Kentucky, 1983).

12. Ibid., 53.

13. Ibid., 9-10.

14. Inis L. Claude, Jr., *Swords into Plowshares* (New York: Random House, 1956), 53.

15. David O. Wilkinson, *Comparative Foreign Relations* (Belmont, Calif.: Dickensen, 1969), 27.

16. Charles Krauthammer, "The Poverty of Realism," *New Republic,* February 17, 1986, 17 (italics added). For an opposing view and a narrower construction of national interest, see George F. Kennan, "Morality and Foreign Policy," *Foreign Affairs* (Winter 1985/86): 205-218.

17. Quoted by William Shawcross, *The Shah's Last Ride* (New York: Simon & Schuster, 1988), 317.

18. Robert L. Rothstein, *The Weak in the World of the Strong* (New York: Columbia University Press, 1977), 127.

19. Seyom Brown, *New Forces, Old Forces and the Future of World Politics* (Boston: Scott/Foresman, 1988), 25. Also see Claude, *Swords into Plowshares,* 23-26.

20. Claude, *Swords into Plowshares,* 35.

21. Ibid., 40; and Brown, *New Forces, Old Forces,* 25-26.

22. Alan Cowell, "Arabs Forming 2 Economic Blocs," *New York Times,* February 17, 1989.

23. Samuel P. Huntington, "Transnational Organizations in World Politics," *World Politics* (April 1973): 333; and Richard W. Mansbach, et al., *The Web of World Politics* (Englewood Cliffs, N.J.: Prentice-Hall, 1976).

24. Huntington, "Transnational Organizations," 338.

25. The classification is based on the table in *The Politics of Global Economic Relations* (3d ed.) by David H. Blake and Robert S. Walters (Englewood Cliffs, N.J.: Prentice-Hall, 1987), 97.

26. Lester R. Brown, *World without Borders* (New York: Vintage, 1973), 213-215; *1983 World Bank Development Report* (New York: Oxford University Press, 1983), 148-149; and *Fortune 500,* May 1983.

27. Quoted in the *New York Times,* December 6, 1985.

28. Samuel P. Huntington, "Religion and the Third Wave," *National Interest* (Summer 1991): 29-42; and Eric O. Hansen, *The Catholic Church in World Politics* (Princeton, N.J.: Princeton University Press, 1990).

29. Neil C. Livingstone and David Halevy, *Inside the PLO* (New York: Morrow, 1990); and Janet Wallach and John Wallach, *Arafat* (New York: Lyle Stuart, 1990).

30. Richard J. Barnet and Ronald E. Miller, *Global Reach* (New York: Simon & Schuster, 1975), 13-15.

31. Hedley Bull, *Anarchical Society* (New York: Columbia University Press, 1977), 271; and K. J. Holsti, *The Dividing Discipline* (Boston: Allen & Unwin, 1985), 137.

32. Kenneth N. Waltz, *Theory of International Politics* (Reading, Mass.: Addison-Wesley, 1979), 93-94.

33. Holsti, *Dividing Discipline,* 137-138.

CHAPTER 4

The Stakes:
The Objectives
of States

POWER POLITICS

The sovereign state is the heart of the state system, and the first and most fundamental prerequisite for any state to survive and remain independent is power. A state may have extensive power or relatively little, but if it is to stay independent, it must have a sufficient amount to ward off potential threats. It may mobilize enough power by itself, or it can join together with other states in alliances. It is because of the pervasive nature of power in international politics that the term *power politics* often is used. Indeed, international politics cannot be anything but power politics.

Strictly speaking, as often as this term is used, it is misused. Power politics is a tautology—that is, it combines two words having the same meanings. Politics is inseparable from power. Whatever a state's objectives or goals, power provides a means to achieve them. Thus, to say "power politics" is repetitious and unnecessary. But one point about the term must be stressed: power is a means to an end; it is not an end in itself. Some analysts claim, however, that the accumulation of power is a continual concern of states. Whatever the ultimate aim, the immediate goal is power. According to this view, power is seen as desirable in itself and may be pursued for its own sake. "Whatever preserves and enhances power must be cherished. Whatever leads to the enfeeblement of power must be avoided." [1] Yet to treat power as an end in itself is analogous to discussing the accumulation of money without any reference to the purposes for which it is spent. An analysis of power must therefore start with a "theory of end." [2] States are not always preoccupied with enhancing power; sometimes they are satisfied with the power they have, and sometimes they will even reduce it. It depends on the objectives they seek and how intensely these are pursued.

Given the priority states attach to their security, for example, it would be better to substitute the term *security politics.*

SECURITY, WELFARE, AND OTHER AIMS

National Security

What are the most common objectives states seek? The first and most basic is *security* against possible external military threats. But a state can expect to realize only some of what it wants. A state can expect a *degree* of security, not absolute security; it can feel only *relatively* safe, not completely safe. There is no such thing as absolute security in a state system composed of many national actors; a state could achieve such security only by universal conquest and the destruction of all other independent states—an unlikely possibility. All states, then, "live dangerously." The only question is how much or how little security does a state feel is enough? Although all states, even great powers, feel some degree of vulnerability, some have more control over their destiny than others. No state, however, is the absolute master of its fate.

The term *security* can be broken down into several categories. At the very least, security means simply *physical survival.* Israel, as noted earlier, was born in 1948. Since then it has been surrounded by states that, at least until 1973, were sworn to its extinction; Arabs refused to recognize Israel's right to exist. Only one state, Egypt, has made peace with Israel (in 1979). No other Arab state has yet formally recognized Israel. But in the wake of the war with Iraq in 1991, there was renewed diplomatic activity under U.S. sponsorship.

A second and more common meaning of security refers to the preservation of a state's *territorial integrity.* Because frontiers may change over time, states may redefine the meaning of this term. Poland, for example, has shifted its eastern and western frontiers westward since World War II; the Soviet frontier also moved westward. The issue of frontiers is particularly troublesome among the developing countries, for, as in Eastern Europe, their territorial integrity may not always correspond to ethnic and linguistic divisions. The new nations inherited their boundaries from colonial rulers, and it is this territorial integrity that some developing countries seek to defend. Other states, however, claim pieces of their territory on the basis of reuniting ethnic groups. Somalia, for example, had claims against Ethiopia that led to fighting in 1978 and to Soviet-Cuban intervention to defend Ethiopia's territorial integrity. Frontiers are part of a nation's identity and dignity. During the peace negotiations after the 1973 war, Egypt demanded the return of the entire Sinai Desert in exchange for peace with Israel. During the 1967 war, Israel seized Syria's Golan Heights to improve its security, but Syria considers the area an integral part of its territory.

A third meaning of security is *political independence,* which refers, negatively, to a state's freedom from foreign control and, positively, to the preservation of its domestic political and economic system. Security involves more than a state's physical survival and territorial security; it also includes the perpetuation of the values, patterns of social relations, lifestyles, and varied other elements that make up a nation's way of life. The threats to the United States in this century were not related to physical danger, for neither Germany during either world war nor the Soviet Union immediately after 1945 had the air power to reach and destroy the United States, or even to invade it across 3,000 miles of ocean. The United States intervened on each occasion because its leaders saw the domination of Europe by a nondemocratic—indeed, *antidemocratic*—great power as a threat to the security of the United States and to the kind of world environment in which the United States could most comfortably exist.

President Franklin Roosevelt explained his decision to aid Britain in 1940 and 1941 by stating that the United States should not become a lone democratic island surrounded by totalitarian seas to its east and west (Roosevelt included Japan's threat in the Pacific in this statement). He meant that, as a *democratic* state, the nation had to preserve an international order in which democracy could flourish. Thus, the United States could not stand by and watch one democracy after another snuffed out by antidemocratic regimes. The result would be a hostile external environment, incompatible with American conceptions of what is just and unjust. That is why the United States today, fifty years later, remains committed to the defense of Western Europe.

External threats to the nation's security have been accompanied by an internal one as well—drugs. Indeed, in 1984 the U.S. Joint Chiefs of Staff declared drugs a threat to the national security because they were undermining the country's social fabric and the discipline of the military services. In 1986, the year U.S. troops were deployed briefly to Bolivia to cut its cocaine production and exports to the United States, President Ronald Reagan also issued a secret directive labeling drug trafficking as a national security threat. (In 1988, while on a visit to Bolivia, Secretary of State George Shultz and his motorcade were the target of a bomb attack, allegedly by drug traffickers.) A "war on drugs" has been officially declared because these imports affect everything from the workplace to lifestyles, from crime to public health. The United States spends billions each year on the war on drugs, but even this sum remains insufficient. And this is a "war" that is not likely to end soon. In 1988, the State Department reported that in most drug-producing countries the production of coca, marijuana, and opium poppy crops had grown substantially and that no single government could control the flood of imports.[3] (The principal sources of coca, from which cocaine is derived, are Bolivia, Chile, Colombia, and Peru, and of marijuana, Colombia, Jamaica, and Mexico.) The report was hardly surprising: as long as demand remains high, there will be supplies. In the meantime, drugs will continue to eat away at the very fabric of American society, a reminder that security needs to be defined in terms broader than military ones.

Economic Security

Even though the issue of security historically has been analyzed within a military context, should it be defined only in terms of the most visible and most obvious threat? The emphasis on a basically military definition of security is perhaps nowhere more clearly demonstrated than in the failure of the United States to protect itself against a sudden disruption of oil imports. Despite the events of the 1970s—the quadrupling of oil prices by the Organization of Petroleum Exporting Countries (OPEC) in 1973-1974, the embargo against the United States for its support of Israel upon its attack by Egypt and Syria, and the further sharp jump in oil prices after the shah of Iran fell in 1979—the nation still lacked an energy policy and remained vulnerable to events overseas, especially in the volatile Middle East-Persian Gulf area. As a result, in 1990, when the oil production and pricing policies of OPEC's Arab members threatened to fall under the control of Iraq's ruthless and ambitious ruler, Saddam Hussein, the United States and other industrial democracies undertook military intervention to ward off this threat to their economic security.*

An even more basic threat to the economic security of the nation was a legacy of the Reagan administration during the 1980s. Coming into office committed to both a huge increase in defense spending and a big tax reduction to stimulate the economy, it ran up the highest deficits in the nation's history. In April 1985, the United States became a debtor nation for the first time since World War I. In 1986, the U.S. debt exceeded those of Brazil and Mexico, the world's two largest debtor nations. The entire federal debt in 1980, accumulated since the founding of the Republic, was three-quarters of a trillion dollars. By the end of the eight years of the Reagan administration, this figure was $3 trillion. To underline the point: Ronald Reagan, an advocate of balanced budgets, had in eight years created a national debt larger than the combined deficits of every administration since George Washington; in 1981, after 205 years, it had totaled almost $1 billion. (By the beginning

---

* Despite the fact that an Iraqi-intimidated OPEC represented a danger to the prosperity not only of all the Western industrial states but also of the developing countries and the fragile new democracies in Eastern Europe—that is, to world economic growth—protests soon started in the United States: "No war for oil." Was the United States risking the lives of its youth because it would not place them in efficient cars? Improving the nineteen miles-per-gallon of the family car by three miles per gallon, it was claimed, would replace all oil imported from Iraq and Kuwait; nine more miles would end the need for any Gulf oil. The protesters seemed to suggest that there was something wrong about defending material interests. Amory B. Lovins and L. Hunter Lovins, "Making Fuel Efficiency Our Gulf Strategy," *New York Times*, December 3, 1990.

of 1993, the figure will probably hit $4.5 trillion.) The budget deficit at the end of Reagan's term in office in early 1989 was reportedly $155 billion. But, in fact, the figure was considerably higher. Creative bookkeeping disguised this higher figure by using the surplus the government had in the huge Social Security fund to reduce the figure and by not adding the huge sums needed to bail out the savings and loan failures. The actual deficit was over $300 billion. Even with such manipulation of the figures, President George Bush, two years in office, had to go back on his election promise not to raise taxes. By the end of the 1990 fiscal year, the official deficit amounted to $220 billion, and, despite a five-year White House budget reduction package, the deficit kept on growing: from $269 billion in 1991 to an expected record $362 billion in 1993, including increased spending for bank and savings and loan failures plus an explosion in Medicare and Medicaid costs. The interest alone on the deficit has become the government's largest economic commitment, ahead of defense and Social Security, as well as health, education, welfare, roads, prisons, and environmental protection.

This meant that the billions needed for education, infrastructure (roads and bridges), environmental cleanup, and the cities and states trying to arrest their declining ability to provide basic services were unavailable; the same was true for the funds needed to help the states of Eastern Europe and the Commonwealth of Independent States (CIS). Much of the world wondered whether the United States could ever get its economic house back in order. The public binge of living beyond its means (that is, beyond the level that it was willing to pay in higher taxes), as true in the private sector as it was in the public one, could not continue without endangering the future of the economy. Yet, while demanding services, the same public continued to resist higher taxes.

As if a debt greater than the total owed by all of the developing countries collectively were not bad enough, the economic security of the nation was even more endangered by its growing uncompetitiveness in the global market. In the late Reagan/early Bush administration days, Congress opposed an American-Japanese deal, supported by the Defense Department, in which the Japanese would upgrade the F-16, the most modern U.S. jet fighter. Its reason: such a deal would give the Japanese the knowledge to build up their own aerospace industry. Why this concern? The United States felt vulnerable. One industry after another had been ravaged by foreign competition, often from Japan (see Chapters 8 and 16). The country faced a huge trade deficit— peaking at $152 billion in 1987 and falling to $66 billion in 1991—and affected industries and labor sought protection against "unfair trade." "Japan-bashing," as it was called, was the reaction. The one American industry that still thrived was aerospace; the United States built most of the world's passenger aircraft and the most modern fighter planes. Thus, Congress insisted that the Reagan administration add more safeguards to the contract so that the Japanese would not be able to "steal" American technology and use it, as in other areas, to then compete and best the last industry in which the

United States excelled. Clearly, the country was becoming aware of its economic decline and weaknesses. And yet because of the belief in free trade, the government refused to adopt an industrial policy to support U.S. companies in their research and development in some of the most modern technologies that would be the basis of tomorrow's economies, national prosperity, and international competitiveness.

Some of the problems of American industry reflected the quality of U.S. labor, which in turn reflected the nation's educational standards (reportedly among the lowest in the industrial world). The United States was graduating fewer engineers and scientists than Japan, which has less than half its population. American children attend school an average of 180 days a year, Japanese children 240 days; the average in Europe is 220 days. Moreover, American children go to school for six and a half hours a day, while the rest of the industrial world requires eight hours. It is hardly surprising in an increasingly technological world in which mathematics represents the cutting edge of research and development—a subject in which American children place lower than children of other industrial countries—that the United States also has difficulties competing in the new high-technology industries. Japanese and German children simply learn more mathematics and science than American children because they are at school longer and do not have a 29 percent high school dropout rate and a 20 percent functional illiteracy rate among high school graduates. Knowledge is the key to future economic competitiveness. Yet despite all the publicity about these shortcomings of U.S. education, they persist. Even among the brightest products of the U.S. educational system, most in the 1980s were drawn not to science and engineering but to corporate law, investment houses, and management consultant firms— that is, to the manipulation of data and money, not to the invention or development of new technologies.

Perhaps symbolic of America's economic decline and the country's new sense of vulnerability was what has been called the "buying into America" or, more aptly, "the selling of America" to the British, Japanese, and Dutch, as well as to others.[4] Foreigners bought up land, buildings, corporations, and financial institutions. From 1974 to the end of the Reagan administration, foreign investments increased from under $20 million to $1.3 trillion, or more than sixtyfold. While such investments have slowed down in order to avoid arousing the ire of American public opinion, this situation has raised deep fears about the future control of the "American" economy—fears that, when expressed by Europeans in the 1960s and developing countries in the 1970s as U.S. multinational corporations invested billions of dollars in their economies, had been discounted. Ironically, the individual states and communities seeking to attract Japanese business helped along this process of "selling America." It is not surprising that U.S. public opinion polls taken in 1988 as the cold war was ending placed economic security ahead of military security and regarded Japan and other economic competitors as a greater threat than the Soviet Union.[5] Indeed, Bloomingdale's in New York, Firestone, Goodyear,

Pillsbury (owner of Burger King), RCA and CBS Records, and Hollywood's United Artists/MGM, RCA, Twentieth Century Fox, and Columbia Pictures are now owned by foreigners; Rockefeller Center, the symbol of American wealth, is now owned by the Japanese. Does this selling of America—for which the blame ought to lie not with the Japanese and others buying, but with those selling—not constitute a security threat? Foreigners are increasingly taking over military-related industries, and the United States is becoming more and more dependent on the latest technologies from Japan for its newest weapons.[6]

Perhaps even more symbolic of the state of the economy, in 1990 President Bush sent the secretaries of state and treasury to America's allies and the Arab oil kingdoms for the money required to support the U.S. military deployment to Saudi Arabia. The country was up to its neck in debt. Unable to help the new democracies of Eastern Europe or the republics of the former Soviet Union with more than small amounts of aid, and on the verge of a recession helped along by the higher oil prices resulting from the Iraqi invasion of Kuwait, the United States could not in effect carry out an operation deemed to be in the national interest unless others helped pay for it. Perhaps because U.S. intervention was vital as well to the interests of the donor countries, the demand that they help pay was legitimate. But what would the United States do if it ever felt compelled to intervene somewhere in the future and its friends disagreed or did not want to become involved for one reason or another? Whatever the answer, there can be little doubt that economic security is also basic to the issue of economic welfare.

National Welfare

Since the French Revolution, which mobilized the masses, and the Industrial Revolution, which introduced mass production, states with sizable populations and industrial capacities have ranked at the top of the power hierarchy. But industry and technology involve more than power; they also involve welfare, the desire of people in all societies for a better material life. Therefore governments—even dictatorial ones—must respond to their citizens' demands. The "revolution of rising expectations" is universal; if it is usually thought of in connection with underdeveloped countries, that is only because they are copying the large Western states, which, as the first to industrialize, have provided their people with the world's highest standard of living.

Until the present concern with environmental problems, mostly the by-products of industrialization, economic growth was the chief, if not the sole, criterion for social policy in the West. Raising everyone's living standards was at the heart of the social policies of all modern Western welfare states, including those of the United States. Attempts to redistribute existing or only slowly growing wealth among different classes or segments of society would have precipitated intense social conflict because one class would have gained at the expense of another. Rapidly expanding the "economic pie" so that everyone could have a larger slice of it made it possible to avoid such conflict and any possible political instability while satisfying the vast majority of groups and people. The 1973-1974 oil embargo by OPEC and its quadrupling of prices was therefore a shock because it demonstrated the vulnerability of Western industrial societies to interruptions in supply and price increases and the degree to which the prosperity of Western economies—income, economic growth, employment, ability to afford social services—was entwined with the fortunes of the international economy and international politics. No country was any longer fully in control of its economy. The 1980s and 1990s, with America's increasing exposure to the global economy, have reinforced this lesson as Western economies have grown even more interdependent.

The desire for the "good life" is not limited to Western states. The drive for even higher economic growth rates and a higher gross national product (GNP)* was shared by the Soviet Union as well. Every few years during the 1950s and 1960s, Soviet leaders promised their long-suffering compatriots that, at the end of this or that five-year plan or decade, their standard of living would be comparable to that of the United States, the nation whose economic and social system they never failed to denounce as exploitive and inhumane. But in the 1970s, because the Soviet Union was falling behind in the second industrial revolution of electronics, especially computers, and because this lag affected all areas of its economy and not just the sector devoted to consumer goods production, the Soviets needed access to Western trade and technology as a "fix" for their own overcentralized, overbureaucratized, and often ideologically hamstrung economy. Such access was believed to be a safer alternative than restructuring the economy and society, with the dangers that this potentially posed for the Communist party's continued monopoly of power and the unity of the Soviet state. Thus, détente was the political price the Soviet leadership was willing to pay to improve its industrial and agricultural economies. But a foreign fix was not enough. The central and critical problem was the Soviet system itself. Even restructuring it, as Mikhail Gorbachev attempted after 1985, failed. During his first five years in power, the economy went from bad to worse, until basic food items had to be rationed, if they could be found in the shops at all. It was not just such staples as bread, butter, fruit, and meat that were in short supply but also soap, sugar, razor blades, and cigarettes. In 1990, pushed by more radical advisers and political figures, a desperate Gorbachev, in charge of a disintegrating economy, committed himself to adopting a market economy, the very economy he and all his predecessors had for seventy-three years denounced as exploitive and inhumane. But in practice, he continued to hold up its implementation. By 1991, as the Soviet Union disintegrated, economic conditions were truly desperate. Emergency ship-

---

* This edition continues to use the term *gross national product* (GNP), the sum of all goods and services produced by a country's nationals, regardless of whether they were produced at home or abroad. GNP is now being replaced by gross domestic product (GDP), which measures only the income produced in the country and excludes foreign earnings. The two measurements are in reality fairly close.

ments of food and medicine from the West were but stopgap measures as the eleven republics of the Commonwealth of Independent States tried to stem the economic decline and lay the basis for an economic recovery through adopting free-market systems. Whether after seven decades of communism, the CIS, having neither a democratic tradition nor free-market experience, could succeed remained questionable.

But, among all nations, it is the developing countries that have been the most bent on modernizing—industrializing and urbanizing—themselves. To attract assistance from the competing cold war superpowers, most of the formerly colonial states pursued a policy of nonalignment. When the cold war turned into détente, they began to press their demands more assertively. OPEC's aggressiveness, attempts to organize other producer cartels to control supplies and prices of resources, and demands in the United Nations for a "new international economic order" all were aimed at changing the distribution of wealth, status, and power between the First and Third worlds. They resulted in confrontation between the "haves" and "have-nots" but failed to reduce the gap between the rich and poor nations. Thus, the "revolution of rising expectations" in much of the Third World has turned into a "revolution of rising frustration." Many Third World nations have turned to market economies in the hope of finally producing economic growth and jobs for their rapidly increasing populations. If these expectations are disappointing, the impact on the international system will likely be highly destabilizing because by the year 2000, 80 percent or more of the world's peoples will be living in the less-developed countries.

National Prestige

A fourth objective important to many states, especially great powers, is *prestige*. Precisely because prestige is closely related to power, especially military power, it may be defined as a nation's *reputation for power* among its fellow states. In a sense, prestige is subjective and intangible because it depends on the perception of other states. Prestige, like love, is in the eye of the beholder. It is, to be sure, acquired as the result of past action. Victory on the battlefield, the ability to detect aggression, or the successful use of economic power gains prestige for a state. Other states note that a state is powerful, that it is willing to use its power to gain its aims, and that it has used its power effectively to achieve what it set out to do. In short, the state's power has credibility. This reputation for power, given the nature of the state system, is not to be sneered at and shrugged off as "mere prestige," however, for a nation's reputation for power may mean it will not be challenged and will thus avoid war. Or a nation may gain compliance with its demands, again without having to threaten or fight. In other words, prestige is a critical possession for a state. Prestige rather than power, it has been correctly said, is the everyday currency of international politics, as authority is to governments domestically. It is the reason that in the conduct of diplomacy and resolution of conflict there is relatively little use of force or the threatened use of force.

Rather, the bargaining among states and the outcomes of negotiations are determined principally by the relative prestige of the parties involved. But behind such negotiations there is the implicit mutual recognition that deadlock at the bargaining table could lead to a decision on the battlefield.[7]

Great powers historically have associated prestige with military power and the successful use of force. Indeed, the Soviet Union's status in the world after 1945 stemmed largely from its military power—and more recently from its strategic nuclear capability. The Soviet Union's victory in World War II and expansion into eastern Europe transformed the Soviet Union into a superpower, even though it did not at the time have an atomic bomb. Over the last forty years, however, the Soviet Union performed poorly in feeding and providing consumer goods for its people and was unable to keep up with the new industrial revolution in electronics and petrochemicals. Moreover, it lost its appeal as a model of development for Third World states and was unable to provide much foreign aid. In addition, Communist ideology was regarded with increasing skepticism and boredom by the Soviet population. Consequently, the Soviet Union's prestige increasingly depended on its military strength.

In Afghanistan, however, the Soviet military met its Vietnam; after eight years of fighting, twice as long as its victorious battle against Nazi Germany, it withdrew its forces by January 1989, unable to suppress the insurgency against the Soviet-imposed government. Thus, its military lost its reputation for invincibility. Worse still, the vast sums the Soviets had spent on the military buildup, nuclear and nonnuclear, finally brought the economy to a halt. Not only had the Soviet Union lost the war in Afghanistan, but also its growing military strength had forged an alliance of the United States, Western Europe, Japan, and the People's Republic of China, thereby surrounding the country. Thus, Moscow had made two cardinal errors: it had invested too much money in the military, starving the rest of the economy, and its buildup had left the country less secure, facing a powerful coalition. The result was a collapse of the economy. Its very efficiency in mass-producing arms thus contributed to the Soviet Union's defeat in the cold war.

The United States too lost a great deal of prestige after its defeat in Vietnam. This emboldened the Soviet Union in the 1970s to extend its influence as its Cuban proxies intervened in several places, among them Angola and Ethiopia. Even Iran, a much smaller power, which was as anti-American as it was anti-Communist, was bold enough to seize the U.S. embassy and its personnel in Tehran in 1979. This completely unprecedented act—the seizure of what was considered "foreign territory"—was something not even Adolf Hitler or Joseph Stalin had tried against their opponents. The Reagan administration tried to restore U.S. prestige by talking "tough" to the Soviets, launching a huge rearmament program, and using force in Grenada and Libya. If a decline in prestige—a nation's reputation for power—is to be avoided, it may at times require force to prevent that decline from happening or, if it has happened, to reverse it. Unlike the interventions in Korea and Vietnam, both of the Reagan administration interventions were quick and caused few casualties. In 1982, however, when terrorists blew up 241 marines in Lebanon, the United States withdrew. It appeared at the time that the United States remained reluctant to use force in any involvements on land that might cause heavy casualties.

Thus, in 1990 in the Persian Gulf confrontation with Iraq, Saddam Hussein reportedly said that the United States, despite the deployment of its troops, did not have the stomach to lose 10,000 troops in one battle.[8] And if it came to war, Iraq, a small country, would, like Vietnam, defeat the United States. The American buildup was therefore a bluff. It was essential then to convey to Saddam Hussein that the United States meant what it said about using force if he did not withdraw from Kuwait. Had the United States failed to do so, its reputation would have sunk to a new low and no Arab state would have felt that it could rely on the United States for its protection. An American failure to achieve the objectives it had set out at the beginning of the crisis would have left Iraq's strongman the dominant force in the area. Thus, to try to make the threat to use force more credible to Saddam Hussein and to add to the pressure on him to withdraw from Kuwait, the United States built up a force of 500,000 troops, a force as large as that maintained in Europe for forty years to oppose the Soviet military and approximately the size of the force that landed on France's Normandy beaches in 1944. In addition, President Bush gained the approval of the United Nations for the use of force if Iraq had not withdrawn from Kuwait by January 15, 1991. Despite these moves, Saddam Hussein continued to believe that the United States would not use force. Based on Vietnam and Lebanon, he had great contempt for the United States, believing it to be a self-indulgent society that was unwilling to pay the price of war.

It was not only the superpowers that were concerned with prestige. Today, such countries as Britain and France, former great powers reluctant to accept their secondary status, and such countries as China and India, trying to establish their status, have all become nuclear powers. Possession of the bomb is—and seems likely to remain—as much a symbol of prestige as empires were in an earlier age. Even smaller countries that do not have memories of past glory or entertain thoughts of future greatness are concerned about prestige. Some of them seek the so-called poor nation's bomb, poison gas; some even seek the means for conducting biological warfare. But what more and more of these states—perhaps as many as 22[9]—are seeking are missiles of various ranges. Capable of hitting distant targets virtually without warning, and almost impossible to destroy in flight, modern-day missiles are perceived not only as symbols of military strength but also, to the extent they are developed indigenously, as technological achievements. And, in turn, missiles are symptoms of these states' determination to play a greater regional and international role. Status symbols in these circumstances become increasingly important.

But prestige, even if largely still related to military power and the effectiveness with which it is used to achieve a state's declared objectives, is no longer identifiable as such alone. Germany and especially Japan, losers in World War II, have reaped considerable prestige and influence because of their economic successes. But Germany, of course, is also an important member of the North Atlantic Treaty Organization (NATO) and has contributed about 500,000 troops to that body. Japan, by contrast, for most of the cold war period spent less than 1 percent of its gross national product on its self-defense forces, as they are known. Only in the last decade did that figure rise to just over 1 percent (admittedly, given Japan's gross national product, that 1 percent buys more hardware than 1 percent of GNP in Germany, Britain, or France). But it is their postwar economic "miracles"—their business efficiency, the quality of their products, and their technological edge—that make German and Japanese goods so appealing to consumers and manufacturers all over the world.

American prestige historically also has been associated with the prowess of American industry, with the country's high standard of living, and, perhaps most of all, with its democratic institutions. It was the nation's reputation for freedom and for granting people equal opportunities to make something of themselves and to rise socially no matter how lowly they were born that drew—and continues to draw—millions of immigrants to these shores. America's triumph in the cold war was widely viewed as a victory for a set of political and economic principles: democracy and a free market. Third World countries, which had rejected both in the past, have now concluded that they are the wave of the future. In short, more than military power and victory is involved. Prestige relates, in the final analysis, to the nature of a society, what it stands for, how well it achieves the goals it has set for itself, and how effectively its government functions.

Ideology

A final goal of states, which some pursue more than others, is the protection or promotion of an ideology. An *ideology* is a set of beliefs that purports to explain reality and prescribes a desirable future existence for society and the world in general. It also defines the role of the believing nation in bringing about this future condition. Revolutionary ideologies in particular, which condemn the present state of existence as evil and intolerable, are expressed in terms of long-range goals that amount to a universal transformation of the state system. Each ideology tends to impart to the revolutionary state a strong sense of mission and commitment to the achievement of humanity's secular salvation. Each, in the name of justice, wishes to create the new Jerusalem here on earth.

Regimes like that of France after 1789 and that of the Soviet Union after 1917 energetically sought to expand their influence and power in the international system to advance their respective faiths. The initial expectation after revolution is that it will spread from one country to another by means of "spontaneous combustion." Leon Trotsky, the first Soviet people's commissar for foreign affairs, did not expect his job to last long. "I will issue a few revolutionary proclamations to the peoples of the world and then shut up shop," he declared.[10] But the proclamations did not spark a global revolutionary fire. Thus, Soviet foreign policy became the instrument for revolutionary expansion.

Ideological passions, however, spend themselves. Communism, which promised to create a new and better just society, fired generations of reformers and revolutionaries and helped spread Soviet influence to all corners of the earth, despite the dismal domestic conditions within the Soviet Union itself. Seventy-four years after the Bolshevik Revolution of 1917, the Soviet state had become highly bureaucratized, and cynicism, corruption, disillusionment, and materialism were widespread. The simplest necessities of life had become hard to find as the economy deteriorated. Shelves were literally bare. Gorbachev himself warned his comrades of the possible collapse of the economy. But the real problem was less economic than political. Unable to provide for its people, the regime lost legitimacy. Ironically, it was the working class, in whose name the Bolsheviks had carried out the revolution in 1917, that delivered a major blow when in 1991 it resorted to widespread strikes that demanded not only economic betterment but Gorbachev's resignation. After communism's seventy years of failing to provide the economic paradise on earth that it had promised, the workers wanted to end the "workers' state." Communism had been a failure.

By contrast, in the nineteenth century, protected by the balance of power in Europe, the United States regarded itself as the New World with a political system morally superior to the regimes of the Old World. The United States chose to isolate itself from possible contamination by the European nations. In the twentieth century, however, it has been increasingly drawn into the Old World's quarrels as Britain's power has weakened. The United States has engaged Germany twice in hot wars and the Soviet Union in a cold war.

In all these struggles, the United States justified its participation by a set of universalist goals. For President Woodrow Wilson in World War I, the aim of the hostilities was to make the world "safe for democracy." President Harry Truman at the beginning of the cold war portrayed the conflict as one between democracy and totalitarianism. And so has every president since that time. The United States was a democracy allied to the two other leading democracies, Britain and France, and fighting first the kaiser's Germany, then Hitler's Germany, and then Stalin's Soviet Union. Thus, such an American presentation was hardly amiss. The survival of democracy was indeed threatened by these undemocratic and antidemocratic systems. But even before the end of the cold war, democracy was spreading to states in Asia and Latin America. With the end of the cold war, a conflict that had been greatly intensified by the opposing ideologies of the two contestants, democracy spread to most of the Eastern European states and made inroads into the Soviet Union itself. Indeed, the democratization of Soviet society and politics was considered the best guarantee of future peaceful Soviet behavior in the world arena.

Since the French Revolution, states have primarily promoted secular ideologies. But Iran, under the Ayatollah Ruhollah Khomeini from 1979 to 1989, advocated an Islamic fundamentalist revolution.[11] Basically a reaction to the Westernization of Iran, which, among other things, displaced the clergy from its prominent role in society, Islamic fundamentalism aims to defend traditional society, with the religious values that govern it, against the encroachment of Western secular values, which are inherent in the concept of modernization.[12] Initially, Islamic fundamentalism was associated with Iranian-sponsored terrorism in Lebanon and other Middle Eastern countries against Western targets, as well as with the Iran-Iraq war, which Iran fought with great zealousness and willingness to sacrifice life for eight years. In 1988, as casualties mounted, oil prices stayed low, and the economy went into debt, the ayatollah finally was forced to call off the war. Iran was exhausted. It too had lost its ardor to export its revolution.

The ayatollah died in 1989, and his successors faced a new situation: Iran was financially drained and politically isolated in the world. During the war with Iraq, Iran had faced the opposition of most Arab states, as well as a Western naval armada in the Persian Gulf. The Iranians also had found that the Islamic fundamentalist message had little appeal in the Arab world, even among fellow Shiites, who identified with Arab nationalism. Iran therefore needed to turn inward, rebuild its economy, and improve its relationship with the West. It began to do so after the Gulf war by reestablishing diplomatic relations with Saudi Arabia, whose regime it had once planned to overthrow, and agreeing to a strategy of moderate oil prices as Islamic zeal began to give way to the urge to prosper. Despite this change, Islamic fundamentalism had by then spread from Pakistan to Algeria, where in late 1991 the Islamic Salvation Front won an overwhelming victory in that country's first free election (but was denied power by the army). From North Africa, where events in Algeria have made neighboring Morocco and Tunisia nervous, it has already spread southward to the Sudan. In the Middle East, Islamic groups are active in Saudi Arabia and other Persian Gulf countries, Egypt, and Jordan; in Africa, they are active in Chad, Niger, and Mali, among others. And who can predict whether a fragile and quarrelsome Commonwealth of Independent States will not someday break up into a Slavic Christian and an Islamic commonwealth (Tajikistan appears to be becoming Muslim)?

Clearly, Islamic fundamentalism is a spreading political and religious force, which may, as suggested, spread to the central Asian republics of the former Soviet Union. Even if Islamic governments do not impose theocracies and Islamic law on nonbelievers as in Iran and wipe out the pluralistic societies that allowed their election, this religious fundamentalism is basically hostile to Western interests and values, as well as to the traditional moderate Muslim, pro-Western Arab governments. Whether Iran's current shift to greater moderation in foreign policy represents a basic shift in policy or a temporary recuperative period, after which it will more energetically seek the leadership of the Islamic world and confront the Great Satan, remains to be seen. In any event, together with the rise of intense nationalism in the post-cold war world, Islamic fundamentalism constitutes one of the major perils to the contemporary system.

Thus, the impact of ideologies on international politics generally has been to enlarge the scope and intensity of conflict between nations with opposing belief systems. It is difficult enough to resolve differences of interest; it becomes infinitely more difficult to reconcile nations with different ideological outlooks, whether they are secular or theological. Each nation sees itself as the representative of truth and morality and opposing states as wrong and immoral. Compromise among states in these circumstances is difficult because it is viewed as treason. How can a state claiming to possess a monopoly of wisdom and morality compromise with the "devil"? A nation believing itself to have a moral mission cannot violate its own principles. It is easier to launch crusades against the "heretics."

'High Politics' and 'Low Politics'

It has become commonplace in recent years to distinguish between the objectives of "high politics" and "low politics." High politics refers to political-security or strategic issues and low politics to welfare or socioeconomic issues. High politics is considered the stuff of international politics and low politics, as implied by the term, a matter of lesser importance. But the proponents of this distinction argue that the process of modernization is transforming the character of foreign policy and the means by which it is carried out. They claim that modernization has elevated low-politics issues to a higher priority than high-politics issues. According to this hypothesis, the increasing popular participation in modern societies means that people are concerned mainly about their standard of living.

> The last century-and-a-half has brought a profound transformation. Governments have become popular and populist even when not democratic. The welfare of the general population . . . is their chief business, and it is to achieving this that they bend their efforts.
> Making war can rarely contribute positively to these goals. In the short run, the mass of the public bears the heavy costs. . . . Welfare-oriented societies typically produce leaders who are attuned to and reflect their societies' goals.[13]

In other words, security has lost its primacy in domestic affairs; economic and environmental issues increasingly rival foreign policy issues for attention and resources. Since few if any societies are economically self-sufficient, fulfilling people's expectations of more jobs, higher pay, and a constantly improving way of life requires nations to cooperate with one another rather than fight. Anarchy and force therefore will be replaced by economic interdependence and cooperation. Inherent in this high-politics/low-politics distinction is the usually unstated maxim "Politics bad, economics good." Politics is concerned with conflict and war and destruction, economics with humans and their welfare—a more positive and obviously more moral area of concern.

The game, then, is claimed to be different in the two realms. High politics remains essentially a zero-sum or adversary game ("What I gain, you lose"); low politics, by contrast, is largely a cooperative game ("We gain or lose together"). The question this distinction raises is not whether interdependence exists, but whether the wrong conclusions have been drawn—namely, that modernization and interdependence are gradually reducing the former priority of security objectives and the role of force in international politics. There is insufficient evidence to support this proposition even in this post-cold war period.

The distinction between security and welfare goals assumes that states place priority on one or the other. States may give primacy to military security, for without security they cannot enjoy other objectives. But the pursuit of security is not without cost. Guns cost money, possibly requiring the sacrifice of other socially desirable goals. Conversely, granting primacy to welfare may require the sacrifice of some degree of security. No country, however prosperous, can maximize both; budgets are finite. Countries have multiple objectives, and in a world of limited resources these objectives compete with one another. What governments must decide is what mix of objectives they seek.

COMPETITION AMONG OBJECTIVES

These then are some, though by no means all, of the principal objectives states seek. The resulting conflict among objectives suggests that *the acquisition of one objective often comes at the cost of another. Objectives are frequently incompatible, and trade-offs must be made.*

Guns versus Butter

One such conflict is between security and welfare or, more colloquially, guns and butter. Realistically, the more a state spends on maintaining military forces, the less it can spend on foreign aid; on the construction of schools, hospitals, and roads; and on education, vocational training, and a "war on poverty." The more taxes it needs to buy bombs, the less the taxpayer has left to buy a new house or car, purchase family insurance, take a vacation, or send the children to college. Nations have limited resources, and they must make choices. The choice is not usually *either* guns *or* butter but how much of each a nation can afford.

A rapidly growing economy could afford a lot of guns and butter. But the slowdown of all Western economies has resulted in a sharper conflict between military spending and social welfare. Already committed to cutting back the government's role in social policies, President Reagan spent almost $2 trillion on defense over eight years (which amounted to $743 million/day, $31 million/hour, $514,000/minute, or $9,000/second) while cutting funds for welfare spending. From the late 1940s to the early 1970s, the U.S. economy grew rapidly enough to afford high wages, a rising standard of living, extensive welfare programs, and large outlays for defense and economic aid. Indeed, President Lyndon Johnson during the 1960s waged the War on Poverty and the war in Vietnam simultaneously (but he soon faced a deficit and had to impose a special tax to pay for the war). Since the late 1960s, however, lower rates of economic growth have, in the absence of increased taxes, sharpened the choice between guns and butter.

Between 1950 and 1969, congressional cuts in the defense budget averaged only $1.7 billion compared with $9.2 billion for nondefense expenditures. For the next six years the balance was reversed, with defense being cut $5 billion while nondefense expenditures were raised an average of $4.7 billion. Defense spending sank to 5 percent of the gross national product, the lowest since before the Korean War. The Nixon-Ford years saw the most sizable reduction in American military strength relative to that of the Soviet Union since the cold war began.[14] President Jimmy Carter began to increase the size of the defense budgets once more by the late 1970s, as congressional post-Vietnam antimilitary sentiment began to weaken in light of the Soviet military buildup. Reagan accelerated the U.S. rearmament effort. But before the end of Reagan's first term, support for further increases had waned; by 1990, the defense budget, which had reached 6.5 percent in 1985, had declined to 5.5 percent. But because the voters did not want to pay for all the government services they wanted, the deficit persisted. As the cold war waned, it was expected that the "peace dividend"—the sizable reduction of the defense budget over a number of years—would help cut this deficit substantially.

Despite the erosion of the Soviet threat, however, the Bush administration initially sought seventy-five B-2 Stealth bombers (said to be almost invisible to radar detection), each costing an incredible $860 million, although it later settled for twenty (at about $2 billion each!) and it terminated the Trident nuclear submarine program after eighteen had been built. These and other strategic weapons acquired during the 1980s had all been intended to deter the Soviet Union. In the wake of the cold war, the debate revolved around the issue of how rapidly and how much the defense budget could be cut. Most in Congress thought that the Bush administration was excessively cautious and slow in its projected cuts of 25 percent over a five-year period in a defense budget of almost $300 billion. Defense savings were expected to be particularly large because of the sizable reductions in U.S. conventional forces in Western Europe and in strategic nuclear weapons. This expectation was fed by the 1990 Soviet-American arms control agreement, which reduced both manpower and weapons levels, and by the 1991 START (Strategic Arms Reductions Talks) agreement, which cut nuclear arms by 30 percent. The promise of further major savings came after President Bush followed up the latter by unilaterally deciding to eliminate all American tactical nuclear arms and suggested negotiating the abolition of all multiwarhead intercontinental missiles. Responding, Gorbachev not only reciprocated but also said that the

Soviets would lower their overall nuclear warhead level on their strategic weapons to 5,000, or 1,000 below the START level, which he hoped the United States would match. He added, however, that he wanted to negotiate a radical reduction of about half in overall strategic weapons after START was ratified by both countries. Because of the subsequent disintegration of the Soviet Union the treaty remains unratified. But the disappearance of the Soviet Union did lead to renewed demands in Congress for far deeper defense cuts and more investments in a recession-weary United States.

Admittedly, the Defense Department resisted deep cuts in its budget. Although America's principal enemy had vanished, the military sought to keep most of its forces by envisioning a limited number of scenarios for potential conflicts that would draw the United States into combat. But they were all relatively minor and not too likely in the near future.[15] It was therefore hard to understand why the administration still wanted to spend $1.5 trillion for "defense" over five years. Nevertheless, given the disappearance of the Soviet Union, the percentage of GNP spent on defense and economic and military assistance in the early 1990s was likely to decline to about 3 percent, the lowest amount spent since 1939, from a peak of 7 percent in 1985.[16]

While U.S. defense spending during the cold war was clearly necessary, averaging below 10 percent of GNP—nowhere near the approximately 25 percent of GNP the Soviets had spent—there can be little doubt that the funding of the military year in and year out over several decades diverted considerable resources away from the serious domestic problems the United States has faced since the 1980s. It has meant less money invested in the nation's industries, once the envy of the world for quality and price, as well as fewer dollars for dealing with such problems as drug abuse, urban crime, and decay in education, public health, and transportation. In an economy whose industries and growth depended on intensive civilian research and development, the diversion of one-third of all engineers and scientists to military research was bound to have negative effects overall. Europeans, spending about 3 percent of GNP on defense, and Japan, allotting 1 percent (and that only since the 1980s), invested their "savings" in the civilian economy.

Because Soviet rulers were unaccountable to public opinion for seventy years, the choice between guns and butter was easy to make. After the 1962 Cuban missile crisis, Moscow began a program of sustained military growth, both nuclear and conventional, but this program came at the cost of a better life for Soviet citizens. Finally, it became clear that the economy could not continue to channel into the military an estimated 25, perhaps even 30, percent of an economy that was probably only one-third of the U.S. gross national product. Moreover, the Reagan rearmament confronted the Soviet Union with a renewed arms race it could not afford. Worse yet, in its Strategic Defense Initiative (also known as Star Wars) program, the United States announced its intention to exploit its technological superiority, the very area in which the Soviet Union was falling further and further behind the West.

Thus, the Reagan arms buildup compelled the Soviets to come to terms with their bankruptcy as a society.

The drawing off of so much capital, skilled labor, and scarce materials from the civilian economy was a key reason for the stagnating Soviet economy. Thus, to obtain the investment desperately needed to revive that economy, Gorbachev had to end the cold war and seek deep arms reductions in arms control agreements. Without an end to the rivalry with the United States and its allies, cuts in the defense budget, and investment of the savings in the civilian economy, as well as perhaps Western technical assistance and economic aid, the Soviet economy was doomed. Whether the former Soviet Union can now recover by adopting the same free-market system that was always so alien to the Soviet Union and czarist Russia before it, and do so while trying to solve its nationality problem, is, of course, the critical issue.

Security versus Democracy

The clash between security and democracy becomes starkly apparent when a democracy allies itself with undemocratic states. Can a democracy associate itself with dictatorial states without undermining its own cause? Or should it confine itself only to allies sharing the same political values, even to the point of jeopardizing its security by failing to take advantage of the strategic position, economic benefits, and added military strength that can be gained from alliance with certain undemocratic states? During World War II, Winston Churchill welcomed the Soviet Union as an ally after Hitler became the common enemy. The Soviet Union might not be a democracy, the prime minister said, but to beat Hitler he would eat supper with the devil—though he did admit that he would use a long spoon. But this alliance had been brought about by Germany's attack on the Soviet Union. Indeed, World War II broke out when Britain, a democracy, went to the rescue of Poland, an undemocratic country. Britain apparently did so because it saw its own security linked to that of Poland, regardless of that country's form of government.

After 1945 and the outbreak of the cold war, the United States made alliances with many undemocratic regimes—Turkey, Greece, Spain, Nationalist China, Brazil, and Portugal, to name some of the more prominent—in the pursuit of the containment of Soviet and Chinese Communist power. Indeed, containment began with the 1947 Truman Doctrine, which somewhat ironically pictured the threat to Turkey and Greece from the Soviet Union as a conflict between democracy and totalitarianism. The Turkish and Greek regimes were hardly models of democratic purity. Were Truman's declaration and American policy hypocritical because they were inconsistent with the values of American democracy, or was the United States acting as the distribution of power after World War II obliged it to act? Truman's action demonstrated clearly that he believed that a democracy can align itself with undemocratic governments in strategically located areas at moments of perceived danger to American security.

The trade-off between security and democracy has been debated frequently. The Congress, the media, and private human rights organizations vigilantly watch the executive when it seeks to align the United States with authoritarian regimes, especially right-wing ones. Or, if the country is aligned already, as occurred frequently during the cold war, they report gross violations of democratic norms such as the arrest of opposition leaders or torture. Such publicity limits the flexibility of the president. On the whole, however, the U.S. government has supported movements toward democracy, as in Greece, Turkey, Portugal, Spain, the Philippines, Chile, and South Korea, because it remains in its self-interest that democratic values flourish in the international system.[17] The United States must remain true to itself. Indeed, in the aftermath of the cold war, it has made observance of democratic norms the basis for American recognition of the former Soviet republics, although how well they understand—let alone practice—these norms remains to be seen.

What Price Security?

This problem of competing objectives and values has continued into the post-cold war period, most poignantly and tragically in the wake of the war with Iraq. The war was fought in part in behalf of Kuwait's right to self-determination. But after its victory, the United States appeared to abandon the principle that had been the justification for every war the nation had fought in this century. Despite the president likening Saddam Hussein to Hitler and despite the barbarous treatment by the regime of the Shiites and Kurds who had rebelled against Saddam Hussein after his defeat—in part in response to President Bush's call for Iraqis to overthrow their leader—the administration refused to intervene in the civil war lest those rebellions lead to the disintegration of Iraq, an outcome it sought to avoid because of its fear of regional instability. Yet this stance was clearly contradictory to the nation's long-standing commitment to human rights and self-determination, which would suggest U.S. intervention in behalf of the Shiites and Kurds. Such interference would have gone far beyond the UN resolutions that had guided the war effort and would have drawn the United States deeply into Iraq's civil conflict and ancient feuds between religious and ethnic groups without any guarantees that the result would have been either a democratic or a united Iraq.[18] Nevertheless, the United States' passive stance while thousands of Kurds and Shiites were being slaughtered by what was left of the Iraqi army—2 million Kurds alone sought refuge in Iran or Turkey—aroused many moral protests.[19]

The fact remains that the United States, like other states, remains basically committed to the principle of national sovereignty. The Kurds, for example, are divided among Turkey, Iraq, Iran, Syria, and the former Soviet Union, all of whom oppose a national state of Kurdistan carved out of their territories. They have enough problems without encouraging Kurdish nationalism and ethnic revolts in their countries. The "national integrity" of Iraq is therefore important to all these states; they naturally fear its disintegration. Similarly, the United States may have supported independence for the Baltic states annexed by

Moscow in 1940, but was reluctant before the August coup against Gorbachev to support the national aspirations of other ethnic groups in the Soviet Union and watch that country, with its huge nuclear arsenal (even after the 1991 START reductions), break up into a series of perhaps squabbling states. Washington has recognized the boundaries of the former Soviet Union since 1933, but, despite its own commitment to national self-determination, it refused to back the moves toward self-government by the various republics until they proclaimed their independence from Moscow.[20] Sovereignty remains the legal basis of the international order, old or new. The central question raised by all these examples of conflicting goals is: *What price security?* [21] Obviously, security and other objectives may clash, as may the objectives and methods by which states pursue their ends. For policy makers, deciding on the exact mix of goals the nation ought to pursue, the means by which to achieve them, and the level of commitment to them is controversial and difficult. This remains true in the post-cold war period.

For Review

1. What are the principal objectives of states?
2. Why is a definition of *national security*—one objective—in military terms not sufficient?
3. Why are economic goals, as well as prestige, so important?
4. What arguments are advanced by proponents of the recent distinction made between the security or "high-politics" objectives of states and welfare or "low-politics" objectives?
5. What are the trade-offs between the different kinds of objectives that states pursue?

Notes

1. Frederick L. Schuman, *The Commonwealth of Man* (New York: Knopf, 1952), 38.
2. Arnold Wolfers, *Discord and Collaboration* (Baltimore: Johns Hopkins University Press, 1962), 89-90.
3. Elaine Sciolino, "U.S. Finds Output of Drugs in World Is Growing Sharply," *New York Times*, March 2, 1988.
4. Martin and Susan Tolchin, *Buying into America* (New York: Times Books, 1988); and Joseph B. Treaster, "Smuggling and the Use of Drugs Are Increasing, U.N. Reports," *New York Times*, January 13, 1992.
5. Daniel Yankelovich and Richard Smoke, "America's 'New Thinking,'" *Foreign Affairs* (Fall 1988): 13.
6. This is especially true for the electronics used in modern U.S. weapons, both for those used in the Persian Gulf war in 1991 and especially for the more sophisticated arms designed today. Martin Tolchin, "Tracking a Foreign Presence in U.S.

Military Contracting," *New York Times* (The Week in Review), January 1, 1989. Also see Theodore H. Moran, "The Globalization of America's Defense Industries: Managing the Threat of Foreign Dependence," *International Security* (Summer 1990): 57-100 for a contrary view.

7. Robert Gilpin, *War & Change* (New York: Cambridge University Press, 1981), 31.

8. "Excerpts from Iraqi Documents on Meeting with U.S. Envoy," *New York Times*, September 23, 1990.

9. Martin Navias, *Ballistic Missile Proliferation in the Third World* (London: International Institute of Strategic Studies, 1990).

10. Quoted in E. H. Carr, *The Bolshevik Revolution 1917-1923* (London: Macmillan, 1953), 16.

11. Said Amir Arjomand, *The Turban for the Crown* (New York: Oxford University Press, 1988); and John L. Esposito, ed., *The Iranian Revolution* (Gainesville: University of Florida Press, 1991).

12. Bassam Tibi, *Islam and the Cultural Accommodation of Social Change*, trans. Clare Krojzel (Boulder, Colo.: Westview, 1990) argues that the resurgence of Islamic fundamentalism is a defensive reaction to the global political and economic changes that they will not be able to participate in unless Islam is "depoliticized" and Islamic countries accept secularism and pluralism.

13. Carl Kaysen, "Is War Obsolete?" *International Security* (Spring 1990): 57-58.

14. John Lewis Gaddis, *Strategies of Containment* (New York: Oxford University Press, 1982), 320-322. Also see the articles by Melvin R. Laird, coauthors Colin S. Gray and Jeffrey G. Barlow, and Robert W. Komer appearing in "The 'Decade of Neglect' Controversy," *International Security* (Fall 1985): 3-83.

15. Patrick E. Tyler, "Pentagon Imagines New Enemies to Fight in Post-Cold-War Era," *New York Times*, February 17, 1992.

16. David Gergen, "America's Missed Opportunities," *Foreign Affairs* (America and the World, 1991/92 issue): 17.

17. Joshua Muravchik, *The Uncertain Crusade* (Lanham, Md.: Hamilton Press, 1986) deals with the Carter administration and the dilemmas it confronted over its pursuit of human rights. Also see Daniel Pipes and Adam Garfinkle, eds., *Friendly Tyrants* (New York: St. Martin's Press, 1991); and Thomas Carothers, *In the Name of Democracy* (Berkeley: University of California Press, 1991).

18. See, for example, Thomas L. Friedman, "Decision Not to Help Iraqi Rebels Puts U.S. in an Awkward Position," *New York Times*, April 4, 1991.

19. Typical was that by conservative columnist William Safire, "Bush's Bay of Pigs," *New York Times*, April 4, 1991.

20. See, for example, Andrew Rosenthal, "Where Do Interests of U.S. Lie: In United or Divided U.S.S.R.?" *New York Times*, July 28, 1991. Also see Bohdan Nahaylo and Victor Swoboda, *Soviet Division* (New York: Free Press, 1990).

21. For an analysis of Israeli views on this, see Joel Brinkley, "A Price for Security," *New York Times Magazine*, September 8, 1991, 42H.

CHAPTER 5

The Security Game

DIFFERENCES BETWEEN DOMESTIC AND INTERNATIONAL POLITICS

The adversary game that nations play is the product of an anarchical international or state system. This does not mean anarchy in the sense of disorder and chaos; rather, it means the absence of legitimate governmental institutions with superior authority. Each state is responsible for its own security and other objectives; no world government exists to provide for each member state's security, prestige, influence, prosperity, or fulfillment of ideological goals. The state system is therefore based fundamentally on the principle of self-help—that is, each state decides for itself how to pursue these objectives, including when and over what issues to resort to force. Thus, the system is always in a state of potential war. The seventeenth-century English philosopher Thomas Hobbes caught the essence of interstate politics and of the adversary game when he wrote,

> Though there had never been any time, wherein particular men were in a condition of war one against another; yet in all times, kings, and persons of sovereign authority, because of their independency, are in continual jealousies, and in the state and posture of gladiators; having their weapons pointing, and their eyes fixed on one another; that is, their forts, garrisons and guns, upon the frontiers of their kingdoms; and continual spies upon their neighbours; which is a posture of war.[1]

It is often said that international conflicts are settled with bullets, and domestic differences are settled with ballots. In international conflicts there is no legitimate central government whose policy decisions are accepted as binding, backed by a common political culture (rules or norms that govern the way a society resolves conflicts peacefully). Admittedly, this distinction between international and domestic conflicts is oversimplified. Not all quarrels between states result in war; most are settled without even invoking the threat of violence. Nor are all domestic clashes of interest settled without force or violent disturbance, even within contemporary Western democracies. Of the 278 European wars fought between 1480 and 1941, 28 percent were civil wars.[2] And the incidence of civil war has risen since World War II, stemming mainly from the large number of new states that have arisen out of the ashes of colonial empires. Many of the developing countries are deeply divided by religious, ethnic, class, and racial differences, often resulting in civil wars and the disintegration of the new states. The frequency with which governments have been overthrown and the recurrence of civil wars and revolutions suggest that, where legitimate governmental institutions and commonly shared political cultures have not yet been achieved, domestic politics tends to resemble international politics. The distinction between domestic and international politics is then not in the use or nonuse of force, but in the fact that national governments normally provide protection for their citizens. Unlike the international system, domestic systems are not usually based on self-help. A central government that is legitimate has the authority or right to ensure that the law is obeyed by its citizens and to use force against any private use of violence.

Role of Governmental Institutions

In some nations, especially the older, more settled Western ones, the role of violence in resolving disputes is considerably less important than the role of international war in the state system. Why? What conditions and processes of conflict resolution within these nations account for their greater capacity to solve inevitable domestic problems?

Executive Branch. One factor is the presence of executive branches of government to enforce the law and keep order. In Western systems, the executive normally holds a preponderance of, if not a monopoly on, the organized force with which it can legitimately enforce the law, protect society, and discourage potential rebels. The executive controls the armed forces and the national police, as well as the citizens of the nation by regulating the ownership of arms and forbidding the existence of private or party paramilitary forces. Domestic peace is therefore always armed. If the executive ever loses this superiority of power, either because all or part of the army refuses to support it—as in Weimar Germany or Spain before the rule of Gen. Francisco Franco—or because of the rise of political parties that possess their own armed forces—as did the Nazis in Germany, the Communist Chinese, the Viet Cong in South Vietnam, and the Sandinistas in Nicaragua—the government may be challenged and the nation plunged into civil war.

Legislative Process. A second factor is that Western political systems also have institutionalized legislative processes through which conflicts of interests within society, articulated by political parties and interest groups, are channeled and peacefully resolved. The term *legislative process* is used instead of *legislative branch* because the latter does not legislate by itself. In every Western political system, it is the leader of the majority party who, as president or prime minister, draws up the legislative program to be submitted for approval to the congress or parliament. Thus, in legislation as well, the executive plays the leading role. The significance of the process of legislation, however, is that law making is essentially synonymous with the issue of domestic war and peace. The most controversial, significant, and bitter conflicts in society revolve around questions of what the law should be. The legislative process is focused on the basic issue of politics, which—as political scientist Harold Lasswell once summed it up—is "who gets what, when, how." [3]

Politics, therefore, is a series of conflicts over the distribution of "goods" such as wealth, status, and power in society. Other political scientists have used more formal terms such as *allocation of values*. The more usual term is *justice*. Although various groups and classes in society define that term differently, they all are concerned with attaining justice—realizing group aspirations and redressing grievances. Should there be a redistribution of wealth? Should minorities be granted full equality in American society, and should discrimination in interstate travel, housing, and employment be banned? Should the poor, the unemployed, the aged, the sick, and the hungry receive assistance? What kind and how much? Should labor be permitted to bargain collectively? Should farmers be subsidized, or should they have to rely on the free market? Should the country have a national health insurance plan, and, if so, what type and at what cost?

These questions are major social issues and arouse strong passions. Yet they are unavoidable; in a pluralistic society new demands are continually being advanced, and people differ on how to resolve the many problems confronting society. A political system that is not very responsive to demands for change and does not provide for sufficient peaceful change will sooner or later erupt in revolution, the domestic equivalent of international war. A political system must either meet the important aspirations of rising and discontented new social groups with sensitivity and sufficient speed or confront violent upheaval. If discontent is widespread enough, the executive's superior power cannot prevent the government's fall because the army and police are recruited from the population. In the ultimate breakdown of society, many soldiers will refuse to fire on their own people; units of the armed forces will instead join the rebellion, as in Russia in 1917 and 1991, in Iran in 1978-1979, and in Afghanistan after the 1979 Soviet invasion, when soldiers defected from the Soviet-imposed government and joined the rebels. The ordinary soldier-citizen will have no more vested interest in maintaining the system than will most other citizens.

Judiciary.   The final factor is that a judiciary, together with the executive and legislative institutions, helps to maintain expectations of individual and social justice. Violence, domestic or international, is normally an instrument of last resort. But, just as there is no international executive with a monopoly of organized force and no international legislative process to provide for peaceful change, the state system lacks an international judiciary with the authority to ensure this sense of justice and bring about peaceful change.

Role of Political Culture

The state system lacks not only effective central political institutions for preserving peace and regulating the behavior of its members but also an international political culture or consensus of political values comparable to those existing within most Western states. A state's political culture includes the shared political values and attitudes of its people related to the general purposes for which society exists and, even more important, the rules or norms by which the domestic "game" is played. The consensus thus comprises both substantive values (agreement on what the country stands for) and procedural values (agreement on how government should be conducted—for example, majority rule and the supremacy of law). Nondemocratic states can proclaim the same substantive goals as democracies. Therefore, it is the way of governing or making political decisions that is critical. If policies were not made according to rules, they would be disregarded and disobeyed; they would lack moral sanction or legitimacy. People obey the law because they agree that the government has the authority or right to govern, not because the government has at its command superior power and the individual is fearful of punishment. "For, if force creates right," the French philosopher Jean Jacques Rousseau wrote in the eighteenth century, "the effect changes with the cause: Every force that is greater than the first succeeds to its right. As soon as it is possible to disobey with impunity, disobedience is legitimate and the strongest being always in the right, the only thing that matters is to act so as to become the strongest." But, Rousseau continued, "the strongest is never strong enough to be always the master, unless he transforms strength into right and obedience to duty." [4] If a government is considered legitimate, even people who disagree with the content of a law normally obey it because they acknowledge that the government has the authority to decide policies for the entire society.

Politics, to sum up, deals with conflicts among groups whose objectives clash. The peaceful resolution of such differences depends on several conditions. First, there must be an executive with superior power, which discourages potentially violent challenges and allows the government to enforce legitimate decisions (according to another teacher of international politics Vernon Van Dyke, "A peaceful country is a policeful country"). Second, there must be a set of governing institutions—executive, legislative, and judicial—that provide for peaceful resolution of conflict and allow most people and organizations to attain justice or what they themselves regard as fair shares of what society has to offer. Third, and perhaps most important, there must be widespread agreement on common purposes and rules of the game so that, even in major disputes, the differing views and needs can be expressed through acceptable political channels and not lead to confrontation and violence. Fourth, this consensus, which serves to legitimize the government, must be reinforced by a deep emotional commitment embodied in nationalism and its various symbols: a flag, national monuments, a national anthem, national institutions, and national celebrations of key events in a nation's history. Such symbols are reminders of national history and the common beliefs and loyalty of a people, as well as of the supremacy of society and the common good.

But instead of such broad agreement, which can buffer and limit areas of conflict so that they do not shred the whole social fabric, the only common agreement on what might be called a minimal "international political culture" is the commitment to the existence of nation-states, their independence, and their security. But this commitment *maximizes* divisions and conflict among nations. The primary loyalty of the nation-state is to itself. The absence of the conditions for peaceful change and accommodation internationally means that the basic condition of the state system is one of potential warfare among its members; at least, there is a higher expectation of violence than in national political systems.[5]

INTERNATIONAL POLITICS AND THE 'SECURITY DILEMMA'

Self-help and the Drive for Power

The primary distinguishing characteristic of the state system follows from the system's decentralized or anarchical nature. *Each state must rely on itself, and only on itself, for the protection of its political independence, territorial integrity, and prosperity.* In what might also be called "politics without government"— perhaps the shortest way of summing up the distinction between international and domestic politics—the issues of who receives what, when, and how are decided, not by a national government recognized as legitimate, but by the interactions of states in a system whose basic rule is "every state for itself." Because a human being's highest secular loyalty is to the nation, policy makers of all states are intensely committed to the maintenance of national security, the prerequisite for enjoyment of the nation's other values—its way of life. If it is further correct that the external environment is anarchical, posing a constant danger to this way of life, policy makers responsible for protecting the nation react fearfully to perceived threats to their country.

More specifically, states living in an environment in which none can acquire absolute security are bound to feel insecure and therefore driven to reduce their sense of insecurity by enhancing their power. As it is with human beings in the Hobbesian state of nature, so it is with states in the state system: they are haunted continually by a fear of violent death.[6] It is the resulting mutual fear and suspicion among states that produce "power politics." When a nation sees its neighbor as a potential foe, it tries to deter potential attack by becoming a little stronger than the neighbor. The latter, in turn, also fears an attack and therefore feels that it too must be strong enough to deter an attack or, if deterrence should fail, to win the resulting conflict. *The insecurity of all states in the system compels each to acquire greater security by engaging in a constant scramble for increased power.* But as each state watches its neighbor's power grow, its own sense of insecurity recurs; it then tries all the harder to gain even greater strength. The result is that each state is continually faced with a "security dilemma."[7]

This is a central problem of international politics. It is not a question of whether one state has aggressive ambitions or not; *both* states can be oriented defensively. Yet this commitment to the status quo is not enough to eliminate the security dilemma. Even if state A explains its increase in arms by saying that it does so only to give itself the added insurance it needs to deter state B, the latter will react by increasing its strength. A will then attribute that reaction to B's offensive intentions, even if the latter also professes status quo aims. After all, did A not declare it was interested only in self-protection? The problem is that B cannot take A's declarations at face value; it is more likely to perceive A's acquisition of new arms as an indication of A's desire to gain military superiority to achieve revisionist goals. Thus, the nature of the system tends to enhance mutual suspicions and distrust, exacerbating already existing conflicts of interests. Even status quo states are compelled to behave like expansionist states because the former cannot afford to allow even states denying revisionist objectives to gain an advantage—just in case they are what they deny they are but are suspected of being. To put it another way, because one state often enhances its security by measures that make other states feel less secure, the assumption that the relations between states that accept the status quo are necessarily peaceful is wrong.[8]

Thus, nations seek power not because simple maximization of power is their goal; they seek it because they wish to guard the security of their "core values," their territorial integrity, and their political independence, as well as their prosperity. And they act aggressively because the system gives rise to mutual fear and suspicion.[9] The dilemma inherent in the state system is essentially kill or be killed, strike first or risk destruction. In this context, it does not take much for one state to arouse and confirm another state's apprehensions and thus to stimulate the development of reciprocal images of hostility, each of which will be validated by the adversary's behavior. Conversely, these images will be hard to dispel even by friendly acts; indeed, such acts may be construed as indications of weakness and may therefore be exploited.

Role of Military Power

Perhaps a more apt way of defining this almost compulsive concern with power shared by all states is in terms of the high potential for violence in the anarchical state system. Threats of violence or actual use of violence are in the end the principal means used by states to impose their demands on other states or, conversely, to resist demands imposed on them by others. It is for this reason that the international system frequently has been characterized as being in a state of potential war; it is war, or the constant possibility of war, that all too often determines who receives what and when. In an environment of conflicting demands in which there are no universally accepted supranational institutions to provide for the nonviolent resolution of differences, the power of the respective adversaries—the power to win a war should it erupt—settles who gains what and who loses what. The actual strength of each party will be clear from the outcome: defeat, stalemate, compromise, peace, or victory. This is not to say that wars are common or even the principal expression of power. War is the instrument of last resort, the ultimate test.

More frequently than war, states use the *threat* of force or coercion. The military power not used may be more potent than the power used. Lord Horatio Nelson, England's famous admiral, reportedly said to a diplomat, "I hate your pen-and-ink men; a fleet of British ships of war are the best negotiators in Europe." [10] And Frederick the Great, Prussia's remarkable ruler and soldier, likened diplomacy without armaments to music without instruments. [11] With force a nation takes what it wants from another state; with diplomacy, supported by the threat of using that force, a nation may persuade another state to make concessions to its demands.

The characterization of international politics as a state of potential war does not therefore seem incorrect historically. Even had there been far fewer wars, it remains true, as Hobbes suggested, that war consists

> not in battle only, or the act of fighting, but in a tract of time ... as it is in the nature of weather. For as the nature of foul weather lies not in a shower or two of rain, but in an inclination thereto of many days together, so the nature of war consists not in actual fighting, but in the known disposition thereto. [12]

Coercion, or the threat of force, generally stands in the background, affecting negotiations among conflicting states, just as the threat of a strike always affects the bargaining between labor and management. Furthermore, the possibility of violence does not mean that it will occur. States do not go to war lightly, for the costs are high, and in the "fog of war" the outcome among evenly matched opponents can rarely be certain, no matter how carefully each has calculated its power and that of its adversary. The knowledge that war is a possibility is more likely to moderate demands and provide a stimulus for other means of conflict resolution such as persuasion, rewards, and coercion. Renunciation of force, in contrast, eliminates the penalty for an uncompromising attitude and gives the advantage to the party willing to invoke violence.

If a nation has prestige, of course, it is less likely to be pressured or attacked and more likely to gain compliance with its demands. Its reputation for power, based on its past effective use of power—especially military power—enhances the possibility of the peaceful resolution of conflicts. Thus, the actual use of violence or explicit threats of violence are not the everyday fare of diplomacy. It is worth emphasizing after the successful war against Iraq that there is no one-to-one relationship between military power and success in achieving a state's objectives. The United States did not defeat North Vietnam. Likewise, American military power could not prevent Iran from seizing U.S. officials as hostages in Tehran in 1979, or terrorist groups loyal to Iran from seizing American and other Western hostages in the 1980s. In Nicaragua, the U.S. government used covert war tactics because public opinion was opposed to the use of America's armed forces. Thus, the possession of military power does not guarantee the fulfillment of foreign policy aims; indeed, there are clearly situations in which it may not even be applicable.

Nevertheless, military power plays a key role in interstate bargaining in peacetime as well as in wartime. It follows that the tendency to think of war and peace as mutually exclusive is wrong. To cite one observation among many, "War means that diplomacy failed, that persuasion did not work, and that bargaining was unsuccessful."[13] It is more accurate to think of war and peace as existing on a continuum along which states have conflicting interests of increasing scope and intensity. Some of these conflicts will be resolvable by peaceful negotiations, but at some point one side will feel that the demands made on it are excessive, that it can no longer offer concessions without endangering its own security. It may calculate that the distribution of power is sufficiently equitable so that it can reject the opponent's demands without war resulting. But the opponent may not be willing to accept this rejection, estimating that the ratio of power favors it. The opponent therefore attempts to intimidate the other state and, when intimidation proves ineffective, resorts to force; or, if the opponent does not initiate the use of force, the side faced with the demands may declare war rather than accept them.

In either case, the outbreak of war does not mean that diplomacy has failed or that negotiations are discontinued until one of the sides has won the war and imposes its terms on the other. War *is* bargaining. As Carl von Clausewitz argues in *On War*, still the definitive book on the subject after a century and a half, war is the continuation of diplomacy or bargaining by other means—that is, force. War does not suspend the political relationship among sovereign states. "How could it be otherwise? Do political relations between peoples and between their governments stop when diplomatic notes are no longer exchanged? Is war not just another expression of their thoughts, another form of speech and writing?" Its grammar—the fighting—may be its own, Clausewitz said, but "not its logic."[14] The logic is that of politics: war erupts because states have conflicts of political objectives that they cannot resolve by persuasion or pressures short of war; they therefore seek to achieve these objectives by combat. The fighting will decide who is the stronger and whether the side demanding a revision of the status quo or the other trying to defend it will achieve its goal.

Peace, in short, is not absolute but conditional. If a state can preserve its security in peacetime, it will do so, but if it cannot, it will invoke force as the instrument of last resort, as Britain finally did when Hitler attacked Poland in 1939. Once fighting erupts it will always continue until one side surrenders conditionally or unconditionally or, more frequently since 1945, until both sides reach a new set of mutually acceptable terms and end the war, an event often symbolized by an official peace conference during which a new postwar balance of power is reached. After the cessation of World War II hostilities, the conflict over the new balance began so quickly that no formal conference was even held. Negotiations between North Vietnam and the United States from 1965 to 1973, for example, could have led to peace at any time, but neither side was willing to accept the other side's terms of peace. The fighting, and the bargaining, thus continued, for they held out the promise to each side of better or more acceptable terms later. *The price of peace was of greater concern than peace itself.*

The axiom "when diplomacy stops, war starts" is therefore untrue. Despite the widespread belief in the United States that war is an alternative to negotiations, it is not; in fact, it is a violent continuation of them. Power, especially military power, is always present. In so-called peaceful negotiations, power stands in the background—"on guard"—and, when needed, is brought to the fore. It is invoked as a threat, and, if that is insufficient, it is used openly. Power is omnipresent. Peace and war therefore have much in common. As Hobbes said, "Covenants without the sword are but words."

Role of Nonmilitary Power

Although the structure of the state system encourages states to be constantly concerned about the ratio of power between themselves and other states, coercion does not always mean the threat of violence. It may mean the use of nonmilitary, especially economic, sanctions that can sometimes be more effective than the threat of force. In the 1970s, members of the Organization of Petroleum Exporting Countries (OPEC) dramatically demonstrated this point to the world. In a system in which, according to all conventional calculations, great powers should be influencing small powers, the reverse seemed to be happening. *One principal characteristic of power is the capacity to hurt.* A state that makes demands on another says, in fact, "Give me what I want, or I will hurt you worse than compliance will hurt." If the other state agrees that compliance will hurt less than resistance, it is likely to submit. If it calculates that the cost of resistance will be less than yielding what is demanded, it is likely to defy the demands made on it. The threat of force is an obvious example of coercion matched by the "reward" of withholding it and not hurting the adversary. The threat of withholding resources vital to a nation's industry or of greatly raising the prices of these resources is also an effective form of coercion. Inflicting violent pain or depriving it of needed resources are just two of the many strategies that can hurt an adversary. The late Chinese leader

Mao Zedong was often quoted as saying that power grows out of the barrel of a gun; OPEC expected power to grow out of a barrel of oil. The military weapon can be replaced by the economic weapon—what Karl Marx called the replacement of the cannon by capital.

Economic means are used not only to achieve national security or high-politics objectives but also for economic or low-politics purposes. Trade is a principal way of obtaining the goods, services, and other resources that a country needs for economic growth, high employment, and a satisfactory standard of living. Oil, for example, can be bought on the international market. If oil-producing countries wish to earn more money, as in the 1970s, they can organize themselves into a cartel and withhold oil or cut back production. This creates shortages and raises prices, which may then create higher unemployment and inflation in oil-consuming industrial countries, threatening them with economic disaster. States pursue their own economic interests as they do their political interests. The very language of international politics—such expressions as economic warfare and aggression, diplomatic fronts, cold wars, crusades for peace, "investment wars," and "trade wars"—is indicative of the contentious nature of the state system and its susceptibility to coercion.

BALANCE OF POWER AS A SYSTEM

Power as a Neutralizer of Power

If states wish to deter potential attackers and ensure their own independence and way of life, they will pursue balance-of-power policies. A balance of power is sought because of fear that if one nation gains predominant power, it may impose its will on other states, either by the threat or actual use of violence. In political scientist Arnold Wolfers's words,

> Under these conditions [of anarchy] the expectation of violence and even of annihilation is ever-present. To forget this and thus fail in the concern for enhanced power spells the doom of a state. This does not mean constant open warfare; expansion of power at the expense of others will not take place if there is enough counterpower to deter or to stop states from undertaking it. Although no state is interested in a mere balance of power, the efforts of all states to maximize power may lead to equilibrium. If and when that happens, there is "peace" or, more exactly, a condition of stalemate or truce. Under the conditions described here, this balancing of power process is the only available "peace" strategy.[15]

The term *balance of power* is often used in loose and contradictory ways. It may refer, for example, to any existing distribution of power between two states, whether it is at an equilibrium, an approximate balance, or an imbalance (meaning either superiority or inferiority of power, as in "the balance has shifted toward Syria" and "the balance has shifted away from Israel").[16] As the term is used here, however, it refers to a *balance-of-power system* in which any shift away from equilibrium in the state system leads to countershifts through mobilization of countervailing power. This definition suggests a mechanism, like the "invisible hand" in the classical free market, that preserves the equilibrium. The systemic nature of the balance of power is further explained by Wolfers:

> While it makes little sense to use the term "automatic" literally, as if human choices and errors were irrelevant to the establishment, preservation, or destruction of a state of equilibrium, there nevertheless is a significant element of truth in the theory of "automatism" which is valid even today. If one may assume that any government in its senses will be deeply concerned with the relative power position of hostile countries, then one may conclude that efforts to keep in step in the competition for power with such opponents, or even to outdo them, will almost certainly be forthcoming. If most nations react in this way, a tendency towards equilibrium will follow it; will come into play whether both sides aim at equilibrium or whether the more aggressive side strives for superiority. In the latter case, the opposite side is likely to be provoked into matching these aggressive moves. Forces appear therefore to be working "behind the backs" of the human actors, pushing them in the direction of balanced power irrespective of their preferences.[17]

In short, states cannot be trusted with power, for they will be tempted to abuse it. *Unrestrained power in the system constitutes a menace to all other member states. Power is therefore the best antidote to power.* The fundamental assumption, of course, is that power will not be abolished, that it is inherent in a system characterized by competition and rivalry, and that the principal task of the international system is thus the management of power.[18] This is not to say that in "real life" all states—especially the great powers—have sought always and everywhere to expand their power. They have not, as demonstrated by the United States' return to isolationism after World War I. Nevertheless, states have sought to enhance their power often enough that one can say that not doing so is the exception and often a cause of wonderment to other states, which may be tempted to exploit the situation. For this reason, even a state wishing to act with restraint usually acts preemptively, knowing that potential adversaries may seek such advantage and that it will then be compelled to react.

Purposes of the Balance

Power thus begets countervailing power. But consider the two aims of countervailing power. The first aim is the *protection of the security of each state*, not the preservation of peace. As noted earlier, most states normally feel secure when they are at peace, but peace is the product of a balance that is acceptable to the leading powers because it ensures their individual security. Peace may be desirable in itself, but it is also only one of several objectives that states pursue. States historically have sacrificed peace to achieve any of these objectives, especially their security. "Peace at any price" has rarely been the aim. To put it simply, peace is the cart, security the horse. To place the cart before the horse is to court disaster. This is easier to conceptualize than to practice, for peace is obviously a desirable value. Most states are reluctant to sacrifice peace, and the difficulty arises in deciding exactly at what point preserving a nation's security is worth the costs of war. If the balance of power is kept, however, the motivation for any state to risk launching an attack may be reduced, if not eliminated.

The second aim of countervailing power is the *protection of the state system as a whole*. The rationale underlying the balance of power is that each state has the right to exist. The way to ensure each state's security and independence is to prevent the emergence of any preponderant state. States are rarely eliminated by other states. To destroy the right of another state to exist is to undermine one's own claim to that right. Thus, at the end of the Napoleonic Wars, despite twenty-five years of fighting, France was neither eliminated nor punished. A lenient peace treaty was signed so that France could once more take its place in the family of European states and contribute to the preservation of the system. A vengeful France might have started another war instead of contributing to the European system's peace and stability.

By contrast, the Treaty of Versailles ending World War I was harsh. Germany considered it punitive, and many regard it as a central reason why Germany remained a threat to the stability and peace of post-1918 Europe. The United States learned from this interwar experience. It signed a generous peace treaty with Japan after World War II and treated West Germany in a spirit of reconciliation. In the postwar containment policy, the United States accepted the premise that the Soviet Union was a permanent player on the international chessboard. The aim of containment was not to eliminate the Soviet Union; indeed, eliminating it would have no more ended the United States' international involvements than had the earlier elimination of Adolf Hitler's Germany. The aim of containment was merely to prevent further Soviet expansion with the expectation that the Soviet Union would eventually "mellow" and coexist peacefully with other states. In short, the Soviet Union's revolutionary ambitions would be subordinated to preservation of the state system. That happened in 1989-1990 when Mikhail Gorbachev made it clear that his country wanted to become part of the emerging global economy and system. President George Bush, in talking about the end of the cold war, emphasized that it was the United States' aim to integrate the Soviet Union into the world community. Instead of gloating over its victory and publicly humiliating the Soviet Union, the United States was seeking to create a more secure Europe and post-cold war international order.

Rules of the Game: Capabilities and Intentions

In a decentralized system, the rules of the balance of power remain the basic norms for states.[19] These rules of the game may be ignored or forgotten only at a nation's peril. They are usually so internalized that those who conduct foreign policy think almost "automatically," as Wolfers has put it, in balance-of-power terms. Policy makers become "socialized" by the system; even revolutionary leaders learn to follow the logic of the balance of power. While behavior patterns vary with the structure of the system—that is, with the number of principal actors or great powers (see Chapter 6)—these rules can be stated in general terms:

1. Watch a potential adversary's power and match it.
2. Ally oneself with a weaker state to restore the balance of power.
3. Abandon such alliances when the balance has been restored and the common danger has passed.
4. Regard national security interests as permanent; alliances must therefore change as new threats rise.
5. Do not treat defeated states harshly through punitive peace treaties. (Today's adversary may be tomorrow's ally.)

The emphasis on the power a state has mobilized, or its capability, is deliberate. In theory, intentions are quickly changeable and a peaceful state today can become a warlike state tomorrow, as leaders' views change or as the leaders themselves change. Capabilities also may vary, but they are not as likely to fluctuate dramatically from one day to the next. The underlying tangible components, such as the number of weapons the armed forces have, do not usually alter overnight; it takes time to produce arms. "Playing it safe"—and what else should a state in the international environment do?—therefore suggests that keeping up with a potential adversary's capabilities, even to anticipating a buildup in order not to be caught napping, is the safest course. While this may aggravate the security dilemma, states have found it better to be safe than sorry. Conversely, it seems wise to play down intentions as unreliable. Capabilities, however, can be measured.

But in real political life, policy makers do make judgments about intentions. Implicit in their concern with capabilities may be an unspoken suspicion that the adversary's intentions are unfriendly and that the buildup had better be matched to serve as a deterrent. During the cold war, American policy makers worried when the Soviets built up militarily but not when Britain did so. Capability analysis cannot really be divorced from some sort of view of intentions. Balancing behavior is set in motion not just by policy makers' assessments of a potential adversary's aggregate or total power, but also by their implicit judgments about whether a state's power is deployed in a militarily offensive mode and, more fundamentally, whether the intentions of that state are unfriendly and, if so, to what degree. For this reason, Stephen Walt, a political scientist, substitutes the term *balance of threats* for balance of power as a more accurate description.[20] During the early 1980s, for example, the Reagan administration depicted the Soviet regime as hostile. It arrived at that judgment by noting the Soviet Union's expansionist behavior in the Third World and continued missile buildup. But after Gorbachev assumed power, American policy makers worried less because he clearly did not share his predecessor's intention to expand further in the name of communism. Rather, after 1987 it became clear that he wanted to call off the cold war and focus on the Soviet Union's economic problems, which entailed arms reductions and a switch to a defensive military strategy.

INTERNATIONAL POLITICS AS A 'MIXED' GAME

Conflict

If in the state system the struggle for security is basic and states perceive one another as adversaries, then as Wolfers points out, "the insecurity of an anarchical system of multiple sovereignty places the actors under compulsion to seek maximum power even though this may run counter to their real desires." [21] The inherent fears and suspicions of states would be reflected even in a situation of general disarmament. States might well be better off if none were armed. But then one state might calculate that, if it armed, it could gain an advantage; it could coerce unarmed opponents or go to war to impose its demands. Precisely because most states fear such a possibility, they not only refuse to disarm but also make sure that they are as strong as potential adversaries, either by being strong themselves or by forming alliances with other states. States are potential enemies, then, not because they are necessarily aggressive or have ideological differences, but because they see that they can harm one another and, being cautious, they view one another as possible enemies.

According to former U.S. secretary of defense Robert McNamara,

> In 1961 . . . the Soviet Union possessed a very small operational arsenal of intercontinental missiles. However, they did possess the technological and industrial capacity to enlarge that arsenal very substantially over the succeeding several years. Now, we had no evidence that the Soviets did in fact plan to fully use that capability. But as I have pointed out, a strategic planner must be "conservative" in his calculations; that is, he must prepare for the worst plausible case and not be content to hope and prepare merely for the most probable. . . .
>
> Since we could not be certain of Soviet intentions—since we could not be sure that they would not undertake a massive buildup—we had to insure against such an eventuality by undertaking ourselves a major buildup of the Minuteman and Polaris [missile] forces. . . .
>
> Clearly, the [subsequent] Soviet buildup is in part a reaction to our own buildup since the beginning of this decade. Soviet strategic planners undoubtedly reasoned that if our buildup were to continue at its accelerated pace, we might conceivably reach, in time, a credible first-strike capability against the Soviet Union. This was not in fact our intention. . . .
>
> But they could not read our intentions with any greater accuracy than we could read theirs. And thus the result has been that we have both built up our

forces to a point that far exceeds a credible second-strike capability against the forces we each started with.[22]

Competition

States engage not only in conflict but also in competition. Great powers are particularly prone to compete with one another, even if they are not at the time in conflict with one another. They are very conscious of their prestige. When possession of an empire was a sign of great-power status, states aspiring to that rank sought colonies. At the turn of the century, Alfred Thayer Mahan, an American naval captain, published a book claiming that a nation's greatness was linked to its possession of a large fleet of battleships—a claim he based on the experience of Britain, an island power and the world's first nation to industrialize. The other powers of Europe, as well as Japan *and* the United States, decided to build navies. But Germany's acquisition of a large battle fleet was seen as a security threat by Britain. Germany was already the Continent's strongest land power, and the kaiser had announced that Germany was about to embark on a world policy beyond Europe. The German navy was therefore a major contributing factor to the increasing tensions between Germany and Britain before World War I.[23] Ironically, the battleship was already passé. It played virtually no role in deciding the outcome of World War I. Had the Germans focused on building more submarines, they might have won the war. In any case, German submarines almost succeeded in starving England into submission, and the battleship remained a symbol of great power until World War II.

The atom bomb has become a contemporary symbol. Whatever its deterrent value, its acquisition is required for great powers seeking to maintain their rank—for example, Britain and France—or for nations such as India and China seeking to acquire such rank. It is not accidental that all the great powers represented on the United Nations Security Council—the United States, Russia, Britain, France, and China—are nuclear powers. Smaller states, seeking regional influence if not dominance, also may seek nuclear weapons. Iraq is an example of this trend.

Cooperation

If, on the one hand, the structure of the system traps states in adversary relationships, states do, on the other hand, cooperate with one another. In their conflicts, states frequently form alliances. Enemies also cooperate; for example, arms control negotiations between the United States and the Soviet Union became almost routine after the 1960s. Even while a war is ongoing, states may cooperate. Prisoners, for example, get mail and food packages via the Red Cross. During the cold war, "limited wars" and confrontations that resulted in crises were kept from escalating only by the superpowers working together despite their simultaneous rivalry.

International politics is thus a mixture of conflict, competition, and cooperation, but much of this cooperation occurs within the context of adversary relations. An

arms control agreement with an opponent may reduce the level of armaments, ease international tensions, and make the world a slightly safer place,
but such agreements have been signed, after all, by such states as the United
States and the Soviet Union, whose weapons were aimed at each other
because they were political rivals. This is true even when states are no longer
potential adversaries. Today, the major European Community (EC) states, such
as France and Germany, are unlikely to go to war with one another, even
though not long ago some of them were bitter enemies. When these Continental states, which were the original members of the European Economic
Community, decided to move toward what they hoped would one day be a
powerful United States of Europe, they did so within the broader context of
the rivalry between the United States and the then-Soviet Union.

Limits of Cooperation

The structure of the state system limits cooperation among states in two
significant ways.[24] First, states concerned about their security or wealth cannot let themselves become too dependent on other states, for they might
become vulnerable to threats to reduce or eliminate any ongoing exchange of
goods and services. For example, the 1973 Arab oil embargo—and price
increases—led the Western oil-consuming nations to seek non-OPEC oil,
develop alternative energy sources, and practice greater conservation.
And after the 1970s, the Soviet Union became increasingly dependent on
the United States for large amounts of grain and desirous of all sorts
of U.S. technology—and the United States encouraged this dependency—but
the Soviet Union also was careful to maintain alternative sources of
supply.

If a state becomes too dependent on another state for any of its critical
needs, it can avoid a reduction or cutoff of supplies only by submitting to the
demands made on it. A preferable strategy therefore is to import critical
resources or goods from several countries or to find several markets rather
than a single one for any products it must export to earn foreign currencies to
pay for imports. Smaller or more poorly endowed states long ago learned that
the price of dependence is a restriction of national freedom and a vulnerability to foreign demands.

Second, even when states cooperate on such critical issues as arms control
because both expect to gain from such cooperation, each worries about the
distribution of benefits and the sharing of costs. Who will come out ahead?
Allowing another nation to gain an advantage might be potentially damaging. Even if President Jimmy Carter had not withdrawn the SALT II (Strategic
Arms Limitation Talks) treaty after the Soviet invasion of Afghanistan in
1979, the U.S. Senate might have defeated it. Many senators thought it an
unequal treaty that benefited the Soviet Union more than the United States.
Even among EC countries, which have grown close during two decades of
economic cooperation, there have been setbacks, delays, and bitter disputes
over the distribution of benefits. Is French agriculture benefiting more than

German agriculture? Are the Continental states gaining more from Britain's annual contribution to the EC than Britain receives from the community?

Most remarkably, given the collective benefits it receives from high oil prices, OPEC weakened itself in the 1980s because of the inability of its members to decide how much wealth each was to earn. Most of them sought to enhance their national earnings by selling more oil than allowed under OPEC's allotment; the results were a surplus of oil over international demand and lower oil prices. In 1986, to retain its share of the market, Saudi Arabia flooded the market, leading to precipitous drops in the price of oil. This in turn has led to renewed efforts to agree on production limits in order to raise the price of oil again, but these efforts have been only partially successful.

Anarchy and the Search for Order

The anarchical nature of the state system, in which each state is concerned about its own national security and welfare, should by now be clear.[25] But, as the preceding emphasis on cooperation makes plain, states also seek a degree of order. Not only are they concerned with their survival and safety, but they also are fated—or condemned?—to live together in the state system and therefore, by necessity, to seek a degree of regularity in their relationships. To minimize the unexpected and undesirable, states have established informal, as well as formal, rules and institutions to guide their interactions. For example, despite their intense rivalry and mutual hostility, the United States and the Soviet Union over the years arrived at certain "rules" to avoid potentially explosive confrontations and make their relationship safer. These ranged from their mutual acceptance of the division of Europe into opposing spheres of influence (which led, for example, to U.S. nonintervention in the 1950s and 1960s when the Soviet satellites in Eastern Europe attempted to throw off the Soviet yoke) to such specific agreements as those aimed at preventing accidents at seas between warships and limiting or reducing nuclear weapons.

More broadly, states need to know what their rights and obligations are with regard to the oceans, airspace, wartime (as belligerents or neutrals), and the exchange of diplomats. International law incorporates the rules that govern the everyday coexistence of states in peace and wartime, and states have agreed to these rules by either consent or custom. Because nations also trade with each other, some degree of predictable order must govern economic exchanges as well. Many states since World War II, mainly Western industrial ones, have subscribed to the General Agreement on Tariffs and Trade (GATT) to avoid the kind of chaos that followed the Great Depression and the resulting economic nationalism of the 1930s, which only worsened everyone's lot. Several former Communist states—including Poland, Hungary, and Yugoslavia—belong to the 108-member organization. China has applied for membership, and the Soviet Union before its disappearance also had expressed its interest in joining GATT.

The first institutional efforts to curb the results of unrestrained sovereignty, as already noted, began in the nineteenth century. The Concert of

Europe followed the defeat of Napoleon and the peace treaty with France in 1815, the League of Nations the surrender of monarchical Germany in 1918, and the United Nations the collapse of Hitler's Germany in 1945. As war has become more destructive and costly, such efforts to manage inter-nation relations in ways that avoid extreme violence have increased. Even if efforts like these eroded after a few years as differences among the victors grew, memories of the wartime alliances faded, and the laws, rules, and institutions to control violence were disregarded when they stood in the way of some nations' ambitions and determination, international politics is clearly not characterized only by conflict and the drive for national power. States, especially the great powers, may enjoy substantial freedom of action, but they also are subject to constraints.

It is precisely because the state system is basically anarchical that order is such a critical issue in international politics—unlike in domestic systems, where order is usually assumed and, as a result, social justice becomes the key issue, as suggested by the modern welfare state.* This does not mean, of course, that the need to preserve international order is necessarily incompatible with just changes.[26] The decolonization of the European empires in the name of national self-determination, a basic Western principle, is proof that order and justice can be reconciled to some degree. Decolonization took place largely because the Western powers, weakened by World War II and recognizing the justice of the colonies' claims to independence, were willing to grant most of them statehood. A few colonies had to fight for independence, but even in those cases, segments of domestic opinion in the Western colonial country favored the "war of liberation" because self-government is a democratic principle.

The cry of revolutionary groups is "Let justice be done," and sometimes they add "though the earth perish" since in their judgment the world is so unjust it deserves to be destroyed if it refuses to change. In fact, revolutionaries do not really expect the earth to perish, but they do expect to succeed, capture power, and then consolidate the gains of the revolution in a "new order." This is as true for the Palestine Liberation Organization, seeking the establishment of a Palestinian state, as it was for the Bolsheviks who captured power in Russia in 1917.

And it is not only revolutionary groups that seek justice; states do as well. As suggested earlier, France in 1789 and the Soviet Union after 1917 considered themselves to be "revolutionary" powers, states that were going to transform the old regimes (monarchy and aristocracy in one case, capitalism in the other) to new orders in the name of justice. Because the old regimes

---

* When that order begins to break down and people begin to feel insecure, they demand "law and order," tougher enforcement of the law, and arms to guard themselves, ranging from home security systems to large dogs to mace. The resemblance to the international system in which each nation has no option but to protect itself then becomes greater.

were alleged to be the cause of poverty domestically and war internationally, their replacement would usher in an era in which people would no longer exploit each other as commodities; instead, they would live together in liberty, equality, and fraternity at home and in peace abroad.

Nevertheless, justice takes a subsidiary place to order internationally for two reasons. The first is the anarchical nature of the state system. Order, meaning the survival and safety of its member states, must be ranked as a basic need. It is, as domestic politics amply demonstrates, the precondition for the realization of justice. The second and closely related reason is that there is no agreed-on moral code among the peoples and governments of the world. Within a nation, the moral code may well be imposed on those who disagree—for example, when laws sanctioning child labor or racial discrimination or the absence of a livable minimum wage are changed by a political process that is recognized as legitimate, and the government enforces the new laws which reflect the nation's conception of justice. Internationally, there is neither an acceptable common moral code (although such norms as national self-determination have received wide acceptance) nor a set of higher institutions that possesses the authority to impose such a code on recalcitrant states.

Thus, with the decentralized nature of the state system also compelling states to seek order, one has come full circle. It is the great powers that historically have been the prime players in the international political game, and each state system has reflected the interests of the dominant powers at that particular time. In a real sense, they provide the closest equivalent to a government within a country. This primacy of the great-power oligarchy has long been recognized not just informally by other states but formally by the status accorded great powers at international congresses and institutions such as the League of Nations and the United Nations. In short, all international systems have international hierarchies or "structures of dominance" of the weak by the strong.[27] Those at the top of the hierarchy are mainly responsible for maintaining some degree of order in the anarchical system in which states live. Because anarchy coexists with the rules that govern the coexistence of states and the common institutions serving them, analysts have used such terms as "anarchical society" and "mitigated anarchy" to underline the point that while the system remains essentially anarchical, it is a qualified anarchy.[28]

CHARACTERISTICS OF THE FIRST LEVEL OF ANALYSIS

Balance of Power

An analysis of the security games that nations play on the level of the state system reveals certain very specific notions of the behavior of states (see Table 5-1). *First, the interactions of states revolve around the axle of the balance of power.* Systemic change affects the behavior of all member states. Whenever the

Table 5-1 The State System

Primary actors

Nation-states
Intergovernmental organizations
  Universal: United Nations
  Regional: Organization of African Unity
  Special-interest: producer cartel, OPEC; "Group of 77"
    (representing Third World countries)
Supranational organization
  Regional: EC
Nongovernmental or transnational organizations
  Multinational corporations; religious, humanitarian groups;
    national liberation groups; terrorists

Characteristics

Decentralized—composed mainly of sovereign and independent
  states
Anarchical—absence of commonly accepted political institutions
  and legitimate rules of the game for allocation of values and
  enforcement of decisions
High expectation of violence—coercion and force as the ultimate
  allocative mechanism or substitute for government
Balance of power—principal mechanism that provides systemic
  stability and individual national restraint

General rules

1. Protect and guard oneself.
2. Be concerned with systemic power distribution.
3. Calculate self-interest rationally on the basis of power,
   not ideology.

system becomes unbalanced, trouble follows. When Britain weakens and can no longer contain a continental power seeking European hegemony, a previously isolationist power, the United States, must step in to play Britain's role. When Germany, in the center of Europe, is defeated, a conflict erupts between two previous allies, both superpowers on the periphery of Europe. Elimination of a troublesome member does not guarantee, therefore, the end of trouble and conflict. Nor can it. To alter the structure of the system is to change everyone's behavior; the new distribution of power merely leads to new alignments. But competition among states continues.

Uniformity of Behavior

Second, the system imposes a high degree of uniformity of behavior on states, regardless of their domestic complexion. The same basic interests and motivations are ascribed to all members. The behavior required by their existence in an anarchical state system overrides different national attributes such as political culture, economic organization, or class structure—or, at least, it is supposed to. The systems analyst will examine internal variables only if they seem to have interfered with how a state should have behaved.

In this connection, note again that the systemic model tends to minimize the importance of ideologies, which are generally used to justify whatever states do. States are motivated by their security interests and are therefore concerned with preserving or enhancing their power. Ideology is viewed as a function of this interest.[29] For example, despite its anticapitalist and antifascist ideology, communism did not prevent the Soviet Union from aligning itself with France in 1935, with Nazi Germany in 1939, and with the United States and Britain in 1941 against its previous ally. And after World War II, the Soviet Union acted very much like czarist Russia: it expanded into eastern Europe and attempted to extend its power into the eastern Mediterranean area. Ideology did not prevent Moscow from behaving in typical balance-of-power terms.

This de-emphasis of ideology suggests that the analyst of world politics need pay little attention to what policy makers *say* about their policies. Clearly, they will say whatever will make their actions look good. They will talk about freedom, national self-determination, liberating peoples from Communist or capitalist slavery, and bringing about a world of peace, law, order, and justice. But such concepts should not be confused with the concrete interests that are the real, underlying reasons for a state's behavior. Indeed, the analyst who assumes that state behavior is the product of an ever-changing distribution of power can, according to Hans Morgenthau,

> retrace and anticipate, as it were, the steps a statesman—past, present, or future—has taken or will take on the political scene. We can look over his shoulder when he writes his dispatches; we listen in on his conversation with other statesmen; we read and anticipate his very thoughts.... We think as he does, and as disinterested observers we understand his thoughts and actions perhaps better than he, the actor in the political scene, does himself.[30]

Whether or not Morgenthau is correct, less emphasis on ideologies and statements of intentions does tend to reduce the probability that international politics will be viewed as a morality tale, a conflict between good and evil, and it refocuses attention on the security dilemma shared by all states living in an anarchical environment in which they see other states as potential enemies and are therefore bound to be concerned about their power vis-à-vis one another.

Limitation of Choice

Third, the system places limits on the policy choices of states. Some observers refer to *system-determined behavior*. Although this term may understate the degree of a state's "free will" or the actual range of its choices, it is a healthy reminder that for states, as for individuals, the available options depend on external realities—in this instance, the distribution of power. As political scientist Hedley Bull has noted, "The choice with which governments are in fact confronted is not that between opting for the present structure of the world and opting for some other structure, but between attempting to maintain a balance of power and failing to do so." [31] The United States again is a perfect example. Each time in this century that the European balance has been upset, the United States has had but two options: to intervene and prevent the continental powers from achieving hegemony or to remain isolationist. The latter course might have been preferable to the American public, but it also might have jeopardized future U.S. security. Three times, therefore, different administrations have rejected isolationism. The United States really had no choice.

Continuity

Finally, and closely related, continuity of policy is a characteristic of many nations. Britain, for example, has had a long history of opposing would-be conquerors of continental Europe—among others, Napoleon, the kaiser, and Hitler. But after World War II, the Conservative party, the guardian of this tradition, lost office to the Labor party, whose slogan was "no enemies to the left." Yet despite the considerable admiration within the Labor party for the Soviet Union (sparked in large measure because the Soviet Union—like the Labor party—represented a new anticapitalist and presumably anti-imperialist order), the Labor government took the lead in organizing European opposition to Moscow as its designs became clear. This meant, above all, mobilizing the power and leadership of the United States, the arch capitalist power, since Britain had grown too weak for this task. This example serves as a useful reminder that the United States too intervened in this century: twice against Germany and once against the Soviet Union. Like Britain's behavior, these U.S. interventions demonstrated a remarkable continuity of policy.

A REMINDER: ANALYSIS AND APPROVAL

All the above observations about state behavior have been deduced from the state-system or balance-of-power framework. While in practice—in "real life" —there will be varying degrees of deviation, construction of such a framework and the deduction of behavior patterns for states are a useful exercise; the conclusions can, after all, be checked empirically. If this method of analysis improves the observer's capacity to understand state behavior, it justifies itself.

Whether the observer personally approves of the "logic of behavior" that a particular framework seems to suggest is not the point. It is one thing to say, as done here, that the state system condemns each state to be continually concerned with its power relative to that of other states, which, in an anarchical system, it regards as potential aggressors. It is quite another thing to approve morally of power politics. The utility of the state-system framework is simply that it points to the "essence" of state behavior. It does not pretend to account for all factors, such as moral norms, that motivate states. As a necessarily simplified version of reality, it clarifies what most concerns and drives states and what kinds of behavior can be expected. Observers may deplore that behavior and the anarchical system that produces it and may wish that international politics were not as conflictual and violent as the twentieth century already amply demonstrated. They may prefer a system other than one in which states are so committed to advancing their own national interests and protecting their sovereignty. Nevertheless, however much they may deplore the current system and prefer a more harmonious world, they must first understand the contemporary one if they are to learn how to "manage" it and avoid the catastrophe of a nuclear war.

For Review

1. Why is anarchy one of the distinctive features of international politics?
2. Why are the balance of power and the "security dilemma" central to understanding the behavior of states?
3. How are war and peace related?
4. What are the rules of the security game that nations play?
5. If anarchy is a principal characteristic of international politics, how can order and hierarchy also be important characteristics?

Notes

1. Thomas Hobbes, *Leviathan* (New York: Collier Books, 1962), 101.
2. Hans J. Morgenthau, *Politics among Nations*, 4th ed. (New York: Knopf, 1967), 490.
3. Harold D. Lasswell, *Who Gets What, When, How* (New York: Meridian Books, 1958).
4. Jean Jacques Rousseau, *The Social Contract* (New York: Dutton, 1947), 6.
5. The domestic system in the United States assumes people will generally obey the law voluntarily. This is clearly shown by the limited number of police (national, state, and local)—certainly not enough to deal with massive resistance to the law and far, far fewer than the number of men and women in the armed forces employed to defend the United States against external aggression. For an interesting analysis in which the willingness of governments to use force against other governments is contrasted with their reluctance, if not unwillingness, to use it against their own populations, see E. E. Schattschneider, *Two Hundred Million Americans in Search of a Government* (New York: Holt, Rinehart & Winston, 1969), 17-22.
6. Hobbes, *Leviathan*, 104.
7. John H. Herz, *International Politics in the Atomic Age* (New York: Columbia University Press, 1959), 231-232.
8. Robert Jervis, "Cooperation under the Security Dilemma," *World Politics* (January 1978): 167-214.
9. John Herz characterizes the effects of such suspicion as follows:

   [The] very realization that his own brother may play the role of a Cain makes his fellow men appear to him as potential foes. Realization of this fact by others, in turn, makes him appear to them as their potential mortal enemy. Thus there arises a fundamental social constellation, a mutual suspicion and a mutual dilemma: the dilemma of "kill or perish," of attacking first or running the risk of being destroyed. There is apparently no escape from this vicious circle. Whether a man is "by nature" peaceful and cooperative, or aggressive and domineering, is not the question.

John H. Herz, *Political Realism and Political Idealism* (Chicago: University of Chicago Press, 1951), 2-3.

10. Quoted in Geoffrey Till, *Maritime Strategy in the Nuclear Age* (New York: St. Martin's Press, 1982), 210.
11. Quoted by Geoffrey Blainey, *The Causes of War* (New York: Free Press, 1973), 108.
12. Hobbes, *Leviathan*, 100. Also see the important book by Robert Gilpin, *War and Change in World Politics* (New York: Cambridge University Press, 1981).
13. Charles W. Kegley, Jr., and Eugene R. Wittkopf, *World Politics*, 2d ed. (New York: St. Martin's Press, 1985), 417.
14. Carl von Clausewitz, *On War*, ed. and trans. Michael Howard and Peter Paret (Princeton, N.J.: Princeton University Press, 1976), 605.
15. Arnold Wolfers, *Discord and Collaboration* (Baltimore: Johns Hopkins University Press, 1962), 83. For contrary interpretations correlating peace with a superiority of power and war with a balance, see A. F. K. Organski, *World Politics* (New York: Knopf, 1956), 325-333; and Blainey, *Causes of War*, 112-114.
16. Discussions of the different meanings of "balance of power" can be found in Morgenthau, *Politics among Nations*, 161-163; Ernst B. Haas, "The Balance of Power: Prescription, Concept, or Propaganda?" *World Politics* (July 1953): 442-447; and Inis L. Claude, Jr., *Power and International Relations* (New York: Random House, 1962), pt. I.
17. Wolfers, *Discord and Collaboration*, 123.
18. Claude, *Power and International Relations*, 6.
19. Ibid., 91.
20. Stephen M. Walt, *The Origins of Alliances* (Ithaca, N.Y.: Cornell University Press, 1990), 17-26.
21. Wolfers, *Discord and Collaboration*, 84.
22. Robert McNamara, "Address to the United Press International, San Francisco," *New York Times*, September 19, 1967.
23. Paul Kennedy, *Strategy and Diplomacy 1870-1945* (London: Fontana Paperbacks, 1984), 109ff.
24. Kenneth Waltz, *Theory of International Politics* (Reading, Mass.: Addison-Wesley, 1979), 105-106.
25. Roger D. Masters, "World Politics as a Primitive Political System," *World Politics* (July 1964): 595-619.
26. Hedley Bull, *The Anarchical Society* (New York: Columbia University Press, 1977), 77-98.
27. Bruce Russett and Harvey Starr, *World Politics* (San Francisco: W. H. Freeman, 1981), 82.
28. Bull, *Anarchical Society*; and Robert J. Lieber, *No Common Power* (Glenview, Ill.: Scott, Foresman/Little, Brown, 1988), 331-332.
29. Morgenthau, *Politics among Nations*, 83-86.
30. Ibid., 5.
31. Hedley Bull, *The Control of the Arms Race* (New York: Holt, Rinehart & Winston, 1961), 49.

CHAPTER 6

The Cold War and Post-Cold War State Systems

Distribution of power is the key to understanding the behavior of states. The first-level (state-system) analysis is based on the assumption that the *structure* of the system conditions this behavior. The structure of the state system is defined by the number of major actors, or *poles*, present and the distribution of power among them. A pole is what is popularly known as a "great power," and the measure of that greatness usually has been military strength.

The structure of the international system and its *stability* are related. Stability is defined as the absence of any nation's predominance, the survival of most member states, and the absence of a major war. The concept of balance of power is based on the assumption that war may have to be invoked as a last resort to preserve systemic equilibrium or to restore it once it has been upset. War, then, is not destabilizing per se, especially if it is infrequent or limited. Major violence, such as a war among superpowers, however, is destabilizing. Thus, a stable system is said to be characterized by minimal violence, the generally peaceful settlement of differences, and a desire to retain the principal features of the system. An unstable system is prone to major violence that may result in the hegemony of one pole; such hegemony will be a threat to the survival of the other major actors.[1]

UNIPOLARITY (STABLE)

Unipolarity requires one state to be dominant and capable of imposing its will on other states. World conquest by one state or a close alliance of states would produce a unipolar system. Obviously, such a system would be stable even if its members were unhappy to be governed by a foreign power and had little say about how they were ruled. The Roman Empire probably has been the closest thing to a unipolar system. Rome—a city-state—ruled more than 100 million people and much of the known world. To the Romans, *empire* meant the inequality of states; those who rebelled against Roman rule were brutally crushed. Relations existed between the empire and the barbarian tribes whom Rome eventually intended to bring within its sphere of military control.

Some analysts have asserted that the immediate post-World War II period was also a unipolar one.[2] That suggestion is dubious. To be sure, France and Britain collapsed after Germany and Japan were defeated, but the Soviet Union was hardly impotent, even though it had been hurt badly and did not yet possess the atomic bomb. Indeed, it was the Soviet Union's great military power, the thrust of that power into the center of Europe, and the attempts to extend that power even farther west that precipitated the cold war. But it was not the division of Europe that was the cause of the resulting American-Soviet conflict. The principal cause was the emergence of two continent-sized states whose power flowed into the vacuum left by the collapse of the historically great powers in Europe, which had until then been the center of international politics. If the postwar system had been unipolar with the United States playing the role of Rome, it is hard to understand why Moscow was not more accommodating on the issue of free elections in Eastern Europe and did not refrain from its expansionist efforts. The fact is that the system after 1945 was bipolar, not unipolar.

These analysts, moreover, remain unconvinced about the uniqueness of unipolarity. They see "long cycles" of about a hundred years' duration, each of which is dominated by a world power. Having won a "global war," such a world power possesses a virtual monopoly on naval power and therefore a global reach and control over world trade. These powers since the fifteenth century have been Portugal, the Netherlands, Britain (which maintained its dominant position for 200 years), and the United States. Each in turn has structured the international political and economic system and maintained order. This dominance or hegemony has maintained the peace. As each hegemony has weakened because the costs and debts it accumulated in maintaining its dominant global position rose faster than its economic capability to support this hegemony, forcing it to cut its naval strength to save money, it has been challenged by a newly rising power, resulting in a series of wars of succession. The next war will erupt, according to the long cycle's founder and chief advocate, George Modelski, in approximately 2030—unless the historic precedent is broken by the presence of nuclear weapons.[3] That prediction, of course, presumed a continuation of the cold war. In any event, apart from predicting the next war for hegemonic control, hegemony theorists have focused principally on the U.S. economy since the economy is the cause of the rise and decline of great powers. Today, the historical cycle is witnessing the decline of the American economy, power, and primacy, and the rise of Germany—not Europe—and Japan.[4] Whether or not these hegemony theorists are correct in these conclusions, it certainly is clear that they reject an explanation of international politics that stresses the anarchical nature of the state system. Analysts who accept this characterization of the state system believe that the balance-of-power phenomenon has, with perhaps rare exception, prevented any single state from achieving systemic hegemony. This fundamental difference in perspectives is specifically the result of the hegemonists' concentration on the hegemonic state's alleged economic dominance—trade, finance, as well as, since the Industrial Revolution, manufacturing—and the balance-of-power theorists' focus on political-military factors.[5]

BIPOLARITY (UNSTABLE)

In a *bipolar* structure, two opposing states or coalitions preserve the balance of power.[6] More specifically, a bipolar system is distinguished by the presence of two actors whose power is so far superior to that of other states that they are called *superpowers.* Secondary powers and a host of lesser states may align themselves with these superpowers, but it is the interactions of the superpowers that are central. In such a bipolar system, conflict is unavoidable, for each superpower regards the other as an adversary—none of the other states can threaten their security. In short, in a two-pole structure *conflict is structurally determined,* and friend and foe are clearly distinguished. Last, and very critical, *bipolarity intensifies international conflict because each of the antagonists tends to see any gain of power and security for the other as a loss of power and security for itself and is determined to prevent this consequence.* Each feels such a high degree of insecurity that each may be said to be driven or compelled to react against the perceived potential threat from the other pole. The balance of power is continuously seen to be at stake. Each side fears that it will be upset, that the adversary will achieve hegemony, and that such hegemony will be irreversible—in short, that the game will be over. Both poles are thus hypersensitive to the slightest shifts of power. Even moves in areas not normally considered of vital interest to the other superpower will be opposed for symbolic and psychological reasons. Each superpower fears a *domino effect:* if one of its allies, friends, protégés, or satellites falls, others will follow and upset the equilibrium.

Thus, *when one power pushes, the other feels compelled to push back.* Each constantly watches the other, and both are "trapped," in a real sense prisoners of the system. Neither can advance or retreat; positions must be held. *Bipolar politics is the politics of confrontation.* When one side challenges the other at some spot and the adversary reacts, a crisis and threats of violence result. Furthermore, a bipolar division of power places a premium on a surprise attack by one side to eliminate the other. If carried out successfully, it leaves one side the clear winner because the only threat to its security has been eliminated. The ancient Greek historian Thucydides, in describing why war had erupted between Athens and Sparta, explained bipolar war in general. The Spartans, he said, attacked Athens because of its growing power and the fear this caused in Sparta. The Spartans, therefore, launched a preventive war.[7]

Is a bipolar system that is both *simple* (because there are only two adversaries) and *rigid* (because most of the allies and friends of the two poles are tied to them and do not shift from one side to the other) stable or unstable? The answer seems clear from the basic rule for behavior in a bipolar structure: oppose any unilateral attempt by the adversary to upset the balance of power. If the opponent pushes, push back. The constant search for allies and friends, the attempts to undermine the opposing "camp" while preventing defections from one's own, and the attendant arms race spurred by the constant fear that the opponent may achieve an irreversible power advantage—and end the game—mean frequent crises, occasional limited wars, and a mutually reinforcing fear. It is because of these characteristics that bipolar systems have usually been judged unstable systems. By definition, the two superpowers are far stronger than any of their allies or friends and therefore cannot be restrained by them.

MULTIPOLARITY (STABLE)

A *multipolar* system, according to most theorists, is composed of at least five approximately equal great powers.[8] Such a system is characterized by more restrained national behavior and is generally more conducive to preserving the peace because, compared with the *simple* and *rigid* bipolar division, multipolarity is *complex* and *flexible.* When the division is simple and the major actors are aligned on one side or the other, friend and foe are easy to determine; this division is rigid because no realignment is possible. But a multipolar structure does not by itself distinguish between friend and foe. Each pole views all other major actors as potential adversaries—and potential allies. *Among a larger number of great powers, each state has the mobility to align and realign itself.* Alliances are created as specific conflicts arise, and they usually last for only short periods, as the equilibrium shifts and alignments change. In contrast to bipolarity's confrontations and crises in which antagonisms are constantly reinforced, *the greater opportunity for shifting combinations under multipolarity reduces the risk of mutually reinforcing hostilities between various "players."* Allies of today may be tomorrow's adversaries—and allies again the day after. Since a state may need its present opponent as an ally in the future, hostilities cannot be allowed to become too intense;[9] indeed, it is a bit more difficult to become aroused about any specific state or cause.

In a particular dispute, for instance, it is claimed that the possibility that an ally may defect acts as a restraint on the other members of the alliance. In a multipolar system, an alliance has the meaning that most people give that term: a collection of states, most of approximately equal power, who by joining together strengthen themselves in the face of a potential common enemy. The loss of one partner is therefore a serious matter because it weakens the alliance. If one member of a defensive alliance tries to persuade its associates to seek a change in the status quo, another member's threat of "de-alignment" is likely to block that effort, for the alliance cannot afford such a loss. Because the state threatening to defect might move into a non-aligned position or even join the opposition, members of the alliance bring collective pressure to bear on the dissenter to moderate its aims. Restraint is thus built into multipolar alliances. Or if one alliance member should enhance its power by increasing its armed forces, a previously unaligned state may throw its weight onto the scales by joining the weaker side. Thus, a multipolar structure, with its inherent flexibility and ability to remedy imbalances, is inherently more stable than a bipolar one. The contrast is striking. If one of the two superpowers in a bipolar system wishes to act in a manner not supported by its allies, they cannot inhibit it. Because of the enormous difference in power between the superpower and its allies, the threat of defection cannot work, for it will not appreciably reduce the superpower's power. Indeed, the situation is quite the reverse: the weaker allies need the superpower's protection more than the superpower needs their support. Bipolar alliances are not, therefore, restrained from within.

One additional argument has been advanced to explain the restraining and peace-preserving characteristics of multipolarity. The more numerous the actors, it has been claimed, the less attention any single actor can give to any other.[10] Whereas in a bipolar system the contestants watch each other unceasingly and are able to devote themselves fully to their quarrels, in a multipolar system, with as many as a dozen great powers, it is possible to avoid major conflicts. Thus, bipolar systems are said to be prone to crises and the eruption of war; multipolar systems, because of their flexibility, are more likely to maintain peace (see Table 6-1).

OR IS BIPOLARITY STABLE AND MULTIPOLARITY UNSTABLE?

The preceding evaluations of bipolarity and multipolarity have not gone unchallenged. Kenneth Waltz argued persuasively that bipolarity is stable and multipolarity unstable.[11] His major reason for this conclusion is that in a bipolar system each state needs to watch only the other one and counter its moves. Both poles may have allies, but, because their allies are lesser powers, the two major actors need pay little attention to their wishes and complaints. The allies are too dependent on their poles' protection. To be sure, a two-pole system means confrontation that can lead to crises. But such crises also suggest that the balance is being kept. War would be much more likely if one power did not respond to the other's challenge. Avoiding trouble when challenged does not mean that war has been prevented, only that it is very likely to come later.

Table 6-1 The Bipolar and Multipolar State Systems

	Bipolar System	*Multipolar System*
Number of powers	Two superior states	Many (usually cited as five to ten) approximately equal states
Nature of system	Simple and rigid	Complex and flexible
Principal characteristics	Unstable: confrontation, crisis, arms competition, preoccupation with adversary's preemptive or first-strike capability, search for allies	Stable: self-restraint and emphasis on negotiating major political differences
Alliance relationship	Cohesive	Rapidly changing

Consistent with this logic, Waltz argued that multipolarity is unstable. Multipolarity's flexibility does not make it stable because fluidity in relationships, with states shifting back and forth among alliances and counteralliances and nonalignment, renders every state's calculations uncertain. Was it not the multipolarity of 1914 that helped precipitate World War I because Austria-Hungary was determined to squash Serbia in the Balkans, and Germany, unwilling to lose Austria-Hungary as an ally, was pulled into the war (admittedly, not at all reluctantly)? When czarist Russia opposed Austria-Hungary, did France, unable to face Germany alone, have any choice but to support its Russian ally? In short, neither Germany nor France felt they could defect, thereby restraining their respective partners.[12] It was the weakest member of each alliance that dragged its stronger partner into what was to escalate into a European-wide war: by pulling in Germany and France, Austria-Hungary and Russia made it impossible to confine the hostilities to the Balkans. Ironically, after the war some German leaders claimed that they would not have gone to war had they known that Britain—which did not have alliances with France and Russia, only ententes—would come into the war (that is, had the system possessed the clarity of a bipolar system).

Are the conventional wisdoms about multipolarity and the stability of the state system and bipolarity and instability then correct or not? Presumably, these causal relationships would not have become conventional wisdoms had there not been a good deal of evidence to support them. Or is Waltz correct? The immediate impression is that he is. The post-World War II forty-five-year-long cold war peace lasted twice as long as the period from the end of World War I (1918) to the beginning of World War II (1939). The absence of another world war certainly suggests that the system has been stable. A quick look at the cold war may reveal what structural reasons, if any, there may be for that stability.

THE COLD WAR: BIPOLAR EXPLANATION

Action and Reaction

The bipolar balance is one of challenge and response, and therefore it virtually maintains itself.[13] Bipolar politics is a zero-sum game—that is, any gain for one is a loss for the other. Thus, the pattern of the cold war was one in which one power sought to improve its position and expand its influence and the other reacted.[14] When after World War II the Soviets sought to turn Iran into a satellite, the United States and Britain countered the effort. And when the Soviets later put pressure on Turkey, Britain initially lent that country its support as well. In the winter of 1946-1947, however, Britain collapsed from the exhaustion of two world wars, leaving the United States to take over Britain's role and become Moscow's chief adversary. The symbol of America's new role was the 1947 Truman Doctrine in which the president committed the nation to the political independence and territorial integrity of both Turkey and Greece. In the civil war in Greece, the Communists received support from Communist Yugoslavia and Bulgaria.

From the eastern Mediterranean, the United States shifted to Western Europe, where both the victors and vanquished were in a state of utter economic and psychological collapse. This led in 1948 to the Marshall Plan, a four-year economic aid plan for the economic revival of Western Europe, named after Secretary of State George Marshall. Soviet pressure on West Berlin, the western half of Germany's former capital which lay surrounded by Soviet-occupied East Germany, was met by an airlift to feed the city. But because Berlin had aroused European uncertainty about American protection while Europe sought to rebuild itself economically, it prompted the United States for the first time in its history to commit itself in peacetime to an alliance, the North Atlantic Treaty Organization (NATO), to safeguard Western Europe's security. Greece and Turkey were later incorporated into the alliance (1952), as was West Germany (1955). The Soviet Union, which already controlled Eastern Europe, formalized that control in the Warsaw Treaty Organization (WTO), shortly after the Western allies admitted West Germany into their alliance. By 1950, Europe's split into two opposing camps was readily apparent.

No sooner had the European situation stabilized than Nationalist China collapsed in Asia as the remnants of the Nationalist Chinese government fled to the island of Taiwan, 100 miles off the Chinese coast. The United States was now intent on balancing this loss with Japan. Just as in Europe, where former enemy West Germany became an ally while the former ally Soviet Union became the United States' chief adversary, in Asia, Japan, the recent enemy, became a desirable ally as Nationalist China, an ally in World War II, became Communist China. Japan signed a mutual security treaty with the United States in 1951. The desire to attract Japan was a key reason why in June 1950 the United States engaged in its first "limited war" when Communist North

Korea invaded South Korea, whose security was intimately linked to that of Japan. When U.S. forces advanced into North Korea, however, Communist China intervened to prevent the elimination of North Korea and protect its own security. The war ended in 1953 back at the thirty-eighth parallel, and to guarantee South Korea against another possible attack, the United States signed an alliance with South Korea the same year.

This pattern of action and reaction continued through the 1950s. Once Korea was over, the United States reacted to the Sino-Soviet alliance of 1950 by seeking to encircle it with additional alliances. In the Middle East, on the Soviet Union's southern border, the United States sponsored the British-led Middle East Treaty Organization (METO). (By staying formally out, the United States hoped that Egypt would be attracted to the West despite its conflict with Israel.) And in southeast Asia, the United States organized the Southeast Asia Treaty Organization (SEATO) to defend South Vietnam after the French defeat in Indochina in 1954. Neither alliance had much support among the countries in these areas and, unlike NATO, were not worth the paper they were written on. In reaction, Egypt and the Soviet Union, both opposed to METO for their own reasons, joined together in an alliance in all but name, leapfrogging and rendering the Western alliance useless. SEATO's main claim to fame was that it dragged the United States into the defense of South Vietnam in 1965 and a losing war, whose principal result—besides loss of life and money and the fall of South Vietnam in 1975—was a weakening of the anti-Communist public consensus in the United States, which for two decades had supported the government's international role.

Indeed, Soviet actions revived U.S. policy and led to the further expansion of U.S. commitments. Soviet-Cuban expansionist efforts in Angola in 1975 and in Ethiopia in 1977 and the Soviet invasion of Afghanistan in 1979 resulted in the Carter Doctrine to protect the vital oil sheikdoms of the Persian Gulf. President Ronald Reagan expanded this commitment to the survival of the Saudi royal family, Saudi Arabia being the non-Communist world's largest oil producer. In 1987, in part reacting to the fear of an expanded Soviet role in the Persian Gulf and Iranian expansion in the Arabian peninsula, Reagan sent the U.S. Navy to protect U.S.-reflagged Kuwaiti oil tankers, which were being attacked by Iran because Kuwait was a virtual ally of Iraq with whom Iran was at war.

Central America also became involved in the superpower rivalry. Before 1979, the United States had intervened intermittently in Latin America to overthrow governments it believed were aligning with the Soviet Union such as Guatemala in 1954, Cuba in 1961 (an unsuccessful operation), and the Dominican Republic in 1965. But, on the whole, the hemisphere to the south suffered from inattention and neglect. America's attention and resources were focused elsewhere: Europe, Asia, and the Middle East. The main thing it wanted in Latin America was peace and quiet. Such "stability" was assured largely by supporting right-wing, often military, regimes. But the collapse of one of these pro-American governments in Nicaragua, stemming from a popular revolution, the consolidation of power by the Marxist Sandinistas after they had displaced their more moderate and democratic allies who had helped them make the revolution, and the prospects of a "second Cuba" in this hemisphere—and the first on the mainland—led the Carter and then the Reagan administration to oppose the Sandinistas. Indeed, Reagan wanted to overthrow the regime, which he claimed also supported the Marxist guerrillas in neighboring El Salvador where the United States supported the government. Regional conflicts and civil wars in the Third World were rarely seen in either Washington or Moscow as having indigenous roots unrelated to the superpower competition. Consequently, their bipolar competition more often than not was superimposed on these regional and domestic rivalries in the ex-colonial and underdeveloped areas of the world.

In summary, in the bipolar structure characterizing the cold war both powers watched each other constantly. Thus, it was easier to ensure that the balance was being kept. A principal means of doing so was alliance formation.

Role of Alliances

The function of alliances in a bipolar structure[15] was, first, to draw lines or frontiers around areas considered vital. By incorporating such areas in alliances, each superpower was drawing attention to their importance and warning the opponent not to invade them if it wished to avoid war. Not all of the United States' alliances have been of equal importance; nor have all survived. METO died the year it was born, although officially it was not interred until after the Iranian revolution of 1979 toppled the pro-American shah. SEATO was buried quietly after the Vietnam War. America's non-European anti-Communist alliances fell victim to the powerful forces of nationalism and social revolution. Even the Latin American Rio Pact, a symbol of America's former hegemony in the Western Hemisphere, has lost any operational significance as nationalism in Latin America has shrunk American influence. Similarly, the Soviet alliance with China ended as the two became enemies. Nevertheless, in Europe, *the area of the two superpowers' principal interests and of direct U.S.-Soviet confrontation,* the alliances survived until the cold war ended. NATO and WTO proved to be significant means of communicating to the opponent which area the other intended to protect even if it meant going to war. The result was forty-five years of peace, Europe's longest in this century.

Outside of Europe, the interests at stake, while important, were secondary and the lines less clear. The Cairo-Moscow axis negated METO, and SEATO drew a line through Vietnam—one that Washington, and apparently Beijing and Moscow as well, regarded as part of the line running around the then Sino-Soviet bloc—but that North Vietnam's leader, Ho Chi Minh, did not. As a nationalist, not just a Communist, he believed that he and his party were the legitimate heirs to French colonial rule. Thus, the civil war resumed, with the United States defending South Vietnam because it regarded the area as much a part of its sphere of influence as South Korea and West Germany.

At least as important as line-drawing in a bipolar division was the power differential between each superpower and its allies. Each superpower was the producer of security; its partners were the consumers of that security. Thus, an alliance within the bipolar structure, with its unequal internal power distribution, was in effect a unilateral guarantee extended by the superpower to its allies, which really were its protectorates. This implied that the United States and Soviet Union needed only to keep their eyes mainly on each other and make policy accordingly, instead of becoming absorbed with holding their respective alliances together and making policy responsive to their allies' interests. On the one hand, such an arrangement allowed the two adversaries to concentrate fully on the management of crises when they occurred so that war could be avoided—particularly important in a nuclear era. On the other hand, if their allies acted in ways that might draw them into a dangerous confrontation, the superpowers could restrain their partners. In an alliance in which each superpower was so much stronger than its allies, who were in effect its dependents, the latter were in no position to exercise similar restraint on the superpower. In an unequal alliance, in short, the superpower could severely limit its allies' freedom to act. Thus, once the United States had decided to oppose the installation of Soviet missiles in Cuba in 1962, its NATO partners could do little but give the United States verbal support while praying that a nuclear clash would not result. They could have protested, but it would not have done much good. Conversely, when Britain and France attacked Egypt in 1956, or when the Nationalist Chinese wanted to attempt an invasion of the mainland in the 1950s, U.S. opposition stopped both. But no one defected. Neither Britain nor France nor Nationalist China had anywhere to go, they all needed U.S. protection. Similarly, in 1958 when Communist China wished to invade Taiwan, unite China, and destroy its Nationalist rival, the Soviet Union, unwilling to risk war with the United States, refused to support Beijing. This caused friction, however, and eventually proved to be the key exception to the rule that alliances within the bipolar division were rigid, not flexible.

While in the key area of Europe the cold war alliances held, there were exceptions in the Third World. The major exception to bipolarity's simplicity and rigidity was the People's Republic of China. It was one thing to prevent the defection of a Hungary or a Guatemala, but China's defection could not have been prevented without a major and costly intervention whose outcome was uncertain. China, in fact, switched sides twice—once from the United States to the Soviet Union and then back again. It was far more normal for Third World states wooed by the two superpowers to shift from one to the other. While most remained nonaligned during the cold war, some did align themselves but eventually switched allegiances—for example, Egypt, Ethiopia, Indonesia, and Somalia.

Indeed, within the overall bipolar structure, with its zero-sum character and self-feeding growth of mutual distrust and fear, these reversals in alignments tended to dampen the adversary relationship. One need but recall that before the Sino-Soviet alliance in 1950 U.S. foreign policy was strictly anti-Soviet, limited to responding to Soviet expansionist moves. After 1950, the United States launched an anti-Communist crusade. Fearful of facing the two largest Communist states together, it forgot to make critical distinctions between primary and secondary opponents or between areas of vital and lesser interest. Erroneously assuming a monolithic Communist bloc, the United States overreacted, especially in Vietnam, where it assumed that the North Vietnamese were Chinese puppets who, if allowed to conquer South Vietnam, would enhance both Chinese and Soviet power. Thus, the United States intervened militarily to prevent a shift in the regional and central U.S.-Soviet balance. After the Sino-American reconciliation, the United States reverted to an anti-Soviet policy, which, despite occasional rhetorical excesses, was largely restrained. Similarly, one reason that Moscow sought a détente in the 1970s was to slow Sino-American reconciliation. The effect, on the whole, was beneficial. Indeed, one analyst has talked of the "salutory role of the smaller powers" in bipolar systems:

> If one of these, say Ethiopia, decides to draw closer to the Eastern bloc, another, Somalia, can approach the West. . . . Chile can cease being governed by a Marxist party while South Vietnam moves steadily towards incorporation with communist North Vietnam. None of these are zero sum conflicts, *for each side gains something in the end.* More generally, with the rise of the new nations in the postwar era, both superpowers sought to gain new adherents with simultaneous gains for both, principally in the Middle East, Asia and Africa. Without the existence of these smaller powers, *it is possible that a more direct confrontation could have occurred.*[16]

Thus, despite the fear in a bipolar system that any loss of even a small country may lead to further losses, and that such a "domino effect" may result in a major shift of power affecting one or the other of the superpowers, this analysis suggests that this concern was exaggerated. The foundations of their respective power did not erode if, for example, they "exchanged" countries such as Ethiopia for Egypt, or if one suffered the loss of a country such as Iran but the other did not pick it up as a gain, or, worse, it did "add" it but the burden became a drain on its resources. Thus, Moscow did not provide large-scale economic aid for Chile in the 1970s or Nicaragua in the 1980s; the Soviets provided the latter mainly with military equipment which it had in abundance. In Afghanistan, the drain was so great that after eight years of fighting, Moscow withdrew.

The 'Long Peace'

There is much to be said for the traditional position that bipolarity is an unstable distribution of power. The zero-sum nature of the two-power conflict, of continual challenge and response, and of each pole seeing even defensive moves as offensive, created tension, mutual suspicion, fear, and intensified feelings of hostility. Ever wary of shifts in the balance and always alert to the possibility of a first strike by the opponent (or the need to beat the latter to the punch), both powers had to think not only of the risks and costs of such an initial blow but also of the risks and costs of *not* doing so. Yet in the specific circumstances of a divided postwar Western Europe, bipolarity produced a high degree of order and predictability in spite of the risks created by a series of Berlin crises. And, more broadly, bipolarity kept the peace. Was it, as Waltz argued, because of the simplicity of the bipolar structure and its characteristic action-reaction pattern; the ability to distinguish clearly between friend and foe, as well as the respective areas of vital interests; the duration of key alliances, their hierarchical structures, and the ability of each superpower to discipline its partners and satellites; and the role that Third World states played in this system? [17]

Similarly, it may be true theoretically that multipolar systems contain more points of conflict; that it is more difficult to know who is aligned with whom at any one point in time; and that this makes balance-of-power calculations more uncertain, allowing a potential aggressor to miscalculate, as Germany did twice for Britain. The first time was before World War I; the other time was before World War II, when Britain had committed itself to the defense of Poland, a commitment Hitler found to be incredible after years of British appeasement. And Germany compounded this error in both wars by not foreseeing that the United States would intervene after the European balance had been upset. Yet, just as one can cite bipolar systems that did lead to war, the most notable and earliest being the war between Athens and Sparta in ancient Greece, there is a good deal of empirical support for the proposition that multipolar systems are more stable than bipolar ones.

Given the unsettled question about whether bipolarity or multipolarity is more stable, another interpretation may be advanced: the stability of postwar Europe must in part be attributed to nuclear weapons. No American, European, or Soviet leaders doubted that a nuclear war would destroy the belligerents. The notion that a war could be won quickly, let alone without major casualties, which had prevailed before both world wars, at least in Germany, did not exist in the age of such unprecedentedly destructive weapons. Bipolarity—its clear division of Europe into two opposing cohesive alliances—as well as the presence of nuclear weapons were primarily responsible for the forty-five years of peace on a continent that had twice in thirty-one years (1914-1945) almost destroyed itself. Thus, Waltz's persuasive conclusion about the stability of bipolarity can be reformulated with the following amended proposition: *nuclear bipolar systems will be stable; nuclear multipolar systems will be unstable* (see especially Chapter 20).

POST-COLD WAR EUROPE: THE UNCERTAIN FUTURE

Did Bipolarity Have Some Virtues?

Will a post-cold war Europe be less stable or more stable? [18] And if less stable, how unstable? It will depend on how events evolve. All former Soviet forces are scheduled to be completely pulled back to the Soviet Union by 1994 when the last troops leave what used to be East Germany. Will U.S. forces also be withdrawn because of the change in Soviet intentions and the retraction of Soviet power from Central and Eastern Europe? This is not wholly certain. Some U.S. forces may remain in Europe: first, to protect U.S. allies against a possible, although unlikely, threat from the East, made even more unlikely by the collapse of the Soviet state after the abortive coup in August 1991; and, second, to reassure the states of Western *and* Eastern Europe fearful of a new German threat. The question is how long those forces can stay. How long will Congress and the American public fund forces that no longer have an enemy to confront? And how long will the new Germany tolerate "occupation" by U.S. forces, even if radically reduced in numbers? Will Germany—since World War II a stable democracy, a loyal NATO ally, and a member of the European Community (EC)—not come to resent its so-called friends who still distrust it? In these circumstances, given the disappearance of the Soviet Union, the reunification of Germany, and the end to Europe's bipolar division, how long can NATO survive?

If both the Soviet Union and the United States then withdraw from Germany, will it lead to a revival of the unstable, interwar multipolar system? The bipolar Soviet-American division of Europe, however unjust to Germany and the Eastern European countries who were denied national self-determination, had several virtues that made the system a stable one. First, after its defeat in 1945 the principal troublemaker in the modern European state system, Germany, was split and each part incorporated as a subordinate component of the two major alliance systems. Neither the Soviet Union nor the United States, as a result, was confronted by any other competitor for power except the other superpower.

Second, the intra-German border had the added advantage, as already noted, of assigning the different European states to an alliance system, each of which was protected by its respective superpower (whether the Poles and others, no doubt glad to be defended against another possible German attack, were always thankful for this protection is another matter). The very clear division of Europe and the extension of American and Soviet deterrence over their respective allies left no doubt in each superpower's mind that if this line of demarcation was crossed the result would be war.

Third, in forming these alliances, the Soviet Union and the United States basically eliminated their alliance members' "security dilemma" in relation to other states in their coalition. In an anarchical system, all states have a security problem. Thus, after 1945 France, for example, would have had to worry about its safety from both the Soviet Union and West Germany had not the United States, through NATO, provided its allies with security against threats made not only by the Soviet Union but also by each other. As the hegemonic power in NATO, which gave France and West Germany a sense of security, the United States eliminated the grounds for a replay of historic quarrels among its allies and dampened the effects of anarchy. Simultaneously, this allowed the two former enemies to cooperate within the NATO alliance and the EC. In short, France did not have to fear renewed German aggression and take measures to contain its former enemy; rather, it could become Germany's principal partner in the creation of an integrated Europe.

Indeed, as long as each alliance faced an external threat from the other, it helped unify the opposing alliance and kept differences of opinion and conflicts of interests within each to a minimum. In addition, the Soviet threat, which also led the United States to seek German rearmament, was responsible for the European integration movement. Besides strengthening the containment policy, it allowed Europeans to restrain German power and use it for Western Europe's collective purpose. In contrast to the intense nationalism that characterized Europe before 1939, and especially before 1914, the nationalism of post-World War II Europe was dampened. Europe's traditional rivalries had stimulated nationalist feelings, but the Europe of NATO and the EC had no need to mobilize nationalist sentiments against one another. Indeed, their own security and prosperity dictated that they submerge their nationalism and jointly create a greater Europe.

In its sphere, the Soviet Union, by its domination of Central and Eastern Europe, also suppressed the nationalist aspirations that had destabilized the area from the Baltics to the Balkans since before World Wars I and II. By incorporating the entire area into its postwar empire, it ended the incessant ethnic feuding over frontiers and political influence which historically have characterized this area and which helped precipitate both world wars.

Revival of the German Problem

But once the former Soviet forces have withdrawn and American forces have either been withdrawn or greatly reduced, will this compel the European states, including a reunified Germany, to engage in their traditional search for security against one another as national differences again rise to the surface? Will they, as before the cold war, again regard one another with suspicion and fear because they can no longer depend on superpower protection against neighboring states? Will the border conflicts and ethnic tensions that used to characterize Eastern Europe—for example, between Romania and Hungary and between Poland and Czechoslovakia—once more disturb the peace of the new Europe? Will the EC's bonds of economic interdependence, forged under the protective security of the United States, erode with the disappearance of the Soviet threat and the reduction of U.S. troops and influence?

Above all, will a new, self-confident Germany—now a country of 80 million people, the world's fourth largest economy with a GNP of over $1 trillion, and a nation no longer constrained by its need for American protection against the Soviet Union—once more reassert its nationalism? Will it unilaterally seek to revise its frontiers with Poland and Czechoslovakia,[19] or acquire nuclear weapons as France and Britain have done, or increase the size of its army beyond the level agreed to by Germany and the former World War II victors at the time of reunification? As Europe's most dynamic and most powerful state with an expansive economy, will Germany, with its postwar democracy, continue to restrain a revival of its former ambitions? Indeed, can the world really be certain that the disintegration of the Soviet empire and decline of Soviet power will not rekindle German nationalism and expansion? Why would Germany, aware of its power and self-confident, not in future years define distant interests and act with the kind of assertiveness that other great powers have done? If that were to happen—and that fear is widespread in Europe, even if for obvious reasons it is not expressed officially—it would surely revive another scramble for security in a multipolar setting.

But another scenario may be more likely. To be sure, Germany will probably become the dominant power in Central and Eastern Europe, filling the vacuum left by the retraction of Soviet power. Indeed, in the absence of a military threat from the East to Germany's security and in its position as Europe's dominant economy, the expansion of German influence eastward is natural. The states of Eastern Europe—including the former Soviet Union—want German capital investment and to reap the benefits of German managerial skills, industriousness, technological sophistication, and quality products. There is nothing illegitimate about such German financial and economic expansion, but there is something ironic about the new Germany achieving "what the Hapsburgs, Bismarck, and Hitler failed to achieve; the Germanization of Central Europe. Through peaceful and laudable means, of course. And by the logic of commerce rather than conquest." [20] Why would the Germans sacrifice the economic benefits, prestige and influence stemming from such a position by trying to convert eager clients into adversaries through seeking to transform an economically superior position into military dominance?

> The forcible methods that traditionally defined and dominated European politics do indeed seem relegated to the past, now that the last great representative of these methods [the Soviet Union] has apparently abandoned them.... [T]he new reality in Europe is not the emergence only of a powerful German state, but of one that, so long as it eschews the old and disastrous ways, is likely to have few constraints placed on its freedom of action. Moreover, the commitment to values of liberal democracy apart, a united Germany has every reason to eschew the old ways, for the new ways hold out the promise of achieving in substantial measure the perennial ends of statecraft.[21]

Moreover, Germany is most likely to achieve these ends within the broader European context. While this comprises East and West, Germany's European anchor remains the EC, initially organized precisely to restrain German power as it remobilized after World War II and to harness that power (used so often in the past to harm Europe) for broader European purposes. Germany has been a loyal member of the EC from the beginning. It values its membership in the association and shares with the other members the twin purposes of the EC: first, the creation of a united Europe from which destructive wars will be banished forever and, second, the building of a new European state that is both prosperous and militarily strong enough to define its own interests and defend them. Admittedly, there is some fear in Europe that Germany, with the largest population and strongest economy in the EC, will eventually dominate that organization. There is also the opposite fear that Germany will become so preoccupied with integrating East Germany into its national fabric that it will lose interest in the EC. Neither of these prospects is too likely. France, Britain, and the other EC members would resist German efforts to dominate the community, and Germany's security and economic welfare depend on its membership in the EC, as well as on its maintaining good relations with the United States, which is remaining in NATO in part to restrain Germany and reassure the other European states. Historically a great power, Russia, too, will be a counterweight to possible German domination when it recovers.[22]

REGIONAL INSTABILITIES OUTSIDE EUROPE: THE IRAQI TEST CASE

Europe was the key front during the cold war. Because vital interests were at stake and the danger of war high if one side intruded into the other's sphere, the two superpowers rechanneled their competition to Third World areas. Each power's motivation was strategic and political, not ideological or economic. The Soviet Union's chief goal was to weaken Western influence; the U.S. aim was basically defensive: to stop the expansion of Soviet influence in developing countries. Neither side was particularly concerned with the domestic character of the regimes it supported as long as they served its purposes.

More specifically this meant that Moscow and Washington tended to support opposing sides in the civil wars that often devastated developing countries, as well as the rival states competing for regional influence if not hegemony (see Chapter 18 on the United Nations). Thus, as the superpowers sought to expand their influence at each other's expense, the conflict was often superimposed on domestic and regional quarrels, and those competing for power internally or externally looked to the superpowers for political support, economic assistance, and weapons. This interaction magnified what otherwise might have been only local disturbances and made them potentially quite dangerous. But the attraction of the two superpowers also placed a lid on these conflicts because neither wanted their confrontations to escalate into a military clash with the attendant danger of precipitating a nuclear war.

The end of the American-Soviet rivalry in the late 1980s, therefore, raised the possibility that more regional rivalries will follow their own dynamics.

The reasons are several: the sources of conflict continue to exist in many areas; the retrenchment of both Soviet and American power will create vacuums that are likely to attract regional rivals; and conflicts among countries in some regions continue to show little chance of resolution. Indeed, many of these countries are still arming. Had the cold war been still underway in 1990, the Soviets would have restrained Iraq, one of the radical states it had supported in the Third World, from invading Kuwait and threatening Saudi Arabia and the other Persian Gulf oil kingdoms on whom the Western industrial democracies are dependent. Given the Soviet-American rivalry, the attempt of a regional power to attain dominance would have been met by a counterbalancing effort. Thus, the United States and the Soviet Union, because of their involvement with their respective client states, would have worked out some sort of diplomatic solution and imposed that on their respective clients, who, in the final analysis, were more dependent on their patrons than the latter were on them. The end of the cold war, therefore, gave Baghdad the freedom of action that it had not had earlier and led it to miscalculate. It is doubtful that Saddam Hussein expected the United States to react as it did when he seized Kuwait.[23]

How will order be kept in the post-cold war era? The problem, when stated in terms of regional rivalries, perhaps fails to underline the two main points: first, the rise of small, radical, potentially reckless states, which seek to play major regional, if not hegemonic, roles, and in some instances, larger international roles, and second, the efforts of these states to acquire, if they do not already have them, weapons of mass destruction (nuclear, chemical, and biological), which when placed atop missiles are capable of hitting targets far beyond their immediate neighbors. That is why the Iraqi invasion of Kuwait became widely known as the first post-cold war crisis. It was clear what Saddam Hussein sought. After his eight-year-long war with Iran, which had ended in victory in 1988, Iraq's economy was in ruins. But Iraq's oil revenues would not even cover current expenditures, let alone the estimated $230 billion reconstruction. Moreover, Saddam had run up a huge $80 billion debt during the war, which affected his credit rating and Iraq's ability to rebuild.[24] Earlier he had sought greater revenues by forcing up the oil prices of the Organization of Petroleum Exporting Countries (OPEC) and threatening Kuwait, which was producing more than the OPEC-set quota and therefore keeping oil prices down. Indeed, prices were already down because of the oil surplus created by Iranian and Iraqi oil coming back on the market. Even after OPEC raised oil prices, however, the Iraqi leader invaded Kuwait. Posing as one who had fought a war to protect all the oil kingdoms against Iran's Islamic fundamentalism, even though he had precipitated that war, Saddam Hussein really wanted all his debts to Kuwait, Saudi Arabia, and others cancelled. In addition, he demanded from them $30 billion. In one sense, then, Saddam Hussein's invasion of Kuwait amounted to simple bank robbery. By gaining control of Kuwait's oil fields and thereby increasing his share of the world's oil reserves to 20 percent, he also sought to increase his

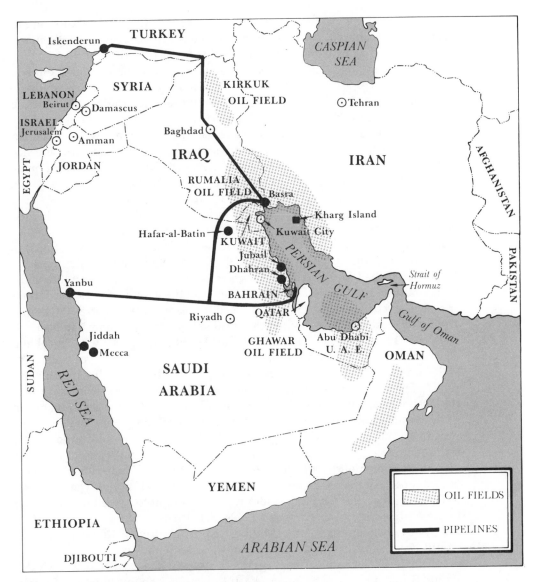

Figure 6-1 Key Oilfields and Pipelines in the Persian Gulf

influence over OPEC production and pricing policies. Indeed, even without invading Saudi Arabia, he would be able to intimidate it and the other smaller oil kingdoms, in effect increasing his control to about half of the world's oil reserves.[25] (See Figure 6-1)

But Saddam Hussein's goals went beyond reducing his debt and enhancing his income. More to the point, he sought to establish his dominance over the

Persian Gulf. Iraq's strongman thought that was his just due because he had defeated Iran's attempt to establish its hegemony. The issue at stake, then, was not just paying a few cents more for gasoline (or as the critics of the Gulf war were fond of saying, American lives were worth more than a nickel increase in gasoline prices). In fact, the real issue was much broader: the availability of the energy needed to fuel the economies of all the industrialized countries, as well as those of the developing countries. Even if the United States had been less dependent on imported oil, Western Europe and Japan, with which the United States trades, would have been badly affected if Saddam Hussein had shut off or slowed the flow of OPEC oil. They were far more dependent on oil imports than the United States, and any effects on their economies would have affected the American economy as well. Thus, control of the OPEC spigot would have given the Iraqi strongman considerable political influence. For better or worse, the world economy is hooked on oil.

Beyond controlling OPEC, Saddam Hussein's goal was to claim leadership of the Arab world, a goal he had sought to achieve by his earlier attack on Iran when he had expected a quick victory because Iran had been in the midst of revolution and turmoil and had alienated the United States, its former friend. The Arab states had long competed for leadership: Egypt, as the largest Arab state, had usually provided that leadership, but Syria and Iraq also had sought that status at times, especially after Egypt made peace with Israel and consequently was for a time isolated in the Arab world. Syria was isolated as well because it had supported non-Arab Iran in the war with Iraq, Syria's rival.[26] There was therefore no one to oppose Saddam Hussein's bid to lead the Arab world. Ultimately, then, he would lead an anti-American alliance in a "holy war" against America's friends: Israel, the oil kingdoms, and moderate pro-American friends such as Egypt and Jordan. He also would undoubtedly try to remove such rivals as Syria's strongly anti-Israeli, anti-American leader. Neither former friends nor foes would be safe from Saddam Hussein, a man of grandiose ambition who appeared to perceive himself not only as successor to Gamal Nasser, the Egyptian leader who had sought to make himself master of the Arab world in the 1950s and 1960s, but also as a modern Nebuchadnezzar. As the hegemonist of the Middle East, in control of its oil wealth, he would become an important world—not just regional—player.

What precedent would Iraq's aggression set for the post-cold war world? Would Saddam Hussein be able to keep Kuwait and go unpunished? Clearly, while Iraq had only 17 million people, it had formidable might at its disposal: an army of 1 million men, including reserves, equipped with thousands of Soviet-made tanks, armored personnel carriers, as well as short-range missiles and chemical weapons. Iraq was the most powerful state in the Middle East with reportedly the fourth largest military in the world. Saddam Hussein, whose entry into politics was as an assassin, and who at age twenty-six was an interrogator and torturer at a prison known as the "Palace of the End,"[27] already had shown his utter ruthlessness and willingness to use all the weapons at his command by his use of poison gas during the war with Iran.

After the conclusion of that conflict, he even used it on Iraq's Kurdish minority. Neither moral qualms nor the possibility of international disapproval restrained him. Presumably, had he possessed nuclear weapons, the acquisition of which had been set back by the Israeli attack on his nuclear reactor in 1981, he would have used them as well had they gained for him the upper hand in the war against Iran. After the American deployment of troops to Saudi Arabia, he initially refused to let American men who were in either Iraq or Kuwait out of the country. Referred to as "guests" of Iraq, they were placed at strategic sites to act as human shields and deterrents against U.S. bombing if war started. His callousness also was evident in Kuwait, which he annexed as Iraq's nineteenth province after the invasion. He also tried to obliterate Kuwait as a nation by terrorizing about half of its citizens into flight using rape, torture, and executions; erasing citizenship records; repopulating it with Iraqis; and looting its banks, hospitals, and museums, as well as the possessions of its citizens, from automobiles to personal computers. If Saddam Hussein were to keep Kuwait, if the coalition organized to oppose him were to fail to compel him to withdraw, what would be the message sent to other ambitious rulers at the dawn of the post-cold war period?

More to the point, what would a man like Saddam Hussein, unrestrained at home where he ruled by fear, who had heavily mobilized his medium-sized country for war, and already started one war in which Iraq had lost over 500,000 lives, do in the future once he had acquired nuclear weapons, as he was expected to do by 1995, or at the latest by 2000? Indeed, the possibility that Saddam Hussein might gain possession of nuclear and even biological weapons was the critical reason that many American analysts declared, "Now or later." It was better to destroy the Iraqi leader and his chemical and potential nuclear capabilities now rather than later when he would be armed even more lethally, including a possible intercontinental-range missile to carry lethal gas or nuclear warheads.* *Thus, the worst possible outcome would be a diplomatic solution.* It would leave Saddam Hussein and his expansionist ambitions in control of Iraq, no internal checks on his power, and all his military hardware intact, and would allow him the time and money to enhance his arsenal. A diplomatic solution would merely postpone the day of reckoning, and when that day did arrive, it would be far bloodier than now.

Put yourself in the Oval Office in 1994. Saddam Hussein moves on Saudi Arabia. The U.S. warns him that means war. Saddam says fine, the first city he will take

---

* In the spring of 1990, an Anglo-American sting operation had led to the seizure in London of forty U.S.-made capacitators, called krytrons, bound for Iraq. Krytrons are used as triggering devices for nuclear weapons. About the same time, European authorities seized parts for a 131-foot gun, planned by Iraq, which had it been built (its Canadian inventor was assassinated by unknown gunmen), would have been able to fire conventional and unconventional explosives up to approximately 1,000 miles.

out is New York. You know he has the means and the will. Bloodshed now is a terrible thing to contemplate. Nuclear war at a time of Saddam's choosing, against a sociopath already to blame for a million deaths, is worse.[28]

As events after the war made clear, that day would have come much sooner than had been expected before the war.[29] What would those states in the Middle East-Persian Gulf area, already intimidated, and those in other areas, affected by Iraq's action and possible control of 40 percent of the world's oil reserves, do if he invaded Saudi Arabia?

The Iraqi invasion of Kuwait therefore posed two central questions: What kind of a world order would be created in the wake of the cold war, and who would organize it? Specifically, how would dangerous regional instabilities be dealt with? Can the world afford to allow states like Iraq to gain possession of weapons of mass destruction? If not, what would the other states do about this dangerous trend? And who would take the lead in organizing concerned states in opposition?

In response to Iraq's action, a coalition comprised of Western states, Arab states, and the Soviet Union formed. The industrial democracies were concerned about what Saddam Hussein's control of oil production and prices would do to their prosperity and the world economy. Even if he did not invade Saudi Arabia, he had already frightened the oil kingdoms, having shown that he was quite willing to invade them and overthrow the royal families if they did not comply with his demands. A majority of the Arab states therefore condemned Iraq's action; they were afraid and knew what Saddam Hussein's hegemony would mean for them if he succeeded. The Soviet Union, trying to demonstrate that the cold war was indeed over and that it wanted better relations with the West, aligned itself with the United States, which took the leadership in organizing the opposition to Saddam Hussein.

It did so by acting through the United Nations to legitimate its action and to set a precedent for dealing with any future regional aggressions. The United Nations condemned Iraq for its invasion of Kuwait, demanded the restoration of the status quo, cut off all arms shipments, and, when Iraq announced that it would annex Kuwait, it imposed an economic embargo and sanctioned its enforcement by naval forces. If the United States had not acted through the international organization, it is questionable whether all the European states would have aligned themselves with Washington. The Arab states, identifying the United States with its support for Israel, would have found such an alignment very difficult, if not impossible, despite their fear of Saddam Hussein. And the Soviet Union's switch from hostility to cooperation with the United States was eased by justifying it as support for the United Nations. While the bulk of the military forces sent to Saudi Arabia were from the United States, there were also contingents from England and France, as well as from Egypt and Syria and several other nations (but not the Soviet Union). It was presumed that if the embargo did not work, force would be used to restore at least the status quo, if not to destroy Saddam Hussein's military machine and perhaps the Iraqi leader as well.

There was no alternative. Saddam Hussein was the first test case of the post-cold war era. If he were not dealt with appropriately, what example would he set for other potential bullies who would like to prey on weaker neighbors except that the ruthless win? How could the United States, after declaring that Iraq must withdraw unconditionally from Kuwait and re-establish its legitimate government, and after having built up its troop strength, pull back before these minimum objectives had been achieved without undermining its own prestige and credibility in the world? Indeed, would the failure to accomplish its goals by economic sanctions if possible, by force if necessary, not discredit the United States, the single remaining superpower, and by doing so encourage other potential regional hegemons to attack their neighbors and seek nuclear weapons? Would not then every Arab country that might fall victim to Saddam Hussein feel that it could not rely on U.S. protection and therefore seek the best deal it could from this utterly callous leader? But, if Iraq were compelled to withdraw from Kuwait, and if its capacity to wage war in the future were destroyed by the use of force, the United States would gain the credibility to deter similar aggressions in the years ahead without sending troops. Washington's warning would be taken seriously. The outcome of the Iraqi confrontation was therefore expected to have a major, if not decisive, influence on whether the new emerging world order would produce unprecedented chaos or a more peaceful world.

For Review

1. What are some of the principal distributions of power in the state system?
2. How do these different systemic structures affect state behavior?
3. Which state-system structure is the most stable or least likely to erupt into a major war?
4. How can one use concepts like "bipolarity" and "multipolarity" to explain the actual conduct of states in the real world, as in the cold war?
5. What is the role of alliances in bipolar and multipolar systems?

Notes

1. Joseph L. Nogee, "Polarity: An Ambiguous Concept," *Orbis* (Winter 1975): 1211-1212.
2. George Modelski, "The Long Cycle of Global Politics and the Nation-State," *Comparative Studies in Society and History* (April 1978): 214-235; Modelski, ed., *Long*

Cycles in World Politics (Seattle: University of Washington Press, 1986); William R. Thompson, "Polarity, the Long Cycle, and Global Warfare," *International Studies Quarterly* (December 1986): 587-615; and Thompson, *On Global War* (Columbia: University of South Carolina Press, 1988). A summary of past works may be found in Joshua Goldstein, *Long Cycles* (New Haven, Conn.: Yale University Press, 1988), 21-147.

3. George Modelski, ed., *Exploring Long Cycles* (Boulder, Colo.: Lynne Rienner, 1987), 1-15, 218-248. A critique of this theory may be found in Richard Rosencrance, "Long Cycle Theory and International Relations," *International Organization* (Spring 1987): 297-301.

4. The most notable book, a bestseller after its publication, was that by Paul M. Kennedy, *The Rise and Fall of the Great Powers* (New York: Random House, 1987). For two of the best critiques, see Samuel P. Huntington, "The U.S.—Decline or Renewal?" *Foreign Affairs* (Winter 1988/89): 76-96; and Richard N. Haass, "The Use (and Mainly Misuse) of History," *Orbis* (Spring 1988): 411-419.

5. Joseph S. Nye, *Bound to Lead* (New York: Basic Books, 1990). See especially Nye's criticisms of the citation of Britain's alleged hegemony in the nineteenth century—even though it ranked third behind the United States and Russia in gross national product and third behind Russia and France in military expenditures—and the use of the analogy of Britain's decline to predict the future course of the United States (22, 48-68), as well as his analysis of America's post-1945 "hegemony" (69-112). For a contemporary opposite view, see Arthur M. Schlesinger, Jr., *The Disuniting of America* (New York: Norton, 1992).

6. There is considerable disagreement about the dangers and virtues of bipolarity. On the dangers, see Hans Morgenthau, *Politics among Nations*, 5th ed. (New York: Knopf, 1972), 346-347; and on the virtues, see Kenneth H. Waltz, "The Stability of a Bipolar World," *Daedalus* (Summer 1964): 881-909; Waltz, "International Structure, National Force, and the Balance of World Power," *Journal of International Affairs* 21 (June 1967): 215-231; and Waltz, *Theory of International Politics* (Reading, Mass.: Addison-Wesley, 1979), 163-176. For a comparative study of the bipolar struggle between Athens and Sparta, see Peter J. Fliess, *Thucydides and the Politics of Bipolarity* (Baton Rouge: Louisiana State University Press, 1966). My own analysis throughout this chapter is heavily indebted to Glen H. Snyder and Paul Diesing, *Conflict among Nations* (Princeton, N.J.: Princeton University Press, 1977), 419-450.

7. Thucydides, *History of the Peloponnesian War* (New York: Oxford University Press, 1960), 46.

8. Morton Kaplan, *System and Process in International Politics* (New York: Wiley, 1957).

9. Karl W. Deutsch and J. David Singer, "Multipolar Power Systems and International Stability," *World Politics* (April 1964): 392-396.

10. Ibid., 396-400.

11. Waltz, "The Stability of a Bipolar World," 163-170.

12. Snyder and Diesing, *Conflict among Nations*, 441.

13. On the general phenomenon of alliance balancing and security cooperation, see Stephen M. Walt, *The Origins of Alliances* (Ithaca, N.Y.: Cornell University Press, 1987).

14. For broad analyses of the beginning of the cold war and American foreign policy during the cold war period, see Louis J. Halle, *The Cold War as History* (New York: Harper & Row, 1967); John Spanier, *American Foreign Policy since World War II*, 12th ed. (Washington, D.C.: CQ Press, 1991); and Joseph L. Nogee and John Spanier,

Peace Impossible—War Unlikely (Boston: Scott/Foresman, 1988).

15. Snyder and Diesing, *Conflict among Nations*, 419-429.

16. Manus I. Midlarsky, *The Disintegration of Political Systems* (Columbia: University of South Carolina Press, 1986), 118ff. Also see Midlarsky, *The Onset of World War* (Boston: Unwin Hyman, 1988), 28-29.

17. Besides Waltz, "The Stability of a Bipolar World," see John Lewis Gaddis, "The Long Peace; Elements of Stability in the Postwar International System," *International Security* (Spring 1986): 99-142.

18. John Mearsheimer, "Back to the Future: Instability in Europe After the Cold War," *International Security* (Summer 1990): 5-56; Jack Snyder, "Averting Anarchy in the New Europe," *International Security* (Spring 1990): 4-41; Stephen Van Evera, "Primed for Peace: Europe After the Cold War," *International Security* (Winter 1990/91): 7-57; Richard H. Ullman, *Securing Europe* (Princeton, N.J.: Princeton University Press, 1991); and Barry M. Blechman, ed., *The United States and Undivided Europe* (New York: St. Martin's Press, 1991), 16-21. Also see Charles Krauthammer, "The German Revival," *New Republic,* March 26, 1990, 16-21; and Andrew C. Goldberg, "Soviet Imperial Decline and the Emerging Balance of Power," *Washington Quarterly* (Winter 1990).

19. After all, the world seems to feel that the Arabs, who lost the West Bank in a war of aggression with Israel, should get it back. Why then should Germany be denied the return of the provinces of Silesia, Pomerania, and Prussia? Krauthammer, "The German Revival," 19.

20. These words were spoken by the first non-Communist Czech ambassador to the United States. Quoted by Krauthammer, ibid.

21. Robert W. Tucker, "1989 and All That," *Foreign Affairs* (Fall 1990).

22. On understanding a reunified Germany's possible foreign policy, see the analysis of forty years of West German foreign policy by Wolfram F. Hanreider, *Germany, America, Europe* (New Haven, Conn.: Yale University Press, 1989).

23. Abdul-Reda Assiri, *Kuwait's Foreign Policy* (Boulder, Colo.: Westview Press, 1990), presents a pre-August 1990 account of what the author appropriately calls a "City-State in World Politics."

24. Efraim Karsh and Inari Rautsi, "Why Saddam Hussein Invaded Kuwait," *Survival* (January/February 1991): 18-30; Shahram Chubin and Charles Tripp, *Iran and Iraq at War* (Boulder, Colo.: Westview Press, 1988); and Anthony H. Cordesman and Abraham R. Wagner, *The Iran-Iraq War,* vol. 2 of *The Lessons of Modern War* (Boulder, Colo.: Westview Press, 1990).

25. On what he calls the "epic quest for oil, money, and power," see Daniel Yergin, *The Prize* (New York: Simon & Schuster, 1990).

26. For an analysis of the Arab states' foreign policies, see Bahgat Korany and Ali E. Hillal Dessouki, *The Foreign Policies of Arab States,* 2d ed. (Boulder, Colo.: Westview Press, 1990).

27. Judith Miller and Laurie Mylroie, *Saddam Hussein and the Crisis in the Gulf* (New York: Time Books, 1990), 24-41, focuses on Saddam's rise to power. Also Efraim Karsh and Inari Rautsi, *Saddam Hussein: A Political Biography* (New York: Free Press, 1991), tells the tale of this particularly violent despot who had few scruples but lots of assets—oil wealth—with which to buy arms and other military technologies from Western countries only too eager to sell them. It was his possession of this wealth that differentiated Saddam Hussein from other equally unscrupulous rulers. Also see Elaine Sciolino, *The Outlaw State: Saddam Hussein's Quest for Power and*

the Gulf Crisis (New York: Wiley, 1991). This *New York Times* reporter covered events in the area.

28. William Safire, "Now or Later?" *New York Times*, August 7, 1990.
29. On Iraq's efforts to become a nuclear power, see the investigative report by James Brooke, Ferdinand Portzman, and Michael Wines, "Iraq's Nuclear Quest: Tentacles in Four Continents," *New York Times*, December 22, 1990. For typical newspaper columns drawing the conclusion that Saddam Hussein's Iraq must be prevented from becoming a nuclear power, see Safire, "Now or Later?" and "Saddam's Bomb," *New York Times*, December 27, 1990; Richard Perle, "Keeping the Bomb From Iraq," *Wall Street Journal*, August 22, 1990; "In the Gulf, the Danger of a Diplomatic Solution . . . ," *New York Times*, August 23, 1990; Daniel Pipes, "War Now—or War Later," *New York Times*, October 23, 1990; Frank J. Gaffney, Jr., "Get It Over With," *New Republic*, December 10, 1990, 19-20; and Karen Elliott House, "The Risks of a Deal with Saddam," *Wall Street Journal*, December 11, 1990. On the postwar evaluation, see Paul Lewis, "U.N. Says the Iraqis Could Have Devised A-Bombs in the 90's," *New York Times*, September 14, 1991.

CHAPTER 7

The Ability to Play:
Calculating Power

PERCEPTION OF POWER

Power, great power, superpower, balance of power—these terms have been used here repeatedly, but at no point has the nature of power been analyzed. In one sense, there hardly seems reason to do so, for *power* is a term with which most people are familiar; it seems so obvious what power is. Everyone knows that some nations are more powerful than others and that international politics generally has been the story of the games played by the stronger members of the state system.[1] Such adjectives as *more powerful* and *stronger* usually refer to military capacity. No one thinks of Belgium or Thailand as powers; their military strength, by either conventional or nuclear standards, is puny. The label *power* historically has been awarded to those states that have won significant military victories. Conversely, a military defeat jeopardizes a nation's reputation for power. There may not even have to be a defeat; the mere fact that a great power is unable to win a conflict with a lesser power hurts its prestige.

There are, of course, variations on this theme of victory and defeat. During the 1960s, when all-out war was no longer viewed as the true test of a nation's power, the "space race" replaced the test of battle. The launch by the Soviets of the first manned satellite to orbit the earth in April of President John Kennedy's first year in office convinced him that a second-rate effort was not consistent with his country's role as a world leader and a great power, whose reputation was based largely on its industrial-technological capabilities. Prowess in space had come to symbolize power. Kennedy immediately ordered a review of various space projects in which the United States could surpass the Soviet Union.[2] The most promising was the landing of a man on the moon, and in May 1961 the president announced that this objective would be achieved before the end of the decade. Indeed, in July 1969 the first men stood on the moon, and, although they talked of having come on behalf of all "mankind," their shoulder patches read *U.S.A.*

Three points about power are very important. The first, generally shared by many citizens and policy makers, is that *power is identified with military capacity*, regardless of whether the estimate of that capacity is based on power overtly applied, peacefully demonstrated (as in parades, maneuvers, and space shots), or held in check during bargaining. When books are written on power, they bear such titles as *The War Potential of Nations.*[3] Because war has been the *ultima ratio* of power in interstate politics, the emphasis on military strength is hardly surprising. Earlier it was suggested that the state system, unlike modern domestic political systems in the West, is characterized by a condition of potential warfare. Each state's continuing concern with its military power is thus understandable.

The second point is that *power is what people think it is.* A distinction thus must be drawn between subjective (perceived) power and objective (actual) power. If power is in the eyes of the beholder, simple calculation of a nation's power is insufficient. If one country believes it is strong enough to deter an enemy, but the latter perceives it otherwise, it may still go to war. Thus, policy makers must concern themselves not only with what the actual balance of power is, but also with how that balance is seen in other capitals. This is a difficult task because access to another state's assessments is not usually available; therefore the best that one can do is guess. Nevertheless, it is a task that must be done.

The third point is that *a reputation for power will confer power*, whether others' estimates of a nation's power are correct or not. If a nation has prestige, it is less likely to be challenged; if its prestige is declining, challenges are likely, not only from powers of equal strength but also from less powerful states. These challengers will think that they can defy that nation's policies with impunity. After Britain's appeasement of Adolf Hitler at Munich in 1938 over the issue of the Sudetenland, Benito Mussolini, Italy's dictator, said: "These men [the British leaders] are not made of the same stuff as Francis Drake and the other magnificent adventurers who created the Empire. They are after all the tired sons of a long line of rich men."[4] Shortly afterward, Hitler seized the rest of Czechoslovakia and began to look hungrily at Poland.

POWER: CARROTS AND STICKS

Power thus may often be identified with military power and may exist only in the mind. But what is power? Probably the most common definition is the capacity to influence the behavior of other states in accordance with one's own objectives. Implicit in this definition is the understanding that, without the exercise of power, other states will not accede to demands made on them.

Power, then, is several things. It is something that a state has; the exact quantity depends on measurement of each of the various components of power (as seen later in this chapter). It is also a means of achieving a state's various ends, or goals. Finally, and most important, power is a relationship. China may be strong relative to India or Pakistan, but it is weak compared to the United States. What matters is not a nation's absolute power but its *relative* power.

It has been argued that power relationships exist when four factors are present.[5] First, *there must be a conflict of values or interests.* If states A and B agree on objectives, B consents freely to A's demands or proposed course of action. Power is not used. One state may be stronger than the other, but, as there is agreement on what to do, power remains latent. Even when there are relatively small differences among states, as perceived by the parties to a dispute, persuasion is very likely all that is necessary to resolve the differences. There is an appeal to common interests, principles, and values; there may be attempts to introduce facts new to one party or interpretations of the situation not yet considered; and the consequences of different courses of action may be pointed out.

Second, for a power relationship to exist, *state B must comply, however unwillingly, with state A's demands.* Compliance is necessary because, though the two states may have a conflict of interest, B may simply stand its ground and not offer any concessions. Then A must either give up its demands or resort to force.

Third, in a power relationship *one of the parties must invoke sanctions that the other regards as likely to inflict "severe deprivation" or pain on itself.* The cost for state B of not accepting state A's demands must be greater than the cost of compliance. B must believe that A's threat of sanctions is credible and not a bluff—that is, that A has both the power and capability, as well as the will, to apply military or economic sanctions. Indeed, and especially between stronger and weaker states, B's knowledge that A possesses both the power and the will often suffices; actual verbalization of a threat should not even be necessary.

This emphasis on sanctions is not meant to imply neglect of promises of *rewards* that A may offer B to promote resolution of their differences. When these differences are too large to be settled by persuasion but not of such magnitude that sanctions must be invoked, holding out rewards and granting them if B complies may be the most effective way to exercise power. A reward might take the form of economic aid, lowered tariff barriers, the sale of high-technology products, or simply the nonuse of force. But a conflict involving deep disagreement may lead one party first to invoke the threat of sanctions against the other and then, in the case of noncompliance, to apply them. There are a wide variety of ways to punish or coerce an adversary: reduce imports, impose embargoes, raise prices, withhold arms (in peace or war), break off diplomatic relations, threaten the use of force, mobilize military forces. U.S.-Soviet relations during much of the cold war included little economic intercourse, but they were characterized by the very visible presence of the military and frequent threats of its deployment.

Fourth, when differences between states cannot be resolved peacefully, *force may be used.* If state B complies when state A exercises coercion, the use of force is, of course, unnecessary; A resorts to force only if state B does not comply with A's demands. But the use of force does not guarantee the attainment of A's objectives. For example, American intervention in Vietnam did not prevent the loss of South Vietnam. *Thus, the use of force may at times result in the loss of one's reputation for power* (see Chapter 14). If sanctions, once applied, do not inflict as severe a deprivation as A's threat had implied, B's future compliance with A's demands is even less likely. Other states also may not comply with A's demands. Thus, knowing that the unsuccessful use of force will likely be very costly to its prestige, state A should exercise extra caution in its use. (War is always a risky enterprise, despite the most careful power calculation. Murphy's Law—if things can go wrong, they will—is especially applicable in wartime; on occasion, states with smaller armies have beaten those with larger armies.) The same caution applies to use of economic coercion. The general rule is—or ought to be—that it is better not to invoke sanctions than use power, whether it is military or economic, ineffectively.

The different degrees of disagreement that lead states to use persuasion, rewards, coercion, and force depend on the parties involved, their demands, their disinclination to comply, and their perceptions of the stakes. Furthermore, these methods of exercising influence may in practice be mixed. If persuasion cannot quite resolve differences, rewards may be held out. Rewards may be enticing, but hints of threats for noncompliance also are useful. A threat may well be more effective if the belief is strong that force will be forthcoming unless agreement is reached. Combinations of carrots *and* sticks may be more useful in resolving differences than either carrots *or* sticks. Carrying a "big stick" but "speaking softly" may be more fruitful than swinging the stick. Finally, coercion and force are more likely to be used against adversaries than against friendly states, but rewards also may accompany such threats if the adversary complies with the demands.

CALCULATING POWER

Most people can list some of the principal components of power. They might include: geography, population, natural resources, economic capacity, military strength, political systems and leadership, and national morale. Several points must be made, however, before taking a brief look at each of these elements. First, any calculation of a nation's power and the power balance must include a mix of *tangible components* such as population, uniformed personnel, and tanks and missiles, and *intangible components* such as morale, efficiency and effectiveness of political systems, and quality of political leadership. The intangible components do not lend themselves to accurate calculations; they are matters of judgment.

Second, when doing such calculations, one must always remain aware of the distinction between *potential power* and *actual capability*—that is, power that has been mobilized. Except for periods of total war, states do not completely transform their economies into war economies or maximize their military strength. There is always a gap between potential and actual power.

Third, an accurate assessment of even the tangible elements is not at all easy. Population figures for different states, for example, can be readily compared, and the rule of thumb "the bigger, the better" tends to be true for the more powerful states such as the United States. Sometimes, however, a large population is a liability rather than an asset. For example, India's huge population is making economic development difficult. Progress is eaten up by the need to feed, clothe, and educate millions of new people.

For all countries, other factors also must be taken into account: age distribution, educational and skill patterns, and ethnic composition, for example. Any one of these factors can complicate the calculation of a single component. For countries deeply divided by various nationalities, religions, or races, a "subtraction" from the calculation may be necessary because in a crisis or war such states may demonstrate low morale or even disintegrate. The developing countries are particularly subject to political fragmentation because of such problems.

Fourth, calculations of any single component of power make sense only when linked with those of other components. Large populations can ensure great-power status only when an industrialized economy is present as well; the marriage of these two elements constitutes power. The power rating is certain to be low in a nation characterized by poverty, a largely agrarian and unskilled population, a high birthrate, and great difficulties in urbanizing and industrializing.

Finally, the balance of power is dynamic, not static. Because various components are always changing, the balance needs frequent recalculation. This makes it particularly difficult to project into the future. Policy makers are obviously concerned about the current balance, but they also must look at the balance five or ten years into the future to be prepared for new relationships with other states, especially adversaries.

Geography

The location and physical size of a nation are clearly very important. The United States and Britain have long been protected from invasion by bodies of water too wide for their enemies to cross easily. The United States was even able to isolate itself from the international political system for more than a century. Similarly, such states as Italy and Spain have been well protected by high mountain ranges—the Alps and the Pyrenees, respectively. Indeed, little of Western Europe's modern culture seems to have crossed the Pyrenees until late in the twentieth century! But small Belgium, not well protected and lying between great powers, was not so fortunate during the two world wars. Switzerland, by contrast, also lying between great powers but very well protected, has remained untouched. The countries on the axis from France to the former Soviet Union all lie on a plain. The Rhine River, separating Germany and France, was of little help in halting repeated German invasions of France. Russia historically has had no natural protection and has been invaded repeatedly from the west. But the same lack of barriers that permitted invasions also allowed Russian expansion into Western Europe, the Middle East, and northern Asia. While Russia has suffered defeats, invaders have found it difficult to conquer because it has used its vast interior space to neutralize invasions. By drawing in the enemy—such as Napoleon or Hitler—the Russians have forced invaders to exhaust themselves trying to conquer such a vast territory, maintain long supply lines, control a large and hostile population, and survive the severe winter weather.

Note the correlation between the world's leading democracies and geographic protection: the United States, Britain, and the northern Scandinavian countries lie off the axis of repeated invasions. The states lying on the axis—France, Prussia/Germany, and Russia/former Soviet Union—know war well, and not surprisingly they have developed large bureaucracies and standing armies to guard themselves. For these countries, notions of individual freedom, rights of opposition, and criticism were luxuries that were subordinated to security and physical survival. Highly centralized governments and authoritarian politics have become the pattern. Even in France, the westernmost of these states, bounded by both the Atlantic Ocean and the Mediterranean Sea and the home of nationalism and democracy since the revolution of 1789, democracy continued to face challenges from the authoritarian tradition until World War II. But democracy was foreign to Prussia and Germany (after Prussia unified Germany in 1871) until after World War II, when it was imposed on West Germany by its conquerors; it was also foreign to czarist and Soviet Russia. And, although there is no suggestion that geography is the primary reason these countries have long been authoritarian, geography surely has been a major contributing factor. The farther east one goes in Europe, the more authoritarian it becomes; the farther west, the more democratic.

The United States, the westernmost power of all, had plenty of time to nurture its democratic roots and no need for large military forces. When drawn into Europe's wars in the twentieth century, the United States was unprepared each time. But, because it was far from the battlefields, it paid no penalty for this lack of readiness; it mobilized its power after war had been declared. The disadvantage of this geographic location and the century-long protection it afforded was that, to come to grips with its enemies, the United States had to project its power over vast distances. Not surprisingly, America's allies and friends often had the jitters because, knowing they were far from the United States, they feared the possibility of being either insufficiently protected or abandoned.

Table 7-1 Population of Major European Powers, 1870-1914
        (in millions)

Year	Austria-Hungary	France	Germany	Britain	Italy	Russia
1870	36	36	40	31	27	82
1890	41	38	49	38	30	110
1900	45	39	56	41	32	133
1910	50	39	64	45	35	163
1914	52	39	65	45	37	171

SOURCE: Adapted from *A Study of War*, I, 670-671, by Quincy Wright, by permission of The University of Chicago Press, copyright 1942 by The University of Chicago Press; and A. J. P. Taylor, *The Struggle for Mastery in Europe* (London: Oxford University Press, 1954), xxv.

In recent years, technology has reduced the significance of geography. After World War II, the United States no longer had the time it had earlier to decide whether its security interests were involved. It was vulnerable to attack and could not afford long indecision; nor could it wait until after it had been challenged to prepare itself militarily. That is why the nation defined many of its interests around the world, signed alliances to communicate these interests to its cold war adversary, and maintained large military forces. Yet obviously geography still profoundly affects the foreign policies of many states, such as Germany, Israel, and the new Commonwealth of Independent States (CIS).

Population

Population figures are good initial indicators of a nation's power ranking and of possible changes in its ranking. Table 7-1 shows how Prussia's unification of Germany in 1871 changed the map of Europe and finally brought the United States out of its isolation. Except for Russia in the east, the Continent's traditional great powers, Austria-Hungary and France, were displaced by Germany. France, which had the largest population (36 million) in 1850, was by 1910 just ahead of Italy, the least populous of the major powers in Europe. Germany's top ranking was underscored by its large-scale industrialization, but Britain had become the world's greatest power by the nineteenth century. Steel production was usually the major indicator of industrial strength because of its association with the production of modern arms. In the first decade of the twentieth century, Germany overtook Britain in steel production (and, by using much of that steel to build a sizable navy, challenged the British navy and drove Britain into closer relations with France and Russia).

Only the United States was a match for Germany. With a population of 76 million in 1900 and 92 million in 1910 and with steel production more than twice that of Germany, the United States clearly would be compelled eventually to abandon its isolationism. In the words of historian A. J. P. Taylor,

By 1914 she was not merely an economic Power on the European level; she was a rival continent. Her coal production equalled that of Great Britain and Germany put together; her iron and steel production surpassed that of all Europe. This was the writing on the wall: economically Europe no longer had a monopoly—she was not even the centre of the world." [6]

In Europe, however, Germany was becoming too powerful for its neighbors. It was acquiring the capability to become the dominant power and a threat to the independence of the other European great powers. World War I and the U.S. participation in it were predictable from population and industrial figures alone. It also was clear that even after Germany's defeat no lasting peace in Europe was feasible without continued American political involvement. A unified Germany remained potentially Europe's most powerful state, despite restrictions on its armed forces. The United States' return to isolationism was certainly one factor responsible for World War II, which again required American intervention.

But population figures can be deceptive. Before 1914, Germany's ally, Austria-Hungary, had a population larger than that of either France or Britain. Composed of a multitude of feuding nationalities who were beginning to demand self-determination, Austria-Hungary was on the brink of dissolution. That is why it was determined to crush Serbia, a Slav state that was fanning the flames of nationalism. Vienna decided that it could avoid death only by risking suicide in a war to eliminate Serbia. Because Russia supported Serbia, Germany supported Austria, and France backed Russia, the result of Austria-Hungary's ethnic composition was World War I.

The coming of World War I illustrates the value of changing population figures, as well as the limitations of looking only at such figures. Current national population figures reveal that Europe and the United States collectively already contain a minority of the world's population (Table 7-2). When these figures are combined with productivity data, the trend toward a *division of the world* between a minority of states that are rich and a growing majority that are poor becomes clear. This potentially very dangerous trend is one reason for growing concern about the North-South confrontation. By the year 2000, the population of the West (including the former Soviet Union) will constitute less than 20 percent of the world's population. [7] The developing nations will have more than 80 percent of the world's population, about half of whom will be under twenty years of age.

Natural Resources

Industrialization married to population gives birth to power, but industrialization cannot produce a nation's goods without natural resources. In the past, Britain, Germany, and the United States were able to industrialize because of plentiful supplies of coal. Today, the United States still has enormous reserves of coal, far more than Saudi Arabia has of oil. The index for economic development in the earlier stage of industrialization was steel,

Table 7-2 Countries with Populations over 50 Million, 1991 (in millions)

Country	Population
China	1,151
India	866
Soviet Union (former)	293
United States	253
Indonesia	193
Brazil	155
Japan	124
Nigeria	122
Bangladesh	117
Pakistan	117
Mexico	98
Germany	80
Vietnam	68
Philippines	66
Iran	59
Turkey	59
Italy	58
Britain	58
France	57
Thailand	57
Egypt	54
Ethiopia	53

SOURCE: Central Intelligence Agency, *The World Factbook, 1991* (Washington, D.C.: Central Intelligence Agency, 1991).

which was used for everything from railroad tracks to cannons to machinery. Iron and coal were key resources. Coal remains a major substitute for oil in the production of electricity, but its use is harmful to the environment.

After World War II, oil replaced coal because oil was cheap until 1973. The whole Western industrial structure and high standard of living have been based on oil. (Would such southern cities as Houston and Atlanta have become great commercial and cultural centers without oil and air conditioning?) The United States, once an oil exporter, now imports much of its oil, as do the other members of the North Atlantic Treaty Organization (although Britain is becoming self-sufficient thanks to its North Sea reserves); Japan imports almost all of the oil it needs.

Table 7-3 shows other imported resources on which the United States is becoming increasingly dependent. Note the higher than 90 percent import levels of cobalt, manganese, and bauxite that are used in manufacturing jet engines, computers, machine tools, tanks, and missiles. The availability of oil and of key mineral resources obviously depends on many factors, including the friendliness or unfriendliness of specific regimes. That is why President Jimmy Carter committed the United States to the defense of the oil sheikdoms on the Persian Gulf after the Soviet invasion of Afghani-

Table 7-3 Key Minerals for Which the United States Is More than 80 Percent Import Dependent, 1980-1983 (average percent of apparent U.S. consumption)

Key minerals are critical to the high-quality production of	Bauxite 95%	Chromium 86%	Cobalt 94%	Manganese 99%	Platinum group 86%
Basic steel					x
Stainless, tools, alloy steels		x	x	x	
Basic aluminum	x				
Aluminum alloys	x			x	
Nickel-based and cobalt-based superalloys	x	x	x	x	
Key minerals are used in such items as					
Ordnance (tanks, fighters, bombers, missiles)	x	x	x	x	x
Power-generating equipment (turbines, controls, transmission)	x	x	x	x	
Electric motors, equipment (locomotives to mixers)	x		x	x	
All electronics (appliances, computers, phones, TV, navigation, controls, telecommunications)	x	x	x	x	x
Nuclear application	x	x	x		
Jet engines, gas turbines (hot parts)		x	x		x
Batteries, fuel cells				x	x
Aerospace (airframes, hulls, rocket engines)	x	x	x		x
Projectiles, gun barrels, machine parts, crankshafts, axles, gears, machine tools		x	x	x	
Mining, drilling (valve stems and systems, drill bits)		x	x	x	
High-tech medical (cryogenics, heart-lung, scanners)	x	x	x		x
Petroleum processing, drilling		x	x	x	x
Chemical processing		x	x	x	x
Glass products			x		x
Pharmaceutical production					x
Food processing, enrichment		x	x	x	x
Synfuel production		x	x	x	x

SOURCES: Adapted from Uri Ra'anan and Charles M. Perry, *Strategic Minerals and International Security* (McLean, Va.: Pergamon-Brassey International Defense Publishers, 1985), p. 4; 1980-1983 figures taken from Department of State, Bureau of Public Affairs, *Atlas of United States Foreign Relations*, 2d ed. (Washington, D.C.: Department of State, 1985).

NOTE: Because effective military technology requires highest possible performance, substitutes are not desirable. Substitutes for purely commercial and civilian items, however, are possible on a mixed basis—recognizing that lower quality and performance would result.

stan, why President Ronald Reagan strengthened this commitment to Saudi Arabia, and why President George Bush defended the latter and was deter-.mined to destroy Iraq's threat to its neighbors.

Western Europe and Japan, America's principal allies, are even more dependent on imported raw materials. Japan, for example, imports virtually 100 percent of its petroleum, bauxite, wool, and cotton; 95 percent of its wheat; 90 percent of its coal and copper ore; and 70 percent of its timber and grain.

Still, Western industry is not as dependent on Third World natural resources as the above suggests for two reasons. First, the industrial states can adjust in several ways if access to one or more supplies were cut off: (1) use substitutes; (2) develop synthetic substitutes; (3) seek alternative Third World resources; (4) develop sources of supply in the industrial states; or (5) conserve resources. Listing the resources Western countries import, then, is not equivalent to dependence.

Second, some nations have developed great wealth or power without possessing all the necessary raw materials. Japan and the newly industrialized countries (NICs) have experienced rapid economic growth; other Southeast Asian countries have undergone somewhat slower growth. Yet none of them has been blessed with an abundance of resources.

Economic Capacity

A common standard for comparison of national power, probably more reliable than population in this industrial age, is wealth or degree of economic development. Wealth is clearly related to military power, for the richest states presumably can afford to buy the most military power. Indeed, wealth can buy power of all kinds, which remains important for distinguishing superpowers from secondary powers. During the cold war, the United States could mobilize both large nuclear and conventional forces, as well as other kinds of power, such as economic and technical assistance, that could serve as diplomatic tools; its allies could not. A nation's gross national product (GNP)—the total value of the goods and services produced by its citizens at home and abroad—thus was used frequently until recently as a relatively accurate and measurable standard for comparing the power of states.*

Still, the GNP figure was not completely reliable. In the United States, at least, it reflected the production not only of automobiles but also of about nineteen different brands of cat food and billions of hamburgers sold through fast-food chains. In the mid-1960s, the Soviet Union, with a GNP of less than half that of the United States, launched a massive arms program; it was able to compete with the United States in arms and aerospace manufacturing because

---

* As mentioned earlier, the gross domestic product (GDP) figure, which in the United States was substituted for GNP in late 1991, excludes foreign earnings, thus giving a somewhat more accurate picture of how a nation's economy is doing by using what is produced inside its borders as a measurement. In this edition, GNP is used predominantly, and GDP is used when it is available.

Table 7-4 Ranking of Economic Capacity among the
Great Powers, 1990 (in billions of dollars)

Country	1990 Gross Domestic Product
United States	5,423
Japan	2,971
Soviet Union	2,042
Germany	1,499
France	1,187
Italy	1,090
Britain	986
China	363

SOURCE: Figures taken from International Institute for Strategic Studies, *The Military Balance 1991-1992* (London: Brassey's, 1991).

it devoted less of its wealth to consumer goods. Soviet cats, no doubt, did not eat as well as American cats. American military spending was about 5 percent of GNP in the 1970s and 6-7 percent in the 1980s, but Moscow was spending on arms 25 percent of a GNP that was about one-third that of the United States.

GNP also did not reflect total production and services. For 1990, the U.S. figure would have been even higher if it had included Mafia activities and the estimated $40-$50 billion Americans spent on drugs that year. Moreover, the GNP did not reflect volunteer work or household chores, for which wages are not paid. More broadly, GNP revealed little about a nation's unity, the stability of its government, its political leadership, its national morale, its military doctrine, and the quality of its diplomacy, which are relevant to an analysis of a nation's power and foreign policy. At best, then, economic productivity—like population and military power—remains a crude indicator of power and a convenient shorthand means of comparison.

Per capita incomes are sometimes used as a standard of wealth. Again, the assumption is that individual income is highest in the most economically advanced nations. The figures for the United States, Western Europe, and Japan are indeed the highest worldwide, but the per capita income of the United States—which long enjoyed the highest standard of living in the world—has slipped below those of Sweden, Switzerland, and Germany. Britain has dropped to a level below that of Italy, which for a long time had the lowest per capita income of the larger European states. In a way, per capita income figures are more accurate indicators of wealth than GNP figures. During the late stages of the cold war, the Soviet GNP was second to that of the United States until Japan overtook the Soviet Union in the 1980s (see Table 7-4); Soviet per capita income was long below that of any major Western country, indicating a much lower standard of living—and that standard has fallen even further since the Gorbachev reforms. Even before its demise, the

Soviet Union was frequently referred to as a Third World country with a nuclear arsenal. The per capita incomes of the developing countries are the lowest.

Finally, two points must be emphasized about economic capacity. First, a nation's economic capacity is enhanced if it possesses strength in the scientific and technological arenas. As political scientist Robert Gilpin has noted, "Whereas, beginning in the latter part of the nineteenth century, control over petroleum resources became essential once naval ships shifted from sail to diesel, so today an independent aerospace and electronics industry, along with the supporting sciences, has become crucial for a nation to enjoy diplomatic and military freedom of action." [8] This is why it is so worrisome that the United States is falling behind Japan in key areas of the new technologies.

Second, the importance of agriculture is often underrated. For much of the postwar period, the developing countries in their eagerness to modernize—by which they meant industrialize—have tended to neglect agriculture, with the devastating results of widespread malnutrition and even starvation for their rapidly growing populations. Although most of the people in these countries live on the land, agricultural production is inefficient and unscientific. By contrast, the United States, with less than 5 percent of its population employed in agriculture, has for much of the postwar period been the breadbasket for the world. A balance between the agricultural and industrial sectors of the economy is clearly desirable and indeed necessary for economic growth and modernization. A move toward a more balanced growth now appears to be occurring.

Military Strength

Because international politics resembles a state of potential war, military power has become a recognized standard of measurement. In the past, every new great power proclaimed its appearance by a feat of arms. The decline of a great power was signaled equally by a defeat at arms, or what other states perceived as a defeat.

A nation's military power is usually measured by the number of people in uniform and by the number of different weapons it has. As might be expected, the countries with the largest populations have the largest armed forces, though not necessarily in proportion to their populations. Table 7-5 shows the military strength of the world's thirteen largest countries as measured by the size of their armed forces in 1991. These figures do not include reserves, nor do they say much about the combat training, morale, and discipline of these forces. The American army in Europe during the 1970s, for example, was often reported to be suffering from a lack of discipline, widespread drug use, and racial strife. In the 1980s, however, with higher educational levels, a volunteer force, and better pay plus improved training, morale was up. Israel, with its population of slightly fewer than 4 million, is obviously not in the same league with the countries listed in Table 7-5. Yet in twenty-four hours it can mobilize 400,000 soldiers to supplement its perma-

Table 7-5 Comparative Military Strength, 1991-1992 (in thousands)

Country (in order of population)	Size of Armed Forces
China	3,030
India	1,265
Soviet Union	3,400 [a]
United States	2,029
Indonesia	278
Brazil	296
Japan	264
Nigeria	94
Bangladesh	106
Pakistan	565
Mexico	175
Germany	476 [b]
Vietnam	1,041

SOURCE: Figures taken from International Institute for Strategic Studies, *The Military Balance 1991-1992* (London: Brassey's, 1991).

[a] In the wake of the Soviet Union's demise, this figure is outdated.
[b] Excludes forces of former German Democratic Republic.

nent army of 164,000, and these forces are highly trained and well led, as four victories in four wars have shown. Switzerland, with slightly more than 8 million people, can mobilize 625,000 troops in forty-eight hours; Swiss reservists train three weeks each summer. Sweden, with roughly the same population, can mobilize 750,000 troops within seventy-two hours. Thus, these countries can almost overnight raise forces as large as the standing cold war armies of Britain, France, or West Germany!

The heavily populated industrial powers also have the largest nuclear arsenals. During the cold war, the United States and the Soviet Union were, of course, in a class by themselves, for they could wipe each other, as well as any other country, off the face of the earth. It is significant that the first five nuclear states (the United States, Soviet Union, Britain, France, and China) were the five great powers whose status was reflected in their permanent UN Security Council membership when the organization was established after World War II. India has since joined this nuclear club.

The two cold war contestants were also producers of huge quantities of conventional arms, as were the Western allies. The adjective *conventional* hardly does these weapons justice. For one thing, they are becoming very accurate; their chance of hitting and destroying the target in one shot has increased to more than 50 percent. One result has been that opposing forces use war material at an ever-faster clip. A war may last only a few days under these conditions; a steady stream of new supplies is needed to continue hostilities. In such circumstances, a superpower's client state cannot be defeated. If defeat appears likely, the allied superpower sends more arms to avert it. As the Soviet Union poured in arms for the Arabs in the 1973 Yom

Kippur War, the United States poured in even more arms for the Israelis, who were badly mauled in the opening phase of the war. Only countries whose opponents have no superpower friends can still win wars. "Wars between small countries with big friends are likely to be inconclusive and interminable; hence, decisive war in our time has become the privilege of the impotent."[9] Also, as Iraq demonstrated in 1991, a country without superpower protection can be defeated—and rapidly with precision-guided munitions.

Weapons balances are not easy to calculate. For example, how does one compare an intercontinental ballistic missile (ICBM) with a single warhead to one with multiple independently targeted reentry vehicles (MIRVs) or several warheads; or a missile with a megaton (million-ton) warhead to one with a 200,000-ton warhead but with extreme accuracy? How does one compare bombers having quite different characteristics or tanks with antitank guns? It is also difficult to compare divisions of different sizes and compositions. In every war Israel's enemies have had more soldiers, guns, tanks, and fighter planes, but the smaller Israeli forces have consistently outfought their enemies. Better leadership, training, discipline, motivation, and tactics have helped them to beat numerically superior forces. In 1940, the stunning German defeat of France was accomplished not by a much larger German army, as has usually been thought, but by forces of about the same size as those of the Allies. The German army won because of its better leadership, its mobility, and its unique tactical combination of tanks and fighter planes.

What is really important is that the soldiers and their political superiors know what kind of war they are entering. "No one starts a war—or rather, no one in his senses ought to do so—without first being clear in his mind what he intends to achieve by that war and how he intends to conduct it."[10] This commonsense advice from Carl von Clausewitz is too often ignored. In the 1960s, a proud American army of half a million, provided with all the latest equipment that American technology could invent, was unable to defeat the Viet Cong and the North Vietnamese army. American military leaders thought that they were fighting a miniature World War II and used essentially orthodox military tactics. The North Vietnamese military leaders, however, were fighting an unorthodox war (see Chapter 14). U.S. leaders did not make that mistake in 1990-1991 in the Persian Gulf. They knew that they could isolate Iraqi forces by cutting their lines of communication with air power and then pound and demoralize those forces before attacking and defeating them on the ground.

Political Systems and Leadership

It is one thing for nations to "have" power, but how that power is used and for what purposes are decided by the leaders of political systems. A nation must ask itself what role it wants to play in the world. What are its objectives and priorities? Can its leaders make decisions with reasonable speed, gain popular approval for their policies, and then carry them out with reasonable effectiveness? Are their policies appropriate to the circumstances? What methods are used to achieve the nation's various aims, and are they compatible with its values? Is the overall foreign policy steady, or does it change from one administration to the next? Are governments stable, or do they fall frequently, to be replaced by new ones?

These questions can be asked about any political system, but there is no attempt to deal with all of them here. In the past, the effectiveness of different types of governments in dealing with the outside world was presented as an issue related to dictatorship, on the one hand, and democracy, on the other. Frequently, the superior effectiveness of a dictatorship was assumed. The reasons were clear-cut: first, decisions can be taken relatively quickly; second, there are no leaks or attempts to head off or dilute policy while it is being formulated; and, third, once a decision has been taken by the top officials, it can be executed immediately. There are no independent parliaments, parties, or interest groups, and no free press or organized public opinion to question, criticize, or oppose. By contrast, making foreign policy in a democracy is like running an obstacle course without any certainty of reaching the end. The policy process is usually slow, and the result almost always embodies a compromise among many conflicting points of view, which may weaken the policy's effectiveness in alleviating the problem at which it is aimed. And, given ultimate dependence on public opinion and support, a democratic foreign policy may—as George Kennan pointed out—be either too little or too much for the issues the nation confronts.

But were dictatorial governments in fact more effective in making policy on issues of war and peace? Clearly not. Neither Hitler nor Mussolini nor the Japanese militarists who were responsible for World War II succeeded; their regimes were all defeated. Nor did the Soviet leaders win the cold war. This raises a fundamental question about the wisdom of their policies. They started wars, hot or cold, that they did not win. Miscalculation, admittedly, is not a vice peculiar to undemocratic regimes; democratic governments miscalculate as well, but perhaps in systems in which policy is debated and criticism must be answered, the substance of policy may more often be wiser and more balanced.[11] Moreover, democratic governments, when they have to, can act speedily with the full support of public opinion. The Truman Doctrine in support of Greece and Turkey, as well as the Marshall Plan for the economic recovery of Europe, were produced in only fifteen weeks in 1946-1947. And President Bush moved quickly after Iraq's invasion of Kuwait—with full public support.

There are also differences among democratic governments. After 1945, as the United States became a world power, American political scientists worried that the constitutional separation of powers would make it very difficult to conduct a coherent, responsible, and steady foreign policy. Quarrels between the president and Congress, the decentralization of the latter into two houses and further into committees and subcommittees, lack of party loyalty and discipline, and the influence of pressure groups exploiting this political fragmentation were expected to result in a paralysis or weakening of policy or at best slow decision making, a change of policies with every administration, and constant pressure reflecting electioneering and the disproportionate influence of all types of interests seeking to impose their narrow demands.[12] The British parliamentary system, with its unity of the executive and legislative branches and its strong party discipline, appeared more likely to meet the requirements of the cold war. But Britain's record in postwar foreign policy has hardly been outstanding. It has been characterized by indecision, procrastination, and mistaken choices (such as its slowness to join the European Community and its maintenance of an "independent" nuclear force at the expense of conventional forces).[13] By contrast, the United States won the cold war.

The wisdom of policy or lack of it can surely be attributed as much to the intelligence, ability, and drive of specific national leaders as to governmental structures and processes. One need only recall the names of some of the twentieth-century leaders whose special qualities have shaped history by electrifying and changing their nations, thereby affecting the course of history: V. I. Lenin, Joseph Stalin, Adolf Hitler, Woodrow Wilson, Franklin Roosevelt, Winston Churchill, and Charles de Gaulle. These men had an impact because they could articulate their nations' purposes, make significant domestic and foreign policy decisions—sometimes drastically changing their nations' directions—pursue their goals with vigor and flair, mobilize support for their courses of action at home, and even inspire their peoples to sacrifice and discipline. One thing is clear: all nations, democratic and otherwise, require leadership.

Perhaps Soviet leader Mikhail Gorbachev was one of those extraordinary leaders. In power from 1985 to late 1991, he had a profound impact both domestically and internationally. He instituted a process of significant reforms at home because the Soviet economy was stagnating and the Soviet Union's status as a superpower was threatened.[14] Indeed, the Soviet economy had been sick for many years. But Gorbachev's predecessors had dealt with the problems in only a piecemeal fashion. He, however, recognized the seriousness of the problems, acted, and therefore deserved the credit he has generally received for withdrawing from Afghanistan, letting Eastern Europe go, permitting the unification of Germany, and calling off the cold war in order to focus the nation's attention and energies on its domestic task. That he might fall victim to the revolution he had started was a possibility from the start. Because of the desperate economic conditions in the Soviet Union, Gorbachev had become very unpopular by the time the Commonwealth of Independent States replaced the USSR. Still, by the time Gorbachev left office just after Christmas 1991, he had helped changed the course of history as few other political leaders have. He had not used the military to squash reforms in Eastern Europe and hold the former Soviet satellites within the Soviet empire; instead, he had withdrawn Soviet forces. He had dismantled the totalitarian system at home and initiated democratic reforms. And he had ended the cold war, signed major arms agreements and, more fundamentally, replaced the historically conflictual Soviet approach to foreign policy with a more cooperative and peaceful approach.

The failure of the inept coup in August 1991 demonstrated how thoroughly Gorbachev's *glasnost* reforms had taken hold of the Soviet people. Led by Russian president Boris Yeltsin, Muscovites did not want a return to an authoritarian past; the taste of freedom that Gorbachev had given the people of the Soviet Union during his six years in office led to a defense of democracy in Moscow, Leningrad, and other cities and republics. As two reporters aptly summed it up, "For the first time since the overthrow of the Czar in 1917, the Soviet Union has been seized by the collective will of its people." [15] This was a truly revolutionary development; it also proved to be the demise of communism in the Soviet Union. For a man whose hand was probably never as strong as it appeared—since he was challenged from the beginning by a party resistant to change, by nationalities threatening the Soviet Union's cohesiveness, and by a rapidly plummeting economy— Mikhail Gorbachev kept the world's attention focused on the dramatic events in his country and Eastern Europe by the initiatives he took. According to Hedrick Smith, a journalist and close observer of Soviet affairs, Gorbachev was attempting to do on a grand scale in one decade something genuinely new on the planet: transform a totalitarian state into a democracy, reversing the more common pattern of men on horseback squashing fragile democracies. [16]

President Bush's leadership, by contrast, was not concerned with the transformation of American society. Yet, from the moment of Saddam Hussein's invasion of Kuwait, the president was determined to undo the Iraqi dictator's aggression. He organized a coalition composed of the United States, the European Community, Japan, several Arab states, the Soviet Union, China, and the United Nations. Had anyone even suggested such an alliance earlier, he or she would have been dismissed as crazy. In successfully mobilizing the American people and the world to support his policy, President Bush created an international consensus behind the condemnation of Iraq; undertook an economic embargo; committed U.S. forces to Operation Desert Shield, thus creating a military option; and then skillfully conveyed America's determination and will to succeed—first, by having the United Nations set a deadline for Iraqi withdrawal from Kuwait, then by virtually doubling the size of American forces, and finally by gaining the support of Congress for the use of force if the UN deadline passed and Iraqi forces had not pulled out of Kuwait.

A focus on personality and leadership, however, should not divorce analysis from the political system in which the leader operates. For example, could Egyptian president Anwar Sadat have held out the hand of peace and accepted the legitimacy of Israel's existence had Egypt been a democracy? Despite popular yearnings for peace, would not opposition party leaders (and possibly also those in Sadat's own party), newspapers, and segments of Egyptian society have opposed his moves, perhaps successfully? If Israel, by contrast, were an authoritarian state, would it not be easier for an Israeli leader to make concessions on the West Bank and Gaza Strip to resolve the Palestinian problem—an important element if a comprehensive peace in that area is ever to be established? Quite apart from Israel's genuine fears of a Palestinian state governed by the Palestine Liberation Organization, which sided with Saddam Hussein in 1990-1991, how can a government based on the intricacies of coalition politics come up with a genuine peace initiative involving Israeli sacrifices? The two major parties are of about equal strength. Likud, the party now in power, is opposed to further "land-for-peace" compromises because it believes the captured West Bank and Gaza Strip—which the Palestinians are claiming as the basis of a Palestinian state—are part of Israel by biblical inheritance. This party has made arrangements with several tiny, even more right-wing parties to ensure its survival in parliament. In doing so, it not only has stiffened the determination of Israel's government (already the most right-wing in its history) to resist any territorial compromises, but also has brought into the cabinet one minister who believes that all Arabs ought to be expelled from Israel. Thus, as the peace process started after the 1991 defeat of Iraq, the only Arab state to be a military threat, Israel's proportional representation electoral system stood as a principal block to a "land-for-peace" deal that could be the basis for peace between Israel and the Arab states and Israel and the Palestinians. And it threatened to separate Israel from the United States because the Israeli government spent $2 billion during 1990-1991 settling the West Bank while seeking Washington's help for a $10 billion loan guarantee to help the 400,000 Russian Jewish immigrants for whom it had little money left over. The political system, in short, appeared unable to help the country decide between spending its money on achieving its ideological goal of a Greater Israel and building a prosperous society for the expected 1 million immigrants, most of them skilled professionals, expected to live within basically the pre-1967 borders.

National Morale

National morale—also often called *national will*—is perhaps best defined as popular dedication to the nation and support for its policies, even when that support requires sacrifice. Examples abound—most occurring in wartime, when identification with one's country is intense. The government, even in undemocratic states, cannot do without mass support, and a people's acceptance of military service, separation of families, and death measures its commitment to the nation. Indeed, whether morale is higher, more intense, or longer lasting in democracies than in undemocratic states is debatable. The German armies fought very well in two wars, despite the Allied blockade of World War I and the heavy bombing of World War II; widespread support for Germany's government lasted until near the end in each instance. Japanese soldiers demonstrated a tenacious fanaticism during World War II, which led them to fight hard for every inch of territory, to sacrifice their own lives freely in the process, and to impose heavy casualties on American marines.

Bombing, which is frequently favored as a way of beating an enemy into submission, appears to be a positive factor in preserving, even raising, morale. Before World War II, it was widely believed that bombing cities not only would destroy the war industries supporting the front-line soldiers but also would break civilian morale. Civilians were not expected to be as tough as soldiers. The Battle of Britain after the German defeat of France in 1940 proved otherwise.

It is difficult to make definitive statements about American morale. The two world wars were fought far away, there was no physical damage to the homeland through invasion or sustained bombing, and civilians were not endangered. The loss of American life was very small compared with that of the other combatants. Moreover, the standard of living at home was maintained at a fairly high level. Sacrifices were minimal and lasted for just over a year in the first war and a bit over three and a half years in the second—compared with four years for Britain and France in World War I and six years for Britain in World War II. The Vietnam War, because it was considered a "limited war" in response to a limited threat, was never popularly perceived to pose much danger to American security, and life went on pretty much as usual in the United States. There was little willingness to sacrifice butter for guns, as during the world wars. The draft of college students was resented, and there was widespread resistance to it; many youths emigrated to Canada and elsewhere. Perhaps it was the nature of that particular war only. There is still no record on how the national morale will hold up when sacrifice is demanded in a real crisis. The peacetime domestic gas crisis of the 1970s demonstrated that Americans do not like to do with less, but the overall twentieth-century evidence remains fragmentary and ambiguous. American society has not really been tested yet.

What seem to be critical components of a high national morale are patriotic feelings that can be rallied when the nation is attacked or insulted, even when the government may not be particularly popular (as in the Soviet Union during World War II), and a belief that the government places the nation's welfare first and pursues policies compatible with the nation's historic role. In the early 1980s, President Reagan was able to mobilize Americans' patriotism and pride in their country, both of which had suffered during the 1970s and the Vietnam era. The country supported his use of force in Grenada (1983), Libya (1981 and 1986), and even Lebanon (1982-1983). In Lebanon, however, the president was forced to withdraw U.S. forces shortly after 241 marines were killed in a suicide terrorist attack on their barracks. He refrained from direct military intervention in Nicaragua because of widespread fears of "another Vietnam." Short, successful interventions with relatively few casualties, such as those carried out by Reagan and Bush against Panama and Iraq, will mobilize popular support; long, unsuccessful ones with heavy casualties will alienate this support.

WAR AND POWER

Overestimating One's Power

A war begins when two or more contestants disagree on their relative power; it ends only when they agree on their relative strengths.[17] In other words, war erupts because one of the nations in an adversary relationship has miscalculated the distribution of power. The fighting clarifies the actual ratio of power, making war a bitter teacher of "reality." More specifically, power calculations—by either underestimating or overestimating the power of the adversary—have influenced decisions to go to war in two ways. The state that has underestimated its opponent's power may be emboldened to make reckless decisions leading to war. The state that has overestimated its opponent's power may become so fearful or cautious that it makes unnecessary concessions or, to avoid later disaster, strikes preventively before the enemy has grown too strong.

Examples are, unfortunately, plentiful. The German kaiser risked World War I in the summer of 1914 because he believed that the war would be over by the time the leaves fell. Among the many miscalculations, the Germans believed that their brilliant but very complicated war plans could be carried out perfectly when, in fact, the experience of war generally supports the wisdom of Murphy's Law. Another miscalculation was to discount intervention by the United States, a country whose power far exceeded that of Germany. Thus, if the initial plans for a quick victory failed, and the war became a war of attrition or exhaustion in which the United States, a democracy and friend of France and Britain, intervened, Germany could not win. Similarly, Hitler started World War II believing that he could attack Poland and that Britain and France would just stand by and do nothing; or that if they did declare war, they would agree to peace after Poland's defeat. When this did not happen and Britain did not surrender after France's defeat, Hitler believed he could attack and rapidly defeat the Soviet Union. Then, discouraged and left without any ally, Britain would either give up or be defeated by a German invasion. This turned out wrong as well because the Soviet Union survived the initial Nazi onslaught, and Hitler found that he understood neither British psychology nor the problems of a large-scale maritime invasion. The Nazi leader thus not only faced a two-pronged war, which he had hoped to avoid, but after Japan's attack on Pearl Harbor he decided to declare war on the United States as well. He had contempt for the United States because it was a racially mixed and thus, in his view, an impure society; and because he believed that Americans were spoiled by their material luxuries. Thus, American armies, perhaps large in numbers but undisciplined and of poor fighting quality, would not be able to prevent Germany's victory. Like the kaiser in 1914, Hitler did not anticipate a long war and, although he ensured U.S. intervention, did not make the type of simple power calculation that would have told him that he could not win if America came into the war.

But it is not just great powers that miscalculate. Iraq's Saddam Hussein did so when he attacked Iran, a country with a much larger population. He expected a quick victory because Iran was caught up in revolutionary turmoil after the overthrow of the shah, the Islamic Revolution's purging of the military's officer corps, and its alienation of the United States. When, despite some initial victories, Iraq failed to win, this war too became a war of attrition in which the two sides sought to exhaust one another. Since Iran had the greater resources, it would presumably win. Thus, Iraq resorted to the use of poison gas to prevent an Iranian victory and demoralize Iranian troops.

Ironically, Saddam Hussein repeated his error when he invaded Kuwait. He expected the Arab world to be intimidated and submit; he certainly did not expect the United States to intervene or many Arab countries to rally behind Washington. And once the United States had taken its stand and sent over 200,000 forces to Saudi Arabia's defense—forces prepared to attack Iraq if it did not withdraw from Kuwait—he did not believe that Washington would go to war, even when Bush doubled the number of forces to make his threat to use force more believable. Like the kaiser and Hitler before him, Saddam Hussein appeared to have great contempt for the United States, believing that it was unwilling to suffer large losses and pay the price of war. Thus, if war erupted and he was able to inflict heavy casualties on the United States, it would "cut and run" and Iraq would win. The one constant in the initiators' miscalculations was therefore the belief in a *quick* victory and the belief that no other state would intervene to support the victim or victims.

Underestimating One's Power

Quite the opposite phenomenon occurred just before World War II. The French and the British, remembering German military prowess in World War I and impressed by Hitler's aggressive speeches and bold international moves, consistently exaggerated German power on land and in the air and were therefore never sure that they could resist him in a war without risking defeat. Thus, they appeased him, only to find that appeasement did not avoid the war they dreaded either.

Israeli policy makers too have consistently overestimated Arab power. Given the history of persecution of Jews, in particular Hitler's policy of extermination, the leaders of the new Jewish state in 1948 felt highly insecure among hostile neighbors who had tried to strangle Israel at birth. In 1956 and 1967, when these neighbors were forming joint commands, talking of war and of "driving the Jews into the sea," boasting of their imminent victories, and parading their Soviet weapons, Israel struck preemptively. Power seemed to be shifting to its enemies. Why leave them the initiative to strike? Why not hit them before they were completely ready? Overestimating an opponent's power and exaggerating one's weaknesses also can result in war.

Even if the attacker correctly understands that it is the inferior in strength, that does not necessarily deter war. When Argentina invaded the Falkland Islands, which it called the Malvinas, it did not think that Argentina was stronger than Britain. In fact, it did not pay much attention to power calculations. If it had, it would have postponed the invasion by a year since Britain was scheduled to sell one of its aircraft carriers to Australia and scrap the other one within a year. The Argentine government, ironically a military government, simply assumed that Britain would not fight to protect a few British sheepherders still living in the Falklands. Britain had given up India and the rest of the empire without a fight, and, anyway, the generals thought of Britain as a declining, decrepit power. What they underestimated was the determination of Britain's prime minister, Margaret Thatcher.

Threat and Vulnerability Analyses

Calculations of balances of power are based on these components. Yet such calculations remain very difficult. In part, this is for the reasons mentioned earlier, such as the difficulties of accurately "counting" each component and "adding" tangible and intangible components. But it stems also in part from the attempt to simplify these calculations and from placing undue emphasis on military power. Thus, in power calculations there is a tendency to emphasize heavily the military factor—the number of troops in uniform, the quality and number of arms, and so forth—in what is often called a *threat analysis*. Using this analysis, Soviet military power, with its plentiful missiles and warheads, its immense army, and its new surface navy and airlift capability, always looked awesome during the cold war.[18] But a concentration on military power overlooked such Soviet weaknesses as its stagnating industrial economy, an agriculture sector unable to feed its people, intra-ethnic differences and demands for greater autonomy by some nationalities, as well as such problems as the questionable loyalty of the states of Eastern Europe. For a careful calculation of the power of another state, it becomes critical that a threat analysis be balanced with what, for want of a better term, might be called a *vulnerability analysis*. It is all too easy to add up the number of soldiers and tanks and not look underneath such figures.

A brief example: one reason the Germans felt 1914 was the right time for a war was that the German General Staff, looking strictly at Russia's population figures and men under arms, was becoming alarmed by the growth of "Russian might." Indeed, some German generals had been advocating a preventive war for several years. If such a war were not undertaken, they said, Germany would be crushed.[19] Incredibly, this threat analysis totally overlooked the fact that Russia, while always possessing forces larger than those of other European states, had just lost a war to Japan (1904-1905) and had not done well in preceding conflicts. After its defeat by Japan, Russia had suffered widespread peasant unrest, a harbinger of the revolution to come. A vulnerability analysis would have shown that Russia's outer strength was matched by internal weakness and that this alleged "military colossus" was in fact an "economic pygmy."

A focus on military power and lack of a vulnerability analysis also may cause those who calculate power to overlook the contextual nature of power.[20]

The usual reason a state fails to attain its declared objectives, it is frequently assumed, is that it did not try hard enough or was not sufficiently skillful, even if it did mobilize greater strength. For example, it has been claimed that the United States did not win the war in Vietnam because political restraints were placed on the military. Had the United States bombed North Vietnam very hard from the beginning and made the war unbearably painful for the North Vietnamese, they would have had reason to sue for peace. No doubt there are occasions when such explanations of failure are correct, and it may be that Vietnam is one such case, but more often such explanations are misleading and prevent one from drawing the correct lessons from the experience.

A better explanation of why a state may achieve success in one situation and encounter failure in another is that the state may have the right kind of power for one but not the other. The variables are the *kind* of power being used or not used, the *purposes* for which it is used, and the *situations* in which it is used. These three factors account for the American failure to win in Vietnam and for its helplessness in preventing OPEC from raising oil prices, a feat that damaged the United States far more seriously than the loss of South Vietnam ever did. A gross assessment of American power cannot explain why a superpower could not avoid defeat at the hands of an inferior power, or prevent a group of small countries, many dependent on U.S. protection, from raising oil prices drastically. Only an analysis of the *specific context* in which the relationship of the United States and Vietnam or the United States and OPEC occurred can do so.

Thus, to reemphasize a key point, power is not just a *possession*, calculated by adding the various components of power, just as a child adds up the coins in a piggy bank; it is also a *relationship*. As aptly explained by political scientist James Rosenau,

> For reasons having to do with the structure of language, the concept of "power" does not lend itself to comprehension in relational terms. Without undue viola-tion of language, the word "power" cannot be used as a verb. It is rather a noun, highlighting "things" possessed instead of processes of interaction. Nations influence each other; they exercise control over each other; they alter, maintain, subvert, enhance, deter, or otherwise affect each other, but they do not "powerize" each other. Hence, no matter how sensitive analysts may be to the question of how the resources used by one actor serve to modify or preserve the behavior of another, once they cast their assessment in terms of the "power" employed, they are led—if not inevitably, then almost invariably—to focus on the resources themselves rather than on the relationship they may or may not underlie.[21]

One final point: in most of the wars started in this century, it is the side that initiated the hostilities that lost the war. The Germans lost the two wars they began, as did their allies, Italy and Japan, in the second one; the United States lost in Vietnam; the Soviets lost in Afghanistan; the Arabs lost all the wars they precipitated against Israel; the Argentinians lost against the British over the Falklands; and the Iraqis lost the war to the United States-led coalition after an exhausting eight-year "victory" over Iran. One of the few exceptions was North Vietnam. But after the unification of Vietnam and its invasion of Cambodia, it was unable to suppress the resistance and, admitting failure, withdrew its forces after several years. This is a terrible record and suggests that great caution should be exercised by states, great and small alike, when making calculations and deciding whether to go to war to achieve their objectives. Miscalculations are obviously all too easy to make. Apparently, this is especially true when confidence in one's own strength and expectations of a quick victory make it even easier to misjudge the opponent's strength and resolve. Balance of power calculations, then, are not as simple as would be suggested by the simple addition of the quantifiable factors. If they were, war would not be necessary, for the contestants would know the outcome ahead of time.

For Review

1. How is power best defined?
2. What are some of the principal tangible components of power?
3. How does one calculate a nation's power?
4. What are some of the key intangible components of power?
5. How can one calculate a nation's power? And what are some of the critical difficulties in making such calculations?
6. How can such calculations help prevent or precipitate war?

Notes

1. Only recently have some analysts questioned the assumption that the great powers are the primary actors. See Stanley Hoffmann, *Gulliver's Troubles or the Setting of American Foreign Policy* (New York: McGraw-Hill, 1968), 26-43. Also see Kenneth N. Waltz, "International Structure, National Force, and the Balance of World Power," *Journal of International Affairs* 21 (June 1967): 161-193.
2. Theodore C. Sorensen, *Kennedy* (New York: Bantam Books, 1966), 589-592.
3. Klaus Knorr, *The War Potential of Nations* (Lexington, Mass.: D.C. Heath, 1970).
4. Quoted by Winston S. Churchill, *The Gathering Storm*, vol. 1 of *The Second World War* (Boston: Houghton Mifflin, 1948), 341.
5. Peter Bachrach and Morton S. Baratz, *Power and Poverty* (New York: Oxford University Press, 1970), 17-38. Also see Charles A. McClelland, *Theory and the International System* (New York: Macmillan, 1966), 68-88; and K. J. Holsti, *International Politics: A Framework for Analysis* (Englewood Cliffs, N.J.: Prentice-Hall, 1967), 191-209.
6. A. J. P. Taylor, *The Struggle for Mastery in Europe* (London: Oxford University Press, 1954), xxxi; and Paul M. Kennedy, "The First World War and the International

Power System," *International Security* (Summer 1984): 23.

7. The U.S. Census Bureau has forecast that the U.S. population will peak in the year 2038 at 302 million and then gradually decline (Richard Berke, "Census Predicts Population Drop in Next Century," *New York Times,* February 1, 1989).

8. Robert Gilpin, *France in the Age of the Scientific State* (Princeton, N.J.: Princeton University Press, 1968), 76.

9. John G. Stoessinger, *Why Nations Go to War* (New York: St. Martin's Press, 1974), 220.

10. Carl von Clausewitz, *On War,* ed. and trans. Michael Howard and Peter Paret (Princeton, N.J.: Princeton University Press, 1976), 579.

11. Bruce Russett, *Controlling the Sword* (Cambridge, Mass.: Harvard University Press, 1990), appropriately subtitled *The Democratic Governance of National Security.*

12. On the difficulties of conducting U.S. foreign policy—for example, the failure to gain ratification of SALT II—see Dan Caldwell, *The Dynamics of Domestic Politics and Arms Control* (Columbia: University of South Carolina Press, 1991).

13. Kenneth N. Waltz, *Foreign Policy and Democratic Politics* (Boston: Little, Brown, 1967).

14. Mikhail Gorbachev, *Perestroika* (New York: Harper & Row, 1987). Also, Robert G. Kaiser, *Why Gorbachev Happened* (New York: Simon & Schuster, 1991).

15. Peter Gumbel and Gerald F. Seib, "Democratic Forces Roll Back Soviet Coup: A New Era May Dawn," *Wall Street Journal,* August 22, 1991.

16. Hedrick Smith, *The New Russians* (New York: Random House, 1990), 560-574.

17. Geoffrey Blainey, *The Causes of War* (New York: Free Press, 1973), 115-119, 122. Also see Jack S. Levy, "The Perception and the Causes of War: Theoretical Linkages and Analytical Problems," *World Politics* (October 1983): 76-99.

18. Andrew Cockburn, *The Threat* (New York: Random House, 1983).

19. Stephen Van Evera, "The Cult of the Offensive and the Origins of World War I," *International Security* (Summer 1984): 58-107; and Paul M. Kennedy, "The First World War and the International Power System," *International Security* (Summer 1984): 7-40.

20. David A. Baldwin, "Power Analysis and World Politics: New Trends versus Old Tendencies," *World Politics* (January 1979): 163-164.

21. James N. Rosenau, "Capabilities and Control in an Interdependent World," *International Security* (Fall 1976): 34.

CHAPTER 8

The Changing State System: A Conclusion

While military power has long appeared to be the most important indicator of a nation's power, the fact is that economic power is the most important. The wealthiest princes could afford the largest armies; industrial capacity has been the critical component since the Industrial Revolution and a key to predicting which states would become great powers and which would lose that status. As some economies grow at a more rapid pace than others, not only does the distribution of wealth change among states but political power shifts as well. Britain, the first nation to industrialize, was the nineteenth century's preeminent power, keeping the balance in Europe while directing most of its energy to its colonial empire. The unification of Germany and its subsequent rapid industrialization changed European politics forever. The traditional great powers such as Austria-Hungary and France, although also industrializing, fell behind Britain and Germany. Russia, despite very rapid economic growth toward the end of the century, was particularly weak as a modern industrial-military power. Germany had become Europe's preeminent power. By early in this century, its steel production was greater than that of Britain, France, and Russia put together.

This transformation of the power equation compelled France and Russia to ally themselves with Britain, their rival in the colonial world. The three countries signed ententes (just short of formal alliances) to form an anti-German coalition. But World War I demonstrated that it was no longer enough for Britain to add its power on the side of the weaker coalition to prevent a continental challenger from establishing hegemony over Europe. After Germany defeated Russia in 1917, it was questionable whether France and Britain alone could have staved off defeat. It was at this point (as described in Chapter 2) that the United States entered the war and became Europe's balancer, for "its economic growth during the preceding two or

185

three decades was probably *the single most decisive shift in the long-term global balances.* . . . [The United States] was growing so fast that it was on the point of outproducing *all* of the European states combined!"[1] Its population was almost 100 million.

Thus, when the United States, after the victory over Germany, withdrew into isolationism, the containment of Germany was left largely to France and Britain. It was a task that proved to be beyond their collective efforts once the appeasement policy had allowed Germany to recover its economic and military strength. Only an American commitment to the defense of the two Western powers—an interwar National Atlantic Treaty Organization (NATO)—might have been able to deter Hitler's Germany. In its absence, war erupted. Germany defeated France quickly, and Britain was saved from the same fate only by the English Channel. Hitler's division of his armies when he invaded the Soviet Union, as well as the severe Russian winter, saved that country. It took the combined power of the Soviet Union and the United States, with the help of Britain as a junior power, to finally bring Germany down in defeat after six years of fighting. With the U.S. army moving eastward and the Soviet army advancing westward, the two met in the center of Europe—where they still were forty-five years later. A bipolar world had emerged.

DECLINE OF THE SUPERPOWERS

U.S. Loss of Economic Competitiveness

In the years after World War II, the United States was the supreme Western power; U.S. technology and productivity were immense. With much of Europe's and Japan's industries destroyed, the United States produced almost half the world's goods and services. The U.S. economy, which from 1940 to 1945 had produced 207,000 aircraft, 86,000 tanks, 15,400,000 small arms, 64,500 landing vessels, and 5,200 larger ships (of almost 53 million tons), now made it possible for the United States to make foreign policy commitments worldwide, build and support powerful nuclear and conventional forces, and vastly expand the domestic welfare state while affording steady increases in wages through the late 1960s and early 1970s.[2] By the 1980s, however, this economy was floundering.[3] Such traditional smokestack industries as steel were especially hard hit because they had become increasingly uncompetitive internationally and had declined. There were many reasons for this decline: U.S. underinvestment in the American economy because of high U.S. wages, the desire of U.S. industry to be nearer overseas markets, and the tariff barriers erected by the European Community (EC) against imports. American industry was going overseas where it could save transportation costs and especially where wages were lower, particularly in Third World countries. American manufacturers also found they could avoid the EC's tariff wall by building factories in Western Europe. Industry considered its actions rational: goods could be produced more cheaply outside of the United States, where large-scale markets and opportunities also were opening up. Goods for consumers both abroad and at home, U.S. industry argued, would be less expensive and more competitive with foreign goods while also increasing corporate earnings.

Another reason was that America's allies and friends, whom it had helped to rebuild or build following World War II, had by the 1970s become major industrial competitors. In some countries, older industries such as the textile, steel, shipbuilding, and automobile industries (in Europe) were rebuilt, and in other countries new industries such as the automobile (Japan) and electronics industries (Japan, South Korea, and Taiwan) were started. Because U.S. industries were accustomed to having the enormous domestic market virtually to themselves, they had not made the necessary investments in research and development. The U.S. textile, steel, shipbuilding, automobile, and even electronics industries became successively unable to compete with goods produced elsewhere by newer technology and at lower wages. Europe and the Far East found new markets in the United States, as American consumers eagerly bought less expensive and better-made products from abroad. Even the high-technology sector of the U.S. economy (computers, machine tools, robotics, and aerospace technology), often acclaimed as the basis for future economic growth and prosperity, experienced difficulties.

By 1987, the U.S. trade deficit (the gap between exports and imports) with Japan was almost as large in electronics as in cars; the $22 billion 1983 deficit had tripled by 1987. The total trade deficit, $25 billion in 1980, had risen to a record-setting $152 billion by 1987—almost a sevenfold increase. Forty-nine percent of that increase was with Japan despite a 60 percent increase in the value of the Japanese yen against the dollar since 1985, which was supposed to raise the price of Japanese products and discourage their importation into the United States, while lowering the cost of U.S. exports. While it has declined since then, the trade deficit with Japan persists, although the trade deficit with Canada fell by more than 50 percent between 1985 and 1989, and the United States had a trade surplus with the EC in the spring of 1990. According to the Council on Competitiveness, composed of 150 of the nation's industrial, labor, and educational leaders, "In field after field . . . foreign competitors have moved into markets pioneered and once dominated by American firms. . . . Often their success was built on exploiting inventions made in American laboratories by American scientists." [4] In the 1980s, as well as the prior decade, American capital investments were among the lowest in the Western industrial world (Canada, Japan, and Western Europe), and the American labor force was declining qualitatively, a reflection of lower educational standards, especially in mathematics and the sciences.

Indeed, by 1990 corporate investment had declined to the point where it was not even keeping up with the rate of inflation.[5] The recession that year, precipitated by the Gulf crisis, cut that amount even further. By contrast, despite a slowdown of the Japanese economy, Japanese corporations continued to pump huge sums into plants and equipment, leaving U.S. and other rivals far behind. In 1990, with Japan having an economy two-thirds that of the United States, Japanese companies invested $675 billion; American investment was $524 billion.[6] Not surprisingly, the Japanese increased their lead in computer research. By contrast, the U.S. government allowed the demise of a microchip consortium for lack of funds and permitted efforts in such areas as high-definition television to languish because the government, in the name of a free market, refused to adopt an industrial policy—that is, to support critical high-tech industries in order to revive or maintain their commercial competitiveness (although the government has done precisely that in such sectors as military aerospace, one of the few areas in which the United States maintains a leadership position). Yet stepped-up research and development, increased investments, and an educated and well-trained labor force were the keys to industrial competitiveness and technological innovation and leadership.

But quite the opposite was happening: American students, having received neither the motivation nor the proper training in the sciences from kindergarten through college, were not going to graduate school. Instead, foreigners, mainly from Taiwan, South Korea, India, and the People's Republic of China, were flocking to U.S. graduate schools in technology and exposing the nation's declining ability to produce its own researchers, scientists, and academicians. Thus, the United States is training its competitors of the future, for most of these highly skilled men and women eventually will return to their countries, and American industry will be deprived of scientists and American universities of professors. In 1990, half of the electrical engineering graduate students and almost all of the civil engineering students at the University of Texas were noncitizens; at the New Jersey Institute of Technology, 734 of 887 full-time students were from Asia.[7] In 1991 at the University of Florida, only 5 percent of the student body were foreign, but foreigners constituted almost half of the students in the Graduate School of Engineering.[8] Over one-third of the faculty teaching these students were foreign-born, and this proportion is likely to grow.

U.S. corporations also placed a premium on quarterly earnings and returns for their stockholders; this contrasted sharply with the Japanese concern with long-term investments of ten, twenty, or even thirty years, as in the computer industry. The common wisdom was that the Japanese thought in terms of decades, the Germans in terms of a few years, and the Americans in terms of a few months.

In short, the relative decline of the American economy was inevitable to a degree as the economies of its allies recovered and grew. America's economic domination after 1945 was unnatural. Some of this decline, however, was caused by complacency and lack of industrial competitiveness because business and labor had for so long had the huge U.S. market largely to themselves and had been protected from foreign competition.[9] The result was a growing gap between the nation's foreign policy commitments and the capabilities to sustain them. Yet while its power base was shrinking, the United States further expanded its commitments after 1979, first to the Persian Gulf, then to Central America. It was as though the nation's leaders were unaware of its so-called imperial overstretch.[10]

Beginning in the early 1970s, however, the United States did try to close the gap between ends and means in a number of ways.[11] First, it reduced the non-Soviet threats to its interests, principally by reconciling with China and, to a lesser extent, by transforming Egypt from a hostile into a friendly state. Second, the United States improved relations with the Soviet Union, primarily by arms control agreements to lower the costs and risks of the nuclear arms race and the Soviet willingness and capability to threaten the United States. Third, the United States sought greater defense contributions from its NATO allies and Japan. But the gap remains. The waning of the cold war and the Soviet threat may save the United States from the more chaotic cuts that would otherwise have been required, especially because in the 1980s the Reagan administration, by cutting taxes while greatly increasing defense spending, turned the United States into the world's largest debtor nation and left it broke in the absence of a tax increase.[12] Mikhail Gorbachev's appearance in 1985 was indeed timely because the end of the cold war permits the defense budget to be reduced over time. But it has resolved none of the fundamental problems of the economy: the lack of savings and investment, the decay of the nation's infrastructure, and the government's refusal in the name of free trade to adopt an industrial policy.

The Collapse of the Soviet Economy

The Soviet economy was in even greater trouble than that of the United States.[13] While American agriculture is so bountiful that it has become dependent on exports, the Soviet Union, a major grain exporter under the czars, imported grain to feed its people during Leonid Brezhnev's years. But a balanced diet that included more meat remained an unrealized goal. By 1990, it was no longer a question of finding meats, vegetables, fruits, and butter in stores; even shortages of bread and potatoes, long staples for Soviet citizens, developed. Industrially, economic growth, after rapid advances in the 1950s and early 1960s, was down to 2 percent by the early 1980s. While the Soviet Union was still the world's leading producer of steel, cement, and many types of chemicals and machinery, and its economy was not devastated by foreign competition, communism was its undoing. In fact, by the mid-1980s the decline of the economy, which was highly centralized and bureaucratized, become particularly notable, especially in the new industrial revolution areas of computers, microelectronics, and petrochemicals.

In short, the Soviet Union, which long had presented itself to the Third World as a model for development, was falling further and further behind in those industries critical for future economic growth. Not only was its industrial sector unable to meet consumer needs, but also the Soviet leadership had to confront the unpleasant fact that the Soviet economy had already fallen from second to third worldwide, behind Japan in GNP, and behind other newly industrialized countries, such as South Korea, in per capita production and rate of economic growth. The first Soviet-supported international investigation of its economy, performed in 1990 by the International Monetary Fund, World Bank, and two major European development organizations, showed that Soviet per capita income in 1990 was roughly equal to that of Mexico, $1,780, or about one-tenth that of the industrial democracies, $17,606. The Soviet figure trails even the $2,465 average for Eastern Europe. While its large manufacturing sector amounts to approximately the same proportion of its GNP as that found for similar industries in Western Europe, the Soviet manufacturing sector is beset by antiquated machinery and technologies, virtually no computerization, and rampant inefficiencies.[14] Communism was clearly not a model for other developing countries.

Even the economic growth the Soviet Union had achieved, evident mainly in the outpouring of weapons rather than consumer goods, had been gained by the enormous sacrifices of its population over several generations. With the Soviets spending, according to several Soviet and American economists, 25 percent of their GNP on the military in the pre-Gorbachev years, Soviet consumers clearly had taken a backseat. Thus, food shortages, even rationing, and lack of consumer goods have long been the lot of Soviet citizens. As former national security adviser Zbigniew Brzezinski has pointed out, never before in history has such a gifted people, with such an abundance of resources, worked so hard for so long to produce so little.[15]

The Gorbachev Reforms.   Gorbachev, who came to power believing that more labor discipline and less absenteeism and drunkenness would revive the economy, realized by 1987 that the problem was a structural one. He therefore sought to reform the Soviet system by launching a program of *glasnost* (openness) and *perestroika* (restructuring). But it quickly became clear that more openness in Soviet society and economic reorganization would not succeed unless accompanied by a restructuring of the political system. At the nineteenth Communist party conference in 1988, Gorbachev called for the removal of the party from the daily management of the economy and other sectors of Soviet life; multiple candidacies and secret ballots in party and legislative elections; a powerful new post of president of the Soviet Union (which he soon made himself); and a partial transfer of power from the Communist party to the popularly elected governmental bodies while still preserving the party's overall authority to determine national policy and its role as the "vanguard" of communism.

But despite Gorbachev's entreaties and reform efforts, there was strong resistance from those with a strong vested interest in the status quo. They feared change because it threatened their jobs and privileges. The Soviet Union had an army of 19 million party and government bureaucrats. The political system that Gorbachev wanted to change might well be described as a system of the bureaucrats, by the bureaucrats, and for the bureaucrats. They were the privileged elite. They also feared that any loosening of central controls might be harmful, if not fatal, in another way: a devolution of power from Moscow might result in greater political self-determination by the non-Russian nationalities. Economic decentralization, in other words, might spill over into political decentralization, thereby threatening Moscow's imperial control over its own vast country.

Thus, Gorbachev felt compelled in 1989 and 1990 to take two revolutionary—and heretical—steps. First, he renounced the Communist party's monopoly of power, stating that the party would have to earn its leadership position in Soviet society by winning the people's trust and votes. But the party's abdication of its claim to sole leadership of the Soviet state left it, in the absence of democratic elections, without legitimacy. Even before the coup in 1991, more than 4 million Communist party members had resigned over the preceding eighteen months. Second, because five years of attempting to restructure the socialist economy had resulted only in empty shelves in the stores, Gorbachev declared a shift from a socialist to a market economy, Thus, just over seventy years after the Bolshevik Revolution, a Soviet leader announced that the socialist system would be replaced by the very system that earlier had been rejected within the Soviet Union. Gorbachev's declared abandonment of Marxism-Leninism was breathtaking, for he had been raised in a country in which private property and business were equated with capitalist exploitation and socialism with virtue. It was all the more remarkable because when he started his reform program, Gorbachev sought to do so through the Communist party and socialist economy. He assumed that when the oppressiveness of the Stalinist system was removed, a revived and robust socialism would emerge.

But Gorbachev had miscalculated, narrowing his options. As the party was losing its authority and the economy was breaking down, protest and opposition spread, including to Moscow and Leningrad, the country's two largest cities, which elected mayors who had quit the Communist party. And in a stunning blow to Gorbachev, Boris Yeltsin, his former protégé and now rival, was in 1989 elected by the Russian legislature to be its president, in effect making him the Russian republic's leader even before he was popularly elected to that office in 1991. Russia spanned two-thirds of the Soviet Union's territory and contained half of its population and most of its oil and natural gas. Yeltsin proceeded to assert Russian sovereignty; he declared that Russian law would take precedence over Soviet law, and that Russia would set the prices of its raw materials and decide for itself its relationships with the other republics. He in effect proposed a loose confederation of Soviet republics. And he pushed Gorbachev hard with a radical plan to transform the Soviet economy into a market economy in 500 days, charging that Gorbachev had procrastinated for five years, tinkering with the economy, only to fail. When Ukraine—the second largest republic with 52 million people, the nation's breadbasket, and a major industrial center, producing most of the Soviet Union's coal and steel—and Byelorussia (now Belarus), the fifth largest republic, declared their sovereignty, asserting their right to conduct their own economic affairs and their own foreign policies, Gorbachev's Soviet Union seemed to be becoming the Soviet Disunion. Eventually, all fifteen republics declared their sovereignty. They may, in turn, splinter further. Russia itself is a federation of sixteen "autonomous republics," which were themselves acquired by conquest and merger. Will any of them—the Tatars, for example— seek independence from Yeltsin's Russia? Gorbachev lost much of his authority and legitimacy as his popularity waned (whereas Yeltsin before his popular election had authority but little power). Despite Gorbachev's verbal embrace of market economics, he continued to procrastinate on radically reforming the economy, thereby in effect reneging on his promise of free-market economic reforms. And despite his renunciation of the Communist party's monopoly of power, he remained reluctant to cede much of the central government's—including his own—power. Anarchy—not government—seemed to prevail. The breakdown in food distribution in 1990, a good harvest year, was itself a symptom of the central government's loss of authority.[16]

Decline and Disintegration of the Soviet Union.

Perhaps still a Communist at heart, Gorbachev concentrated on preserving the territorial integrity of the Soviet Union and salvaging the central government's powers. To do this, he turned to the traditional instruments of power—the military, secret police, and Communist party bureaucracy—to help stem the challenge of the republics' nationalism. The question was whether falling back on the most reactionary and xenophobic elements of the pre-Gorbachev era, all of which opposed private property and a free-market economy, would allow Gorbachev to form a government that possessed both power and authority while also preserving the union. In December 1990, Soviet foreign minister Eduard Shevardnadze resigned in protest against Gorbachev's apparent abandonment of reform and democracy, and he warned against the possibility of a new dictatorship. The central question now was how could Gorbachev continue to manage a country on the verge of disunion, whose problems had gone beyond empty food shelves, interethnic violence, and a struggle between the remnants of the old order and the new political forces to the very heart of national existence— namely, the legitimacy of Soviet political institutions and the identity of the Soviet people.[17] Gorbachev's major challenge, in short, was less economic than political. Symbolically, in Russia, Yeltsin, the advocate of decentralization and democratic reform, became the first popularly elected president in its thousand-year history. While he won every major city, taking Moscow with 72 percent of the vote, his Communist opponent, a former Soviet prime minister, failed to win any major city.[18] Even more symbolically, a majority of the citizens of Leningrad favored changing its name back to St. Petersburg, a rejection of the founder of Soviet communism for the czar who had built the city.

Faced at this moment of weakness, however, with calls from his new right-wing allies for his ouster from office, Gorbachev, ever the shrewd tactician, once more swung toward his old allies of reform. He finally made his peace with the republics by agreeing with the presidents of nine republics, including Yeltsin (who, after his popular election, gained greater prestige and bargaining power with Gorbachev, who had not submitted himself to a free election), to turn the Soviet Union into a voluntary union of republics, with all republics having the right to join (or not join) the new federation, as well as to choose their own forms of government (implicitly recognizing the right of six of the republics to secede). There would be a new constitution and a newly elected central government. The Kremlin, however, would cede most of its powers over industry, natural resources, and foreign trade. Gorbachev also reportedly asked the West to participate in the planning of the transformation of the Soviet command economy into a free-market economy and to assist with $100 billion in aid to be given over a number of years (see Chapter 15 for further discussion of this issue).[19]

As hard-liners in the party continued their resistance, two things happened. First, Gorbachev warned them that they were destroying the party from within and that the party would lose future elections. He rejected Marxist-Leninist "dogma" as no longer able to guide the country and proposed a new charter for the transformation of the party into a broad-based one committed to democratic reform. Without reform, the party would lose any claim to participation in the country's political life.[20] Second, on the eve of the signing of the so-called All-Union Treaty, the "old guard" struck. As Gorbachev's reforms were taking on the appearance of inevitability, the hard-line Communists, about to fade into history as the Soviet state and Communist party were on the verge of losing much of their authority to the republics, felt that they had to strike before it was too late. But the coup failed.[21]

The results were to transform the Soviet Union as the world had known it for seventy-four years. First, it led to rapid and spreading assertions of independence by more and more republics (see Figure 8-1). The three Baltic republics were quickly recognized internationally as new nations. It was thought that, at best, a loose political confederation composed of many, but not necessarily all, of the republics might survive. The republics needed to cooperate with one another economically. But the desire for self-determination, coexisting with historic fears of Russian domination, strengthened the centrifugal momentum.

Second, with the Communist reactionaries discredited and disgraced and no longer able to block reforms, the democratic forces led by Boris Yeltsin, who had courageously led the opposition to the coup and raised his prestige and reputation in the Soviet Union and the world to an all-time high, were now in charge and in a position to push hard for the more radical political and economic reforms needed to make the Soviet Union a democratic and free-market society. Significantly, the crowds in Moscow that had defied the coup and its unconstitutional seizure of power had yelled for Yeltsin, not for

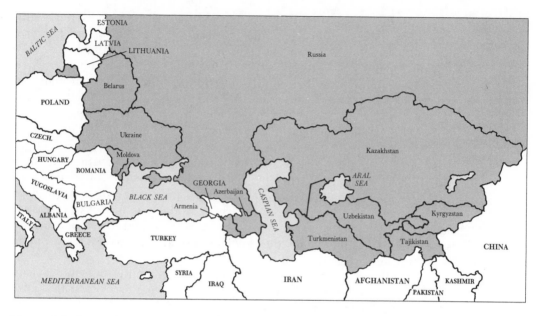

Figure 8-1 Commonwealth of Independent States, 1992

Gorbachev. Yeltsin, freely elected, had become the most powerful figure in the Soviet Union during the coup in which Gorbachev was overthrown by his own appointees. It was the Russian president, responding to the anger and demands for change sweeping the country, who now led the movement against the old order by taking sweeping measures against the Russian Communist party, closing all its newspapers and offices.

Gorbachev, correctly sensing that his authority was slipping, sought to recover some of that authority by resigning as the party's general secretary, disbanding its leadership, and ending the party's watchdog role in the military, secret police, and government offices. For all practical purposes, the banning of the once all-powerful party from its governing role, which it had maintained despite Gorbachev's officially ending its monopoly of power, killed it once and for all. Seven decades after the revolution, the Communist party had destroyed itself and, as it turned out, any kind of association that retained a central government; democracy and radical economic reforms now appeared to be the wave of the future in most republics.

Throughout the nation, the once sacred statues of Marx, Lenin, and other Communists, including the founder of the Soviet secret police, the embodiment of Communist totalitarian rule, were torn down. In Russia, the prerevolutionary flag designed by Peter the Great was raised over the Russian Supreme Soviet, replacing the hammer and sickle, and Leningrad regained its old name, St. Petersburg. It probably was only a matter of time until Lenin's body would be removed from the mausoleum in front of the Krem-

Table 8-1 Soviet Leaders, 1917-1991

Leader	*Years in Power*
V. I. Lenin	1917-1924
Aleksei Rykov	1924-1930
Vyacheslav Moloto	1930-1941
Joseph Stalin	1941-1953
Georgi Malenkov	1953-1955
Nikolai Bulganin	1955-1958
Nikita Khrushchev	1958-1964
Leonid Brezhnev	1964-1982
Yuri Andropov	1982-1984
Konstantin Chernenko	1984-1985
Mikhail Gorbachev	1985-1991

lin. Other republics followed. The week of August 19, 1991, a week that shook the world, saw the destruction of the Communist empire, initiating a stampede toward disintegration that destroyed even the possibility of the survival of a weak confederation. No central authority appeared acceptable; the bickering over the shape of a new union was endless. It was in these circumstances that the three Slavic states finally declared the old Soviet Union dead and formed a new commonwealth. On December 25, 1991, the USSR died. As the familiar red and gold Communist flag over the Kremlin was lowered, the Russian flag was hoisted in its stead, and Yeltsin moved into the Kremlin offices occupied by Gorbachev, the last Communist leader to occupy them. In summary, the "old guard" that had for seven decades governed the Soviet Union, and had hoped to recapture its power when it launched the coup, could be prevented from blocking basic political and economic reforms only by eliminating the all-union institutions through which it ruled. And this could be achieved only by destroying the Soviet Union.

Rise of Japan and the 'Others'

Notwithstanding its relative decline, the United States remains the non-Communist world's strongest military power. The dollar is still the international currency, weakened as it is, and English remains the international language. Yet, unlike right after World War II, no European or Japanese today is likely to utter this prayer:

> Sam be thy name.
> Thy navy come,
> Thy will be done,
> In London, as it is in Washington.

Yet, as Brzezinski has emphasized, "The change in America's global economic position is neither the consequence of an antagonistic competition nor the result of a hostile rival for global primacy gradually displacing America. Instead it is the outcome of a cooperative policy initiated and sustained by the United States itself." [22] Brzezinski is saying that the rise of Japan and the "others" is the result of the postwar American programs of reconstruction. One of those helped was Europe, and today the European Community's economic potential is enormous. As Hedley Bull commented during the cold war, "The countries of Western Europe are superior to the Soviet Union in population, wealth, technology, and military potential, and the idea that Russia is the naturally dominant power in Europe, against which Europe itself can construct no counter balance without importing outside [U.S.] help, is a rather recent one." [23] The question confronting Western Europe is whether its member-nations can complete their economic and financial union after 1992, remain in step with technology, and move toward greater foreign and defense policy coordination. Without greater political cohesion, Europe cannot play a great-power role.

But the real economic dynamism at present is in Asia. During the 1980s, China appeared to be progressing along its path of agricultural growth and industrial development. In 1984, for example, the growth in China's gross national product (GNP) exceeded the total GNP of one of Asia's fastest growing economies, South Korea.[24] But China underwent a significant economic *perestroika* but no *glasnost*, precipitating widespread popular dissatisfaction and vehement student protests in the late 1980s against widespread corruption, the privileges of the Chinese leadership, and major inflation. The 1989 crushing of the students' pro-democracy movement by the regime set back China's economic development, but only temporarily. As the 1990s began, the government once again stressed economic growth and the private sector rather than ideological and economic orthodoxy.

The current Asian economic dynamo is, of course, Japan. Its economy, together with those of Singapore, Hong Kong, South Korea, and Taiwan, is the reason why the future has been called by some the Pacific Century. These "little Japans," two of which are city-states, are all major economic actors. South Korea and Taiwan, "now world-class industrial and manufacturing centres, need to be thought of not so much as the 'new Japans,' but as the 'new Frances' or the 'new Italys.' " [25] Export-led development has transformed backward, agrarian countries into modern, dynamic ones.

Japan may in fact become the world's number one economic power.[26] It already has overtaken the former Soviet Union, and the gap between the Japanese and U.S. GNPs is closing gradually (see Table 7-4 on page 170). Japan has made its mark in such areas as textiles, steel, shipbuilding, automobiles, and electronic products (from calculators, cameras, stereos, televisions, and microwave ovens for consumers to office equipment), although it now finds itself competing in some of these areas with the other newly industrialized Asian countries, whose labor costs are lower than Japan's. Japan is moving steadily toward gaining the lead in the sectors that will be prominent in the twenty-first century: computers, especially the supercomputers, and computer software, as well as robotics. It also is investing in biotechnology, pharmaceuticals, and telecommunications, and may move into aerospace.[27] Where Japan will not be number one, it is likely to be number two.

In 1951, Japan's total GNP was one-third that of Britain and one-twentieth that of the United States. Four decades later, Japan's GNP was twice that of Britain and half that of the United States.[28] Complementing this miraculous achievement, since 1985 Japan also has been the world's chief financial power (and America's leading creditor nation), a position until recently occupied by the United States, now the world's largest debtor nation. As the 1990s began, the world's six largest banks were all Japanese; the top seventeen were all foreign.[29] Citibank, America's largest bank, ranked eighteenth worldwide. In 1986, Japan's capital outflow was more than twice that of all the OPEC nations combined at the height of their wealth.[30] Among the world's largest insurance companies, Japanese companies are numbers one, four, and five; Prudential Life and State Farm are numbers two and three, respectively. The largest stock brokerage firm in the world is Japanese, and Japan is a major presence on Wall Street.

How can the United States—and Western Europe—cope with this "economic attack" on the traditional industrial, high-technology, and service sectors? The Soviet competition had been easier to deal with, for it had been a political and military threat that included weapons and troops, but the Japanese competition has revealed no visible threat or loss of blood. Nevertheless, it represents a challenge to the very organization of the societies, values, work habits, and educational practices of the older democracies. It is not merely a matter of more U.S. research and development, better business management, and closer management-labor practices, as crucial as these are. The Japanese challenge is more fundamental. Indeed, increasingly it will be an Asian challenge as the other newly industrialized countries progress as well. If the Pacific Rim countries continue to grow at current rates of 5 percent per year until the year 2000, they may exceed the combined GNP of the United States and Europe, possess the world's most modern stock of capital, and become the world's largest source of credit and technological innovation. According to a 1988 article in the *New York Times*, "Japan may achieve a clear lead in four key technologies (semiconductors, advanced structural materials, manufacturing technology, and biotechnology), rough parity in two (telecommunications and data processing) while lagging in three (aircraft, space, and nuclear power)."[31] Perhaps symbolic of this broader U.S. loss of technological and industrial competitiveness is the decimation of the U.S. semiconductor industry.* In about twenty years, virtually an entire industry has moved across the Pacific.[32]

---

* The United States was so worried in the late 1980s by the prospect of American weapons, satellites, and supercomputers becoming dependent on foreign corporations for microchips that the Defense Department planned to invest several billion dollars to help the U.S. electronic industry recover (Andrew Pollack, "U.S. Sees Peril in

(Footnote continues)

American industries, including defense industries, thus have become increasingly dependent on Japanese technologies. In the 1989 book *The Japan That Can Say "No"* coauthored by the chairman of Sony and a former novelist turned politician, the latter asserted rather stridently that had it not been for Japanese semiconductors, the United States would not have been able to increase the accuracy of its missiles. He added, "It has come to the point that no matter how much they [the United States] continue military expansion, if Japan stopped selling them the chips, there would be nothing more they could do." Indeed, if Japan had decided to sell them instead to the Soviet Union, that would have upset the entire military balance.[33] This statement, while no doubt exaggerated, displayed a new and more assertive, if not arrogant, Japanese nationalism (and growing contempt for a United States that had allowed itself to become so weakened). But it did point to a dangerous trend in the high-tech area: a 1991 analysis of new patents demonstrated all too clearly how U.S. industrial and technical vigor was rapidly losing ground to Japan in engineering, computer science, electronics, communications, and robotics (see Figure 8-2).[34]

Indeed, Japanese computer and electronic companies, rich in cash, are now establishing research centers in the United States and hiring the nation's top computer scientists away from the leading computer science departments in American universities. Universities are unable to match the substantially greater salaries offered by the Japanese firms. Thus, American scientists could end up helping Japan compete economically against the United States in what is a not-too-subtle form of economic warfare. While Japanese firms are plowing much of their profit back into long-term research and development, in the United States nonmilitary research and development has dropped to only 1 percent of GNP—the lowest in over twenty years—and research laboratories increasingly are focusing on short-term goals.[35] Overall, the Japanese economy, despite a 1992 slowdown, has sufficient momentum that it threatens to outdistance the Western economies sometime in the 1990s or, at

---

Japan's Dominance in Chips," *New York Times,* January 5, 1988). Indeed, the worry about U.S. technological leadership is so great that the Defense Department has been advised by experts in and out of government to take a more assertive role in setting economic policy, not just in stimulating advances in specific military technologies. The lack of U.S. competitiveness, inadequate research and development, and increasing foreign ownership of U.S. companies, which affect the whole economy, also affect the weapons manufacturers (John H. Cushman, Jr., "Pentagon Is Urged To Be More Active in Economic Policy," *New York Times,* October 19, 1988). The critical high technologies for national security, listed by the U.S. government, may be found in Martin Tolchin's "Crucial Technologies: 22 Make the U.S. List," *New York Times,* March 7, 1989. But the Bush administration, in the name of the free market and the government's inability to "pick winners and losers", rejected government support to maintain U.S. high-technology industries, cutting the funds to a consortium of corporations who were trying to make the U.S. semiconductor industry more competitive with that of Japan.

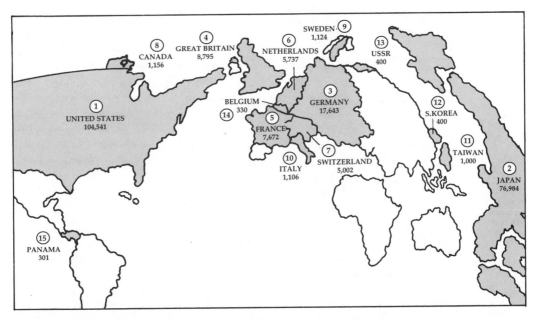

Figure 8-2 The New World Order Based on Share of Leading Patents

NOTE: A nation's size corresponds to its technical strength as measured by an index based on the number of influential patents it holds. The index number is circled, and only the top fifteen countries are ranked. Scores for Taiwan, South Korea, and the Soviet Union are estimates.

the latest, by the early part of the next century. Since 1985, its economy has grown by the equivalent of one France or South Korea every four and a half years. Its trade surplus has started to rise again, hitting a record $100 billion, and is expected to rise even further in 1992. In late 1991, a majority of Americans participating in public opinion polls thought Japan would surpass the United States as the world's leading economic superpower by early in the twenty-first century: in a CBS/*New York Times* poll also conducted in late 1991, only 36 percent thought the United States would retain that role.[36]

In the 1980s General Motors, once the model for automobile mass production and the world's largest multinational corporation, closed eleven older plants and trimmed eight assembly plants. Then, almost symbolically, GM announced in 1991 that it would close twenty-one more plants and cut over 70,000 more jobs in what was tantamount to a retreat to a smaller market share, most of it lost to Japanese cars. Indeed, GM had been the very model of the successful American corporation that had made America the world's premier industrial power. As the 1990s began, the plight of GM, Ford, and Chrysler had become the symbol of the nation's struggling manufacturing base; they were hardly alone as many of America's leading industrial and financial corporations, from IBM to Chemical Bank, laid off blue-collar and white-collar workers in a "restructuring" process that was unlikely to see them reemployed by their industries when the recession ended. Japan's prime minister summed it up aptly. GM, he said, "is like the Stars and Stripes to the

United States. So it comes as a great shock to Americans that GM has been defeated by Japanese cars, which in twenty years have captured one-third of the U.S. car market." [37] An interesting footnote to this story of Japan's economic ascent and America's decline is that while Japanese automobile chief executive officers make an average of $300,000—$400,000 a year, sixteen times the average salary of their workers (and they are expected to take a voluntary pay cut if company profits decline), U.S. CEOs make 160 times the average salary of their workers, continuing to earn well over $2 million a year while their companies' profits sink and plants close.[38] The retired GM chairman makes over $1 million a year in retirement earnings—presumably for presiding over GM's huge loss of the U.S. car market share.

FROM BIPOLARITY TO 'UNIPOLYCENTRISM'

If bipolarity has ended, what has taken its place? What conclusions about the shape of the new post-cold war system can be drawn from the changing economic indicators that affect the relative power positions of states? One conclusion points to the relative decline of both superpowers. Of these, the Soviet Union's decline was the most precipitous. As it declared chapter 11, it was economically and ideologically bankrupt. In these circumstances, even before it vanished from the world's map, the Soviet Union was no longer able to play a major role in the international system.

The United States, however, remains a military superpower, although the country has been weakened by its own economic problems: a continuing budget deficit; a low savings and investment rate; an educational system that stubbornly resists improvement; and states and cities marked by declining public services, homelessness, crime, AIDS, and drugs. The Persian Gulf crisis in 1990 was an apt characterization of American power. On the one hand, in an impressive display of its military strength and reach, the United States quickly deployed over 100,000 personnel and materiel to the defense of Saudi Arabia. Eventually, the buildup capped at just over 500,000. On the other hand, it sent the secretaries of State and Treasury, tin cups in hand, asking its allies for contributions to pay for the expedition. It is not that the United States, protecting its own interests as well as those of its allies (who were in fact even more dependent on Gulf oil than the United States), was wrong in asking them to share the burden. This was long overdue. Nevertheless, the demand for financial assistance, especially from Germany and Japan, America's wealthiest allies, both of whom cited constitutional reasons for not sending any soldiers,* was a sign of the nation's weakness.

---

* Germany claimed it could not send military forces outside the NATO area, but after several months it did send a squadron of jet trainers to help bolster Turkey's defenses against Iraq—the German fighters, however, did not have the range to hit Iraq. Indeed, the German government did not even announce that the fighters would be

In an earlier day, Washington would not have asked for economic and financial support. It did not do so, for example, during the Korean and Vietnam wars; the United States was able to foot those bills itself. But by 1990, on the edge of a recession, it could not carry out a military operation clearly in its own interest, not just that of its allies, without their paying for much of it! Would it in future contingencies have to ask Germany or Japan for permission to act at all? This is neither a facetious nor a far-fetched question. Will the United States, after selling off one asset after another—from Rockefeller Center to its most famous movie and recording studios to urban real estate and cattle ranches—to British, Dutch, Japanese, and other buyers, be in command of its own destiny and be able to act according to its conception of the national interest?

The Persian Gulf war also demonstrates how difficult power calculations have become. First, the United States was clearly the only power left in the world that could immediately bring its military power—which, despite forecasts to the contrary, remained important—to bear and deter Iraq from invading Saudi Arabia. Second, President George Bush skillfully organized a coalition of the Soviet Union, Western allies, and Arab states to act collectively against Iraq through the United Nations. By mobilizing the United Nations and having it denounce Iraq's invasion of Kuwait as an act of aggression, as well as impose an economic embargo and legitimate its enforcement on the high seas and in the air, the United States demonstrated that it was still the largest possessor of not only what Joseph Nye has called "hard power"—in this case, military power—but also "soft power," the ability to co-opt other nations because of its leadership, ability to forge consensus, and values.[39] Third, after the war erupted in January 1991, American prestige shot up as a result of the rapid destruction of Iraqi military power and the decisive use of U.S. power in ending the war in forty-three days. By the time the ground forces were sent in, air power had demolished and demoralized the Iraqi forces to such an extent that the ground war became a mopping-up operation.

By contrast, Germany and Japan, for all their vaunted economic power and financial clout, demonstrated that their power was one-dimensional. Neither

---

used in defense of Turkey, a NATO ally, because German public opinion opposed any involvement in the war, even though polls showed that a majority favored the use of force against Iraq and was ashamed of German help that had made Iraq the power it had become.

Because after World War II the United States had insisted that Japan's constitution include a provision against Japan ever again going to war, the country has only a small self-defense force. When, because of U.S. pressure, the Japanese government proposed sending some troops to the Gulf in a noncombat role, public pressure forced it to abandon the plan. But there are reasons to question these constitutional invocations as reasons for not sending troops. See, for example, Donald Hellmann, "Japan's Bogus Constitutional Excuses in the Gulf," *Wall Street Journal*, February 6, 1991.

could have organized the collective action against Iraq. If the United States had not taken the initiative, the Arabs would never have found the courage to stand up to Saddam Hussein, nor would the Saudis have asked for U.S. intervention and cut off the Iraqi oil pipeline running through their country. Without Washington, Kuwait would have remained just another victim of aggression, much like the hapless states left as victims in the 1930s. Indeed, none of the European powers would have taken the lead. While they, like the United States, had to be concerned about the consequences of the precedent for a new post-cold war order of aggression, and the impact on their economies if Iraq commanded OPEC production and pricing policies, they waited for the Bush administration to define the response to Iraq's aggression and then closed ranks behind Washington. As dependent on the United States as during the cold war, they also permitted the United States to continue assuming the principal risks and burden. Only it was willing and able to project sufficient power. The limits of the power of America's principal allies were clearly evident—and this only a short time after they had felt growing self-confidence stemming from their economic success to act more independently on the world scene in the new post-cold war era.

This is not to belittle Germany's and Japan's postwar economic accomplishments or the critical importance of the economic component of power. But it does demonstrate the one-dimensional nature of the power of the two states widely said to be the principal challengers to American dominance. In the past, great powers usually not only were leading military powers and diplomatic actors, but also had the economies needed to sustain those roles as well as an ideological-cultural attraction. Even the Soviet Union at one time possessed wide appeal when capitalism collapsed in the Great Depression of the 1930s and the belief that a Communist society would provide both full employment and social justice for all members of society grew. Later, the Soviet Union's heroic wartime resistance was greatly admired in the West. But this ideological appeal vanished when the Soviet economy failed to provide either economic abundance or freedom, bringing scarcity and repression instead.

By contrast, America as a free society remains a model for much of the world as democracy and free markets have spread. Moreover, its popular culture, from movies to rock music and blue jeans, is widely admired and imitated. In fact, the United States remains a player in the key diplomatic, economic (as the world's largest economy, it still has approximately 25 percent of the gross global product), and ideological-cultural areas, as well as in the areas of strategic nuclear power and conventional military power. And it is still the chief player in each area.

In contrast to other countries, the United States ranks extraordinarily high in almost all the major sources of national power: population size and education, natural resources, economic development, social cohesion, political stability, military strength, ideological appeal, diplomatic alliances, technological achievement.... At present, no country can mount a multidimensional challenge to the United States.[40]

In one sense, then, and despite everything said earlier and the rarity of its occurrence, the state system has become unipolar! At a time when the ideological appeal of American political and economic institutions is growing, the demonstration in the Persian Gulf of the nation's refurbished military power, the will to use it, and the effectiveness of its use against Iraq underlines this primacy, which, in the flush of victory, some considered to be evidence of a new *pax Americana*.[41]

But the world also might be characterized as a "uni/multipolar" one. While the United States is the only power that can be truly called a superpower, the Soviet Union's successor state, Japan, Germany, England, and France, as well as China, are major actors, with specific strengths and weaknesses. In addition, it also must be noted that power has become widely diffused to an unprecedented degree in the contemporary system. There are today many national and other actors who assert their interests and demands. Since the international system is not composed of approximately equal powers, it cannot be characterized as multipolar; perhaps the more accurate descriptive term is polycentric or, given the U.S. status in the system, *unipolycentric*.

The Iraqi crisis suggests, in fact, the relationship between the end of bipolarity and the rise of this polycentric world. The relative decline of the superpowers has made it easier for regional rivalries to erupt, and left the field clear for aspirants to regional hegemony, because the former cold war contestants no longer seek to recruit or maintain "client states" or to encourage and support local quarrels in order to enhance their own influence at the expense of the other. Nor is it any longer the case of each superpower having to restrain its respective clients to prevent local conflicts from escalating into a superpower confrontation and a possible nuclear holocaust. Thus, the weakened state of the former cold war adversaries coexists with regional balances of power, which are at times likely to be unstable because of the actions, not necessarily military, of regionally influential states. The evolution of the state system away from bipolarity—the fragmentation and regionalization of power—is perhaps best symbolized by the proliferation of modern weapons technology, from chemical and nuclear weapons to short- and middle-range missiles.

Still, as was the case for polarity, the changing nature of power in the post-cold war era is perhaps more ambiguous than suggested. It is true that with the disappearance of the Soviet threat the military power that played such a prominent role during the four decades of the superpower rivalry is likely to play a lesser role. The currency of power that will be displayed more and more is economic.[42] The disintegration of the Soviet Union, the relative decline of U.S. power, and the rise of Germany and Japan particularly (and, after 1992, possibly the EC) are evidence of the changing roles played by military and economic power. While the influence of Germany and Japan on economic and financial issues is obviously high—so much of the world wants their goods and capital investments—neither the Japanese yen nor the German mark, for all their vaunted power versus the much-weakened dollar, can deal with a Russian missile or Iraqi poison gas. Economic power is obviously a necessary condition for a nation to become a great power, but it is not a sufficient condition. Economic power does not automatically translate into geopolitical influence. Neither of the two powers widely reputed before the invasion of Kuwait to be America's rivals and pillars of a new multipolar world has yet defined its political role.

During the Iraqi crisis, both Germany and Japan tried to remain uninvolved, neither sending any military assistance. They limited themselves to contributing several billion dollars to support Turkey, Jordan, and Egypt—nations hurt by the embargo against Iraq—and to supporting the U.S. military effort in Saudi Arabia. But actually they gave little relative to their GNPs, and what they gave they gave slowly, causing great resentment in the United States. Germany, to be sure, has been preoccupied with the task of reviving the East German economy, as part of a reunified country at the center of Europe where East meets West, and of managing its conflicting obligations to the EC and to Eastern Europe, to which it is attracted. But as a key member of the EC, Germany will find that its future is really that of the broader community, and only the future will tell whether the 1992 "last push" to European economic and political integration will succeed. Will the EC move increasingly toward common foreign and defense policies? Will the new Europe define a role for itself beyond a strictly commercial one, either by itself or together with the United States?

Japan's foreign policy since its defeat in World War II has been one of trade and not alienating any potential customers. Frequently referred to in the past as Sony Inc., suggesting that it is more a trading company than a nation, Japan has been extremely reluctant to define a political role for itself. Unlike Germany, which at least has come to grips with its past and has found a place for itself in the Western European "family," Japan has largely avoided discussing the war and, proud of its uniqueness as a nation, has remained culturally isolated. Not a member of any larger group of nations, it tends to deal with other countries as patrons and clients rather than as nations with whom it shares mutual interests and with whom it must compromise and mesh its own interests. Japan is obviously an economic superpower. Worldwide, it has the second largest economy, is the second largest exporter of manufactured products, and is the largest creditor. But in the Gulf confrontation in 1990-1991, Japan (like Germany) was a conscientious objector. The crisis also underlined once again Japan's vulnerability because of its high dependence on imported resources, particularly oil. Thus, there are real limits to Japan's status as a great power.

Why then are Americans so worried about Japan? Why do they see that country, a cold war ally, as a growing threat while they view the former Soviet Union as a waning one? The reasons are fairly obvious, and the public reaction demonstrates that the American people have the right instinct about the nature of power: superior economic performance generates superior economic power. The public is as right to be concerned about the rise of Japanese economic power as it was to worry about the growth of Soviet power during the cold war. The reasons are at least threefold. First, in the fairly narrow sense of the term *national security*, the United States is becoming increasingly dependent on Japan for key technologies in its weapon systems. In 1989, the Defense Department said Japan had a significant lead in six of the twenty-two technologies crucial to the long-term qualitative superiority of U.S. weapons systems.[43] The brilliant performance of U.S. high-technology weapons against Iraq in 1991— although some were already dated technologically—does not change this increasing dependence on Japanese microelectronics, optics, superconductivity, and information systems technologies.[44] Second, in the broader sense of the term *national security*, the public clearly understands that the growth of Japanese economic power threatens U.S. markets and jobs; in short, it will hit America's economic well-being. Third, and most profound of all, the increase in Japanese economic power translates into an increase in Japanese influence in the world and a decline in that of the United States. Thus, while the two nations are allies, their trading relations are increasingly taking on the appearance of economic warfare. Despite the interdependence viewpoint which says that economic relations tend to be mutually beneficial—as generally supported by the free trade perspective prevalent in the United States—economics also can be the "continuation of warfare by other means." [45]

In the context of the current international system, then, two conclusions are reasonably clear. The first is that although the United States may be declining economically while Germany and Japan are ascending, neither one seeks to replace the United States as the West's leading power.[46] At least, up to this point, there is no reason to believe that we are witnessing another of the repetitive historical cycles in the rise and fall of the great powers. The second is that the redistribution of economic power points to a more collective management of the world's political and economic affairs among these three states, for, economically, it might be said that the world is tripolar. Even if, militarily, it is unipolar, the United States asserted the need for its allies to share the burden during the Persian Gulf involvement. It was right to do so. But burden-sharing requires another obligation: power-sharing. The United States cannot act unilaterally—define the issues and objectives and decide if, when, and how force is to be used—and then expect its allies and friends to simply fall in line and help pay the costs; that would be perpetuating the cold war relationships in which Washington led and Japan, Germany, and others followed. The post-cold war world, marked by a greater diffusion of power or pluralism, is therefore likely to be characterized by greater collective responsibility and security. This assumes, however, that Germany, the EC, and Japan will gradually define a political role for themselves, and that their growing economically interdependent relationship will not split apart as a result of increasingly bitter trade rivalries.

In this respect, the Iraqi crisis may have set a pattern: the great powers acting in concert. In that instance, they acted through the United Nations in order to legitimate the action against Iraq and enlist the assistance of Arab states, which, had it not been for the UN cover, might not have been able to align themselves with non-Muslim Western states, one of whom was Israel's closest friend. The United Nations also made it easier for the Soviet Union to cooperate with its former NATO adversaries. But in future instances, the United Nations may not be the best organization through which to act. Other issues, such as the Israeli-Palestinian problem, which led to several anti-Israeli resolutions during the Iraqi confrontation, may stress a UN coalition. The United States, the leader of the coalition against Iraq, had to tread very warily between preserving its Arab alliance and maintaining the relationship with Israel. An alternative to the United Nations might be NATO, if it survives the end of the cold war and the withdrawal of Soviet troops from Central and Eastern Europe, as well as the dissolution of the Warsaw Pact.[47] Or it might be the European Community.

The Arab-Israeli peace conference, which first met in Madrid in late 1991, suggests that this collective approach will be useful in other ways as well—not just for dealing with disturbances in the post-cold war system. The United States was clearly the prime mover in getting all the parties to the table and initiating what are likely to be long, often vitriolic, and somewhat sporadic negotiations, which could last years before the Israeli-Palestinian and Arab-Israeli differences are resolved. The end of the cold war and the decline of Soviet power left the United States the dominant power in the Middle East. The more moderate Arab regimes were indebted to the United States after its opposition and defeat of Iraq, which, at least for the time being, is no longer a major actor in the Arab world. The hard-line Arab regimes (especially Syria, which in the past could always count on Moscow for diplomatic support and weapons), no longer able to play off one superpower against the other, were trying to warm up to Washington (the reason Syria sent forces to Saudi Arabia against Iraq). Israel, highly dependent on the United States for political support, economic assistance, and high-tech arms, and no longer as strategically important as it had been during the cold war, had to take Washington's position about negotiating a compromise peace more seriously than in the past when it rejected outright any kind of "land-for-peace" deal. None could afford to alienate the United States, the only military superpower left. So they all showed up, some more reluctantly than others. But they all showed up: none wanted to be the first to walk out and be singled out as having undermined possibly the last chance for peace in the area. The same has been true for subsequent meetings.

But the United States was not the only nonregional power at the table; the Soviet Union, and after its collapse, Russia, was the cosponsor. Although it was no longer a rival and its power was declining, it had some remaining influence with the more radical regimes and the Palestine Liberation Organization (Russia became the cosponsor at a January 1992 meeting of all the parties in Moscow). The European Community and the United Nations also were represented at the Madrid conference. Even though it was the principal power at the conference, the United States was in no position to impose a solution on the participants. It could cajole, pressure, shame, make helpful suggestions, mediate if called upon, but not dictate. Nor could any of the other nonregional actors present. The regional actors had their own strongly held views on whether and how to resolve the over forty-year-old dispute; they also possessed the means to resist coercion.

THEORY AND REALITY

The post-cold war era was supposed to be different. It was supposed to be multipolar. Economics was supposed to replace military power. And transnational and subnational forces were supposed to tie nations together in an interdependent web, replacing an anarchical system in which nations were divided by nationalism. No one would have predicted that less than a month after NATO leaders in July 1990 proclaimed the end of the cold war, a country of only 17 million people would precipitate a crisis that would bring together in opposition a concert of the great powers and bring about the first post-cold war conflict. But more than that, the Persian Gulf crisis demonstrated that the nature of international politics had not changed as much as had generally been predicted.

From the moment of the Iraqi invasion of Kuwait, it was clear that the United States was the dominant post-cold war power. The Soviet Union acquiesced to its leadership in opposition to Saddam Hussein.[48] Germany (reunified as a single country in October 1990) and Japan stood on the sidelines. It also was evident that military force, which had played a prominent role during the cold war, was hardly an obsolete instrument of power. A dictator of a relatively small nation, who had used his country's oil wealth to build one of the world's largest and best-equipped armies and had shown that he was willing to use it, demonstrated dramatically that the use of force was not yet a thing of the past. Finally, while the post-cold war period certainly saw states moving toward greater interdependence, especially the industrial states, the nationalism that in the wake of the retreat of Soviet power from Eastern Europe broke up the Soviet Union and other countries such as Yugoslavia while reuniting Germany, had not yet been so weakened that the decentralized nation-state system in which military power remained the ultimate arbiter was dead—or even dying.

It is, in addition, ironic that at a time when it was expected that the terms of the emerging post-cold war system would be the product of East-West negotiations, the consequences of the confrontation with Iraq appeared to be even more important because it might set a destabilizing precedent. Saddam Hussein was a very familiar historical phenomenon: a locally powerful and ambitious ruler making a bid for regional hegemony. It can be anticipated that we shall see a lot of this regional imperialism in the new era: the greater freedom of action for middle powers following the ending of the superpowers' global rivalry; the opportunities created by the centrifugal and centripetal effects of unleashed national, ethnic, and religious passions; the greater availability of sophisticated weapons—all of these will encourage it. And if Saddam gets away with even half a success in the current confrontation, his example will be followed by neighborhood toughs around the world.[49]

What is hopeful is that in this new world the United States will exercise its influence not only to stop blatant aggression that would have profound potential consequences, but also to reconcile old enemies to prevent future crises and wars. Yet the limits of American influence are also clear. In helping the transition of the states of Eastern Europe and the republics of the Commonwealth of Independent States to more pluralistic political systems and reconciling them to the post-cold war international system, the United States has had to act in partnership with its allies. Indeed, their economies—especially the German economy—have meant that they, not the United States, have taken the initiative and exercised the corresponding influence.

For Review

1. Is there one component of power more important than all others in any analysis of which nations are rising to the top of the international state hierarchy, and which are declining?
2. What are some of the external causes and internal causes responsible for the relative decline of U.S. power and the rise of Japan to economic superpower status? Which—external or internal—were more important?
3. What are some of the other countries that we must focus on to explain the changing nature of the contemporary hierarchy of states?
4. Describe what is meant by the term *unipolycentric view of the world*.
5. Why is power in the post-cold war period said to be more complex and ambiguous than before, thus complicating the calculation of power relationships between states?

Notes

1. Paul M. Kennedy, "The First World War and the International Power System," *International Security* (Summer 1984): 23. On Britain's decline, see Aaron L. Friedberg, *The Weary Titan* (Princeton, N.J.: Princeton University Press, 1988).
2. Paul M. Kennedy, *The Rise and Fall of British Naval Mastery* (Malabar, Fla.: Robert E.

Krieger, 1982), 309-310.

3. Among other works, see Paul M. Kennedy, *The Rise and Fall of the Great Powers* (New York: Random House, 1987), 413 ff. For a briefer analysis, see the section entitled "The Pacific Century" in *Newsweek*, February 28, 1988, 42-63. For a response, see Henry R. Nau, *The Myth of America's Decline* (New York: Oxford University Press, 1990).

4. Martin Grutsinger, "U.S. Edge in Technology Is Slipping," *Gainesville Sun*, September 8, 1988. For a view that Japan may be taking the lead in technology, see Clyde V. Prestowitz, *Trading Places* (New York: Basic Books, 1988). Especially important for his case studies of several U.S. industries is Lester Thurow, *Head to Head: The Coming Economic Battle Among Japan, Europe, and America* (New York: Morrow, 1992), 153-218.

5. David E. Sanger, "In Computer Research Race, Japanese Increase Their Lead," *New York Times*, February 21, 1990.

6. "The Outlook: Japan Slows but Firms Still Invest Heavily," *Wall Street Journal*, April 22, 1991; and William J. Broad, "Research Spending Is Declining in U.S. as It Rises Abroad," *New York Times*, February 21, 1992.

7. Anthony DePalma, "Foreigners Flood U.S. Graduate Schools," *New York Times*, November 29, 1990.

8. *Independent Alligator* (University of Florida, Gainesville), January 10, 1991.

9. For a catalog of what the author believes to be the errors of U.S. "self-indulgence" in the 1980s and a belief that the United States will regain its competitive stature in the 1990s, see Alfred L. Malabre, Jr., *Within Our Means* (New York: Random House, 1991). Indeed, the weak dollar and lower labor costs relative to those of Japan and Germany had led to a boom in manufactured exports by 1990. Whether this presages a turnaround in U.S. industry in general remains to be seen. Sylvia Nasar, "Boom in Manufactured Exports Provides Hope for U.S. Economy," *New York Times*, April 21, 1991.

10. Paul M. Kennedy, "The (Relative) Decline of America," *Atlantic Monthly*, August 1987, 29-37.

11. Samuel P. Huntington, "Coping with the Lippmann Gap," *Foreign Affairs* (America and the World, 1987/88 issue): 456-458.

12. "The Pacific Century" *(Newsweek)*, 62.

13. Marshall I. Goldman, *Gorbachev's Challenge* (New York: Norton, 1987); and Edward A. Hewett, *Reforming the Soviet Economy* (Washington, D.C.: Brookings, 1987).

14. Michael Putzel, "Report: Soviet Economy Backward," *Gainesville Sun*, December 23, 1990; Peter Truell, "Western Study Says Soviet Aid May Be Futile," *Wall Street Journal*, December 24, 1990. Also see Henry Rowen and Charles Wolf, eds., *The Impoverished Superpower* (San Francisco: Institute for Contemporary Studies, 1989), especially for the military burden on the Soviet economy.

15. Zbigniew Brzezinski, *Game Plan* (Boston: Atlantic Monthly Press, 1986), 99-144.

16. Bill Keller, "Soviet Food Short for Many: Others Find Ways to Cope," *New York Times*, December 12, 1990.

17. A very good summary analysis of Gorbachev's problems and the dilemmas he faced from the revolution he unleashed is presented by Dimitri Simes, "Gorbachev's Time of Troubles," *Foreign Policy* (Spring 1991): 97-117. Also see John Dunlop, "Why Gorbachev Is Cracking Down," *National Interest* (Spring 1991): 24-32; and Stephen Sestanovich, "Fiddler on the Roof," *New Republic*, May 27, 1991, 19-22; and Robert G. Kaiser, *Why Gorbachev Happened* (New York: Simon &

Schuster, 1991).

18. Serge Schmemann, "Yeltsin Is Handily Elected Leader of Russian Republic in Setback for Communists," *New York Times,* June 14, 1991.

19. Peter Gumbel, "In the Soviet Union, Infighting Gives Way to a Fragile Optimism," *Wall Street Journal,* May 21, 1991; and Fox Butterfield, "Soviet and U.S. Economists Discuss a Bailout for Moscow," *New York Times,* May 21, 1991.

20. From the *New York Times,* see Francis X. Clines, "Soviet Reformers Agree to Form an Anti-Communist Opposition," July 2, 1991; Esther B. Fein, "Gorbachev Warns Hard-liners Risk Communist Demise," July 4, 1991; and Serge Schmemann, "Leadership of Communists Approves Gorbachev Plan," July 26, 1991, and "Gorbachev Offers Party a Charter That Drops Icons," July 27, 1991. On Gorbachev's rise, decline, and survival, see Robert G. Kaiser, *Why Gorbachev Happened* (New York: Simon & Schuster, 1991).

21. Jeremy R. Azrael and Sergei Zamascikov, "The Enemies Within," *New York Times,* August 4, 1991.

22. Zbigniew Brzezinski, "America's New Geostrategy," *Foreign Affairs* (Spring 1988): 693.

23. Hedley Bull, "Europe's Self-Reliance," *Foreign Affairs* (Spring 1983): 878.

24. "The Pacific Century" *(Newsweek),* 45. Also see the speeches by Under Secretary of State for Political Affairs Michael H. Armacost, "China and the U.S.: Present and Future," June 1, 1988, and "The United States in the Changing Asia of the 1990s," June 6, 1988, *Current Policy,* nos. 1078 and 1079, respectively, published by the Bureau of Public Affairs, Department of State.

25. Bernard K. Gordon, *Politics and Protectionism in the Pacific* (London: International Institute of Strategic Studies, 1988), 10.

26. Erza Vogel, "Pax Nipponica?" *Foreign Affairs* (Spring 1986): 752-767; Thurow, *Head to Head,* 113-151; and Kennedy, *Rise and Fall of the Great Powers,* 458-471. For a case study of the rise of Nissan (Datsun) and decline of Ford as examples of the efficiency of the Japanese automobile industry and the inefficiency of its American competitor, see David Halberstam, *The Reckoning* (New York: Morrow, 1986). Ironically, right after the book was published, Ford made a major comeback while Nissan slumped. Only in 1989 with new models did Nissan rebound.

27. William J. Broad, "Novel Technique Shows Japanese Outpace Americans in Innovation," *New York Times,* March 7, 1988; and David E. Sanger, "A High-Tech Lead in Danger," *New York Times,* December 18, 1988.

28. Kennedy, *Rise and Fall of the Great Powers,* 467.

29. Nathaniel C. Nash, "Japan's Banks: Top 10 in Deposits," *New York Times,* July 20, 1988. By 1991, it was only the top six.

30. Kent E. Calder, "Japanese Foreign Economic Policy Formation: Explaining the Reactive State," *World Politics* (July 1988): 520.

31. Broad, "Novel Technique"; and see the editorial "The Art and the Grasshopper," *New York Times,* January 9, 1989, subtitled "Why Is U.S. Prosperity Eroding? Japan's Lessons."

32. Kenneth Flamm, *Mismanaged Trade?* (Washington, D.C.: Brookings, 1991). On the broader relative U.S. economic decline, see Robert Gilpin, *The Political Economy of International Relations* (Princeton, N.J.: Princeton University Press, 1987).

33. Akio Morita and Shintaro Ishihara, *The Japan That Can Say "No"* (Kobunsha: Kappa-Holmes, 1989), 3-4. A later version of this book by Ishihara himself, published in 1991 by Simon & Schuster, is much more critical of Japan and less so of the United

States.

34. William J. Broad, "In the Realm of Technology, Japan Looms Ever Larger," *New York Times*, May 28, 1991. Also see William S. Dietrich, *In the Shadow of the Rising Sun* (State College, Penn.: Pennsylvania State University, 1991).

35. Gina Kolata, "Japanese Labs in U.S. Luring America's Computer Experts," *New York Times*, November 11, 1990.

36. R. W. Apple, Jr., "Majority in a Poll Fault Bush for Foreign Focus," *New York Times*, October 11, 1991; and Karel van Wolferen, "An Economic Pearl Harbor?" *New York Times*, December 2, 1991.

37. Steven R. Weisman, "The Deal Gap: What Bush Needs and Tokyo Can't Give," *New York Times*, December 29, 1991.

38. Jill Abramson, "High Pay of CEOs Traveling with Bush Touches a Nerve in Asia," *Wall Street Journal*, December 30, 1991.

39. Joseph S. Nye, Jr., *Bound to Lead* (New York: Basic Books, 1990), 29-35.

40. Samuel P. Huntington, "The U.S.—Decline or Renewal?" *Foreign Affairs* (Winter 1988-1989): 91. Also see Charles Krauthammer, "The Unipolar Moment," *Foreign Affairs* (America and the World, 1990-1991 issue): 23-33.

41. Joshua Muravchik, "At Last, Pax Americana," *New York Times*, January 24, 1991. Muravchik concludes that the result will be not only the joys of jeans and Big Macs, "but also our concept of how nations ought to be governed and to behave."

42. See, for example, Catherine McArdle Kelleher, "The Changing Currency of Power," *Adelphi Papers* (Winter 1990-1991), on the changing roles of military and economic power. Also see Thurow, *Head to Head*.

43. Martin Tolchin, "Technology Report Finds Japan Leads in 6 Areas," *New York Times*, May 16, 1989.

44. Andrew Pollack, "In U.S. Technology, a Gap between Arms and VCR's," *New York Times*, March 4, 1991.

45. Samuel P. Huntington, "America's Changing Strategic Interests," *Survival* (January/February 1991): 8-11.

46. Robert Gilpin's *War and Change in World Politics* (New York, N.Y.: Cambridge University Press, 1981) argues not only that uneven economic growth rates produce shifts in the power distribution among states but also that these changes result in conflict and, on occasion, war as the rising states assert themselves and the declining states try to preserve the status quo. This has not yet happened among the Western allies, however, largely because of cold war pressure for collective self-defense. Whether it will happen in the post-cold war period remains a matter of dispute.

47. Indeed, to the degree that the former Soviet Union cooperates with the NATO powers, it has been suggested that NATO may wish to offer membership to its former enemy in "NATO Mark II." Coral Bell, "Why Russia Should Join NATO," *National Interest* (Winter, 1990-1991): 37-47.

48. See Graham E. Fuller, "Moscow and the Gulf War," *Foreign Affairs* (Summer 1991): 55-76, on the struggle in the decision-making process in Moscow.

49. Owen Harries, "Of Unstable Disposition," *National Interest* (Winter 1990-1991): 103-104.

Part Three

THE SECOND
AND
THIRD LEVELS:
FOREIGN POLICY

C H A P T E R 9

National and Elite Styles in Foreign Policy: American and Soviet Perceptions and Behavior during the Cold War

CONCEPT OF STYLE: INSULAR AND CONTINENTAL STATES

In the previous chapters, the game of international politics was analyzed in terms of the international system's structure and the interactions among states. It was assumed up to this point that states have similar interests, motivations, and internal structures and that their behavior is the product of the state system. Thus, at the first level of analysis, there was no reason to look inward—except in those instances in which states have not behaved as expected. Although the assumption that states are identical in nature is useful conceptually, it clearly does not suffice. To analyze and more fully understand the actual behavior of states, one must look not only at their interactions but also at individual states and their foreign policies—that is, their perception of themselves, their role in the world, and their behavior.

Nations develop distinct personalities or "styles" that affect the manner in which they conduct themselves in the international arena, whether they take the initiative or react to what other states are doing. This style reflects a country's historical experience, geographical position, political values and organization, and economic resources. Nations have unique histories; each reads its own past and draws certain lessons from it—or misreads it and learns the wrong lessons. Each state develops a certain picture of the system and possesses a repertoire of acts and responses derived from its domestic and foreign experiences. Each, to put it another way, perceives "reality" selectively from its particular *Weltanschauung* (worldview) or "cognitive map"; in practice, each has a corresponding "operational code" or national style.

In no two states has this been more obvious than in the United States and the former Soviet Union; their styles during the cold war could not have been more different. The United States was a product of its long isolationism. Surrounded by fish to the east and west and weak neighbors to the north and south, the United States had had no security problem for most of its history. It had taken security for granted. In its early days, the country possessed only a small army and, until the turn of the twentieth century, a small navy; the military and its values were generally despised and felt to be the antithesis of the nation's democratic values. Indeed, when needed, the army was drawn primarily from citizen-soldiers or militia. The nation's main task was internal; domestic concerns held absolute priority. It is no wonder then that in an *insular* or island nation like the United States (and to a lesser extent in Britain, protected so long by the English Channel) foreign and domestic policies were thought to be entirely distinct. Events overseas appeared to have little to do with the development of democracy at home. European *continental* powers, bordering one another, could never afford to think of the domestic and foreign arenas as separate or independent. Unable to take security for granted, they gave priority to the conduct of foreign policy.[1]

For the United States, the stark contrast between the intense conflicts, violence, and often perceived immorality (sometimes disapprovingly referred to as Machiavellianism) of international politics, and the law and order, consensus, and generally peaceful change of democracy reinforced this tendency to separate international anarchy from domestic affairs. This insular, democratic distinction between international and domestic systems, the result of the country's foreign and domestic experiences, led Americans to draw a further distinction between policies of "choice" and "necessity." The American approach to international politics was based on two beliefs: (1) that the United States had a choice about whether it would participate in international politics; and (2) that if it did, it could apply the same moral principles that governed domestic affairs. Americans, once they had gained independence from Europe, told themselves that they were different from the Europeans (Continental Europeans, anyway), who were addicted to power politics. Americans tended not only to associate the behavior of the European states with the character of their class societies but also to see a causal relationship between them. Conflict and war were associated with Europe's aristocratic or undemocratic governments; the United States, an overwhelmingly middle-class society whose outlook was liberal and democratic, was peaceful in its behavior. Almost a century of experience seemed to support the belief that democracies were peaceful in their foreign policies.[2]

Rejecting the power politics approach (an unsocialized attitude according to the state system's rules of the game), American political leaders were concerned primarily with realizing proven democratic principles in foreign policy as the United States became involved internationally. This contrasted with the Continental tradition. Influenced mainly by geography, European leaders spoke of the "necessities of state" and learned to cope with the conflict between morality and "reasons of state." They were in no position to accept the American assumption that nations' leaders did not have to act out of necessity. Living far from Europe, Americans, as democrats, believed that they had freedom of choice and that, in fact, they could choose the moral path in their foreign policies as they did in their internal ones. The resulting American approach has often smacked of excessive moralizing, if not self-righteousness, in the conduct of external affairs. Indeed, the pursuit of policies believed to be inconsistent with democratic and moral principles arouses a sense of guilt and subjects these policies to moral condemnation.

The Soviet approach to international politics in the seven decades before Mikhail Gorbachev was quite different. Perhaps it is more appropriate to say *Russian* approach here because Russia was an old country before the Soviet regime came to power. Unlike the United States, Russia had a long history of invasions. It was attacked by, among others, the Mongols, Turks, Poles, Swedes, French (1812), Japanese (1904-1905), and Germans (1914-1917 and 1941-1945), and was defeated by many of them. Russia's leaders, like most leaders of the Continental states, had always felt vulnerable. Not protected by any natural barriers—oceans, channels, rivers, or mountain ranges—Russia had been invaded and beaten, or almost, so many times that its leaders had been rendered virtually paranoid about security. They did not assume the good neighborliness of surrounding states but their natural enmity. Peace was only a period that started after the last war and served as a time of preparation for the next one. The Russian state historically dealt with its security problem by centralizing power in an authoritarian state, possessing large armies, and pushing outward and keeping foreign threats as far away as possible.

Not all of Russia's expansion over the centuries, however, could be considered defensive. The same lack of natural barriers that did not stop invasions also could not prevent Russia's outward thrust of power for offensive purposes. Russia was the world's largest territorial state, covering one-sixth of the earth's surface. It no more became that large merely by repelling invasions than a man becomes rich by being constantly robbed. Indeed, Russia's history had been one of sustained territorial expansion, leading its neighbors such as Japan, which attacked Russia at the turn of the century, to regard it as a threat. Russia's advantage was that it lay at the crossroads of Europe, Asia, and the Middle East. This strategic location allowed it to probe all along its borders for weak spots and expand where these existed. According to Zbigniew Brzezinski, President Jimmy Carter's national security adviser, Russia historically was a "persistent aggressor" against its neighbors rather than their victim. That expansion, of course, alarmed Russia's neighbors and, instead of increasing Russian security, *de*creased it because those neighbors reacted by strengthening themselves. Thus, even if Russian foreign policy was interpreted as mainly defensive, a cycle was established: "Insecurity generated expansion; expansion bred insecurity; insecurity, in turn, would fuel further expansion."[3]

Russia's leaders understood only too well the meaning of the phrase "reasons of state" and recognized that foreign policy frequently had to be given priority over domestic policy. Democracy with its decentralization of power, as practiced in the United States, had not taken root in Russia; an American-style neglect of military power would have been an open invitation to foreign threats and would have negated opportunities for expansion when they arose. Soviet leaders inherited this historical experience when they came to power. They merely carried on in the traditional way, with its emphasis on conflict and struggle, the potential enmity of other states, the importance of military power, and self-reliance. Communism was to accentuate these attitudes many times over.

These examples of the contrasting styles of an insular democratic state and a continental undemocratic state suggest that the concept of style can be very useful in clarifying the ways in which a nation and its policy makers are likely to view a specific situation, alternative courses of action, and the course selected. If, for example, a certain nation has acted repeatedly in a particular fashion in similar situations, one could then suggest that it has demonstrated certain distinctive characteristics in its foreign policy outlook and behavior patterns.[4] The examination of U.S. foreign policy that follows will clarify this point. Indeed, the value of this second-level approach is even more dramatically demonstrated by Gorbachev's Soviet Union, which is analyzed later in this chapter, for what brought the cold war to a conclusion was the change in its domestic character and the new leadership's radically different ways of viewing the world and defining Soviet interests.

AMERICAN NATIONAL STYLE

The U.S. national style is distinguished by seven characteristics of its external behavior that are uniquely "American."[5]

Isolationism versus Interventionism

Fundamental to the American experience is the nation's lengthy isolation from the quarrels of the great European powers. For almost a century, the United States was able to devote itself to domestic tasks: strengthening the bonds of national unity, expanding westward, absorbing the millions of immigrants attracted by its opportunities, and industrializing and urbanizing an entire continent. But this freedom to concentrate on internal affairs cannot be explained entirely by the presence of the Atlantic Ocean and weaker neighbors to the north and south, the preferences of the electorate also must be taken into account. Citizens in a democracy are concerned primarily with their individual and family well-being.[6] Thus, government demands for service in the armed forces or for higher taxes to finance international obligations are bound to be viewed as burdens. Foreign policy is then, on the whole, considered a distraction from primary domestic tasks.

Given its profound inward orientation, it is not surprising that the United States has turned its attention to the outside world only when there has been a danger so obvious that it could no longer be ignored. This point cannot be overemphasized: the United States rarely has initiated policy; the stimuli responsible for its foreign policy usually have come from beyond its frontiers. The result historically has been both reactive and discontinuous U.S. foreign policy, a series of impatient responses to external pressures whenever there has been a "clear and present danger" and of returns to more important domestic affairs as soon as that danger has passed. Not surprisingly, long-range commitments and foreign policy planning have tended to be rare.

U.S. involvement in both world wars serves to demonstrate this pattern of isolation-intervention-isolation. The unrestricted German submarine campaign in 1917 led the United States into World War I. After Germany's defeat, the United States returned to its traditional isolationist stance. But the Japanese attack on Pearl Harbor in 1941 brought the United States out of this posture again. After the victory over Germany and Japan, the country attempted to withdraw once more. Britain took the first steps in containing the Soviet Union; the United States, considering itself a friend of both, attempted to mediate impartially between the two! Only after Britain, exhausted by the second world war in this century, collapsed in the winter of 1946-1947 did the United States engage in the cold war.

Moralism and Missionary Zeal

The American attitude is further characterized by a high degree of moralism and missionary zeal arising from the nation's perception of itself as a unique and morally superior society. The United States was the world's first democracy, committed to improvement of the lot of ordinary people. Americans regarded themselves as the "chosen people." The New World stood for opportunity, democracy, and peace; the Old World for poverty, exploitation, and war. Abraham Lincoln phrased the point aptly when he said that the United States was "the last best hope on earth." Woodrow Wilson during World War I and Franklin Roosevelt during World War II expressed much the same view. Just as in 1861 the United States had not been able to remain half free and half slave, so in 1917 and again in 1941 Americans thought that the world could not continue half free and half slave. Each war was considered an apocalyptic struggle between the forces of darkness and the forces of light.[7] Moralism in foreign policy reflected the awareness and pride of a society that believed it had carved out a better domestic order, free of oppression and injustice.

Isolation from European power politics, therefore, was basically a means of safeguarding American morality and purity from the undemocratic domestic institutions and foreign policy behavior of the European states. Withdrawal from the state system and providing the world with an example were the only correct course. But once in the twentieth century it became impossible to remain aloof, the country went to the other extreme and launched crusades to destroy the nation—Germany—that had made it necessary to emerge from its isolationism. As a self-proclaimed superior country—morally and politically—the United States could remain uncontaminated only by eliminating those that might infect it. Once provoked, the nation acted as a missionary power and sought to make the world safe for American democracy by democratizing or Americanizing it. American crusading and American isolationism sprang from a single source.

America's wars fitted the pattern. Kaiser Wilhelm II's Germany in World War I (1914-1918) was a semiabsolutist monarchy; Adolf Hitler's Germany in World War II (1939-1945) was a fascist totalitarian regime; and Joseph Stalin's Soviet Union in the cold war (after World War II) was a Communist totalitarian state. They were all antidemocratic, evil systems led by evil men, and they had to be destroyed (or, at least, contained). American power was "righteous power." Either it was not to be used at all, or it was to be used totally in a moral cause—in defense of democracy. The German submarine campaign in 1917 was regarded as more than a series of attacks on American ships. President Wilson called it "warfare against mankind. This is a war against all nations.... The challenge is to mankind." Also, according to Wilson,

> The right is more precious than peace, and we shall fight for the things which we have always carried nearest our hearts—for democracy ... [and] for a universal dominion of right by such a concert of free peoples as shall bring peace and safety to all nations and make the world itself at last free.[8]

Similar words, although perhaps not quite so eloquent, were used during World War II and the cold war. For example, these thoughts were contained in President Harry Truman's 1947 speech, which became known as the Truman Doctrine:

> At the present moment in world history nearly every nation must choose between alternative ways of life.... One way of life is based upon the will of the majority.... The second way of life is based upon the will of a minority forcibly imposed upon the majority ... [and] it must be the policy of the United States to support free peoples who are resisting attempted subjugations by armed minorities or by outside pressure.[9]

Almost every succeeding president spoke similar words at some point during his term.

Depreciation of Power Politics

A third characteristic of the American national style follows from the liberal democratic values on which the nation was founded and the resulting high moralism: a depreciation of power politics, with its connotations of conflict, destruction, and death. Strife is considered abnormal and only transitory; harmony is viewed as the normal condition among states. The use of power within the national political system is legitimate only in the service of democratic purposes; its employment in the state system can be justified only in the service of a moral cause. Specifically, in the state system power cannot be employed, at least without arousing guilt feelings, unless the nation confronts a morally unambiguous instance of foreign aggression. And when that happens, the United States must eradicate the immoral enemy that threatens the nation and its democratic principles. The presumption is that democracies are peaceful states because the people, who elect their rulers, do not like to go to war and suffer the resulting hardships and losses in lives and property. Therefore, the eruption of hostilities is attributed to authoritarian and totalitarian states whose rulers, unrestrained by democratic public opinion, wield power for their own personal aggrandizement. Their removal becomes a precondition of peace and the end of power politics itself. If the struggle for power cannot be avoided, it is to be abolished.

The American experience appears to support this belief in the normality of peace. Because the United States was a democracy and had enjoyed a long peace during the nineteenth century, lasting until 1917, the association was logical. Americans never asked themselves whether democracy had been the cause of peace or whether that peace had been the product of other forces. The frequent wars of Europe seemed to provide the answer, and European societies were viewed as undemocratic. It was because of this contrast that the United States had cut itself off from the Old World; the nation had to guard its democratic purity and virtue.

Distinction between Peace and War

Arising from both this moralism and the depreciation of power is a fourth characteristic of the U.S. national style: the tendency to draw a clear-cut distinction between peace and war. Peace is characterized by harmony among nations, and war and power politics in general are considered atypical. In peacetime, little or no attention need be paid to foreign problems. Indeed, such problems would divert people from their individual, materialistic concerns and upset the scale of social values.

But once Americans are angry and the United States has to resort to force, its use can be justified only in terms of the universal moral principles with which the nation, as a democratic country, identifies—with the goal of the complete destruction of the immoral enemy that threatens the integrity, if not the existence, of these principles. Since American power has to be "righteous" power, only its full exercise can ensure salvation or absolution from sin. The national aversion to violence thus becomes transformed into national glorification of violence, and wars become ideological crusades to make the world safe for democracy—by converting authoritarian adversaries into peaceful, democratic states and banishing power politics for all time.[10] Once that aim has been achieved, the United States can again withdraw into itself. Although foreign affairs are annoying diversions from more important domestic matters, such diversions are only temporary; maximum force is applied to aggressors or warmongers to punish them for provocation and to teach them that aggression is immoral and will not be rewarded. As a result, American wars are total wars, fought to achieve total victory and the enemy's unconditional surrender. "There is no substitute for victory," said Gen. Douglas MacArthur in Korea. To stop short of victory is to fight "a half-war." There can be no compromise with the enemy. Only its total defeat is acceptable.[11]

Divorce of Diplomacy from Force

The United States not only considers peace and war two mutually exclusive conditions but also divorces diplomacy from force, so that in wartime political considerations are subordinated to military considerations. Once the diplomats have failed to keep the peace through appeals to morality and reason, military considerations become primary. During wartime, the soldier is in charge. The United States rejected the traditional concept of war as a political instrument; war was not the continuation of politics by other means. Instead, it was regarded as a politically neutral operation that should be conducted according to its own professional rules and imperatives. The military officer was a nonpolitical technician who conducted the campaign in a strictly efficient, military manner. And war was a purely military instrument whose sole aim was the destruction of the enemy's forces and its despotic regime, so that after its defeat the people could be democratized.

The same moralistic attitude that is responsible for the American all-or-nothing approach to war also militates against the use of diplomacy in its classic sense: to compromise interests, to conciliate differences, and to moderate and isolate conflicts. Although Americans regard diplomacy as a rational process for straightening out misunderstandings among nations, they also have been extremely suspicious of diplomacy. If the United States is by definition moral, it obviously cannot compromise, for a nation endowed with a moral mission can hardly violate its own principles. If it did, national interests would be undermined and the national honor stained. Moreover, to compromise with the immoral enemy is to be contaminated by evil. To reach a settlement with the enemy instead of wiping it out is to acknowledge American weakness. This attitude toward diplomacy, viewed as an instrument of compromise, reinforces the American predilection for violence as a means of settling international problems. War allows the nation to destroy its evil opponent, while permitting it to pursue its moral mission uncompromised.

Belief in U.S. Omnipotence

In both world wars the United States successfully dealt its enemies total defeat, thereby highlighting a sixth characteristic of the American national style: the belief that the United States is omnipotent and, once engaged in a conflict, can "lick anyone in the system." [12] Indeed, even earlier in the history of the country American actions had met with quick success whenever the United States had been drawn into the international arena. Furthermore, the United States had never been invaded, defeated, or occupied (as most other nations had been). It had made mistakes, to be sure, but with its great power, it usually had been able to rectify them. For a nation that had the confidence to promise "the difficult today, the impossible tomorrow," failure would be a new experience.

Thus, before the cold war, American history had included only victories; the unbroken string of successes seemed evidence of national omnipotence. This belief in American invincibility tended to be reinforced by domestic successes. Historically, the United States was unique in that, with the single exception of the Civil War, it had never experienced national tragedy. Few other states have managed to avoid defeat and conquest. American policy makers usually have not been deterred by thoughts of failure, but had failure in fact occurred, they could have expected a major political reaction because in a country that is believed to be all-powerful, the public will understand failure or defeat only as the result of national incompetence or treason. The nation cannot admit that its situation may not be resolvable through the proper application of force.

Pragmatism

A seventh and final characteristic of the U.S. national style is generally known as pragmatism. Again, it has been part of the nation's experience that when problems have arisen, they have been solved using whatever means were at hand. Americans have prided themselves on their problem-solving abilities. Europeans invented radar and the jet engine, but Americans refined and developed these inventions, produced them on a large scale, and marketed them more effectively than the countries of origin. All problems have seemed solvable; they are only matters of know-how. The question is not *whether* but *how*—and how quickly at that. This approach to foreign policy may be called the engineering approach.[13]

More specifically, the United States tends to tackle each problem as it arises. In the abstract, this approach may make sense. After all, until a situation has occurred and the "facts" are in, how can one react? The trouble is that by the time sufficient facts are in, the situation may well be so far developed that it is too late to do much about it, or if one tries, difficulties abound. The American quest for certainty is usually carried too far. Policy making involves tackling problems early enough that influence can still be brought usefully to bear. Often, however, it can only be brought to bear when there is still insufficient information. By the time the situation is clear, it may be too late for any effective action short of applying military power; it may even be too late for that. Pragmatism thus reinforces the reactive and discontinuous nature of American foreign policy, along with the emphasis on the immediate and short run to the detriment of longer-term policy consideration.

AMERICAN POLICY AFTER WORLD WAR II

The American approach to international politics, then, reflects a series of simple dichotomies: domestic policy versus foreign policy, good peace-loving nations versus bad aggressor nations, isolationism versus crusading, war versus peace, force versus diplomacy. But fundamental to all these is the self-image of the United States as the epitome of democracy and the defender of the democratic faith. The United States, the shining "beacon lighting for all the world the paths of human destiny" in peacetime (in the words of Ralph Waldo Emerson), has been like a democratic St. George battling against evil aggressors.

During World War II, this moral attitude led the United States to divide nations into those that were "peace-loving" (the United States, Soviet Union, and Great Britain) and those that were "aggressors" (Germany, Italy, and Japan). The former had to destroy the latter and thus sought unconditional surrender. The Western democracies crusaded for total victory. Once that objective had been achieved, the aggressors were to be entirely disarmed and peace preserved through the cooperation of peace-loving nations within the new United Nations. Power politics would be ended. Alliances, spheres of influence, and balances of power, President Roosevelt said shortly before his death, were to be replaced by an international organization, which would furnish an alternative and better means for preserving peace. As the evil nations had been defeated, no new aggressors were expected. The Soviet Union, an ally, was certainly not expected to become an adversary.

Although Soviet behavior had already changed by the time hostilities ceased, a period of eighteen months was to elapse before U.S. policy toward the Soviets was reassessed. The American public attitude toward the Soviet Union was still generally friendly and hopeful for peaceful postwar coopera-tion. The United States wished to be left alone to occupy itself once more with domestic affairs and the fulfillment of American social values. The end of the war presumably signaled the end of power politics and the restoration of harmony among nations. The emphasis was therefore on rapid demobiliza-tion. Only when Britain pulled out of the eastern Mediterranean and there was no longer any countervailing power on the European continent—and only after continued Soviet denunciations and vilifications of the United States and Britain—did America's leaders again commit themselves. For this commitment to be made, a major external stimulus was needed.[14]

Cold War Crusade and Intervention in Vietnam

American identification of the Soviet Union as the new enemy and aggressor stemmed from Soviet actions in Eastern Europe, Iran, and Turkey. Because international conflict was viewed as a contest between good and evil states instead of a competition among states who all had legitimate interests, the American-Soviet struggle became transformed into another moral crusade. The Korean War, and especially the Chinese Communist intervention in it, turned a conflict that previously had been limited to Europe and aimed against the Soviet Union into a "global" conflict against communism. The contrast between American democratic values and the Soviet Communist values of what Washington saw as a united Sino-Soviet bloc, was striking. It was a clear instance of good against bad, and it fitted the traditional dichotomy between New World democracy and Old World autocracy.

The impact on policy was readily visible. For example, during the cold war years of 1946-1969 American policy makers put off any attempt to achieve a major political settlement with the Soviet Union until after communism had "mellowed"—that is, changed its character. Until then, negotiations were thought to be useless not only because of the expansionist aims of the Soviet leadership but also because such diplomatic dealings with the devil in the Kremlin would be immoral. Recognition of Communist China after Nationalist China's collapse became impossible, and mainland China's intervention in Korea only confirmed the American appraisal of Communist regimes as evil, even though the United States itself had precipitated this intervention with its march up to the Chinese frontier with North Korea.

If communism per se were the enemy, then the United States had to oppose it everywhere or, at least, wherever it seemed that counterbalancing American power could be applied effectively. Thus, the United States built up alliances in Europe (North Atlantic Treaty Organization), the Middle East (Middle East Treaty Organization), and Asia (Southeast Asia Treaty Organization) around the Sino-Soviet bloc and fought two limited wars on the Asian continent. It also supported numerous anti-Communist regimes, mostly outside of Europe, whether they were democratic or not. Most of them were right-wing; Chiang Kai-shek (Nationalist China) on Taiwan and Ngo Dinh Diem and Nguyen Van Thieu (and several between them) in South Vietnam were typical of the dictators receiving U.S. support. Viewing communism as truly wicked, Americans counted all Communist states as uniformly evil. The recognition of differences among Communist states—and the exploitation of these divisions—was therefore difficult. Nationalism as a divisive factor within the Communist world was played down because of the belief that all such states were equally immoral. Above all, every issue of foreign policy tended to be framed as part of a universal struggle between democracy and totalitarianism, freedom and slavery. The expansion of any Communist country's power was viewed in Washington as an expansion of Soviet power, and, since a gain of power and security for the Soviet Union was equated with a loss of power and security for the United States, it is not surprising that the possible loss of Vietnam was viewed in terms of a domino effect. If Vietnam fell, the rest of the dominoes in Southeast Asia were expected to fall, thereby profoundly altering the regional balance of power. That had to be prevented.

This international logic was reinforced by domestic politics as the anti-Communist justification for American foreign policy came back to haunt the policy makers. In Europe, communism was contained, but when Nationalist China collapsed, the Truman administration was attacked as "soft on communism." Indeed, the unquestioned assumption that the United States was omnipotent suggested that the American failure in China had been caused by treason within the U.S. government. If the nation was supposed to be omnipotent, then it could not be lack of strength that accounted for its "defeat."

Such setbacks appeared to have resulted from American policies.

It was argued that China had fallen because the "pro-Communist" administrations of Roosevelt and Truman had either deliberately or unwittingly "sold China down the river." This charge, which came primarily from the strong conservative wing of the Republican party (including Joseph McCarthy and Richard Nixon), was simplicity itself. American policy had ended in Communist control of the mainland. Administration leaders and the State Department were responsible for this policy. The government must therefore be harboring Communists and Communist sympathizers who were "tailoring" American policy to advance the global aims of the Soviet Union.[15] Low morale among the Nationalist Chinese, their administrative and military ineptitude, and repressive policies that had alienated mass support were ignored, as were the superior Communist organization, direction, morale, and ability to identify with popular aspirations. When supposed omnipotence failed, conspiratorial interpretations were the result.[16]

The effects on American foreign policy makers were several. Above all, they wanted to avoid being accused of "having lost" country A or B or of "appeasing communism." The Democrats, accused by the Republicans during the 1952 presidential election (which the Democrats lost) of having lost China, were supersensitive to such charges. The principal result was to make American policy more inflexible and interventionist than it might otherwise have been. This was especially true of policy in Asia where one consequence was the inability of any administration to recognize Communist China and exploit Sino-Soviet differences before Nixon's visit to mainland China in 1972. That visit took place after the Vietnam War had weakened America's anti-Communist consensus, and Nixon, a conservative Republican, who could hardly be accused of being "soft on communism," had been elected.*

The ultimate cost of this crusading policy was not the failure to recognize Communist China or exploit the Sino-Soviet split but the intervention in Vietnam. As the situation in Vietnam worsened in late 1961, it is not surprising that President John Kennedy introduced American military "advisers," particularly after the Bay of Pigs fiasco in Cuba and American inaction at the time of the erection of the Berlin Wall. Kennedy did not want the Democrats accused of being the party that had "lost Indochina," as it had "lost" China.

---

* The irony is that until 1988 it was conservative Republicans, claiming to be strongly anti-Communist, who could be more accommodating in policy toward China and the Soviet Union than liberal Democrats. In 1979, Jimmy Carter could not get the Strategic Arms Limitation Talks (SALT) II agreement through the Senate; in 1988, however, Reagan was able to mobilize support for the Intermediate-range Nuclear Forces (INF) treaty and had he completed the Strategic Arms Reduction Talks (START) agreement, he could have gained support for it as well. In fact, the Soviets let it be known that Gorbachev wanted to sign an agreement on strategic weapons before the end of Reagan's term precisely because Reagan could attract the support needed whereas his successor, especially if he were a liberal Democrat, might fail.

The military advisers temporarily kept the situation in Vietnam from deteriorating. Kennedy's successor, however, had to deal with forestalling a defeat of the South Vietnamese. He intervened with American forces, the logical culmination of his predecessor's actions. From Truman on, each president had done just enough to prevent the loss of South Vietnam.

For each post-World War II president, increasing involvement in Indochina led to a major military intervention calculated as *less costly* than doing nothing and disengaging from Vietnam. In the context of American domestic politics, acquiescence in defeat was unacceptable.[17] The basic rule was "Don't lose Indochina." Each time the American administration came face to face with the possibility of disaster, it escalated the involvement and commitment not to lose Vietnam. Note the negative nature of the goal: to prevent a disaster. It was hoped that if the North Vietnamese found they could not win, they would finally just give up.

Post-Vietnam Withdrawal

The United States, seduced by the "illusion of omnipotence," was reasonably optimistic that it could win in Vietnam. After all, where had American power ever failed? As hostilities in Vietnam dragged on and as American casualties and impatience grew,[18] American domestic politics became divided between those who advocated further escalation in the hope of attaining a clear-cut military victory and those who proposed withdrawal because victory seemed elusive. Indeed, these alternative responses sometimes were put forth by the same people, and President Lyndon Johnson found himself increasingly subject to opposing political pressures. To appease those calling for escalation, mainly conservative and hawkish elements in Congress, he did in fact escalate U.S. involvement. This decision was temporarily popular but backfired when it failed to achieve victory. The other pressure was to withdraw, but to do this was to risk the charge of "appeasement." If he chose the middle course of neither expansion nor retreat, domestic opinion would split further, leaving the center weaker than ever. Whatever he did, the president was trapped, and he could count on little aid from his deeply divided party.

Not only did this all-or-nothing attitude erode Johnson's support, leading him to forgo seeking a second term and producing a Republican victory in the 1968 presidential election, but it also led to widespread American disillusionment with foreign policy and the use of power, especially the use of force. Power politics, it has been suggested, historically has been considered wicked, to be engaged in only by the states of the Old World. American power was supposed to be righteous power. The Vietnam War, watched nightly on television in "living color," seemed to prove only that, in the exercise of power, the nation had forsaken its moral tradition. Driven by anticommunism, which exaggerated the cohesiveness and threat of the Sino-Soviet bloc, tempted to intervene in many places and to make widespread commitments in the name of anticommunism, and aligning itself with many a disreputable reactionary regime in the name of freedom, the United States appeared to have violated its own democratic and liberal principles. This use of power in Vietnam created guilt feelings. Power was viewed as a corrupting factor. It seemed better to concentrate on domestic affairs and to return to a historic duty: to complete the unfinished tasks of American society—that is, create a truly democratic nation in which the gap between aspiration and performance would be minimal and would serve as an example for people everywhere.

Whereas power is viewed as evil and its exercise as tantamount to abuse, providing an example of a just and democratic society to the world is considered the moral thing to do. According to such liberal critics as former senator William Fulbright, chairman of the Senate Foreign Relations Committee until 1974, power had made the United States "arrogant." He counseled that the United States should focus its attention and resources "to serve as an example of democracy to the world" and to "overcome the dangers of the arrogance of power." More specifically, "the nation performs its essential function not in its capacity as a *power* but in its capacity as a *society*." [19] Similarly, Ronald Steel, in appraising *Pax* Americana, said the same thing more eloquently:

> It is now time for us to turn away from global fantasies and begin our perfection of the human race within our own frontiers.... America's worth to the world will be measured not by the solutions she seeks to impose on others, but by the degree to which she achieves her own ideals at home. That is a fitting measure, and an arduous test, of America's greatness.[20]

The optimistic faith that the United States, with its power and missionary zeal, could improve the world was thus replaced by a mood of disillusionment because, in the wake of the Vietnam War, it appeared that the wicked world outside could not be quickly or totally reformed and that the attempt would corrupt the nation. The characteristic swing pattern, which began with an attempt to reform the world, ended with the fear that the nation would forfeit its soul in the effort. Setting an example for the rest of the world, instead of corrupting its own purity with power politics, was said to be the American task.

In this context, foreign policy was replaced by domestic policy, and power by virtue. According to the critics, America's influence was to be derived solely from the United States' moral standing as a good and just society; it was not arms, alliances, and spheres of influence but a redistribution of income, racial justice, environmental concerns—worthy ends in themselves—that counted. In making this shift from military services to social services, the critics were characteristically American in their assessment of foreign policy. They viewed policy in terms of dichotomies: between peace and war, abstention and total commitment, no force and maximum force, and passionate crusading and disillusioned withdrawal.

Détente I and Its Collapse

Because of this mood of isolationism, the détente of the 1970s was largely a tactic. President Richard Nixon and his national security adviser, Henry

Kissinger, recognized two opposing forces.[21] One force was the popular desire to limit American involvement in the world because the country was weary of its cold war role, a weariness reinforced by the shock of OPEC's actions and oil price increases. The country had been shown that it was not militarily invincible; now it was also clear that it was economically vulnerable. The other force was the Soviet Union's achievement of strategic parity with the United States. Moreover, the Soviet Union had considerably upgraded its conventional capabilities, developing a sizable surface fleet plus airlift capability. Czarist and Soviet Russia had always been essentially a Eurasian, or continental, power. Now, for the first time in its history, its capacity to project its conventional power beyond Eurasia had grown. Would the Soviet Union in these new circumstances continue to expand its influence only on land and in territory contiguous to its own? Or would it feel a new confidence and take greater risks, challenging the United States in new areas farther away from the Soviet Union? At the very moment when the United States was experiencing its greatest doubts about its own international role and seeing its strategic superiority which had helped it to "contain" the Soviet Union erode, the question became how could the United States contain the Soviet Union now? How could it be induced to follow a path of self-restraint? Were there nonmilitary levers to supplement, or even to replace, the military one? [22]

The Republican administration found the levers in exploiting the Sino-Soviet schism and enticing Moscow with trade and technology. Détente then was not so much a rejection of the cold war but a continuation of it by other means until the pendulum would swing back and the United States could once more assert its power internationally. The Soviets too had their tactical reasons for pursuing détente. Perhaps the chief one was economic. The Soviet Union's agricultural and industrial problems predated Gorbachev, but General Secretary Leonid Brezhnev was unwilling to risk *glasnost* and *perestroika* to reinvigorate the economy. The possible consequences in terms of domestic upheaval and the security of the Communist party's monopoly of power were too frightful. Brezhnev therefore wanted to import Western food, industrial plants, and modern technology rather than risk the structure of Soviet power. To gain time and credit, he needed a period of relaxation internationally. The Soviet desire to slow down the Sino-American reconciliation and realignment, to legitimate the postwar European status quo, and to obtain arms control agreements reinforced the need for détente.

Détente I was undermined when the Soviets also sought to exploit the resulting relaxation of tensions. Not that the United States did not seek to make some unilateral gains itself, but Moscow, which replaced virtually all of its strategic missiles *after* SALT I in 1972 as it continued its massive nuclear and conventional military buildup, undertook expansionist efforts that were more sustained and deliberate. Moscow believed the 1970s to be a period of shift in the global balance of power from the United States to the Soviet Union. Therefore, it was disposed to exploit this situation. It also saw a new radicalism rising in the Third World, and it hoped to attract new and reliable

Marxist allies for the Soviet Union as former colonial states were detached from the imperialist camp. American reaction would be deterred by the Soviet attainment of nuclear parity. The United States, it believed, would have no choice but to face this "new reality" and accept these changes in alignment, whether it liked them or not.

> The international order was now viewed as being conducive to a pro-Soviet bandwagon, in which Soviet gains could cumulate rapidly. . . . [T]he Soviet leaders went through a period of high expectations about their ability to gain the advantages from détente, including the avoidance of confrontation, without sacrificing their commitments to exploit the rapidly growing opportunities for competitive gains in the Third World.[23]

By 1979—the year of the Soviet invasion of Afghanistan, the collapse of Gen. Anastasio Somoza Debayle in Nicaragua and his replacement by the pro-Soviet Marxist Sandinistas, and the fall of the shah in Iran and the emergence of a militant Islamic anti-American regime—détente had collapsed.

The failure of détente I also spelled the end for Democratic president Jimmy Carter, who in 1976 defeated incumbent president Gerald Ford (successor to Richard Nixon, after he had resigned his office in the wake of the Watergate scandal). The Carter administration had reflected the nation's mood of withdrawal and guilt about the misuses of American power. Until the Soviet invasion of Afghanistan, it had rejected power politics. Had not this approach been responsible for America's involvement in Vietnam? The Carter administration therefore de-emphasized the East-West struggle and focused its attention on the Third World and the problems of nationalism, self-determination, racial equality, human rights, and poverty. Balance-of-power politics was being transformed into "world order" politics. In the dawning new age of interdependence among states, security as the primary issue was being replaced by a concern with welfare, the hierarchy of nations by greater equality, and the use of force by more peaceful cooperation among states to advance the greater good of all nations, with special emphasis on human welfare and individual dignity. Presumably, the wicked days of power politics were over. A more peaceful and just world was within grasp.

Humiliation and the Reassertion of U.S. Power

In late 1979, the Iranian seizure of American diplomatic personnel in Tehran as hostages sharply shifted the nation's mood again. The 444 days that the hostages were held were considered a national humiliation. One month after the attack on the embassy, the Soviets invaded Afghanistan, and again the United States felt helpless. It was not just that the other superpower felt it could act without considering U.S. reactions; even a middle-range power such as Iran, in the midst of revolutionary turmoil, thought it could act against American interests with impunity.

All nations could see that in the wake of Vietnam the United States was determined to play a lesser role in the world. Congressional restraints on the president's ability to use the armed forces and Central Intelligence Agency for overt and covert intervention raised questions about America's will and capability to act. As a further demonstration, defense budgets plummeted from 8.2 percent of the gross national product in fiscal 1970 to 5.2 percent in fiscal 1977, the lowest figures since before the Korean War. With the Soviets spending what at the time was estimated to be 15 percent of GNP on defense (but, in fact, this figure turned out to be 25 percent), this meant that the 1970s witnessed the largest reduction in American military strength relative to that of the Soviet Union of the entire postwar period.[24] Large defense requests citing the continual and enormous growth of Soviet military strength were dismissed by Congress as a "Pentagon scare tactic" in the annual budget fight. When the sharp increases in Soviet missiles were noted, the response was that the Soviets were just "catching up." When they caught up, the reaction was that now they would stop. When they did not stop, the excuse was that the Soviets, after all, confronted not only the United States and NATO but China as well. And as Soviet military power continued to grow steadily year after year, it was pointed out that the Soviets suffered from paranoia because of past invasions. Finally, as Soviet strength in strategic and conventional weapons grew beyond any conceivable defense needs—as Washington saw it—the ultimate excuse was that force no longer played a role in the post-Vietnam War world. The Soviets were wasting their money, and apparently they were too stupid to realize that the forces they were buying were no longer useful. In this political atmosphere, is it really surprising that the multiple indications of American impotence led to the humiliation at Tehran? Or that this slap in the face would once more arouse the nation to reassert itself?

President Carter's reaction to Afghanistan was twofold: the Carter Doctrine, committing the United States to the defense of the Persian Gulf oil kingdoms, and the imposition of economic sanctions on the Soviet Union. But despite Carter's belated recognition of the Soviet threat and the fact that power politics was not quite dead, Ronald Reagan, the former governor of California, was the beneficiary of this change of public mood. Why reelect Carter, the belated convert to the "hard line," when Reagan had been the genuine hard-liner all along? The pendulum had swung at least part of the way back to involvement and the reassertion of American interests and power in the world.

In 1980, President Reagan refocused the nation's attention on the Soviet Union, the East-West struggle, and the central issue of American security. He sought support for his reapplication of the classical containment policy in characteristic American style by depicting the East-West struggle as a moral conflict. According to Reagan, the Soviet Union was "the focus of evil in the modern world." And he told a Baptist convention, "There is sin and evil in the world and we're enjoined by Scripture and the Lord Jesus to oppose it with all our might."[25] Reagan also stimulated and exploited a renewed pride in the nation and frequently praised the military and its service to the country.

The Reagan administration's policies were intended to exact a cost for the Soviet Union's military buildup and expansionist activities in the Third World. They did so in three ways.[26] The first was by increasing America's military power, which was expected to create incentives for the Soviets to negotiate. The proposed strategic modernization program was intended to devalue the intercontinental ballistic missiles (ICBMs) on which the Soviets had spent so much for so long; the MX and Trident II missiles and the B-1 bomber, to be followed by the Stealth B-2, were all counterforce weapons. The Strategic Defense Initiative (SDI) to be developed and deployed for defensive purposes only, according to President Reagan, was seen in Moscow as fitting within a broader offensive, preemptive counterforce strategy whose purpose was seen as "prevailing" in a nuclear war. Unable to defend the United States from a full-scale Soviet nuclear attack, SDI would be able to protect the country against a retaliatory Soviet strike crippled by an initial American disarming attack. In addition, the American intermediate-range nuclear forces (INF), deployed to counter the large-scale Soviet deployment of modern intermediate-range ballistic missiles, threatened Soviet territory from Western Europe. The Soviet Union was therefore confronted not only with greater military vulnerability and insecurity but also with a high tech arms race it could not afford at a time when huge capital investments were needed at home.

Second, the Reagan administration also bargained very hard by appearing uninterested in arms control negotiations. Indeed, it initially blamed arms control for what it considered to be America's weakened military position. The arms control positions it advanced were strictly propagandistic, intended to ward off public pressures. But when in its second term the administration did begin to negotiate seriously, it "hung tough," insisting on deep cuts in, not upper limits to, the weapons to be deployed. The proposed cuts, moreover, were not to be even. Since the Soviets had more weapons, the administration insisted on asymmetric Soviet reduction, far greater than any of its predecessors had demanded, and on verification procedures for arms agreements far more intrusive than those the Soviets had in the past consistently rejected. But with a collapsing economy, the Soviets could not afford to do so any longer. Gorbachev needed to pursue arms control agreements involving not only INF but also—and more important—strategic arms reductions and conventional arms reductions in Europe.

Third, the administration aimed to undo the results of Soviet expansion during the 1970s in Afghanistan (where Carter had begun helping the resistance), Angola, Nicaragua, and Cambodia. All four had become Marxist states, but all faced resistance movements. Assuming that the Soviets had overextended themselves, that the balance of power was shifting back to the United States, that the Soviet Union had critical domestic problems (even before Gorbachev acknowledged this fact), and that except in Afghanistan only peripheral Soviet interests were involved, the Reagan administration believed that Moscow would not risk a confrontation with the United States. In Afghanistan, American military supplies allowed the resistance to the Soviet armed forces to survive until Moscow, tiring after eight and a half years of war, decided to withdraw. In Angola, fighting and negotiations continued until 1988 when a settlement was reached. In Nicaragua, the administration failed because the American-supported contras failed to win a popular base in the country and the Congress and public opinion, fearing another Vietnam, opposed the "covert" war the United States was waging to overthrow the Sandinista government.* In Cambodia, the Soviet-supported Vietnamese, tired of never-ending fighting, agreed to withdraw as well. The imperial outposts that had looked so promising only ten years earlier had lost their luster, and sustaining proxies like the Cubans and Vietnamese was too expensive. Gorbachev had no choice but to recognize what Marxists have always prided themselves on recognizing: objective reality. With a structurally unsound economy, surrounded by a Western coalition of NATO, Japan, and China, driven together by the Soviet Union's expansionist foreign policy, Gorbachev was compelled to recognize the need for rapprochement with the United States.

It is ironic that by the end of his second term President Reagan had forged a new détente with the Soviet Union, retracted his statements about the "evil empire," and embraced Gorbachev's efforts to reform the Soviet Union. The administration had in 1987 negotiated an Intermediate-range Nuclear Forces treaty which abolished this entire class of missiles, and the two powers had made significant progress on a strategic arms agreement that would radically cut such offensive weapons. The Reagan administration's achievements in arms control were substantial, in part because of its negotiating tactics, in part because of the need of the Soviet Union to slow down the arms race, and in part because SDI proved to be an especially potent bargaining chip at a time when Moscow wanted to avoid a costly arms race. Although Reagan had been accused of stirring up a new cold war during his first years in office, he and Gorbachev had in fact inaugurated détente II. A new era of Soviet-American relations had begun. Détente I in the 1970s had been the product of Vietnam and America's loss of will to continue its containment policy. Détente II was the result of Soviet weaknesses, especially internally, at a time of a revival of American pride and military strength.

---

* But in 1990, under pressure from the Central American presidents and Gorbachev to hold free elections, the Sandinistas, believing they could control the election, legitimate themselves, and deprive the contras of any further U.S. support, risked an election and were voted out of office by a public fed up with the war, inflation, and arbitrary Sandinista rule.

SOVIET ELITE STYLE

The Communist 'Ruling Class'

Because foreign policy decisions are made not by nations but by a few decision makers, some analysts have suggested that perhaps the styles or operational codes of the political elite, the small group that makes policy, may be more useful analytically. The United States frequently has been called a one-class society; the basic values of American society have been essentially those of the liberal middle class. For this country, it can be argued, the policy elite and the masses share a fundamental set of beliefs, values, and attitudes: democratic liberalism. In other countries, where class differences are more obvious and the political elites are clearly separated from the mass of the population, the beliefs and values of the elites are usually easily identifiable. Even in such countries as the Soviet Union, which reject class distinctions and claim to be classless societies, the political elites are much more visible and far fewer in number than in Western societies, even those with clear-cut class structures. In the Soviet Union, the Communist party had, until Gorbachev monopolized all power, controlled both the government and the economy. This control made it the privileged "Soviet ruling class" or *nomenklatura* (this name derives from the secret system by which the party controlled all appointments to political, administrative, military, police, and other jobs that it thought to be politically sensitive). The party admitted and promoted within its ruling class, which theoretically did not exist. The *nomenklatura* was estimated at about 750,000 or, with families, approximately 3 million or just over 1 percent of the population. But those who were its highest members and who ran the party and state in Moscow and the provinces numbered about 100,000. Powerful and privileged, they lived in exclusive apartments, shopped at special stores, went to vacation resorts reserved for them, and had their own medical clinics and doctors. Their wealth came from the possession of power, in stark contrast to the widespread Western pattern in which power stemmed from the accumulation of wealth. This top elite of the Communist class, who also were called "partocrats," [27] had an obvious interest in preserving the status quo and resisting any changes that threatened its status, power, and privileges. For that reason, they launched a coup against Gorbachev in August 1991.

Ideology, Perception, and 'Operational Code'

In what ways did Soviet ideology affect the various elites in the party, military, secret police, and economic ministries, all members of the *nomenklatura*, before Gorbachev (and, as the 1991 coup attempt showed, even during Gorbachev's tenure)? In a specific situation, they certainly did not rush to the Kremlin library and search for guidance in the works of Marx and Lenin. There was no one-to-one relationship between ideology and policy. Indeed, from a practical point of view the ideology appeared largely irrelevant. Policy makers act in terms of threats to their security, opportunities for enhancing their influence, domestic politics, and other conditions. But the ideology was not irrelevant in the sense that it provided the Soviet leadership with a way of perceiving and interpreting "reality"—with *their* model of the world.* Ideology in this context is what earlier was called an analytical framework that "organized reality" for its devotees. It is through ideological lenses that policy makers selectively perceive the world and understand it, define the "national interest," and decide how to act.[28] Alexander George, a political scientist, has referred to this general Marxist-Leninist orientation to the world as an "operational code."[29] At its core are certain questions about political life: What is the "essential" nature of politics? Is it basically one of harmony or conflict? What is the fundamental character of one's opponents? What are the prospects for victory and should one be optimistic or pessimistic? How much control does one have over historical development, and how can one move it in the desired direction? What is the role of "chance"? And what are the best tactics to most effectively achieve one's goals? It is the answers to these questions that constitute the operational code, and it is the resulting set of attitudes toward international politics that all Soviet leaders shared.

Briefly, the basic tenets of Marxism-Leninism are:[30]

- Economic forces are fundamental. The organization of the production and the distribution of wealth is the foundation, or substructure, on which society is built.
- The capitalist superstructure consists of (1) the owners of the means of production and wealth, and (2) those who work for them and are exploited by them. Class relations are based essentially on opposing interests and conflict. According to Marx, all history is the history of class struggle between the rich and the poor—between the slave owners and the slaves, the feudal, land-owning nobility and the peasantry, the capitalist owners of industry (the bourgeoisie) and the working class (the proletariat).

---

* Ideology here is analyzed differently than at the first level where it was viewed merely as justification for what leaders believe they must do to preserve and enhance their security interests in the state system. Ideology is an instrument for rationalizing what would have been done anyway. Ideology, therefore, is not a motivating force. All leaders, including Soviet leaders, think in terms of "national interest"; it is this interest that motivates the behavior of nation-states. Ideology did not lead the Soviets to adopt any policy that the Soviet national interest did not demand. It was merely a means of promoting that interest. The manipulation of ideology to justify any and every change of foreign and domestic policy only "proves" that it is too flexible to be a guide to action. See Samuel L. Sharp, "National Interest: Key to Soviet Politics," in *The Conduct of Soviet Foreign Policy*, ed. Erik P. Hoffmann and Frederic J. Fleron, Jr. (Chicago: Aldine-Atherton, 1971), 108-117.

- The capitalist political system, like the class structure, reflects the nature of the economic system. The owners of wealth control the state and use its instruments—the army, the police, and other levers of government power—to keep control. They also can manipulate other means of control, such as the legal and educational systems and religion, to maintain their power.
- This type of system cannot be reformed. Superficial, or cosmetic, changes may be attempted in order to "buy off" the underprivileged and the exploited, but they cannot save the system. Contemporary capitalism is based on private property and the profit motive. Their abolition is the prerequisite for the productive use of industry for the benefit of the many instead of the luxury of the few. But the nature of capitalism cannot be changed; attempts to create a socialist society will be resisted.
- The injustices of capitalism will come to an end, however, with the proletarian revolution. This revolution will occur when the proletariat has become the majority and is politically conscious of its own exploitation. This day of reckoning is historically inevitable.
- Lenin explained the failure of this "inevitable" revolution to occur in the Western industrial countries by imperialism and the massive capitalist exploitation of non-Western, or colonial, peoples. This global exploitation was so profitable that some of the profits trickled down to the industrial proletariat so that its standard of living was improved, its revolutionary consciousness eroded, and its vested interest in capitalism strengthened. Domestic revolution was thus avoided by means of a policy of imperialism.
- The Marxist class struggle within the capitalist states was projected onto the global plane. The rich are now defined as the Western industrial states, the poor and exploited as the developing countries. This worldwide class struggle has become the critical conflict in the world.
- Only when the industrial states lose the cheap raw materials previously provided by the developing countries and the economic growth rate slows, so that unemployment increases and the standard of living declines, will the domestic proletariat again recognize that its interests clash with those of the bourgeoisie. Then the class conflict will resume and will end in the proletarian revolution.

What is striking, and what shall be emphasized below, is that this ideology was fully compatible with—indeed, reinforced—the realist perspective of leaders of states socialized by the state system. The Communist emphasis was on conflict and change; all political relationships were viewed in terms of struggle, including war. Specifically, the general ideological outlook, with its total critique of capitalist society and way of analyzing the world, defined the foe for Soviet leaders in the past, the ultimate aim, and a commitment to help history along to its predestined end. By positing the Soviet relationship with capitalist states as one of enmity and continual struggle and by attributing to the latter hostile intentions, Moscow's sense of insecurity was heightened even beyond traditional concerns; the external world was always viewed as unremittingly threatening. The resulting determination to rely mainly on oneself, not allies, to be strong, especially militarily; to not relax one's guard; and to distrust the enemy's professions of peaceful intent—all these are attitudes hardly unknown in the realist's world.

Definition of the Enemy and Revolutionary Aims

However weakened the hold of Marxist-Leninist ideology on Soviet leaders before German unification, it did in the past provide them with a set of core beliefs and attitudes that profoundly influenced their views of the state system; the nature of politics, including international politics; and who their enemies were. Most of all, it defined their principal enemy and the historically appointed task of helping to bring about the new, postcapitalist order. But this ideology did not merely embody a critique of contemporary capitalist society; it also projected communism as the desired state of existence for humanity.

Domestic justice and international peace could be realized only if the old capitalist order were swept away throughout the entire state system; all people were to be liberated from the social tyranny of capitalism and the scourge of war. After 1917, this purpose transformed Russia, a traditional great power, into *Soviet* Russia, a revolutionary state, committed to the secular mission of eliminating world capitalism. Soviet leaders historically denied the legitimacy of what they regarded as the prevailing international capitalistic order. Their ideology was thus contrary to the basic assumption of the balance of power: that each state has the right to exist, regardless of its domestic structure. The balance is supposed to protect all members of the state system. But the revolutionary state is revolutionary just because it *claims universal applicability for its values and ways of organizing domestic society and makes the domestic structures of all other states the central issue of international politics.*

No state in a pluralistic system can feel absolutely secure; yet each, though greatly concerned with its security, normally does not feel *so* insecure that it seeks universal domination to eliminate threats from all other states. It seeks security within a balance-of-power system that provides for its survival, as well as for the survival of other states. Conflicts are therefore *limited* and *pragmatic;* no state seeks another's elimination. Each recognizes the right of the others to exist. Communist ideology, by repudiating the legitimacy of capitalist states, however, transformed the international struggle between the revolutionary power and its adversaries into a *total* and *ideological* conflict. If one state felt compelled to destroy the domestic structures of other states and to transform them according to its own ideological values, that state had to seek dominance or hegemony so that it could impose its will on them.

George Kennan described how this revolutionary approach to foreign policy made a "mockery of the entire Western theory of international relationships, as it evolved in the period from the seventeenth to the nineteenth centuries."[31] He went on to say,

> The national state of modern Europe, bitterly as it might feud with its neighbors over the questions of *relative* advantage, was distinguished from the older forms of state power by its abandonment of universalistic and messianic pretensions, by its general readiness to recognize the equality of existence of other sovereign authorities, to accept their legitimacy and independence, and to concede the principle of live and let live as a basic rule in the determination of international relationships....
>
> It was this theory that the Bolsheviki challenged on their assumption of power in Russia. They challenged it by the universality of their own ideological pretensions—by the claim, that is, to an unlimited universal validity of their own ideas as to how society ought to be socially and politically organized. They challenged it by their insistence that the laws governing the operation of human society demanded the violent overthrow everywhere of governments which did not accept the ideological tenets of Russian Communism, and the replacement of these governments by one that did....
>
> There were, in those initial years of Soviet power, some very significant differences between anti-Sovietism in the West and the hostility which the Soviet leaders entertained for the Western powers. This hostility from the Communist side is preconceived, ideological, deductive. In the minds of the Soviet leaders, it long predated the Communist seizure of power in Russia. Anti-Sovietism in the West, on the other hand, was largely a confused, astonished, and indignant reaction to the first acts of the Soviet regime. Many people in the Western governments came to hate the Soviet leaders for what they *did*. The Communists, on the other hand, hated the Western governments for what they *were*, regardless of what they did. They entertained this feeling long before there was even any socialistic state for the capitalists to do anything to. Their hatred did not vary according to the complexion or policies or actions of the individual noncommunist governments. It never has....
>
> Had the Soviet leaders contented themselves from the outset with saying that they felt that they knew what was good for Russia, and refrained from taking positions on what was good for other countries, Western hostility to the Soviet Union would never have been what it has been. The issue has never been ... the right of the Russian people to have a socialistic ordering of society if they so wish; the issue is how a government which happens to be socialistic is going to behave in relation to its world environment.[32]

The upshot of this new long-range mission that Soviet rulers assumed after 1917 was to reinforce historic Russian expansionism. Russian leaders had a right to feel insecure, given the frequency of invasions; the Soviet leaders' insecurity was even greater, given their ideological perception of the outside world as hostile. Indeed, this perception was so strong that they maintained a "garrison state" at home. No doubt, Soviet leaders also found the enmity of the capitalist world a convenient rationalization for preserving a totalitarian state and legitimizing their monopoly of political power. But their perception of states beyond their borders, especially in Europe, as bourgeois and dangerous, on top of a sense of historic vulnerability, appeared to them to demand constant vigilance and central control to deal with their enemies, whom they saw everywhere, abroad and at home. Even if offensive reasons for expansion are ignored, the unique combination of the Soviet Union's great, almost paranoid, insecurity and its great power, the result of its sizable population, rich resources, and large industrial base, led to a policy of constantly seeking to enhance Soviet influence in order to maximize Soviet security.[33] But this search for virtually absolute security came, as Brzezinski suggested earlier, at the price of the insecurity of other nations, and as the latter took measures to increase their security, the cycle began again.

Commitment to Struggle and Caution

Indeed, once Marxism-Leninism had committed the Soviet leadership after 1917 to elimination of the old order, the conflict between the Soviet Union and the Western industrial states, all of which were regarded as capitalist, became total and irreconcilable. For Marx, the basic "fact" of history was the condition of unending conflict between classes; for Lenin, it was the struggle between states controlled by antagonistic classes. For the Soviets then, politics was not a means of ultimate reconciliation. It was instead a bitter and unending series of campaigns to defeat the capitalist enemy. The only question was *kto, kovo?* (Who, whom?—meaning "Who will destroy whom?"), though history had already predicted the outcome.[34] Between adversaries, agreements can be only temporary, each only a tactical move in the struggle.

This struggle had to be prosecuted with persistence; to end this historically ordained struggle would have been tantamount to betrayal of the revolutionary mission. Victory over capitalism was the *raison d'être* of the movement. But while the goal was constant, the tactics were flexible. Opportunities for advancement of Soviet power were not to be forgone, but they were to be pursued only after the most careful calculation of the possible benefits versus the likely risks and costs. Soviet doctrine rejected adventurism, and it counseled knowing when to stop pushing to expand and even to retreat before superior power. There was no special emphasis in Communist doctrine on the use of force, as there was in Nazi doctrine.[35]

Soviet doctrine also accepted the tactical need for periods of relaxation of tensions or détentes to recoup strength for the next phase of the struggle. It also accepted negotiations and agreements such as arms control accords to prevent a suicidal nuclear war (see Chapter 13), as well as measures to advance the purposes of the Soviet state in some other ways such as attracting Western trade, technology, and credits to help modernize the economy. This did not mean, however, that the struggle against capitalism was abandoned. Indeed, rather than postponing it, such agreements may have served to further it if, for example, they defused the enemy image, drove a wedge between members of the opposing coalition (such as between Europeans and Americans), or relaxed the enemy's guard by feeding its hopes that the conflict was over.

Soviet doctrine was therefore very cautious.[36] Force was used only where vital interests were at issue, Soviet intervention promised a quick solution at moderate costs, and the United States was unlikely to intervene. Even in Hungary in 1956 and Czechoslovakia in 1968, Soviet intervention was hesitant despite the obviously critical importance of preventing defections from the Warsaw Treaty Organization. They intervened neither in Yugoslavia when Stalin threw it out of the Soviet bloc in 1948, nor later in Romania when it showed independence in foreign policy, nor in China when relations tensed in the late 1960s, nor in Poland, where the regime's authority was being undermined in 1980-1981. All these states were close to or bordered on the Soviet Union. Only in Afghanistan did Moscow make a miscalculation. Soviet behavior clearly reflected the memory of the awful losses and destruction of World War II and a keen awareness of the catastrophic impact a nuclear war would have. Although the Soviet Union used force only against its allies and friends, it was nevertheless repeatedly willing to challenge and test American commitments and resolve. But while willing to raise tensions, it always very carefully and unfailingly left itself an escape route if the United States and the West reacted firmly; if not, it took another step forward.

According to the Soviet viewpoint, at least before Mikhail Gorbachev in 1985, good will was a quality absent from such an adversary relationship. Capitalist states did not possess decent intentions; by nature, their motives were hostile. Western conciliatory gestures and peaceful professions were dismissed as either hypocritical or propagandistic. When Western states signed arms control agreements, it was not because they sought genuine mutual accommodation but because they recognized the superiority of Soviet power and had no choice but to be compromising. Thus, Western acts of moderation and expressions for a better relationship provided Moscow with a rationale for further arms buildups and continued pressure; the more arms, the more accommodating the West would be. In over thirty years, Kennan once wrote, he had never known a single instance of a non-Communist government being credited with a "single generous or worthy impulse." [37] All actions responsive to Soviet interests were attributed to "bowing to necessity," yielding to "outraged opinion," or some ulterior motive.

The Soviet Style, World War II, and the Beginning of the Cold War

Not surprisingly then, the ideological perceptions of Soviet leaders enhanced the regime's insecurity and reinforced the traditional Russian approach to international politics. That approach consisted of relying on oneself, not allies or professions of peaceful intent from potential adversaries; of regarding the outside world with deep suspicion, if not hostility; and of always being strong militarily to defend oneself and not relaxing one's vigilance. In the constant struggle of international politics, one result of these attitudes was deepening suspicion and fear among the states coexisting with the Soviet Union. Perhaps the most significant characteristic of Soviet leaders' thinking was their insistence on their superior insight into history. They claimed that Marxism-Leninism had given them a greater ability to understand political events as a manifestation of an objective underlying reality defined by basic economic and social structures. Thus, Soviet leaders convinced that they had an unsurpassed theoretical comprehension of the past, present, and future, were bound to see the international environment as extremely hostile and to regard with deep distrust any Western state, however benevolent its expressed intentions or conciliatory its approach. Indeed, since the Soviet Union assumed that the Western states were out to destroy it—as it had been bent on destroying the Western states—the Soviets' attitude toward what they regarded as a capitalist-dominated system bordered on paranoia.

Consequently, it was immaterial during World War II whether Stalin personally liked Roosevelt. Roosevelt's expressions of hope for peace and cooperation after the defeat of Germany were dismissed as "sentimental gestures" not reflecting "reality." Stalin *knew* that the deeper objective forces of the economic substructure, on which the prevailing social and political superstructure rested, would determine Roosevelt's actions. In his view, the American president was merely a puppet—though perhaps a likable puppet—of Wall Street interests. Governmental decisions simply reflected the law of capitalism. How could anyone have persuaded Stalin otherwise, when he, like all other Soviet leaders, was absolutely convinced of his deeper insight into history, arising from his Marxist-Leninist training?

This suspicion of capitalist states was constant after 1917.[38] When any state defines another as an enemy long enough and acts on that assumption, it will come to see confirmation for its suspicions in the reaction of the other state, whether that reaction is firm or conciliatory. For example, the intervention by Russia's former World War I allies after the Bolshevik capture of power in 1917 was seen as an attempt to restore the czar and the old order. The French attempt to contain Germany between the two world wars by means of an alliance with Poland and several other eastern European countries was viewed as an effort to keep the Soviets out of Europe. The appeasement of Hitler was perceived as a move to turn Nazi Germany away from an attack on the Western states to an attack on the Soviet Union. Appeasement "opened the gates to the East." During World War II, from 1941 to 1945, Moscow viewed the United States only as a temporary ally. Once Germany had been defeated, the United States, the strongest Western capitalist power, would become the Soviet Union's principal enemy in the continuing struggle against capitalism.

Ironically, given Stalin's expectations, the war years had created a great reservoir of good will toward the Soviet Union in the United States and in Western Europe. The Soviet Union had borne the brunt of the German armies, and the heroism of the Red Army and the Soviet people was acclaimed everywhere. Stalin, the dictator who had collaborated with Hitler in 1939-1941, became "Uncle Joe." In the United States and Britain, hopes for the postwar period were high. By and large, the Soviet Union was described in glowing terms—virtually as a democracy—just as it was later depicted in almost satanic terms. Concerned as the Soviet Union was about its security in Eastern Europe, in this atmosphere it should have been easily reassured.

Had the Soviet Union left Bulgaria, Hungary, Poland, and Romania to govern themselves domestically while securing control of their foreign policies, as it did in postwar Czechoslovakia, it could have avoided arousing and alienating the United States and Britain. The Western states accepted the Soviet contention that Eastern Europe was the Soviet Union's security belt, but they argued that freely elected coalition governments that included Communists could be friendly to both the Soviets *and* the West. President Eduard Benes of Czechoslovakia seemed a symbol of this model for Eastern Europe, for the Czech Communists had, in a free election, won a plurality of the vote and were therefore the dominant partner in the coalition government. But even that kind of coexistence was unacceptable to the Soviet Union. Non-Communist parties by nature were regarded as anti-Communist because they allegedly represented class enemies. They thus had to be eliminated from the Czech government, as they already had been in the rest of Eastern Europe. The Soviets overthrew the coalition government in Prague.

It may be that Soviet expansionist policy in the wake of the retreating German allies can be explained in terms of state-system behavior. Russian leaders long ago had been socialized by this system and it can hardly be doubted that this traditional power politics outlook was intensified greatly by later Soviet leaders' ideological perceptions. Since Stalin was suspicious of the capitalist states' professions of peace and friendship as tricks to deceive the Soviet Union and lower its guard and because he could not believe that President Roosevelt's statements of good intentions and good will were not genuine, he could not abstain from exploiting weaknesses to the south and west of the Soviet Union in an effort to extend socialism to a larger area. The relative security that the Soviet leader could have gained for his country by acting more cautiously was squandered because of his ideological thinking and behavior. This aroused British and then American opposition.

Effects of Ideology on Communist State Relationships

Communist ideology not only intensified the suspicions that already existed in the state system, helping to break up the Soviet Union's alliance with the Western states and precipitating conflict with them, but also impeded the formation of smoothly working alliances with other Communist states. The Soviet Union's suspicions of other Communist states were revealed when, right after the war, Stalin expelled Yugoslavia's Marshal Tito—a loyal Stalinist until then—from the Soviet bloc. Soviet suspicion was revealed even more dramatically in the Soviet Union's relationship with Communist China; it simply proved impossible for these two giants of the Communist world to maintain a long-term, mutually beneficial alliance. Conflicts among Communist nations—all of which professed to be classless societies—were supposed to be nonexistent, for antagonism among states was ostensibly the result of the competing interests of their dominant classes. But, in fact, the Soviet Union was no longer the only powerful Communist state, and its monopoly of "truth"—that is, its total control of decision making—was being challenged.

In part, Kremlin leaders had only themselves to blame for this undermining of their authority. One of the functions of Communist ideology was to legitimate those who held authority. Communist ideology, therefore, was designed to legitimate Soviet leaders both as rulers of the Soviet Union and—when the Soviet Union was the only socialist state—as directors of the international Communist movement. Just as there can be only one pope, there can be only one source of ideological pronouncements in a secular movement like communism. Moscow was this infallible source. But Beijing's leaders challenged this authority and the Soviet monopoly of political wisdom. In the resulting interparty conflict, each contender claimed the correct interpretation of history and the true interpretation of party theology. Within years of Stalin's death, each country was denouncing the other for heresy. Claiming to be fundamentalists, the Chinese saw themselves as remaining true to Marxism-Leninism, which they believed the Soviets had betrayed. Moscow, the Communist Rome, and Nikita Khrushchev, the new Communist pope (and later Leonid Brezhnev), were thus challenged by Mao Zedong's Eastern orthodox church.

Compromise on common policies between the *Communist* Soviet Union and *Communist* China was to pose an insuperable obstacle. In matters of doctrine, when the purity of ideology is at stake, does not a policy of give-and-take represent contamination? How can mutual adjustments be made between two members of a movement in which differences of emphasis become issues of loyalty to the faith? How could the primacy, infallibility, and doctrinal purity of the Kremlin leaders be reconciled with Chinese claims to an equal voice, Maoist infallibility, and ideological fundamentalism? The Western allies, themselves pluralistic societies, could cope with pluralism and diversity. Communist states could not, for their parties imposed uniform domestic patterns in accordance with their ideological interpretations. Each was a totalitarian society precisely because the Communist party claimed to be the bearer of revealed "truth," which must be imposed on society. Heresy had to be ruthlessly eliminated. How then could two such states, each convinced that its interpretation of the truth was the only correct one, coexist? With ideology so intimately linked with power, as it was in Communist policy and decision making, there could be only one "correct" answer.

The resulting bitterness between Soviet and Chinese leaders over who was orthodox and who was heretical led to decades of extreme and vitriolic denunciations, worse than those each had ever aimed toward the United States. Compromise was blocked by the insistence on doctrinal purity. A "correct" answer demanded a single center of political authority and ideological orthodoxy. *Any relationship between Communist states, therefore, had to be hierarchical in nature; it could not have been one of equality.* Either Moscow or

Beijing had to be the center of Communist theological interpretation *and* the source of policy for most, if not all, issues. Thus, it was not wholly surprising that the Sino-Soviet break occurred after the border clashes in 1969; nor was it surprising that Chinese fears of Soviet intervention led Beijing to look to Washington for protection and brought about a Sino-U.S. coalition and the encirclement of the Soviet Union.

CONTINUITY AND CHANGE IN STYLES

Continuity: Détente in the 1970s

The above analyses of American and Soviet styles reveal how little their fundamental outlooks changed from 1917 until the closing years of the cold war. Nowhere was this more visible than in the collapse of détente in the 1970s.[39] Basically, the cause of this collapse was less a question of personalities or individual policies than of the sharply contrasting styles and perceptions of the two superpowers.

American Search for an End to Conflict

In their perception of the nature of politics—especially their image of conflict—Americans historically have emphasized an international harmony of interests, which has stood in stark contrast to the emphasis in the state system on the inevitability of conflict and differences of interest among states. Moreover, Americans have viewed conflict as an abnormal condition, whereas the Soviets viewed harmony as an illusion. Before World War I, the United States, long isolated from Europe and therefore not socialized in the state system, did not accept the reality and permanence of conflicts among members of that system. Differences between states were not considered natural and certainly not deep or long-lasting. Instead, they were attributed to wicked leaders (who could be eliminated), authoritarian political systems (which could be reformed), and misunderstandings (which could be straightened out if the adversaries approached each other with sincerity and empathy). Once these obstacles had been removed, peace, harmony, and good will would reign supreme.

Thus, every change of Soviet leadership during the cold war years aroused hopes in the United States for an end to the cold war. Perhaps, it was said, a more moderate leader would succeed, a more peaceful man. Terms such as *liberal* and *dove* were used frequently, in contrast to *conservative* and *hard-liner*. Or, it was believed, the Soviet system would be transformed from within. Again and again, the Soviet Union was expected to behave with restraint either because it needed Western economic assistance (right after World War II and again during the détente of the 1970s), or because its own industrialization would make the totalitarian regime superfluous, or because Soviet leaders, to satisfy their people's hunger for a higher standard of living, would have to shift resources from the military sector to investment in consumer goods.

If evil men were not replaced or evil systems were not fundamentally changed, there was always the hope that any "misunderstandings" that might have given rise to the superpower struggle would be corrected, especially at summit conferences. There American leaders could prove to their Soviet counterparts that they were sincere when they talked of peace and demonstrated their good will. The goal was to reduce Soviet leaders' suspicions of American intentions and, if possible, win their friendship. If the leaders could just talk to each other face to face and realize that none of them were devils with horns but just ordinary mortals, they could more easily see each other's points of view and, given good will, resolve their differences. The problem, then, appeared merely to be Soviet misperception of American leaders' desires for peace. Conflict could be resolved by correcting this misperception. In this way, the search for a cooperative, stable relationship with the Soviet Union could go on, regardless of past disappointments. An adversary relationship remained unacceptable to Americans; conflict and war were signs of failure.

Thus, it was hardly surprising that the United States became disenchanted so frequently, as it did with détente shortly after it was launched in the early 1970s. If the cold war was over, peace and a moderation of conflict should have been the consequence. "Negotiations rather than confrontations" were to be the rule. But Soviet activities in Vietnam, Cambodia, Angola, Somalia, Ethiopia, South Yemen, and Afghanistan were seen as incompatible with the "spirit of détente." Americans expected Soviet leaders to restrain themselves—that is, to behave unlike Soviet leaders. Soviet ideological perception, however, made acceptance of the status quo impossible. Changes in Soviet leadership tended to bring changes of emphasis in policy or tactics, but they did not, until Gorbachev and the collapse of the Soviet economy, change the *fundamental* perception of the United States as the enemy and of a commitment to a long-term struggle. The United States remained the enemy.

Revisionist Explanation of U.S. Foreign Policy

Perhaps the most telling symptom of the American style in conducting foreign policy is the appearance after every major war of works reinterpreting the country's participation. The *revisionist* histories have certain common themes: the conflicts in which the nation had been entangled had not in fact threatened its security interests; or politicians had seen a menace where none existed, and this mistaken perception had been promoted by propagandists— soldiers with bureaucratic motives and, above all, bankers and industrialists (the "merchants of death" of the 1930s, the "military-industrial complex" of the 1960s)—who expected to benefit from the struggle. Also according to the revisionists, the United States' engagement in two world wars in this century (and in the cold war) had been a mistake; these wars had really been unnecessary, immoral, or both. Yesterday's apparent aggressor thus had not represented a threat to American security after all; on the contrary, the threat really came from within. Except for certain domestic forces, the United States could have continued to isolate itself from international politics.

Such revisionism is perhaps the deepest symptom of the American aversion to power politics. The distinguished American diplomatic historian Dexter Perkins wrote that revisionists always seek to convince the public that "every war in which this country has been engaged was really quite unnecessary or immoral or both; and that it behooves us in the future to pursue policies very different from those pursued in the past." [40] What is most striking about the revisionists' claims that the cold war was avoidable (based on second-level analysis) is that they really believe that, had it not been for the United States' purported anticommunism and lack of sensitivity to Soviet interests, the conflict between the superpowers would not have erupted. It was American policy that aroused Stalin's fears and suspicions and led him to react aggressively and angrily. Stalin's ambitions were limited to Eastern Europe, where the Soviet Union had legitimate security interests. Thus, the cold war could have been avoided had the United States, animated by anticommunism, acted less provocatively.[41] A change in *American* behavior has therefore been seen as the remedy. Such a revisionist attitude, which seeks to deny the reality of international struggle and suggests that it can be avoided, has not in the past been found among the characteristics of Soviet style.

Soviet Focus on Conflict

The Soviet emphasis during détente I, totally unlike that of the United States, was on the inevitable and irreconcilable struggle with capitalist states. Conflict was attributed not to wicked capitalist political leaders—they might be very decent and likable—but to the system they represented. Genuine peace and harmony could come only after capitalism, the real cause of rivalry between states, had been eliminated and replaced by world communism. Until then, it was only natural, indeed imperative, to exploit existing opportunities in the Third World to advance Soviet influence. Soviet leaders claimed not only that history was inevitably going in their direction, but also that they had a superior—indeed, exclusive—insight into this historical process and that they were obligated to help history along.

In contrast to the United States, which expected détente to result in modification of Soviet behavior, Soviet leaders never believed or said that détente was incompatible with continued struggle. When Americans became disillusioned with détente and cynicism about Soviet intentions replaced the initial confidence, the Soviets claimed not to understand why Americans were so disappointed in détente. They were not doing anything very different from what they had been doing all along. The United States seemed to be overreacting. There had been no understanding between the two powers on freezing the status quo—and therefore no violations. The United States and the Soviet Union clearly perceived détente differently and had quite divergent expectations. The United States assumed détente would result in mutual restraint. The Soviet Union perceived that détente was the result of the new strategic parity; the loss of U.S. strategic superiority because of the massive Soviet missile buildup "compelled" the United States to behave with greater restraint.

Détente, then, was seen as a symptom of America's growing weakness vis-à-vis the Soviet Union; the growth of Soviet strategic power was "forcing" the United States to behave with "moderation." Because of its military power, the Soviet Union regarded itself, and was regarded by the world, as a superpower. And because the Soviets also believed that their newfound strength had led to a less confrontational posture by the United States, the logical step was to add more. Military power "paid off." Thus, in the 1970s, while U.S. defense budgets declined significantly, the Soviets continued to invest heavily in the military, despite having overtaken the United States in numbers of missiles, and despite the fact that this investment came at the cost of improving the Soviet people's standard of living and of reversing the continuing stagnation of the Soviet economy. This cost was willingly paid by the regime because military might was a measure of Soviet standing and political achievement in the world.

Above all, the contrast in the attitudes of the two countries toward power could not be more striking. The United States had always considered itself a morally and politically superior society because of its democratic culture. Its attitude toward the use of international power had therefore been dominated by the belief that the struggle for power need not exist, can be avoided through isolation, or can be eliminated. Moralism in foreign policy meant that power was to be employed only in confrontation with unambiguous aggressors, at which point the United States would fight in behalf of a righteous cause. Power internationally, just as domestically, could be legitimated only by democratic purposes; otherwise, its exercise was evil and necessarily aroused guilt.

The Soviet belief in unceasing and irreconcilable conflict meant acceptance of power as an instrument of policy, dedicated to the pursuit of Communist ends. But this power was to be used with care and restraint. As Kennan observed in 1951,

> [The Kremlin] has no compunction about retreating in the face of superior force. And being under the compulsion of no timetable, it does not get panicky under the necessity for such retreat. Its political action is a fluid stream which moves constantly, wherever it is permitted to move, toward a given goal.... But if it finds unassailable barriers in its path, it accepts these philosophically and accommodates itself to them. The main thing is that there should always be pressure, increasing constant pressure, toward the desired goal. There is no trace of any feeling in Soviet psychology that the goal must be reached at any given time.[42]

For the Soviets, power was the raw material of international politics, to be applied discriminatingly and cautiously in the effort to achieve specific objectives and to probe for soft spots in the adversary's positions. Its use aroused no guilt; the only requirement was that it successfully advance Soviet goals. "Adventurism" and "romanticism," which might have provoked the enemy and endangered the base of the world revolution, were to be avoided.

Americans, believing that peace is a natural condition and that differences between states usually can be resolved through demonstrations of sincerity and good will, could not comprehend an attitude so dedicated to struggle. Soviet leaders, because of their commitment, never hesitated to sacrifice opportunities to win good will in exchange for strategic gains. The expansion and consolidation of Soviet power in Eastern Europe, which helped to undermine the wartime alliance, were not the only instance of the Soviets torpedoing good relations with the West. In 1955, the summit conference and the "spirit of Geneva" quickly fell before the Soviet arms deal with Egypt, which helped to precipitate the Suez War a year later. And the ink was hardly dry on the first strategic arms limitation treaty when the Soviets supplied Egypt with the offensive arms that led to the Yom Kippur War in 1973 and nearly resulted in a military confrontation with the United States. During all the years of negotiations on SALT II, the Soviets never hesitated to extend their influence in Africa. Even while the Senate was debating SALT II and the survival of the treaty was in doubt, the Soviets expanded their influence to the Indian Ocean and Persian Gulf areas, intervening with their own troops in Afghanistan. Believing in economic determinism and irreconcilable class struggle, they rejected the idea that opportunities for advancing their cause should be passed up; good will among enemies locked in a deadly struggle seemed to them an illusion anyway.

Change: Gorbachev's 'New Thinking' and the End of the Cold War

Yet clearly significant changes in the mutual perceptions of the two superpowers occurred after Reagan and Gorbachev assumed their respective offices. When he came into office in 1981, Ronald Reagan denounced the Soviet Union as an "evil empire." Furthermore, making the point that democracy and freedom were the waves of the future, he questioned the legitimacy and longevity of communism as a social and political system in both Eastern Europe and the Soviet Union. Simultaneously, he presided over a $2 trillion rearmament program, the largest of any administration in postwar history, and during the first term rejected any serious arms control efforts. By the end of his second administration, however, he had forged a new détente. Having denounced the first one, he met with his Soviet counterpart more times than Nixon had met with his, signed an arms control agreement that for the first time eliminated an entire class of nuclear weapons, and was negotiating a 50 percent reduction in strategic arms when he left office. Just over forty years after an English prime minister spoke in the United States of an iron curtain coming down over Europe, the American president expressed his hope in

London that it was being lifted and that a "new era" in U.S.-Soviet relations was about to begin. "What about your 'evil empire' talk?" Reagan was asked while walking around in Moscow's Red Square at the 1988 summit conference. He retracted the statement, saying it belonged to a different time—pre-Gorbachev.[43]

Reagan was right. For Gorbachev, terminating the cold war was a matter of necessity. It is easy—and has become commonplace—to say that the Soviet Union defeated itself. Its economy brought it down. Communism, in short, was the cause of the self-inflicted defeat not too many years after Soviet fortunes had appeared at their height with the acquisition of strategic parity and outposts in the Third World and its principal adversary had withdrawn from Vietnam and no longer seemed to have the will to compete. But this view overlooks the contribution of American policies and pressures in the 1980s and the policy of containment in general. At the beginning of the cold war, the conceptual architect of the containment policy, George Kennan, argued that the United States had

> it in its power to increase enormously the strains under which Soviet policy must operate, to force upon the Kremlin a far greater degree of moderation and circumspection than it has had to observe in recent years, and in this way *to promote tendencies which must eventually find their outlet in either the breakup or the gradual mellowing of Soviet power. For no mystical, messianic movement—and particularly that of the Kremlin—can face frustration indefinitely without eventually adjusting itself in one way or another to the logic of the state of affairs.*[44]

In retrospect, these words appear prophetic. Containment achieved its aim of basically containing Soviet power and by doing so compelling it to "mellow" or moderate its behavior.

The first sign that the Soviet Union was asking for a cease-fire in the cold war came in 1987, the year Gorbachev realized that the economy could not be cured by greater labor discipline and less absenteeism and drunkenness at work, and that the stepped-up military campaigns in Afghanistan and Angola could not end those increasingly draining conflicts. After years of insisting that the Soviet Union could deploy intermediate-range nuclear forces in Europe while the United Sates could not deploy any, as well as walking out of all arms control negotiations unless the United States and its European allies accepted Moscow's one-sided position, Gorbachev resumed negotiations and accepted virtually the entire American position: all intermediate-range nuclear forces, as well as short-range missiles, should be eliminated globally, not just in Europe; and the agreement was to be verified by a mutual inspection system of nuclear facilities in both countries.[45] This was followed by the Soviet withdrawal from Afghanistan and a Soviet confession that its intervention in Afghanistan had been illegal and in violation of Soviet law and international norms of behavior (this was followed by another extraordinary confession that the Soviet Union had violated the 1972 Antiballistic Missile treaty, just as the United States had been contending).[46]

In the meantime, Gorbachev also had made a number of important pronouncements on foreign policy. Whereas the historic Russian/Soviet pattern had been one of concern for only Soviet security, with neither sensitivity nor concern for the security of its neighbors or other states, Gorbachev talked of "common security," suggesting that he understood that Soviet restraint was a necessary prerequisite to producing and sustaining more friendly U.S. policies, which, after all, profoundly affected Soviet security—in contrast to the 1970s détente, which was torpedoed largely by Soviet expansionist efforts in the Third World.[47] Less security for the United States was not in the Soviet Union's interest, he said. Unlike his predecessors, Gorbachev recognized the implications of the security dilemma. The unilateral Soviet pursuit of security led only to greater distrust and instability as it compelled the United States to arm itself further. This was a significant shift from the prior Soviet view which held that security required the Soviet Union to be stronger than the United States.

Other shifts in viewpoint were evident as well. Force and the threat of force would no longer be instruments of foreign policy; security would be achieved by political means and disputes resolved by compromise. "Reasonable sufficiency" would be the yardstick for Soviet military strength. Its forces in Western Europe, organized for a surprise attack and a lightning or *blitzkrieg* strike toward the English Channel, would be reorganized in a "nonoffensive defense" or "defensive defense" so that NATO could feel reassured. Negotiations between NATO and the Warsaw Treaty Organization would reduce the levels of manpower and arms, and, wherever there were asymmetries, the one ahead—such as the Soviet Union, for example, in tanks and personnel carriers—would reduce down to the level of the other side rather than the latter building up.

These pronouncements, so contradictory to long-held doctrine and positions, together with Soviet actions, all suggested how profound a transformation of perceptions and outlook were occurring in the Soviet Union. But perhaps the most startling statement was that the "all-human value of peace" took precedence over the class struggle, meaning that the unilateral pursuit of advantage to extend socialism could jeopardize the peace. The global struggle against the West, therefore, had to be ended. Lenin, the father of the class struggle against the West and cited by every one of his successors for seventy years to legitimate that struggle, was suddenly transformed into a man who had in fact given priority to human values and survival above class conflict!

In reality, this was another indication, as was the abandonment of the party's monopoly of power, that Communist ideology was no longer operationally meaningful. This issue was critical to ending the cold war because the character of the Soviet state, together with bipolarity, had been one of the causes of the American-Soviet rivalry. From the beginning of the cold war, the central concern of the United States and its Western allies had been Soviet motives and objectives. Soviet actions, although they were not always by themselves necessarily threatening, tended to be seen in the context of what were perceived to be the Soviet Union's larger aims. Governments do not always know the intentions of their adversaries; they therefore infer them. In assessing Soviet rhetoric, Washington and its allies often found that it suggested universal and unlimited goals. The erosion of Marxism-Leninism therefore was a significant factor in changing Western perceptions of the Soviet Union; it was no longer an adversary.

The first sign that the cold war might be over sooner than anyone had expected occurred in 1989 in the area where it started. The cold war, as noted earlier, had begun with the thrust of Soviet power into the center of Europe after World War II. But the economic burden of supporting the failing economies of Eastern Europe and the danger that suppressing further revolts posed for his *perestroika* program (stemming from mass dissatisfaction with lack of food and other basic necessities of life), led Gorbachev to accept a more traditional sphere of influence. It started in Poland, where in 1989 the first free elections since World War II repudiated the Communist party and endorsed Solidarity, the trade union that had expressed the general unhappiness of the workers and of the Polish people at the beginning of the decade and had been outlawed as a result. Solidarity now formed the first non-Communist government in postwar Eastern Europe. It continued in Hungary, where the parliament removed the word *People's* from People's Republic and renamed the country the Republic of Hungary. At the same time, the Communist party, readying itself for a free election in 1990 in which other parties would be allowed to run, relabeled itself a social democratic party in the hope of surviving the elections. And all this boiled over into East Germany. Initially, tens of thousands of refugees, mainly younger people, had left through Hungary for West Germany. This was followed by spontaneous mass demonstrations in several East German cities demanding change. In what was truly a people's revolution, the old party and government leaders were replaced, and the new Communist party leader promised radical reforms, including free elections. As a token of the changes to come, he declared an end to restrictions on emigration and travel to the West. Hundreds of thousands of East Berliners then swarmed across the Berlin Wall in a mass celebration of their new freedom. The thaw resulting from Gorbachev's reforms in the Soviet Union had become a flood in Eastern Europe.

If any act could spell the transformation of the cold war, it was the destruction of the Berlin Wall on November 9, 1989. It had been built in 1961 to keep a people in, to prevent their escape to a better and freer life in West Germany. The opening of the wall was therefore symbolic of a new freedom. As Communist states in Eastern Europe were subjected to increasing domestic pressure for *perestroika*, it became clear that Eastern Europe was in the process of "de-Communizing." Communism as a social, economic, and political system had failed because it had been unable to provide its citizens with either a decent standard of living or freedom.

Reunification of Germany

Of all the countries in Eastern Europe, East Germany posed a special problem. If East Germans in a free election were to vote out the Communist party and move toward political pluralism and a market economy, what would be the rationale for East Germany's continued existence? The German Democratic Republic was a Communist-controlled country; only as such would it have a reason for maintaining its independent status. A democratic and free-market East Germany that truly lived up to its name of German Democratic Republic would seek unification with the larger and richer (and democratic) Federal Republic of Germany. The collapse of the Berlin Wall and free elections, which were won by followers of West German chancellor Helmut Kohl, therefore, ensured reunification—if Moscow agreed.

To make a united Germany acceptable to Moscow, which increasingly— although reluctantly—accepted the notion that German reunification was not only inevitable but also imminent, the West proposed that a united Germany be a member of NATO. This proposal contained two types of reassurances for Moscow: first, that no Western armies, including German troops assigned to NATO, would be stationed on what used to be East German territory since Moscow was certain to oppose the expansion of the Western alliance up to the Polish border; and, second, to reassure the Soviets during the three- to four-year transition period, that the 380,000 Soviet troops could remain on what had been East German soil (but now a reunited and sovereign Germany that was a member of the NATO alliance and that would pay for the upkeep of these troops!). Germany also would guarantee its neighbors' borders, restate West Germany's pledge that it would not seek to acquire nuclear weapons, and accept a limit of 370,000 on the size of Germany's armed forces, below West Germany's 474,000 level of 1990 and well below the 667,00 level of the two Germanies.

Why did the Western powers insist on German membership in NATO? No longer really needed to defend Western Europe against the Soviet Union, that organization justified its continued survival by the need to restrain a reunified Germany and to reassure both Western and Eastern Europeans about their future security. Thus, NATO was transformed from an alliance basically deterring the Soviet Union from war, although that remained a residual function given the strength of the Soviet Union even after a withdrawal to Soviet territory and the possibility that Gorbachev might someday be replaced by a less conciliatory figure. NATO's new function was to maintain stability in Central Europe—that is, to contain German power, something that for diplomatic reasons none could say publicly. America's allies, remembering that there had been no security in Europe in this century without the presence and engagement of the United States, did not want to see it leave Europe either. The new post-Communist Poland, Hungary, and Czechoslovakia also favored Germany's inclusion in NATO, increasing the pressure on Moscow to accept this solution.

Gorbachev initially resisted, remembering that the Germans had defeated czarist Russia in World War I and that while the Soviet Union had thrown back the German invasion in World War II, the cost had been a staggering 20 million lives. He therefore insisted that a reunited Germany had to be a neutral, disarmed state. But this was unacceptable to virtually everyone else, who wondered whether a united but neutralized Germany would become once more as self-centered and nationalistic as in the past, trying to play East and West off against one another, thereby dangerously destabilizing the continent? Gorbachev, however, continued to resist the Western solution to the German problem. Quite apart from the memory of two German invasions, the collapse of East Germany also spelled the end of a central Soviet cold war goal: hegemony over Europe.

Even more humiliating, a reunited Germany would likely emerge as the financial and economic center of Europe and become the dominant power in Eastern Europe and the principal source for capital and machinery for the Soviet Union. During the cold war, because of its far superior military strength, the Soviet Union had been the dominant power; in the post-cold war period, when economic considerations and power were more significant and the Soviet Union needed German help, the Soviet-German relationship was likely to be reversed, resembling that before both world wars. But in July 1990, only four months after declaring that German membership in NATO was "absolutely out of the question," Gorbachev bowed to the inevitable; he accepted a reunited Germany in NATO. His acceptance was made easier by the promise of $8 billion in German credits to help the failing Soviet economy.

Gorbachev's acquiescence to German membership in NATO clearly revealed who had lost and who had won the cold war. Indeed, the American insistence of Soviet acceptance of Germany's admission to NATO appeared in large part to reflect the need to clarify this issue. Although *July 16, 1990*, had none of the drama of a VE or VJ day marking the ends of the war in Europe and the Pacific in 1945, *it will be remembered in the history books as the day the Soviet Union surrendered in the cold war.* It was not until November, however, that in the Charter of Paris for a New Europe the cold war was declared officially over as the opposing alliances (or what was left of the Warsaw Treaty Organization) met, together with all the other European nations to sign an arms control agreement for Europe in which the Soviet Union, long far superior in conventional armaments, renounced that superiority.

AMERICAN FOREIGN POLICY IN THE POST-COLD WAR ERA

With the disappearance of the Soviet Union and its replacement by the Commonwealth of Independent States (CIS), its members will be preoccupied with sorting out their relationship whether the CIS collapses, survives, or eventually leads the eleven republics to restore some kind of central government so that they can more effectively cope with their economic and other problems. Russia, the successor state to the Soviet Union, however, will at a minimum pursue further arms reductions with the United States (see Chapter

13) and seek economic assistance from the West. But, short of restoration of some kind of dictatorship should Yeltsin fail, its foreign policy is likely to remain accommodating, not adversarial.

Now U.S. policy makers confront a world in which its principal adversary has withdrawn from the field of battle. If communism is dead, so to speak, so is anticommunism. As the latest crusade ends, should the country retreat once more into its traditional isolationist posture? Voices on both the Left and the Right advocate such a course. They want to bring back the troops from Europe because Europe can now take care of itself. As for the Third World, it is basically not a vital interest. Thus, America should come home and take care of itself. But the course of American foreign policy in the twentieth century suggests otherwise.

The principles dictating what the American national interest should be are reasonably clear.[48] First, the United States remains opposed to the emergence of another great power whose ideology and political and social values are hostile to its own. While at the moment no such threat exists, history did not end with the end of the cold war, as the confrontation and war with Iraq demonstrated. In a policy study leaked early in 1992, the Defense Department specifically asserted that the U.S. mission in the post-cold war era is to prevent the emergence of a superpower rival in Western Europe, Asia, or the territory of the former Soviet Union.[49] When the study was leaked, the Bush administration repudiated it, largely out of embarrassment. Second, and closely related, the nation's security and prosperity remain intimately tied to those nations who share its values. NATO may not survive, but U.S. bonds to the democracies of Western Europe, the Pacific, and other areas remain. Indeed, it has been suggested by some observers that the spreading of democracy should be at the core of future U.S. foreign policy.[50] Circumstances will dictate the strength of these ties.

Third, America's relations with other nations will largely be decided on a case-by-case basis. Countries that are in the process of changing their internal arrangements to more democratic ones are likely to have friendlier relations with the United States than those that do not. But, by and large, whether this nation has friendly, cool and correct, or hostile relations with another country will depend on that country's attitudes and policies and whether it threatens what are believed to be American security or economic interests or both, as Iraq did in the sands of Kuwait. If a nation displays hostile intentions, they will presumably be returned.

> We are still a world power and have every intention of remaining so. This means that a traditional kind of isolationism is out of the question. But we are now a world power that is no longer compelled by an adversary to be interested in every part of the globe. We are now free to pick and choose and assemble a coherent agenda. In short, we are now free to define our national interest, instead of having it defined for us.[51]

Fourth, the United States also has an interest in the kind of international order that will succeed the cold war one.[52] Clearly, as the Iraqi crisis also demonstrated, the United States is the only power now capable of leading efforts to preserve the peace. Instead of organizing alliances against the specific threat of the Soviet Union and its friends, as it had done for forty-five years, it will mobilize different coalitions against states that disturb the peace, whomever they are. It may not oppose each and every aggression in the name of maintaining the "international order"; its own tangible interests will have to be at stake as well. Nevertheless, in playing this role, the United States will be identifying this peace-keeping role with the broader international system. The war with Iraq was not just about liberating Kuwait or weakening Iraq's offensive military power to threaten its neighbors, but also about establishing the "rules of the game" for the post-cold war state system. Operations Desert Shield and Desert Storm were to be lessons for other potential regional bullies.

The question is whether the American people will accept their role as the "world's policemen" or a "global 911." It is not the glamorous role of defending freedom and launching moral crusades that they assumed in the two world wars and the cold war; rather, it is a more nebulous role, in which the enemy will not necessarily be easy to portray as evil, like Saddam Hussein, yet that enemy will threaten U.S. interests. It will therefore be harder for the public to grasp the causes of the conflict and in turn more difficult for the president to mobilize and sustain public support once the initial "rallying round the flag" disappears—especially if future confrontations and hostilities do not end as quickly as the 1990-1991 conflict. In fact, American foreign policy continues to be characterized by moralism. The country continues to want to justify its behavior in the world arena by such slogans as "resisting aggression," "fighting oppression," "protecting human rights," and supporting the "right of self-determination." Yet the country acts in the spirit of political realism. "We don't always resist aggression, or fight aggression, or act to protect human rights, or recognize a right to self-determination. Everything depends on circumstances. Sometimes we do and sometimes we don't. . . . Prudence always has been, and always will be, the mark of authentic statesmanship in foreign policy." [53] Given the fact that the United States is presently the only power to maintain some degree of order in the international system, and that the isolationist impulse in the wake of the end of the cold war may resurface, the key question is whether American political leaders can mobilize public support without invoking the historic American approach to foreign policy.

Thus, the future role of the United States is one of increasing disengagement from the cold war commitments—such as the withdrawal of most of the U.S. forces that have long defended Europe and Asia—and selective interventions where material and moral considerations warrant. The end of the cold war means that the United States can change its priorities. Indeed, the end of the conflict with Moscow means that Washington has been given a rare opportunity to reorder its priorities from foreign to domestic policy and deal with the vast domestic agenda: drugs, crime, education, the budget deficit, industrial competitiveness, and urban decay. "The United States had never been less threatened by foreign forces than it is today. But the unfortunate corollary is that never since the Great Depression has the threat to domestic well-being been greater." [54] Without question, because U.S. power is rooted in American society and economy, in the coming years the nation's central foreign policy priority and its central domestic priority must be the same: strengthening the economy.

For Review

1. What is meant by "styles" in foreign policy?
2. How have American isolationism and democracy shaped American perceptions and foreign policy behavior?
3. How have Russia's history and Communist ideology affected pre-Gorbachev Soviet views of international politics, its enemies, and its objectives? .
4. How did American and Soviet styles contrast during the cold war?
5. How did Soviet domestic reforms change Soviet foreign policy behavior?
6. How is U.S. post-cold war foreign policy likely to change and why?

Notes

1. Arnold Wolfers and Laurence W. Martin, eds., *The Anglo-American Tradition in Foreign Affairs* (New Haven, Conn.: Yale University Press, 1956), ix-xxvii.
2. Louis Hartz, *The Liberal Tradition in America* (New York: Harvest Books, 1955).
3. Zbigniew Brzezinski, "The Soviet Union: Her Aims, Problems and Challenges to the West," in *The Conduct of East-West Relations in the 1980s* (London: Institute of Strategic Studies, 1984), 1:4; and Richard Pipes, *Survival Is Not Enough* (New York: Simon & Schuster, 1984), 37-44.
4. Alexander L. George, "The 'Operational Code': A Neglected Approach to the Study of Political Leaders and Decision-Making," *International Studies Quarterly* (June 1969): 190ff.
5. An exhaustive analysis of the American "style" can be found in *Gulliver's Troubles, or The Setting of American Foreign Policy*, by Stanley Hoffmann (New York: McGraw-Hill, 1968), 87-213. Also see Hans J. Morgenthau, *In Defense of the National Interest* (New York: Knopf, 1951); Robert E. Osgood, *Ideals and Self-interest in America's Foreign Relations* (Chicago: University of Chicago Press, 1953); George F. Kennan, *American Diplomacy 1900-1950* (Chicago: University of Chicago Press, 1951); and John Spanier, *American Foreign Policy Since World War II*, 12th ed. (Washington, D.C.: CQ Press, 1991). For an application of this style—and Soviet style—to nuclear strategy, see, for example, Colin S. Gray, *Nuclear Strategy and National Style*

(Lanham, Md.: Hamilton Press, 1986). For a quite different interpretation of U.S. foreign policy, see Michael Parenti, *The Sword and the Dollar: Imperialism, Revolution, and the Arms Race* (New York: St. Martin's Press, 1988); or Gabriel Kolko, *Confronting the Third World* (New York: Pantheon Books, 1988).

6. The hypothesis about democratic behavior offered by Klaus Knorr and others and discussed in Chapter 2 is generally supported by Gabriel A. Almond, who, in *The American People and Foreign Policy* (New York: Holt, Rinehart & Winston, 1960), strongly emphasizes the "extraordinary pull of domestic and private affairs even in periods of international crises." See particularly Chapter 3, with Almond's summation of the American value orientation.

7. Paul Seabury, *The Rise and Decline of Cold War* (New York: Basic Books, 1967), 39-45, offers some fitting quotations, especially a poem by Archibald MacLeish celebrating *Pax* Americana as a preamble to the *pax humana* of World War II. The moralism of Secretary of State John Foster Dulles is discussed by William L. Miller, "The 'Moral Force' Behind Dulles' Diplomacy," *Reporter*, August 9, 1956.

8. Quoted by Arthur S. Link, *Wilson the Diplomatist* (Baltimore: Johns Hopkins University Press, 1957), 89.

9. Quoted in Joseph M. Jones, *The Fifteen Weeks* (New York: Viking, 1955), 272.

10. Robert E. Osgood, *Limited War* (Chicago: University of Chicago Press, 1957), 28-45, focuses on this point in explaining the difficulties the nation experiences in conducting limited wars.

11. John Spanier, *The Truman-MacArthur Controversy and the Korean War* (Cambridge, Mass.: Harvard University Press, 1959), 221-238.

12. Denis W. Brogan, "The Illusion of Omnipotence," *Harper's*, December 1952, 21-28.

13. Robert Tucker, *The Soviet Political Mind* (New York: Holt, Rinehart & Winston, 1963), 181-182.

14. For a contrasting analysis of the American "empire," comparing U.S. and Soviet roles after 1945 and arguing that the American style has been given too much emphasis, see Ger Lundestad, *The American Empire and Other Studies of U.S. Foreign Policy* (New York: Oxford University Press, 1990).

15. Tang Tsou, *America's Failure in China* (Chicago: University of Chicago Press, 1963), 538-541. For a study of the accusation of a leading State Department figure by Sen. Joseph McCarthy, see McGeorge Bundy, *The Pattern of Responsibility* (Boston: Houghton Mifflin, 1952), 201-220.

16. The repetitious pattern of conspiracy charges in American political life has been explored by Richard Hofstadter, *The Paranoid Style in American Politics* (New York: Vintage, 1967).

17. Leslie H. Gelb and Richard K. Betts, *The Irony of Vietnam* (Washington, D.C.: Brookings, 1979), 220-226.

18. Larry Elowitz and John W. Spanier, "Korea and Vietnam: Limited War and the American Political System," *Orbis* (Summer 1974): 510-534; and John E. Mueller, *War, Presidents and Public Opinion* (New York: Wiley, 1973). Mueller comes to the startling conclusion that the war had no *independent* impact on President Lyndon Johnson's declining popularity, though the rate of the decline was the same as that for Truman during the Korean War. Also see Milton J. Rosenberg et al., *Vietnam and the Silent Majority* (New York: Harper & Row, 1970).

19. J. William Fulbright, *Arrogance of Power* (New York: Vintage, 1967), 256-258.

20. Ronald Steel, *Pax Americana* (New York: Viking, 1967), 353-354.

21. Henry Kissinger, *White House Years* (Boston: Little, Brown, 1979), 115-130.

22. For analyses of the feasibility of economic leverage in the 1970s, see Samuel P. Huntington et al., "Trade, Technology and Leverage," *Foreign Policy* (Fall 1978): 63-106; and Herbert S. Levin, Francis W. Rushing, and Charles Movit, "The Potential for U.S. Economic Leverage on the USSR," *Comparative Strategy* (1979): 371-404.

23. George W. Breslauer, "Ideology and Learning in Soviet Third World Policy," *World Politics* (April 1987): 436; Stephen D. Hosmer and Thomas W. Wolfe, eds., *Soviet Policy and Practice Toward Third World Conflicts* (Lexington, Mass.: Lexington Books, 1983); and Andrzej Korbonski and Francis Fukuyama, eds., *The Soviet Union and the Third World* (Ithaca, N.Y.: Cornell University Press, 1988).

24. John Lewis Gaddis, *Strategies of Containment* (New York: Oxford University Press, 1982), 320.

25. Quoted in *The Russians and Reagan* by Strobe Talbott (New York: Vintage Books, 1984), 113.

26. For a more detailed analysis of the ending of the cold war and U.S. terms for an end to "hostilities," see Spanier, *American Foreign Policy Since World War II*, 345-376.

27. Michael Volensky, *Nomenklatura*, trans. Eric Misbacher (New York: Doubleday, 1985); and Ilya Zemstov, *The Private Life of the Soviet Elite* (New York: Crane, Russak, 1985). For the roster of Soviet civilian and military officials, see Albert L. Weeks, *Soviet Nomenklatura*, 3d ed. (Washington, D.C.: Washington Institute Press, 1991).

28. Joseph L. Nogee and Robert H. Donaldson, *Soviet Foreign Policy Since World War II*, 4th ed. (New York: Macmillan, 1992), 13-39.

29. Alexander L. George, "The 'Operational Code': A Neglected Approach to the Study of Political Leaders and Decision-Making," in *The Conduct of Soviet Foreign Policy* ed. Erik P. Hoffmann and Frederic J. Fleron, Jr. (Chicago: Aldine-Atherton, 1971), 165-190. Also see Nathan Leites, *A Study of Bolshevism* (New York: Free Press, 1953).

30. Arthur P. Mendel, *The Essential Works of Marxism* (New York: Bantam, 1961); Alfred G. Meyer, *Communism*, rev. ed. (New York: Random House, 1967); V. I. Lenin, *Imperialism, the Highest Stage of Capitalism*, rev. ed. (New York: International Publishers, 1939); and Joseph Stalin, *The Foundations of Leninism* (San Francisco: China Books, 1965).

31. George F. Kennan, *Russia and the West Under Lenin and Stalin* (Boston: Little, Brown, 1961), 179.

32. Ibid., 180-183 (emphasis in original). Used by permission of the publisher.

33. John Lewis Gaddis, "The First Fifty Years," in *Shared Destiny*, ed. Mark Garrison and Abbot Gleason (Boston: Beacon Press, 1985), 19-39.

34. Leites, *Study of Bolshevism*, 27-63.

35. Kennan, *American Diplomacy 1900-1950*, 118.

36. Hanes Adomeit, *Soviet Risk-Taking and Crisis Behavior* (London: George Allen and Unwin, 1982); Jan F. Triska and David D. Finley, *Soviet Foreign Policy* (New York: Macmillan, 1968), 310-349; and Stephens S. Kaplan, *Diplomacy of Power* (Washington, D.C.: Brookings, 1981) for a thorough analysis of the 190 incidents in which Soviet armed forces were used to achieve foreign policy aims.

37. Kennan, *American Diplomacy 1900-1950*, 182.

38. For World War II and the beginning of the cold war, see Adam B. Ulam, *Expansion and Coexistence*, 2d ed. (New York: Holt, Rinehart and Winston, 1974), 314-455; Ulam, *The Rivals* (New York: Viking Compass, 1971), 3-151; Voitech Mastny, *Russia's Road to the Cold War* (New York: Columbia University Press, 1979); William Taubman, *Stalin's American Policy* (New York: Norton, 1982); and Hugh Thomas,

Armed Truce (New York: Atheneum, 1987).

39. Mike Bowker and Phil Williams, *Superpower Détente* (Newbury Park, Calif.: Sage Publications, 1988).

40. Dexter Perkins, "American Wars and Critical History," *Yale Review* (Summer 1951): 682-695.

41. For some of the revisionist histories that place the responsibility for beginning the cold war on the United States, see D. F. Fleming, *The Cold War and Its Origins*, 2 vols. (Garden City, N.Y.: Doubleday, 1961); Gar Alperovitz, *Atomic Diplomacy: Hiroshima and Potsdam* (New York: Vintage, 1967); William A. Williams, *The Tragedy of American Diplomacy* (Cleveland: World, 1959); Gabriel Kolko, *The Politics of War: The World and United States Foreign Policy, 1943-1945* (New York: Random House, 1968); and Thomas G. Paterson, *Soviet-American Confrontation* (Baltimore: Johns Hopkins University Press, 1973).

  Evaluations of the Fleming-Alperovitz thesis, in which American anticommunism is blamed directly, may be found in Arthur Schlesinger, Jr., "The Origins of the Cold War," *Foreign Affairs* (October 1967): 22-52; J. L. Richardson, "Cold War Revisionism: A Critique," *World Politics* (July 1972): 579ff.; and John Spanier, "The Choices We Did Not Have: In Defense of Containment," in *Caging the Bear*, ed. Charles Gati (New York: Bobbs-Merrill, 1974), 128ff. The Gati book provides a discussion of Kennan's analysis and the policy of containment twenty-five years after the latter's anonymous article, "The Sources of Soviet Conduct," in *Foreign Affairs* (July 1947): 566-582, later republished in *American Diplomacy 1900-1950*, 107-128. In that article Kennan had provided the Truman administration with a rationale for its containment policy. Finally, for an assessment of economic interpretations of American policy, see Robert W. Tucker, *The Radical Left and American Foreign Policy* (Baltimore: Johns Hopkins University Press, 1971). For an analysis that suggests either poor scholarship or a deliberate distortion of the documents, see Robert J. Maddox, *The New Left and the Origins of the Cold War* (Princeton, N.J.: Princeton University Press, 1973).

42. Kennan, *American Diplomacy 1900-1950*, 118.

43. Steven V. Roberts, "U.S.-Soviet Tension Is Now Receding—Reagan Declares," *New York Times*, June 4, 1988.

44. Kennan, *American Diplomacy 1900-1950*, 127-128 (emphasis added).

45. For the political battle over intermediate-range nuclear forces in Europe, see Jeffrey Hex, *War by Other Means* (New York: Free Press, 1991); and Jonathan Haslam, *The Soviet Union and the Politics of Nuclear Weapons in Europe, 1969-1977* (Ithaca, N.Y.: Cornell University Press, 1990).

46. For the dramatic change in Soviet policy toward the developing world under Gorbachev, see W. Raymond Duncan and Carolyn McGiffert Ekedahl, *Moscow and the Third World under Gorbachev* (Boulder, Colo.: Westview, 1990).

47. Seweryn Bialer, "'New Thinking' and Soviet Foreign Policy," *Survival* (July/August 1988): 291-309; and David Holloway, "Gorbachev's New Thinking," and Robert Levgold, "The Revolution in Soviet Policy," *Foreign Affairs* (America and the World, 1988/89 issue): 69-71 and 83-98, respectively. Also, Daniel Deudney and G. John Ikenberry, "The International Sources of Soviet Change," *International Security* (Winter, 1991-1992): 74-118; and Richard K. Hermann, "Soviet Behavior in Regional Conflicts: Old Questions, New Strategies, and Important Lessons," *World Politics* (April 1992): 432-465.

48. For a sample of different points of view, see Alan Tonelsen, "What Is the National

Interest?" *Atlantic Monthly* (June 1991): 35-52; Graham E. Fuller, *The Democratic Trap* (New York: Dutton, 1992); and Robert J. Art, "A Defensible Defense: America's Grand Strategy after the Cold War," *International Security* (Spring 1991): 5-53; and Richard Nixon, *Seize the Moment* (New York: Simon & Schuster, 1992).

49. Patrick E. Tyler, "U.S. Strategy Calls for Insuring No Rivals Develop," *New York Times*, March 8, 1992.

50. See, for example, Joshua Muravchik, *Exporting Democracy* (Lanham, Md.: American Enterprise Institute Press, 1990).

51. Irving Kristol, "In Search of Our National Interest," *Wall Street Journal*, June 7, 1990. Also see Kristol, "Defining Our National Interest," *National Interest* (Fall 1990): 16-24.

52. Among other works, see the one on U.S. foreign policy in a "world transformed" edited by Nicholas X. Rizipoulos, *Sea-Changes* (New York: Council on Foreign Relations Press, 1989).

53. Irving Kristol, "Tongue-Tied in Washington," *Wall Street Journal*, April 15, 1991.

54. William G. Hyland, "Downgrade Foreign Policy," *New York Times*, May 20, 1991; and Robert D. Hormats, "The Roots of American Power," *Foreign Affairs* (Summer 1991): 132-149.

C H A P T E R 10

The Developing Countries: The Primacy of Domestic Concerns

FOREIGN POLICY AS A CONTINUATION OF DOMESTIC POLITICS

During the cold war years, the term *Third World* was used to describe the formerly colonial, mostly non-Western, largely nonwhite, poor or developing countries. But these nations did not constitute the unitary bloc implied by the label. There was considerable diversity among them: in history and experience, religion and culture, population and resources, and ideology and political and economic systems. Some nations were more developed than others. Some had very large populations; many had small populations. Some possessed sizable resources; others were not well endowed. Some were governed by religious tradition (especially in the Islamic world), but most were secular. What united the majority of them was their past colonial history, their poverty, a determination to modernize, and a desire to fulfill the "revolution of rising expectations." In these respects, they were distinct from the First World (Western industrial nations) and the Second World (Soviet-led Communist nations). In their foreign policies, the Third World states generally preferred nonalignment—that is, independence from the two rival global power blocs—in the initial period of being "newcomers" in the international system, and they were very much aware of their lack of influence and status in that system.

The status of the developing countries becomes even clearer by taking a look at the economic gap between the First and Third worlds or between the rich North and poor South.[1] The term *South*, like *Third World*, claims more than it should. Tanzania and Uganda are *South*, but Australia and New Zealand are *North*; South Korea and Taiwan are in between as newly industrialized countries (NICs). Geographically erroneous as it may sometimes be, the

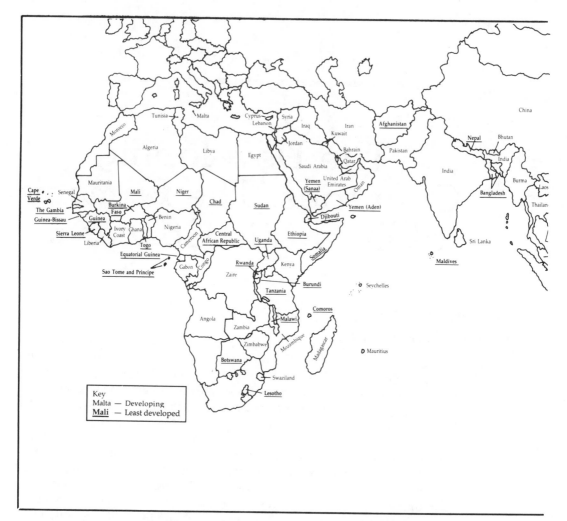

Figure 10-1 Developing and Least-developed Countries

term *North-South* does have the advantage of emphasizing the frustration of most developing countries over the continued division of the world between rich and poor nations (see Figure 10-1). This division between rich and poor nations is, to be sure, somewhat oversimplified; a continuum between very rich and very poor is probably a more accurate image. While the distance between the extremes is growing, that between the developed countries and the top rank of the developing countries—the OPEC countries and NICs—is narrowing. Nevertheless, these countries constitute a minority of the developing nations.

As the 1980s began, the North, including Eastern Europe, had a quarter of the world's population and four-fifths of its income; the South, including

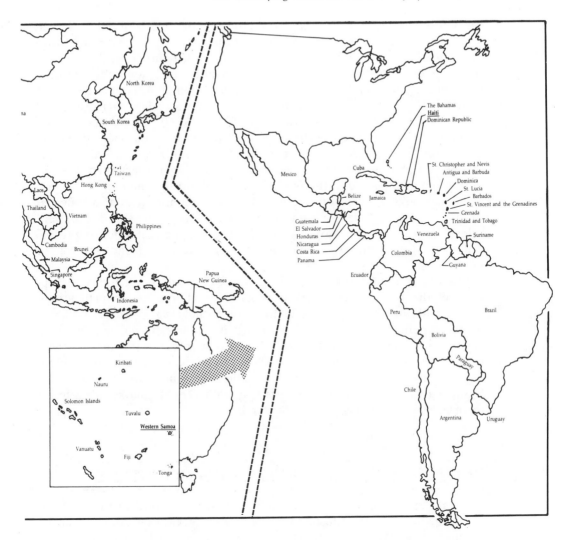

China, had three-quarters of its population and one-fifth of its income. Thus, as the term *less-developed countries* (LDCs)—or developing countries—suggests, their principal motive is to achieve a higher standard of living and to abolish the abject poverty and misery of past centuries. In the economically developing countries, people have continued to live on subsistence agriculture because they have not possessed the modern tools—factories, machinery, computers, and so forth—with which to increase productivity. A vast increase in productivity was the essence of the Industrial Revolution and the means for the "great ascent" out of poverty. Equally important, the developing countries have lacked the cultural values, social structures, and political order necessary for industrialization. But developing nations do not necessarily lack natural resources. They can in fact be divided between those that possess plentiful resources (for example, the oil states) and those that control either less desirable raw materials or very little of nature's wealth. But the hallmark of a developing country is its inability to attain self-sustaining economic growth and a higher per capita income. A large number of developing countries still have per capita incomes of less than $400, and many more have incomes that range from $400 to $1,600. By contrast, the per capita incomes of Japan, the United States, and Western European democracies range from $10,000 to just over $20,000.² Children under the age of thirteen in the United States spend more ($230 per year) than the 380 million poorest people in the world.³ But the dividing line between developed and developing countries is not only economic; it is also reflected in differences in infant mortality, life expectancy, general health and calorie intake per person, availability of consumer goods and housing (especially bathing facilities and living space), education, and sources of energy.

The desire to modernize, in short, molds the developing nations' perceptions of the world. Their foreign policies reflect this preoccupation with nation building. It has been said that, for a "new state, foreign policy is domestic policy pursued by other means; it is domestic policy carried on beyond the boundaries of the state." ⁴ This remained true in the 1980s and into the 1990s as confrontation proved counterproductive and more developing countries turned for help to multinational corporations for capital and technology and experimented increasingly with Western market ideas to lift themselves out of poverty (see Chapter 16).

'WESTERNIZATION' OF THE DEVELOPING COUNTRIES

The right to national self-determination, a notion conceived in the West but denied by the Western industrial powers to their overseas territories, became a key issue after World War II. Throughout Asia and Africa, former colonies sought national independence and most gained it. The common denominator of this global nationalist revolution was a fundamental urge to be free from the control of former colonial powers. From the beginning, therefore, colonialism contained the seeds of its own destruction. Humiliation and resentment of foreign domination stirred a "reactive nationalism" that asserted itself in terms of the very values by which the Westerners justified their rule—national self-determination, dignity, and equality. Thus, the role of the Western industrial nations in forging the nationhood of these countries cannot be ignored.

Territorialization

Territorialization by the colonial powers usually defined the present frontiers of the developing countries. The Western powers drew arbitrary lines on the map, often straight through tribal or ethnic boundaries, and then imposed administrative and legal structures on the resulting territories. All who lived within a particular structure were treated as if they belonged to a single nation. Thus India, in its quarrel with China over precisely where the Sino-India boundary lies in the Himalayas, has defined its claim by the line drawn by British colonizers.

Infrastructure

Another byproduct of colonialism has been the construction of harbors, roads, railroads, airports, telephone and telegraph lines, and factories, as well as the development of natural resources. These facilities have provided what economists call the infrastructure or capital overhead, the prerequisite for any major industrialization.[5] To be sure, Europeans did not undertake such projects for the benefit of the natives. The roads and railroads were used to carry resources and crops from the interior to the harbors; they also were used to move troops to quell uprisings and riots. Furthermore, the impact of these projects on the traditional native economy and society was disruptive. The traditional patterns of life and expectations of the vast majority of peasants who had migrated from the land were altered in the cities. European-built centers of government, business, and communications offered the peasants who came there to work a new way of life and values. Urban life provided the "demonstration effect." [6] Europeans lived better and longer. Why, the natives wondered, could they not live as well and as long? They could hardly avoid awareness of the technical and scientific knowledge, tools, and skills that had given the Europeans their higher material standards, as well as their power. Why, the natives asked themselves, could they not learn these secrets? One point was especially noteworthy: Europeans believed that life could be improved here on earth and that poverty need not be accepted as one's fate.

Education

The urge to transform backward societies into modern societies thus began with the European introduction of urbanization, industry, wage-labor forces, and exchange economies. But the most significant contribution of Western colonialism was education of the social groups determined to lead their shackled nations into freedom and modernity. A relatively small and youthful group, this secular nationalist intelligentsia produced the leadership of revolutionary movements in the developing countries. Its members were doctors, journalists, civil servants, and lawyers; they had in common their "Westernization." Educated in Europe or the United States, or in Western schools in their own countries, they had learned Western ways. Even more significant, in the course of their professional training they had learned to think in characteristically Western rational and secular terms. This had revolutionary implications: for the Third World intelligentsia, this thinking provided an escape from the traditions, customs, and privileges that had held their societies in the tight grip of economic, social, and political backwardness. Its simple but powerful message that human beings can be the masters of their own destinies was exhilarating, a promise of intellectual liberation from religious superstition, substituting rationalism for obsolete traditions and institutions.

Education then was the chief means by which Western political and social thought was diffused to non-Western peoples. As one political analyst has observed, "The future will look back upon the overseas imperialism of recent centuries, less in terms of its sins of oppression, exploitation, and discrimination, than as the instrument by which the spiritual, scientific, and material revolution which began in Western Europe with the Renaissance was spread to the rest of the world." [7] It was this Westernization that transformed members of the intelligentsia into leaders of the nationalist and modernist movements of their own countries. [8]

But, as intensely aware as the first generation of leaders and their successors were of the underdeveloped condition of their countries and as determined as they were to initiate development, they faced almost insuperable obstacles to the necessary economic "takeoff" and self-sustaining economic growth. Lack of national cohesion, rapidly growing populations, insurmountable hunger and malnutrition, a dearth of capital, and traditional social structures and values all have impeded the modernization of most of their societies, with grave foreign policy implications.

OBSTACLES TO DEVELOPMENT

Absence of National Unity

The first obstacle encountered in creating cohesive societies in developing countries is a lack of national unity. Leaders of the new nations have had to construct the very nations in whose names they once revolted against colonial domination. They have had to be "nation builders." The lives of the citizens of the new nation have been rooted in smaller communities, and their first loyalties are to tribes, regions, or religious, racial, or linguistic groups. [9] Loyalties are parochial, and attitudes are particularistic. These stand as formidable barriers to the formation of a national consciousness and devotion to national symbols and may, in fact, reach such intensity that civil war breaks out. Disunity, not unity, is the spirit of most new nations. The communities created by the colonial powers may have become "national" in the sense that the people living in them rid themselves of foreign rulers. But their common resentment and aspiration to be free often have not developed into a shared allegiance to nations with artificial boundaries drawn earlier by Europeans.

Indeed, upon the departure of the colonial rulers that united them, the new nations have tended to fall apart. When the British maintained order and public security in India, the Muslims, Hindus, and Sikhs could coexist; once

Britain withdrew, their fear and hatred of one another led to disintegration and bloodshed. The groups composing a new nation realize how little they have in common—indeed, how many things divide them. The issue facing new nations then is not whether they will develop economically, but whether they will survive as national entities. When people obey racial, religious, or tribal authority instead of legitimate national authority, secession and civil war may result. Ironically, the new nations face the task of nation building at a time when some Western states such as Belgium, Ireland, and Spain are confronting similar demands for independence and greater self-government. Of those new nations that have managed to remain united, many have had to cope with demands for greater autonomy, if not independence. For example, civil wars plagued the Sudan, Ethiopia, and Sri Lanka until recently.

Race.   Integrating diverse masses into a new nation, forming a national consensus, is therefore crucial. Race is one element impeding this "integrative revolution." For example, many of the countries of Southeast Asia, such as Malaysia, contain many large minority groups, chief among them the ethnic (overseas) Chinese. In Singapore, they constitute the majority. Almost everywhere in Southeast Asia the Chinese act as distributors of consumer goods, bankers, investors, and shopkeepers. But while dominating Southeast Asian economic life, they have retained their language and customs, tending to isolate themselves; they remain foreigners in the nations in which they live. Centuries of Chinese invasion and conquest have left a residue of suspicion that is only intensified by this cultural separatism. The result is fear, jealousy, discrimination, accusations of "alien exploitation," and occasionally, as after the abortive Indonesian Communist party coup in 1965, the slaughter of the Chinese population. Another example is the cruel expulsion of the Chinese from Vietnam in the late 1970s. The majority were forced out on unsafe boats after most of their money had been taken from them, and many drowned on the high seas. Most of these "boat people"—some of whom were still seeking refuge over a decade later—found refuge in other Southeast Asian countries. Vietnam's anti-Chinese sentiment was one of the factors contributing to the brief Vietnamese-Chinese war in 1979.

It is not just the inhumanity of such behavior that is notable but also its counterproductiveness. In non-Communist states, such minorities play a critical role in the process of development. And, as noted, in some traditional societies, such as in Southeast Asia, the Chinese minority comprises the entrepreneurs. In Africa, this role is often played by the Indian-Pakistani community. Hostile or discriminatory actions, such as expelling this minority, which happened in Uganda, or rioting and attacking their shops, which occurred in Kenya, are likely to hurt economic growth.

Religion.   A second element is religious animosity. When Britain partitioned India in 1949 into Hindu India and Muslim Pakistan because the Muslim minority wanted its own nation, the division was accompanied by a great blood bath in which more than half a million people died.[10] In the middle of all this were the Sikhs. Their prosperity stemming from India's agricultural revolution had led them to forget their religious background. This, in turn, resulted in a counterrevolution as young radicals, often from well-to-do families, were attracted to religious fundamentalism and the idea of establishing a Sikh nation in the Punjab, India's breadbasket. During the 1980s, this spilled over into violence as the Sikhs' convictions grew that they were being discriminated against by the Hindu-dominated national government. One victim was Indira Gandhi, India's prime minister, who was assassinated by her Sikh bodyguards after she ordered Indian troops to attack the Sikhs' sacred Golden Temple, where militants had fortified themselves. In 1990, India, whose population of 880 million was 82 percent Hindu, and Pakistan almost came to blows over Kashmir, the only Indian state with a Muslim majority, which wanted to secede from India. Characterized by religious and political violence and terrorism, 1990 was the most violent year in the four decades since India had become independent. Rajiv Gandhi, who had succeeded his mother in office until he lost an election, was its most prominent victim; he was assassinated in the midst of the 1991 election in which he was seeking to lead India once more. The assassination was reportedly plotted by a Sri Lankan separatist group because Gandhi had sent the Indian army to that island nation in the 1980s in an unsuccessful attempt to help squash Tamil separatism. In the election itself, the second largest party was a fundamentalist Hindu party, which threatened not only the Muslim minority but also the secular nature of the Indian state.

Religious divisions have tended to be disastrous. Internal religious differences have hampered nation building in Lebanon, where religious and political hostilities among Maronite Christians and other Christian sects, as well as Druse, Shiite, and Sunni Muslims, all but destroyed the country. While their impacts have not been as devastating as in Lebanon, religious conflicts have occurred in other countries as well. In Nigeria, for example, the religious differences between the Muslim Hausas and the Christian Ibos fueled modern Africa's bloodiest civil war, which lasted three years and reflected tribal, regional, and economic divisions; over a million lives were lost. In the Sudan, conflict erupted between the black Christian south and the Arab Muslim north when the government tried to impose the Islamic laws on the Christians. This conflict, combined with millions of refugees from Ethiopia and rioting in response to the government's removal of food subsidies, led to the overthrow of the government. But the fighting continued.

Regionalism. Regional differences are a third divisive element, particularly when they are accompanied by the uneven distribution of resources and wealth. "Regionalism is understandable because ethnic loyalties can usually find expression in geographical terms. Inevitably, some regions will be richer than others, and if the ethnic claim to power combines with relative wealth, the case for secession is strong."[11] In India, this is the basis for the Sikhs' demands for greater autonomy, if not independence. When Pakistan was born and split between East and West Pakistan, separated by over a thousand miles, it was West Pakistan that became more prosperous, even though many of the resources were located in East Pakistan. This fueled the latter's resentment and revolt, which led to the establishment of Bangladesh and the further division of Pakistan.

Ethnicity. Ethnic or tribal divisions also contribute to disunity. Indeed, African tribal chieftains may invoke the same claim of national self-determination that the intelligentsia originally invoked in behalf of their nations. Moreover, because Europeans often split up tribal groups when drawing their artificial boundary lines in the conference rooms of Berlin, London, and Paris, the new nations' frontiers have tended to be unstable. Tribes freely cross frontiers in search of water and grazing lands; one part of a tribe may even try to break away from its "nation" to join the rest of the tribe in the neighboring nation. The result may be a frontier war such as that between Ethiopia and Somalia in 1977, when Somalia tried to unite with its ethnics in Ethiopia who sought to secede and join Somalia. One consequence was that the Soviets were forced to choose between two friends, Ethiopia and Somalia; together with 10,000 Cuban troops, the Soviets intervened on the side of Ethiopia, the larger nation. But $12 billion later and after a virtual cutoff of Soviet aid in 1991, the Marxist government of Ethiopia fell to its Marxist civil war opponents, among whom were the Eritreans who had sought independence since World War II.

Tribalism also affects domestic politics. In some countries, such as Burundi, tribal warfare breaks out from time to time between the minority Watusis, who rule the nation, and the majority Hutus. In 1988, one of these eruptions resulted in the death of an estimated 20,000 people in one week; in 1972, 100,000 Hutus had been massacred. One major reason for the civil war in Angola during the 1970s was the exclusion of the largest tribal group, the Ovimbundu, from the Soviet- and Cuban-supported government.

Sometimes problems related to race, religion, regionalism, and ethnicity occur simultaneously. For example, the war against Iraq in 1991 was fought to destroy its military power, which represented a threat to the entire area. But a defeated Iraq also may present a danger: domestic conflict and the nation's dismemberment by its neighbors. A nation drawn by the British at the end of World War I, Iraq encompassed three regions of the Ottoman Empire: Kurds in the north, Shiite Muslims—tied culturally and religiously to Iran—in the south, and Sunni Muslims in the center. These dissimilar groups were held together first by a British-supported monarchy and, after its overthrow in the 1950s, by a series of military governments. The Kurds, about a third of Iraq's population, have long suffered as a result of the government's policies, including the gas attack by Saddam Hussein after the war with Iran ended in 1988. They have long sought their own state, based economically on Iraq's main oil fields, which are on their territory. The Shiites, the largest group in Iraq, have been treated badly as well by Saddam Hussein's government because of its fear of Shiite collaboration with Iran during the Iran-Iraq war. Even more frightening than the threat of civil war are the appetites of Iraq's neighbors. Turkey has had claims on the northern oil region of Iraq since the breakup of the Ottoman Empire; Syria and Iraq have long been bitter enemies; and Iran, a state larger than Iraq but defeated by it in their eight-year war, undoubtedly wished to reassert its power and influence in the Gulf if the circumstances were right. The most likely beneficiaries of an Iraqi defeat, Syria and Iran, might well replace Iraq as threats to the postwar stability of the region. The U.S. goal therefore had to be not just the ejection of Saddam Hussein from Kuwait and the destruction of his offensive capabilities, but also the establishment of a regional balance after hostilities had ceased.

Language. The lack of political and cultural cohesiveness faced by new nations is symbolized by the language problem, the fifth element in their disunity. Language is one of the most important factors in forming and preserving a sense of nationality. Uniformity of language not only helps people communicate with one another but also promotes common attitudes and values. Group consciousness and common interests are stimulated in turn; people learn to think in terms of "we" as opposed to "they." Yet in many developing countries several languages are spoken, and any attempt to impose a single language is resisted. The prospects for national cohesion in these circumstances are not promising.

In India, a nation with fifty major regional languages, fourteen of which are recognized officially, the government has tried to make Hindi the official language. The fact is that English, the colonizer's language, has become the preferred language of many urban Indians, especially India's educated, rapidly expanding middle class. English is also the language of commerce, computers, finance, science, and social sciences, as well as of the leading newspapers, advertising, and growing television network. Even though it is emerging as the nation's first language, English is spoken only by about 150 million Indians, reflecting what may well be a schism between modern India and traditional India. Since the key decisions that affect most Indians' lives and the important discussions carried on in the news media are in English, most Indians may be increasingly cut off from public life. Yet efforts to make Hindi the national language have led to repeated rioting and violence. In neighboring Pakistan, the national language, Urdu, is spoken only by a minority.

Overpopulation

The second problem encountered in modernizing developing countries is overpopulation. Not all such countries have this problem, but where it exists, overpopulation casts doubt on whether a country can make any economic progress at all. In 1987, the world population passed the 5 billion mark and is increasing at an annual rate of just over 2 percent. Even as population growth in the Third World, with the exception of Africa, began to slow down in the period from 1980 to 1985, it was still 2.02 percent, while the annual rate of population growth in the developed world was 0.64 percent. Africa had the highest rate (3.01 percent), followed by Latin America (2.30); South Asia, including India (2.20); and East Asia, excluding Japan (1.20). Despite this slowing of population growth, the figures for the population growth of specific countries remain startling. For example, in 1950 Mexico's population was 27 million; in 1987 it hit 83 million. China's population of 547 million in 1950 has since passed the billion mark. India will likely overtake China early in the next century. Kenya has the highest population growth in the world: its 6 million people in 1950 had almost quadrupled by 1988; at a growth rate of 4 percent, its 23 million population will reach 79 million in thirty years. Nigeria's population of 112 million, growing at a rate of 3 percent, will total 274 million in three decades.[12] In 1900, there was one European for every two Asians; in 2000, the ratio will probably be one to four. It is also estimated that by 2000 there will be two Latin Americans for each North American—and this is based on a 300 million population figure for the United States.

There is then a population explosion. World population first reached 1 billion in 1830, and by 1930 it had doubled. In 1960, the total was 3 billion people, nearly half of whom were under twenty years old. The fourth billion took only another fifteen years. Currently at 5 billion, world population is expected to exceed 6 billion by the year 2000, and by 2025 it will be 8.5 billion. Moreover, the inhabitants of Third World countries (including China) will constitute more than 80 percent of the world's population. Fewer than 20 percent—perhaps only 15 percent—of the rest of the world's citizens will live in North America, Europe, the former Soviet Union, and Japan. Can this crowded earth continue to sustain such enormous increases in population—of over 1 million people every five days—despite the recent decrease in population growth in the Third World (see Table 10-1)?

Disturbance of Malthusian Checks. The developing countries have come face to face with the realities of the Malthusian problem: the constant hunger and grinding poverty that result when the population grows faster than the means of subsistence. More than 150 years ago the Reverend Thomas Malthus, a British cleric who was also an economist, predicted this fate for the Western world—unless population growth was limited by "positive checks" (such as wars and epidemics) or "preventive checks" (such as sterilization and contraception). The great economic progress of the West—despite the huge population increase since 1800—had seemed to refute the Malthusian prediction. Agricultural production increased to provide a plentiful supply of food, and industrial production raised the standard of living to new heights. For years, therefore, Malthus's dire warning was ignored by all save diehard pessimists.

Ironically, the pattern in the developing countries to a significant degree has been brought about by the colonial powers. In the precolonial period, the Malthusian "positive checks" had, in their own cruel way, contributed to some sort of balance between population and resources. But the Western colonial

Table 10-1 Population Estimations, 1950 and 1980, and Projections, 2000-2100 (in millions)

	1950	1980	2000	2025	2050	2100	Total Fertility Rate 1980[a]	Year in which NRR = 1[b]
Selected Countries								
China	547	980	1,198	1,397	1,414	1,426	2.3	2005
India	350	675	1,001	1,361	1,605	1,778	4.7	2020
Indonesia	80	146	216	297	351	388	4.4	2020
Brazil	53	118	177	239	274	297	3.9	2015
Bangladesh	42	89	156	259	342	412	6.3	2035
Nigeria	32	85	169	329	472	600	6.9	2040
Pakistan	40	82	148	249	329	394	6.4	2035
Mexico	27	69	115	166	197	214	4.8	2015
Egypt	20	42	64	88	104	115	4.6	2020
Kenya	6	17	40	84	122	153	8.0	2030
Regions								
Developing countries								
Africa	223	479	903	1,646	2,297	2,873	6.4	2050
East Asia	587	1,061	1,312	1,542	1,573	1,596	2.3	2020
South Asia	695	1,387	2,164	3,125	3,810	4,328	4.9	2045
Latin America	165	357	543	748	868	944	4.1	2035
Subtotal	1,670	3,284	4,922	7,061	8,548	9,741	4.2	2050
Developed countries	834	1,140	1,284	1,393	1,425	1,454	1.9	2005
Total world	2,504	4,424	6,206	8,454	9,973	11,195	3.6	

SOURCE: Robert S. McNamara, "The Population Problem," *Foreign Affairs* (Summer 1984): 1113. Reprinted with permission.

[a] Total fertility rate is the number of children an average woman would have during her lifetime.

[b] NRR (net reproduction rate) refers to a level of childbearing in which each couple on average replaces itself in the next generation. This column thus projects a decline in the level of fertility to just a replacement level.

states, by introducing modern medicine, upset the balance: more of the newborn survived, people lived longer, and populations began to increase at much greater rates. The AIDS epidemic, growing rapidly in the developing countries and becoming the leading killer of adults in their most productive years, may affect this population growth, however; 40 million people by the year 2000—90 percent of whom will live in the developing world—are expected to be infected.

Hindrances to Birth Control.   Children in many of these countries are a religious, social, and even economic necessity. In India, for example, Muslims believe that children are the "gift of Allah," and the childless couple is pitied or despised; a woman does not even establish herself with her husband or his family until she has borne a son. A Hindu man needs a son to perform certain rituals after his death, and during life he needs sons to fight in village feuds or in tribal warfare. Furthermore, there is a fear of having *too few* children, for they may be needed to work in the fields and support their parents as the latter grow older. Children are in this sense a substitute for the social security payments or endowment policies common in the West. People, in short, are not poor because they have large families; they have large families because they are poor. Birth control can be economically disastrous in these circumstances. The family is also the hub of life for Indian villagers. Weddings and births are festive social occasions, important village events. A woman's prestige may even be measured by the number of children, especially sons, that she bears. A voluntary reduction in the size of her family would in these circumstances strike at the very basis of her life.

Fertility, then, once the key to survival, seems to have become the curse of humankind (see Table 10-2). Despite a slight decline in its growth rate since 1970, the world population continues to rise. A UN Children's Fund (UNICEF) report in 1990 forecast a peak 149 million births in the year 2000, compared to 142 million in 1990, before starting a gentle decline. The fertility rate in the Third World fell from 6.1 births per woman in the late 1960s to 4.2 in the late 1980s (compared with 1.9 in the United States). Yet at the 1984 UN International Conference on Population, despite a World Bank study that predicted that even with the declining birthrate the world's population will double by 2050, the United States took a strong stand against abortion and family planning. Since 1974, U.S. law has prohibited the use of foreign aid for abortion, reflecting the domestic controversy over family planning. President Ronald Reagan's administration, strongly influenced by pro-life groups, administered the law strictly, withdrew its contribution to the UN Fund for Population Activities in 1986, and cut off all funds for nongovernmental organizations working in family planning if they supported abortions. Planned Parenthood, for example, had to cancel programs in eighteen African countries, despite the fact that only an estimated 30 percent of couples in developing countries outside of China use contraceptives. Remarkably, Secretary of State George Shultz could still say, "Rampant population growth underlies the third world's poverty, and poses a major long-term threat to political stability and our planet's resource base."[13] This was an accurate assessment, but U.S. policy during the Reagan years guaranteed a more crowded planet, and the Bush administration has continued this policy.

Yet there is some glimmer of hope. Despite the U.S. stance, there has been a largely unnoticed contraceptive revolution. As the 1990s began, Third World women were averaging 3.9 births and more than 50 percent of women were using some means of contraception, according to UN estimates. This contrasts sharply with six children and only 8 percent of women using contraceptives in 1965. Some of the most notable successes have been in Thailand, Indonesia, Mexico, Colombia, Brazil, and Bangladesh (in sub-Saharan Africa and the Islamic world contraception remains low and fertility

Table 10-2 Population and Economic Growth Rates of Selected
Developing Countries, 1991 (in percent)

Country	Population Growth Rate	Economic Growth Rate
Angola	2.7	2.0
Brazil	1.8	-4.6
Egypt	2.3	1.0
Honduras	2.9	0.0
India	1.9	4.5
Ivory Coast	3.9	-1.2
Kenya	2.6	4.0
Malawi	1.8	4.8
Malaysia	2.4	10.0
Mexico	2.2	3.9
Morocco	2.1	2.5
Nigeria	3.0	2.7
Zaire	3.3	-2.0

SOURCE: Central Intelligence Agency, *The World Factbook 1991* (Washington, D.C.: Central Intelligence Agency, 1991).

high). If in this decade a sufficient investment is made in family planning, the world's population of 5.4 billion might stabilize between 10 and 12 billion by 2045, according to UN projections.[14] And in a Malthusian way, the AIDS epidemic mentioned earlier may affect this population growth.

Consequences for Political and Social Stability. For the developing countries, the following maxim may yet be painfully true: *industrial revolutions may be defeated by Malthusian counterrevolutions.*[15] In developing countries that have achieved economic growth, population increases may cancel most, if not all, of the hoped-for increase in living standards or savings for capital investment. How can these developing countries possibly provide adequate food, housing, education, health care, and jobs for all their people? The Aswan Dam, planned in 1955 and completed in 1970, added 25 percent to Egypt's arable land, but in those fifteen years, Egypt's population increased by 50 percent to more than 30 million. By the year 2000, the Egyptian population will double to more than 64 million if the present rate of growth continues. Mexico, with a population in 1980 of 69 million people and projected to add 50 million by the year 2000, must create 700,000 new jobs per year if its already high unemployment rate is not to increase even more, but the prediction is for only 350,000 jobs a year. In 1988, the UN Population Fund warned that within ten years the developing countries would have to increase their capacity to provide social services by 65 percent just to maintain their present living conditions. As it is, many Third World governments cannot cope with the current demands for jobs, education, housing, health services, sanitary systems, and other social services brought on by the shift of their ever larger populations from the land to the city.

By the year 2000, more than half the world's people will live in over-crowded cities; and four of the six largest cities will be in the Third World.[16] Mexico City may be the world's largest city, growing from the present 15 million to 26 million; São Paolo, Brazil, will be 24 million; and Calcutta and Bombay, both in India, will be 17 and 16 million, respectively (Tokyo also will be the third largest city with 17 million, and New York City will have just over 15 million). The masses of people will strain, if not collapse, the already inadequate social services and facilities such as transportation, sanitation, education, and housing. Of the top thirty-five cities in the year 2000, twenty-five will be in the developing countries. They may come to resemble huge slums surrounding small inner-city enclaves of middle-class dwellers and may, in turn, become the breeding grounds of political radicalism and social turmoil. In the words of Robert McNamara, former president of the World Bank,

> Rapid population growth, in sum, translates into rising numbers of labor force entrants, faster-expanding urban populations, pressure on food supplies, ecological degradation, and increasing numbers of "absolute poor." All are rightly viewed by governments as threats to social stability and orderly change. Even under vigorous economic growth, managing the demographic expansion is difficult; with a faltering economy it is all but impossible.[17]

Malnutrition and Hunger

The third problem impeding modernization in the Third World is inadequate food supplies and growing malnutrition. The paradox of the developing countries is that, although the overwhelming majority of their populations live on the land, the peasants do not produce enough food. The emphasis instead has been on industrialization and such visible projects as steel factories and automobile plants with the hope that replication of at least the outward symbols of industrial society will raise living standards. This usually has led to the neglect of agriculture, which requires costly long-term investment in land reclamation and irrigation projects, fertilizer plants, and extension services. Furthermore, to the leaders of these countries, agriculture has meant poverty; it has been a constant reminder of colonial subjugation and of their continued status as suppliers of raw materials. But industry has symbolized freedom and national dignity. Given the continued swings in the prices of agricultural commodities, investing more money in food has been viewed, not surprisingly, without enthusiasm.

Yet food production must be raised to feed the rapidly growing populations. *An industrial revolution requires a prior or simultaneous agrarian revolution.*[18] Instead of being separate and distinct processes, agricultural development and industrial development are intertwined. An industrial revolution cannot occur without the provision of extra food to feed the urban population, and raising food production above the subsistence level requires the application of science and technology to farming. Britain, the first nation to industrialize, also had the highest agricultural productivity at the time. By contrast, most developing countries have to spend their hard-earned currency on *importing* food.

Food imports stem from the dilemma facing developing countries: cheap food for urban workers means keeping prices down, but low prices provide little incentive for farmers to raise production. Higher prices for farmers, however, may lead to trouble, even rioting or a coup d'état. Most Third World governments, therefore, have failed to provide farmers with the necessary economic incentives to provide more food; few governments have had the courage to stake their own survival on this issue. Cheap food is used to curb economic and political unrest because high food prices are dangerous when wages are low and many people are unemployed or underemployed. Government policy, in short, has been a principal stumbling block to food production, leading several former "breadbaskets" to become empty baskets, no longer able to feed themselves and forced to import food.

Yet the Green Revolution, so-called because of its use of high-yield strains of grain and rice to increase production per acre, has been remarkably successful in several countries. Between 1954 and 1973, the food supply in the Third World increased sufficiently to feed an extra 1.3 billion mouths. India, once the recipient of American food aid, became self-sufficient in food and has even begun to export wheat. Thus, more and more developing countries have begun to realize that the rush to industrialize and the neglect of agriculture were wrong, and agricultural development finally is receiving the emphasis reserved in the late 1950s, 1960s, and 1970s for industrialization. Like India's, China's impressive increase in food production—50 percent in just the eight years from 1976 to 1984—is evidence of a change that points to the farmer, instead of the industrialist, as the key figure in pulling the developing countries up out of poverty and hunger. Together with large surpluses of food in North America and Western Europe, this suggests that Malthus's contention that population increases will outgrow the world's ability to feed its inhabitants may be wrong.

But despite the increases in food production since 1950, during the 1980s an estimated 700 million people, according to the World Bank, still confronted the prospect of malnutrition. Africa and South Asia fall within the area of fastest population growth, suggesting that even India's claim to self-sufficiency may only mean the maintenance of a subsistence diet and that tens of millions of India's population remain undernourished. Thus, one-third of the population of the Third World does not consume sufficient calories to sustain an active working life, and one-fourth of the populations of Africa and South Asia do not receive enough calories to prevent stunted growth and health problems. Sizable increases in food production are therefore needed just to sustain the current population, let alone future growth. In the longer run, whether food production can be accelerated to keep up with future population growth remains questionable, unless there is significant progress toward limiting such growth. On occasion, however, as in Ethiopia, two other factors account for malnutrition: civil war and governmental callousness.

Ethiopia's Soviet-style collectivization of land by its late Marxist rulers had already created hunger and malnutrition before 1985, the year an extended drought brought death to millions. Incredibly, despite its people's starvation, Ethiopia spent $100 million the same year on the tenth anniversary celebration of its 1975 revolution which had abolished the monarchy. Had it not been for a foreign photographer, who sold his film to Western television, the widespread starvation accompanying the drought might not have become known outside of Ethiopia. The government had suppressed the news in favor of glorifying "Ethiopian socialism." Even after trucks and food had been shipped to Ethiopia, the regime gave priority to unloading Soviet arms over Western food and used the trucks for military purposes rather than for the transport of food to the starving. The government, moreover, would not allow food distribution in rebel areas. In any event, it was only the outcry in the West that compelled the Ethiopian regime to pay some attention to its starving people, and it was largely private Western relief agencies that transported the food, often in the face of government obstruction and incompetence. In 1987-1988, drought and civil wars (in Ethiopia, Sudan, and Mozambique) again produced famine in central and southern Africa. But in Ethiopia, hard hit once more, the government refused to allow foreign relief agencies to distribute food in certain areas because of the continuing internal strife. Thus, the donated food piled up as millions were threatened with starvation. Despite the government, however, resourceful agencies got food through to the needy and avoided a repetition of the starvation of 1985. In 1991, civil war, not drought, placed millions at risk of dying from famine. Matters did not improve much after government forces were defeated by the rebels in the Ethiopian civil war and the government collapsed. More than 100,000 refugees fled to neighboring nations, and 300,000 more, mostly soldiers loyal to the old government, were left without any means of subsistence.

Ethiopian indifference to the suffering of its people unfortunately is not unique.[19] Today, developing country governments aware of food crises can call on the reserve food supplies that Western governments put aside each year if their harvests are plentiful. If developing country governments do not possess the administrative skills and organization for emergency relief, international relief organizations are available to help. The fact, however, is that governments for various reasons, including the desire not to publicize failures that reflect poorly on them, may not care about the feeding of their peoples—for example, in China from 1959 to 1962 in the wake of the "Great Leap Forward," a disastrous economic experiment in which several millions were believed to have starved; in Nigeria, where from 1967 to early 1970 the government encouraged starvation to bring the rebel province of Biafra back into the national fold, at the cost of perhaps 1 million ethnic Ibos who lived there; in East Pakistan in 1970, when the government, located in West Pakistan, responded slowly in the aftermath of a typhoon, resulting in no only about 100,000 deaths but also secession and the creation of the new state of Bangladesh; in Ethiopia, where the emperor, before his overthrow in 1974, tried to conceal news of a famine; in Afghanistan, where after 1979 Soviet forces deliberately destroyed crops to force hungry peasants either into the Soviet-controlled towns and cities or out of the country; and in the Sudan, where in 1990-1991, government forces attacked those delivering food to the southern part of the country in order to end the civil war between the Arab Muslim north and the Christian African south.

Even if sufficient food were made available by providing farmers with the incentive of higher prices, many people in developing countries could not afford to buy food, especially if prices rose.[20] During the 1974 world food crisis, for example, there was enough food to go around. The cause of hunger was simple: poverty and poor income distribution in the affected areas. The higher the price of food, the more widespread hunger will be because the poor already spend 60-80 percent of their income on food. Even in those countries where the Green Revolution increased food production—India, Pakistan, Bangladesh, and Mexico—malnutrition remains. The sub-Saharan region will continue to be a chronic food-deficit area, with a limited food supply and too many people. The key to reducing malnutrition and eliminating starvation is therefore an agricultural *and* industrial revolution.

Accumulating Capital for Modernization

A fourth overwhelming problem of backward, even stagnant, economies is how to accumulate the capital needed to escape a past as "raw-material appendages" to the industrial powers. New nations recognize the need to build industrial economies to banish poverty, end economic dependence on the former colonial powers, and achieve international standing.

Developing countries are exporters of raw materials. Fifty nations rely on single commodities for export; others rely on two or three resources. Altogether, ninety-three developing countries rely on the export of crops or natural resources other than oil for more than 50 percent of their export earnings (see Table 10-3 for examples of developing country exports). Theoretically, these countries should be able to earn sufficient capital from their exports to carry out large-scale industrialization because, ideally, as Western industrial nations continue to consume more, their demand for raw materials should rise. In practice, however, it usually has not worked out that way. The developing countries' dependence on exports of raw materials has limited their earning capacities. One reason is that their exports reflect every fluctuation in the Western business cycle. For example, as Western industrial economies approach full employment, the demand for and prices of materials rise. When these economies turn downward, as they did in the 1970s and economic growth remains low as in the 1980s, demand and prices decline. A drop of just one cent in coffee or copper prices can result in the loss of millions of dollars, sometimes tens of millions of dollars, for developing countries. As the Mexicans used to say, "A sneeze in the American economy can lead to

Table 10-3 Selected One-Commodity Countries

Latin America	Iraq	Comoros	Rwanda
Bahamas	*Crude petroleum*	*Cloves*	*Coffee*
Petroleum products	Kuwait	Congo	Seychelles
Bolivia	*Crude petroleum*	*Crude petroleum*	*Copra*
Natural gas (1983)	Oman	Gabon	Somalia
Colombia	*Crude petroleum*	*Crude petroleum*	*Live animals*
Coffee	Qatar	The Gambia	Uganda
El Salvador	*Crude petroleum*	*Groundnut products*	*Coffee*
Coffee	Saudi Arabia	Guinea	Zaire
Jamaica	*Crude petroleum*	*Bauxite*	*Copper*
Alumina	South Yemen	Lesotho	Zambia
Mexico	*Petroleum products*	*Diamonds*	*Copper*
Crude petroleum	Syria	Liberia	
Netherlands Antilles	*Crude petroleum*	*Iron ore*	**Asia/Pacific**
Petroleum products	United Arab	Libya	Brunei
Suriname	Emirates	*Crude petroleum*	*Petroleum*
Alumina	*Crude petroleum*	Mauritania	*products*
Trinidad and Tobago		*Iron ore*	Fiji
Petroleum	**Africa**	Mauritius	*Sugar*
products	Algeria	*Sugar*	Indonesia
Venezuela	*Crude petroleum*	Niger	*Crude petroleum*
Crude petroleum	Angola	*Uranium*	Papua New Guinea
Middle East	*Crude petroleum*	Nigeria	*Copper concentrate*
Iran	Botswana	*Crude petroleum*	Vanuatu
Crude petroleum	*Diamonds*		*Copra*
	Burundi		
	Coffee		

SOURCE: United States Department of State, *Atlas of United States Foreign Relations*, 2d ed. (Washington, D.C.: Department of State, 1985), 54.

NOTE: Based on 1980-1983 export average; market economies only. One-commodity countries are those for which one commodity provides more than 50 percent of export earnings.

pneumonia in Mexico." * Commodity prices during the last decade were the lowest in fifty years! A second reason for the limited earning capacities of exports is that advanced Western industrial technology has, in many instances, made it both possible and profitable to develop synthetics and other substitutes for Western-imported raw materials. The demand for resources by industries no longer dependent on certain natural raw materials then decreases and prices drop. A final reason for developing countries' difficulties in earning money through their exports is their practice of producing more to

---

* In Colombia, dependent on coffee exports for legal income, a 40 percent drop in coffee prices, stemming from a 1980s U.S. suspension of an international coffee agreement, drove more farmers to produce and process coca. Yet Washington was simultaneously urging Colombia to eliminate its cocaine industry. An international price support program for coffee was clearly needed if farmers were to make a living.

compensate for low prices. The result is a glut on the international market, which drives prices even lower. For example, for Chile or Zambia, dependent solely on copper exports, the drop in price from $1.34 per pound in 1980 to 65 cents in 1985 was a disaster; the same has been true for Ghana and cocoa, Uganda and coffee, Cuba and sugar, and Chad and cotton.

The dilemma of many developing countries is agonizing. They desperately need capital, and they rely on their raw material exports to earn it. But the harder they work to enlarge the volume of these exports to enhance their earnings, the less they may earn. At the same time, because of their frequent difficulties in producing enough food for their rapidly growing populations, they must buy food. They also must import the Western machinery required to boost their industrialization, the price of which is usually rising. The "terms of trade"—the developing countries' earnings from their exports versus the cost of their imports—are thus against them. Exports of raw materials then do not seem a likely route of escape from poverty for the non-OPEC developing countries dependent on commodity exports. Faced with higher oil prices, a sharp drop in commodity prices, and shrinking Western markets because of the increase in oil prices, many developing countries began to borrow heavily in the 1970s, only to accumulate huge debts (see Chapter 15). The declining foreign aid from Western countries reinforced this trend. Banks, given the debts, were not eager to loan more money. As a result, in the 1980s developing countries eagerly sought relationships with multinational corporations (MNCs), as aid and trade failed to bring in sufficient capital. But the MNCs often repatriated their profits rather than reinvesting in the countries in which they were earning their money; indeed, even the initial capital outlays may have come partly or wholly from local sources, diverting capital from native investments. Certainly, with debt repayments, more capital was by the mid-1980s flowing from the poor South to the rich North than the other way around.

Newly Industrialized Countries

The international economy is, however, in the process of major change (see Chapter 8). While in the past the developed states imported raw materials and agricultural products from the developing countries, they are now increasingly importing finished goods. This change stems in part from a vast increase in the activities of multinational corporations (see Chapter 16). During the 1960s, the international economy began to be turned on its head as MNCs invested in the low-wage nations to produce manufactured goods for export to the industrial nations. The latter now export agricultural goods to the poor states, a startling change from the previous pattern. In the 1970s, political observers Richard Barnet and Ronald Müller called this phenomenon the "Latinamericanization of the United States":

> Production of the traditional industrial goods that have been the mainstay of the
> U.S. economy is being transferred from $4-an-hour factories in New England to

Table 10-4 Profile of Eight Newly Industrialized Countries, 1991

Country or City-State	Population (millions)	Infant Mortality Rate (per thousand)	Life Expectancy	Literacy Rate (%)	Per Capita Income
Hong Kong	5.8	7	77 men 84 women	77	$11,000
Indonesia	193.6	73	59 men 63 women	77	490
Malaysia	18.0	29	65 men 71 women	78	2,460
Philippines	65.8	54	62 men 67 women	90	700
Singapore	2.8	8	72 men 77 women	88	12,700
South Korea	43.1	23	67 men 73 women	96	5,600
Taiwan	20.7	6	72 men 78 women	91	7,380
Thailand	56.8	37	66 men 71 women	93	1,400

SOURCE: Central Intelligence Agency, *The World Factbook 1991* (Washington, D.C.: Central Intelligence Agency, 1991).

30 cents-an-hour factories in the "export platforms" of Hong Kong and Taiwan. Increasingly, as the cars, televisions, computers, cameras, clothes, and furniture are being produced abroad, the United States is becoming a service economy and a producer of plans, programs, and ideas for others to execute. . . .

The United States trading pattern is beginning to resemble that of underdeveloped countries as the number one nation becomes increasingly dependent on the export of agricultural products and timber to maintain its balance of payments and increasingly dependent on imports of finished goods to maintain its standard of living. . . . (Unlike poor countries, however, the U.S. also exports "software"— i.e., technical knowledge.) [21]

This turnaround presently involves only a handful of nations: Hong Kong and Singapore, both city-states; South Korea and Taiwan; as well as Singapore's ASEAN colleagues Malaysia and Thailand, and a few nations in other regions, such as Brazil in Latin America. Table 10-4 reveals the higher per capita incomes, higher life expectancy and literacy rates, and lower infant mortality rates of these nations in contrast to those of the more typical developing countries shown in Table 10-5. Indeed, a look at these figures raises the question of whether Hong Kong and Singapore can still be classified as developing countries, even if they are more rapidly developing ones.

Table 10-5 Profile of Eight Typical Developing Countries, 1991

Country	Population							Economics			Type of Government
	Total (millions)	Growth Rate (%)	Infant Mortality Rate (per thousand)	Life Expectancy	Literacy Rate (%)	Ethnic Groups	Religious Groups	GNP (billion dollars)	Per Capita Income		
Brazil	155	1.8	68	62 men 68 women	81	Portuguese Italian German Japanese Amerindian Black	Roman Catholic	388.0	2,540	Federal republic
El Salvador	5.4	2.0	47	63 men 68 women	73	Mestizo	Roman Catholic	5.1	940	Republic
Ethiopia	53	3.1	114	50 men 53 women	62	Oromo Amhara Tigrean	Muslim Ethiopian Orthodox Animist	6.6	130	Communist state
India	866	1.9	87	57 men 59 women	48	Indo-Aryan Dravidian	Hindu Muslim Sikh	254.0	300	Republic
Kenya	25	2.6	69	60 men 64 women	69	Kikuyu Luhya	Protestant Catholic	8.5	360	Republic
Nigeria	122	3.0	118	48 men 50 women	51 30	Hausa Fulani Yoruba Ibo	Muslim Christian	27.2	230	Federal republic
Pakistan	117	2.5	109	56 men 57 women	35	Punjabi Sindhi Pashunt Baluch Mahajir	Muslim	43.3	380	Islamic republic
Saudi Arabia	17.9	4.2	69	65 men 68 women	62	Arab	Muslim	79.0	4,720	Monarchy

SOURCE: Central Intelligence Agency, *The World Factbook 1991* (Washington, D.C.: Central Intelligence Agency, 1991).

But can the NICs, especially the Asian NICs whose population is less than 5 percent of the entire Third World, serve as a model for the other developing countries? If they can take off economically, should not the other developing nations able to produce textiles, clothing, simple consumer electronics, and such products as shoes and toys take their place on the lower rungs of the development ladder? Probably not.[22] Potential NICs, like the commodity-exporting nations, confront a shrinking international economy. The 5 percent growth in the 1950s and 1960s fell back to 3 percent in the 1970s and fell further to just over 2 percent in the 1980s. In short, the rapid growth of the international economy through the 1960s permitted room for newcomers, but this may now be at an end. Indeed, the very presence of South Korea and Taiwan may be obstacles to the entry of new Koreas and Taiwans. Moreover, as Western industries decline and unemployment grows, protectionist pressures grow. In fact, the more successful developing countries are at exporting—for example, textiles, clothing, and shoes—the more likely they are to face rising trade barriers. Not surprisingly, the Third World has stopped growing since the early 1980s; many developing nations have even slipped backward. It is therefore doubtful that, for their development, they can rely on the export strategies adopted earlier by the NICs. Yet whether a strategy oriented toward production for the domestic market will be more successful for most developing countries also remains to be seen. Ironically, Communist China—which has been shifting to capitalist market methods—may become the new model for many of the nonexporting developing countries, if the quashing by its leaders of the pro-democracy movement in 1989 does not set the country back.

Cultural Transformation

The term *economic development* suggests a one-dimensional picture of the transition process from a traditional rural society to an advanced modern nation. Economic development implies that the only requirement for this process is industry, that industrialization follows automatically from the formation of capital, and that mobilizing capital is therefore the crucial problem. Even when agricultural growth is included, as it must be, the term *economic development* is an oversimplification—indeed, a distortion—of the complex realities of modernizing a traditional society. Modernization is more than simply building steel mills and constructing dams. It means, above all else, changes in values, aspirations, and expectations. The necessary changes are not simply economic, but also political, social, and cultural. Modernization is multidimensional; it aims at the complete transformation of society.

Traditional societies have not usually regarded economic activity as a prime concern. Even in Western history, money making was not always the chief pursuit. In the Middle Ages, for example, religion was the principal concern. The church condemned the charging of interest—a necessity in a monetary economy—as usury. The desire for profit was equated with greed, and economic competition was simply not part of the accepted way of life. This attitude toward interest and profits was, of course, inimical to business. A major break with this medieval attitude came with the introduction of the Protestantism of John Calvin in the sixteenth century. In contrast to Catholicism, it gave priority to earthly works. Industriousness, profits, savings, and investments were in this way legitimated by religion. Thrift, character, and hard work represented the earthly trinity.

It is hardly surprising that this "Protestant ethic" and capitalism became closely identified.[23] It was but a short way from Calvin to eighteenth-century British economist Adam Smith, whose theory of capitalism was based on recognition of the acquisitive passion that the Roman Catholic church had earlier condemned. Smith accepted the desire for gain as a fact of life, calling it "enlightened self-interest." *Laissez-faire* capitalism was merely to harness this acquisitive instinct to the public welfare.

In the contemporary world such a process of secularization is also critical. Today, the NICs embody this "Protestant" ethic with their "this world" attitude, their energetic and active orientation as opposed to contemplative life, and their positive view toward accumulating wealth, which is combined with a willingness to postpone gratification, thereby gaining savings for further investment and capital accumulation.[24] This secularization has not gone unchallenged, however. Islamic fundamentalism, which has spread throughout much of the Middle East and West Asia since the late 1970s, is essentially an "other world" religion, a reaction against Westernization, and an attempt to uphold traditional society and values—and the status of the mullahs or religious leaders.[25] The process of modernization brings with it a "foreign" way of life, whose external manifestations such as rock music, dancing, public displays of affection between couples, and pornography are often as shocking for old societies as ostentatious displays of wealth by the newly rich (which are in striking contrast to the lifestyles of the ordinary people) and the omnipresence of foreigners doing business. Critics of modernization have called it "Westoxication."

Psychologically, modernization means recognition of the inferiority of both the old ways and old society and the superiority of the foreigner's—the Westerner's—way. Thus, it was the inferiority of the traditional society and its way of life that made it possible for Western states to conquer these "backward" areas. The colonialists were the first to erode traditional society. Westerners may have been able to colonize the non-Western world because they had the guns, but to the natives guns were a symbol of a more advanced society.

Not unnaturally, the West considered itself to be the model of what an advanced, modern society should be; where it led, others would follow. It was not a matter of coercion but of preference. Islamic fundamentalism is the most profound, most widespread, and angriest reaction to this phenomenon. It also has been violently anti-American until recently because the United States represents the most advanced secular Western society and is the most powerful Western state. Islamic fundamentalism asserts the dignity and worth of the ways of Islam, and it provides the mass of people untouched by the prosperity of Westernization—indeed, often displaced by it when, for example, people are driven off the land into urban shantytowns—a sense of belonging and spiritual and emotional comfort. In Iran, this movement was led by the mullahs, the traditional religious leaders whose property had been confiscated by the shah and whose role in a modern secular society would have been much less important than that of other groups. Not only has Islam gained a firm grip in Iran, but rulers in other states from Pakistan to the Sudan and Egypt have either adopted Islamic laws or become sensitive to them. Its potential to spread among Muslims in other Arab countries, the Israeli-occupied West Bank, and even the former Soviet Union north of Afghanistan is a matter of concern to many.

But the reaction to the cultural transformation inherent in modernization occurs even in those societies that have achieved economic development and cultural changes. It is less severe, obviously, than in Iran, but Westernization spurs ambivalence about the price of success even in such a city-state as Singapore. Because traditional society with its emphasis on community values and hierarchy gives away in a modern society to individualism, achievement, reward, and social mobility, loss of "core Asian values" and preoccupation with self at the cost of the larger group became a concern of Singapore's former prime minister, Lee Kuan Yew, and his succesor. In Singapore, English is the primary language being taught in the schools, and business has brought in its wake Western television, books, magazines, and other cultural influences. What then is a Singaporean? [26]

NATION BUILDING AND CIVILIAN AND MILITARY AUTHORITARIANISM

Building a nation that is in the initial stages of modernization is thus enormously difficult and complex, requiring a number of tasks. First, the new state must achieve national cohesion. Second, a set of legitimate governmental institutions must be created through which conflict can be channeled peacefully and compromise achieved. Otherwise, coups d'état, riots, revolutions, assassinations, and civil wars will remain the methods of resolving differences.[27] The third task is economic development. For new nations, the response to the "revolution of rising expectations" is important for humanitarian and political reasons and for the cause of nation building itself. The degree to which expectations are satisfied will be proof of the effectiveness of the new national government. Economic development produces a better life for each citizen; its significance is its *political* payoff. The leaders of a new nation not yet solidly knitted together must prove to the people that what they, the leaders, are seeking to establish will benefit the people. Otherwise, why should the people transfer their loyalty to the new nation? Economic development can in this way strengthen the fragile bonds of national unity and give a new nation legitimacy.

But how does the leader of a new nation deal with these tasks? One way is to "nationalize" the people—that is, to inculcate in them national consciousness and loyalty and recognition of the national government as *their* government, its laws reflecting *their* adherence. The majority must acknowledge that they are citizens of one nation and that the national government has the legitimate authority to make decisions on behalf of the entire population. Such popular consciousness cannot be developed overnight. An entire people must, in a sense, go to school—to learn their nation's language and history (much of it mythical, devised for the purpose of fostering national identification) and to be brought into the mainstream of national life. Only then will national symbols stimulate deep emotion and a national community emerge.

After independence, many new developing countries were held together by their leaders, who more than anyone else symbolized the new nation.[28] If they had led the nationalist movement before independence, they had agitated for freedom for years, propagated national mythology, and served time in jail as a result. They and their nations were thus in a very real sense identical. As the founders of these nations, they provided a kind of symbolic presence. Loyalty can usually be felt more keenly toward individuals who incorporate an idea such as the "nation" than toward the idea itself. The heroes in the new nations were transitional figures in transitional societies. They served the indispensable function of encouraging a shift from the traditional, parochial loyalties to tribe or region to broader loyalties to the impersonal nation-state. Moreover, these heroes usually had charisma—"a quality of extraordinary spiritual power attributed to a person ... capable of eliciting popular support in the direction of human affairs." [29] They were, in fact, *substitutes* for their nations and for the national institutions that had yet to be built; they also conferred legitimacy on the new nations and their governments.

They were usually supported by a single party as the principal instrument of national integration. Unlike Western political parties, which primarily represent the various interests within a nation, the single party in a developing country has a double rationale. First, it is a means of socializing the traditionally "tribalized" people on a national basis, instilling in them a sense of identification as citizens of a distinct national community. Just as the charismatic leader replaces the traditional chieftain, the nation is supposed to replace the tribe. The party claims to represent the nation. The second rationale of one-party rule is its alleged efficiency in mobilizing the economic and human resources of a nation for the purpose of modernization.[30] By American standards, such a one-party system is, of course, undemocratic. In the United States, the opposition is a loyal opposition whose allegiance is to the same nation and values as the governing party. But in a new African nation, for example, the opposition's allegiance is often regional and tribal, and it thus represents the centrifugal forces in society. In these circumstances, a change in the form of government favoring greater democracy could result in disintegration of the state. The choice is *not* between democracy and dictatorship but between nationhood and disintegration. The problem is not one of restraining power to ensure individual freedoms, but one of accumulating sufficient power to ensure that the government will be obeyed.[31]

Because of the tenuous nature of the bonds holding a new nation together and the immense difficulties inherent in modernization, civilian one-party governments often give way to military governments. For example, during the first decades of their existence more than half the nations in Africa were governed by the military. By late 1988, thirty-eight of the forty-five sub-Saharan governments were one-party or military governments. Overall, more than two-thirds of the countries of Asia, Africa, the Middle East, and Latin America have experienced varying levels of military intervention since 1945.[32] The trends away from or toward military governments vary by region and circumstance. In the late 1970s, thirteen of Latin America's twenty republics were governed by generals, Haiti by a family dictatorship, and Cuba by a Communist dictator. But that had changed by the early 1990s because the vast majority of countries had by then turned toward civilian democratic rule. Several of the new civilian governments remain fragile, however, in large part because of the debt problem. The army remains visible in the background. Even in Africa, after years of mismanagement, corruption, and economic collapse, by 1991 many of the entrenched authoritarian leaders were being challenged by pro-democracy movements, including those in Zaire, Ghana, Kenya, Zambia, and Zaire.[33]

FOREIGN POLICY IN THE BIPOLAR ERA

Because the leaders of the new states confronted problems that were so vast and seemingly insoluble, they were tempted to play dramatic and popular roles on the international stage rather than concentrate on their nations' domestic needs. Indeed, foreign policy helped them accomplish their various internal aims.

Nationalization of Their People

First, leaders used foreign policy to help them "nationalize" their people. Often the only force that initially united the people was hatred of the former colonial power, but this "reactive nationalism" tended to lose its force as a socially cohesive factor soon after independence. Thus, the only way to arouse people and keep them united was to continue the struggle against European colonialism or "imperialism" in general. The more tenuous the bonds uniting the members of a society, the more ardent was the campaign against the "vestiges of imperialism." By asserting that the nation was once more the victim of the West, leaders sought to arouse the people and unite them against a common external danger. Anticolonialism thus did not end with the achievement of national independence. The struggle against "neocolonialism" had to be continued until a measure of national unity and economic progress had occurred. "Anti-colonialism is a cement that holds together otherwise incompatible domestic factions. The cohesive function of the 'common enemy' must be perpetuated even when the foreign 'enemy' is no longer a real threat. . . . This, perhaps, is the reason why opposition to colonialism frequently grows more intense *after* independence." [34] Foreign policy thus served as *a continuation of the revolution against colonial rule to preserve the unity of the new nation.*

Search for Identity, Status, and Dignity

Second, and closely related, the foreign policy of developing countries involved a search for identity, status, and dignity. Many of these countries were new nations, former colonies, with no national history, no commonly accepted political institutions, no domestic unity, and almost no strong national commitment among their populations. Even if they had a glorious past and were at present independent, the feeling that they were still subject to Western influence led to an assertive foreign policy:

> In short, the state's legitimacy is more easily asserted through its foreign policy than through its domestic policies and it is more apparent when performing on the international than on the national stage. Domestic issues divide the nation and disclose how little developed is its consciousness of itself; foreign issues unite the nation and mark it as a going concern. [35]

Foreign policy, therefore, was also *an effort* to *discover and establish the new state's personality and to affirm its identity as a nation separate from the former colonial power.*

Assertion of Equality

The new states were very conscious that the history of the international system was the history of inequality. By and large, as developing states they were aware of their lower places in the hierarchy of states dominated by the Western industrial states (including Japan). While the leaders of the developing countries vigorously asserted their equality as legally equal sovereign states in the United Nations, they bristled at being excluded from conferences and institutions that dealt with issues that affected their countries, particularly economic and financial ones. The developing countries tended to see themselves as the West's "dependencies" who did not control their own destiny. Thus, a third aim of foreign policy was *to secure greater participation in decisions that had an impact on their societies, and, more generally, to play a more influential role in the state system.*

Maximization of Foreign Aid

A fourth aim of the foreign policy of developing countries was *to attract the external funds necessary for their domestic transformation from rural, economically backward societies to urban-industrial societies with high standards of living.* Bipolarity favored this quest. As political scientist Robert Good observed in 1962, at the height of the cold war,

> The possibility of "blackmail" is built into the very structure of Cold War competition. But from the point of view of the excessively dependent, relatively impotent new state, this is not blackmail. It is the equally ancient but more honorable art of maintaining political equilibrium through the diversification of dependence, the balancing of weakness—in short, the creation of an "alternative" lest the influence of one side or the other become too imposing. The attraction of Communist aid is enhanced for radical governments whose wariness of the intentions of the former metropole extends to the "capitalist-imperialist West" in general. Yet [even] conservative governments are receptive to Communist aid. They want it partly to placate their radical oppositions and to hasten development, but also, one suspects, to pursue the first requirement of operational independence—the creation of a rough equilibrium among foreign influences in the life of the country. Conversely, radical governments that have developed extensive relations with the Communist bloc may seek the re-establishment of compensatory links with the West.[36]

Preservation of Power

Fifth, because nationalist leaders wanted to stay in power, they frequently sought to divert popular attention from domestic problems. At home only painfully slow progress could be made—the task of development was bound to be long and arduous—and the masses tended to become restless and dissatisfied. The gap between their rising material expectations and satisfaction seemed unbridgeable as increasing numbers of people became politically conscious and demanded that their needs be met. The pressure on national leaders to improve living conditions and build the new nation then was unrelenting. If these demands remained unsatisfied, the revolution of rising expectations might turn into a revolution of rising frustration, and the leaders and their governments might suffer declining prestige and support. The tendency to political fragmentation remained ever present.

To preserve or recapture the people's support, stay in power, and stabilize the government, leaders were tempted irresistibly to assert themselves in foreign policy. In circumstances of economic stagnation, cultural alienation, and governmental insecurity, political leaders might try to preserve their power by externalizing domestic dissatisfaction; foreign scapegoats would be required to relieve internal stresses and strains. It was easier for leaders to play prominent and highly visible international roles—at the United Nations, at meetings of the nonaligned states, during visits to Moscow or Western capitals, for example—than to undertake the difficult work of modernizing their nation. Foreign policy, therefore, also served the *purpose of exporting domestic dissatisfaction and mobilizing popular support for the government.*

CHARACTERISTICS OF NONALIGNMENT

A foreign policy of nonalignment during the cold war favored the implementation of all these aims. Bipolarity made nonalignment feasible. By taking an in-between position, a new state could maximize its appeal to both the Soviet Union and the United States, as well as to their respective allies. The two superpowers acted as though they were suitors seeking to win the same woman. By occasionally hinting at a commitment, a new nation could gain leverage, despite its lack of power. Each suitor was then compelled to demonstrate its serious intentions, usually with large amounts of foreign aid. The further a new state moved away from the West, the more eagerly the Communists offered it assistance; the closer it moved to the West, the greater the number of Western loans or grants offered.

Although bipolarity favored nonalignment, not all non-Marxist, non-aligned countries implemented this policy in the same way. The Yugoslavs considered themselves nonaligned, as did the Egyptians, Indians, Ethiopians, Malaysians, and Tunisians. Yet the dispositions of these countries ranged from pro-Soviet to pro-American. In a way, the problem of classifying the varieties of nonalignment was one of *time*. A regime could be looking eastward one moment and yet normalize its relations with the West the next. Ethiopia was pro-American one year; then the new Marxist regime shifted toward the East. But in Somalia, the Marxist government, once close to Moscow, shifted toward the United States when the Soviet Union switched its support from Somalia to Ethiopia, with which Somalia was in conflict. Egypt for many years seemed to be a Soviet pawn—indeed, in 1971 it formalized its association with a treaty of friendship and cooperation—but a year later it threw out its Soviet advisers and within two more years its president had reestablished diplomatic relations with the United States, called Secretary of State Henry Kissinger (who is Jewish) his "good friend and miracle worker," and denounced the treaty of friendship with the Soviet Union. Similarly, in the early 1970s India under Indira Gandhi signed a friendship treaty with the Soviet Union. But a few years later, after she had been defeated in a general election, her successor declared that his government would adopt a foreign policy of "proper nonalignment" and that the Indian-Soviet friendship treaty would not be allowed to interfere with India's relations with other countries—presumably the Western states. Upon reelection, Gandhi shifted again somewhat toward the Soviet Union, and, after she died, her son continued to stress the Indian-Soviet link.

Nonalignment was even more a matter of *issue areas*.[37] One such area was military. Egypt and India received vast amounts of military equipment from the Soviet Union, but Singapore was willing to make its naval base available to the West in the event of hostilities, and Tanzania once relied on the military forces of its former mother country (Britain) to restore domestic order. Yet all these countries consider themselves nonaligned. Some even sought and gained military aid from both sides. The same was true for other issue areas such as economic assistance and trade, diplomacy, and ideology. For example, country A may have appeared to lean toward the West because it placed high priority on democratic values, received most of its military hardware from the West, received about equal amounts of economic aid from both sides, and gravitated more toward Western than Soviet diplomatic positions. (An exception was India, which, democratic tradition notwithstanding, often gravitated toward the Soviets.) Country B, in contrast, was politically sympathetic to the East, a recipient of its military hardware; obtained much of its economic aid and trade from the West; and leaned notably toward the East on diplomatic issues. In this category Egypt was an exception. A one-party state, Egypt, with its "Arab socialism," switched from a pro-Soviet stance toward rapprochement with the United States. It also dismantled much of its brand of socialism to stimulate private initiative and attract foreign investments while retaining some public ownership of certain sectors of the economy.

Even when a nonaligned country seemed to lean more toward the Soviet Union or the United States, however, one had to be careful about classifying it one way or another. The term *pro-Soviet* might have reflected the general attitude and preference of national leaders (for example, the Sandinistas in Nicaragua), but it also might have indicated positions that those leaders would have taken even in the absence of a cold war—if they had been opposed to colonialism or apartheid, for example, which the Soviets also opposed. The same was true of a country that seemed pro-American. For example, Anwar Sadat was first an Egyptian nationalist. When he made overtures to the West, it was because he knew U.S. leaders could better help him achieve his goal of recovering Egyptian lands lost in 1967 because they had influence in Israel and the Soviets did not. On balance, however, nonalignment more often than not seemed—especially during the 1970s—to be pro-Soviet because of strong anti-Western attitudes.

The developing countries attributed all sorts of ills—from their continued role as raw material suppliers for Western industries to conditions in South Africa—to the West's "neocolonial" control. The conviction that the distribution of power between the First and Third Worlds was stacked against them and that the West thereby kept them poor and dependent led the nonaligned countries to take increasingly anti-Western stands. If the many countries of Asia, Africa, and Latin America could have been considered a cohesive bloc, it was because they shared this set of attitudes.[38]

FAILURE OF DEVELOPMENT: INTERNAL OR EXTERNAL CAUSES?

Initial Western Development Models

Forty-seven years after World War II, much of the Third World remains poor, illiterate, hungry, and unhealthy, despite an economic growth rate higher than that of the First World. The difficulty is that, because these countries started so far behind in per capita income, it has been virtually impossible for them to catch up. For example, a person earning $200 in a developing country receives $220 when that income rises by 10 percent; another earning $20,000 in the United States receives a $2,000 increase. In short, the income gap between rich and poor states widens, even if the poorer nation has a faster rate of economic growth. Some of the developing countries, to be sure, have managed surprisingly well, especially the resource-rich (particularly oil-rich) countries and the export platforms.

Nevertheless, many of the developing countries have remained just that, developing. This result has been contrary to the early models of development drawn up by Western social scientists as more and more colonial countries achieved independence. Essentially, it was said, nations went through certain stages of development. In this process, as in the development of individuals as they progress from childhood to old age, nations passed, according to the economists, through several "stages of economic growth," and, according to the political scientists, through a number of "stages of political growth." [39] At the end of their growth, the new nations would look like Western states: politically pluralistic, democratic, stable, and industrialized, with a high standard of living and a relatively equitable distribution of income. Peaceful was another characteristic often added, although sometimes it was left implicit. Development, thought mainly to be the economic transformation of a traditional rural society into a modern urban-industrial one, was therefore also called *Westernization*. Having no models of global development to work with, Western social scientists, not surprisingly, looked back at their own societies and generalized about their evolution into modern societies. The paths the European states had trodden seemed likely to be the ones the new states of Asia and Africa would walk along. The West, then, held itself up as the model for the rest of the world.[40] This was an ethnocentric view, but it was also an optimistic one. In effect, it promised that the developing countries, no matter how backward, would *inevitably* develop; they would make it, just as the countries of Europe and North America had.

It was in this context that the United States and other Western states began to provide the developing countries with economic aid. Nations living at the poverty level, it was pointed out, could not squeeze the required capital out of their low-paid work force; foreign funds were therefore necessary to fan the fires of development. But aid did not help the vast majority of developing countries realize self-sustaining growth. Finding their status as recipients of Western "charity" rather humiliating, their slogan became "Trade, Not Aid." In an industrial world, they expected orders for their natural resources to earn the funds they needed for capital investment. This would enable them to diversify their economies and become less dependent on single commodities for exports. This too failed as Western states protected their industries against developing country imports.

Increasingly, therefore, the First and Third worlds took opposite views of why the developing countries had not been able to modernize. The Western industrial countries argued that the Third World's problems were primarily internal. They arose from overpopulation; ethnic, religious, and racial divisions; lack of natural resources; lack of professional training; government corruption and mismanagement; the low priority given agriculture; a hostile attitude toward private capital investment; and the expulsion or mistreatment of productive minorities. The developing countries argued that they could not modernize because they were the victims of an international economy dominated by the industrial West. The causes and cures of their underdevelopment, they claimed, were not internal but external. Specifically, they asserted that the reason for their economic backwardness was international capitalism.[41]

Developing Country Dependency and World Capitalism

The difficulties that most developing countries face in earning money in the international market have already been noted. They are too dependent on single resources, and the prices of these resources fluctuate with the Western industrial economies. Competition among resource producers tends to lead to an oversupply, forcing prices downward. When Western industries substitute other resources or synthetics, prices are further depressed. In the meantime, the manufactured goods bought in the West tend to rise in price. The terms of trade do not favor the developing countries.

It is in this context that the developing countries have generally claimed that their relations with the industrial West have not changed much since colonial days. Formerly the colonies were governed directly from London, Paris, or other Western capitals. Since independence, the former colonies have achieved self-government but, they insist, their independence is only formal, not meaningful. Indeed, this formal independence masks the fact that *real* self-government does not exist. The developing countries remain tied to their former masters by the same economic chains that characterized the colonial era. These chains keep them dependent on the capitalist West. Politically independent in name only, the majority remain in *neocolonial* bondage as raw material suppliers for Western industry.

As a result, they claim, their economies are not oriented toward their national needs, toward improving the lives of their own people. Their resources were originally developed by the West and then used by Western industry for the production of goods that have raised the *Western* standard of living to the highest in the world. Decisions about their economies were, in brief, decided by foreigners for the benefit of foreigners. That is why the West (the exploiters) grew rich while the developing countries (the exploited) remained poor. Even today, the former colonies still provide Western industry with cheap raw materials—except oil. The United States, Western Europe, and Japan are said to benefit enormously from this

Western-dominated international economy. They are the *core countries* of world capitalism. The developing countries constitute the *peripheries*. Thus the free market, which in theory benefits all nations, actually favors the strong and keeps the developing countries in a subordinate position.

Dependency is a relationship characterized by asymmetry, in which the economic growth of the developing countries is conditioned by events in the industrialized nations' economies. (Interdependence, in contrast, is characterized by greater symmetry.) The developing countries' dependency takes several forms. One is trade dependency; the developing countries depend on the industrial states for markets in which to sell their commodities and are obviously both sensitive and vulnerable to levels of demand. Another form is investment dependency. Western investors control key sectors of Third World economies: production of natural resources and any manufacturing that may have been developed. Foreign aid creates yet a third form of dependence.

A more radical version of this dependency thesis asserts that these economic chains are supplemented by Western political alliances and by military and police links to the developing countries' ruling elites, who have a vested interest in preserving this dependency relationship. These governing elites owe their social status, political power, and wealth to this exploitive arrangement. They are the "fronts" for Western capitalists; their survival depends on the preservation of the status quo. By the same token, these elites have no strong ties to their own people. Ruling on behalf of foreigners, they are domestically unpopular and, as a result, resort to authoritarian regimes. If their power were threatened, covert or overt foreign intervention—usually by the United States since it is the world's most powerful capitalist state—might occur. U.S. foreign policy is therefore counterrevolutionary according to this viewpoint. Despite its verbal commitment to democracy, the United States in fact suppresses democracy abroad. In this way, the developing countries are "managed" by the United States and its Western partners, who are the real beneficiaries of the free market. Note that in this dependency argument underdevelopment is not a stage preceding the "stages of economic growth" but is the outcome of the international economy.

To sum up the overall developing country case: (1) the current old international economic order favors the Western industrial capitalist states that organized it; (2) the ex-colonial, now neocolonial states, occupy a subordinate and underdeveloped status because of international capitalism, not internal problems; and (3) a new international economic order is needed to right past injustices and bring about a more equitable distribution of wealth, status, and power among the nations of the First and Third worlds. More specifically, the hegemony of the Western states, which left the developing countries helpless pawns in the international economy, unable to better their individual lots by their own efforts, required a fundamental structural change.

CHANGING THE INTERNATIONAL ECONOMY: REVOLUTION OR REFORM?

Those who believe that the old international economic order is not only unfair but also permanent and that the global inequality of wealth is directly attributable to an inherently exploitive capitalism prescribe a strategy of revolution as a solution. Because the United States and its Western allies are the preeminent capitalist states, and their domination of the international economy is viewed as the prerequisite for the continued exploitation of the peripheral states, a strategy of liberation must be used to destroy this link and America's role in the world economy. In theory, the best solution would be a revolution within the United States itself in which capitalism would be replaced with a socialist economy. By definition, a socialist United States would not exploit the developing countries and would allow them to live in political *and* economic freedom (under socialism, people no longer exploit each other, domestically or internationally, for profit). In practice, however, this is an unlikely solution. A more feasible course, it is suggested, would deprive the United States and its capitalist associates of Third World markets and resources. Cutting the economic links that bind the developing countries with the core states is an alternative strategy that can be achieved by revolutions that overthrow the capitalist puppet regimes in the Third World. Such revolutions may well involve guerrilla war, as in China and Vietnam. However the revolution is brought about, violence is the only way of gaining true national liberation.

The reformist approach agrees that an exploitive relationship exists between the Western industrial states and the raw material-producing developing countries but explains it differently. Instead of attributing the cause to capitalism and advocating a revolutionary solution because imperialism is a necessary expression of capitalism, the reformers blame the structure of the state system. In other words, the cause of the division between rich and poor nations is the inequality of power between states with advanced economies and those with less-developed economies, not the inherent nature of capitalism. The solution thus is to reduce this inequality of wealth and power. Initially, the prescription was "import substitution." The developing countries had to develop their own industries. They should not import the industrial and consumer goods they needed but produce them themselves. This required the temporary protection of their "baby industries" until they were able to compete internationally. Unfortunately, this solution, which tended to make industries uncompetitive behind their protective barriers, did not prove to be the correct one. It was in this context that in 1974 the new international economic order was offered as a solution.

The political objective of the developing countries was to change the international economy so that wealth would be more equitably distributed. Thus, they had seven goals:

1. Higher and more stable commodity prices (to provide steady income "decoupled" from Western economic fluctuations) so that they can plan for several years ahead, diversify their economies, and become less dependent on the sale of single resources.
2. Protection of their purchasing power through "indexing," linking the sale of resources to Western inflation rates and rising prices for Western machinery, weapons, and food.
3. Doubling or tripling of foreign aid and capital contributions from such institutions as the International Monetary Fund and the World Bank, and more influence in these organizations.
4. Preferential Western tariffs for developing country exports, which would give them a competitive edge and enhance their earning capacity.
5. A voice in controlling the levels of production and prices of alternative sources of minerals, such as those found in the seabeds.
6. Deferral of their debt, which had stood at $142 billion in 1974, but was to shoot up in succeeding years.
7. Greater control over the multinational corporations.

Although satisfaction of these demands would not constitute a revolutionary transformation of the international economy, it would constitute a new international economic order in which the Western states' perceived control of the economic rules of the game would be reduced.[42] The developing countries' demands reflected their struggle to end past humiliations and their determination to participate actively in shaping their futures.

Developing countries are deeply resentful of their past treatment and present lot in the system. It may be said that the poor and plentiful people of the southern half of this planet are no longer willing to be the "hewers of wood and drawers of water" for the rich states of the northern half. This attitude was the main reason the poorer developing countries, though the hardest hit by OPEC policies, continued to support OPEC during the 1970s. The louder the rich Western countries squealed, the greater the delight of the Third World countries. As William Wordsworth wrote of the French Revolution, "Bliss was it in that dawn to be alive/But to be young was very heaven." A Third World poet might have written those lines in the winter of 1973-1974. If OPEC were successful, other developing countries could organize cartels for their raw materials and control production and prices—that is, lower production and raise prices.

Throwing off the alleged chains of economic dependence was the critical task for the developing countries. Clearly, though economics can be discussed rationally, the issues being negotiated in the 1970s and early 1980s were only partly economic. The discussion of the terms of trade was deeply symptomatic of a general assertion of non-Western nationalism against the West. The economic bargaining took place, therefore, between parties who were all too frequently deeply separated by wide psychological and cultural barriers.

Insisting that their poverty was the result of Western exploitation, the developing countries were really claiming that the West owed them a moral debt for past colonial sins, which it must pay off in more earthly coin. Charging that the West had plundered them in the past and continued to do so, they repeated over and over that such "imperialistic exploitation" was wrong. Presumably, in their view, Western political organization, economic ideas, scientific inventiveness, and technological skills have had little to do with creating Western prosperity.[43] The attempt to induce a sense of Western guilt for past behavior was a shrewd tactic, however, because many Westerners feel ashamed and morally culpable for what their forebears did, even though the political standards and moral codes were quite different in the colonial age. Reparation for past errors seemed the right thing to do; helping the poor by narrowing the gap between them and the rich constituted, for those Westerners, a morally worthy cause, a way of gaining national redemption and of living up to the promise of a democratic way of life. The developing countries had little leverage, but by charging Western exploitation they hoped to place the West on the defensive. Morality, no less than arms, can be a weapon used by the weak against the strong.

Vanishing Communist Model

Marxism-Leninism had widespread appeal to many of the early developing country leaders. They had associated colonialism with capitalism and imperialism, and, as a result, they continued to regard the West and multinational corporations as exploiters. Their strategy for transforming their countries into rich modern societies was to emphasize government-supervised industrialization at the expense of agriculture, replacing imports with domestic production, and protecting infant industries from foreign competition. At the heart of this process was the belief that government should guide this economic development.

Yet even before the collapse of socialism in the late 1980s fewer and fewer developing countries were attracted to the Soviet model. The Soviet Union's continual problems in providing its citizens with a balanced diet, its failure to produce a sufficient number and variety of quality consumer goods, and its inability to keep up with Japan and the United States—or even South Korea—in the new industrial revolution made the Soviet economy more and more inappropriate as a model. It was Soviet citizens, after all, who carried the banners in Moscow in 1989 proclaiming "72 Years of Getting Nowhere." Those nations outside the Soviet bloc that had followed this model—such as Ethiopia, Cuba, and Nicaragua—themselves became examples of mismanaged economies. Soviet-style communism's main attraction for Marxist leaders and groups remained its ability to seize power by using its ideology to attract supporters and to organize them for revolutionary warfare (China, Vietnam, Nicaragua), as well as to provide its friends engaged in civil wars with Soviet and Soviet-bloc advisers, weapons, and troops (largely Cuban). But as an economic model for increasing food or industrial production, it was increasingly useless. In short, the Soviet Union could help its friends in the seizure and consolidation of power but not in the modernization and management of their economies. Gorbachev too recognized that the Soviet Union could no longer be a model for modernization of the developing countries. He spoke of "market socialism," as the Soviet Union repudiated the Communist organization of its economy and tried to switch to a free-market economy.

Communist China had years earlier turned away from what a Chinese leader called the "radical leftist nonsense" of Mao Zedong and had moved toward a more flexible economic system that encouraged some private enterprise and property ownership.[44] Largely abandoning the collective farm, China experienced a "great leap forward" in food production. The widespread slogan, "To get rich is glorious," appealed to the Chinese. "Marx died 100 years ago," said Beijing's *People's Daily*. "There have been tremendous changes since his ideas were formed.... So we cannot use Marxist and Leninist works to solve our present-day problems."[45] (See Chapter 7.) And China's leader, Deng Xiaoping, said that it did not matter whether a cat was black or white (Communist or not), as long as it could catch the mouse. Until the 1989 crushing of the pro-democracy movement in China, the contrast with the Soviet Union was striking: in the latter, *glasnost* (political openness) was not accompanied by *perestroika* (economic restructuring), but in China *perestroika* was not accompanied by *glasnost*.. Ironically, the suppression of demands for a more open society did not set China back economically because it maintained its shift toward the private sector.[46] Of the four hard-line Communist regimes left by 1991, only Cuba and North Korea remained faithful to the ideology; Albania and Vietnam declared in favor of democracy and free-market economics, respectively. The Communist form of command economics had failed. It has even been rejected in the former Soviet Union, and it is disappearing in the Third World.

Latest Prescription: Western Free Markets

The declining appeal of Soviet communism as a model for development among the many non-NIC developing countries coincided with the end of the 1970s era of confrontation with the West and the beginning of a more reflective and pragmatic attitude toward economic development. The demands for a new international economic order had gained little. The first half of the 1980s saw the economic growth rates of the developing countries decline sharply and the average incomes in most Latin American and sub-Saharan states drop while their debts accumulated. Commodity prices remained low. The South's lot, despite some significant exceptions, had not improved. In a more chastened mood, the developing countries were willing to look at other prescriptions.

The key to development is still capital accumulation. Economists, including those in the Third World, have found that considerable capital resources exist in the developing countries, especially in the more developed states in Latin America. But that capital is wasted by governments whose leaders indulge in

Rolls Royces and Mercedes or villas on the French Riviera or in Miami, whose bureaucracies are so oversized that they are a drain on the economy, and whose military forces spend too much on weapons. The solution to such economic mismanagement is a return to the standard capitalist prescription: an emphasis on internal savings, austerity, and investment in economic growth. Government, while taxing consumption heavily, should encourage industrial and agricultural development.

Critical to this 1980s shift was a growing endorsement of the private marketplace. President Ronald Reagan's view of the "magic of the market-place," which initially met with skepticism, seems to have gained support and placed on the defensive the more traditional view that free-market economies were inappropriate and that state-directed economies were the answer. Even more surprising, the developing countries were not alone in recognizing the importance of the market; during the 1980s, as noted, Communist China began experimenting with the profit motive and greater political decentralization.

In fact, more governments in all areas were showing a new interest in private enterprise—in large part because their state-controlled economies were going broke—and Asian capitalism was their model. Japan, of course, as well as South Korea, Taiwan, Hong Kong, Singapore, Malaysia, and Thailand, were all growing rapidly and providing their people with better health and nutrition, lower infant mortality, longer life expectancy, higher literacy, and more income. Certainly, the grinding poverty once so visible in much of the Third World is no longer seen in these societies. The average per capita income in Taiwan was $7,380 by the beginning of the 1990s (up from $500 in 1949); South Korea's was $5,600 and Singapore's was $12,700. Moreover, and very important, if any societies can be called "dependencies," these can. South Korea and Taiwan have been very dependent on the United States; Hong Kong has been dependent on Britain; and Singapore has been a small cog in the international capitalist economy. Even Japan's development was initiated during the American occupation after World War II. Yet this dependency status has not prevented these countries from achieving successful economic growth and development far beyond the dreams of most developing countries.

Japan and its East Asian neighbors are, interestingly, "neo-Confucian" societies; they are relatively homogeneous in population, with a strong belief in the work ethic and a commitment to education. The governments of these nations have played a strong role in their development, guiding their economies by setting economic priorities. Unlike in U.S. capitalism, they work closely with corporate leaders to encourage their countries' export strategies, carrying out land reforms and rural development (while avoiding the "urban bias" of most developing countries) and investing heavily in education and human capital.[47] Above all, these governments have worked with and not against the market; government intervention has been based on market forces, thereby spurring private enterprise and economic efficiency and productivity. Whether, of course, the NICs are likely to be the model for other developing countries seeking to improve their lots remains—as noted—problematic because of their dependence on a growing world economy.[48] Nevertheless, Third World countries are widely turning toward economic reforms and welcoming the foreign investments and trade often regarded with suspicion in the past. As India's finance minister said in 1991, "Everybody is convinced it is time for fresh thinking." [49]

THE END OF THIRD WORLDISM?

Much about the Third World remains painfully familiar. With the exception of East Asia, many countries are still unable to meet their peoples' "revolution of rising expectations." The 1980s was for them a time of diminishing economic aid, as well as a time of enormous debt to Western countries from which they had borrowed money in order to continue their modernization after oil prices first shot up (see Chapter 15). The upshot was that the repayment, to the extent that developing countries kept up with their payments, resulted in a net capital outflow of billions of dollars from the South to the North. In Latin America, where significant progress in industrialization had been made from the end of World War II through the 1970s (albeit at the cost of accumulating the largest debt), this meant a severe depression and drop in the standard of living. Africa, however, remained the worst off. Thus, as the 1990s dawned, the world remained divided into a minority of rich nations and a majority of poor nations trying to sustain over 80 percent of the world's population. This is a formula for massive instability.

In this connection, explosive population growth remains an especially critical problem which increasingly is affecting the developed states. It already has produced massive migration to the West. As populations overwhelm the capabilities of governments to provide housing, food, education, health care, and employment, such mass migrations could turn into tidal waves as desperate people try to escape from their misery. The United States took in more immigrants during the 1980s than in any other decade in its history. In Western Europe, especially France and the newly reunified Germany, immigration, mainly from North Africa, not easily absorbable into the population, has given rise to some extreme right-wing reaction. In addition, the clearing of forests, for example, to make extra room for people or for industries and farms, may result in severe and perhaps irreversible environmental damage that affects all nations.

Thus, the fates of the developing and developed worlds are intertwined. No problem showed this more keenly than the de-Communization of Eastern Europe and the Soviet Union. At the very time that a reversal of the transfer of wealth from the developing to the developed states was needed, the developing countries were concerned that the Western democracies would focus their aid on Eastern Europe and, later, the former Soviet Union to the neglect of the Third World. Clearly needed are long-term, sustained Western assistance and cooperation between the less-developed and developed countries.[50]

Yet Third Worldism too was dying as the 1990s began. It had risen as a result of several factors. The first was the post–World War II eruption of the cold war with its fairly cohesive First and Second world blocs, together with Western decolonization and the high birthrate of new nations. Another factor was new nations' association of capitalism with imperialism and their own colonial subjugation. A closely related factor in the rise of Third Worldism was the availability of an alternative system, socialism, in which the state, unlike in capitalism, would own the principal means of production and industry would be used to benefit all human beings in society, not just the few owners of industry who became rich at the cost of the many. Finally, Third Worldism arose from those nations' intense sense of nationalism, which led the new and underdeveloped nations to share a common identity. This identity found its outlet for the first time at Bandung in 1956 when they decided collectively to be active on the world stage, articulate their grievances and demands for assistance, and, by and large, pursue a course of nonalignment between the two warring blocs.

By the 1990s, the widespread belief that the developing countries had been placed in a structurally inferior position in a Western-dominated international economy and were therefore unable to develop had been doubly challenged. The first challenge came from the failure of Soviet socialism, which had appealed to so many developing country leaders and had led them to adopt similar command economies and centralized controls throughout the cold war years. Indeed, the end of the bipolar cold war competition, which had allowed the developing countries to play one superpower off against the other, enhancing their foreign aid contributions, was bad news. The second challenge stemmed from the experience of the export-driven East Asian countries, who had convincingly demonstrated that poor countries could modernize and benefit their peoples. In addition, during the Reagan years the United States preached a policy of free markets and free trade, thus ensuring, despite its growing trade deficit, access to the huge American market for developing countries' products (although protectionist forces limited this access for sugar and textiles).

The decade of the 1980s also witnessed the spread of democracy as tolerance and support for authoritarian Third World regimes wore thin. The justifications for one-party rule, which all too often had deteriorated into corrupt dictatorial rule, had not been balanced by sufficient economic growth and improvements in the standard of living. Promises of future rewards were no longer credible. Again, presidential rhetoric in the United States, if not a catalyst for change, was consistent with a number of free elections held in Latin America, the Philippines, and elsewhere in the Third World—although many of these democracies remained fragile with the military watching in the wings—in addition to the erosion of totalitarianism in China and the Soviet Union and the collapse of the latter's Eastern European allies.[51]

Only one issue remains on which the less developed countries continue to show a relatively united front to collectively increase foreign aid from the West: the environment. The developing countries' first priority continues to be economic growth, and they regard it as unfair that those countries that were the first to industrialize—and continue to be the largest consumers of the world's resources and generators of the world's pollution—now want the poor countries to develop without further inflicting irreparable environmental damage. If the West wants them to pursue "sustainable development," they assert—and the West's efforts to fight pollution will come to naught if the less developed states do not follow suit—it will have to provide funds. At the 1992 Earth Summit, the West did in fact commit itself to increasing foreign aid to Third World countries but, unhappily from the perspective of the latter, it refused to commit itself to a specific timetable.

Apart from that single, although prominent issue, however, the developing countries show increasingly fewer common characteristics as they pursue divergent national and regional interests.

For Review

1. How did the colonial experience shape the new states?
2. Why does the possibility of national disintegration continue to be perhaps the basic problem for many developing countries?
3. How are rapidly growing populations threatening the future of the developing world?
4. What has prevented most developing countries from following the successful example of the newly industrialized nations?
5. How can one account for the Third World's past dominant pattern of civilian and military authoritarianism?
6. How have bipolarity and nation building affected the developing countries' foreign policies?
7. In the developing countries' continued search for development, which countries have served as their models, and which model do they appear to be adopting?
8. Why can we perhaps talk of "the end of Third Worldism"?

Notes

1. Brandt Commission, *North-South* (Cambridge, Mass.: M.I.T. Press, 1980), 32.
2. Specific figures are available in Central Intelligence Agency, *The World Factbook*

1991 (Washington, D.C.: Central Intelligence Agency, 1991).

3. Alan Durning, "How Much Is Enough?" *World Watch* (December 1990): 2.

4. Robert C. Good, "Changing Patterns of African International Relations," *American Political Science Review* (September 1964): 638.

5. The disruption of traditional colonial society by the economic behavior of the Western industrial nations is analyzed in *The Emerging Nations,* ed. Max F. Millikan and Donald L. M. Blackmer (Boston: Little, Brown, 1961), 3-17; and in Immanuel Wallerstein, *Africa: The Politics of Independence* (New York: Vintage, 1961), 29-43.

6. Barbara Ward, *The Rich Nations and the Poor Nations* (New York: Norton, 1962), 54.

7. Rupert Emerson, *From Empire to Nation* (Cambridge, Mass.: Harvard University Press, 1960), 6.

8. According to Klaus Mehnert,

> The term "intelligentsia" is used to denote specifically those intellectuals who are experiencing internal conflict between allegiance to traditional cultures and the influence of the modern West. Within these terms of reference it is not the amount of knowledge or education that determines membership in the intelligentsia. . . . No man, no matter how learned, is classified as a member of the intelligentsia if he has retained his identity with his national background. As long as he remains integrated in his society and accepts the values of that society as his own, he is likely to remain essentially a conservative without that revolutionary spark which . . . would class him as a member of the intelligentsia. If, on the other hand, he is an intellectual who has felt the impact of Western civilization and has been drawn into the vortex of conflicting ideas, he enters the ranks of the intelligentsia. . . . Within the intelligentsia, however, rebelliousness is a common characteristic. Beset with doubts about traditional cultural values, its members have felt a driving need to search for something new.

> Klaus Mehnert, "The Social and Political Role of the Intelligentsia in the New Countries," in *New Nations in a Divided World,* ed. Kurt London (New York: Holt, Rinehart & Winston, 1964), 121-122.

9. See particularly Emerson, *From Empire to Nation,* 89-187, 295-359; Clifford Geertz, "The Integrative Revolution," in *Old Societies and New States,* ed. Clifford Geertz (New York: Free Press, 1963), 105-157; and Walter Connor, "Nation-Building or Nation-Destroying?" *World Politics* (April 1972): 219ff.

10. Michael Brecher, *Nehru: A Political Biography* (New York: Oxford University Press, 1959), 362-363.

11. Wallerstein, *Africa,* 88.

12. Anastasia Toufexis, "Too Many Mouths," *Time,* January 2, 1989, 48.

13. *New York Times,* July 25, 1985.

14. Steven W. Sinding and Sheldon J. Segal, "Birth-Rate News," *New York Times,* December 19, 1991.

15. Alexander Gerschenkron, *Economic Backwardness in Historical Perspective* (New York: Holt, Rinehart & Winston, 1965), 28.

16. John T. McGowan, "Third World to Lead Surge in Growth," *USA Today,* May 9, 1986.

17. Robert S. McNamara, "The Population Problem," *Foreign Affairs* (Summer 1984): 1119. Also see Lester R. Brown, *In the Human Interest* (New York: Norton, 1974).

18. W. Arthur Lewis, *The Evolution of the International Economic Order* (Princeton, N.J.: Princeton University Press, 1978).

19. Nick Eberstadt, "Famine, Development and Foreign Aid," *Commentary*, March 1985, 25-31; and Arch Paddington, "Ethiopia: The Communist Use of Famine," *Commentary*, April 1986, 30-39. In 1991 in Sudan, the government even sold pre-drought grain to earn money to buy weapons from China for use in the civil war. Jane Perlez, "African Dilemma: Food Aid May Prolong War and Famine," *New York Times*, May 12, 1991.

20. Francis Moore Lappé and Joseph Collins, *Food First* (Boston: Houghton Mifflin, 1977); and John Warnock, *The Politics of Hunger* (New York: Methuen, 1987).

21. Richard J. Barnet and Ronald E. Müller, *Global Reach* (New York: Simon & Schuster, 1975), 216-217; and Lewis, *Evolution of the International Economic Order*, 34-37.

22. Robin Broad and John Cavanaugh, "No More NICs," *Foreign Policy* (Fall 1988): 81-104.

23. See R. H. Tawney, *Religion and the Rise of Capitalism* (Baltimore: Penguin, 1947).

24. Peter L. Berger, *The Capitalist Revolution* (New York: Basic Books, 1986), 161-170.

25. Robin Wright, *Sacred Rage* (New York: Linden Press, 1985).

26. Steven Erlanger, "In the Global Village, Seeking an Exit," *New York Times*, November 5, 1988.

27. Samuel P. Huntington, *Political Order in Changing Societies* (New Haven, Conn.: Yale University Press, 1968), 1.

28. Wallerstein, *Africa*, 98.

29. Ibid., 99.

30. See, for example, Julius Nyerere, quoted in *The Ideologies of the Developing Nations*, by Paul E. Sigmund, Jr. (New York: Holt, Rinehart & Winston, 1963), 199.

31. Wallerstein, *Africa*, 96.

32. General analyses of the role of the military in new nations are found in: Morris Janowitz, *The Military in the Political Development of New Nations* (Chicago: University of Chicago Press, 1964); S. E. Finer, *The Man on Horseback*, rev. ed. (Baltimore: Penguin, 1976); John J. Johnson, ed., *The Role of the Military in Underdeveloped Countries* (Princeton, N.J.: Princeton University Press, 1962); Huntington, *Political Order*, 192-263; Edward Feit, "Pen, Sword and People: Military Regimes in the Formation of Political Institutions," *World Politics* (January 1973): 251ff.; and Feit, *The Armed Bureaucrat* (Boston: Houghton Mifflin, 1973). For the dominant role the military played in Latin America from 1962 to 1973, see Alain Rouquié, *The Military and the State in Latin America*, trans. Paul Sigmund (Berkeley: University of California Press, 1988).

33. Kenneth B. Noble, "Despots Dwindle as Reforms Alter Face of Africa," *New York Times*, April 14, 1991; Carl Lancaster, "Democracy in Africa," *Foreign Policy* (Winter 1991-92): 148-165; and Samuel P. Huntington, "How Countries Democratize," *Political Science Quarterly* (Winter 1991-92): 579-616.

34. Robert C. Good, "State-Building as a Determinant of Foreign Policy in the New States," in *Neutralism and Nonalignment*, ed. Laurence W. Martin (New York: Holt, Rinehart & Winston, 1962).

35. Ibid., 8-9.

36. Ibid., 11.

37. Cecil V. Crabb, Jr., *The Elephants and the Grass* (New York: Holt, Rinehart & Winston, 1965), 20-38.

38. For the evolution of nonalignment from 1955 to 1983, see Robert A. Mortimer, *The Third World Coalition in International Politics*, 2d ed. (Boulder, Colo.: Westview Press, 1984).

39. W. W. Rostow, *Stages of Economic Growth* (New York: Cambridge University Press, 1960); and A. F. K. Organski, *The Stages of Political Development* (New York: Knopf, 1965).

40. Tony Smith, "Requiem or New Agenda for Third World Studies?" *World Politics* (July 1985): 533-544.

41. Ibid., 544-558; Brandt Commission, *North-South*; Barbara Ward, Lenore D'Anjou, and J. D. Runnalls, eds., *The Widening Gap* (New York: Columbia University Press, 1971); Mitchell A. Seligson, ed., *The Gap between Rich and Poor* (Boulder, Colo.: Westview Press, 1984); and Gabriel Kolki, *Confronting the Third World* (New York: Pantheon Books, 1988).

42. Stephen D. Krasner, *Structural Conflict* (Berkeley: University of California Press, 1985).

43. For a critique of dependency, see Robert Gilpin, *The Political Economy of International Relations* (Princeton, N.J.: Princeton University Press, 1987), 263ff. For a rebuttal of this view, see Nathan Rosenberg and L. E. Birdzell, Jr., *How the West Grew Rich* (New York: Basic Books, 1985).

44. *New York Times*, February 21, 1985.

45. Orville Schell, *To Get Rich Is Glorious* (New York: Pantheon Books, 1985).

46. Nicholas D. Kristof, "Hard Line in Beijing Fails to Kill Boom," *New York Times*, December 17, 1991.

47. Gilpin, *Political Economy of International Relations*, 301-302.

48. Ibid., 303-304.

49. Sylvia Nasar, "Third World Embracing Reforms to Encourage Economic Growth," *New York Times*, July 8, 1991. Also see Bernard Wieraub, " 'India Is Now in a New Ball Game,' " and Sanjoy Hazarika, "India Retreats from Socialist Path," *New York Times*, July 8 and July 25, 1991, respectively; and Thomas Kamm, "South Americas Push Sales of State Assets in Swing to Capitalism," *Wall Street Journal*, July 9, 1991.

50. Richard N. Gardner, "The Comeback of Liberal Internationalism," *Washington Quarterly* (Summer 1990): 32-34.

51. Richard Bissell, "Who Killed the Third World?" *Washington Quarterly* (Autumn 1990): 23-32. Robert S. Greenberger, "With Cold War Over, Poorer Nations Face Neglect by the Rich," *Wall Street Journal*, May 14, 1992.

CHAPTER 11

The Games Policy Makers Play

A FOCUS ON DECISION MAKERS

Whereas the first level of analysis (the state system) focuses on external explanations for nations' foreign policies, the second and third levels of analysis emphasize domestic explanations. The difference between the second and third levels is that the second level identifies how the character of the state and its political/ideological style affect state behavior; the third level, however, zeroes in on the individuals who make specific decisions. It is one thing to learn from the second level of analysis what one nation's "operational code" may be and use it to analyze and understand the general thrust of its policy, but it is another to know that insular and continental states, for example, show different patterns of behavior. Moreover, within each category states act differently, and one can use the decision-making approach to account for these differences in state behavior.

The decision-making approach to understanding the foreign policy of a country is based on a close look at the specific personnel officially responsible for making foreign policy.[1] When one speaks of a state doing this or that, one is really speaking of those officials, the policy decisions they make, and how they implement them. The state, in short, equals the official policy makers whose decisions and actions constitute its policies. Decisions are the "output" of the domestic political system. By focusing on decision makers, this approach emphasizes, first, how they *see* the world. What is important is not what the international system is like objectively, but how policy makers perceive it. It is based on their perceptions that these officials act or, for that matter, do not act; reality does not exist outside of policy makers' definitions of it.

As noted earlier, a balance-of-power analysis could have explained what British prime minister Neville Chamberlain should have done to counter

Adolf Hitler in the 1930s, but not what he did. Without studying the prime minister and his advisers and without analyzing their perceptions of Hitler, the goals of Nazi Germany, and the Versailles peace treaty, first-level analysts could not tell why the British did not choose another course of action, or why they bungled it and brought on the war they had hoped to avoid. Thus in this situation, a first-level analysis was not very helpful. A useful analysis would have included Chamberlain's misperception of Hitler as simply a German nationalist who, while seeking some territorial adjustments, had otherwise only limited ambitions. Such an analysis also would have focused on the pacifist nature of British public opinion, still guided by memories of horrible losses during World War I. The strength of this opinion acted as a constraint on British political leaders, even had they wished to contain Germany.

Rational Actor Model

One model of decision making—the *rational actor model*—is central to the first-level analysis. Each state is viewed as a unitary actor, and each calculates by what means it can best achieve its ends or objectives. It does this in four clearly separate steps: (1) selecting objectives and values, (2) considering alternative means of achieving them, (3) calculating the likely consequences of each alternative, and (4) selecting the one that is most promising. Henry Kissinger wrote in 1957 that if American policy is to seek security and peace, it cannot be based on a strategy of massive retaliation against the Soviet Union when confronted with limited challenges. To respond in this manner would only ensure American suicide; not to respond at all would be tantamount to surrender. Both courses are therefore irrational. The only rational option in these circumstances is "limited war." [2] This rational model underlies not only analyses of international politics and specific foreign policies but also other spheres of decision making. In the competitive games nations play, with their informal rules, each player creates a strategy designed to lead to "victory." There are usually several options, and players must decide at points during the game which play is the best in terms of the ultimate goals.

Governmental Politics Model

The other model of decision making is the *governmental politics model*. It focuses on the executive branch of government and especially on the bureaucracies whose official responsibility is to formulate and execute foreign policy. Indeed, this model is usually referred to as the *bureaucratic politics model*. The term *governmental politics* is used here because it must also include the legislature, at least in free countries, as well as interest groups, the mass media, and the various publics that together constitute public opinion. The bureaucracy, in short, is viewed in its broader governmental and societal setting. The emphasis is on the *pluralistic nature of decision making* in which, in general, the actors' views reflect their organizational positions and interests. For example, a foreign service officer in the State Department sees the world quite differently than a military officer. And in the Defense Department, an army officer is likely to define what U.S. defense policy should be quite differently than a navy or air force officer. Policy makers' perceptions of the national interest depend on the position in government they occupy. This emphasis on the roles individuals play as officials has been aptly summed up by the phrase *"Where you stand depends on where you sit."* Policy in these circumstances is formulated through conflicts among many actors with different perceptions, perspectives, and interests, but also through reconciling these differences. These two elements of the policy struggle will determine who receives what and when.

Political scientist Graham Allison has illustrated the difference between rational and bureaucratic policy making.[3] When in the late 1950s the Soviet Union tested its first intercontinental ballistic missile (ICBM), American leaders became very concerned about a possible "missile gap" favoring the Soviets. Following the rational model, they concluded that the Soviet Union would exploit this technological breakthrough, mass-produce ICBMs, and use them to pressure the United States to concede territorial changes in central Europe, specifically in the symbolically significant western half of Berlin. In terms of the balance of power, the Soviets had achieved a major technological breakthrough, which, if fully exploited before the United States could test and deploy an ICBM, could give them superior power. Rationally, in terms of the rules of the game of the international system, that is what the Kremlin leaders should have done—at least, that is what American policy makers expected them to do. Had the United States been the nation to test the first ICBM, it would have gone into large-scale production, which would have strengthened the American hand in relation to the Soviet Union. It would have seemed the logical thing to do.

If the same American policy makers had used the governmental politics model, however, they would have been more cautious in drawing this conclusion. The Red Army controlled the missiles, and it was unlikely to abandon suddenly the traditional definition of its role on the ground in favor of intercontinental strategic deterrence with ICBMs. The very thought would be alien to an organization preoccupied with land defense and a role limited to Eurasia. Indeed, a dramatic shift of deterrence from the army to another service certainly would have been accompanied by an observable policy struggle. The development of a large ICBM force would have required a vast transfer of funds to that other service, creating interservice rivalries and quarrels. The different models, then, offered grounds for quite different assessments of what the Soviets would do and implied quite different American defense and foreign policies. The incoming administration of John Kennedy, acting on the rational model, initiated a more numerous intercontinental missile deployment than it would otherwise have done. It was not until after the Cuban missile crisis in 1962 that the Soviets began the extensive buildup that resulted in the achievement of strategic parity. And the dangerous confrontation in Cuba occurred because the Soviets sought to reduce the imbalance in strategic weapons by placing intermediate-range missiles (of which they had plenty) in Cuba.

Before these two decision-making models are examined in more detail, it must be noted that, although these models can be used in explaining other countries' foreign policies, American examples and the American policy process are used here because of readily available materials, the many decisions that have been made in Washington since World War II, and the greater familiarity of American readers with latter-day U.S. history.

CRISIS DECISION MAKING: CUBA AND IRAQ

The rational actor model is probably the most relevant to explaining and understanding crisis decisions. A crisis is characterized by a number of features: decision makers are taken by surprise; they feel that they must make decisions rapidly; and they perceive that vital interests are at stake.[4] In these circumstances, decisions cannot be made in the routine manner characteristic of bureaucracies. The element of surprise is likely to forestall use of standard operating procedures in management of the crisis.

In the international system, when vital interests of one state are threatened by another *major* actor, a crisis erupts because one party threatens the status quo and the other is determined to defend it. Indeed, a crisis is called that in the first place primarily because of the *heightened expectation of violence* it raises. A crisis exists at the crossover point between peace and war; if the international system is defined, as it was earlier, as a system in a state of potential warfare, then at the moment of crisis that potential becomes a reality. Moreover, the possibility of escalation to war becomes ever greater as the crisis goes on. It is this fear that drives policy makers to act quickly and to try to resolve the issues at hand before the crisis gets out of hand. Time is therefore of the essence. During the cold war, crises were particularly dangerous because an escalation could result in a nuclear war that would obliterate both of the superpowers. A crisis, then, involved the likelihood that the United States itself would be attacked and destroyed beyond any hopes of quick recovery.

In that sense, the Iraqi crisis of 1990 was not a crisis. To be sure, there was great fear in both Washington and the Saudi Arabian capital that Saddam Hussein would try and seize the oil kingdom of Kuwait, which was followed by the rapid deployment of U.S. forces after this fear was realized on August 2, 1990. The "crisis" then dragged on for five and a half months until, after Iraq's refusal to withdraw from Kuwait, hostilities erupted. Clearly, the American-Iraqi confrontation was not comparable to an American-Soviet crisis. The 1962 Cuban missile crisis, for example, by its very nature confronted both states with the possibility of extinction. That *was* a crisis in every sense of that word, and the longer such a face-off lasted, the greater was the likelihood that a misstep by one or the other party would lead to a dangerous escalation. That kind of danger was only a potential in the Iraqi instance. It was precisely because Iraq might some day acquire nuclear arms that some observers—and probably some policy makers—felt that war to destroy Saddam Hussein was better now than later. If left in power and able to develop nuclear and perhaps biological weapons on top of his chemical warfare arsenal, he would be far more dangerous to face down, let alone defeat, at a "reasonable" cost at some future point. Thus, a potential crisis loomed if not headed off. Not that an actual crisis did not already exist, however, for the Iraqi leader was perceived to be threatening U.S. and Western vital interests. Not only had he increased his own share of oil by assuming control of Kuwaiti oil wells, but also if the militarily vulnerable Saudi Arabia and the other Gulf oil kingdoms knuckled under to his threats, Saddam Hussein would have virtual control of OPEC's decision making on the supply and price of oil, on which all Western industrial economies depended. His invasion of Kuwait therefore did represent a real crisis, even though Iraq was hardly a superpower.

Rise of Decision Making to the Top

The need for quick decisions in crises limits the number of officials involved. Above all, the perception that vital interests are at stake quickly centralizes the decision making and takes it to the top—the first characteristic of crisis decision making. At the top in the United States is the president and the chief presidential advisers.

In terms of the decision-making process, the various characteristics of a crisis listed earlier tend to be highly functional. The usual drawn-out haggling over differences in policies between different bureaucracies, the separation of powers between the executive and Congress, and all the efforts of interest groups to influence policy, if not to undermine it, are, in crises, short-circuited. The different ways in which crises are managed by the government means that the policy process works speedily and efficiently, free of the traditional domestic pressures, for the short duration of crises. And the fact that crisis decisions flow upward to the top officials has another important consequence: the careful and cautious management of superpower crises. A crisis obviously results in stress and anxiety, and there is always the possibility of rash or impetuous actions. Another possibility is that policy makers may not examine all the options and may choose the wrong one because some officials are reluctant to express doubts about the policy being adopted.

Psychologist Irving Janis has argued that conformity is especially common within a relatively small circle of leading officials because there is a great deal of pressure to conform to "groupthink."[5] "Dovish" views tend to be suppressed within a group whose members are trying to impress one another with their toughness. The more cohesive the group, the greater is the inclination of its members to reject a nonconformist; the greater the desire to remain in the group, the more likely an individual with doubts about a proposed policy will suppress them and go along with the majority. If others too suppress their reservations, the so-called consensus on policy will clearly be a superficial one. More serious, however, is the possibility that, because searching questions about the policy are not asked, the nation will mismanage the crisis. Nevertheless, although in the past policy mistakes were made when U.S. policy makers had to confront what they believed to be a second- or third-rate opponent, they were very cautious and keenly aware of the dangers of a miscalculation when facing the Soviet Union. The risks and costs of not examining all alternatives, and not scrutinizing the assumptions on which they were acting, were all too clear—and a clear antidote to groupthink.

In the case of Cuba, Kennedy's advisers considered all the various options of how to get the Soviets to take their missiles out of Cuba *without* having to go to war once the president had made that the American objective. They had the rare luxury of time, thanks to photos taken by a U-2 spy plane, and took the better part of a week to consider their alternatives—from taking the issue to the United Nations to a "surgical strike" on the missiles. In choosing a blockade to prevent further shipments of missiles, Kennedy and his advisers underlined the seriousness of the U.S. demand that the missiles be removed, although the blockade could not remove the ones already in Cuba. But it left any further escalation of pressure to achieve this objective to later. Whether the United States would increase this pressure thus depended on what the Soviets did. In the meantime, the blockade was not too risky a course and placed the responsibility for the next step—whether to escalate or de-escalate—on Moscow.

While the management of the Cuban missile crisis was the very opposite of groupthink, George Bush's handling of the Iraqi crisis was, like many key foreign policy decisions in the Bush administration, limited to a few individuals: the president, the secretaries of state and defense, the national security adviser, and, in this case, the chairman of the Joint Chiefs of Staff.[6] The secretary of state was equally restrictive in whom he talked to in his department. These four individuals and the president appeared to agree on the fundamentals, thus reinforcing their thinking on policy rather than examining its bases. This inner war cabinet was part of what was dubbed the "Big Eight" which included, in addition to the so-called war cabinet, Vice President Dan Quayle; Robert Gates, deputy director of the National Security Agency; and John Sununu, White House chief of staff. Like Kennedy's Executive Committee during the Cuban crisis,[7] this inner circle took over from the more formal National Security Council.[8] During crises, presidents tend to favor being surrounded by an informal network of advisers and friends and to cut out the policy makers mandated by law.

Indeed, it is not uncommon for policy makers who assume power with strong convictions to ignore or downgrade the best advice available within the government from the bureaucrats in the different foreign, defense, and intelligence agencies. They are the experts based on their knowledge and experience; those who win power or are appointed to high office by the president are "generalists." They may be "the best and the brightest," but they usually lack the expertise the bureaucrats possess. This does not mean, however, that the bureaucrats are always right and the generalists are usually wrong. The experts often cannot see the forest for the trees, and bureaucracies, wedded to their policies, tend to resist policy changes, even when the president seeks those changes. The point is that the generalists should consult the available experts in the government—and sometimes former officials and academics outside the government—before making critical decisions.[9] The reason the generalists often do not is that when presidents and their advisers enter office they have great confidence in their own political judgments. They do not feel that they need defer to the political analyses of the bureaucracies, whose policy preferences are, after all, also reflections of their political judgments.

Central Role of the President

A second characteristic of making crisis decisions is the central role of the president, who interprets events and evaluates the stakes in the crisis. Kennedy's "reading" of the situation he confronted during the Cuban missile crisis, the consequences this situation might have for American security, and his political future and ability to lead the nation were responsible for his actions. (The latter two factors can hardly be separated, for the external challenges, as the president sees them, do not really leave a choice of accepting a loss of personal prestige without a loss of national prestige. For the president of the United States, personal and national cost calculations tend to be identical.)

Kennedy saw the installation of Soviet missiles in Cuba as a personal challenge with potentially damaging national effects. In response to earlier congressional and public clamor about possible Soviet offensive missiles in Cuba—as distinct from ground-to-air or ground-to-ship defensive missiles—Kennedy had publicly declared that the United States would not tolerate offensive missiles on an island ninety miles off the Florida coast. Intended primarily as a declaration to cool domestic criticism that had come largely from Republicans, Kennedy's statement also had led Soviet leaders to respond that they had no intention of placing missiles in Cuba. Kennedy thus was pledged to act if the Soviets lied—as it turned out they had—unless he wished to be publicly humiliated. If he did not act, Soviet leaders would not believe the other pledges and commitments the president had made or inherited from his predecessors. At least, that is how Kennedy perceived the situation.

He saw the consequences as very dangerous because he feared that Soviet premier Nikita Khrushchev had interpreted previous acts—the abortive 1961 Bay of Pigs invasion of Cuba and the inaction of U.S. troops when the Berlin Wall went up the same year—as signaling a lack of will, an absence of sufficient determination to defend American vital interests. Khrushchev spoke openly of an American failure of nerve. It was not so much the effect of the Soviet missiles on the military equation between the two powers that mattered, although that was important; it was the political consequences of the *appearance* of a change in the balance of power that were deemed critical by Kennedy. The Soviet Union was supposed to be on the short end of the missile gap, but Kennedy feared that American inaction would persuade the world that Soviet claims of missile superiority were accurate. This would lead allied governments to fear that, in the new situation in which the United States would be vulnerable to nuclear devastation, they could no longer count on this country to defend them. Above all, it might tempt the Soviets to exploit the situation and to seek to disrupt American alliances—especially the North Atlantic Treaty Organization. Khrushchev already had restated his determination to eject the Western allies from West Berlin. If Khrushchev succeeded in Cuba, why should he take Kennedy's pledge to defend West Berlin seriously? And if he did not, would not Soviet and American troops soon be clashing in an area where they would be hard to separate?

The real irony of the Cuban missile crisis was that Kennedy also was determined to seek a stabler, more restrained basis for coexistence with the Soviet Union during his years in office. This long-range goal, which hardly had the massive support it would have later, could not be realized if Khrushchev did not take Kennedy seriously and tried to push him around. Then serious negotiations, in which each party would recognize the other's legitimate interests, would be impossible. A major change in the cold war atmosphere was at stake, in addition to the United States' reputation for power and willingness to keep commitments. Domestically, of course, another "defeat" in Cuba, discrediting Kennedy's foreign policy, was bound to affect his personal standing with his party, Congress, and the public. It also would lead to strong right-wing Republican pressures to be more forcible in foreign policy and would give less priority to the president's liberal domestic reform program. Thus, the foreign policy and domestic pressures for Kennedy to act were overwhelming.

The dominant role of the president in crises was reaffirmed by President George Bush during the Iraqi confrontation from August 1990 to March 1991. From the beginning, he interpreted the Iraqi invasion of Kuwait as an attempt by Saddam Hussein to make Iraq the dominant power in the Gulf, thereby able to control OPEC oil production and pricing policies; to establish Iraq as the hegemonic power in the Middle East, eliminating moderate pro-Western Arab leaders; and to position Iraq as leader of an anti-Israeli and anti-American campaign. These goals had to be opposed, all the more so because Saddam Hussein's conquest and rape of Kuwait would set a bad precedent in the newly emerging post-cold war period for other potential aggressors if he went unpunished. In making his decision to oppose the Iraqi strongman, to apply sanctions, and to use force if necessary to evict him from Kuwait, the president was guided by two powerful convictions. The first, derived from Bush's World War II experience in which he served as the navy's youngest fighter pilot, was that aggressors had to be stopped in their tracks; appeasement was folly. The president viewed Saddam Hussein's threat in terms similar to Hitler's threat in the 1930s. The horror stories of the brutal behavior and atrocities committed by the Iraqis in Kuwait only reinforced his belief that the Iraqi leader, like the Nazi one, was an evil, immoral man who had to be stopped. The second conviction was Bush's continuing belief in the worth and purposes of American power. Unlike many of his fellow citizens, especially within the Democratic party, Bush had not lost confidence in both after Vietnam. Indeed, the president told an interviewer, "Because of the role of the United States in the world, we have a disproportionate responsibility." [10]

The president's role as leader throughout the events that followed has been widely recognized and praised. Having decided at the outset that the occupation of Kuwait "will not stand," he kept his eye on the central strategic issue, which in fact was neutralizing Saddam Hussein as a threat to the entire Middle East. He then proceeded to organize an unbelievable coalition of disparate nations: the Soviet Union, such key Western allies as Britain and France, and important Arab states, including Egypt, Syria, and Morocco, in addition to the threatened Gulf states. Bush also proceeded to mobilize the United Nations in support of his aim of getting Iraq out of Kuwait. This certainly made it easier for the Soviet Union and several of the Arab states to justify cooperating with the United States, their former cold war rival and friend of Israel. It also gave legitimacy to the U.S. goal of ejecting Iraq from Kuwait and the application initially of economic sanctions to achieve that goal, and, when these were not successful, the setting of a deadline for an Iraqi withdrawal, which, if not met, would lead to the use of military force. Bush's domestic handling of the crisis was equally skillful. He mobilized public opinion in support of his actions despite cries of "Vietnam." Thus, the initial buildup of 250,000 troops met little opposition. The Democratic party, which since its trauma in Vietnam had become an essentially pacifist party, at first supported the president in his use of economic sanctions. Only later, when the president doubled this military force in an effort to convince Saddam Hussein that if he did not get out of Kuwait voluntarily he would be forced out, did the Democrats oppose Bush, arguing that they were committed to the same goal as Bush but preferred to avoid the heavy casualties that a war against a million-man Iraqi army might involve. At least, they said, give economic sanctions a year, eighteen months, perhaps two years, to work. Iraq would have to comply because its loss of oil revenues would bring it to economic collapse. The Democrats demanded that the United States not go to war except as constitutionally mandated—that is, with congressional support, and Bush eventually did go to the Congress for support. The United Nations had already given its support for military action. Would the Congress be the one exception? It was a gamble, but despite the almost wholesale opposition of the Democrats, Bush squeaked by in the Senate where the issue had been in doubt.

Once the deadline for an Iraqi pullout had passed on January 15, 1991, Bush did not hesitate and ordered the war to start. It lasted forty-three days. The initial weeks saw only an air battle. Indeed, air power basically won the war, destroying Iraq's capability to become a great regional power by building up its weapons of mass destruction; it also pounded the Iraqi army in Kuwait and southern Iraq mercilessly. Nevertheless, the critics urged the president to continue the fight in the air; they pleaded that he avoid a ground war. But when his generals told him that they were ready for action on land, he gave them the permission they needed. In less than 100 hours it was all over. U.S. casualties for the entire war were only an astonishing 148 on the ground, including 35 caused by "friendly fire." On the Iraqi side, however, the vaunted Iraqi army was only too glad not to fight and surrender or retreat.

But it was Bush's diplomatic performance that dominated the war. First, he prevented the split-up of the coalition that Saddam Hussein thought he could achieve by attacking Israel with missiles. Saddam expected Israel to retaliate, thereby forcing the Arab states out of the war, but the Israelis showed remarkable restraint and did not (allied, including Saudi, planes were diverted to finding and destroying Iraqi missile launchers). Moreover, all Arab members of the coalition remained in place, and their peoples did not rise up in anger against their governments for joining in an attack on a fellow Arab state—despite widespread predictions that this would happen by many experts on the Middle East besides Saddam Hussein.

Second, and more important, Bush prevented an outcome that would have saved face for Saddam Hussein and preserved much of his conventional fighting capability. As it became obvious that a ground war was required, Mikhail Gorbachev tried to end the war by getting the Iraqi leader to withdraw from Kuwait and save the former Soviet client, as well as to position himself as a major postwar player at the bargaining table. Saddam Hussein agreed to pull out, seeking to lure Gorbachev from the coalition, but on terms unacceptable to Bush: economic sanctions would have to be ended before the Iraqi withdrawal was complete; no economic reparations would be imposed on Iraq for its pillaging and mistreatment of tiny Kuwait, most of whose oil wells the Iraqis set on fire at the last moment; and Saddam Hussein would not be required to formally disavow Iraq's annexation of Kuwait. In addition, without a ground war the United States could not ensure the destruction of the Iraqi army, especially Saddam Hussein's elite and loyal Republican Guard forces. Bush thanked Gorbachev but told him the terms did not go far enough. Instead, he cut short a potentially troubling diplomatic situation—which could have delayed the ground war and been troublesome for the alliance's cohesion—by giving Saddam Hussein a twenty-four-hour ultimatum to get out of Kuwait or face a ground war. Once the ground war started, again right after the Iraqi leader had ignored another deadline, Saddam Hussein accepted Soviet terms more favorable to U.S. demands; he even announced Iraq's withdrawal without any conditions.

But Bush, with a rout of Iraqi forces in sight, would have none of these maneuvers. The added ground sweep around all of the Iraqi forces in Kuwait, especially the Republican Guard, whose strength had to be destroyed before the fighting ceased, remained his top priority. Saddam Hussein's threat to the area had to be ended; that had been the central strategic aim from the beginning of the crisis. Restoring Kuwait was the subsidiary goal. All in all, the commander in chief's performance was widely hailed in what turned out to be a very popular victory viewed closely in living rooms across America because of the extensive television coverage. Americans' pride in their armed forces and in their country was at an all-time high. Bush's job approval rating was almost 90 percent, the highest of any president in nearly a half century and the second highest since public opinion polls had begun.

Role of the Bureaucracy

The third characteristic of crisis decision making is the subordination of bureaucratic interests to the need to make a decision to safeguard the "national interest." The crisis is accompanied by a sense of urgency, as well as by policy makers' perceptions that the nation's security is at stake and that war looms. Thus, although decision making has risen to the top levels of the government, and the men and women in those positions reflect their departmental points of view, they do not necessarily feel limited to representing those points of view. Organizational affiliation is not a good predictor of those points of view. Senior participants in crises behave more like "players" than like "organizational participants." For example, Secretary of Defense Robert McNamara did not reflect the Joint Chiefs' readiness to bomb and invade during the Cuban missile crisis (just as late in the Vietnam War he was to disagree increasingly with their views and recommendations); he became the leading proponent of the blockade. Other players in that crisis did not even represent foreign policy bureaucracies—the two men closest to the president, the attorney general and the president's special counsel, along with the secretary of the treasury and a former secretary of state, for example, represented only themselves. The bureaucratic axiom that "you stand where you sit" is thus not necessarily correct, at least during a crisis.

The bureaucracy's principal role in a crisis is carrying out the policy. This especially applies to the military because the threat of force, if not some limited application of force, becomes quickly visible in such a confrontation. Military organizations, like all organizations, operate according to certain standard operating procedures. While these serve the purpose of the organization, they may not serve the policy makers' goals of preventing a dangerous escalation and preserving the peace. Thus, the air force, when asked about the possibility of a "surgical strike" on the Cuban missiles, dusted off old plans drawn up for an invasion of Cuba and simply added the missiles to hundreds of other targets—that is, the air force produced a disproportionate response, which might have led Moscow to respond differently if it had suspected the goal was not only the withdrawal of Soviet missiles but, despite the president's words, the elimination of Castro as well. And the navy wanted the blockade to be imposed outside the range of Cuban-piloted Soviet MIG fighters, while Kennedy wanted the blockade pulled in to give Khrushchev extra time to think about his next move. Both goals were legitimate, but obviously they were incompatible. The risks of war by inadvertence, then, are real. No one wants war, but loss of control in the implementation phase of a crisis may well provoke an unintentional escalation. It is, therefore, imperative that in such situations presidents ensure that their political goals remain primary and that military operations do not jeopardize them.

Indeed, military operations can tend to drive policy. They can set deadlines for political action, foreclosing diplomacy and determining the nation's course. In Vietnam, the U.S. military became disillusioned by the gradual escalation of pressure and the restraints imposed on the conduct of the war. In the Persian Gulf, the officers in charge of the campaign against Iraq, led by Gen. Colin Powell, chairman of the Joint Chiefs of Staff and a Vietnam veteran, believed in gathering sizable forces so that if hostilities erupted, the United States could act with overwhelming force and, unhampered by political constraints, try to win quickly with few lives lost. Thus, the initial commitment to defend Saudi Arabia was over 250,000 U.S. troops, in addition to Saudi and other countries' forces. It also was hoped that such a large commitment would convey to Saddam Hussein the seriousness of the American determination to defend the oil kingdom and deter a possible Iraqi attack. But as the Iraqi buildup continued, the U.S. military sought to reach greater strength for its offensive punch if war came. Admittedly, political objectives were also present—communicating to Iraq's leader that if he did not withdraw from Kuwait he would be forcefully ejected. But the U.S. military's purpose in doubling its forces, including tank divisions from Germany where they had long faced the Soviets, was to have the capabilities needed to seize the initiative at the outset of a war, to destroy immediately all key military targets in Iraq, and to contain Iraqi forces in Kuwait while cutting their supply lines. While no one could promise a quick victory and few casualties, the military planned on obtaining as quick a victory as possible and holding casualties down by attacking with large forces and exploiting U.S. technology to the hilt.

But once Operation Desert Shield, as it was called, reached full strength, the critics feared that the military option might become unstoppable. Once the forces were in place, war would become hard to avoid; they could not be kept in place month after month, much of the time in the desert heat. Moreover, a long stay by Western "infidels" in Saudi Arabia might jeopardize the monarchy, especially if those troops were still there when the faithful visited Mecca in the late spring when the searing hot desert weather returned. Thus committing military forces, particularly such large ones, might limit, if not undermine, any possible diplomatic efforts to resolve differences peacefully. Admittedly, the likelihood of war might just give Saddam Hussein the incentive to withdraw from Kuwait. But the hope for that solution was never high. The annexation of Kuwait as a province of Iraq did not suggest that Saddam Hussein would withdraw even if in return he were granted certain objectives such as access to the Gulf. And his firm belief that America would not fight meant that President Bush's warnings and deployment of troops to Saudi Arabia may have been dismissed as a bluff. Thus, while the military buildup probably did place a time limit on diplomatic efforts, the likelihood of a peaceful settlement of the issue of Kuwait was never high.

Once hostilities began, the main emphasis was on the air war, although it was recognized that eventually a ground war might be needed to eject the Iraqi army from Kuwait. Air power has never won a war by itself, but U.S. Air Force planners argued that the carpet-bombing of Iraqi troops and the cutting of supply lines could perhaps destroy up to half of the well-dug-in land forces and demoralize and starve the rest. Air Force officers claimed that no war had ever been more winnable because the desert, unlike the jungles of Vietnam, would allow no concealment unless troops stayed on the defensive in entrenched positions. Subsequently, the war planes, flown by U.S. Air Force, Navy, and Marine pilots, as well as British, French, Saudi, and Kuwaiti pilots, softened up the land forces before the ground engagement. The principal issue was one of time; the air war had to be given sufficient time. And this position was supported by those in Congress and outside experts who wished to minimize U.S. and allied ground casualties. The problem, some critics believed, was that the war was being planned by army officers—the chairman of the Joint Chiefs of Staff, General Powell, and the commanding officer in Saudi Arabia, Gen. Norman Schwarzkopf. Quite naturally, army officers believe that only ground forces can capture territory and dislodge enemy forces—that is, that wars are won on land. They were quite correct in this estimation, but despite their belief, they in fact waged essentially an air war, consisting of over 100,000 sorties, to destroy and demoralize the Iraqi forces in Kuwait. By the time the army rolled in, the ground war had become a quick mopping-up operation! Thus in this superbly planned combined arms operation, the army planners did not act parochially, as might have been expected, largely because the reorganization of the Joint Chiefs of Staff had eliminated much of the previous interservice rivalry by making the chairman of the Joint Chiefs its most powerful member. He was directly in touch with the local theater commander, General Schwarzkopf in this case, depriving the other chiefs of much of their authority.[11]

Role of Congress

Finally, decision making in a crisis is characterized by congressional noninvolvement. Congressional leaders usually are called in and informed of the president's decision just before it is announced publicly. This form is followed as a matter of courtesy. But their advice is not requested. Presidents consider themselves more representative of the country than any senator or House member and as representative as Congress as a whole. Interestingly, Kennedy, after informing a congressional delegation of his decision to blockade Cuba, did ask for its opinions. When the response was to question the utility of the blockade and to propose an air strike instead, Kennedy reacted angrily. After the members left, he consoled himself by saying that had they had more time to think it over they also would have decided on the blockade. If presidents assure themselves like this, why indeed consult members of the legislative branch? In any event, in American-Soviet crises the Congress has generally supported the president.

But one characteristic of a crisis is its brevity. There is not sufficient time to develop criticism and opposition. And even if there were disagreement, there is a great reluctance to voice it in the early stages of the confrontation. Rather, the country "rallies round the flag." Time is the critical factor. If a crisis does not end quickly, however, congressional opposition many grow. During the confrontation with Iraq, Congress initially fully supported the president's goals and actions. But after the substantial increase in forces in November 1990, three months after the first deployment, questions about the future course of events multiplied. Did the military buildup make war inevitable? Had economic sanctions been given enough time to work? What about diplomatic efforts to resolve the Kuwaiti issue without resorting to force? If war came, how would the war be conducted? Would the emphasis be on a long air war, relying mainly on air power to win the war, or would the focus, after a short air campaign, be on the ground engagement? Would the result be heavy U.S. casualties? Even if war were unavoidable and it ended quickly without many U.S. deaths, would the aftermath of a war in which Westerners again killed Arabs further destabilize the Middle East, making America's Arab friends more vulnerable and poisoning relations with the Arab world for generations to come? Even if Iraq were defeated, would this not result in Iran once more seeking to become the hegemon in the Gulf, with Syria resuming its drive for Arab leadership?

Thus as war threatened, the Congress, having been witness to presidential uses of force time and time again during the cold war, began to insist on its authority to declare war. Given the institutional rivalry between the executive and legislative branches (if not also between the House and the Senate) and partisan differences, with one party much of the time occupying the presidency and the other the Congress, it was not easy for the United States to confront its adversary with unity at home. Since Vietnam, it has become increasingly clear that, short of an attack on the United States or on U.S. forces overseas, Congress is unlikely to overwhelmingly support any use of force. Bush declared repeatedly in public that he would like congressional support if he felt it necessary to use force against Saddam Hussein, but unless Congress gave him overwhelming support he would rather do without it. A close vote would send the wrong signal to Iraq, confirming its dictator's belief that the United States was too divided to go to war against him. With the UN vote sanctioning the use of force if Iraq did not pull out of Kuwait by January 15, 1991, Bush believed that as commander in chief he already possessed the authority to go to war. But at the last minute, probably assuming that Congress would not dare undermine the president of the United States, he did seek a congressional equivalent to a declaration of war and got it. Despite the opposition of the entire Democratic leadership, he attracted just enough Democrats to his side to slide past in the Senate and win comfortably in the House (for more details, see Chapter 14 on limited war).

In short, there may be a period of "rallying round the flag" initially after the outbreak of a crisis or hostilities, but that support will erode the longer the fighting lasts and as the casualties mount. One has to suspect that even in the Cuban missile crisis the overwhelming support President Kennedy had mobilized would have eroded after a two- to three-month congressional and public debate about whether getting a few missiles out of Cuba was worth the cost of a nuclear war, and about how flexible or inflexible the president should have been in negotiations with Soviet leader Khrushchev while peace activists, as they called themselves, led demonstrations in major cities.

Finally, one reason for the post-Vietnam involvement in only relatively short wars has been to hold congressional involvement to a minimum. It is notable that even against Iraq, Bush called off the war as soon as the Iraqis had been driven out of Kuwait with minimal U.S./UN casualties. He rejected driving to Baghdad not only because he believed that Iraq's nuclear facilities had been destroyed, but also because he felt that assuming responsibility for governing Iraq and becoming drawn into its civil war would prolong U.S. involvement and raise casualties. As it is, the later revelations that Iraq's nuclear facilities had not been destroyed (as had been believed before a defector informed the United Nations of secret nuclear sites) led to criticism of the quick ending of the war before Saddam Hussein had been deposed in Baghdad. But Bush was probably right. Had the hostilities lasted six months, possibly a year, and, above all, had casualties ranged upward from 5,000 to 20,000, with perhaps 2,000 dead, he would have faced a growing peace movement and increasing criticism from Congress. In brief, congressional involvement in crises is simply a reflection of time.

NONCRISIS DECISION MAKING AS A PLURALISTIC POWER STRUGGLE

Multiple Actors

The governmental politics model of decision making is characterized first by multiple institutional actors: the three branches of the federal government. In foreign policy matters, the principal participants are the executive and legislative branches. Within these institutions, there are a multitude of departments, organizations, staffs, committees, and individuals concerned with foreign policy. Within the executive branch, there are (1) the president, the national security adviser, and the adviser's staff; (2) the senior foreign policy departments—the State and Defense departments and the Central Intelligence Agency (CIA); (3) the junior departments—the Agency for International Development (AID), U.S. Information Agency (USIA), and Arms Control and Disarmament Agency (ACDA); and (4) the departments with domestic jurisdictions that occasionally deal with foreign policy issues falling within their areas of expertise—the Departments of the Treasury, Commerce, and Agriculture. On the legislative side, both the Senate and the House are divided into many different party groupings, committees, and subcommittees.[12]

This institutional pluralism is supplemented by organized groups representing many economic, ethnic, racial, religious, and public interests. But they are less involved in security policy than in domestic/intermestic affairs. The reason is easy to understand. Interest groups have abundant knowledge of and experience in internal affairs, but on foreign policy issues they rarely have comparable information and skill. In addition, interest groups are consulted regularly by the respective executive departments while domestic/intermestic legislation is being drawn up, but in foreign policy the departments tend to be their own constituencies and spokespersons. The responsible agencies have their own experts and are in contact with other experts, be they at the RAND Corporation or at Harvard University. Although there is a fairly stable structure of societal interest groups concerned with domestic/intermestic policies, the comparable structure in the traditional area of foreign policy concerned with security issues is weak and at times even ephemeral. Business groups and labor may be interested in particular tariff issues when certain industries and their employees are exposed to foreign competition, or an ethnic group may be stimulated by disputes involving a specific country, such as Israel or Greece. Yet continuing concern with foreign policy as a whole is usually lacking; it is largely intermittent and tied to special issues. This is generally true as well for public interest groups and nonethnic, one-issue groups concerned with such specific issues as the Panama Canal or an arms control agreement, although from time to time these groups may exert considerable influence on such issues.

In short, the main differences between foreign and domestic policy making are that domestic policy making involves more participants in both the executive and legislative branches and receives more attention from interest groups and the public. The larger the number of actors and the more important the stakes that key legislators, committees, and lobbyists perceive to be at issue, the more difficult it is to arrive at policy decisions (see Table 11-1). Negotiations are long and difficult, and compromises acceptable to so many parties are not reached without immense effort, if they can be arranged at all. In these circumstances, the president's ability to initiate, lead, and maneuver is seriously circumscribed. For the traditional security issues where no immediate tangible interests are perceived to be at stake, the president is generally—although not always—acknowledged to have greater expertise. In contrast, domestic issues involve many concerns, especially material ones, that arouse many actors who believe they are just as expert and experienced as the executive. Presidential involvement, therefore, does not guarantee successful domestic negotiations. On key issues, presidents, lacking votes, may be reluctant to enter the policy arena at all, lest failure and an impaired reputation for getting things done result. The contrast to the foreign policy realm is striking; there presidents can normally count on achieving their aims, building successful records, benefiting their political parties, and presumably helping the nation.

Table 11-1 Policy Characteristics

Type of Policy	Chief Charac- teristics	Primary Actors	Principal Decision Maker	Role of Congress	Role of Interest Groups	Relations among Actors
Crisis	Short run; bureaucracy & Congress short- circuited	President, responsible officials, individuals in & out of government	Executive (president- ial preemi- nence)	Postcrisis legitimation	None	Cooperation
Noncrisis (security)	Long run; bureaucratic- legislative participation	President, executive agencies, Congress, in- terest groups, public opinion	Executive bureaucracy	Congres- sional parti- cipation	Low to moderate	Competition and bar- gaining
Domestic (welfare)	Long run; bureaucratic- legislative participation	President, executive agencies, Congress, interest groups, public opinion	Executive- congres- sional sharing	High	High	Competition and bar- gaining

SOURCE: This table is modeled on one in Randal B. Ripley and Grace A. Franklin, *Congress, the Bureaucracy, and Public Policy* (Homewood, Ill.: Dorsey, 1976), 17.

Conflict

A second characteristic of the governmental politics model of decision making is conflict among actors. Because the president is both the nation's chief diplomat and the commander in chief of its armed forces, this conflict occurs primarily within the executive branch, among executive departments that are responsible for formulation and implementation of foreign policy (although conflict between the executive and legislative branches of government also occurs—in fact, the two branches rarely speak with a single voice).[13] Conflict may arise, for example, between the State and Defense departments. And within the State Department, the head of the bureau for European and Canadian affairs may express a view quite different from those of the heads of the Inter-American or African bureaus. In the Defense Department, the position of the air force may differ from those of the army and navy. Indeed, within each service there are differences, as between the Strategic Air Command and Tactical Air Command, or as among the surface navy, strategic submarine navy, and aircraft-carrier navy. In the Senate, the Foreign Relations Committee may clash on a specific issue with the Armed Services

Committee, and subcommittees of each committee may disagree with one another. This situation must be multiplied by the other committees and subcommittees in both houses. Each of these institutions, bureaucracies, committees, and interest groups develops intense organizational identifications, and all are determined not only to survive but also to expand their influence in the policy-making process. Furthermore, each, viewing a problem from a special perspective, is likely to develop strong convictions about the content of policy, especially when "national interests" are involved and the organization or department thinks that it has a vital contribution to make. Institutional struggles between the executive and legislative branches, as well as within each branch and within executive departments, are consequently the norm.

This kind of policy-making process is often condemned as "parochial," on the assumption that more comprehensive—more "correct"—solutions to all policy problems could be found were it not for the selfish and narrow points of view of the various participants in the policy process. Adherents to this view ignore the fact that in any pluralistic institution, diverse convictions compete. Different policy recommendations are offered as solutions to the problems being considered, and these recommendations represent a fairly broad spectrum of choice. Just as in a democracy different groups and individuals have the right to articulate their values and interests, so the various parts of the executive and legislative branches have the right to articulate their own policy views and seek to protect their own interests. The issue is not which policy positions and recommendations are correct; clearly, there is no single correct policy. *The issue is how to reconcile conflicting interpretations of what the correct policy ought to be.* This reconciliation of the policy preferences of the various "players" is complicated by the many players outside the executive branch.

Consensus Building

The third characteristic of the governmental politics model of decision making, stemming from the first two, is reconciliation of these different points of view to build a consensus or majority coalition so that decisions can be made. Negotiating thus occurs throughout the executive branch as officials and agencies in one department seek support in another or attempt to enlist the aid of the president or the White House advisers to achieve their goals. The process is one of widening the base of support within the executive branch and then seeking further support in the two houses of Congress, gaining allies through continual modification of the proposed policy. The official policy "output" that emerges represents the victory of one coalition formed across institutional lines over an opposing coalition of the same kind.

More specifically, a coalition across institutional lines can be, for example, an alliance among the personnel of a particular desk in the State Department, of a specific service in the Defense Department, of various bureaus in the Departments of the Treasury and Commerce, or of several committees in Congress. It may be opposed by the personnel of other desks, services, bureaus, and committees in the same or other departments or in the legislative branch. Such a coalition usually holds together only for the specific issue being considered. A different issue requires mobilization of a different coalition. The reason is that in the United States political parties are undisciplined, and party loyalty cannot be counted on automatically for any given presidential policy. Great energy must be expended on this task. *Policy is therefore not only a matter of which point of view seems to have the most merit and pertinence, but also a matter of who has power and exercises it the most effectively.* The resulting intragovernmental policy struggle is every bit as intense and persistent as intergovernmental conflicts.

Incrementalism and Crisis

A fourth characteristic of the governmental politics model of decision making is the effect of conflict and coalition building on policy output. One of the most important results of the continual bargaining within the "policy machine" is that policy in any area moves forward one step at a time and tends to focus on fleeting concerns and short-range aims.[14] This is usually called *incrementalism.* Another word is "satisficing." Policy makers, as this word suggests, do not sit down each time they have to make a decision and go through the rational procedure of decision making. They do not try to isolate which values and interests they wish to enhance, examine all the means that might achieve these goals, calculate the consequences of each, and then select the one most likely to be successful. Policy makers have neither the time nor resources to go through this process. Instead, they pick a policy such as the containment one that was successful in the past. Why then not take another step forward on the same path and apply that policy to the changed circumstances of today?

The presumption is that what worked in the past will work now, as well as in the future. There are good reasons for this. For one, bureaucracies gain vested interests in their own policies and they therefore defend them; a change in policy may lead to a decline in their influence and increase in clout for other bureaucracies. Thus, they resist policy changes when a current or new administration decides on a major shift in policy. In addition, most administrations do not suddenly shift policy. They are constrained by previously existing policy and commitments. Such incrementalism has advantages. It allows policy makers to adjust policy to changing circumstances; it also permits retreat in policy if the incremental change did not work. And it avoids brawls and struggles within the policy-making community. Once a majority coalition of the actors involved in the decision-making process has been forged after a hard struggle and probably much bloodletting, it will normally prefer modification of the existing policy to another major fight. The presumption is, of course, that a policy will result, which is not necessarily true. Negotiations among different groups with conflicting perspectives and vested interests can produce a stalemate and policy paralysis.

As a result, policy tends to vacillate between incrementalism and crisis, either because incrementalism is not adequate to a developing situation or because stalemate produces no policy at all. It may be said with reasonable certitude that during "normal" periods, low external pressure on the policy machine favors continuation of existing policies; during crises, high pressure tends to produce innovative reactions, perhaps because a stalemated policy machine must have an *external trigger* to undermine the coalition supporting the status quo. A crisis may break up coalitions, awaken a sense of danger great enough to dampen the pluralistic struggle (even if only for a short time), and create a feeling of urgency—and therefore a common purpose—among the various participants in policy making. In addition, as suggested earlier, crisis policy is decided in an inner circle, composed of the president and a few top officials and trusted advisers; at a time of perceived danger, these officials function relatively free of departmental points of view and interests. The usual process of consensus or coalition building is thus short-circuited.[15] There are, then, two policy processes: the pluralistic advocacy system and the crisis management system, the latter involving top officials (assistant secretaries and up), the former a broader mix of interests.

Because the U.S. political system, with its multiple actors, often tends to produce a stalemate, it is during crises that policy makers can most easily shift policy. For example, it took the bombing of Pearl Harbor in 1941 to harness the strength of the United States and direct it toward warding off German and Japanese threats to the nation's security. Before December 7, 1941, President Franklin Roosevelt had taken only intermittent measures to help England survive after the defeat of France because he had faced constant opposition at home. After Japan's attack, however, the president, who had called himself "Dr. New Deal"—the physician called in to cure a sick economy—became "Dr. Win the War"—the physician who could mobilize the nation's full resources to defeat its enemies. Similarly, after World War II it was the overwhelming Soviet threat that allowed Truman to mobilize the country for containment. Before the threat became so obvious that it could no longer be ignored, Truman had been unable to take the necessary countermeasures. And, again, it was Castro and his attempts to stir up anti-American revolutions in Latin American countries that allowed President Kennedy to mobilize support for the Alliance for Progress, which was intended to help relieve some of the potentially revolutionary problems in the Southern Hemisphere.

Need for Time

A fifth characteristic of this policy-making process, implicit in the analysis thus far, is its time-consuming nature. Incrementalism suggests a policy machine in low gear, moving along a well-defined road rather slowly in response to specific short-run stimuli. Normally, a proposed policy is discussed first within the executive branch. It then passes through official channels, where it receives clearances and modifications as it gathers a broader base of support on its way "up" the executive hierarchy to the president. Constant conferences and negotiations among departments clearly slow the pace. The process takes even longer when the policy requires extensive congressional participation and approval. On domestic/intermestic policy particularly, potential opponents can use any one of many "veto points" to block legislation within Congress. Such veto points are the numerous House and Senate committees and subcommittees that hold hearings on legislation and the floor debate and votes in both chambers. Should both houses of Congress pass the legislation, the differences between the two versions must be compromised and resubmitted to both houses for final approval. Only then does the legislation go to the president for a signature. Should the president veto it, it will go back to Congress, which can override the presidential veto, but only by a two-thirds vote. The advantage of this slow process lies with those who oppose specific pieces of legislation, for it is difficult for legislation to jump all the hurdles along the route to final approval and enactment. But, admittedly, this process is applied more to domestic policy than to foreign policy because of the president's greater responsibility and freedom to make foreign policy.

Given this slow negotiating process, the formidable obstacles, and the great effort needed to pass a major new policy, old policies and the assumptions on which they are based tend to survive longer than they should. For example, policy based on the assumption that the Communist world was cohesive continued even after the Sino-Soviet conflict had surfaced in the late 1950s, and a preoccupation with strategic deterrence persisted long after the need for a limited war capacity had been painfully demonstrated in the Korean War.

Appealing Packaging and Shared Images

A sixth characteristic of the governmental politics model is the premium placed on attractive and appealing policy packaging and advertising arising from the competition among groups involved in the policy-making process. This means that rather than presenting complex and sophisticated reasons for a particular policy position, proponents will try to make it more acceptable by oversimplifying the issues, tying their "product" up with a pretty moral ribbon, and selling it by insisting that it will definitely solve the buyer's problems. The sellers may indeed exaggerate these problems to enhance the buyer's feeling that he or she absolutely needs the policy product being offered.[16] In foreign policy making during the cold war, the presentation of issues in terms of anticommunism versus communism, good against evil, hardly promoted understanding of the real issues involved and made it difficult to adjust policies to a changing international environment and a changing Communist world. The threat of Russia, simply as a great power, was real enough; that it was Soviet Russia constituted an even greater threat. Nevertheless, the menace of "international communism" was exaggerated, partly because it was an effective device for persuading various government agencies to accept certain policies, and partly because it helped mobilize majority support in Congress and the country for those policies.

More specifically, the commonly shared assumptions on which decision makers operate—their shared biases or images—help determine which decisions are made. If anticommunism is the bias, those who try to "sell" their preferences in terms of these "shared images" have a good chance of putting together a majority coalition. Those whose preferences are not in line with these assumptions, however, lose out.

Public Debate

The seventh characteristic of this model is the usually public nature of American foreign policy making. In a democracy, public involvement is inevitable. Although policy may be made primarily by the executive, its limits are established by public opinion. No British government before 1939 could have pursued a deterrent policy toward Hitler, and no American government before the fall of France in 1940 could have intervened in Europe to preserve the balance of power. In general, however, public opinion tends to be permissive and supportive as far as presidential conduct of foreign policy is concerned.[17] The public is aware that it lacks information and competence in this area, which is remote from its everyday involvement, and it looks to the president for leadership, information, and interpretation of that information. Only when setbacks arise or painful experiences pinch the voters will public opinion on foreign policy be expressed, the limits of public tolerance broadly clarified, and perhaps the party in power punished. Even though most of the time public opinion does not function as a restraining factor, policy makers are always aware of its existence, however amorphous it may be. Because mass opinion does not tend to take shape until *after* some foreign event has occurred, it can hardly serve as a guide for those who must make policy. Nonetheless, the latter will take into account what they think "the traffic will bear" because they know that if a decision is significant enough, there is likely to be some crystallization of opinion and possibly retribution at the polls.

Reflecting public opinion, Congress was—at least until the Vietnam War— usually *supportive* of the president's foreign policy. Throughout most of the post-World War II period, Congress had followed the president's lead, and its role had been essentially reactive and peripheral. The executive initiated and devised foreign policies, which Congress rarely rejected. Primarily, its role was to legitimate those policies in either the original or amended form.[18] The record of American foreign policy from 1945 to the mid-1960s shows clearly that all major presidential initiatives were accepted and supported by Congress.[19]

This situation has changed since the Vietnam War, however, as Congress, reflecting the erosion of the previous cold war consensus, has become both more skeptical of presidential wisdom in foreign policy and more assertive on the many international issues facing the United States. This assertiveness was evidenced in the congressional passage of legislation in 1973 to restrict the president's use of force and subversion. But more than anything else, the

Vietnam War itself raised the congressional sense of confidence and competence in foreign policy. It surely could do no worse than the executive branch. Issues were more thoroughly debated, executive judgments were accepted less readily and evaluated more critically, and restraints were imposed on the president's ability to use the armed forces and overt intervention, as well as the Central Intelligence Agency and covert intervention, without legislative knowledge and consent. Thus, President Ronald Reagan, restrained by Congress from lending military assistance to the contras fighting to overthrow the Marxist government of Nicaragua, sought to bypass Congress and the Constitution by seeking private funding of such assistance, thereby initiating the so-called Iran-contra scandal. Particularly important since Vietnam has been the shift in the role of the media from one of communicating and explaining official policy to one of questioning and criticizing policy. In this more adversarial role, the press, and especially the television news, have unquestionably affected and influenced public debate and opinion on foreign policy issues. In summary, amid an absence of consensus on what the role of the United States should be in the world, partisan conflict, and institutional rivalry, as well as a disbelieving press, it has become increasingly difficult for the president to provide the leadership the country needs.

THE POLITICS OF STRATEGIC DEFENSE: FROM ABM TO SDI

The seven characteristics discussed in the preceding section by no means exhaust the characteristics of the foreign policy process in the federal government, but they are the most obvious and are reflected in the following case study of the politics of strategic defense. In 1983, President Reagan proposed his Strategic Defense Initiative (SDI), or "Star Wars," as his critics dubbed SDI, because it relied largely on space-based defenses. This program is still being funded. It has survived the end of the Reagan presidency, the end of the cold war, and the end of the Soviet missile threat against which it was originally founded. It was therefore ironic that, despite its gutting by Congress, SDI received a new boost from the fear that such states as Iraq, hostile to the United States, would develop long-range missiles, thereby forcing Washington to worry increasingly about the use of chemical- or nuclear-armed warheads against friendly states, if not the United States itself. How did it survive the very threat against which it was proposed?

A look back at the original antiballistic missile (ABM) decision made by President Lyndon Johnson during the 1960s will place SDI in some perspective. That decision provides a keen insight into governmental decision making and is especially important because the ABM treaty, incorporated into Strategic Arms Limitations Talks (SALT) I, became part of the controversy over SDI. In the 1960s, the United States' deterrent policy was based on a retaliatory capability (see Chapter 13). It was generally assumed that a defense of either the missiles or the U.S. population was unnecessary. The deterrent forces were supposed to be invulnerable to a first strike, and, if they were, it was assumed that the people in the cities were also protected; no enemy would be foolish enough to attack America's cities if the United States could retaliate in kind. A first strike made sense only if the U.S. retaliatory capability could be destroyed; therefore, as long as this force was invulnerable, the enemy would be deterred.

From time to time, however, the defense of either the population or America's land-based deterrent forces has been proposed and debated publicly. The first time was in 1967 when Secretary of Defense Robert McNamara made a speech that seemed to make no sense because it included contradictory themes. On the one hand, he denounced the ABM—designed to knock down incoming missiles or warheads before designated targets were hit—as an expensive venture that would stimulate another round of the arms race and leave the United States less secure in the end; on the other hand, he proposed building a "small" ABM system against the Chinese (who were verbally more radical and militant than the Soviets but had few ICBMs)! To say the least, it was a strange speech, but it reflected the opposing views on defense within the government.[20]

Antiballistic Missile: Contestants and Arguments

On the anti-ABM side were McNamara and Secretary of State Dean Rusk, as well as the Arms Control and Disarmament Agency. All believed that the decision to deploy ABMs would mean a spiraling and costly arms race and would destroy all chances for stabilization of the American-Soviet deterrent balance. McNamara believed that such deployment would virtually preclude any possibility of initiating arms limitations talks with the Soviets. He was also skeptical of the technical feasibility of the proposed ABM. The secretary, however, was in the minority within his own department on this question. The Pentagon's Office of Defense Research and Engineering, concerned with development of modern weapons, and its Office of Systems Analysis both supported deployment of ABMs. Within the Defense Department, only the Office of International Security Affairs agreed with McNamara.

The principal bureaucratic supporters of the ABM were the armed services, which, in contrast to their situation on most defense issues, were united in their support. Although the army, navy, and air force each "saw a different face of ABM and reached different conclusions,"[21] the very fact of this interservice agreement is worth noting. Earlier, McNamara had exploited divisions among the services to prevail on issues of defense spending. Their united front, however, compelled him to go above the services and to appeal directly to the president. Different departments and, indeed, different bureaus within the various departments thus all saw different "faces" of the same ABM problems and had different stakes in the issue.

Congress too had interests and stakes in the ABM debate. Supporting the services were several senior members of the Senate Armed Services Committee, including Chairman Richard Russell, John Stennis, and Henry Jackson. These Democratic senators were supporters of Johnson's Vietnam policy and had been friends of the president when he served as the Democratic majority leader in the Senate during the administration of Dwight Eisenhower. Indeed, Johnson had served with them on the Armed Services Committee and trusted their judgment. He was particularly close to Russell.

In arguing their case, proponents and adversaries often emphasized different factors. Supporters stressed that the Soviets had already developed such a system, that it threatened the U.S. deterrent capacity, and that the ABM would save American lives. They argued that an ABM would provide Americans with an extra bargaining chip in any negotiations on a mutual defensive weapons limitation. Opponents, however, were less concerned about the Soviet deployment of ABMs than about the potential for a new arms race. Another factor that concerned them was the price tag. Estimates of the cost of an ABM system ranged from $30 billion to $40 billion.

View from the Presidency

In the face of these opposing pressures, no decision below the presidential level was possible. But a president's stake in any given issue is always greater than that of anyone else, and the White House perspective is different from that of any other player. For one thing, unity in the administration is a primary goal. Thus, Johnson sought to avoid, if at all possible, a direct break with McNamara. They were already at odds over the war in Vietnam, but the president still valued his secretary of defense too highly to reject his advice out of hand. McNamara viewed the ABM choice as a direct confrontation between himself and the Joint Chiefs of Staff, and he would have seen a decision to deploy the system as a rejection. In addition, a president also needs congressional support for foreign and domestic policies. A negative decision on the ABM would have alienated key senators who were also longtime friends and colleagues and whose opinions and convictions Johnson respected. But presidents are more than the chief officers of their administrations and chief architects of legislation to be submitted to Congress. They are also the heads of their political parties and concerned with reelection and their parties' fortunes at the polls. The Republicans were already talking of an ABM gap, threatening to do to the Democrats what Kennedy and Johnson had done to Nixon in 1960—use the potentially powerful charge of neglecting the nation's defenses. Johnson, who had not yet decided to forgo a reelection bid, had to be worried about the possible impact of such an accusation.

But presidents must take other considerations and pressures into account as well. They know that in the final analysis they are responsible for the country's security and protection. Others can advise them, but only presidents can make the required decisions, and it is they who will be judged not only by the people but also by history.[22] And that judgment is their ultimate stake. They will be compared to others: George Washington, Thomas Jefferson,

Abraham Lincoln, Theodore Roosevelt, Franklin Roosevelt, Harry Truman. No one who occupies the White House (or its equivalent in other countries) can possibly ignore his or her historical reputation. Johnson, whose involvement in Vietnam was already arousing popular and congressional criticism and casting doubt on his place in history, was keenly interested in a major arms limitation agreement with the Soviet Union to help his standing at that time and in the future; he needed a major breakthrough in the area of international reconciliation.

Minimal Decision Making

In this situation, given the "pitfalls" he saw in the ABM issue and the stakes he had in it, yet buffeted by conflicting pressures, the president would have preferred to make no decision at all and to allow the proponents and opponents of ABM to reach some kind of compromise among themselves. The problem of gaining presidential support for one side or another thus is not limited to reaching presidents, but also includes persuading them to make decisions. Their tendency is to procrastinate or to make only a "minimal decision." "How to decide without actually choosing" is the way political observer Warner Schilling aptly put it in connection with another important presidential decision:

> The President did make choices, but a comparison of the choices that he made with those that he did not make reveals clearly the minimal character of his decision. It bears all the aspects of a conscious search for the course of action which would close off the least number of future alternatives, one which would avoid the most choice....
>
> One of the major necessities of the American political process [is] the need to avert conflict by avoiding choice. The distribution of power and responsibility among government elites is normally so dispersed that a rather widespread agreement among them is necessary if any given policy is to be adopted and later implemented. Among the quasi-sovereign bodies that make up the Executive the opportunities to compel this agreement are limited.[23]

Truman put this need to gain support to decide policy in fewer and more picturesque words: "They talk about the power of the president, how I can push a button and get things done. Why, I spent most of my time kissing somebody's ass."[24]

The critical question thus became: What will be the nature of the ABM compromise? At least part of the answer became clear in a meeting between Johnson and McNamara and Soviet premier A. N. Kosygin in Glassboro, New Jersey, in June 1967. Johnson pressed the Soviets for a date for the opening of arms limitation talks. This declaration would allow him to postpone the decision on the ABM. But Johnson did not receive an answer. Kosygin described the Soviet ABM system as defensive and therefore unobjectionable. As a weapon that would save lives, it was, in the Soviet premier's judgment, a good weapon that would not destabilize the arms balance and was not a proper subject for strategic arms limitation talks. McNamara's principal objection to the ABM had been refuted by the Soviets. Consequently, Johnson no longer saw the ABM as a possible stumbling block to beginning arms limitations talks.

Johnson then made his minimal decision: to adopt a small anti-Chinese ABM system. McNamara announced the decision in his contradictory speech. He said, on the one hand, that the most effective way to overcome a Soviet ABM was to saturate the defense with offensive missiles, suggesting that the Soviets could do that to the United States as well. On the other hand, should the Chinese be as irrational as their militant revolutionary rhetoric suggested, a "thin" or small ABM system might help to deter a strike. In one sense, McNamara had won a victory against the Joint Chiefs of Staff and ABM supporters in Congress, who favored a "thick" or nationwide anti-Soviet (and more expensive) ABM system. The very fact that he made the speech showed that he had by no means suffered a major defeat on this issue. He could view the president's decision as leaving open the possibility that the system would never be deployed at all if the Soviets would later agree to limitation of mutual defensive weapons. The administration had come out *not* in support of deployment but only in support of increased funding for the procurement of certain ABM parts that would require a long lead time. But the administration had publicly changed its position, and that represented a victory for ABM supporters in Congress and the Joint Chiefs. Proponents of the more extensive system viewed the change in the administration's position as a hopeful sign and expected that they could accomplish their goal later. There were as yet no "winners" or "losers." Compromises had prevented that.

The fight over ABM continued into the Nixon administration. At the time, the large Soviet missile buildup, which overtook the United States in the number of ICBMs and to which there seemed no end in sight, was perceived as an increasing threat to U.S. ICBMs. The fear was that the number of missiles plus the number of warheads the Soviets would place on them over the coming years would give the Soviet Union a first-strike capability. President Nixon, therefore, switched the ABM from defending cities to defending ICBMs. This would counter the possibility of a successful Soviet strike and help keep the mutual deterrent balance stable.

Nixon also wanted a bargaining chip for the Strategic Arms Limitation Talks. There had been no U.S. missile buildup, so he could not trade some of them against the larger number of Soviet missiles. The ABM might be the only thing the United States could trade. As it turned out, the SALT treaty placed a low limit on ABMs (the Soviets had already deployed about sixty around Moscow), so low that the United States abandoned it. At the same time, the two powers agreed to freeze all offensive systems for a five-year period during which they would negotiate mutually acceptable ceilings on all strategic systems.

Neither Johnson nor Nixon was strongly committed to a strategic defense. Johnson was concerned that the Republicans would make the lack of an ABM defense a key issue in the next presidential election, and he was also worried about his relations with his own secretary of defense and several senators whose friendship and support he needed for his Great Society domestic reform program. Nixon, in his turn, wanted a trade-off between defensive and offensive systems at a time when the public and Congress were in an antimilitary mood and the defense budget had reached its lowest percentage of the gross national product since 1950, *before* Korea.

Star Wars

President Reagan, by contrast, was committed to a strategic defense and did not think of SDI as a bargaining chip.[25] Moreover, Reagan's advice on some sort of defensive system had come from outside the government, primarily from Edward Teller, the "father" of the hydrogen bomb. There was no pressure within the executive branch, including the Defense Department, or Congress for SDI. Indeed, at the time of the president's speech proposing it, the Defense Department's assessment of a strategic defense was that it was not feasible. Many in the administration were surprised by the president's speech, especially since the SDI conclusion had been added by the president at the last moment. The idea had not been submitted to the relevant departments for their examination, analysis, and recommendations.

This is not to say that SDI reflected a momentary whim. Ronald Reagan had expressed concern both before and immediately after he became president that the U.S. population was not being defended. The strategic balance when he assumed the office of the presidency was, in his judgment (although not that of most experts), shifting in the Soviet Union's favor. Whether or not it was, the president worried about the long-term consequences of a deterrent balance that depended on the threat of wiping out millions of Russians. He had little faith in deterrence. Nuclear weapons, instead of preventing war, would produce Armageddon, the biblical prophesy of the end of the world. Would it not be better to build deterrence on a defense that would shoot down incoming missiles and protect, rather than incinerate, the civilian populations of *both* countries? And, if the Soviets were behind the United States technologically, he offered to share SDI technology with them.

The security of the United States was not Reagan's only reason for advancing SDI; domestic politics was another. The president was seen by many as a militant anti-Communist crusader. He and other members of his administration had made a number of careless comments about nuclear war. Moreover, members of the administration had talked of *nuclear war fighting*, of *limited nuclear war*, and of *prevailing* in a nuclear exchange, not of deterrence. Partly because of all this talk, partly because détente had ended and the United States was embarking on a major modernization of its strategic forces, and partly because the administration was clearly opposed to arms control, many people feared a nuclear war. The media, physicians, Catholic and Methodist bishops, and other groups made constant reference to a "nuclear winter" and "the day after." The nuclear freeze movement gained a large public following. In these circumstances, the president was on the defensive, especially against the bishops who denounced the immorality of using, if not possessing, nuclear weapons—which, in effect, was tantamount to saying that nuclear deterrence was immoral. SDI placed the president back in charge and gave him the initiative in the nuclear debate. If nuclear war was bad for the nation's health and bad for Americans' souls, why not propose a nuclear shield that would protect the population? Why not seek mutual assured survival instead of mutual assured destruction? "War-monger" Reagan thus stole his critics' antinuclear thunder. There was something profoundly ironic about the most conservative president in postwar history adopting the nuclear abolitionist stance of the most left-wing nuclear disarmers.

Strategic Defense Initiatives 1-3

In his speech the president proposed that SDI be able to render missiles "impotent and obsolete." A three-phase system, SDI would try to shoot down missiles while they were in their initial boost phase, lasting about five minutes. It would then try to destroy the multiple warheads after they had separated from the missiles in mid-phase flight (an infinitely more difficult task because of the far larger number of targets). And, last, a terminal defense would try to destroy the warheads that had escaped. Nevertheless, SDI was controversial from the beginning. However shrewd a move in the context of American politics, it also suddenly undermined the deterrent basis on which U.S. and Western security had rested for four decades. Deterrence assumed that the threat of retaliation and extinction was sufficient to prevent an attack; SDI assumed that deterrence would fail. Moreover, it turned out that there was not one but three SDIs. SDI 1—the president's proposed nonnuclear population defense shield based in space—was quickly dismissed by most technologists and arms controllers. Such a futuristic system was deemed so complex and technically demanding that it was doubtful that it could offer the 100 percent protection the president had promised. Even if it were 80-90 percent effective—which was doubtful—enough Soviet missiles would be able to penetrate the "space shield" to still destroy the United States. The point was that no matter how good U.S. technology might be eventually— and no one was likely to know that for a decade or two—it was questionable whether SDI would work perfectly the first time it was needed. Indeed, because no full-scale test of all the components could be carried out beforehand, the congressional Office of Technology Assessment thought SDI would be a "catastrophic failure."[26]

To make matters worse, because the Soviets were hardly likely to accept the president's assurance that the United States would share this new technology with them so that both powers could substitute SDI for their offensive missiles simultaneously—as Gorbachev sarcastically remarked, the Americans would not even share their oil-drilling technology with the Russians—SDI was likely to stimulate not one but two arms races. One way the Soviets could seek to overcome SDI was by flooding it with more warheads than it could possibly handle. This meant a further Soviet offensive buildup, just as the United States had responded to the Soviet ABMs in the 1970s by multiplying the warheads on its missiles to inundate and thereby overwhelm any Soviet defenses. Simultaneously, the Soviets would accelerate their own SDI research. Thus, the critics said, SDI would result in offensive and defensive arms races, which would be enormously expensive and in the end leave both powers less secure than before.

SDI 2 did not create such intense controversy. Relying largely on then- or soon-to-be-available technology (fundamentally ground-based), SDI 2 was limited to missile protection. Given the large numbers of Soviet missiles and increasingly accurate warheads with their potential for a first strike, SDI 2 had some appeal. It would reduce the potential vulnerability of land-based missiles, thereby stabilizing the deterrent balance. Because such a defense was not based mainly on exotic space-based technologies, it also would be more affordable and feasible. And, unlike a population defense, a defensive capability of 50 percent would suffice. If a potential attacker knows that even half of the enemy's missiles will survive to retaliate against it, it will remain deterred. Not surprisingly, many military officers, including the Joint Chiefs of Staff (who hoped for an only 30 percent shoot-down rate) and members of Congress, skeptical about SDI 1, were attracted to SDI 2, and the Senate Armed Services Committee specifically went on record favoring this more attainable goal.

One critical difference distinguished SDI 1 from SDI 2. It was assumed that with the deployment of SDI 1 offensive missiles would be eliminated. They would become "impotent and obsolete" and therefore could be scrapped. With SDI 2, however, it was assumed that offensive missiles would remain; deterrence, rather than being abolished, would be made safer by sending the message to the other side that it cannot prevent a devastating second strike—even if it struck first. SDI 2 was also compatible with further arms control efforts.

SDI 3 was the *Soviet* perception of the president's proposal as an offensive, not defensive, system. If SDI 1 could not be made "leak-proof" against an attack by thousands of warheads, a certain number of which would still be able to penetrate it to create enormous destruction, it could be effective against a retaliatory blow already weakened by the opponent's first-strike capability. This, the Soviets claimed, was what the Reagan administration was really seeking. Interestingly, the Soviet objection to SDI was the same as the U.S. objection to Soviet ABM deployment in the early 1970s. Washington had viewed the Soviet ABM as part of a first-strike strategy, since Soviet military doctrine had emphasized a preemptive strike if nuclear war appeared likely and destruction of as much of the U.S. retaliatory capacity as possible to limit damage to itself. The ABMs might then further weaken the retaliatory blow by the remnants of the crippled U.S. forces, reducing the damage to the Soviet Union even further. But in fact, SDI's aims remained defensive, although the military sought to promote the use of lasers offensively against satellites.[27]

Incentive or Obstacle to Arms Control?

The Reagan administration, worried that U.S. ICBMs were becoming more vulnerable to a Soviet attack, had from the outset sought a radical reduction in Soviet ICBMs and warheads to reduce this danger. But it had little to offer the Soviets in return. SDI thus proved, no doubt to Reagan's surprise, a powerful counter. In part, this stemmed from the Soviet fear of SDI as part of an offensive strategy. It stemmed as well from the fear of the Soviet leadership—beset with a stagnating economy at home and already unable to keep up with Western technological advances—that SDI research would result in a quantum leap forward in the very area in which the United States had a successful past and the Soviet Union did not: technological innovation. The consequences of such a leap forward would be even further setbacks for the Soviet Union technologically. Moreover, the expense of a Star Wars race would have profound consequences for the already low Soviet standard of living.

Thus, the Soviet interest in preventing SDI deployment, or at least in slowing it down and allowing Soviet science to catch up, was intense. The research could continue in the laboratories; that could hardly be prevented. But there was to be no testing or deployment of any SDI technology in space, as the two powers had agreed in the 1972 ABM treaty. SDI had thus given the Reagan administration the lever with which to gain a radical reduction in the Soviet first-strike capability. SDI, like the U.S. ABM, was potentially a very powerful bargaining chip. But while Richard Nixon had been willing to use the ABM that way, Reagan was unwilling to do so. The president clung to his vision, speaking of SDI as if it were already a reality instead of a research program that could only in ten to twenty years reveal whether SDI was even technologically feasible. Unwilling to accept any limitations on U.S. research and *testing*, Reagan rejected Gorbachev's "grand compromise" of a 50 percent cut in offensive weapons, even as his secretary of state and others were seeking to negotiate such an agreement and make it so attractive that neither the president nor other SDI supporters could turn it down.[28]

Thus, instead of being a bargaining chip, SDI became an obstacle to an arms control agreement on strategic weapons. The Soviets repeated over and over that they should not be expected to greatly reduce the numbers of their strategic missiles when they did not know whether they had enough to cope with SDI. Again, they were merely repeating President Nixon's argument that he could not accept limits on U.S. offensive missiles until he knew whether the Soviets intended to deploy a nationwide ABM system. If the Soviets were going to deploy such a system, Nixon had said, the United States would need large numbers of missiles to penetrate this defense; if not, the United States was willing to accept an upper ceiling on missile deployment. Now Gorbachev presented Reagan with the same argument, but the president would not accept the linkage between the offensive and defensive arms races that had made SALT I possible in 1972.

It was hard to understand why the president was not more compromising on SDI because he was not being asked to abandon his vision, and the Soviets were willing to make him a good offer while SDI research could continue in the laboratories. But what the Soviets were unable to achieve, Congress did. SDI stimulated governmental politics in the form of an executive-legislative confrontation. The Congress—especially the Democrats, who controlled the House and, after the 1986 midterm election, the Senate as well—had never been enthusiastic about SDI, about whose purposes, feasibility, and costs even the administration appeared to be divided. The enormous cost of SDI at the time of a huge budget deficit was an additional factor inciting congressional resistance. Finally, there was the arms control impact; the likelihood that SDI would accelerate the defensive and offensive arms competition was very critically regarded by members of Congress who favored arms agreements. Indeed, there was a good deal of skepticism about the shift from deterrence to defense. The Senate specifically insisted that SDI concentrate on protecting missiles, contending that protection of the population was impossible. The result was that Congress cut funding for SDI every year after 1985.

The biggest skirmish in this battle, however, came over the 1972 ABM treaty.[29] The Reagan administration, determined to go ahead with SDI, wanted to test elements of SDI in space rather than just confine its research to the laboratories. Thus, it asserted a "broad" interpretation of the treaty that would allow such testing. This led to a confrontation with Congress, especially the Senate and Sen. Sam Nunn, who had become chairman of the Senate Armed Services Committee after the Democrats regained control of the Senate in 1986. Nunn, a Georgia Democrat and the Senate's leading expert on military affairs, reviewed the record of the ABM treaty negotiations and found that the Senate had consented to the "narrow" treaty submitted by the Nixon administration. Thus, for the administration to unilaterally change the treaty that had been signed with Moscow and ratified by the United States would lead to a "constitutional crisis" with the Senate. Just to make sure, the Senate Armed Services Committee voted an amendment to the 1988 defense authorization bill which blocked any testing activities that violated the traditional reading of the ABM treaty.

Faced with congressional reductions in funding and a confrontation with the Senate over the ABM treaty, Reagan tried to commit his successor and the Congress to SDI by pushing for early deployment with currently available technology by the mid-1990s, even though it would not be the SDI the president had proposed and early deployment required a lowering of the system's performance requirements. A Senate study showed that it would stop only 16 percent of the warheads fired in a full-scale attack. Even a report by a 1987 panel of the American Physical Society, composed of leading physicists on exotic weapons technologies—all of whom had access to the research and development being done on SDI—did not deter the administration. That report stated that it would be ten or more years, perhaps the next century, before it would be known whether these technologies were even feasible.[30]

Reagan was clearly concerned that if deployment had not started before the end of his administration, SDI would be downgraded after he left office, becoming a bargaining chip and a long-term research program.

Even before the 1988 election results were known, Gen. James Abrahamson, the air force general in charge of the SDI research program, resigned, declaring that a new administration would want to take a fresh look at SDI. The resignation probably symbolized the end of the idea of a comprehensive space-based missile shield deployment. This was not stated, but what was offered almost simultaneously was a vastly scaled-down version of the 1987 plan for early deployment. Within the executive branch, the opposition of the Joint Chiefs remained strong. They were very worried that the enormous expense of even the original space-based deployment plan, estimated at $115 billion (even without the research and development cost of the more exotic future technologies), would eat up the resources needed for virtually all other military programs in a period of budgetary restraints. In fact, there were cheaper alternatives: shifting more land-based missiles to sea; making greater use of the mobile missiles on land; and, most of all, concluding a strategic arms control agreement that cut the number of missiles by as much as half.

Back at the White House, one of the biggest remaining unknowns about SDI was domestic politics, which had been largely responsible for its origin and which continued to haunt it. Precisely because SDI had been a vision rather than a strategic program, and because it had been so bitterly criticized (especially by Democrats) for accelerating the nuclear arms race rather than abolishing the likelihood of nuclear war, the Reagan administration had made support for SDI a loyalty test. SDI thus became a "Republican weapon." Michael Dukakis, the 1988 Democratic presidential candidate, had denounced the entire program, and, although he backtracked on SDI research, he declared SDI a waste of the money needed badly for more pressing domestic programs. The 1988 election of George Bush to succeed Reagan in the White House therefore gave SDI at least a partial new lease on life. Conservative Republicans remained loyal to SDI, and they were a strong faction within the Republican party. Bush, however, remained subject to the same constraints as his predecessor: the technical-scientific limits; the opposition from the still Democratic-controlled Senate, especially Senator Nunn who favored only a limited system against accidental launches; and the huge Reagan-inherited budget deficit. Thus, Bush was in a good position to achieve the "grand compromise" deal on missiles if he downgraded SDI from a vision to a long-term research program on the feasibility of the exotic technologies involved and perhaps limited any development to ground-based interceptors to protect missiles and bombers (although even that was questionable if Bush were to shift to mobile ICBMs).[31]

In fact, that was the deal the Soviets offered the administration soon after it came into office: a 50 percent cut in strategic forces. A prior agreement on SDI would not be necessary as long as the United States did not violate the 1972 ABM agreement. This would allow the Strategic Arms Reduction Talks

(START) to be completed, permit Gorbachev to avoid a high-tech arms competition that would interfere with his transfer of military resources to his failing civilian economy, and allow Bush to claim that he had not sacrificed SDI. Gorbachev, of course, knew that Congress, already lukewarm in its support of SDI, would be even less likely to fund it after a START agreement reduced U.S. concerns about a Soviet missile threat to American forces—concerns that had largely disappeared anyway because of the changed atmosphere of Soviet-American relations in the wake of the cold war.

Thus, SDI, after a $24 billion investment, seemed largely a dead issue—until the war with Iraq erupted in January 1991. In that war, the Iraqis used Soviet-made SCUD missiles to attack Saudi and Israeli urban targets; the missiles, a product of 1960s technology, were too inaccurate to use against military installations. In response, the American ground-to-air Patriot missile had dramatic successes, destroying many of the incoming SCUDs against Saudi Arabia and Israel. The Patriot, adapted by the army during the Reagan years from an antiaircraft system to shoot down missiles, admittedly was not perfect in its performance, but even its high success rate did not mean that a Patriot defense was equivalent to a Star Wars defense against Soviet ICBMs. A SCUD travels at five times the speed of sound; an ICBM warhead flies at twenty times the speed of sound. SCUDs come one at a time; Soviet warheads and their multistage missiles would come in the thousands and at a high altitude. Nevertheless, the Patriot's performance suggested that U.S. industry might be able to solve the problem of shooting down a missile with another missile. A test firing in January 1991—of a ground-based interceptor—destroyed a mock warhead 100 miles up in space.[32]

The point is that the Iraqi attacks, launched mainly against urban targets, raised the question of whether U.S. civilians did not deserve equal protection against the possibility of a future missile attack by states able to obtain chemical, nuclear, and biological warheads, as well as long-range missiles. The C.I.A. has conservatively estimated that fifteen nations will acquire ballistic missiles by the year 2000 (see Chapter 20). Will the threat of retaliation in these circumstances continue to deter an attack by weapons of mass destruction? Will the Saddam Husseins, Muammar al-Qaddafis, * and other such rulers refrain from using their arsenals of modern weapons as Soviet leaders did, or will their missionary ambitions lead them to take risks that less ambitious and more cautious and rational leaders would not? Should the nation therefore deploy or not deploy a defensive system so that the United States can do more than just watch such incoming missiles land?

The issue of strategic defense, in short, remains very much alive in the changing strategic environment of the post-cold war world. Only its focus may

---

* When U.S. planes attacked Libya in 1986 in retaliation for what was believed to be Libyan-inspired terrorism against U.S. service personnel in a West Berlin discotheque, Qaddafi reportedly said that if he had possessed a missile with the range to hit New York City, he would have fired it. Sen. Malcom Wallop, "Patriots Point The Way," *New York Times,* January 31, 1991.

change: a mix of ground- and space-based interceptors against a small attack of up to 100 enemy warheads by a Third World state.[33] In the words of President Bush's 1991 state-of-the-union address, Star Wars should be "refocused on providing protection from limited ballistic missile strikes—whatever their source." This was something that some members of Congress, including the influential chairman of the Senate Armed Services Committee, Sam Nunn, had long favored.[34] In 1991, the program cost just over $4.6 billion for SDI; $1.7 billion more than 1990. More specifically, a new generation of interceptor was to emphasize two missions. The first mission would extend the range of an antimissile defense so that a larger area can be protected from missiles moving at greater heights and speeds than SCUDs. The second mission would create separate, mutually supporting layers of defense so that a missile that evades one layer can be attacked by another. Such a backup system is particularly critical when the hostile warheads may be nuclear and even one miss spells catastrophe for the city at which it is aimed. The Senate Armed Services Committee version also would concentrate 100 interceptors against 100 enemy warheads, but unlike SDI it would be based on land. Star Wars would thus come back to earth, as envisaged in the original ABM conception.[35] Congress authorized the deployment of the land-based system by 1996; but that date will be delayed by more thorough testing of the interceptors.

Two further developments encouraged the likelihood of eventual deployment. One was Bush's 1992 proposed elimination of all land-based and a substantial number of sea-based multiple warhead missiles and, on the heels of the collapse of the Soviet Union, Russian president Boris Yeltsin's proposal of even deeper cuts in U.S. and Russian multiple warhead missiles. (Although the two countries may never realize President Reagan's goal of complete nuclear disarmament, they appear to be heading for substantial cuts.) The other development was Yeltsin's proposal that the United States and Russia cooperate in the new post-cold war era of "friendship and partnership" by establishing a joint ballistic missile early warning center and possibly sharing Star Wars technology to devise a global antimissile shield to protect the world from further nuclear proliferation.[36] He also reportedly said that the ABM treaty might need to be modified. Indeed, SDI researchers were apparently eager to buy critical technologies from the former Soviet strategic defense program to speed up the deployment of the limited U.S. anti-missile defense shield.[37]

AMERICAN POLITICAL PROCESS
AND FOREIGN POLICY DECISION MAKING

'Where You Stand Depends on Where You Sit'

This slogan sums up the decision-making approach. In contrast to the first-level analysis in which each state is considered a unitary actor, at the decision-making level each government is viewed as a composite of multiple actors. Instead of regarding foreign policy as the product of a rational choice among several options that maximize a chosen value such as security, analysts focus on the many conflicting values, perspectives, and interests that result in a specific policy.[38] The "games nations play" are the result of the "games bureaucrats play" to enhance their personal influence, as well as that of their own agencies. The same can be said of nonbureaucratic players, although the center of decision making remains in the executive branch.

President Johnson's decision to go ahead with the anti-Chinese ABM system is not easily explainable in terms of the rational actor model. The decision might not have been made had it not been for congressional and bureaucratic pressures, for the president really was primarily interested in starting the SALT talks and avoiding an expensive and possibly destabilizing arms race. But even for a president, there are constraints. Specifically, Johnson wanted to avoid a break with influential senators, as well as with his own secretary of defense, over ABM. The political costs of such breaks were greater than he was willing to pay. He also had to consider the probable electoral costs if he decided to avoid any ABM decision. So he compromised—he made a minimal decision, satisfactory to all the chief actors, who thought that they had "won" the president over to their position. In fact, he had kept his options open for a more definitive decision in the future.

The president was merely one of many players. To be sure, he may have been the "first among equals," but his ability to impose his decisions was limited by the other players. Johnson did not want an ABM but was pushed into taking the first minimal step toward acceptance of it. He could not ignore the Joint Chiefs' coalition with powerful leaders in the Senate. The president, according to the organizational charts of the executive branch, may be the "boss" and presumably can order the Joint Chiefs, for example, to do or not to do what he or she chooses, but in reality, the relationship is more equal, and the participants bargain with one another. A close relationship between military leaders and a powerful congressional committee and ranking legislative leaders or the threat of resignation by military leaders (which reportedly occurred during the Vietnam War) forces the president and the secretary of defense to persuade their subordinates.

As the ABM case illustrates, the "foreign policy" decision that emerges from this bureaucratic system, which in turn is set in the broader governmental system,

> is not necessarily "policy" in the rational sense of embodying the decisions made and actions ordered by a controlling intelligence focusing primarily on our foreign policy problems. Instead it is the "outcome" of the political process, the government actions resulting from all the arguments, the building of coalitions and countercoalitions, and the decisions by high officials and compromises among them. Often it may be a "policy" that no participant fully favors [for the system is] more responsive to the internal dynamics of our decision-making process than to the external problems.[39]

Presidential Initiative and Leadership

The case of the ABM reveals the constraints, especially within the executive branch, on presidential leadership and initiative in foreign policy.[40] The SDI scenario, however, illustrates why the presidential perspective is usually preeminent in what political scientist Robert Art has called "innovative policy." First, presidents can seize for themselves certain specific policy areas, such as Nixon and SALT I, détente with the Soviet Union, and reconciliation with China; Carter and SALT II and the Israeli-Egyptian peace negotiations; and Reagan and the "space shield." "The ability of bureaucracies to independently establish policies is a function of Presidential attention. Presidential attention is a function of Presidential values. The Chief Executive involves himself in those areas which he determines to be important." [41] Whereas the bureaucratic politics model emphasized policy as the product of intrabureaucratic bargaining, it is probably more correct to say that, to a large degree, bureaucratic influence is a function of presidential, as well as congressional and public, inattention. The bureaucracy plays its largest role in routine daily affairs—for example, the military service organizations normally decide which weapons they want to develop—its smallest during crises or arms decisions seized by the president. On SDI, for example, the Defense Department bureaucracy had already decided against a space shield, believing it to be an impractical idea.

A president also can structure the organization for making foreign policy decisions. Nixon did so by making Kissinger his national security adviser, a kind of supersecretary of foreign affairs, giving him a fairly sizable staff and clearly ignoring the established bureaucracy or subordinating it to the White House. Kissinger's staff asked the established bureaucracy for policy papers on certain areas or policies, gathered them together, evaluated the alternatives, and, once the president had selected the best policy, sent the decision back to the bureaucracy for implementation.[42] Foreign policy decisions resulting from primarily bureaucratic infighting and compromise, rather than from rational responses to perceived external challenges and problems, were to be avoided as much as possible. Bureaucratic interests were to be subject to presidential perspectives and interests.

Reagan's problems in foreign policy during his two terms, especially the Iran-contra affair, often stemmed from disorganization. In contrast to Nixon who had one national security adviser, Ford who had two, and Carter who had one, Reagan had six! Moreover, the first four had little competence or experience in foreign policy. Worse, the president set broad directions but showed little interest in the details of policy or in close involvement on a daily basis (except for monitoring the U.S. hostage situation in Lebanon and the contra war in Nicaragua). Thus, there was no one to resolve key conflicts, especially between the secretaries of state and defense until the latter resigned in 1987.

A president also chooses cabinet officials. And, although they do represent the various bureaucracies and agencies in government, they also normally reflect the president's general views and values, for they owe their places in the history books to the person who appointed them and they are likely to feel some gratitude. They know too that the president, if displeased, can fire them and that most of them are expendable. Moreover, the president can ignore them; the president decides whom to listen to and whom to exile from the policy-making circle. Kennedy chose to heed Secretary of Defense Robert McNamara rather than Secretary of State Dean Rusk. During the Vietnam War, Johnson dismissed powerful and respected men such as McNamara from his administration when they increasingly opposed his bombing policy, and he simply did not listen to others. During his first term, Nixon listened to his national security adviser and paid little attention to his secretary of state. Reagan, for most of his eight years, listened to Secretary of Defense Caspar Weinberger; only in the last years did Secretary of State George Shultz gain the president's ear.

Partisanship, Domestic Politics, and Executive-Legislative Conflict

As both ABM and SDI demonstrated clearly, bureaucratic politics, by focusing on the executive branch, tended to downplay the importance of party politics, domestic political considerations, and the role of Congress in the policy process. Nevertheless, in ABM, Democrats feared that Republicans would use accusations of an "ABM gap" and weakness on defense against them in the next election. And SDI was Reagan's attempt to neutralize the antinuclear movement he himself had stirred up by his huge military buildup, militant anti-Soviet rhetoric, and declarations of nuclear warfighting instead of deterrence. While it is correct that before the Vietnam War, Congress generally supported the president's policy, largely because it shared a set of common anti-Communist images, electoral politics and executive-legislative conflict nevertheless permeated the conduct of foreign policy. The most prominent example, with perhaps the most negative impact on the conduct of U.S. foreign policy, was the nation's Asian policy after Nationalist China's collapse and Communist China's birth. The Republican attacks on the Democrats paralyzed even President Dwight Eisenhower, the moderate Republican, but particularly Democratic presidents remained fearful of improving relations with Communist China and, more broadly, of any "appeasement of communism." Knowing the great difficulties that they would have with Congress if they defied it, these presidents were afraid to assume anything less than strong positions against Communist China. When President Johnson was informed that South Vietnam was collapsing, he responded that he was not going to be the president who saw Southeast Asia go the way of China.

The price of all this was very high. Had China been recognized in early 1950, the Truman administration might have more accurately assessed how the Chinese would react to U.S. intervention in Korea. Had American observers been stationed in Peking (now Beijing), the Kennedy and Johnson administrations would have known that the war in South Vietnam was not part of

Chinese Communist expansion and U.S. involvement might have been avoided. Better relations with China might have been established earlier and the increasing Sino-Soviet conflict exploited to bring about a parallel reduction in American-Soviet tensions.

With the erosion of the U.S. consensus on containment after Vietnam, executive-legislative conflict has affected virtually the whole range of American foreign policy. Congressional questioning and criticism of presidential policy grew during the 1970s and 1980s.[43] The Vietnam War discredited the leadership of the executive branch and its expertise in foreign policy; the Watergate scandal and revelations about the CIA and Federal Bureau of Investigation (FBI) added to congressional determination to be more assertive in foreign policy in a period in which there was no new consensus on which to base policy. In the early days of détente, when Kissinger wanted to supplement the military stick with economic carrots to induce more restrained Soviet behavior, the Senate added the Jackson-Vanik amendment on Jewish emigration from the Soviet Union to a commercial treaty. Because of this attempt at interference with its domestic affairs, Moscow rejected the treaty, thus reducing the economic leverage the United States might have gained. The Senate also failed to vote on SALT II, which effectively killed it.[44] Congress as an institution was more splintered than ever before: party loyalty had further declined; the authority of committee chairs had been reduced; and subcommittees had become more numerous and influential. Given this now high degree of decentralization, pressure groups have gained increased access to congressional policy makers. Especially active are such ethnic groups as American Jews, who have made it difficult for American administrations to take an even-handed position on Middle East affairs. Whenever in the past the executive has pressed Israel to be more conciliatory in peace negotiations, Congress—itself pressured by a pro-Israeli lobby that is probably the most potent ever organized by a foreign government[45]—has undermined the effort. In the regional peace talks, which started in October 1991, will the president and secretary of state be able to wrench concessions from an Israel that even before negotiations began announced it will not exchange the land it captured in the 1967 war for peace with its neighbors and the Palestinians living in these captured territories? Simply put, since Vietnam it has become more difficult for a president to mobilize Congress on foreign policy issues; obstructing, delaying, changing, and even emasculating policy have become considerably easier.

Congress has become especially sensitive to any presidential use of force, and in 1973 it passed the War Powers Act over President Nixon's veto to avoid more Koreas and Vietnams. This resolution required the president to consult with Congress before using American forces and required Congress to approve presidential use of force after sixty days (or the troops would have to be withdrawn).

By and large, presidents since Nixon have refused to invoke the War Powers Act. They have considered it an encroachment on their commander-in-chief powers and, politically, they have feared—as Reagan did in 1987 in the Persian Gulf—that if they invoked it, Congress would seize the opportunity to end American involvement at the first sight of heavy American casualties. Eisenhower resorted to covert means to overthrow Guatemala's government in 1954, and Kennedy used Cuban refugees to invade Cuba in 1961. But Reagan's attempt to use proxies in Nicaragua was unsuccessful. Congress opposed the intervention, and the continual headlines in the press and leadoff stories on the television news made a charade of the term *covert.* Congress, fearful of another Vietnam, thus had placed restraints on the presidential conduct of foreign policy. Not that Congress was opposed to all interventions, but it had become far more selective and discriminatory in those it would support. It expected the president to make a strong case that such interventions would promote national security. As already noted, when President Bush reluctantly asked Congress for the functional equivalent of a declaration of war against Iraq in early 1991, he received only narrow congressional support.

DECISION MAKING AND INTERNATIONAL NEGOTIATIONS

The governmental politics model holds several important implications for international negotiations. One implication is how difficult such negotiations are likely to be, quite apart from the substantive complexity of the problems being negotiated. Misunderstandings, failures of communication, disappointed expectations, and even failed negotiations between two countries may easily result when each set of national policy makers for foreign affairs is so deeply engaged in its own bureaucratic and governmental "games" that it does not pay sufficiently close attention to the other side. Even between countries as close as Britain and the United States, negotiations can break down because the Londoners are negotiating with other Londoners and Washingtonians with other Washingtonians in trying to formulate policy. "Their self-absorption is a day-and-night affair; it never flags. They calculate accordingly and act to suit. So do their counterparts inside the other government. . . . Comprehension of the other's actual behavior is a function of their own concerns." [46]

Another implication is that in negotiations between two highly bureaucratized governments, the international negotiations are only one of *three* simultaneous sets of negotiations; the other negotiations are those between the governments and those among the various participants within each government. Kissinger used to complain that it was easier to negotiate with the Soviet leaders than to negotiate an agreed-upon policy in Washington. This complaint may be common in many capitals. [47]

For Review

1. What is the governmental politics decision-making model and how does it differ from rational decision making?
2. How does the governmental politics decision-making model explain different types of policies?
3. What are the chief characteristics of both crisis and noncrisis policy decisions?
4. What does a case study of the Strategic Defense Initiative reveal about the American political process, especially the roles of the president and the Congress?
5. How can this American model of decision making be applied to other countries and international negotiations between states?

Notes

1. See Roger Hilsman, *To Move a Nation* (Garden City, N.Y.: Doubleday, 1967); Graham T. Allison, *The Essence of Decision* (Boston: Little, Brown, 1971); Morton H. Halperin, *Bureaucratic Politics and Foreign Policy* (Washington, D.C.: Brookings, 1974); Halperin and Arnold Kanter, eds., *Readings in American Foreign Policy* (Boston: Little, Brown, 1973); and David C. Kozak and James M. Keagle, eds., *Bureaucratic Politics and National Security* (Boulder, Colo.: Lynne Rienner, 1988).
2. Henry A. Kissinger, *Nuclear Weapons and Foreign Policy* (New York: Harper & Row, 1957).
3. Graham T. Allison, "Conceptual Models and the Cuban Missile Crisis," *American Political Science Review* (September 1969): 716.
4. Oran Young, *The Politics of Force* (Princeton, N.J.: Princeton University Press, 1968), 6-15; Charles F. Hermann, ed., *International Crises* (New York: Free Press, 1972); and Phil Williams, *Crisis Management* (New York: Wiley, 1976).
5. Irving L. Janis, *Victims of Groupthink* 2d ed. (Boston: Houghton Mifflin, 1982).
6. Michael R. Gordon, "Cracking the Whip," *New York Times Magazine*, January 27, 1991, 16ff. Bob Woodward, in *The Commanders* (New York: Simon & Schuster, 1991), claims that the chairman of the Joint Chiefs of Staff preferred continuing economic sanctions to military action in the early phase of the confrontation with Iraq.
7. For the Cuban missile crisis, see Elie Abel, *The Missile Crisis* (New York: Bantam Books, 1966); Alexander L. George et al., eds., *The Limits of Coercive Diplomacy* (Boston: Little, Brown, 1971); Robert F. Kennedy, *Thirteen Days* (New York: Norton, 1967); James G. Blight, *The Shattered Crystal Ball* (Savage, Md.: Rowman & Littlefield, 1990); Blight and David Welch, *On the Brink* (New York: Farrar, Straus, 1989); and Michael R. Beschloss, *The Crisis Years* (New York: Harper Collins, 1991).
8. Gerald W. Seib, "How President Bush Deftly Orchestrated Swift Victory over Iraq," *Wall Street Journal*, March 1, 1991.
9. On mainly domestic issues, see Walter Williams, *Mismanaging America* (Lawrence: University of Kansas Press, 1990).

10. Fred Barnes, "The Hawk Factor," *New Republic*, January 2, 1991, 8-9. Also see Paul A. Gigot, "Bush's View: This Is Still America's Century," *Wall Street Journal*, January 24, 1991.

11. Kurt M. Campbell, "All Rise for Chairman Powell," *National Interest* (Spring 1991): 51-60.

12. For elaboration, see John Spanier and Eric M. Uslaner, *American Foreign Policy Making and the Democratic Dilemmas*, 5th ed. (Pacific Grove, Calif.: Brooks/Cole, 1989).

13. See Samuel P. Huntington, *The Common Defense* (New York: Columbia University Press, 1961), 123ff., for formulation of defense policy.

14. Charles E. Lindblom, "The Science of Muddling Through," *Public Administration Review* (Winter 1959): 79-88.

15. Theodore J. Lowi, *The End of Liberalism* (New York: Norton, 1969), 160-161.

16. Ibid.

17. Francis E. Rourke, "The Domestic Scene," in *America and the World: From the Truman Doctrine to Vietnam*, ed. Robert E. Osgood (Baltimore: Johns Hopkins University Press, 1970), 147-188; William R. Caspary, "The 'Mood Theory': A Study of Public Opinion and Foreign Policy," *American Political Science Review* (June 1970): 536-547; and James N. Rosenau, "Foreign Policy as an Issue Area," in Conference on Public Opinion and Foreign Policy, *Domestic Sources of Foreign Policy* (New York: Free Press, 1965).

18. Former secretary of state Dean Acheson offers some amusing and somewhat sarcastic comments on the way Sen. Arthur Vandenberg helped to legitimate presidential policy during the crucial days after 1945. See *Present at the Creation* (New York: Norton, 1969), 223.

19. James A. Robinson, *Congress and Foreign Policy-making*, rev. ed. (Homewood, Ill.: Dorsey Press, 1967). For the early postwar period, see Daniel S. Cheever and H. Field Haviland, Jr., *American Foreign Policy and the Separation of Powers* (Cambridge, Mass.: Harvard University Press, 1952), 106ff. For the post-Vietnam days, see John Spanier and Joseph L. Nogee, eds., *Congress, the Presidency and American Foreign Policy* (Elmsford, N.Y.: Pergamon Press, 1981).

20. This section relies heavily on the account by Morton H. Halperin, "The Decision to Deploy the ABM: Bureaucratic and Domestic Politics in the Johnson Administration," *World Politics* (October 1972): 62ff. For the development of the ICBM, see Edmund Beard, *Developing the ICBM* (New York: Columbia University Press, 1976).

21. Halperin, "The Decision to Deploy the ABM," 67-69.

22. Halperin, *Bureaucratic Politics and Foreign Policy*, 81-82.

23. Warner R. Schilling, "The H-Bomb: How to Decide without Actually Choosing," in Halperin and Kanter, *Readings*, 253, 255.

24. Quoted in *Time*, January 25, 1968.

25. For the background of SDI, see Lou Cannon, *President Reagan* (New York: Simon & Schuster, 1991), 319ff.; Ashton B. Carter and David N. Schwartz, eds., *Ballistic Missile Defense* (Washington, D.C.: Brookings, 1984); and Philip M. Boffey et al., *Claiming the Heavens*, subtitled *The New York Times Complete Guide to the Star Wars Debate* (New York: Times Books, 1988). Two anti-SDI books are those by Sidney Drell, Phillip Farley, and David Holloway, *The Reagan Strategic Defense Initiative* (Cambridge, Mass.: Ballinger, 1985); and Robert McNamara, *Blundering into Disaster* (New York: Pantheon, 1986). Two pro-SDI books are those by Zbigniew Brzezinski et al., *Promise or Peril* (Lanham, Md.: University Press of America, 1986); and Keith

B. Payne, *Strategic Defense* (Lanham, Md.: Hamilton Press, 1986). Also see Harry Waldman, *The Dictionary of SDI* (Wilmington, Del.: Scholarly Resources, 1988) for the terminology of SDI. For historical and Soviet perspectives, among other issues, see Samuel F. Wells, Jr., and Robert S. Litwak, *Strategic Defenses and Soviet-American Relations* (Cambridge, Mass.: Ballinger, 1987). The congressional Office of Technology Assessment reports, the second one of which is very critical, may be found in *Strategic Defense Initiative* (Princeton, N.J.: Princeton University Press, 1988). The economic aspects are examined in Rosy Nimroody (for the Council on Economic Priorities), *Star Wars* (Cambridge, Mass.: Ballinger, 1987).

26. Warren E. Leary, "Report Depicts 'Star Wars' as an Unworkable System," *New York Times*, April 25, 1988.

27. William J. Broad, "U.S. Promoting Offensive Role for 'Star Wars' " and "Military to Ready Laser for Testing as Space Weapon," *New York Times*, November 27, 1988, and January 1, 1989, respectively.

28. See Strobe Talbott's *The Master of the Game* (New York: Knopf, 1988) for details of the "grand compromise" negotiations and the progress made during the Reagan administration. Also see Cannon, *President Reagan*, 163-171, 287-292, 219-333, for Reagan's early obsession with strategic defense.

29. William J. Durch, *The ABM Treaty and Western Security* (Cambridge, Mass.: Ballinger, 1987); and Gerald M. Steinberg, *Lost in Space* (Lexington, Mass.: Lexington Books, 1989).

30. William J. Broad, "The Star Wars Program Prepares for a Year of Reckoning," *New York Times*, November 29, 1988.

31. Talbott, *Master of the Game*.

32. William J. Broad, "In Test, 'Star Wars' Hits Warhead in Space," *New York Times*, January 30, 1991.

33. William J. Broad, "A New Course for 'Star Wars' from Full to Limited Defense," and Eric Schmitt, "Republicans Split over 'Star Wars,' " *New York Times*, January 31 and June 15, 1991, respectively.

34. "President Bush's State of the Union Message to the Nation," *New York Times*, January 30, 1991. Yet questions about the success of the Patriot missiles began to surface after the war. See, for example, Bob Davis, "Patriot Missile, High Tech Hero in Gulf, Comes under Attack as Less than Scud's Worst Enemy," *Wall Street Journal*, April 15, 1991; and Theodore A. Postol, "Lessons of the Gulf War Experience with Patriot," *International Security* (Winter 1991/92): 119-162.

35. William J. Broad, "As Anti-Missile Era Dawns, Planners Eye Panoply of Weapons," and "Anti-Missile Plan Exploits Controversial Technology," *New York Times*, February 5 and July 30, 1991, respectively. The Senate plan would require renegotiation of the 1972 ABM treaty. For Senator Nunn's defense of the Armed Services Committee plan, see "Needed: An ABM Defense," *New York Times*, July 31, 1991. Also see Broad, " 'Star Wars' Plan to Be Delayed Because of Risk," *New York Times*, June 6, 1992.

36. Michael Wines, "Bush and Yeltsin Declare Formal End to Cold War; Agree to Exchange Visits," and Thomas L. Friedman, "U.S. and Russia See New Arms Accords for a July Summit," *New York Times*, February 2 and 19, 1992, respectively.

37. John Noble Wilford, "U.S. Is Seeking Soviet Expertise for 'Star Wars,' " and William J. Broad, "U.S. Moves to Bar Americans from Buying Soviet Technology," *New York Times*, February 8 and March 1, 1992, respectively.

38. Halperin and Kanter, *Readings*, 3.

39. I. M. Destler, *Presidents, Bureaucrats, and Foreign Policy* (Princeton, N.J.: Princeton University Press, 1972), 64, 74.

40. For the critique that follows, I am indebted to Robert J. Art, "Bureaucratic Politics and American Foreign Policy: A Critique," *Policy Sciences* 4 (1973): 467-490; and Stephen D. Krasner, "Are Bureaucracies Important?" *Foreign Policy* (Summer 1972): 159-179.

41. Krasner, "Are Bureaucracies Important?" 168. Krasner's emphasis on the state as a unified actor pursuing its "national interest" is elaborated in his *Defending the National Interest* (Princeton, N.J.: Princeton University Press, 1978).

42. Destler, *Presidents, Bureaucrats, and Foreign Policy*, 118-152. For a more recent and favorable assessment, see Robert J. Strong, *Bureaucracy and Statesmanship* (New York: University Press of America, 1986). Also see Alexander L. George, "The Case for Multiple Advocacy in Making Foreign Policy," *American Political Science Review* (September 1972): 751ff.; and Janis, *Victims of Groupthink*.

43. Spanier and Nogee, *Congress, the Presidency and American Foreign Policy*; John T. Rourke, *Congress and the Presidency in U.S. Foreign Policymaking* (Boulder, Colo.: Westview Press, 1983); and William P. Quandt, *Camp David* (Washington, D.C.: Brookings, 1986).

44. Dan Caldwell, *The Dynamics of Domestic Politics and Arms Control* (Columbia: University of South Carolina Press, 1991).

45. Mitchell G. Bard, *The Water's Edge and Beyond* (New Brunswick, N.J.: Transaction Publishers, 1991).

46. Richard E. Neustadt, *Alliance Politics* (New York: Columbia University Press, 1970), 66.

47. For the Reagan administration's internal fights on arms control, see Strobe Talbott, *Deadly Gambits* (New York: Knopf, 1984), and *Master of the Game*.

CHAPTER 12

Foreign Policy: A Conclusion

FOCUS ON PERCEPTION

The single thread that runs through the preceding chapters is *perception:* the way nations, political elites, specific bureaucracies, and individual leaders see the world, and the way they define vital issues and the international roles their countries should play. It quickly becomes clear that although states see the same "reality," they view it differently. During the cold war, the United States and the Soviet Union saw their conflict with each other as the primary one; the threat each posed to the other was the key to their foreign policies. National security was their critical concern. The developing countries view the struggle for modernization and a more equitable distribution of status and wealth in the state system as the chief issue. Their focus is on North-South tensions. The resulting emphasis in international politics on conflicts of interests should not therefore be surprising. Individual policy makers often view the world through the lenses of their own organizations, and their policy recommendations tend to reflect their organizations' interests. The result is a conflict of interest within government as well and competition among multiple versions of what is truly in the national interest. Even presidents are subject to constraints in pursuing their policies.

Policy makers, whether their views are filtered through national, elite, or bureaucratic lenses, are persuaded that the way they see the world is correct. It is the *other* policy makers in the other states who see the world incorrectly. Each nation can justify its perceptions and policies and marshal an impressive array of facts and historical analyses. Do the facts not speak for themselves? After all, facts are facts. Or are they? The truth is that a fact as such does not possess any meaning. What gives it meaning is the observer's perceptual framework, influenced by personal experiences, beliefs, and interpretations of history. This image of the world leads the observer to select a specific fact from the thousands available. But why was that particular fact chosen? The answer is selective vision. It not only allows one to pick out some facts and ignore others—those picked tend to be consistent with one's way of viewing the world—but also gives meaning to those selected, thereby allowing a better understanding of the world. This is as true for nations as it is for individual policy makers (or outside observers) and bureaucracies.

Misperception and Conflict

The cold war illustrated certain objective geopolitical realities. The U.S. objective before World War II, as afterward, was to prevent the domination of Eurasia by any hostile power. The Soviet Union, which after the collapse of all the prewar great powers was the only great power remaining in Europe, already spanned all of Eurasia. American power was the only power able to balance Moscow's. The Soviet Union, with its fresh memories of Germany's invasion—the second in this century—and its enormous losses, was determined that this pattern not be repeated. It therefore pushed outward into Eastern Europe to keep the enemy, whoever it might be, as far away from Russian soil as possible. Thus, as so often before, two great powers, allied to defeat a common enemy, fell out with one another and became adversaries. The momentum of great-power rivalry, as old as history itself, then became an additional factor. Sparta versus Athens, Rome versus Carthage, France versus England (plus the rest of Europe at various times), England versus Germany— all preceded the post-1945 conflict. Influence, status, and power were the stakes; each considered the other a security threat. These "structural" causes of the cold war—causes inherent in the decentralized nature of the state system—were intensified by the ideological and cultural differences between the two societies, such as the individualist versus collective philosophy, democracy versus authoritarianism, private enterprise versus state ownership of property. Thus, the roots of the U.S.-Soviet conflict, in terms of both interests and values, were real and not easily resolvable. Even though the superpowers in the Gorbachev era no longer viewed each other as "mortal enemies," and the Soviet Union's successor state, Russia, under Boris Yeltsin was committed to amicable relations with the United States, Russia remains a potential rival. If Russian attempts at democracy fail and a new nationalistic dictatorship gains power, this would be especially likely.[1]

The *subjective* reality of Soviet leaders after World War I—their perception of reality—made it virtually impossible to work out a postwar modus vivendi or mutually acceptable working arrangements, as in 1815 when czarist Russia, also trying to protect itself from another invasion, pushed outward and seized control of the then Duchy of Warsaw, much to the consternation of Russia's fellow victors. George Kennan has argued that this post-1917 subjective reality stemmed from Soviet ideology, which tended to see the United States as only a temporary ally during World War II. As a capitalist state, the United States was viewed as an enemy, and what were intended to be American declarations of good intent and hopes for postwar peace were interpreted as mere rhetoric, which, if anything, was intended to deceive and relax the Soviet Union's guard. Thus, the Soviet Union's

> own aggressive intransigence with respect to the outside world began to find its own reaction. . . . It is an undeniable privilege of every man to prove himself right in the thesis that the world is his enemy; for if he reiterates it frequently enough and makes it the background of his conduct he is bound eventually to be right.[2]

The American reaction to the Soviet perception of the United States as the enemy took on the character of a crusade. With its tendency to see the world in terms of friend and foe, moral and immoral, U.S. foreign policy, initially limited to reacting to specific Soviet moves, soon spilled over into a global anticommunism. These differing perceptions and behavior patterns accounted for much of the intensity and bitterness of the superpower competition, the failure of a détente to emerge before the 1970s, and the collapse of détente I. They accounted as well for the refusal of the United States to recognize the new mainland Chinese government for thirty years after it proclaimed its existence, to exploit the growing Sino-Soviet schism after 1956, and to intervene with U.S. forces in Vietnam in 1965.

John Stoessinger, a longtime student of the effects of perceptions on nations, has noted the frequent gap between image and reality. Therefore, nations "live in darkness," he has argued. "Great nations struggle not only with each other, but also with their perceptions of each other."[3] In saying that perception may be almost as critical a factor in accounting for a state's behavior as objective reality, he and other analysts are implicitly, if not explicitly, drawing a line between correct perceptions and misperceptions. These misperceptions can aggravate or prolong, if they do not cause, conflict, as well as make peaceful resolution difficult, if not at times impossible.

Thus, even though both the United States and Soviet Union had good reasons for wanting détente in the 1970s, it did not last long because each one understood its meaning differently and therefore held different expectations. The Soviets assumed that the United States was interested in a relaxation of tensions and agreements with Moscow because of the Soviet Union's new military strength. Therefore, Leonid Brezhnev and the Kremlin felt that they could exploit opportunities for expanding Soviet influence with impunity. The United States would have to accept the resulting changes in the status quo. The men in the Kremlin at no point saw such behavior as incompatible with détente or believed that their own behavior would once more aggravate tensions and bring on a new cold war. In exaggerating the constraints on the United States, the Soviets badly miscalculated, for with the Soviet invasion of Afghanistan, the United States did an about-face in policy.

American disillusionment with détente had grown over the years. Détente was supposed to restrain the Soviets and reinforce the status quo, but Soviet actions helped bring Ronald Reagan, a hard-liner, and critic of détente, into power. The Soviet Union's unilateral search for advantage was thus counterproductive and led to a new confrontation for which the country no longer had the sustaining power. To Mikhail Gorbachev's credit, he recognized this. He also recognized, unlike his predecessors, that Soviet behavior affected America's behavior, just as the latter's behavior affected that of the Soviet Union. He therefore changed Soviet foreign policy by calling off the cold war.

Causes of Misperceptions

Why do national leaders so often misperceive the true nature of the world they face? The reasons are multiple. Both the British prewar and American wartime experiences showed, as already noted, how reluctant democracies are to recognize threats—in both cases from revolutionary states. Traditional states assume one another's right to exist; they are therefore at a disadvantage when a revolutionary state appears. Wishing to preserve peace and maintain their own tranquillity rather than face serious threats to their national security which entail costly rearmament programs and risks of war, democracies prefer to believe that the revolutionary state is really like themselves—that is, it has only limited, legitimate objectives, which can be satisfied by patience, good will, and compromise.[4] In other words, democracies are tempted to interpret their challengers' demands and behavior in familiar, favorable, and recognizable terms as if revolutionary states were in fact traditional states like themselves. Thus, the British thought Adolf Hitler was just another German nationalist, while the Nazi dictator justified every move he made in terms of the principle of national self-determination, the basis of the Western-imposed peace treaty at the end of World War I. Claiming that the Western powers had violated their own principles, he undermined the legitimacy of the territorial settlement and disguised his ultimate intentions of making Germany the dominant world power while paralyzing the will of Britain and France to oppose him. They recognized Hitler's claims as just and could not be sure that he was merely exploiting the principle of self-determination until he violated it. In the hope of preserving peace, they wanted to believe him when he said that his claims were limited and that he too wanted to preserve peace.

American history and experience reinforced this democratic unwillingness to admit the existence of international conflict and the U.S. stake in the outcome. In both world wars, the United States stayed out until its enemies attacked. In 1917, the United States would not have declared war had not the Germans launched their unrestricted submarine campaign to starve Britain into submission and, in the process, sunk American ships. Had Hitler not stupidly declared war on the United States after the Japanese attack on Pearl Harbor in 1941, the American war effort would have been directed only at Japan, and Germany, the greater threat, might have defeated Russia and Britain. In fact, it is questionable whether the United States, with a divided public, could have declared war on even Japan had it not been for the Japanese attack on Pearl Harbor. The ultimate decisions to go to war were made by Germany and Japan, not by the United States, even though the balance of power in Europe and Asia was at stake.[5] Unable to act wisely, the United States was saved by its enemies from the consequences of its behavior. Thus, it is not surprising that during World War II American leaders were generally optimistic about postwar relations with the Soviet Union. Just as the British had thought of Hitler as another Otto von Bismarck, who after unifying Germany in 1871 had declared that Germany would support the status quo, American policy makers thought of Joseph Stalin as another czar concerned only with securing historic *Russian* goals.

More specific explanations of misperceptions vary from policy makers' misreading of history to their personalities. In a biography of Dean Acheson, President Harry Truman's secretary of state during the early days of the cold war, Gaddis Smith, a historian, argued that underlying Acheson's thought and policy advice was "an extraordinarily articulate expression of thoughts which guided American foreign policy for a third of a century after the outbreak of the Second World War. An appraisal of Acheson must therefore be an appraisal of the nation's behavior in world affairs for an entire generation."[6] According to Smith's interpretation, Acheson's general image of the world and what ought to be the American role in it was shared by his successor, Dwight Eisenhower appointee John Foster Dulles, as well as by Presidents Truman, Eisenhower, Kennedy, Johnson, and Nixon. All were heavily influenced by their generation's experiences and perceptions. Postwar U.S. leaders had been tempered in the crucible of the 1930s; the career of Hitler and the appeasement at Munich, as well as the Nazi-Soviet pact, had made deep impressions on them.

Even more specifically, this generation had learned from the interwar period that the American isolationist stance had helped bring on World War II and that American participation in the defense of Western Europe after World War I would have helped deter Hitler. Isolationism no longer seemed a feasible policy; expansionistic totalitarian movements, whether Nazi or Soviet, had to be contained. A second lesson was that appeasement only whets a dictator's appetite—it is better to stand firm against demands and "present arms." Soviet policy was expansionist and aggressive and had to be resisted, by force if necessary. Driven by "the ghost of Hitler,"[7] of concessions made from a position of weakness, and of failure to match the adversary's military strength, this generation had learned that peace could not be preserved solely by good intentions. Military power and, if necessary, force were required.

Acheson and a host of postwar American policy makers therefore approached American-Soviet relations as a deadly contest. Soviet totalitarianism had to be contained and its expansionist attempts dammed, until some day that nation mellowed. Inflexible American policies, distrust of all Soviet and other Communist states, and an inability to recognize the diversity within the Communist world were the results, as was the unnecessary prolongation of the cold war.[8] President George Bush, a product of World War II, thought of

Saddam Hussein's aggression in similar terms. He likened the Iraqi dictator to Hitler and was determined not to appease Saddam's aggression.

Whereas Smith and other analysts have attributed misperceptions to drawing the wrong lessons from history, political scientist Ole Holsti has attributed them to other factors. For example, Holsti pointed to the rigid personality and equally inflexible anti-Communist view of Secretary of State John Foster Dulles.[9] Holsti argued that Dulles drew a distinction between the Soviet state and the governing Communist party, between Soviet national interests and Marxist-Leninist ideology with its universal revolutionary goals, and between the Soviet people and Soviet leaders. The consequence of these distinctions, Holsti claimed, was that in Dulles's mind the American quarrel was with the Soviet leaders, whose aims reached beyond legitimate and limited Soviet interests. The United States was not in conflict with the Soviet people, who, had they been represented by a democratic rather than a totalitarian government, would have pursued only limited national interests and not global expansionism. Soviet expansionism, in Dulles's view, was the cause of the cold war. The United States had to prevent the spread of "atheistic communism" and be constantly on guard against Communist attempts to lull the West.

Given Dulles's black and white image of the world—which is of central importance to the misperception approach—all incoming information had to be filtered through his particular perceptions: what fitted his preconceived image was accepted, and what did not fit was filtered out. The image thus remained intact. *Psychologic* is the term sometimes used to describe this tendency to see what we want to see and to reject contrary evidence; psychologists call it a "reduction of cognitive dissonance." On the basis of Dulles's public statements, Holsti argued that various Soviet pronouncements and moves, including a major reduction in the size of the Soviet army during Dulles's tenure as secretary of state, were not recognized as possible concessions and attempts to relax tensions. They served only to reinforce his preexisting views of the Soviet Union and were interpreted as signs of Soviet weakness and attempts to win a respite to recoup strength for a more effective and successful struggle with capitalism. A more flexible, less suspicious personality, Holsti has suggested, might have been more receptive to new and conflicting information. Presumably, this kind of person also might have made a more serious and sustained effort to test Soviet intentions and perhaps to bring about what is now popularly known as détente.

Correct Perceptions: World War II and the Cold War

If misperceptions may cause, magnify, or prolong conflict, then it follows that correct perceptions will either prevent or restrain conflict; at least, they will not blow it out of proportion to the interests at stake. But this is not necessarily true either. States that perceive each other all too correctly also go to war. For example, it was while Neville Chamberlain misperceived the nature of Hitler's aims that Britain tried to appease him.

Once the prime minister's perceptions had been proved erroneous by events, however, and he saw Hitler for what he really was, Britain declared war on Germany. The British prime minister's incorrect perception of Hitler and his attempts to come to an understanding thus avoided conflict for several years, giving Nazi Germany time to build up its armed forces and expand its strategic position.[10] Had Chamberlain understood Hitler's aims earlier and risked war before Germany strengthened its military and expanded its territory, the world might have been spared a war—or, at least, a long war.

During World War II, President Franklin Roosevelt, in characteristic American wartime fashion, focused U.S. policy on Germany's defeat and a total victory. Once the war was over, "normalcy" would be restored. Roosevelt was confident he could win the Russian leader's trust and cooperation. Typical of the American approach that to win a friend one had to be a friend, the president simply projected his domestic experience. At home he dealt constantly with other politicians; as a democratic politician, socialized in the arts of negotiation and compromise, he believed that all problems were solvable. Stalin was just another politician, and, as reasonable men, he and Stalin could compromise differences and avoid conflict. But Stalin was the product of a different political culture. While Roosevelt was optimistic about the future, as were the majority of Americans, Stalin's policy was based on the assumption of the inherent antagonism between capitalism and Soviet socialism.

The irony was terrific. While Roosevelt basically viewed Stalin as a Russian Roosevelt, Stalin saw Roosevelt as a capitalist Stalin! To Stalin, the president was the leader of an imperialist state, a tool of Wall Street. Also to Stalin, there was no fundamental difference between Roosevelt and Hitler, who too was a leader of a capitalist state. No real distinctions between Nazi fascism and American democracy existed. All capitalist states were believed to be hostile; Nazi Germany was simply the most extreme capitalist state. After Germany's defeat, the United States would take its place, and the conflict of the two social systems would continue. Thus, Stalin dismissed all of the president's professions of peace and good will. Capitalist leaders, he *knew*, possessed no such feelings for the Soviet Union. They were merely using words of good intentions to lull the Soviets into relaxing their guard. Roosevelt—and Churchill—were "adversaries who would do unto him approximately what he would do unto them, assuming they got the opportunity." [11]

Had Roosevelt understood that he and Stalin held opposite conceptions of what the postwar world would be like, he might have advocated different policies opposing Stalin, and Truman might have resisted demobilizing U.S. military strength once the war was over. The enormous conventional power of the United States—it did not need to use the threat of the atom bomb— could have provided the political leverage that Stalin would have understood. Protests over Stalin's brutal "satellization" of Eastern Europe were disregarded as the Soviets, after Germany's defeat, established themselves in the center of Europe and then attempted to expand into Iran, Greece, and Turkey. It was President Truman's accurate perception of Soviet behavior, as exhibited in these events, that led to the Truman Doctrine and the containment policy.

Misperceptions thus ensured the occurrence of World War II and the cold war; probably neither was avoidable. *Correct perceptions by Britain and the United States finally led each to recognize the stakes at issue and take a firm stand.* Had they done so earlier, they would have been in a stronger position for their respective conflicts. But democracies appear reluctant to acknowledge that there are states that wish them ill. Rather than confront enemies, it is more comforting to explain away enemies as unfortunate victims of past history (invasions, mistreatments), or to believe that no vital interests are threatened.

Correcting Misperceptions

Thus, misperceptions can cause conflicts and possibly wars; they also can prevent states from recognizing emerging threats and acting to forestall them. How can such misperceptions be corrected? Of all the ways, disaster appears to be a chief one. Policy (as Chapter 11 revealed) tends to be incremental; what worked yesterday will work today and tomorrow. As long as a particular policy appears to be successful, it will not be questioned, even if circumstances change. Policy makers and bureaucracies, as already noted, see what they want to see and reject contrary evidence. It is only when policy fails disastrously that it tends to be reexamined. For example, Britain's appeasement policy appeared to be successful in avoiding another war until 1938; when events then demonstrated Germany would continue its expansion, British policy began to shift and oppose German moves. But by then it was too late to contain German expansion peacefully. As another example, the American-Soviet alliance during World War II began to come apart over Soviet control of Eastern Europe; postwar Soviet pressure on Iran, Greece, and Turkey finally shifted the relationship from recent allies to adversaries. President Franklin Roosevelt's efforts to establish an era of Soviet-American cooperation after Germany's defeat lay shattered. It was the collapse of the wartime expectations that led to the containment policy. Soon spilling over into an anticommunism crusade, it lasted for two decades—until the Vietnam disaster.

Yet despite this anticommunism, the possibility of committing mutual suicide had already led the United States and Soviet Union to initiate arms control negotiations and agreements even before Vietnam. In the early 1970s, these were extended to the central strategic systems of the two superpowers as President Nixon pursued a policy of détente toward the Soviet Union and rapprochement with China. Perhaps no better proof exists that even before the occurrence of disaster, perceptions can and often do change as circumstances change. Nuclear weapons, precisely because of their awesome nature

358 The Second and Third Levels: Foreign Policy

and the certainty that their use would be catastrophic, have been a greater teacher of reality.

During the 1950s, Nixon had been a militant anti-Communist. In the 1970s, he pursued a flexible, nonideological, pragmatic balance-of-power foreign policy. Moreover, China's revolutionary and anticapitalist posture and rhetoric did not stand in the way of improving relations with the United States when the Soviet Union seemed a growing threat. The philosophies of Marx and Mao were simply subordinated to the balance of power. In 1989, the most anti-Communist American president in four decades ended his years in office having endorsed his Soviet counterpart and his reform efforts, signed the INF treaty, and made major advances toward a 50 percent reduction in strategic arms.

But the most dramatic turnaround came when Gorbachev decided that the Soviet Union's future as a superpower was in danger unless he could shake up the stagnant Soviet economy.[12] His references to "common security" were a significant departure from past Soviet thinking about Soviet defense policies. The Soviet leader admitted that in the past the Soviet search for military security had produced American feelings of insecurity and reactions, which in turn jeopardized Soviet security. Thus, the original Soviet policy was counterproductive. Both the Soviet Union and the United States, he said, needed to be more sensitive of the impact of its defense policy on the other. That would have been novel for Moscow, whose constant, almost paranoid scramble for more security had in the past subscribed to the maxim that the more power gained, the greater Soviet security. Conversely, the less power and security the adversary had felt, the better. What was surprising was not only the emphasis on defense policy, but also the underlying willingness to admit that Soviet policies might be responsible for the conduct of other nations. This was simply unheard of. The collapse of détente I, according to Gorbachev's predecessors, was not attributable to the continued Soviet military buildup in the 1970s or to Soviet interventions in Angola, Ethiopia, and elsewhere; these activities were merely cited as pretexts by anti-Soviet U.S. cold warriors who wanted to torpedo détente. This Soviet admission of an action-reaction pattern may in fact have been a prelude to the end of the cold war. What led the new leader of the Soviet Union to see the world differently? One factor was the disintegration of the Soviet economy, which stimulated Gorbachev's "New Thinking" and the shift in priority from foreign to domestic policy. The Soviet leader signed in turn a series of arms control measures and indicated his willingness to accept the de-Communization of Eastern Europe. A second factor was Gorbachev's recognition that Brezhnev's military buildup and the effort to exploit it politically, while successful in the short run, were counter-productive overall because they led to American rearmament and the encirclement of the Soviet Union by the U.S.-led NATO alliance, Japan, and the People's Republic of China. In short, its security had been reduced, not raised, despite the vast sums spent for over two decades on military hardware.

BACK TO THE LEVELS OF ANALYSIS

All this being said, the perceptions of leaders cannot be divorced from the larger context. Before World War II, British public opinion was pacifist, and the prime minister accurately reflected this feeling. Further indicating Britain's desire for peace, Winston Churchill's warnings were ignored, and he did not become a member of the government until the war broke out; indeed, he did not become prime minister until after the initial disasters of the war. During that war, President Roosevelt's hopes and attitudes represented U.S. opinion. And after that war, most Americans wanted to believe that there were no basic conflicts between the United States and the Soviet Union. According to Gen. Dwight Eisenhower, "The ordinary Russian seems to me to bear a marked similarity to what we call an 'average American.'"[13] How, given such views, could the United States have initiated an anti-Soviet policy against an ally who had borne the brunt of the fighting and whose wartime courage and endurance were much admired? The democratic nature of England in the late 1930s and the United States in 1945-1946 thus prevented these nations from formulating policies that would have contained their enemies more effectively. In short, the misperceptions of Chamberlain and Roosevelt have to be explained in terms of the larger social setting.

They also have to be explained in terms of their adversary's deceptive tactics of taking only limited steps, each one of which appeared reasonable and legitimate in terms of security or Western principles of national self-determination, thereby catering to the democratic state's belief that no basic threat existed and that all problems were negotiable and resolvable. British and American policy makers may have preferred to believe that good relations were possible with Germany and the Soviet Union—in fact, the latter nations made it a point to continually reassure the democratic states that they shared the desire for peaceful and harmonious relations.

Because the issue of perception cannot really be separated from the broader state system context, what are some of the key issues that policy makers' perceptions, bureaucratic and governmental politics, and public opinion must heed if they are to deal intelligently with the threats and opportunities that every government faces in advancing its national interests?

Defining the National Interest

It should be fairly obvious by now that the notion of "national interest" is of little help analytically. No political leader, bureaucrat, legislator, or interest group spokesperson is likely to advocate a policy that is *against* the national interest. To maximize the appeal of the policy solution they are advancing, these individuals wrap up their advocacy with the suggestion that their particular preferences are in the nation's best interests. There is no objectively defined national interest. But geography, for example, may instill in succeeding generations of policy makers similar ideas about how they should define their country's security interests in geographical terms. Thus, both czars and commissars showed an interest in Eastern Europe because of its importance for Russia's security, as will the new Russian leaders, despite the withdrawal of the former Soviet Union from the area. Yet Bismarck's interpretation of German "national interest" differed from Hitler's, and Chancellor Helmut Kohl's interpretation of the reunited Germany's national interest is different yet.

American leaders in the nineteenth century consistently defined U.S. security in terms of hegemony over Latin America, or at least over Central America. When in the twentieth century the Sandinistas took control of the government in Nicaragua, a country of only 3 million people, did that country then constitute a threat to American security? Should it have been overthrown because it considered itself an implacable foe of "U.S. imperialism" and had ties to Havana and Moscow? Or was it enough to ensure that the Sandinistas did not export their revolution to their neighbors and that they committed themselves to not allowing a Soviet base to be built in their country from which the Soviet Union could threaten the United States (as in Cuba in 1962)? Clearly, there was considerable disagreement over whether Nicaragua constituted a threat to the United States and, if so, how much of a threat.

While there are answers to all these questions, they are anything but clear in most cases. This would be true even if policy makers' parochial interests did not influence their perceptions and policy preferences. Normally, only in a crisis does a government appear united in its stance. But everyday policy decisions, security or economic, have to be forged from a set of diverse views and conflicting opinions.

Who Threatens These Interests?

It is not enough to define what a nation's interests are; it is also important to clarify who threatens them and how, or who may do so in the future and under what conditions. Indeed, the two issues are inseparable, for the specific interests to be defended or advanced can be selected only in the context of specific relationships with other countries. In part, the answer stems from a potential or actual adversary's power. This power, as already noted, is hard to calculate because of the number of its components, the mixture of tangible and intangible elements, the fact that these components are rarely static, and the difficulties incurred in "adding" them up (see Chapter 7). Moreover, depending on the specific situation, only some elements of power are even relevant and applicable, while others are totally useless. But even more difficult than calculating another nation's power is calculating another state's intentions.

At the heart of the Reagan administration's initially hard anti-Soviet line and emphasis on large-scale rearmament was a judgment about Soviet intentions and the meaning of the Soviet military buildup. Thus, despite the quantifiable nature of weapons, such calculations may not by themselves say much more than that they exist. But what does their existence mean? For example, what was the purpose of the enormous strategic and conventional military buildup begun by the Soviets in 1964? Was it to catch up with the United States, behind whom they had lagged so long? Was it to achieve parity militarily, as well as psychologically, and attain recognition equal to that of the United States? Was it undertaken because the Soviet Union needed larger forces to confront NATO to the west and China to the east? Was defense the primary motive for a country that had been invaded repeatedly throughout history? Or was the correct impression, widespread in the West, one of a new Soviet arsenal—including airlift and sealift capabilities developed over a decade and at huge cost—that was offensive and far larger than anything required for defense? Counting weapons, therefore, is not enough; more important is what people believe the weapons mean.

The question of intentions becomes even more difficult in the economic realm because it is America's allies who are the threat. Are America's economic problems largely the result of its own doing or the result of the unfair tactics of its allies in dumping goods on the international market and protecting their home markets? Are the Japanese, as some Americans charge, pursuing economic domination of world markets and doing so with the same energy, determination, and ruthlessness that they once sought by military victory over the United States? Or are the Japanese correct when they say that the United States' Japan-bashing is part of an effort to blame others for America's economic problems rather than accepting responsibility for them? Whatever the judgment, given the interdependent relations among the Western countries and their fierce competition economically, what should and can be done when they need one another politically and militarily? Can any Western country, as angry as it may be with the others, really afford to alienate them?

What Is Domestically Feasible?

Whatever the rational and intelligent response to a particular foreign policy situation, domestic politics and opinion will determine how much maneuverability a government will have. A pacifist British public opinion and an isolationist mood in the United States during the 1930s meant that both governments were constrained in what they could do. It was not accidental that Churchill, who had warned of the folly of appeasing Hitler, was out of power and out of favor during the "gathering storm." Nor was it accidental that President Roosevelt retreated back into passivity after his 1937 speech advising the democracies to quarantine dictators was met with a storm of criticism.

Similarly, during the cold war years the anti-Communist consensus limited the flexibility of U.S. foreign policy, such as recognizing Communist China. Vietnam dispersed this consensus into three belief systems: (1) cold war internationalism, essentially the continuation of the old cold war consensus, which focused on the bipolar East-West struggle and saw security as the main issue of international politics; (2) post-cold war internationalism, which focused on North-South issues and saw social and economic issues as primary; and (3) semi-isolationism, which focused on domestic issues and viewed the Soviet Union as a minor threat (the first two belief systems are detailed in Table 12-1).[14]

The cold war internationalist position was generally identified with the Republican party in the post-Vietnam era, and the post-cold war internationalist position with the Democrats. These positions did not, of course, correspond perfectly, given differences within and between each party, and the related rivalry between the presidency, occupied by the Republicans from 1969 to 1989 (with the exception of the single term of Jimmy Carter), and the Congress, mainly controlled by the Democrats. Thus, conflict and controversy between the executive and legislative branches, influenced by the effects a policy can have on a party's fortunes in the next election (the next election being never more than two years away), became the norm. Presidential leadership, once assumed, was no longer taken for granted; legislative support, almost automatic for over two decades (except on Asian policy), was no longer assured. The use of force by presidents had come to be regarded with great suspicion by the Congress. "No more Vietnams" haunted this generation of Americans, much like "Munich" and "appeasement" haunted their predecessors. As the party that involved the United States militarily in Vietnam, the Democrats have been especially opposed to military interventions since that time.

This Democratic antipathy to military intervention, publicly displayed when President Bush announced in early November 1990 the doubling of U.S. forces in the Gulf to give them an offensive capability, and again on the congressional vote permitting the president to use force after the January 1991 deadline for an Iraqi withdrawal from Kuwait had passed, led one of the few Democratic members of Congress to state the case for war before his party:

> The Democrats must ponder the political consequences of a reflexive refusal to even consider the use of force. The party has suffered in too many elections from the popular perceptions that it is categorically and emotionally unwilling to use force under almost any circumstances other than a direct attack on the United States itself. If Democrats are not prepared to support the use of force in a situation like this when the aggression is so unambiguous, the international community is so cohesive, and the stakes so great, how can anyone expect the Democratic Party to support the use of force in defense of vital American interests in the far more common circumstances of confusion, ambiguity, and uncertainty?[15]

In early January 1991, only 20 percent of the Democrats in the Senate (only one north of the Mason-Dixon line) and 30 percent of the Democratic members of the House supported a resolution in support of the UN resolution authorizing the use of force if Saddam Hussein had not withdrawn from Kuwait by January 15, 1991. In other words, 80 percent of Democrats in the

Table 12-1 Two Foreign Policy Belief Systems in the Post-Vietnam Years

	Cold War Internationalism	*Post-Cold War Internationalism*
Nature of the international system		
Structure	Bipolar (and likely to remain so) Tight links between issues and conflicts	Complex and interdependent (and becoming more so) Moderate links between issues and conflicts
World order priorities	A world safe from aggression and terrorism is necessary precondition for dealing with other issues	International regimes for coping with a broad range of issues, with high priority on North-South ones
Conception of interdependence	Encompasses security issues ("domino theory")	Encompasses economic/social issues
Primary threats to the United States	Soviet and Soviet-sponsored aggression and terrorism Military imbalance (favoring Soviet Union) Soviet ability to engage in political coercion based on nuclear blackmail	North-South issues (for example, rich-poor gap) which threaten any prospects for world order International environmental problems Danger of nuclear war
Soviet Union		
Nature of the system	Model totalitarian state	Great power
Driving force of foreign policy	Aggressive expansionism	Seeks parity with United States Defensiveness (exaggerated view of defense needs may create further tensions)
Appraisal of recent foreign policies	Highly successful	Moderately unsuccessful
Soviet-American relations		
Nature of the conflict	Genuine conflicts of interest Largely zero-sum	Some real conflicts of interest but exaggerated by hard-liners on both sides Largely non-zero-sum
Appraisal of détente	A dangerous delusion	Some useful first steps
Appraisal of SALT process	Skeptical; dangerous as conducted in the past	Some useful first steps

Table 12-1 —Continued

	Cold War Internationalism	Post-Cold War Internationalism
Primary dangers of war	Military imbalance will lead Soviets to threaten vital U.S. and Western interests Recent successes will make Soviets more aggressive, perhaps recklessly so	Uncontrolled arms race Both sides equally likely to misperceive other's actions, leading to unwanted war
Linkages	Vital to link issues	Decouple issues
Third World		
Role in present international system	Primary target of Soviet and Soviet-inspired subversion and aggression	Primary source of unresolved social/economic problems that must be resolved to create a viable world order
Primary source of Third World problems	Subversion and aggression by Soviet Union and its proxies (Cuba, Libya, etc.) Left-wing authoritarian governments	Legacies of western colonialism and imperialism Right-wing authoritarian governments Structural flaws in the international system
Primary U.S. obligations	Help provide security from aggression and terrorism, but on a selective basis (to strategically important ones: oil producers, etc.)	Economic and other forms of nonmilitary assistance Play a leading role in structural systemic changes (new international economic order, etc.)
Prescription for American foreign policy	Rebuild military strength to regain a position of parity with the Soviet Union Rebuild collective security system Active U.S. role in the world is a necessary but not sufficient condition to create a stable and just world order	Stabilize relations with the Soviet Union in order to free energy and resources for dealing with North-South and other high-priority issues Active U.S. role in the world is a necessary but not sufficient condition to create a stable and just world order

SOURCE: Ole R. Holsti and James N. Rosenau, "Consensus Lost: Consensus Regained? Foreign Policy Beliefs of American Leaders, 1976-1980," *International Studies Quarterly* (December 1986): 380-381.

upper chamber and 70 percent in the lower chamber, including the party's senior leadership, voted against what was in effect the functional equivalent of war: they voted instead to give sanctions more time. While they declared that they shared the president's goal of freeing Kuwait and that they would be willing to employ force if sanctions failed, these declarations were not credible. Quite apart from the question of whether the fragile UN alliance would hold over a year or longer while the world waited to see if economic sanctions would work, did Democrats who favored sanctions over force really believe that force would be used as the 1992 presidential campaign began in the fall of 1991? Was not a vote in favor of sanctions a vote not to use force, period, and to accept the new status quo in preference to the risks and costs of war? The Democratic party remained essentially "Vietnamized." It had made one mistake in committing the country to war; it did not want to do so again. But more profoundly, Vietnam had affected the Democratic leadership's ability to grasp the facts of power internationally. It retained a powerful distaste for the military and the use of force as an instrument of national statecraft, reflecting its post-Vietnam beliefs that America was more often a corrupting influence in the world than a force for good—giving the party a profound aversion to the exercise of American power—and that conflicts were essentially the result of misunderstandings, making such exercises unnecessary.[16] It remains to be seen whether in the wake of the American triumph against Iraq a new consensus will form about the U.S. role in the post-cold war era—including a legitimate role for the use of force as an instrument of policy.[17]

By What Methods?

Even if policy makers agree on the aims they wish to pursue and mobilize legislative and public support, the question of how best to achieve these objectives remains, and that itself can become a matter of intense debate. Because the cold war is over (indeed, the Soviet threat evaporated even before the Soviet Union disappeared), is the United States now permitted to withdraw from Europe and Japan to focus on its domestic problems? More specifically, to deal with its economic problems, should it resort to protectionism of its surviving industries? In short, is isolationism now possible again now that the Soviet military threat to the United States and its principal allies has passed? Indeed, are America's economic security and welfare not the nation's primary interest? Or should the country maintain its old commitments in order to deal more effectively with post-cold war political instabilities, such as the disintegration of the Soviet Union and other Eastern European countries, as well as the economic competition among the long-term allies? How should it deal with the potential new regional threats such as Iraq and the proliferation of weapons of mass destruction: unilaterally or through multilateral organizations such as the United Nations? As for dealing with the proliferation of nuclear weapons—whether unilaterally or multilaterally—should the United States rely mainly on diplomacy, on the application of economic sanctions, or on the use of force? And if the latter, should it act preventively before the Iraqis acquire nuclear, chemical, and biological weapons, or should it wait until they act? In summary, how in the contemporary world should the United States protect and advance its political and economic interests?

For Review

1. Why are the perceptions of nations, political elites, specific bureaucracies, and individual leaders so important in the conduct of foreign policy?
2. What are some of the causes of their misperceptions?
3. How do the correct perceptions of policy makers affect the likelihood of conflict and war?
4. How can misperceptions be corrected?
5. How do perceptions relate to the key issues all policy makers face?

Notes

1. Seweryn Bialer, " 'New Thinking' and Soviet Foreign Policy," *Survival* (July/August 1988): 303; Josef J. Joffe, "Entangled Forever," *National Interest* (Fall 1990): 36-37; and Richard Nixon, "The Challenge We Face in Russia," *Wall Street Journal*, March 11, 1992.
2. George F. Kennan, *American Diplomacy 1900-1950* (Chicago: University of Chicago Press, 1951), 111-112.
3. John G. Stoessinger, *Nations in Darkness* (New York: Random House, 1971), 5; and Stoessinger, *Why Nations Go to War* 5th ed. (New York: St. Martin's Press, 1989).
4. Henry A. Kissinger, *Nuclear Weapons and Foreign Policy* (New York: Harper & Row, 1957), 317-320.
5. Robert A. Divine, *The Illusion of Neutrality* (Chicago: University of Chicago Press, 1962), 280-281.
6. Gaddis Smith, *Dean Acheson* (New York: Cooper Square, 1972), 414.
7. Ibid., 423.
8. Gaddis Smith, "The Shadow of John Foster Dulles," *Foreign Affairs* (January 1974): 403-408. Also see Townsend Hoopes, *The Devil and John Foster Dulles* (Boston: Little, Brown, 1973). Others invoke generational attitudes that later were attributed to the Establishment, all of whose members believed in the need for U.S. leadership of the world and *pax Americana*. See, for example, Godfrey Hodgson, *The Colonel* (New York: Knopf, 1990), a book about "the life and wars of Henry Stimson, 1867-1950," in the words of the book's subtitle.
9. David J. Finlay, Ole R. Holsti, and Richard R. Fagen, *Enemies in Politics* (New York: Rand McNally, 1967), 25-96.
10. Williamson Murray, *The Change in the European Balance of Power, 1938-1939* (Princeton, N.J.: Princeton University Press, 1984).
11. William Taubman, *Stalin's American Policy* (New York: Norton, 1982), 39.

12. Bialer, " 'New Thinking,' " 298.

13. Dwight D. Eisenhower, *Crusade in Europe* (New York: Doubleday, 1952), 457, 473-474.

14. Ole R. Holsti and James N. Rosenau, "Consensus Lost: Consensus Regained? Foreign Policy Beliefs of American Leaders, 1976-1980," *International Studies Quarterly* (December 1986): 380-381.

15. Stephen J. Solarz, "The Stakes in the Gulf," *New Republic*, January 7 and 14, 1991, 25.

16. On the Democrats' abandoned heritage in foreign policy, see, for example, George Weigel, "Defining the Moment," *American Purpose* (Washington, D.C.: Ethics and Public Policy Center, April 1991), 26-27.

17. Richard A. Melanson in *Reconstructing Consensus* (New York: St. Martin's Press, 1991) appears optimistic, but despite the book's publication date, it omits the entire Iraqi experience and the party division on whether to go to war.

Part Four

HOW TO PLAY— POLITICALLY, MILITARILY, ECONOMICALLY

CHAPTER 13

The Balance
of Terror

THE NUCLEAR REVOLUTION AND BALANCE OF POWER

Expansion of Violence

The noted English political observer E. H. Carr once wrote, "War lurks in the background of international politics just as a revolution lurks in the background of domestic policies."[1] Ironically, democracy, which was expected to abolish war—and still is expected to do so—greatly enhanced the power of nations and made war more terrible than ever before. One democratic assumption used to be that only irresponsible rulers were belligerent; for them, wars were merely an enjoyable and profitable "blood sport." In this view, it was the people who paid the price of wars with their lives and their taxes. If peace-loving people could hold their rulers accountable, wars would be eliminated and peace secured. Democracy would then bring an era of good will—of individual freedom and social justice at home, of peace and harmony abroad. The world would be safe for democracy because it would be democratic. Government by the people, of the people, and for the people would ensure perpetual peace.[2]

Instead, democracy became tied to nationalism, and the two gave birth to the "nation in arms." Once people were freed from feudal bondage and granted the right to some form of self-government, they came to equate their own well-being with that of their nation, and it seemed only reasonable that the nation should be able to call on them—the citizens—for defense. Not surprisingly, it was the 1789 French Revolution that brought people into contact with the nation-state. One result was the first system of universal military service. When the supreme loyalty of citizens was to their nation, the nation in arms followed logically. Democracy and nationalism thus enabled France to mobilize fully for total war and destroy its opponents completely.

This change was one reason why in 1815 the Congress of Vienna reacted with such horror to the revolution, which had unleashed mass passions and all-out war. Previous wars had been restrained because men had identified not with nations but with smaller units, such as towns or manors, or with universal entities, such as that embodied in the Roman Catholic church. The armies of the *ancien régime* were composed largely of mercenaries and such lowly elements of society as debtors, vagrants, and criminals—men who were animated neither by love of country nor by hatred of the enemy, but who fought because they were paid or compelled to do so. States lacked sufficient economic resources to maintain sizable armies. Indeed, their tactics were determined by the need to limit expenses. And to keep casualties low the emphasis was on maneuver rather than on pitched battle. The revolution enlisted popular support, however, and mass armies aroused by nationalism began to fight in defense of their countries. Frenchman Bertrand de Jouvenel described this "new era in military history" as "the era of cannon fodder." [3]

It remained only for the Industrial Revolution to produce the instruments that enabled men to kill one another in greater numbers. Modern military technology brought total war to its fullest realization.[4] Mass armies were equipped with mass-produced weapons that were ever more destructive, making it possible for nations to inflict progressively greater damage on one another in shorter and shorter periods. In the seventeenth century, it took thirty years for the states of central western Europe to slaughter half the population of central Europe. In the second decade of the twentieth century, it took only four years for them to bleed one another into a state of exhaustion and, for some, collapse. But the atomic bomb, and especially the hydrogen bomb, made it possible to inflict catastrophic damage in minutes (or at most hours) that previously had taken years, and this catastrophic damage was tantamount to near destruction. Ironically, the atomic bomb's enormous destructive power disciplined the use of power. Instead of leading to World War III between the two global rivals that emerged from World War II, it was a principal reason for four decades of peace between the United States and the Soviet Union and their respective allies. Historically, the great powers have been the chief cause of war. The bomb had a revolutionary impact: it eliminated war among them.

Destructive Nature of Nuclear Weapons

With the ascendancy of strategic air power and nuclear weapons, human beings had then the means with which to accomplish their own extermination. Cities—indeed, whole nations—could be laid waste in a matter of hours, if not minutes. The effectiveness of that kind of strategic air power against a highly urbanized and industrialized society is no longer a matter of dispute. Nuclear bombs are so destructive that they make World War II bombing attacks appear trivial by comparison. Atomic bombs, such as those dropped on

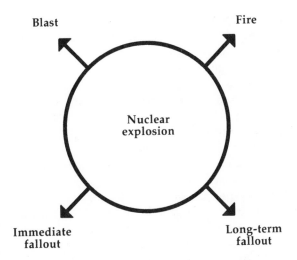

Hiroshima and Nagasaki, were surpassed in destructive power within a few years by the new hydrogen bombs. Kilotons were replaced by megatons (1 megaton equals 1 million tons of TNT). A single U.S. Strategic Air Command B-52 bomber can carry 25 megatons of explosive power—or 12.5 times the explosive power of all bombs dropped during World War II, including the two atomic bombs![5]

A nuclear explosion has four physical effects: blast, fire, immediate radiation, and long-term radiation. The blast, or shock wave, is the almost solid wall of air pressure produced by an explosion, creating a hurricane-type wind. The blast from a low-altitude bomb exploding in a city will collapse all wooden buildings within six miles of ground zero for a 1-megaton bomb, within fourteen miles for a 10-megaton bomb, and within thirty miles for a 100-megaton bomb. For brick buildings, the figures for the same bombs are four, nine, and eighteen miles, respectively, and for sturdier buildings, the distance ranges from three to twelve miles.

The thermal impact of a bomb can be heightened by a higher-altitude explosion or airburst. The heat generated by a 1-megaton bomb is tremendous, producing second-degree burns of the skin up to nine miles from ground zero; a 10-megaton bomb has the same effect up to twenty-four miles; a 100-megaton bomb up to seventy miles.[6] Furthermore, the heat in most instances would ignite wooden houses and other combustible objects (from plastics and furniture in homes to gas lines and furnaces) over the same range. World War II demonstrated that the real danger from fire, even when started with ordinary incendiary bombs, is the fire storm.[7] In a fire storm the intense heat from the fire rises, heating the air in turn. As the difference in pressure between the hot and colder air sucks in fresh oxygen to feed the hungry flames, the process builds in intensity. Air rushes in at ever greater speeds until wind velocity surpasses gale force. The flames, whipped by the wind and fed further by the gas, oil, and other incendiary materials of the homes and streets of the burning city, leap upward, stabbing high into the air, enveloping the stricken area. Everything burns in this tomb of heat and flame. There is no escape. Those who have not yet been crushed in their shelters are asphyxiated by lack of oxygen or by carbon monoxide poisoning; if they seek to escape into the burning streets, their lungs are seared, and their bodies, exposed to the intense heat, burst into flame. During the 1943 attack on Hamburg, the fire storm caused a ground temperature of 1,400 degrees Fahrenheit. Indeed, near the center of the fire storm the temperature exceeded 2,200 degrees Fahrenheit.

The third and fourth effects of a nuclear explosion, the radiation impact, can be maximized by a surface burst or a low-altitude explosion. The resulting fireball—a large, rapidly expanding sphere of hot gases that produces intense heat—scoops up debris and converts it into radioactive material. The fireball of a 10-megaton bomb has a diameter of six miles. The heavier particles of debris fall back to earth within the first few hours. Besides the immediate radiation in the area of explosion, longer-term, lighter particles "fall out" during the following days and weeks over an area the size of which depends on the magnitude of the explosion, the surface over which the explosion occurs, and meteorological conditions. The American 15-megaton thermonuclear explosion of 1954 in the Pacific Ocean caused substantial contamination over an area of 7,000 square miles (equivalent to the size of New Jersey). Under more "favorable" conditions, the fallout could have covered an area of 100,000 square miles (equivalent to the areas of New Jersey, New York, and Pennsylvania).

Fallout can emit radiation for days, months, and even years. The power of this radiation depends on the amount absorbed by humans and animals.[8] A dose of 100-200 roentgens causes radiation sickness, a combination of weakness, nausea, and vomiting that is not fatal, although it can result in disability. At 200 roentgens, radiation becomes very dangerous: disability is certain, and death can come within a month. The possibility of death increases until, at 500 roentgens, it is certain for 50 percent of those exposed to the radiation. Above 600 roentgens, the number of deaths continues to mount, and deaths occur more rapidly.[9] Radiation also has two other effects: cancer and genetic transmutations that may affect subsequent generations.

Considering the overwhelmingly destructive character of a single nuclear weapon and the large number of them that the United States and the Soviet Union possessed during the cold war, a coordinated nuclear attack on a nation's major urban and industrial centers would be catastrophic, reducing everything to rubble and leaving the population dead or injured, with little hope of help. Most hospitals, doctors, nurses, drugs, and blood plasma would be destroyed, as would the machinery for the processing and refrigeration of food and the purification of water. Medical "disaster planning" for a nuclear war is meaningless (not surprisingly, nuclear war has been called "the last epidemic"). In addition, there would be no transportation left to take survivors out of the smoldering ruins and into the countryside; most, if not all, of the fuel would have burned up. Estimates of casualties in such a coordinated urban strike range from 30 percent to 90 percent of the population, depending on the yield of the bombs, the heights at which they were exploded, the weather, civilian protection, and preparations for coping with the aftermath of such an attack.[10]

If cities were the main targets in a nuclear war, former Soviet premier Nikita Khrushchev's remark that the survivors would envy the dead appeared all too true. A 1977 Department of Defense study estimated that 155-165 million Americans would be killed if all explosions were detonated at ground level and no civil defense measures existed. If half the explosions were airbursts, the casualties would be reduced to 122 million.[11] Other studies showed equally high figures, although some differed by 20 million fatalities or so. Even "low" figures such as 55 million dead are staggering and unprecedented in the history of human existence, particularly when it is recalled that these were only the casualties that would occur immediately and within thirty days of the attack. Deaths occurring afterward from injury, radiation, starvation, and general economic chaos were not included. Total fatality figures would be much higher.

Today, we are more aware of some of the side effects of nuclear explosions. In 1983, some scientists issued a warning that nuclear war may destroy the ozone layer in the stratosphere.[12] This layer protects all living things from ultraviolet solar radiation, which destroys protein molecules. In addition to death, destruction, and radiation, therefore, extensive ozone depletion could destroy the food chain of plants and animals on which humans and animal life depend for survival. As if this were not bad enough, these scientists also concluded that fires from large-scale attacks on Soviet and American cities in a nuclear war would create so much smoke that it would filter out sunlight, thereby creating a "nuclear winter." The Northern Hemisphere, for example, would be plunged into darkness by plumes of dust and soot suspended in the stratosphere. This would cause extensive freezing of the earth's surface, including lakes and rivers, even during the summer, leading to the extinction of a major portion of plant and animal life. Such a freeze might last weeks, months, possibly even years. The implications of a nuclear winter were twofold: (1) even if the initiator of a nuclear war could launch a surprise attack and destroy most of the opponent's retaliatory capability, the first-strike state would be the victor only briefly because the nuclear winter would soon cripple it as well; and (2) because the nuclear winter would spread from the Northern to the Southern Hemisphere, the human race could become extinct. Scientists continue to debate whether in fact nuclear war would unleash such a deep freeze and how long it would last. But clearly the environmental effects of a nuclear war can no longer be considered secondary to the results of blast, fire, and radiation.

Nuclear Impact on the Balance of Power

The impact of this awesome power on the conduct of international politics has been revolutionary.[13] Before 1945, war was still considered a rational instrument of policy, despite the rapidly increasing costs of modern warfare. States usually preferred to accept these costs rather than submit. Nuclear weapons, however, endanger the very substance of national life. Rather than helping preserve civilization, the new instruments of violence promise to destroy it through the "assured destruction" of society. What possible goal could be "worth" the cost of self-immolation? How could a nation defend its political independence and territorial integrity if, in the very act of defense, it could be sacrificing itself? Nuclear war can know no victors; all the contestants will be losers. *Total wars may have been compatible with weapons of limited destructive capacity, but they are incompatible with "absolute weapons."*

The conclusion to be drawn from this general principle is that the main function of strategic military strength in the nuclear age is *deterrence* of an all-out attack. Deterrence protects a nation's security by preventing an attack rather than by defending the nation after an attack. The opponent is threatened with such massive retaliation that it dare not attack. The assumption is that, faced with the risk of virtual suicide, the enemy will desist. Mutual deterrence between two states, each seeking to protect its own security interests, thus becomes a matter of conflict resolution. "I won't destroy you, if you don't destroy me" is the offer of each side to the other. "We shall both lose if you attack me because I shall retaliate" is the answer.

In this extraordinary situation the role of nuclear power is that it is *not* to be used. Its primary value is in peacetime; if war erupts, it will have failed. The decisive test of arms is no longer vanquishing the enemy in battle; it is not having to fight at all. Furthermore, deterrence must be perpetual. There can be no margin for error. The frequency of war throughout history suggests how often deterrence has failed. But because no weapon was so destructive that failure spelled extinction, such mistakes were not irreparable. The critical issue for the military was not whether it could prevent the outbreak of hostilities but whether it could win on the battlefield. But later this was no longer true. The superpowers after World War II possessed overwhelming power yet were completely vulnerable to attack and destruction. Thus, modern nuclear warfare would be irrational. Nuclear technology has so vastly augmented the scope of violence and destruction that total war can destroy the very nation that wages it and can do so in a matter of hours, not years.

In sum, the balancing of power historically has had two purposes: (1) protection of individual states and (2) protection of the state system as a whole. Peace has not been the chief aim. When states have been secure, peace has followed; when states have not been secure, they have gone to war. The philosophy of "peace at any price" has been rejected by states. But nuclear weapons have changed all that; security can no longer be given priority over peace. Security and peace have become virtually identical. The deterrent function of the balance has therefore become supreme. To fight a war—a total war—is no longer feasible.

HOW ARMS CONTROL DOCTRINE HELPED PREVENT NUCLEAR WAR

Rationale

For a state to deter its opponent, it must have the forces to launch a massive retaliation. Before World War II, states normally had military forces with which they hoped to prevent an enemy attack, but these forces were never nearly as strong as the forces that could be mobilized if war actually broke out. Since war was not fatal, there was no reason to keep large, expensive forces always ready. Plowshares were to be converted into swords after the attack. This attitude was particularly prevalent in the United States. Protected by two oceans and thus not subject to invasion or even air attack, it had time to mobilize its vast power after it entered a war. But nuclear deterrence required peacetime readiness of all the forces required for retaliation if an enemy attack occurred. If deterrence were to be permanent, the enemy must never doubt that it would be committing suicide should it strike first.

The need for a wartime offensive capability was thus constant and required unfailing concern with effective delivery systems. But this was a difficult problem because of the rapid technological changes that occurred every few years after 1945. These changes became critical in determining the stability of the nuclear balance of power. For example, the ability of fast bombers to execute surprise attacks tended to destabilize the postwar equilibrium. Deterrence depended on the threat to drop enough bombs to wipe the Soviet Union off the map. But this threat would have been meaningless if most American bombers could have been destroyed in a surprise attack. The surviving bombers would not have been able to retaliate with sufficient destructiveness. Thus, the vulnerability of bombers to a nuclear Pearl Harbor rendered the balance of power unstable because the side that delivered the initial blow gained an enormous advantage. Possessing only bombs was insufficient to ensure that war would not result. The possibility of eliminating the opponent's retaliatory bombers—bombers above ground were considered "soft" targets—constituted a powerful incentive to attack. The consequent balance was therefore a delicate one.

What conditions might instigate an opponent's first strike against one's own retaliatory force? And what could be done to prevent such an attack and "stabilize" mutual deterrence? [14] These questions preoccupied students of arms control in the late 1950s and 1960s. Proponents of arms control rejected the feasibility of general disarmament and assumed that neither conflicts among states nor nuclear weapons would be abolished. Instead, the best hope for earthly salvation seemed to lie in the "control" of armaments. In a competitive state system, deterrence was recognized as the only feasible policy. It had to be improved, however, to be made "safe."

Preemptive and Preventive Strikes.   Arms control came to be considered the verso of more traditional defense policies, as its aim was identical: to protect the national security by deterring war. Whereas disarmament stressed the reduction of a nation's military capability, either completely or partially, arms control emphasized the elimination of American and Soviet incentives to strike first. Two presuppositions underlay arms control: (1) despite the continuation of their political conflict, both nuclear powers shared a *common interest in avoiding nuclear war*, and (2) both possessed delivery systems that raised tensions by providing a strong and *independent incentive* for a first strike.[15] Of paramount importance was hitting first because, in the nuclear age, to come in second was to lose. Policy makers thus might have been tempted to launch a first strike.

It is useful here to recall the first law of preservation in the state system: Be suspicious. One side's gain—and any proposal by a potential adversary is assumed to have advantages for itself—is usually considered the other side's loss. The fear of loss is particularly acute in the military sphere, where each party is hypersensitive to the possibility of being inferior. Few arms agreements have existed in history precisely because states, driven by their sense of insecurity, preferred to add arms to their already existing arsenals to ensure that they would not find themselves lacking. *Arms control thinking, however, was based on the assumption that one side's gain was not necessarily the other's loss; both sides gained simultaneously.*

If the only defense was indeed an offense, then a *preemptive strike* was a particular danger during crisis periods. It differed from a *preventive strike*, in which the aggressor coolly planned the strike beforehand with confidence that it could obliterate the opponent—that is, the attacker picked a specific date and then sent its forces on their way, regardless of possible provocation. In a preemptive strike, however, the attack was launched to forestall a strike by the enemy. In this instance, the aggressor believed that the opponent was about to strike; it therefore struck first to destroy the enemy's forces before they could take off. The attack resulted from moves on the other side that were interpreted as menacing.[16]

The role of a possible miscalculation in precipitating a preemptive strike was clear. The signs that an opponent was about to launch an attack were likely to be ambiguous. The opponent might simply be taking measures to make its own strategic force less vulnerable and thereby enhance its deterrent stance. For instance, during the years the United States and Soviet Union possessed mainly bombers, the opponent might have sent many of them into the air to avoid having them caught on the ground; by making them less vulnerable to sudden destruction, the opponent tried to prevent the other side from launching an attack. But the action itself could easily have been misinterpreted as the prelude to an attack. In a situation of mutual vulnerability, in which the "nice guy" finished last, delay could prove fatal. Offensive action might therefore be the only wise course.[17] What was important, in short, was not what state A intended to do but state B's perception of state A's intentions. Even defensive actions, intended merely to enhance one's deterrent power, might have intensified international tensions or touched off nuclear conflagration. Paradoxically then, the very weapons intended to deter nuclear war may have well precipitated it.

Stabilizing Mutual Deterrence. How then could a preventive war and especially a preemptive strike be forestalled? The answer was to make each side's retaliatory or second-strike forces invulnerable. *A second-strike force was one that could absorb an initial blow and still effectively perform its retaliatory mission.* The deterrent force that mattered was that part likely to be left after an initial enemy attack; the size of the force before the attack was less relevant. In the bomber era, an invulnerable deterrent force was impossible. The solution was twofold. First, instead of relying on one weapons system for deterrence, several systems were to be developed so that if one became vulnerable as technology changed, the others would still be safe and deterrence would be assured. It was best to err on the side of safety. Thus, the United States and the Soviet Union developed a triad consisting of bombers, intercontinental ballistic missiles (ICBMs), and submarine-launched ballistic missiles (SLBMs). Second, solid-fuel missiles that could be fired instantly became the backbone of the deterrent forces. They could be dispersed more easily than bombers, which were generally concentrated at a relatively small number of bases, the location of which was easily discoverable. Missiles, unlike bombers on the ground, could also be hardened, or placed in underground concrete silos that could withstand the enormous pressure from the blast of a nuclear explosion. Most important, sea-launched missiles—in contrast to stationary ICBMs—could be concealed and made mobile by placing them in nuclear submarines whose exact locations were not known to the enemy.

This dispersal, hardening, mobility, and concealment of missiles deprived a surprise attack of its rationale. The entire justification for a first strike had been to surprise the opponent with its bombers on the ground and to destroy them. But when the opponent's retaliatory power was basically invulnerable, obliterating the enemy's cities would benefit the aggressor very little. Surprise no longer conferred any significant advantage to the side that hit first because the enemy's first strike could not destroy the ability to strike back. The fact that a second-strike force would remain was the best guarantee against war. *Invulnerable deterrents stabilized mutual deterrence.*[18] Once the advantage of an initial attack had been greatly reduced, if not eliminated, the incentive to strike at all and the possibility of war also disappeared.

Characteristics of Arms Control

U.S. arms control thinking was composed of three critical elements. First, the number of nuclear weapons needed to achieve the "assured destruction" of the other society determined how many weapons each side needed, not the number of weapons possessed by the opponent. Second, deterrence required urban areas to be left vulnerable to attack as "hostages." And third, second-strike forces had to be invulnerable, so that the enemy could never believe that it could destroy enough forces to survive a retaliatory strike.

Parity in Numbers of Weapons.   *The balance of capability did not necessarily require equal numbers of bombers and missiles.* A balance was achieved when each side, after absorbing an initial blow, had a second-strike force able to destroy the opponent's homeland. The best size for such a second-strike force varied quite a bit in the views of U.S. and Soviet leaders. For example, SALT I, the 1972 agreement on offensive arms, froze the strategic missiles of the United States at 1,054 ICBMs and 656 SLBMs. The Soviet Union was permitted to have 1,618 ICBMs and 740 SLBMs. The treaty seems to have given the Soviets a hefty advantage of 2,358 missiles to 1,710, although it seems less unequal when it is noted that approximately 450 U.S. bombers, as opposed to 150 Soviet bombers, were allowed.

According to U.S. leaders' arms control thinking, even if most U.S. land-based missiles had been destroyed in their silos by Soviet ICBMs, the sizable bomber fleet plus nuclear submarines, each one armed with sixteen to twenty-four multiwarheaded missiles, would have remained. Could Moscow therefore really have risked launching a strike on the assumption that it might have been able to destroy enough of the U.S. second-strike force to prevent the latter from inflicting overwhelming retaliatory damage on the Soviet Union? Would not such a move have represented a reckless gamble—a "cosmic roll of the dice," as Harold Brown, President Jimmy Carter's secretary of defense, called it—even if the total Soviet strike force was larger than that of the United States by several hundred missiles? [19]

Thus, although the superpowers were capable of destroying each other, they early on reached a plateau—variously called *parity, sufficiency, mutual deterrence, nuclear stalemate,* and *balance of terror*—in this capability. The nuclear balance, or mutual deterrence, was not sensitive to numerical variations if each side retained an invulnerable deterrent force capable of the assured destruction of the enemy's society. Parity then could have been defined as a relationship in which each superpower was able to destroy the other, regardless of who struck first—in short, what has usually been described as mutual assured destruction. [20]

Vulnerable Populations and Economies.   *Urban industrial areas were deliberately left unprotected as hostages.* In 1964, the Soviets began to deploy an antiballistic missile (ABM) system around Moscow. By itself, the Soviet ABM constituted no problem. The problem lay in the possibility of an extensive ABM deployment to protect the Soviet urban population. If such ABMs were capable of shooting down a large percentage of missiles in a retaliatory strike—or if the Soviets believed they could—it might weaken the U.S. capability to deter.

Deterrence depended on the ability to hold the adversary's population hostage: a Soviet ability to greatly reduce America's capacity to inflict unacceptable losses on Soviet cities might, by eliminating the possibility of suicide, have tempted the Soviets to risk launching a preventive or preemptive strike. Anything that detracted from the superiority of the offense to inflict assured destruction on the opponent tended to destabilize mutual deterrence, which was based on a *vulnerable population and invulnerable offensive forces.* Thus, an ABM protecting cities was a "bad" weapon in the sense that it could endanger nuclear deterrence.[21] In SALT I, for all practical purposes, the United States and Soviet Union abandoned the ABM and left their cities vulnerable to each other.

Invulnerable Retaliatory Forces. Because invulnerable second-strike forces were the key to the stability of mutual deterrence, *the weapons produced and deployed had to be the "right" kind.* Whether a weapon was right or wrong, good or bad, depended on whether it would help stabilize the balance or destabilize it; these terms had no moral connotations in this context.

Bombers, when they constituted the backbone of deterrence, were bad because they were vulnerable to attack. Missiles, because they could be dispersed, protected in silos, or moved around and concealed underwater, were good; it was not so easy then for a surprise attack to destroy one's retaliatory capacity. Indeed, in the early 1960s it was believed that once both powers possessed invulnerable missiles, peace would be guaranteed because there would be no point in attacking. Moreover, it was expected that once each power had reached the level it needed to retaliate, the arms race would end.

MAD and Technological Innovation

It was these ideas that led the United States and Soviet Union during the 1970s to stop pursuing strategic defenses and to first freeze their offensive forces for a five-year period in SALT I, before negotiating equal ceilings in SALT II and proceeding to significant reductions in SALT III, or the renamed START I (see Table 13-1). In short, SALT was viewed as a process—a series of agreements that would be negotiated over time. But by the time SALT II was agreed on in 1979, arms control concepts were being undermined by technological innovations[22] and changes in military doctrines.[23]

Just as technology had stabilized mutual deterrence with single-warhead missiles that were not especially accurate (they were accurate enough to hit cities but not accurate enough to hit missiles in their silos), so technology in the 1970s appeared to be undermining this stability, first with multiple warheads (or MIRVs, multiple independently targeted reentry vehicles), and then with increasingly accurate guidance systems. MIRVs once more made it possible for both superpowers to strike first. If both the United States and the Soviet Union had, for example, 1,000 ICBMs with single warheads, a surprise attack on the other would not be feasible. On the assumption that it takes two warheads to destroy one missile, it would take 2,000 ICBMs to eliminate the opponent's 1,000 ICBMs. If, however, one side had three warheads per missile

Table 13-1 Provisions of SALTs I and II

	SALT I (1972)		SALT II[a]
	U.S.	USSR	U.S. and USSR
Total of all strategic delivery systems	1,710	2,358	2,250 (including bombers)
Intercontinental ballistic missiles (ICBMs)	1,054 (550 with MIRVs)	1,618 (minus 210 older ICBMs which could be scrapped and replaced by SLBMs)	820 (all with MIRVs: Soviets could keep 308 heavy missiles such as the SS-18 allowed by SALT I)
Submarine-launched ballistic missiles (SLBMs)	656 (496 with MIRVs)	740 (plus 210 SLBMs)	1,200 (SLBMs *and* ICBMs with MIRVs)
Bombers	(450, excluded under SALT I)	(150, excluded under SALT I)	1,320 (SLBMs, ICBMs with MIRVs, plus bombers with ALCMs)
			930 (single warhead ICBMs, SLBMs, and bombers without ALCMs)

NOTE: MIRVs = multiple independently targeted warheads or reentry vehicles; ALCMs = air-launched cruise missiles.

[a]Unratified by the United States. The Reagan administration, however, observed its limits until 1986.

and the other eight, then the latter gained the capability to destroy the former's missile sites with a fraction of its ICBM force. It would have ICBMs to spare. Missiles that had that capability were called counterforce weapons.

In fact, the United States had over 2,300 ICBM warheads, 1,500 of them on 500 Minuteman III missiles plus 500 on an additional 50 MX missiles. The Soviet Union had 1,400 ICBMs; 308 of these were the gigantic SS-18s, most with 10 warheads on each missile, and 350 were SS-19s with 6 warheads apiece, for a total of more than 6,000 warheads. Either the SS-18s or the SS-19s could destroy most of the 1,000 U.S. ICBM launchers by aiming five warheads against each silo.[24] Soviet military doctrine in the nuclear age heavily stressed striking first. If war was about to erupt, the Soviet Union would try to destroy as much of the U.S. retaliatory force as possible before it could be launched. It did not stress absorbing the first blow and then retaliating. Such a preemptive blow was usually referred to as a disarming or damage-limitation strike.

This trend toward counterforce attacks, as distinct from countercity or countervalue attacks, was worrisome for two reasons. First, for each side it placed a premium on striking first, "to use 'em [the ICBMs] or lose 'em," especially in a time of crisis when the superpowers confronted one another toe-to-toe. * Second, if both powers really believed that they could limit their strikes to the opponent's military forces and prevent an escalation to all-out nuclear war, they might have risked a nuclear attack in the belief that they could avoid mutual annihilation. Otto von Bismarck, the Prussian chancellor who united Germany in 1871, defined the so-called security dilemma well when he said that no "government, if it regards war as inevitable even if it does not want it, would be so foolish as to leave to the enemy the choice of time and occasion and to wait for the moment which is most convenient for the enemy"—even if a preventive war was, as he also called it, "committing suicide from the fear of death." [25]

Strategic Arms Control Record

If counterforce was not really compatible with stable mutual deterrence, what did that mean for arms control? There can be no question that arms control was popular with the public because of the association with better Soviet-American cold war relations. But the record of arms control regimes has been mixed (see Table 13-2).[26] Liberals were disillusioned with the high ceilings that they found incompatible with arms limitation. They charged that SALTs I and II allowed the arms race to go on; the agreements merely codified the existing forces each possessed and modernization plans. Indeed, they often pointed out that after more than a decade of arms control negotiations following SALT I, the superpowers' arsenals were much larger than they had been in 1972. Conservatives were upset because the SALT negotiations had not prevented the Soviet achievement of parity in the early 1970s or the modernization that increasingly threatened U.S. deterrent forces after 1972. They also accused Moscow of systematically violating the agreements it had signed in its continual quest for strategic superiority and a war-fighting and war-winning capability. But in fact, liberals and conservatives alike exaggerated both the promise and danger of arms control.

By establishing ceilings, arms control reduced the uncertainty each superpower had in estimating the other side's buildup. Not sure of the opponent's plans, each tended to make "worst-case" assumptions. The likely overestima-

---

* An illustrative situation occurred in 1988 in the Persian Gulf when the captain of the U.S. cruiser *Vincennes,* believing that an Iranian jet fighter armed with missiles was flying toward his ship, and recalling an earlier incident in which the U.S.S. *Stark* had allowed an Iraqi jet to get too close—resulting in the death of thirty-seven of its crew and a near sinking when the jet mistakenly attacked that ship—decided to fire his missiles. He destroyed instead an Iranian civilian airliner with 290 people on board. Trying to protect his ship, acting on available information, and having just three or four minutes to make a decision, the captain made the only rational decision he could in that compressed amount of time and in circumstances in which he had just been engaged in a fight with three Iranian attack boats and sunk two of them.

Table 13-2 Objectives of Nuclear Arms Control and Relevant Agreements

Objective	Agreement	Year
Quantitative and qualitative limits	SALT I ABM agreement	1972
Ceilings on strategic delivery systems	SALT I interim agreement on offensive arms	1972
	Vladivostok guidelines	1974
	SALT II[a]	1979
Reduction of strategic delivery systems including all land-based MIRVed ICBMs	START I[b]	1991
	Russian-American agreement[c]	1992
Eliminating all intermediate nuclear forces (INF)	INF agreement	1988
Direct communication between U.S. and Soviet leaders during crises	Hot-line agreement	1963
	Hot-line modernization agreement	1971
Barring nuclear weapons from specific regions	Antarctica treaty[d]	1959
	Outer-space treaty[d]	1967
	Seabed treaty[d]	1971
Discouragement of nuclear proliferation	International Atomic Energy Authority[c]	1954[b]
	Nonproliferation treaty[d]	1968
	Nuclear Suppliers' Club	1975
Limiting of nuclear tests	Limited test-ban treaty[d]	1963
	Threshold test-ban treaty[a]	1974[a]
	Peaceful nuclear explosion treaty[a]	1976[a]
Banning nonnuclear weapons of mass destruction	Biological weapons convention	1972

[a] Signed but not in force because of Senate refusal to ratify.

[b] Signed but not ratified by either the United States or the Soviet Union before its collapse.

[c] Russia.

[d] Multilateral agreements.

tion of what the opponent may have acquired—based on "it's better to be safe than sorry"—then resulted in overbuilding. This in turn caused the opponent to react, if not overreact, in an ever-upward cycle. Arms agreements therefore contributed to a more predictable atmosphere. This may in fact have been SALT's principal contribution to arms control regimes. For the United States, this was especially important because its knowledge of Soviet plans was bound to be less than Soviet knowledge of U.S. plans. In fact, Washington, using worst-case assumptions, thought it was facing "gaps" in bombers in the 1950s and missiles in the 1960s. Thus, the SALT process was a recognition by both superpowers of the dangers of an unconstrained arms race and of the need to moderate the security dilemma.

SALT also sought to preclude the defensive-offensive arms linkage. The development and deployment of defensive weapons would only escalate the offensive arms race in order to overwhelm any defensive shield and to still impose assured destruction on the enemy. Indeed, an effective defense that could protect the latter's population might lead to a first strike by the adversary. Deterrence would fail. The ABM treaty specifically recognized this defensive-offensive linkage; without a restriction on defensive weapons, restraining the offensive arms competition would be difficult. In one sense, then, the 1972 ABM agreement was the prerequisite for the SALT process, which included first freezing these forces in SALT I, establishing equal offensive ceilings in SALT II, and then reducing them in SALT III (which the Reagan administration retitled START for Strategic Arms Reduction Treaty).

Unfortunately, by the time SALT I had been negotiated, the United States had already begun to deploy multiple warheads. Thus, the defensive-offensive linkage helped *destabilize* a process whose central concern was the stabilization of mutual deterrence. MIRVs were the U.S. response to the Soviet deployment of an ABM system around Moscow, which, Washington believed, might be the prelude to a nationwide deployment. By multiplying the warheads on its missiles, the United States could overwhelm any Soviet defensive system and still destroy Soviet society. Had the SALT negotiations started in 1968, as they were supposed to, and had they not been delayed first by the Soviet invasion of Czechoslovakia and then by a change in American administrations, the use of MIRVs might have been stopped.[27] But by 1972 it was too late. The long-term impact of MIRVs was destabilizing. Ironically, the Reagan administration's START proposal was to cut the numbers of strategic launchers and warheads by 50 percent in order to reduce each side's counterforce capability, a capability that neither would possess but for MIRVs. But even more ironically, President Ronald Reagan had by this time introduced the Strategic Defense Initiative (SDI) to counter the threat of Soviet missiles to America's population and its ICBMs. Unlike SALT, however, START lacked a framework; there was no agreement within the administration, as noted earlier (Chapter 11), on the role of defensive systems in the deterrent equation. The president, indeed, clung to his vision of SDI and sought to substitute it for deterrence. Others in the administration wanted SDI to strengthen deterrence. Thus, the START treaty was concluded by President George Bush in 1991.

Because MIRVs were the cause of the rapid multiplication of U.S. and Soviet warheads and the subsequent destabilizing trend, why did the United States not give them up after 1972 when the SALT I treaty had ensured that America's single-warhead ICBMs could get through to deliver their assured destruction punch? The principal reason was the same one that had made arms control negotiations so difficult: in the bipolar competitive game, the side that gained what it believed to be a major technological breakthrough sought to exploit its perceived advantage.

Perhaps the best evaluation of the SALT process is the following:

> What is most striking about the arms control experience . . . is what it did not do. Those who hoped arms control would bring about major reductions in existing or planned inventories or slow the introduction of new and more capable technologies have little grounds for satisfaction. Nor do those who looked to arms control as a means for constraining the emergence of a large, modern Soviet arsenal capable of destroying a significant proportion of U.S. strategic retaliatory forces. Even the contributions of the ABM Treaty, arms control's chief accomplishment, are of uncertain durability. The treaty may merely have codified the postponement of a race in defensive systems until advancing technologies made effective defenses possible.
>
> What emerges above all is the modesty of what arms control has wrought. [It] has proved neither as promising as some had hoped nor as dangerous as others had feared.[28]

This conclusion should hardly be surprising. The fact that the two superpowers managed to negotiate arms control agreements at all is surprising. Historically, states have enhanced their security by unilateral measures, largely arms buildups. The idea that a nation that has become vulnerable should seek to supplement traditional military measures by cooperating with the adversary who threatens its security to *decrease* that security threat is a novel one. Cooperation among enemies is *not* the norm.[29] When it does happen, it is subjected to all the competitive pressures that made them rivals in the first place.

One of the ironic results of arms control regimes was their rechanneling of the arms competition from the weapons controlled to newer technologies. SALT I froze missile launchers because silos and submarines were easy to count; this constraint shifted the new race to multiple warheads. Just as in the Darwinian theory of natural selection, limitations on weapons simply stimulated the evolution of species not restrained.[30] Some of the most successful arms control agreements, taken to stabilize mutual deterrence, were not in fact formal bilateral agreements producing treaties but unilateral moves, such as the U.S. shift from bombers to the triad. Arms control became unavoidable in the nuclear age, but obviously it was not a magic cure for the arms race and the political rivalry that fed it. Yet it eased that rivalry, while also serving as an indication of improved superpower relations.[31]

THE POST-COLD WAR REVERSAL OF THE ARMS RACE

The ending of the cold war helped reverse the arms race. First, the START agreement cut the most destabilizing forces—Soviet land-based missiles with their multiple warheads—by 50 percent, thereby reducing the threat to the survival of American ICBMs. While the overall cut in strategic weapons was not 50 percent, the originally declared goal, but closer to 30 percent

Table 13-3 Outline of START I

Total (U.S. and Soviet) strategic delivery systems (ICBMs, SLBMs, bombers)	1,600
Total (U.S. and Soviet) strategic weapons (carried on delivery systems)	6,000[a]
Total (U.S. and Soviet) ballistic missile warheads	4,900
Reduction in Soviet heavy ICBMs	50%
Reduction in Soviet ballistic missile throw-weight (size of warhead)	50%

[a]If the cut had been approximately 50 percent for both countries.

SOURCES: Max M. Kampelman, "START: Completing the Task," *Washington Quarterly* (Summer 1989): 5-16; and Robert Einhorn, "Strategic Arms Reduction Talks: The Emerging START Agreement," *Survival* (September/October 1988): 387-401.

for the Soviet Union, cutting its warheads from 11,000 to 7,000, and 25 percent for the United States, cutting its warheads from 12,000 to 8,500, * reductions per se were not the objective. *Stabilizing reductions* was the aim (see Table 13-3).[32] President Bush also has proposed in a follow-up agreement with Russia that the two sides eliminate their MIRVed ICBMs and return to single-warhead missiles. Since the Russians have the most missiles with multiple warheads and the United States holds the advantage at sea, the Russians have asked for sizable cuts in SLBMs.

Second, President Bush followed up START I by unilaterally removing all tactical nuclear air, naval, and ground weapons in Europe and Asia. Simultaneously, he ended the 40-year-old 24-hour alert of U.S. bombers and the 450 ICBMs slated for elimination under START and suggested negotiations on the elimination of all MIRVed mobile ICBMs.[33] Soviet leader Mikhail Gorbachev responded with similar steps, saying the Soviet Union would lower the START I warhead levels to 5,000. And he proposed radically cutting strategic arms levels by about half after both countries had ratified START.

The collapse of the Soviet Union after August 1991 and its replacement by the Commonwealth of Independent States (CIS) ended the Soviet military threat. Although Russia inherited the former Soviet Union's nuclear arsenal, the possibility of a left- or right-wing government rising to power cannot be totally dismissed if the pro-democratic and economic market reforms should fail.

Nevertheless, at the first Bush-Yeltsin summit in June 1992, the United States and Russia struck what was undoubtedly the best deal in the history of arms control: additional radical cuts of all long-range missile warheads, and,

---

* Excluded from START were 3,000 U.S. and 1,800 Soviet bombs and short-range missiles carried by bombers and sea-launched cruise missiles.

most significantly, the elimination of all multiwarhead land-based missiles, plus a 50 percent reduction of U.S. MIRVed SLBMs. Thus, the two presidents cut the START treaty levels, agreed to in 1991, by about half—to 3,000-3,500 by the year 2003 or by the year 2000 if the United States offers additional assistance to Russia in dismantling its missiles and warheads—for a total cut of two-thirds from pre-START levels.* By abolishing the most threatening former Soviet nuclear weapons and deactivating all SS-18s immediately (the heart of the Soviet Union's arsenal), as well as the far smaller U.S. MIRVed ICBM force composed of 50 MXs and removing two of the three warheads on the Minuteman III, the two leaders eliminated the weapons that had most threatened the stability of mutual deterrence.[34] Although the United States and Russia were no longer enemies, and President Yeltsin had declared that Russian missiles were no longer aimed at the United States, the nuclear balance now reverted to the mutual deterrence of the pre-MIRV era. The U.S. nuclear triad, instead of being based on the approximately equal capabilities of its three components, would be based primarily on submarines and bombers, with relatively few on ICBMs. Clearly, the reversed arms race had accelerated to unbelievably low levels in what Bush and Yeltsin have called the new era of "friendship and partnership founded on mutual trust and respect and a common commitment to democracy and economic freedom."[35]

In Retrospect: Mutual Vulnerability and Mutual Cooperation

The nuclear peace between the United States and Soviet Union held for three reasons.[36] First, the enormous destructive power of each nuclear weapon, multiplied by their huge stockpiles (even after a 50 percent reduction of both superpowers), meant that nuclear war risked national survival. Even if a nuclear exchange had begun with attacks primarily restricted to bomber bases and missile fields, it is likely that such a "limited nuclear war" would have in the heat of battle escalated to attacks on cities.[37] Second, if either side had ever been tempted to undertake a preemptive strike, many things probably would have gone wrong operationally, so that such a first strike would not have succeeded in destroying most of the opponent's ICBM/bomber retaliatory capability. The likelihood that a small percentage would have survived to be used in a retaliatory blow meant that a first strike became too great a risk to take. Third, this risk was even greater because of the large size and diversity of strategic forces. There was safety in both the numbers of weapons and the possession of the triad, which complicated an attacker's effort to destroy its adversary's deterrent forces and made it more difficult to defend against a retaliatory blow.[38] Submarines, especially the American ones, remained the most invulnerable. As the range of their missiles increased, they roamed over

---

* Because the Soviets had run out of money, Congress had already voted $400 million from the Defense Department budget to help dismantle and destroy Soviet nuclear and chemical weapons. U.S. experts were sent over to the four nuclear republics (Russia, Ukraine, Belarus, and Kazakhstan) to assist.

larger areas of the ocean, making themselves ever harder to find. In fact, if necessary, they could have fired from their home ports and reached their target—as could have the latest Soviet submarines. Altogether, then, the likelihood of committing suicide remained much too high for either side to risk launching a first strike.

The fear of a nuclear Armageddon, a fear shared by both the United States and the Soviet Union, had thus been the best guarantee of peace. For better or worse, regardless of specific weapons systems or military doctrines, the post-1945 world had been a MAD one. In the words of Thomas Schelling, "I like the notion that East and West have exchanged hostages on a massive scale and that as long as they are unprotected, civilization depends on the avoidance of military aggression that could escalate to nuclear war." [39] With nuclear weapons, it had no longer been a question of seeking victory. A preemptive strike had been much too risky; if it had failed, the result would have been a catastrophe. And that was really the basic point: victory had been very unlikely, annihilation virtually certain. Thus, neither superpower's leaders had risked taking the steps that might have escalated into a nuclear war.

In these circumstances, the avoidance of nuclear war had been the only sensible course. But neither power could by taking only unilateral measures make itself more secure. U.S.-Soviet security had become interdependent; each one's security had become dependent on what the other did. While each power continued to take unilateral steps to improve its security, they had to be supplemented by bilateral cooperation. Realist theory may focus on the conflict of interests between states, but as these arms control negotiations suggest, cooperation among adversaries was required as well. The U.S.-Soviet relationship had increasingly become an *adversary partnership*. [40] Despite their long rivalry, their desire to survive also compelled them to cooperate on arms control. Their rivalry accounted for the difficulties encountered in both arriving at and maintaining agreements. Suspicion that one or the other might be cheating to gain an advantage was inherent in their adversarial relationship. That they continued to negotiate on arms control despite their conflicts, often angry feelings, and bitter words of denunciation, testified to the powerful impact of nuclear weapons. Cooperation among adversaries, it is worth repeating, is not normal in international politics; the security dilemma is more often the norm. But confronted by the threat to their existence, the Soviet Union and United States had little choice but to collaborate, for neither power could ensure its survival by going to war. Indeed, that virtually guaranteed their complete destruction. Thus, at a time that nuclear war could serve no rational purpose, arms control agreements were tantamount to mutual antisuicide pacts. International politics is essentially a zero-sum game—"what I gain in power or security, you lose." But nuclear weapons mitigated the great powers' security dilemma in the post-World War II international system and helped keep the peace.

For Review

1. What are the principal effects of a nuclear explosion?
2. What impact have nuclear weapons had on warfare, traditionally the ultimate instrument of persuasion?
3. What were the requirements of deterrence?
4. How did arms control help "stabilize" mutual deterrence?
5. What was the record of U.S.-Soviet arms control negotiations?
6. What were the basic reasons that the United States and Soviet Union were able to avoid a nuclear war?

Notes

1. Edward H. Carr, *Twenty Years' Crisis, 1919-1939* (London: Macmillan, 1951), 109.
2. See, for example, Immanuel Kant, *Perpetual Peace,* trans. Carl J. Friedrich in *Inevitable Peace* (Cambridge, Mass.: Harvard University Press, 1948), 251-252.
3. Bertrand de Jouvenel, *On Power,* trans. J. F. Huntington (Boston: Beacon Press, 1962), 148.
4. The interrelations between war and industrial power are well treated in *War and Human Progress* by John U. Nef (Cambridge, Mass.: Harvard University Press, 1950); and in *Men in Arms,* rev. ed., by Richard A. Preston and Sidney F. Wise (New York: Praeger, 1970), 176ff. For the impact of democratization and industrialization on U.S. military performance, see Walter Millis, *Arms and Men* (New York: New American Library, 1956).
5. Arthur T. Hadley, *The Nation's Safety and Arms Control* (New York: Viking, 1961), 4.
6. Ralph E. Lapp, *Kill and Overkill* (New York: Basic Books, 1962), 37; and Scientists' Committee for Radiation Information, "Effects of Nuclear Explosives," in *No Place to Hide,* ed. Seymour Melman (New York: Grove Press, 1962), 98-107. Also see Richard Rhodes, *The Making of the Atomic Bomb* (New York: Simon & Schuster, 1988).
7. A vivid account of a fire storm is given in *The Night Hamburg Died* by Martin Caidin (New York: Ballantine, 1960), 80-105, 129-141. The German estimate of those killed by British bombers in Hamburg was 60,000. The U.S. B-29 attack on Tokyo, March 9-10, 1945, burned up sixteen square miles and killed 84,000 people, most of whom were burned to death or died from wounds caused by fire. The Hiroshima atom bomb killed 72,000 people. The most destructive attack ever, however, was the two-day Anglo-American bombing of Dresden in February 1945: 135,000 people were killed. On this attack, see David Irving, *The Destruction of Dresden* (New York: Holt, Rinehart & Winston, 1964). For the origins of the city bombing undertaken by the United States and what the author critically calls "the creation of Armageddon" in the subtitle, see Michael S. Sherry, *The Rise of American Air Power* (New Haven, Conn.: Yale University Press, 1987).
8. Lapp, *Kill and Overkill,* 53-54.
9. Ibid., 77.
10. Office of Technology Assessment, *Effects of Nuclear War* (Washington, D.C.: Gov-

ernment Printing Office, 1980), 159.

11. Ibid., 159.

12. Paul R. Ehrlich, Carl Sagan et al., *The Cold and the Dark* (New York: Norton, 1984). In the same genre, with no pretense at being "scientific," see Jonathan Schell, *The Fate of the Earth* (New York: Avon Books, 1982). For a critical appraisal of the "nuclear winter" and its impact on nuclear strategy, see Albert Wohlstetter, "Between Unfree World and None," *Foreign Affairs* (Summer 1985): 962-994; and for an appraisal of its scientific basis, see Stanley L. Thompson and Stephen H. Schneider, "Nuclear Winter Reappraised," *Foreign Affairs* (Summer 1986): 981-1005; and a *Path Where No Man Thought*, appropriately subtitled *Nuclear Winter and the End of the Arms Race* (New York: Random House, 1991), another gloomy assessment of the future despite the end of the cold war.

13. Glenn H. Snyder, "Balance of Power in the Missile Age," *Journal of International Affairs* 14 (1960): 21-34.

14. This continuing concern with different strategies and changing weapons systems is discussed by William W. Kaufmann, *The McNamara Strategy* (New York: Harper & Row, 1964). For overall views of U.S. strategy and arms control, respectively, see Lawrence Freedman, *The Evolution of Nuclear Strategy* (New York: St. Martin's Press, 1981); Gregg Herken, *Counsels of War*, rev. ed. (New York: Oxford University Press, 1987); and Charles L. Glazer, *Analyzing Strategic Nuclear Policy* (Princeton, N.J.: Princeton University Press, 1991).

15. Fine introductions to the field of arms control can be found in Hedley Bull, *The Control of the Arms Race*, 2d ed. (New York: Holt, Rinehart & Winston, 1965); and Thomas C. Schelling and Morton H. Halperin, *Strategy and Arms Control*, 2d ed. (Elmsford, N.Y.: Pergamon-Brassey, 1985).

16. In Schelling's words:

    The "equalizer" of the Old West [the pistol] made it possible for *either* man to kill the other; it did not assure that *both* would be killed. . . . The advantage of shooting first aggravates any incentive to shoot. As the survivor might put it, "He was about to kill me in self-defense, so I had to kill him in self-defense." Or, "He, thinking I was about to kill him in self-defense, was about to kill me in self-defense, so I had to kill him in self-defense." But if both were assured of living long enough to shoot back with unimpaired aim, there would be no advantage in jumping the gun and little reason to fear that the other would try it.

    Thomas C. Schelling, *Strategy of Conflict* (Cambridge, Mass.: Harvard University Press, 1960), 232-233 (emphasis in original).

17. Ibid., 231.

18. Ibid., 232.

19. For an early discussion of the lack of payoff that the Soviet Union might achieve from a position of strategic superiority, see Benjamin S. Lambeth, "Deterrence in the MIRV Era," *World Politics* (January 1972), 221ff.

20. David Holloway, *The Soviet Union and the Arms Race*, 2d ed. (New Haven, Conn.: Yale University Press, 1984), 49. McGeorge Bundy, *Danger and Survival* (New York: Random House, 1988), 606-607.

21. Jerome B. Wiesner et al., *ABM: An Evaluation of the Decision to Deploy an Antiballistic Missile System* (New York: Signet, 1969); and Johan J. Holst and William Schneider, Jr., eds., *Why ABM? Policy Issues in the Missile Defense Controversy* (New York: Pergamon Press, 1969).

22. Matthew Evangelista, *Innovation and the Arms Race* (Ithaca, N.Y.: Cornell University Press, 1988).

23. Derek Leebaert, ed., *Soviet Military Thinking* (Boston: Allen & Unwin, 1981); and Joseph D. Douglas, Jr. and Amoretta M. Hoeber, *Soviet Strategy for Nuclear War* (Stanford, Calif.: Hoover Institution Press, 1979). For the United States, see Desmond Ball and Jeffrey Richelson, *Strategic Nuclear Targeting* (Ithaca, N.Y.: Cornell University Press, 1988).

24. Robbin F. Laird and Dale R. Herspring, *The Soviet Union and Strategic Arms* (Boulder, Colo.: Westview Press, 1984), 53-54.

25. Quoted by Fritz Fischer, *The War of Illusions* (New York: Norton, 1975), 377, 461.

26. Albert Carnesdale and Richard N. Haass, eds., *Superpower Arms Control* (Cambridge, Mass.: Ballinger, 1987).

27. Raymond L. Garthoff, "SALT: An Evaluation," *World Politics* (October 1978): 20-21.

28. Carnesdale and Haass, *Superpower Arms Control*, 1,355; Condoleezza Rice, "SALT and the Search for a Security Regime," in *U.S.-Soviet Security Cooperation*, ed., Alexander L. George, Philip J. Farley, and Alexander Dallin (New York: Oxford University Press, 1988), 293-306; and April Carter, *Success and Failure in Arms Control Negotiations* (New York: Oxford University Press, 1982).

29. Rice, "SALT and the Search for a Security Regime," 302.

30. Bruce D. Berkowitz, *Calculated Risks* (New York: Simon & Schuster, 1987).

31. Alan B. Sheer, *The Other Side of Arms Control* (Winchester, Mass.: Allen & Unwin, 1988). See Michael Mandelbaum, *The Other Side of the Table* (New York: Council on Foreign Relations, 1990), for the Soviet side of arms control negotiations.

32. Robert Einhorn, "Strategic Arms Reduction Talks: The Emerging START Agreement," *Survival* (September/October 1988): 390; and Max M. Kampelman (the Reagan administration's START negotiator), "START: Completing the Task," *Washington Quarterly* (Summer 1989): 5-7.

33. Andrew Rosenthal, "U.S. to Give Up Short-Range Nuclear Arms: Bush Seeks Further Cuts and Further Talks," and Michael R. Gordon, "The Nuclear Specter," *New York Times*, September 28, 1991.

34. Michael Wines, "Bush and Yeltsin Agree to Cut Long-Range Atomic Warheads; Scrap Key Land-Based Missiles"; and Thomas L. Friedman, "Reducing the Russian Arms Threat," *New York Times*, June 17, 1992.

35. Michael Wines, "Bush and Yeltsin Declare Formal End to Cold War: Agree to Exchange Visits," *New York Times*, February 2, 1992. Also from the *New York Times*, see Andrew Rosenthal, "Bush and Yeltsin Propose Deep Cuts in Atomic Weapons," January 30, 1992; Serge Schmemann, "Yeltsin Describes His Cutbacks in Arms," January 30, 1992; and Thomas L. Friedman, "U.S. and Russia See New Arms Accords for a July Summit," February 19, 1992.

36. Robert Jervis, *The Illogic of American Nuclear Strategy* (Ithaca, N.Y.: Cornell University Press, 1984); and Spurgeon M. Keeny and Wolfgang K. H. Panofsky, "MAD vs. NUTS: The Mutual Hostage Relationship of the Superpowers," *Foreign Affairs* (Winter 1981/82): 287-304.

37. Desmond Ball, "Can Nuclear War Be Controlled?" (London: International Institute for Strategic Studies, 1981). Also see Paul Bracken, *The Command and Control of Nuclear Forces* (New Haven, Conn.: Yale University Press, 1983); and Bruce G. Blair, *Strategic Command and Control* (Washington, D.C.: Brookings, 1985). But for the devastating consequences of even a limited nuclear war, see William Daugherty, Barbara Levi, and Frank von Hippel, "The Consequences of 'Limited' Nuclear

Attacks on the United States," *International Security* (Spring 1986): 3-45.

38. Michael M. May, "The U.S.-Soviet Approach to Nuclear Weapons," *International Security* (Spring 1985): 487; Joseph S. Nye, Jr., "Farewell to Arms Control?" *Foreign Affairs* (Fall 1986): 1-20; and Nye, "The Role of Strategic Nuclear Systems in Deterrence," *Washington Quarterly* (Spring 1988): 50.

39. Thomas C. Schelling, "What Went Wrong with Arms Control?" *Foreign Affairs* (Winter 1985/86): 233.

40. Interesting reinterpretations of Soviet deterrence can be found in Raymond Gerthoff, *Deterrence and the Reduction in Soviet Military Doctrine* (Washington, D.C.: Brookings Institution, 1990); and Michael MccGwire, *Perestroika and Soviet National Security* (Washington, D.C.: Brookings Institution, 1991); and Charles L. Glazer, "Nuclear Policy without an Adversary: Planning for the Post-Soviet Era," *International Security* (Spring 1992): 34-78.

CHAPTER 14

The Use
of Force

LIMITED WAR: RESTRAINT IN THE NUCLEAR AGE

Nuclear weapons made all-out war suicidal for the superpowers; only a "limited war could be used safely to advance their purposes." [1] Although the use of total force was considered irrational, it did not follow that *any* use of violence was irrational. The two superpowers could directly, or indirectly through allies and friends, pursue their goals through limited wars, conventional or unconventional. Even after World War II when the United States enjoyed virtual immunity from attack, it was not rational to fight a total war in response to a limited provocation. The credibility of commitments is related to the importance of the interests at stake. A power may risk a major war in defense of itself and its principal allies but not of lesser states in areas of secondary concern. The ineffectiveness of threats of all-out war in deterring limited Soviet probes was clearly demonstrated when North Korea attacked South Korea in June 1950. The Soviets were apparently quite willing to acquiesce in, if not initiate, this use of force by an ally, despite the United States' overwhelming strategic superiority. Obviously, they did not expect direct U.S. retaliation in response to North Korea's invasion of South Korea. The subsequent war in Korea became a model for the only kind of warfare possible between the nuclear powers and, in this respect, was an additional reason why, despite the post-1945 superpower rivalry, an all-out war was avoided. But at the same time because Korea—like Vietnam later—was a protracted conflict and, therefore, costly in lives, and because the possibility of escalation involving the superpowers was always present, the end result was to reinforce the reluctance to use force to advance the United States' interests. The Soviets, too, before the end of the cold war learned that in the post-1945 world, contrary to traditional power calculations, big nations did not win small wars.

Definition of Limits

In the post-1945 world, a limited war was a war fought for limited political purposes.[2] In contrast to the aims of total war, which generally included the complete destruction of the enemy's military forces and government, perhaps the most obvious goal of limited war was the capture or recapture of strategically located or economically important territory. In the Korean War, for example, the North sought to take over the South and to establish Communist control over the entire Korean peninsula; the North then would have, in the metaphor used by the Japanese, "pointed the Korean dagger straight at Japan's heart." After Nationalist China's collapse, the United States needed Japan as an ally. It thus had to defend South Korea; otherwise Japan would have been neutralized.

Another reason for U.S. intervention in Korea was to preserve the recently formed North Atlantic Treaty Organization. Europeans remembered America's retreat into isolationism after World War I. Was the United States' just-proclaimed commitment to Western Europe's defense then a credible one? Through the United Nations, the United States had sponsored an election that had brought the South Korean government into power and then had assisted the new government with military and economic aid. Would the United States defend its protégé or abandon it? The United States had little choice but to defend South Korea to keep the confidence of its NATO allies.

Moreover, the United States was concerned with a broader goal. President Harry Truman recalled that during the 1930s the democracies had not moved to halt the aggressions by Germany, Italy, or Japan. This failure to do so eventually led to World War II. The United States wanted a postwar world free from aggression. Failure to act in South Korea might encourage further Communist inroads.[3]

All these objectives could be ensured by defending South Korea; they did not require, as in past American wars, the complete defeat of the enemy. In short, U.S. goals were limited and compatible with restoring the status quo. They did not require the enemy's unconditional surrender or the removal of its government. To forget the goal was to risk escalating the war.

The Victor's Restraint and the Opponent's Survival. In limited war the existence of the opponent's state could not become the issue—the first constraint of limited war. Halting the opponent's violations of one's interests was the issue. Unconditional surrender or total victory could not be the goal. The "winner" on the battlefield therefore had to forego winning a total victory; the "loser" would then not be compelled to escalate the conflict by, for example, calling on friends to intervene. The Korean War again provides a good example of this situation. The United States at first sought only the restoration of the status quo. But once the North Korean forces had been driven back to the thirty-eighth parallel, the United States, seeing an opportunity to unify all Korea and to destroy a Soviet satellite regime, changed its objective. But by turning around the dagger once aimed at Japan and thus endangering the political survival of the North Korean regime, the United States provoked Chinese intervention.[4] China's entry into the conflict intensified the fighting and risked escalating the war even more. Leaders in Washington, afraid that striking back against China *in* China would trap the United States into a full-scale war on the Asian mainland or precipitate World War III, reverted therefore to their original aim. They had learned the consequences of what could occur in the nuclear age if the United States followed its historic policy of seeking a total victory on the battlefield.

Noninvolvement of Major Powers.   The forces of the cold war rivals also had to avoid engaging each other directly if a war was to be limited. Even their participation in combat increased the difficulty of controlling the conflict. The United States and the Soviet Union seemed to be well aware of this second constraint. They were extremely careful about where they confronted each other, as in Western Europe. Incidents involving direct clashes between American and Soviet forces were scrupulously avoided.

It is significant that the Korean War occurred outside of Europe and in an area from which U.S. forces had been withdrawn. After the U.S. intervention, the fighting was between the troops of North Korea, the Soviet Union's ally, and the troops fighting under the flag of the United Nations. The Communist Chinese troops that later intervened were not sent officially by the Chinese government. The government in Beijing never declared war and never accepted responsibility for the Chinese troops in Korea who were declared to be "volunteers." Nor did the United States declare war on North Korea or on Communist China; U.S. troops were regarded as part of the UN force fighting a "police action." The absence of a declaration of war and the use of volunteers may seem rather obvious fictions, yet such fictions help keep wars limited.

Geographical Constraints.   A third constraint was geographical: limited wars generally were confined to the territory of a single nation. The Yalu River served as the frontier between North Korea and China during the Korean War, and even after the Chinese intervention the war was not extended beyond it. Bombers were not sent to hit targets in Manchuria. The Korean War was thus fought only in Korea (see Figure 14-1). Moreover, each side allowed the other some clearly demarcated "privileged sanctuaries"—inviolable areas for reserve troops, supplies, and air and naval bases. In a limited war, to attack these areas was to risk removing one of the constraints on the scope of the conflict. Manchuria was such a sanctuary for the Communists during the Korean War, although many in the United States demanded that it be bombed. The United States also possessed privileged sanctuaries within the actual area of the fighting. For example, no air attacks were launched against either Pusan or Inchon, the two largest ports through which most of the supplies for the UN forces were channeled. If either port had been bombed frequently, UN operations might have been seriously hampered. Similarly, Communist Chinese jet fight-

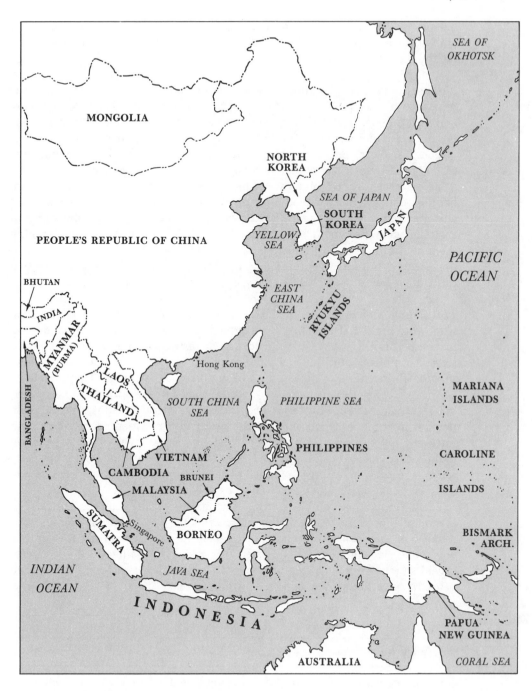

Figure 14-1 Far East and Southeast Asia

ers did not attack UN troops in the field, American air bases in South Korea, or aircraft carriers off the coast; instead, they were limited to the Yalu River area, defending the bridges.

Nonuse of Nuclear Weapons.   A final constraint on limited wars was the refusal to use tactical or battlefield nuclear weapons. If these weapons were employed, the critical dividing line between conventional and nuclear weapons would have been crossed and a dangerous precedent set. Once a small "tactical" nuclear weapon is used, escalation is unavoidable, for by what logic can larger "strategic" weapons be refused if they can be used more efficiently against larger targets? Nuclear weapons of any kind were also a political liability. The stigma attached to their use was such that whatever military advantage they might have offered would have been offset by the storm of criticism their use would have aroused worldwide, even from allies, making them politically counterproductive. This would especially have been the case if nuclear weapons had been used again against Asians, stirring accusations that the United States used them only against nonwhite races.

Limitations and Escalation.   When these principal constraints were present, wars were limited. The belligerents agreed to these limits by *tacit* bargaining on the battlefield. However ridiculous such restrictions might have appeared from the military point of view, the principal aim of observing them was to provide an incentive to the enemy to accept similar restraints. The limitations had to be clearly drawn; precisely because they were *not* formally negotiated but tacitly agreed on, the terms had to be qualitatively distinguishable from possible alternatives. Frontiers and the distinction between conventional and nuclear weapons were so crystal clear that it was relatively easy to agree on them tacitly; once these limits had been violated, however, it was far more difficult to draw new lines. Nonuse of tactical nuclear arms was simple and unambiguous, easily understood and observed.[5]

These limitations, moreover, tended to reinforce one another; conversely, the more that were violated, the more tenuous the limitation. Because the removal of each constraint tended to weaken the capacity to limit the conflict, when one side did escalate, this step was taken only after the most careful consideration. After each step up the escalation ladder, cautious leaders had to pause to see whether the opponent would desist.[6]

GUERRILLA WARFARE

Guerrilla conflict, even more than conventional limited war, reflected the restraints imposed on the use of force by nuclear weapons. The Soviets called these kinds of conflicts wars of "national liberation." In the developing countries, guerrillas aimed to capture state power in an effort to use it to completely transform the social and political structures and economic organizations of their country.

One advantage of such wars over conventional limited wars was that they did not raise the issue of aggression and the response to that aggression (as in Korea) as clearly; the initiators remained free of the stigma *aggressor*. There was no single moment when a major attack commenced across a well-defined frontier. David Galula, an expert on such conflicts, compared conventional warfare and revolutionary warfare:

> In the conventional war, the aggressor who has prepared for it within the confines of his national territory, channeling his resources into the preparation, has much to gain by attacking suddenly with all his forces. The transition from peace to war is as abrupt as the state of the art allows; the first shock may be decisive. This is hardly possible in the revolutionary war because the aggressor— the insurgent—lacks sufficient strength at the outset. Indeed, years may sometimes pass before he has built up significant political, let alone military, power. So there is usually little or no first shock, little or no surprise, no possibility of an early decisive battle. In fact, the insurgent has no interest in producing a shock until he feels fully able to withstand the enemy's expected reaction.[7]

Guerrilla wars also tended to be lengthy. If the guerrillas were as strong as, or stronger than, their opponent, they would seek quick victory in conventional battle. But their very weakness compelled them to whittle away at the enemy's strength bit by bit. This process of attrition could go almost unnoticed in the outside world until the last stage of the war, when the guerrillas were poised to defeat their weakened and demoralized opponent. By then it was usually too late for effective countermeasures, especially military intervention by a friendly external government seeking to help the local government. Thus, in the nuclear age waging guerrilla warfare was considerably safer than fighting a regular war.

Guerrilla Strategy and Tactics

In the initial phase of a revolutionary war, the weaker guerrillas are strategically on the defensive; tactically, however, they are always on the offensive. To wear down the enemy they adopt *hit-and-run* tactics. Mobility, surprise, and rapid military decisions characterize their operations. They fight only when there is a good chance of victory; otherwise, they do not attack and, if engaged, quickly disengage. Their attacks are swift, sudden, and relentless. There is no front line in such a war. The front is everywhere, and the guerrillas can strike anywhere. Guerrilla tactical doctrine is perhaps most aptly summed up in Mao Zedong's well-known formula: "Enemy advances, we retreat; enemy halts, we harass; enemy tires, we attack; enemy retreats, we pursue."[8]

Rather than inflicting major defeats on the enemy, these tactics result in harassment, confusion, and frustration. The guerrillas do not engage in conventional battle until the last stage of the war because they are too weak throughout most of the hostilities. Physical violence is important, but it is the *psychological impact* of the war that is decisive. Although the enemy cannot be beaten physically, its *will to fight* can be eroded in two ways. First, the regular army can be demoralized. Suffering one minor defeat after another, rarely engaging the enemy directly in battle, and forced increasingly on the defensive by the guerrillas' tactics, the army loses its offensive spirit as it finds its conventional tactics useless. The determination to stay and fight declines, and stamina is sapped.

Second, and even more important in undermining the enemy's will to fight, are measures taken to isolate the government either by capturing the support of most of the population or by neutralizing popular support for the regime in power. Control of the population is essential if the guerrillas are to achieve their objective of internal conquest. The populace provides them with recruits, food, shelter, and, above all, intelligence. To surprise the enemy, guerrillas must know where to strike and when. To be able to choose favorable moments to fight and then to escape when government reinforcements suddenly arrive, they must know all their opponent's moves.

Victory is one way of impressing the people. As government troops become demoralized and defensive and as they increasingly appear unable to provide the population with elementary security in daily life, the government loses whatever allegiance it has had. It is the peasants—the majority—who are most concerned about their future. If they think the guerrillas will win the war, they are unlikely to antagonize them but will cooperate instead. Selective terrorism also helps to elicit cooperation. Its aim is to reaffirm the weakness of the government by attacking mainly local government officials. Obviously, wholesale and indiscriminate terrorism would alienate the very people whose support the guerrillas seek to win, although on occasion massive execution or the burning of an entire village is used to influence other villages and towns. The guerrillas have made their point vividly when they can show the peasants that the government is not able to protect even its own officials.[9] Furthermore, by eliminating these officials, often with all the villagers forced to watch, the guerrillas break the link between the government and the majority of the people, restricting the government's authority largely to the cities.

Guerrillas, however, achieve popular support mainly because of an effective *social strategy* in which they identify themselves with a popular cause or grievance.[10] Thus, Communist guerrillas, for example, would not usually present themselves as Communists, nor would the people support them because they are Communists or because they desire establishment of a Communist state. Guerrillas present themselves simply as representatives for existing social causes and aspirations. If the people are resentful of a despotic native government, the guerrillas take up the cry. If certain classes seek social and economic justice, the guerrillas demand it in their behalf. The guerrillas identify themselves as liberators and reformers, promising that they can satisfy rising expectations. In South Vietnam, for example, the Viet Cong appealed to the peasants by pointing out that they were working in the landowners' rice fields for the landowners' benefits. When the landlords fled to the cities, the Viet Cong told the peasants that they no longer had to pay exorbitant and exploitative rents (or taxes); the peasants owned the land, and the Viet Cong would protect them if anyone sought to take it away. The result was a deep schism between the government in Saigon and the peasantry.

This social strategy is basic to the guerrillas' revolutionary warfare. Although the military component is important, it is neither the most significant nor the most distinguishing characteristic of this particular kind of war, especially as it has been waged by Communist parties whose entire social outlook was based on a class analysis and class struggle. Indeed, the struggle begins before the military phase of the war begins. In each village and hamlet the revolutionary party establishes its cells, seeks local control and support, and thus diminishes the base of popular support for the government. That a large proportion of the population tends to be neutral in the war, waiting to see who is likely to win, is partly the result of this *preemptive* social strategy. Whereas the revolutionaries' maximum goal is to mobilize the population to fight with them against the government, their minimum aim is to prevent the population from fighting on the government's side.

As the war goes on, the government becomes increasingly isolated socially and weakened militarily, so that only a final blow is needed to topple it. This last step involves conventional battle unless, as in Cuba and South Vietnam before American intervention, the entire governmental structure and authority have already disintegrated. The defeat of the French forces at Dien Bien Phu in Indochina in 1954 broke France's determination to hold onto its old colony, yet the French garrison at Dien Bien Phu consisted of only one-fifteenth of the total number of French troops in Indochina. The French suffered 12,000 casualties, including prisoners, but the estimated Vietminh casualties were greater—15,000. Since its total force was not as large as that of the French, the Vietminh clearly had been badly hurt. Nonetheless, this single battle sapped France's will to resist.[11] The French decided to end the long and—for them—futile fighting.

Guerrilla warfare may at times seem militarily primitive, for guerrilla weapons do not begin to compare with the highly intricate weapons in Western arsenals. Guerrillas may receive sophisticated weapons, but their success does not depend on them. Politically, however, guerrilla warfare is "more sophisticated than nuclear war or . . . war as it was waged by conventional armies, navies, and air forces."[12]

Primacy of Political over Military Factors

No counterrevolutionary war can be won by conventional military means alone: *a purely military solution is impossible.* Interestingly, the successful guerrilla and counter guerrilla leaders of the past two decades have not been military men.[13] In China, Mao—a student, a librarian, and subsequently a professionally trained revolutionary—defeated Chiang Kai-shek, a professionally trained soldier. In Indochina, Ho Chi Minh, a socialist agitator, and Gen. Vo Nguyen Giap, a French-educated history teacher, defeated four of France's senior generals. Fidel Castro was a lawyer, and Ramón Magsaysay, who led the counter guerrilla war in the Philippines, was an automotive mechanic turned politician. In short, the orthodox military officer has generally been unable to cope with the unorthodox nature of guerrilla warfare.

In the final analysis, the government can win its war against the revolutionaries only if it alleviates the conditions that led the peasantry to support the revolutionary party in the first place. For example, in Malaya (now Malaysia) the British promised independence during the war there from 1946 to 1960. Because they had already granted independence to India, Pakistan, and Burma, their word was credible, and the Malayans had a stake in the government's struggle. The Communists were thus stripped of their guise as liberators from colonialism. Many Malays fought alongside British troops. The contrast with the situation in Vietnam is striking. In the first Indochina War from 1946 to 1954, the people supported the Vietminh as national liberators because the French refused to grant them full independence. Ho Chi Minh became a symbol of Vietnamese nationalism. Anti-Communist Vietnamese who had fought with the French against the Vietminh (as anti-Communist Malays had fought with the British) were never able to compete with Ho for this nationalist identity. After 1954 they appeared to many—including many in the West—as puppets of France. This image was reinforced by their lack of social conscience and concern. Indeed, the government's suppression of political opponents, critics of the war, and advocates of settlement with the Viet Cong only fortified this image.[14]

Popular confidence, then, is the indispensable condition for successful antirevolutionary warfare. Military countermeasures alone are never adequate; troops trained in the tactics of unconventional warfare must be supported by political, social, and economic reforms.[15] The major task of antirevolutionary warfare is thus fundamentally *political*. Guerrillas are a barometer of discontent, which must be ameliorated, as it is the decisive element in victory or failure. Perhaps the French experience in Algeria offers the clearest evidence. By 1960, the French had actually won the military war against the Algerian guerrillas. The Algerian National Liberation Army no longer possessed even a battalion-sized unit. And by the end of the war in 1962, the Algerian guerrillas had, according to French army sources, fewer than 4,000 troops left (10,000, according to other, more sympathetic French sources) out of a total of almost 60,000 three years earlier.[16] French military tactics therefore had been as effective in Algeria as they had been ineffective in Indochina. Nevertheless, the French lost the war because it could not be won *politically*. The Algerian population was hostile; so were France's NATO allies and the nonaligned states. The suppression of a nationalist movement was politically unpalatable and infeasible in an age in which the right of all former colonies to rule themselves was almost universally recognized and asserted. In such circumstances, the use of conventional military force may be self-defeating.

THE UNITED STATES IN VIETNAM AND THE SOVIET UNION IN AFGHANISTAN

Vietnam War

The preceding analysis should largely explain why in the second Indochina War from 1965 to 1973 it was difficult for the United States to cope with guerrilla warfare in Vietnam.[17] American military leaders had been trained traditionally. They saw this war, like other wars, as essentially a military, not a political, undertaking.[18] All that was necessary, they believed, was to apply American technology and know-how to the problem. Could the world's mightiest nation, with its huge army led by well-trained officers and supported by the might and knowledge of American industry, not defeat a few thousand black-clad Asian guerrillas? It was easy to indulge in the illusion of omnipotence. The United States had, after all, beaten far greater powers. France's earlier failure was blamed on the alienation of the Vietnamese nationalists and on an army that was not well equipped or led and had poor air support. Presumably, none of these factors would hamper the United States. It, after all, was a *superpower*. Precisely because of that, the United States—like the Soviet Union later in Afghanistan—overestimated its power and underestimated that of its adversary.[19] If the superpowers could match each other, they surely would overwhelm small opponents.

Hubris (the Greek word for overweening pride), then, proved a great impediment for the United States in understanding on which kind of a war it was embarking and how it could prevail in such a conflict, if that was in fact possible. In effect, the United States was so powerful and so sure of success that it believed it could fight a guerrilla war simply by changing the rules and fighting according to the American concept of war.[20] This concept emphasized fighting a conventional war in Vietnam and achieving victory through the attrition of the enemy's forces.[21] The soldier's concern was strictly military; politics was not the military's business. This division of labor suggested that the crucial political reforms would be postponed until after the guerrillas had been defeated. The additional advantage, according to the military, was that the United States would be fighting the war, thereby avoiding the difficulties and frustrations of cooperating with the ineffective South Vietnamese army, which was expected only to stay out of the way. But this policy and ordering of priorities guaranteed failure. Surely the war could not be won primarily by foreign troops; instead, an indigenous army with a will to fight and support from a sizable portion of its people was required. Indeed, how could the South Vietnamese government establish its own identity and claim the allegiance of its people if it was seen as essentially an American puppet, completely dependent on the United States politically, militarily, and economically?

U.S. Military Strategy and the Erosion of Public Support. To defeat the North Vietnamese forces sent into South Vietnam, the U.S. military adopted a conventional offensive strategy of "search and destroy." While the American military focused on the task of decimating the North Vietnamese forces, the Communist government in Hanoi matched the military buildup in South Vietnam. *America's aim was physical attrition; North Vietnam's was psychological exhaustion.*[22] The United States was irrevocably committed to a seemingly interminable war that eventually eroded the patience of the American public. Indeed, the search-and-destroy strategy that left the cities essentially undefended was an invitation to a Viet Cong attack. The dramatic Tet offensive of 1968 in which the Viet Cong infiltrated many South Vietnamese cities and towns not only revealed the folly of U.S. strategy but also forced Americans to ask whether the war could be brought to a successful political and military conclusion at all.[23] Psychologically, the Tet offensive was the beginning of the end for the United States in Vietnam, as the American public, increasingly beset by doubts about the wisdom and costs of a war that seemed to have no end, became more and more disillusioned. Tet sapped American will and determination. But it was not an American military defeat. Quite the contrary, the Viet Cong suffered such an enormous defeat that the North Vietnamese bore the burden of the fighting thereafter.

Americans like to win their wars quickly. Within one year Americans were fed up with "Truman's war" in Korea and the continuing, apparently futile loss of American lives. This mood contributed to the defeat of the Democrats in the 1952 presidential election, as it did again in 1968 following the Vietnam War. A long-drawn-out, indecisive engagement did not fit the traditional American all-or-nothing approach, and guerrillas could exploit this impatience by simply not losing.[24] In total war, when the public perceived a serious threat to the nation, it was willing to mobilize fully and make sacrifices; guns were automatically placed ahead of butter. Indeed, when the national security was seen as directly and greatly threatened, people were willing to accept tax increases, a draft, rationing, and inflation. But in a limited war, where by definition the security threat was a limited one, the public did not automatically give priority to the prosecution of the war. Neither in Korea nor in Vietnam did the United States mobilize fully. Because the aim was not the total defeat of the enemy, most men were not drafted and industry was not generally converted to military production. For the vast majority of Americans, life went on pretty much as before, and guns had to compete with the continuing demands for butter by the many interest groups in society.

The erosion of public support for these wars testified to the fact that in a guerrilla war such as that waged in Vietnam there were two battlefields: "one bloody and indecisive in the forests and mountains of Indochina, the other essentially nonviolent—but ultimately more decisive—within the polity and social institutions of the United States."[25] The Viet Cong could not invade the United States, nor could they militarily defeat American forces in Vietnam. Their entire strategy was one of protracted conflict to wear down the adversary's *will.*[26]

Orthodox military doctrine thus led to the adoption of a counterproductive strategy. American officers had not heard the axiom that a conventional army in a guerrilla war loses if it does not win, whereas guerrillas win if they do not lose. They could not grasp the fact that the United States could win all the battles, yet lose the war. Winning this kind of war demands a strategy that does not downgrade the political and psychological factors. The United States military, however, selected a strategy guaranteed to lose and then blamed its lack of success on the flow of men and weapons from North Vietnam. In this way, military leaders could avoid acknowledging their faulty strategy in the South, the main place where the war could be won, and could argue for more intensive bombing of the North. While this bombing had only a limited effect in Vietnam before 1972, it had a major impact in the United States.

The bombing, more than any other issue, deeply divided the American population and antagonized even friendly Western nations. It made the United States appear a bully and North Vietnam the underdog. It aroused international sympathy and support for the Hanoi government, and it stirred many an American conscience. The fact that the bombing brought many people out for anti-American demonstrations all over the world was as significant as the actual battles—and seemingly more decisive. It made it even more difficult to handle the war "politically at home and diplomatically abroad."[27] And it shifted the onus of the war from Hanoi to Washington as well as intensified the U.S. desire to get out of a war in which there was no light at the end of the tunnel. In 1973, the United States withdrew militarily from the war, although ground forces already had been replaced increasingly by the South Vietnamese army.

Why Vietnam Won. In the final analysis, the North Vietnamese won the war in 1975 even though the 1973 settlement had left the South Vietnamese government with a reasonable chance of survival.[*] The North won for three

---

[*] The question of winning may need rethinking in view of post-1973 events. One was that many of the so-called boat people, who were Vietnamese of Chinese origins, immigrated to the United States where, together with so many other Asians, they enriched the nation's educational and cultural life. The North Vietnamese, however, upon taking over South Vietnam found themselves incapable of running the new unified national economy. Thus, they, like other developing country leaders, turned to capitalism, and Japanese and European—but not yet American—entrepreneurs are combing the country for business opportunities. See Karen Elliott House, "Help Vietnam and Ourselves: Normalize Ties," *Wall Street Journal*, December 18, 1991. Note her conclusion:

Note continues

reasons. First, the American public had had it, and, when North Vietnamese forces invaded South Vietnam openly in 1975, the United States refused to intervene again. Second, the South Vietnamese regime fell, not only because of its military errors and panic but also, more fundamentally, because of its political weakness in mobilizing broad popular support throughout South Vietnam. And third, the North Vietnamese were absolutely determined to win, unify, and govern all of Vietnam, regardless of the cost.

To put it another way, the Vietnam War revealed the limitations of traditional power analysis. By conventional standards, the United States was far stronger than North Vietnam, even when the latter received help from the Soviet Union and China. American forces should have won the war. But it was exactly because the United States was so superior in strength that it was complacent and fought according to the orthodox military doctrine intended for a different kind of warfare. And it was precisely because North Vietnam was so much weaker and vulnerable that its political and military leaders had the incentive to create an unorthodox military doctrine that brilliantly exploited its enemy's commitment to fighting a conventional war. While the American approach to warfare stressed capabilities, North Vietnam's guerrilla warfare placed power in its political-economic-social context. Not only did it supplement the military conduct with a social strategy, but it also innovatively extended the battlefield to the enemy's homeland.

If Vietnam demonstrated anything, it was the outright uselessness of employing force in unfavorable political circumstances. The fact that in 1963—two years before the U.S. intervention in Vietnam—President John Kennedy acquiesced in the South Vietnamese military's overthrow of Ngo Dinh Diem was evidence of the political bankruptcy and catastrophic failure of American policy. After the first Indochina War between the Vietminh and French, Gen. Walter Bedell Smith, head of the American delegation to the 1954 Geneva conference, reportedly said that any second-rate general should be able to win in Indochina if there was a correct political atmosphere. Without such an atmosphere, not even a first-rate general could win. According to Smith, "Sound politics in Vietnam was the precondition of military victory, not that military victory was the precondition of sound politics." [28] Military intervention by an external power in the unfavorable political circumstances of a corrupt and incompetent ally can result only in political failure and the loss of that power's prestige. And failure on the battlefield inevitably stimulates increasing domestic opposition to a war that drags on with great sacrifice of life and money but without a victory in sight.

With the passage of time there's less reason for Americans to view their sacrifice in Vietnam as a failure. It was precisely U.S. intervention that bought the rest of Asia time to develop stability that has led to the economic and political liberalization that Vietnam now tentatively seeks to emulate.

Soviet Experience in Afghanistan

It took eight years for the United States to learn that lesson, and almost nine years for the Soviet Union to do the same after it intervened in Afghanistan in support of its Communist government. Having seized power in 1978, the Communist party in Afghanistan had alienated much of the population with its Marxist and antireligious policies in a profoundly Muslim society. The Soviets intervened in 1979 to prop up the government whose forces were losing the resulting civil war.

Soviet policy also failed. The Soviet military thought it too could disregard the rules of guerrilla warfare with firepower and mobility, but it believed that it would succeed where the Americans had failed. Earlier, Mao, recognizing the guerrilla strategy of separating the government from the people and winning their support for the guerrillas' cause, had used the analogy of fish (guerrillas) in water (the people) to underline the guerrillas' need for the people's support. The Soviets, with 115,000 troops in Afghanistan, reassessed Mao's strategy. Because the Afghan resistance, also known as the *mujahedeen* or holy warriors in this Muslim society, was based on popular support, "the easiest way to separate the guerrillas from the population [was] to empty the fish bowl and capture its contents. In other words, an effective counterstrategy in the face of guerrilla action involves massive reprisals, sometimes including the extermination of a large part of the population." [29] Underlying this approach was the assumption that "the war would be won by the side that succeeded in making terror reign." [30] The indiscriminate use of Soviet airpower was especially effective, destroying most Afghan villages. More than 5 million refugees—about a third of Afghanistan's population of 15 million before the invasion—fled to Pakistan and to Iran during the war. Two million people were "internal refugees." Historically, the size of the Afghan refugee flow is unprecedented.

For a while it appeared as though Soviet power would grind down the resistance, as heroic as it was. But beginning in 1986, American-supplied, hand-held Stinger antiaircraft missiles and similar British missiles made a difference because they neutralized Soviet air dominance. Losing more than one aircraft a day, the Soviets had to abandon their helicopter gunship raids, which had been effective against the guerrillas. Once this occurred, the war turned around, and the resistance gained control of about three-quarters of the countryside, confining the Soviets and their Afghan allies to the major cities and towns and the roads connecting them. It was also true that Soviet attention focused almost exclusively on military considerations, neglecting the Marxist approach to analyzing problems in terms of social, economic, and ethnic factors. The Soviets failed therefore to grasp that their intervention would unite and strengthen the opposition. Thus, the Soviet military's reported promise in December 1979 that the "boys would be home" by the time of the Summer Olympics in 1980 or, failing that, by the time of the Communist Party Congress in early 1981, could not be kept.[31] When *glasnost* or openness was allowed by Gorbachev in 1987-1988, the public mood quickly registered opposition to continuing the war. Like Vietnam in the United States, Afghanistan divided Soviet society and helped transform opposition to the war into opposition to all things military. This was more significant than in the United States, for since World War II the Soviet Union had praised its military as its savior.[32]

Although Moscow had limited its commitment of troops to one-fifth of the number of U.S. forces in Vietnam, and it had no protests in the street or a critical media reporting unfavorably on the war, the Soviet Union finally decided after over eight years of fighting to pull out from what Gorbachev called a "bleeding wound." If the Soviet Union, after fighting the *mujahedeen* twice as long as the Nazis, could not win the war, it was better to desist. Resources had to be conserved for solving the severe economic problems at home. Thus, the Soviets, like the United States, apparently lost a war against guerrillas at an officially admitted cost of 13,000 dead and 35,000 wounded (but in fact these figures are probably higher). An estimated 1 million Afghans also died. Interestingly, the Soviet Communist party implied in a secret circular that the decision to send troops into Afghanistan was an error; other Soviet commentators more bluntly stated that this decision reflected an excessive tendency in Soviet foreign policy to use force.[33] In short, both superpowers, highly industrialized and possessing large military forces and huge nuclear arsenals, were defeated by guerrillas in peasant societies. After the Soviet withdrawal, however, peace did not come to Afghanistan. Only in 1992 did the guerrillas drive the formerly Soviet-supported government from power. Then, the various ethnic and religious guerrilla factions began quarreling and killing one another in jockeying for power.

WAR BY PROXY

Because nuclear weapons made nuclear war too costly to fight, the use of force, as distinct from the threat of using force, was safe only in limited wars. It was not accidental that the age of suicidal weapons witnessed this revival of a more limited form of conflict, or that the superpowers, anxious to control the risk of escalation, were inventive in coming up with a variety of ways of engaging each other without direct confrontation. One of these ways became especially prominent during the 1970s—war by proxy. The Soviets used it in both Angola and Ethiopia by supplying military advisers, arms, and large numbers of Cuban troops to fight on the side of the government. In addition, to ensure governmental control of these self-proclaimed Marxist regimes, the Soviets supplemented troops with East German policemen and other Soviet-bloc personnel.

Proxies were used to avoid direct superpower confrontation. Employing a "stand-in" made the attempt to change the status quo less provocative to the other side. Thus, rather than confronting the United States directly, which might be perceived by Washington as a direct challenge to U.S. interests (thereby requiring some sort of American reaction), Moscow presented its challenge by means of a proxy, thought to be viewed by Washington as less provocative. The main benefit of proxies was that Moscow could keep a lower profile than if it intervened itself. There was another benefit as well: someone else did most of the dying. Proxies, then, substantially reduced the danger of a possible superpower confrontation and represented another refinement of the techniques devised in the nuclear era.

Under the so-called Reagan Doctrine, the United States during the 1980s actively supported guerrilla movements against Marxist regimes—especially in Angola, Afghanistan, and Nicaragua—to reverse what it saw as Soviet expansion in the 1970s. These proxy wars provided an alternative to the open use of American forces. By resorting to war by proxy in the age of absolute weapons, the superpowers shifted their conflict to the lower levels of the spectrum of violence when they used force at all. Such conflicts were therefore often referred to as "low-intensity conflicts."

Still, that did not mean that this strategy was "cheap," even if there was no risk of a direct confrontation. For the Soviet Union, there was a double cost. First, preserving its new empire proved costly in terms of life, as well as rubles. That expense was in addition to a defense budget that devoured 25 percent of the Soviet Union's gross national product. Second, it sacrificed the détente it had achieved with the United States, leading to the election of Ronald Reagan, a huge American rearmament program, and hard-line policies, particularly during the first four years of the administration. Mikhail Gorbachev therefore withdrew Soviet troops from Afghanistan, helped settle the principal regional conflicts in Angola and Cambodia, and placed pressure on the Sandinistas in Nicaragua to test their fate in a free election. The Reagan Doctrine, by contrast, was inexpensive. It raised the Soviet cost of maintaining Leonid Brezhnev's new colonies in the Third World and undoubtedly contributed to the decision of Brezhnev's successor, Gorbachev, to reduce the Soviet Union's commitments in the underdeveloped regions of the world and to turn to domestic reform. While the Soviet Union was spending an estimated $10-$20 billion a year to hold the positions under attack by U.S.-supported guerrillas, the United States was spending under a billion dollars a year on the Reagan Doctrine. Furthermore, there were no casualties. The only failure was in Nicaragua, where the support of the contras did not lead to the collapse of the pro-Soviet Marxist government (although one could argue that it was U.S. pressure that made the plan of the Central American presidents for a free election possible or, alternatively, made Gorbachev pressure the Sandinistas).

THE STRONG AND THE WEAK: LESSONS FROM IRAQ

Two conclusions may be drawn from the above analysis. One is that nuclear weapons had the effect of restraining the superpowers' use of power. Neither the United States nor the Soviet Union was willing to risk an escalation that might lead to a nuclear confrontation. Notably, the Korean War was a one-time affair. The danger that such limited hostilities might become "unlimited" was ever present and too dangerous. Guerrilla and proxy wars were safer. The other conclusion is that the power relations on the battlefield did not reflect traditional power calculations. The great powers' military strength did not translate into corresponding political influence.

This requires serious reconsideration of the terms *strong* and *weak*. The Vietnamese fought the French and the Americans—and won. The Afghan rebels fought the Soviets—and won. These great powers, who lost their respective wars as much in Paris and Washington as on the battlefield, were unable to impose their will on the weaker states. France also had withdrawn from Algeria, even though militarily the French had done well. The United States, after suffering 241 casualties in a suicide attack on U.S. marines participating in a peace-keeping force in Lebanon, withdrew, fearing more casualties.

Clearly, the strong no longer dominate and the weak no longer submit. In war, the domestic arena has become as important as the international scene, if not more so. Generals must not only plan how to fight wars but also keep looking over their shoulders to be sure that popular support at home does not erode. A political time clock starts to tick, and a deadline becomes apparent from the moment military forces are placed in harm's way.[34]

It is not surprising that after Vietnam the U.S. military insisted that before any future U.S. intervention there should be a reasonable assurance of congressional and public backing. Generals and admirals can no longer think in purely military terms as they did in the past. Symbolically, after supporting President Bush's initial deployment in August 1990 of 250,000 U.S. forces to Saudi Arabia, Democrats in Congress reacted to the president's doubling that force three months later by insisting that he gain the legislature's authority to declare war before he launched an offensive against Iraq. The Democrats, who controlled both the House and the Senate, also let him know that they thought economic sanctions should be given from nine to eighteen months or longer to work and that the president should not rush into war.

The constitutional problem, therefore, posed its own dilemma. If the Congress supported the president, it might make his threat to use force against Saddam Hussein more credible and enhance his incentives to withdraw from Kuwait and restore the legitimate government without war. But if it refused to support the president and instead voted to give the embargo more time to work, in effect putting off any use of force, American diplomacy would be weakened. This would be true even if congressional advice were sound. But by advertising to the world that it disagreed with the president, even if it disguised that disagreement by declaring that it supported the president but simply wanted to ensure that American lives would not be lost until it was clear that economic sanctions would not work, Congress also would undercut the president's efforts to make the threat of war believable to Saddam Hussein.

It was frequently said during the Gulf crisis that Saddam Hussein, while ruthless, was not suicidal. If he really believed that war was imminent, he would withdraw rather than face defeat. But the American political system, with its checks and balances and the Republicans in charge of the White House and Democratic majorities in the Congress, made it difficult to use the threat of force in a credible way in order to try and avoid having to fight a war. The Democrats remained traumatized by Vietnam, a war in which they had intervened. Basically, the Democratic party had become an antiwar party. Saddam Hussein tried to manipulate this by, among other things, releasing the several thousand foreign hostages, including American ones, he had held. In confessing that holding them had been against "established norms," he specifically thanked Senate Democrats, who in hearings of the Armed Services and Foreign Relations committees had concluded that economic sanctions needed to be given more time to work. Saddam Hussein clearly hoped that his action would increase the "restraints on the intentions and decisions of the evil ones, who are led in their evil intentions and steps by the enemy of God, Bush!" [35] More broadly, Saddam Hussein expected to exploit America's reluctance to fight another protracted war and suffer heavy casualties—even though President Bush had tried to reassure the nation that if war erupted, the United States would not fight "another Vietnam."

President Bush, therefore, was initially reluctant to go to the Congress. Instead, he tried another tack to communicate U.S. resolve. He sought—and got—a UN Security Council resolution declaring that if Iraq did not obey the earlier resolutions demanding that it withdrew unconditionally from Kuwait by January 15, 1991, force might be used to eject it. The vote in the Security Council also conveyed to Saddam Hussein that the coalition against him was holding fast. Especially important was that the United States and the Soviet Union stood together. In wooing Gorbachev to support the authorization to use force, Secretary of State James Baker at one point was asked the central question by the Soviet leader: Did he understand that if a resolution authorizing force were passed and Saddam Hussein did not pull out of Kuwait, the United States would have to use force? Baker replied that President Bush understood "perfectly." [36] A high British official put the same thing this way: If Saddam Hussein refused to leave Kuwait by January 15 and the allied forces did not act, Iraq's opponents would suffer a humiliation equivalent to a military defeat. [37] The UN deadline for Saddam Hussein was thus the international equivalent of a declaration of war.

Only after he had received the United Nations' authorization to use force after mid-January did Bush focus on mobilizing domestic support for the UN decision. He did so first by offering to "go the extra mile" diplomatically. He proposed receiving Iraq's foreign minister in Washington and sending the secretary of state to Baghdad. If these talks did not result in Iraq's withdrawal from Kuwait, Bush expected to isolate his critics and thereby muster the country's and Congress's backing for the use of force. Indeed, the talks came to nothing. Iraq and the United States could not even agree on a date for Secretary Baker to visit Baghdad. Saddam Hussein also insisted on linking the Kuwaiti issue to settlement of the Palestinian problem (although at no time did he offer a pullout from Kuwait as a quid pro quo). The only U.S.-Iraqi contact was a meeting in Geneva between the secretary of state and the Iraqi foreign minister. There each side restated its position, but the result was unproductive. Again, the Iraqi foreign minister did not even mention the central issue of Kuwait; he talked only of the Palestinians and Israel, as if Iraq had invaded and savaged Kuwait in order to free the Palestinians.

It was only after the failure of the Geneva meeting that President Bush asked the Congress for authority to use force after January 15. It did so, although by only a slim 52-47 majority in the Senate—three votes could have turned the whole thing around—and by a 250-183 majority in the House. Overwhelmingly, Democrats voted against the authority to use force and for reliance on economic sanctions. The Democrats had placed themselves in a precarious position. If there were no war, their votes would not matter much. But if there were a war and it resulted in a quick victory, the Democrats risked reviving the electorate's memory that they were "soft on national security" just as the 1992 presidential campaign began. But if the war dragged on and the casualties mounted—prewar estimates ranged from 5,000 to 20,000—the Democrats could say that they had warned the country against going to war and had advocated instead peaceful means of compelling Saddam Hussein to withdraw from Kuwait. Bush, of course, was aware of these calculations. A long, drawn-out war would make him a one-term president; politically, he needed a short war and a quick victory.

What is striking is the contrast in the U.S. efforts to mobilize international and domestic support and the narrowness of the margin of victory in the congressional vote for the use of force. Clearly, for democracies, and especially the American democracy, the use of force has become increasingly difficult. As Vietnam and, indeed, Afghanistan had demonstrated, public support for intervention is lacking in most of the major powers because of the fear that hostilities will be long and casualties heavy. Thus, in the Iraqi confrontation Saddam Hussein sought to turn the conflict into a prolonged one. By adopting a defensive strategy and surviving the American onslaught for several months, he could portray himself to the Arab masses as invincible. In the meantime, he would absorb the initial blows inflicted on Iraq by allied air power, which he was in no position to challenge, and wait for the ground battle. Then with his sizable and well-equipped forces, experienced in defensive warfare (and perhaps using poison gas), he expected to inflict heavy casualties on American forces in a war of attrition. This would, he assumed, encourage a growing peace movement in the United States. Saddam Hussein was quite willing to accept any level of casualties for his own military, a million or more if necessary, as long as American television showed a continual stream of body bags being unloaded in the presence of grieving family members at airports all over the country. He, like North Vietnam's leaders, was very much aware of the sensitivity of the American media, Congress, and population to the loss of American lives. Also like his North Vietnamese counterparts, he was quite indifferent to his losses. And he was not totally in error. The preference for economic sanctions, and once hostilities had begun for continued air warfare, was a reflection of the desire to avoid what many expected to be a costly ground war. It was even said that the chairman of the Joint Chiefs of Staff initially favored prolonged economic sanctions.

Thus, as in Iraq, a president risks political career and reputation when deciding to resort to war. Yet in an anarchical system in which there is no supranational institution to mediate conflicts between states and police the system and maintain order, it is the great powers that keep order. In the unipolar post-cold war system, this burden has fallen principally on the United States. If order is not kept, smaller states will gain greater freedom to attack their neighbors in their search for regional hegemony, creating an unstable post-cold war world. As things turned out, the war against Iraq was short and avoided the erosion of public support. Indeed, the war, because of the splendid performance by U.S. forces and their weapons systems, proved immensely popular, reviving both great pride in the leading and decisive role of the United States and American patriotism. Moreover, Saddam Hussein, unlike Ho Chi Minh during the Vietnamese war, was such a "bad guy" that he helped President Bush's efforts to mobilize and maintain American public opinion. And once Desert Shield turned into Desert Storm, *the United States, not having to worry about Soviet intervention, could use its full power from the beginning and it did.* Unlike North Korea and North Vietnam, who had the backing of the communist world, Iraq and Saddam Hussein had to confront the United States alone.

He did not have a chance in the new unipolar post-cold war world. The defensive nature of Iraqi strategy, which had worked so well against Iran, and the absence of any air power to protect Iraqi positions or attack allied forces, left the Iraqi army in Kuwait and southern Iraq a sitting duck. According to Colin Powell, chairman of the Joint Chiefs of Staff, allied military forces would isolate Iraqi forces and kill them. Communications and supply lines were heavily bombed, and then, when the forces in Kuwait were cut off, the weight of the air war turned against them. By the time the ground war was launched, the Iraqis were only too happy to surrender; those who could not surrender retreated or would not fight. Even the elite Republican Guard turned out not to be the formidable force it had been portrayed as being. The war lasted forty-three days. The Iraqis suffered an estimated 100,000-120,000 deaths during the air and ground campaigns—primarily the former—and at least 60,000 Iraqis were taken prisoners of war during the 100-hour land offensive. That is twice the number of deaths the United States suffered during eight years of the Vietnam War. U.S. ground combat deaths were 148, 38 of which resulted from "friendly fire." *

Does this mean that the above comments about the relationship between the strong and the weak no longer apply? Was the UN-U.S.-Iraqi war the beginning of a new trend in which the strong will play their historic role? Or were the allies just lucky that the Iraqis fought so incompetently (other potential powers might have better war plans and their armies might be better led, like the Vietnamese forces)? Would the war have gone as well and seen so few casualties had, for example, Iraqi forces not stopped at the Kuwaiti-Saudi border in early August 1990? Using the forces it was flying in, most of which were initially lightly armed, the United States would have had to fight against what at that time was a much larger Iraqi army. Or if the Iraqi leadership had treated its men better, feeding and clothing them properly, would not this sizable army have given a better account of itself despite its lack of air cover? Or, what if the Iraqi army had Moscow's support and Soviet satellite information on allied troop movements so that its forces could be redeployed to meet the attack? Whatever the answers to these questions, it appears that one result of the quick Western victory over Iraq has been to whet the appetites of Third World nations for more advanced weapons with greater accuracy and technological sophistication. It they acquire such weapons, it raises the prospects that future Third World wars will be vastly more destructive, even if they are the conventional types of conflict U.S. forces are trained for—unlike guerrilla wars, of which Vietnam may not have been the last one.[38]

For Review

1. What was a "limited war"?
2. What were the constraints that kept a limited war from escalating?
3. How does guerrilla warfare differ from conventional warfare?
4. Why did the United States lose in Vietnam and the Soviet Union lose in Afghanistan?

---

* Iraq has not announced any death totals. U.S. estimates may be too high because it is still not known how many Iraqi troops were mobilized initially or how many deserted—some say 150,000—or were wounded and were evacuated. The U.S. estimate of 540,000 Iraqi troops in or near Kuwait was based on the number of Iraqi divisions. But Iraqi prisoners have suggested that many divisions were undermanned and that as many as half their troops deserted at various points in the war. There may have been only 350,000 troops with 100,000 desertees by the time the ground campaign began. See Walter S. Mossberg and David Rogers, "Iraqi Troop Deaths Totaled at Least 100,000, U.S. Says," *Wall Street Journal,* March 22, 1991. Also see Patrick E. Tyler, "Iraq's War Toll Estimated by U.S.," *New York Times,* June 5, 1991.

5. What are the lessons of the limited wars fought by the United States, Soviet Union, and other Western powers, and what do they reveal about the relationships of the stronger industrial states to weaker Third World states? Did the recent war with Iraq confirm these lessons? If so, why? If not, why not?

Notes

1. The two best introductory books on limited war are those by Henry A. Kissinger, *Nuclear Weapons and Foreign Policy* (New York: Harper & Row, 1957); and Robert E. Osgood, *Limited War* (Chicago: University of Chicago Press, 1957).
2. Kissinger, *Nuclear Weapons*, 140.
3. See Harry S. Truman, *Years of Trial and Hope*, vol. 1 of *Memoirs* (Garden City, N.Y.: Doubleday, 1958), 332-333.
4. See John Spanier, *The Truman-MacArthur Controversy and the Korean War* (Cambridge, Mass.: Harvard University Press, 1959), 84-134; and Allen S. Whiting, *China Crosses the Yalu* (New York: Macmillan, 1960).
5. Thomas C. Schelling, *Strategy of Conflict* (Cambridge, Mass.: Harvard University Press, 1960), 75; and Schelling, *Arms and Influence* (New Haven, Conn.: Yale University Press, 1966), 137-141.
6. Herman Kahn, *On Escalation* (New York: Holt, Rinehart & Winston, 1965), 38-41. On controlling escalation, also see Richard Smoke, *War* (Cambridge, Mass.: Harvard University Press, 1978).
7. David Galula, *Counterinsurgency Warfare* (New York: Holt, Rinehart & Winston, 1964), 9-10.
8. *Mao Tse-tung on Guerrilla Warfare*, trans. Samuel B. Griffith (New York: Holt, Rinehart & Winston, 1961), 103-104. For the Vietminh's seven rules for the conduct of guerrilla warfare, see Otto Heilbrunn, *Partisan Warfare* (New York: Holt, Rinehart & Winston, 1962), 78-79.
9. On Viet Cong terror, see Guenter Lewy, *America in Vietnam* (New York: Oxford University Press, 1978), 272-279, 454.
10. Jeffrey Race, *War Comes to Long An* (Berkeley: University of California Press, 1972), 141ff.; Heilbrunn, *Partisan Warfare*, 145-146; and George K. Tanham, *Communist Revolutionary Warfare* (New York: Holt, Rinehart & Winston, 1961), 143. On the different components of strategy, see Michael Howard, "The Forgotten Dimensions of Strategy," *Foreign Affairs* (Summer 1979): 975-986.
11. Tanham, *Communist Revolutionary Warfare*, 32, 97.
12. Griffith, Introduction to *Mao Tse-tung on Guerrilla Warfare*, 7.
13. Charles W. Thayer, *Guerrilla* (New York: Harper & Row, 1963), 42-60.
14. Bernard B. Fall, *The Two Viet-Nams*, 2d ed. (New York: Holt, Rinehart & Winston, 1964); Denis Warner, *The Last Confucian* (New York: Macmillan, 1963); and Stanley Karnow, *Vietnam* (New York: Viking, 1983), 128-239.
15. Quoted in Heilbrunn, *Partisan Warfare*, 34. On the decisiveness of civilian loyalties, see Chalmers A. Johnson, "Civilian Loyalties and Guerrilla Conflict," *World Politics* (July 1962): 646-661. Also see Johnson, *Autopsy on People's War* (Berkeley: University of California Press, 1973).

16. Fall, *Two Viet-Nams*, 346-347. The Algerian example also clearly demonstrates that counterterror is not effective in ending guerrilla warfare.

17. This section is not concerned with judgments on whether the United States should have intervened in Vietnam, only with the manner in which force was used. Judgment is, of course, implicit in such an analysis. Ultimately, it reflects on the issue of the original intervention, for, if the conclusion is that force was exercised ineffectively—indeed, counterproductively—it also may be deduced that the intervention should have been avoided in the first place. This judgment, to be sure, is pragmatic, not moral. For moral and legal judgments on the war, see, among others, Telford Taylor, *Nuremberg and Vietnam* (New York: Bantam Books, 1971); and Richard A. Falk, Gabriel Kolko, and Robert J. Lifton, eds. *Crimes of War* (New York: Vintage, 1971). For a contrary point of view defending the war's legality, see Lewy, *America in Vietnam*, 223-270, 343-373. My own pragmatic judgment on Vietnam is much the same as Donald Zagoria's in *Vietnam Triangle: Moscow, Peking, Hanoi* (New York: Pegasus, 1967), xiii—namely, that American strategy and tactics raise "serious doubts in my mind whether we as a nation have the wisdom, the skills and the manpower to cope with civil wars."

18. Gen. Lewis W. Walt, assistant commandant of the U.S. Marine Corps, confessed in 1970 that when he visited Vietnam in 1965 he thought of it as a conventional war like the Korean War (*New York Times*, November 18, 1970). Gen. Earle Wheeler, chairman of the Joint Chiefs of Staff, held the same opinion, as reported by Roger Hilsman, *To Move a Nation* (Garden City, N.Y.: Doubleday, 1967), 426.

19. On Lyndon Johnson's intervention and escalation in Vietnam, see Brian Vandermark, *Into the Quagmire* (New York: Oxford University Press, 1990). Also see Larry Berman, *Planning a Tragedy* (New York: Norton, 1983); and Berman, *Lyndon Johnson's War* (New York: Norton, 1989).

20. Robert Thompson, *No Exit from Vietnam* (New York: McKay, 1969), 13-17; and Lewy, *America in Vietnam*. Both authors stress that the United States, by waging a conventional conflict, was guilty of misconduct of the war.

21. The most vigorous defense of Vietnam as a conventional war may be found in Harry G. Summers, *On Strategy* (New York: Dell, 1984). The best critique of this position, besides that by Lewy (*America in Vietnam*), is by Andrew T. Krepinevich, *The Army and Vietnam* (Baltimore: Johns Hopkins University Press, 1986).

22. Henry A. Kissinger, *American Foreign Policy* (New York: Norton, 1969), 104.

23. Thompson, *No Exit from Vietnam*, 40-74; and Don Oberdorfer, *Tet* (Garden City, N.Y.: Doubleday, 1971). For intelligence failure preceding Tet, see James Wirtz, *The Tet Offensive* (Ithaca, N.Y.: Cornell University Press, 1992).

24. Andrew J. R. Mack, "Why Big Nations Lose Small Wars: The Politics of Asymmetric Conflict," *World Politics* (January 1975): 175-200. Also see John E. Mueller, *War, Presidents, and Public Opinion* (New York: Wiley, 1973); and Larry Elowitz and John Spanier, "Korea and Vietnam: Limited War and the American Political System," *Orbis* (Summer 1974): 510-534.

25. Mack, "Why Big Nations Lose Small Wars," 177.

26. Fall, *Two Viet-Nams*, 113.

27. Townsend Hoopes, *The Limits of Intervention* (New York: McKay, 1969), 82. For an assessment of "coercive violence" in Vietnam, see Wallace J. Thies, *When Governments Collide* (Berkeley: University of California Press, 1980), 349-374.

28. Theodore Draper, *Abuse of Power* (New York: Viking, 1967), 29, 30. For balanced interpretations of why the war was lost, see Timothy J. Lomperis, *The War Everyone*

Lost—and Won (Washington, D.C.: CQ Press, 1987), 176. Also see Lawrence E. Grinter and Peter M. Dunn, eds., *The American War in Vietnam* (Westport, Conn.: Greenwood Press, 1988).

29. Claude Malhuret, "Report from Afghanistan," *Foreign Affairs* (Winter 1983/84): 427. On Soviet intervention, see Thomas T. Hammond, *Red Flag over Afghanistan* (Boulder, Colo.: Westview Press, 1984); and Rosanne Klass, ed., *Afghanistan, The Great Game Revisited* (New York: Freedom House, 1988).

30. Malhuret, "Report from Afghanistan," 428.

31. Jeanette Voas, ed. (*1990 Sea Power Forum*), *Soviet Intervention in Afghanistan: Never Again?* (Alexandria, Va.: Center for Naval Analyses, 1990), 2.

32. Ibid., 2-3.

33. Bill Keller, "Secret Soviet Party Document Said to Admit Afghan Errors," *New York Times*, June 17, 1988. Also see Oliver Roy, *The Lessons of the Soviet Afghan War*, Adelphi Papers 259 (London: International Institute for Strategic Studies, 1991).

34. See, among many works, Michael I. Handel's last chapter, entitled "The Future of War: The Diminishing Returns of Military Power," in *War, Strategy and Intelligence* (Totowa, N.J.: Frank Cass, 1989), 485-500.

35. "Iraqi Leader's Message to National Assembly," *New York Times*, December 7, 1990.

36. Thomas L. Friedman, "How U.S. Won Support to Use Mideast Forces," *New York Times*, December 2, 1990.

37. Craig R. Whitney, "British Say Allies Must Erase Doubts," *New York Times*, December 5, 1990.

38. Michael Wines, "Third World Seeks Advanced Arms," *New York Times*, March 26, 1991; and Patrick E. Tyler, "As Fear of a Big War Fades, Military Plans for Little Ones," *New York Times*, February 3, 1992.

CHAPTER 15

The International Political Economy and Statecraft

The effects of changes in the international economy on the distribution of wealth and power among the great powers were discussed in Chapter 8. Even if the post-cold war world—characterized by President George Bush as the "new world order"—is less prone to violence than in the past, conflicting interests among states are not likely to disappear. If this thesis is correct, what may increase as the currency of national power shifts from military to mainly economic means is the use of economic instruments of statecraft.[1]

NATIONAL INDEPENDENCE AND SELF-SUFFICIENCY

. . . In Wartime

Sovereign nation-states guard their independence jealously, even when they believe the world is becoming more interdependent. In pre-World War I Europe, most professional soldiers thought that no war could last very long precisely because of the high degree of economic interdependence found there.[2] Countries would not be able to mobilize large armies and pay for such a war without risking mutual bankruptcy and social revolution. War plans aimed at quick victories, but the opposite happened. Once they realized that the war was not going to end quickly, the industrial economies demonstrated their enormous potential power by mobilizing for the long haul. The war lasted four years before Germany's exhaustion led to the end of hostilities.

The fate of Britain during World War I underlines why it has so long been believed that the great powers should be as self-sufficient as possible. Even though it was the first nation to industrialize, the world's most powerful country for most of the nineteenth century, and the country that demonstrated that a prerequisite for the Industrial Revolution was an agricultural revolution, Britain neglected its production of food, while industry demonstrated its capacity to increase the country's wealth and power. By World War I, Britain had become a food importer. Moreover, as a resource-poor state, Britain had to import the raw materials needed for the manufactured products it exported to earn a living. A new weapon, the submarine, thus became a threat to Britain's lifelines. Using submarines, the Germans, who had built only a small fleet (like the British, they had spent most of the money allocated for the navy on battleships), almost managed to starve Britain into submission. But by declaring an unlimited submarine campaign against all shipping to England, including neutral American ships, the Germans provoked the United States into entering the war.

During World War II, the German threat to British lifelines was even greater. After France's defeat in 1940, when Britain was left alone to carry on the fight against Germany, the Battle for the Atlantic became critical for Britain's survival as well as the prerequisite for an ultimate victory over Germany. Especially after the United States declared war against Germany in December 1941, this battle was waged fiercely until the Allies won it in May 1943. Once the sea lanes to Britain were secured, U.S. troops, landing craft, and other supplies needed for the invasion of France could be shipped to the British Isles.

Just as the Germans used submarines, the British tried to use the naval blockade during World War II to defeat Germany by slow strangulation.[3] But it was a strategy doomed to failure. German industries produced synthetic oil, rubber, and wool; the neutral states—such as Russia (until Germany attacked it), Sweden, and Spain—supplied materials Germany needed; and, of course, Germany conquered most of Europe and looted it for whatever it wanted. Without these supplies, Germany would have been vulnerable to a blockade. It instead built up its military forces quickly and then rapidly conquered the raw material and financial base needed for a long war.[4] Indeed, as an industrial state, especially a continental one with railroads and access to the harbors of neutral states, Germany was not particularly vulnerable to sea blockades. It was vulnerable to air power, however, which is able to destroy a nation's industries and transportation systems.

. . . In Peacetime

Because states are not generally self-sufficient and must obtain what they need through trade in the absence of conquest, one of the economic tools they frequently use in conflict is the embargo. An embargo prevents the shipment of certain products or even all products to the targeted country. During the cold war, in what might be called economic warfare or a strategy of denial, the United States regulated exports to the Soviet Union. All products that might have had some sort of military application or could have contributed to the economic strength of the Communist state were placed on the embargo list.

Although America's allies in the North Atlantic Treaty Organization (NATO) were somewhat less restrictive in the goods they embargoed, the overall consequence was that the economies of the West and the East remained separate and independent. There is no evidence, however, that these Western attempts at coercion resulted in Soviet political compliance, and the cold war years until 1962 were among the most tense and conflict-filled of the postwar era.

As the cold war gave way to détente in the 1970s, U.S. diplomatic strategy sought to make the Soviet economy more dependent on that of the United States. One tactic was use of the productivity of American industry and agriculture to offer the Soviets "carrots." The Soviet economy even then had stagnating industrial and agricultural sectors. But because the Brezhnev regime judged fundamental structural reforms of its centrally controlled and directed economy to be too risky politically, Soviet leaders turned logically to the West for technology, food, and credits with which to buy what they needed. Secretary of State Henry Kissinger and, after him, President Jimmy Carter were quite willing to offer the Soviet leaders economic "rewards" if they acted with greater restraint in foreign policy.

Thus, the U.S. government used trade with the Soviet Union as a political lever. More specifically, Kissinger attempted to create a *tactical linkage* that utilized trade to change Soviet international behavior. The Soviets were asked to pay not only an economic price for what they wanted but also a political price. When they acted with self-restraint in ways acceptable to the United States, they were to be rewarded; when they did not, they were to be punished. The economic spigot was to be turned on and off. The sanctioning state's assumption was that if the adversary's needs were sufficiently great, it would behave in the desired manner to avoid a cutoff of trade. In other words, the Soviet Union would contain itself!

Limitations of Using Trade as a Political Lever

Practice, as distinct from theory, quickly revealed the limitations of using the Soviets' need for computers, oil drilling equipment, and wheat as a political lever to reward their restraint and punish their expansionism.

U.S. Domestic Resistance. One limitation soon became clear; the United States could turn the economic spigot on but could not turn it off so easily.[5] American farmers let President Gerald Ford know in 1975 that if he expected their votes he had better not try a grain embargo against the Soviet Union. He did not. But in 1979, after the Soviet invasion of Afghanistan, President Carter embargoed 17 million tons of grain, most of it earmarked for Soviet livestock feed. Presidential candidate Ronald Reagan promised farmers that he would end the embargo if elected (despite his tough anti-Soviet rhetoric). He received the farm vote.

Clearly, the eagerness of U.S. banks, corporations, and farmers to trade with the Soviet Union and the pressures that they could exert on Washington meant that this kind of leverage could not be used frequently. Indeed, the Soviets were able to manipulate U.S. economic interests more skillfully than American leaders because American interest groups sought to avoid confrontation and "unpleasantness" to protect their profits. (So much for capitalist enmity toward communism!) All this then revealed that if the cost of sanctions to domestic interests is too high, public support for sanctions will erode. The lesson was clear: shooting oneself in the foot is not painful for the targeted nation.

Availability of Alternative Supplies. A second limitation was that the Soviets could buy technology and wheat from Western Europe, Japan, and other countries. Trade and credits are satisfactory bargaining tools only when the items that an adversary needs cannot be obtained elsewhere. Even if the U.S. government were to stand firm, foreign businesses and farmers overseas would be all too happy to receive the contracts. The Soviet Union could, in fact, have played one Western country off against another and gained economic benefits despite its political behavior. Cold War embargoes then, tended to be leaky when Western countries needed markets for products.

USE OF AID AND TRADE AMONG THE GREAT POWERS AND THEIR ALLIES

In the difficult years that followed World War II, the United States, Soviet Union, and their respective cold war allies took economic measures to strengthen their political positions. The United States created the Marshall Plan, several Western European states formed an economic union, and the Soviet Union created economic ties with Eastern Europe and other allies. As the cold war ended, the relative decline of both superpowers was symbolized by the former donors becoming recipients of economic aid.

Marshall Plan

The United States resorted to economic means to advance its foreign policy goals from the very beginning of the cold war. It was, in fact, the economic collapse of Western Europe—short of food and fuel, with its cities and factories destroyed—that finally made it impossible for the United States to return to isolationism, as it had done after World War I. Most of what Western Europe needed for reconstruction—wheat, cotton, sugar, coal, machinery, and trucks—could be obtained in sufficient quantities only from the United States. But the United States, in contrast, was so well supplied with everything that it did not have to buy much abroad, leaving Europeans unable to earn the dollars they needed to buy the goods required for their recovery. Consequently, the term *dollar gap* became as ominous a term as *cold war* was shortly after World War II because it denoted Western Europe's collapse and the utter dependence of the Old World on the New World.

This collapse posed a fundamental question for the United States: Was Western Europe vital to America's security? The answer was never in doubt, for Western Europe ranked second behind the United States in industry, productivity, skilled labor, scientists, and engineers. These assets could not be allowed to shift toward the Soviet Union. Two world wars had made it unambiguously clear that U.S. and European security were inseparable; Western Europe's collapse simply reaffirmed it. The U.S. commitment was demonstrated by the grant of billions of dollars in Marshall Plan funds to stimulate economic recovery and by the establishment of the NATO military alliance. Only an aid program could restore Western Europe's prewar agricultural and industrial production and stimulate a revival of European *élan vital*, political stability, economic prosperity, and military strength. Such a revived Europe would be not only a trading partner for the United States but also an ally in containing Soviet expansion into the center of Europe.

Integration of the European Economic Community

But based on its own continental-sized market free of the internal trade barriers that divided Europe into smaller national markets that lacked American-style mass-production industries, the United States made its aid conditional on European economic integration. Such integration was considered necessary for Europe's recovery and long-term prosperity. As imaginative as the Marshall Plan infusion of funds was, however, the subsequent French use of economics was revolutionary. After its experience with Germany in 1871, 1914, and 1939, France was alarmed by the rebirth of Germany's economy and power as part of European recovery. If for the United States the problem was one of containing Soviet power—a task that required reviving Germany's power, potentially the strongest in Western Europe—for France the problem was one of containing German *and* Soviet power. Since the unification of German power in 1871, France had attempted to deal with its militaristic and aggressive neighbor by forming alliances with nations to its east. But neither that with Russia before 1914 nor that with the Soviet Union before 1939 had prevented World Wars I and II.

The failure of the traditional balance-of-power technique, by which an inferior power seeks to balance a stronger one, led France to adopt a revolutionary means of exerting some control over German power: European integration. Through the creation of a supranational community, to which Germany would transfer certain sovereign rights, German power would be controlled. Only in this manner would German strength be prevented from harming the rest of Europe and instead channeled into support for European welfare and security. European integration into a "United States of Europe" led by France also would eventually create a third superpower that would permit France to regain the major influence it sought but did not possess either in NATO or on the world stage.

France made its first move in the direction of a united Europe in May 1950, when it proposed formation of the European Coal and Steel Community

(ECSC), to be composed of "Little Europe" or the "Inner Six" (France, Germany, Italy, Belgium, the Netherlands, and Luxembourg). The French showed great political astuteness in their selection of heavy industry as the first to be integrated. Coal and steel are the basis of the entire industrial sector, a sector that cannot possibly be separated from the overall economy. Thus, according to French thinking, the success of the ECSC would exert pressure on the unintegrated sectors of the economy, and, as the benefits of pooling heavy industry became clear, such sectors as agriculture, transportation, and electricity would follow suit, leading then to the creation of a single European market and efficient mass-producing industries. Industry, labor, and agriculture would all benefit. The ECSC was thus the forerunner of the European Common Market (later known as the European Economic Community, or EEC), formed in 1958. The EEC was designed to integrate the entire economies of its members and serve as the basis of a "United States of Europe," whose core was the French-West German relationship.

The Common Market, now known simply as the European Community (EC) presently has twelve members. In 1992, it is slated to make its final push for full economic and financial integration (see Chapter 19 for an analysis of the process of integration and current status). Former Soviet satellites in Eastern Europe and countries in Western Europe—including such neutral states as Austria and Sweden—are seeking full EC membership. The present twelve members of the EC, with a population of over 330 million, constitute the world's largest market. Germany's chancellor expressed the optimism of many in Europe when he exulted that the 1990s would be the decade of Europe. Europe, it was expected, would once more become a world player economically, politically, and militarily.

Ironically, although it was the United States that made the revival of Europe possible by offering its protection for over four decades, providing the funds for the initial post-World War II revival, insisting on European integration, and creating the international free-trade environment that led to prosperity for all the Western industrial nations, today it is the United States that is the economically troubled player with little spare capital to invest at home, let alone in key states in Latin America, Eastern Europe, or elsewhere. Nothing symbolized the current status of the United States better than Operations Desert Shield and Desert Storm, which, on the one hand, demonstrated its superb military capability and yet, on the other hand, its economic weakness and need for financial bailout.

United States as Aid Recipient: Petrodollars into Pentagondollars

During the Iraqi crisis of 1990-1991, the oil-producing countries threatened by Saddam Hussein also were the big economic beneficiaries of the higher oil prices and the increased production incurred to compensate for the loss of Iraqi and Kuwaiti oil after the invasion of Kuwait. The economic losers, of course, were the United States, Japan, Western and Eastern Europe, and all oil-importing developing countries. Other losers were Turkey, which had shut off the Iraqi oil pipeline running to a Turkish port, and such countries as Egypt, which lost money from the pay workers sent home from the oil fields, and Jordan, which lost trade with Iraq as well as aid from the oil producers because it sided with Iraq.

But, as noted, America's economic problems made it imperative that the United States, which organized the defense of Saudi Arabia and supplied the bulk of the military forces, receive financial assistance. Turkey, Egypt, and several other states also needed economic aid. From August to the end of December 1990, Saudi Arabia and the other Gulf states committed almost $9 billion to a fund to aid countries hurt by the crisis. Japan and Germany stated that they would give $2 billion and $1.3 billion, respectively, and $2 billion each to support the U.S. military operation. The Arab states, including the Kuwaiti government-in-exile, also financially supported Desert Storm. But American officials, especially members of Congress, felt that neither Saudi Arabia, given the size of its profits, nor Japan and Germany, given their wealth and dependence on imported oil, were contributing their "fair shares," especially because neither contributed any troops. Actually, despite its windfall profits, Saudi Arabia had to borrow $3.6 billion from international banks in early 1991, a step it had not taken since the early 1970s. By early 1991, the war had already cost the Saudis $48 billion.[6] Its commitments were extensive: aid to such countries as Turkey and Egypt, funds to support U.S. and other military forces as well as its own increased military outlays, the cost of increasing its production to make up for the shortfall stemming from the embargo on Iraqi and Kuwaiti oil, and the cost of cleaning up the environment after Iraq released several hundred million gallons of oil into the Persian Gulf. These commitments to the United States and other coalition partners continued for the duration of the war, and some beyond. In the meantime, the initially steep rise in oil prices immediately after Iraq's invasion of Kuwait settled back quickly to near pre-invasion levels. As for other commitments, the Saudis and other Gulf states extended $5 billion in aid to Moscow, inducing it to join the anti-Saddam Hussein coalition. They also paid for all the fuel the allied forces used.

But the brunt of the criticism was reserved for Japan and Germany—dubbed the "Checkbook Powers" by columnist William Safire.[7] Given Japan's $2.8 trillion gross national product and Germany's $1.4 trillion economy, their contributions to the war were considered minimal. Even then, Japan's aid to Turkey, Egypt, and Jordan was in the form of loans, not grants, as had been expected. Some of Germany's aid to the United States was in the form of castoff gear from the defunct East German army. At a time of strained trade relations, these countries' failures to support wholeheartedly U.S. efforts to protect the oil on which they were far more dependent (in fact, what they finally did give appeared to be forthcoming only because of U.S. pressure) raised already existing tensions in the alliance relationships.[8] In the end, however, for the period January 1-March 31, 1991, a period during which war was expected and costs were predicted to shoot up dramatically, Kuwait pledged $13.5 billion, and Saudi Arabia promised to match that sum. Washington hoped that its costs would be no more than 20 percent, and Tokyo did respond by saying it would raise its contribution to $9 billion, although it faced considerable domestic opposition. Other allies were asked for the remaining 60 percent. Germany said it would contribute an additional $5.5 billion, bringing its total to almost $9 billion since August 1990, the same amount as Japan whose GNP was twice as large. Britain and France, both with troops in Desert Storm, contributed most of the rest. Altogether, the allies pledged $55 billion (not all of which has been collected), money that otherwise would have had to be borrowed from private investors overseas and added to the deficit. The cost of the war for the United States may yet be zero. Although in 1991 the U.S. budget director still expected the final total cost of the war to be $60 billion, this figure included the replacement of all equipment destroyed or damaged, which is unlikely to occur in the scheduled defense build-down.[9]

Clearly, judging from the Iraqi experience, future large-scale U.S. interventions will not be carried out unilaterally. The country, for all of its military power, cannot afford to do so. Burden-sharing, however, will require power-sharing. Other nations will demand a say in the decision-making process, possibly constricting America's initiative and freedom of maneuver.

Disintegration of COMECON

The Soviets had a different way of organizing the economies of Eastern Europe after World War II. They founded the Council for Mutual Economic Assistance, known in the West as COMECON. When Joseph Stalin died, his successors decided to treat all of Eastern Europe as a single economic region, in which each country would produce certain items for the whole region. Poland would mine bituminous coal, East Germany would produce lignite and chemicals, and Czechoslovakia would manufacture automobiles. If each country were specialized, all countries would have to cooperate. The aim was to link the political and economic interests of the Communist countries and to create a high degree of interdependence among them. Economic specialization was to be the means of making Eastern Europe dependent on the Soviet Union and of isolating the Soviet bloc economy from the West. (After 1962, Mongolia, Cuba, and Vietnam joined COMECON and were integrated into the Soviet bloc.)

But such specialization began to be resisted as states sought to be self-sustaining in areas they thought important. Although the regimes in Eastern Europe before 1989 were for forty years kept in power by the Soviet army, their increasingly nationalistic outlooks gave them a degree of legitimacy. Economic improvements, such as those in Hungary in the early 1970s, helped strengthen this legitimacy, just as economic failure, as in Poland in the 1980s and elsewhere, weakened the authority of the regime.

Ironically, the inability of Moscow to provide substantial assistance during the 1970s and 1980s compelled the six countries of Eastern Europe—whose growth rate in the first half of the 1970s of over 4 percent fell drastically to virtually zero after that—to turn to the West, including the United States. By the end of 1987, Eastern Europe's debt had grown to $81 billion. By 1989, all of Eastern Europe was potentially explosive.[10] It is striking that the collapse of the regimes in the area resulted from spontaneous mass movements, epitomized by the trainloads of fleeing East Germans and the massive demonstrations in the cities by those who stayed. The Soviet-imposed governments had alienated virtually the entire population of Eastern Europe.

Faced with staggering economic and ethnic problems at home, Mikhail Gorbachev decided to unburden himself of the political and economic costs of supporting Communist regimes that, despite their efforts to enhance their legitimacy, remained hated by the people they had for so long oppressed. Instead of intervening militarily to deal with any explosions and trying to maintain the Soviet-imposed Communist governments in power, as his predecessors had done, Gorbachev decided not to use force and to accept the results of what can only be called genuine people's revolutions first in Poland, then in Hungary, East Germany, Czechoslovakia, Romania, and Bulgaria. He was willing to permit his Warsaw Treaty Organization (WTO) allies to "de-Communize" and move toward democracy and economic market reforms (except Romania and Bulgaria, which reelected so-called reformed Communists under new names) as long as they stayed in the alliance. One result, however, of allowing free elections was the demand by the successor governments in Czechoslovakia, Hungary, and Poland for the withdrawal of Soviet troops. Thus, the Warsaw Treaty Organization eroded anyway. East Germany disappeared as it became part of a reunified Germany, and the other Eastern European states turned away from the Soviet Union and sought closer relations with the European Community. Indeed, Poland, Hungary, and Czechoslovakia all applied for association agreements with the EC while pressing for eventual full membership. COMECON, like WTO, died officially in 1991 with the end of Soviet hegemony over Eastern Europe.

The real problem was how these former satellites, especially Czechoslovakia, Hungary, and Poland (as well as East Germany, now a problem for what used to be West Germany), could be shifted toward free-market economies and democratic societies. Neither would be easy after forty years of communism and totalitarian regimes. All were in economic turmoil, with crumbling infrastructures, outdated factories (many of which were closing and laying off their employees), and considerable environmental damage. Only Czechoslovakia had had experience with democracy before World War II, and the introduction of democracy elsewhere led to protests against widespread unemployment and spiraling inflation, making the transition to a market economy much more difficult. The lot of the Eastern European countries was made even worse when Moscow announced that starting in 1991 it would no longer subsidize oil shipments. Eastern Europeans would have to pay for Soviet oil in hard currency (dollars or German marks, with which the Soviet Union could then buy goods in the West). But that of course, would make it extremely difficult for Eastern Europeans to buy goods from the West. Long dependent on the Soviet Union for cheap fuel and raw materials and for the purchase of most of their finished products, they produced few items competitive on the international market. Thus, they were severely handicapped not only in earning hard currency but also in surviving economically.[11]

The United States and the Western European states all extended aid. American assistance was relatively small because of the budget deficit; indeed, it was a long way from the Marshall Plan. Germany, Europe's most prosperous state, offered far more. The EC too extended aid packages, and France's president called on Europeans to establish the European Bank for Reconstruction and Development. They did so with $13 billion in capital, to be used to encourage profitable ventures and the development of a private sector in Eastern Europe in the wake of the failed Communist economies. But as those economies teetered, that sum seemed increasingly insignificant in view of the enormity of the task. Indeed, after the failure of the 1991 coup in the Soviet Union and the subsequent collapse of that country, their lot worsened, for the Soviet Union had been their largest trading partner.

Aid for the Soviet Union: Bailing Out a Former Enemy?

But it was the Soviet Union that proved to be the country most in need. By the late 1980s, the central government's authority in Moscow was being challenged openly by republics that considered themselves sovereign and their law superior to that of the Soviet Union. Indeed, at least five republics sought statehood. Its economic troubles worsened as well, in part because of Gorbachev's dwindling authority, in part because of the resistance of the Soviet bureaucracy, and in part because of the difficulties encountered in replacing seventy years of communism with a market economy—Gorbachev's declared goal.

As the 1990s began in the Soviet Union, the fear of hunger was widespread. The Soviet government's ability to impose its will was declining, and Gorbachev was becoming increasingly unpopular. Not surprisingly, then, President George Bush and the other Western leaders were concerned about Gorbachev's survival, in whom they had a vested interest. It was Gorbachev who had called off the cold war, who had allowed the Eastern European countries to de-Communize, who had signed the largest conventional arms reduction treaty in history (and was about to agree to a major strategic arms control agreement that cut the most destabilizing weapons by 50 percent), and who had helped resolve several regional conflicts. Germany, which was particularly grateful to Gorbachev for letting German reunification proceed and which had between 1989 and 1991 pledged $34 billion in credits and subsidies (including $13.5 billion to help pay for the upkeep of Soviet troops until they were withdrawn in 1994), sent potatoes, an item not earlier in short supply. The EC as a whole gave the Soviet Union $1 billion in emergency aid and authorized an additional $1.4 billion in technical assistance for 1991-

1992.[12] In 1990, the United States extended $1 billion in loans, enabling Moscow to buy food, and it extended a further $1.5 billion in agricultural credits in 1991. Other Western states sent food as well, although the big question was whether that food would reach Soviet consumers since the Soviets could not even get their own food from the field to the kitchen. More to the point, in a study commissioned by the industrial nations at their 1990 economic summit, the International Monetary Fund concluded that, short of the Soviet Union making a decisive change from its centralized command economy, economic aid to the Soviet Union would be wasted.[13]

But wishing to see Gorbachev remain in power was not the only goal. The second goal was reconciliation with the defeated power and its integration into the state system that it had so long rejected and sought to replace. The United States had not treated its former World War II enemies in a vengeful manner as the allies had done with the harsh peace settlement they had imposed on Germany after World War I. Instead, it had helped them get back on their feet economically and welcomed them into the Western alliance of democratic nations. Similarly, having won the cold war, the United States did not intend to gloat over the Soviet Union's defeat. Rather, it sought to attract it as a partner in the creation of a more secure Europe and post-cold war political and economic international order.

The third goal was to prevent, or at least reduce, indigenous causes of future conflict. Eastern Europe was a hotbed of ethnic, nationalist, and border disputes. All the old nationality problems, suppressed for so long by the Soviet presence in all countries but Yugoslavia (which for most of the postwar period was held together by its revered wartime leader, Marshal Tito), seemed to be bursting out anew with even greater intensity. Fifteen—or more— probably squabbling countries emerging out of the Soviet Union would intensify this instability. Moreover, the fledgling democracies of Eastern Europe could easily fall victim to this strife and bigotry as in Yugoslavia. What was likely to accentuate these divisions was economic failure; it certainly had fed the demands of the various Soviet republics for independence or greater sovereignty. Only in a situation of economic growth in which all or most groups prospered could political and economic instability be avoided. Such economic failure would be even more visible and more troublesome if the ideological wall that had earlier separated Europe became an economic one. Poland's first non-Communist premier voiced these thoughts when he told European leaders in 1990, "Our common future may be darkened by the sinister clouds of resurging conflicts of bygone days unless the split into a rich and a poor Europe, an 'A' class and a 'B' class Europe, is overcome." [14]

In the case of the Soviet Union, economic failure would be compounded if it led ultimately to the resurrection of some sort of angry authoritarian regime. Given its still formidable nuclear and conventional forces, the decay of the Soviet superpower was therefore a matter of concern. But the issue was not just military. The Western states had to be concerned about the flood of immigrants from the Soviet Union to Western Europe if the economy continued its downward spiral. For the Soviet Union as well as Eastern Europe, the linking and eventual integration of their economies to those of the EC and, more broadly, to those of the West as a whole, were expected to be beneficial to their economic growth and political stability, as well as those of the European and world economies. Indeed, the problems of the Soviet Union were so much greater than those of its former allies—and the consequences of failure so much more serious—that the West began to consider whether it should provide economic aid comparable in scale to the Marshall Plan to help Gorbachev and the reformers maintain popular support during the difficult transition period toward a free-market economy.

Indeed, it was Gorbachev in 1991 who sought Western help in drafting and financing a plan for extensive reform, including the creation of a market economy, political decentralization (giving the republics control of their natural resources, industry, and foreign trade), and privatization.[15] The figures widely quoted ranged from $30 billion to $50 billion a year for five to six years, to be given collectively by all the major industrial Western powers. Some U.S. analysts thought the exchange of Western aid for political and economic changes in the Soviet Union to be a "grand bargain."[16]

Just as after World War II, American policy makers—as well as European and Japanese ones, since today the United States cannot afford this kind of money all by itself—had to ask themselves two questions. The first was whether helping the Soviet Union transform itself into a democratic, free-market society and helping Gorbachev stay in power—as opposed to the possible establishment of a right-wing dictatorship or the disintegration of the country into squabbling republics—were worth this kind of economic effort, given their own financial problems and commitments to domestic policies, many of which needed more money as well. Over four years, the United States had spent $5 billion a year (2 percent of its GNP) on the Marshall Plan. The equivalent today for the seven major industrial powers would be about $200 billion, a figure considerably below that suggested by Gorbachev.

The U.S. contribution was estimated at $3-$4 billion, a manageable figure. Admittedly, *perestroika* was in trouble. Changing a society over to totally new ways of economic and political organization could fail, reactionary forces might try to stop this process and reestablish a dictatorship, and the country might still fall apart. But, as emphasized earlier, not humiliating a defeated power—which is what the Soviet Union was—and extending a helping hand were said to be the best means of ensuring future stability and peace. It would be a gamble. But was it not worth such a "grand bargain" to ensure the transformation of an enemy into an ally or, at worst, a neutral state— especially when the cost could be more than made up from the sizable cuts in defense that a friendly Soviet Union would allow and the aid extended would benefit U.S. farmers and manufacturers?[17] Was this not especially so if the democracies really believed that democratic countries could pursue peaceful foreign policies?

The second and, as it turned out, more critical question was what the chances of success would be. The assumption was that such a radical domestic restructuring was possible even though the bureaucrats in the party, army, secret police, and economic ministries remained in power—unlike in Eastern Europe, where the *nomenklatura*'s elimination was a precondition for the introduction of democracy and the free market. Without the removal of those wedded to the status quo, would the "grand bargain" not turn out to be a "grand illusion," leaving the United States and the West just pouring money down the proverbial bottomless sinkhole (as they had done earlier with their loans to the still-Communist Eastern European states in the 1980s)? Did Gorbachev—an unelected and increasingly unpopular leader who had been talking about economic restructuring since 1988, only to reject previous radical plans for introducing a free-market economy—have the will to push through the revolutionary changes required against the formidable domestic opposition? Surely the Western powers would not advance large sums of money without first seeing Gorbachev carry out substantial economic reforms.[18] Otherwise, would they not be strengthening the very forces that were opposed to the free market? And should not such reforms also include substantial military cuts in Soviet offensive capabilities, as well as a cut in the still multibillion dollar annual aid for Cuba? [19] *

Keeping in mind the West's caution about committing large sums of money before the Soviet Union had done more to demonstrate its will to carry out the transformation to a market economy, Gorbachev—with the support of nine republic presidents—went to a meeting in 1991 of the world's seven leading capitalist states (the so-called G-7) and, publicly at least, did not ask for funds (he also did not provide a more detailed economic plan, committing himself in only general terms). The Soviet Union was offered special associate status in the capitalist world's International Monetary Fund and World Bank (it then applied for full membership, which it received in 1992, even though it had not yet adopted a free-market economy). That status would enable it to draw on the expertise of those institutions as well as money for planning the transition, and initiate a linkage to the world economy. The Soviets also hoped to obtain substantial technical assistance in converting their economy from a military to a civilian one and improving its food distribution, rebuilding its oil economy, and making its transportation system more efficient.

---

* The decline in the Soviet aid on which Cuba had so long depended, leading to severe austerity on the island, raised the question of whether Cuban leader Fidel Castro—who stubbornly declared that he would continue his socialist ways—could long survive. In September 1991, Gorbachev announced that Soviet military personnel would be withdrawn from Cuba and that future economic relations would be based on free trade, thus ending the roughly $2 billion annual subsidy, which from 1961-1988 had totalled $39.6 billion and in 1989 had still amounted to $4.5 billion. Thomas L. Friedman, "Gorbachev Says He's Ready to Pull Troops Out of Cuba and End Castro's Subsidies," *New York Times*, September 12, 1991.

(Indeed, as Gorbachev reportedly suggested, private corporations might wish to invest in such areas as oil and gas, transportation, information technology, light industry, and the conversion of arms factories to consumer goods production as part of Gorbachev's program of demilitarizing the Soviet economy.) While Gorbachev thus did not "crawl," as he had put it, for aid from the leaders of the Western industrial nations once it became clear that no large-scale aid would be offered, his very presence at the G-7 meeting and his request for help in reforming his failed and bankrupt economy were clear indicators of the failure of communism and its defeat in the cold war.[20] Whether the Soviet Union was defeated or not, the failed coup attempt shortly after the G-7 meeting weakened further the reactionary forces in the party, military, secret police, and military-industrial complex who had waged the cold war and strengthened the democratic ones.

After the coup, the calls for the West to reconsider extending large-scale aid to strengthen the movement toward a politically more pluralistic society and to ease the transition to a free-market economy became more urgent. But the problem now was that it was unclear what political structure would replace the federation of quasi-autonomous republics originally envisaged in the All-Union treaty. On the one hand, the political changes resulting from the breakup of the Communist party's grip on power were hopeful, for they removed the biggest obstacle to reform. On the other hand, economic improvement of a centerless economy would prove difficult. Would there be a commonwealth of genuinely independent states, each with its own currency and taxing and spending plans, that would quarrel over trade and borders, or would the republics, despite their differences, be able to agree on maintaining a single economy and currency and cooperate on essential economic, military, and political issues? How many republics would join such a "union"? Indeed, did it make much sense to offer any assistance until it became clear what kind of political structure, if any, would emerge?[21] In the meantime, did it not make more sense to provide in-kind assistance, such as food, to alleviate critical shortages during the winter of 1991-1992 and, more important in the long run, technical assistance to improve the Soviet distribution system so that the food does not rot between field and table, or to establish a banking system, or to convert a defense economy to a civilian economy, or to improve the yield of Soviet oil fields?[22] But there was one thing all Western states agreed on: they all had a stake in supporting the reformers.

The question became even more critical as the Soviet Union was declared officially dead and the new Commonwealth of Independent States (CIS) took its place. In the words of the director of the Central Intelligence Agency,

> All of the former Soviet republics face enormous economic, social and political problems that will make the transition to democracy and a market economy difficult and potentially dangerous. The economy is in a free fall with no prospects for reversal in sight. Severe economic conditions, including substantial shortages of food and fuel in some areas, the disintegration of the armed forces and ongoing ethnic conflict will combine this winter [of 1991-1992] to produce

the most significant disorder in the former U.S.S.R. since the Bolsheviks consolidated power."[23]

Bush administration secretary of state James Baker, emphasizing that the West's security interest would be deeply affected by the outcome of what was happening in the Soviet Union, said,

> If during the cold war we faced each other as two scorpions in a bottle, now the Western nations and the former Soviet republics stand as awkward climbers on a steep mountain. Held together by a single rope, a fall toward fascism or anarchism in the former Soviet Union will pull the West down, too. Yet a strong, steady pull by the West now can help them to gain their footing ... [and] anchor [the CIS] firmly in ... the democratic commonwealth of nations.[24]

In short, the West and a huge stake in the success of the new association.

If the CIS faltered in its efforts to build peaceful, democratic, and economically stable societies—and especially if Russia reverted to its internally repressive and externally aggressive one—it would have harmful effects on future Western relations with the commonwealth. The West could not risk an economic collapse and possible restoration of a dictatorship in a country still equipped with thousands of nuclear weapons. Would not aid to assist a shift away from militarization and toward a free economy more than make up for the long-run savings from defense budgets cuts? According to the administration, however, the United States, burdened by its enormous deficit, could not afford much assistance. This position was harshly criticized by former president Richard Nixon. Comparing the historical significance of the democratic revolution in Russia to the defeat of Napoleon at Waterloo in 1815, the Versailles peace treaty in 1919, and the creation of the Marshall Plan and NATO in the late 1940s, he argued that the "stakes are high, but we are playing it as if it were a penny-ante game."[25] Stung by this criticism and reminded that the secretary of state had already made the same case for aid, the administration committed itself to a collective Western aid plan. In President Bush's words, "Together [with our allies] we won the cold war, and today we must win the peace."[26]

Yet two questions hung over the entire aid issue. One was whether the CIS would survive the same divisive nationalist, ethnic, and economic forces that had destroyed the Soviet Union. CIS members seemed unable to maintain a single economic market with a single currency—the basis for their economic recovery—to which they initially had committed themselves. They also disagreed about maintaining a joint military force. The core of the CIS was Russia and Ukraine. But these two republics appeared almost from the beginning to be heading for a divorce as Ukraine, asserting its nationalism, sought its own currency and armed forces. In response, Russia too established its own Ministry of Defense, providing for its own security if and when the commonwealth collapsed.[27] (A subsidiary issue was whether the republics, especially Russia, could manage to avoid further subdivision.)

The second major question was whether Russian leader Boris Yeltsin would survive the population's unhappiness at the steep price increases, continued shortages, and rising unemployment as he began his free-market conversion? Could the 1992 announced Western aid package of $24 billion, if it is delivered, make more than a marginal contribution? After two years in which it had already received over $40 billion in aid, Russia's prospects—and those of the other republics—seemed as dim as ever. Germany's continuing sizable and greater-than-expected investment in the former East Germany suggested that Russia probably would require trillions of dollars over a number of years, although the International Monetary Fund estimated that Russia and the fourteen other republics of the former Soviet Union would require $100 billion over the next four-year period to help achieve the desired results.[28] In the final analysis, then, the success of a transition to democracy after hundreds of years of autocracy and a free market after seventy years of a Soviet centralized economy appeared to depend on the population of Russia and the other republics.[29]

THE GREAT POWERS VERSUS THEIR SECONDARY ADVERSARIES: QUOTAS, BOYCOTTS, AND EMBARGOES

Economic pressures are used by the great powers in dealing not only with one another and their chief allies but also frequently with other conflicts. The examples described here involved the United States and countries in Latin America and the Middle East.

Cuba, Panama, and Iraq

Cuba. After Fidel Castro assumed power in Havana in 1959, Cuba's relationship with the United States grew more contentious. Evidence of Cuban alignment with the United States' principal enemy led the administration of Dwight Eisenhower to try to both punish and warn Castro by suspending imports of 700,000 tons of sugar that remained unshipped out of Cuba's total 1960 U.S. quota of approximately 3 million tons. (A quota is an import level for a particular product established by the importing government for a specific period. This amount can be sold at a price higher than the international market one.) For Cuba, whose entire economy was based on sugar production, this suspension was a form of pressure. The United States was trying to punish Castro, if not to eliminate him. But despite the loss of a sure American market, Cuba was not deterred from turning toward the Soviet bloc, even after the United States embargoed all exports to the island (except food and medicine).

Panama. In 1988, the United States tried to use its economic power against a nearby target—Panama.[30] If great-power primacy in the international system, or for that matter American hegemony in this hemisphere, meant anything, it should have been a simple matter to eliminate Gen. Manuel Noriega, the head of Panama's armed forces who had been indicted by two Florida grand juries for drug-running. The Panamanian economy was very vulnerable to American pressure. Indeed, the U.S. dollar was Panama's currency. By freezing all Panamanian government assets in American banks, withholding payments of canal revenues and taxes by American companies doing business in Panama, and depositing these monies instead into an escrow account to be used by a post-Noriega government acceptable to the United States, Washington caused a severe cash shortage. Banks could not meet payrolls, and the financial system, already badly managed and debt-ridden, was brought close to collapse. The then severely damaged Panamanian economy, together with the mass demonstrations against Noriega, which had already been going on for some time, were expected to force him out of office within a few weeks. How could Noriega govern if he had no cash?

But Noriega could not have cared less about the hardships of the Panamanian people. He consolidated his power by replacing officers not completely loyal to him and strengthening his links to Cuba, Nicaragua, and the Medellin drug cartel in Colombia. Above all, Noriega made the United States look— to paraphrase Richard Nixon's comments on Vietnam—like a pitiful, helpless giant, an impotent superpower. President Ronald Reagan had declared that this "tin horn" dictator had to go, and Noriega successfully stood up to him as all of Latin America and the rest of the world watched.

In 1989, the failure of the United States to aid in a coup attempt by some of Noriega's fellow officers after President Bush had encouraged such a coup appeared to underline U.S. impotence and Noriega's defiance. But force was ruled out because of the precedent of using U.S. armed forces stationed in a foreign country to overthrow its government and even more because of Latin American fears of "Yanqui intervention" and because of opposition to such intervention. Ironically, given the popularity of the antidrug cause at the time and U.S. support of the Colombian government's efforts to suppress the Medellin drug barons, there was strong congressional support for the use of force. It was only after the failed coup attempt that Noriega, cockier than ever, taunting the United States and harassing American personnel stationed in Panama, provoked U.S. military intervention, resulting in his own ouster.

Iraq. If any embargo should have worked, it was the one against Iraq after it had invaded Kuwait in 1990 and then annexed the country, declaring it to be a province of Iraq. By this action, Saddam Hussein was sending the world the message that he would not retreat (a message that he reinforced by giving up all the gains from the long war with Iran to concentrate his forces against the Western forces gathering in Saudi Arabia). Having surrendered the gains paid for with so much blood, could he retreat a second time?

Applied to compel Iraq to pull out of Kuwait and restore its legitimate government, the embargo against Iraq was a good test case of the effectiveness, as well as the limits, of this economic tool for several reasons. First, the Iraqi action was denounced and opposed by the United States, its NATO allies, the Soviet Union, and most Arab nations. Thus, there was considerable collective support for the embargo. Second, the embargo was endorsed by the UN Security Council. Countries that might not have supported the embargo had it been organized by the United States were willing to do so because the United Nations gave their action legitimacy. The United Nations also gave its blessing to enforcement of the embargo by American and other Western warships and aircraft. And, third, Iraq, almost totally dependent on oil export earnings for its living, was very vulnerable to economic sanctions, so much so that it was hoped that they alone would suffice, making the use of force unnecessary.

The embargo deprived Iraq of approximately $1.5 billion a month in revenues. To implement the embargo, Turkey and Saudi Arabia shut down the oil pipelines that ran across their territories, and a naval blockade stopped shipment of oil through the Persian Gulf. Iraq depended on imports for much of its food; the country produced only about one-quarter of its needs. Food imports too were cut off. Iraqi industry, in addition, needed a steady supply of foreign supplies and raw materials, and power-generating plants, irrigation works, and petrochemical industries all needed Western machinery and spare parts. Finally, the economy required foreign experts and labor to keep it running. While Iraq was forcing these technicians to stay and work, the cutoff of imports of supplies left them little to do. Foreign laborers were used especially on farms, but most of the 1 million Egyptians who had worked there fled the country.[31]

Thus, Iraq faced bankruptcy, a total breakdown of its economy, and food shortages. It should have worked. The Western industrial states defending Saudi Arabia appeared willing to bear the burden of the daily shortfall of 4 million barrels of oil, which, although made up quickly by increased production by Saudi Arabia and other states, led to a steep (but brief) rise in oil prices, fueling inflation and deepening a recession—particularly in the United States. Moreover, no major leaks appeared in the embargo, although smuggled goods continued to enter from Turkey, Iran, Syria, and Jordan.[32] Iraq, formerly one of the radical states the Soviet Union had supported in the Third World, had no alternative sources of supply or markets. Even Iran stated its support of the embargo, although it voiced its displeasure at the presence of U.S. forces in the area. And the majority of Arab states were steadfast too.

Indeed, the embargo reportedly had major effects. Several serious food shortages occurred after some months, and prices rose sharply.[33] Supplies of chlorine compounds to purify drinking water ran low. As Soviet advisers left, the maintenance and combat readiness of Soviet-supplied aircraft and air defense radar and missiles were affected. Thus, many voices in the United States, especially Democratic ones in the Congress, argued that if sanctions were given time—estimates ranged from nine to eighteen to twenty-four months—war would be unnecessary. But Saddam Hussein remained as tough as ever, restating that Kuwait had become a permanent province of Iraq. The loss of oil revenues and the pain from the sanctions did not have the desired effect of compelling him to withdraw from Kuwait.

Conclusions. What conclusions can be drawn from these three examples? In Cuba, U.S. economic pressure was unsuccessful. In fact, the eventual elimination of the sugar quota strengthened Castro's popularity at home, diverted Cuban attention from the regime's failures, and allowed Castro to use the United States as his scapegoat while simultaneously urging his people to work harder and rally to his cause. Attempted economic coercion also brought him admiration throughout Latin America precisely because of his successful defiance of the United States. Probably no amount of U.S. economic aid could have dissuaded Castro from enacting his role as a revolutionary leader. Thus the lesson to be learned: economic sanctions may serve only to arouse nationalism and to rally public support for the targeted regime. In short, they can have effects opposite of the ones sought.[34]

Another lesson can be drawn from the Cuban experience: if alternative sources of supplies and export markets are available, sanctions inflict only temporary pain. A nation is vulnerable only if it is largely dependent on one product and trades mainly with one country. Castro was able to simply switch markets. Cuban sugar was sold to the Soviet bloc, which also became the source of products that Cuba had previously imported from the United States. Given the diversity of available markets, any targeted regime can survive with very little discomfort.

During the application of economic sanctions, a population that supports its government will tend to bear a lot of hardship. Moreover, if the regime has tight control of the population, it really does not matter very much if the population grumbles about its deprivations. In such regimes as those in Panama and Iraq, both controlled by the military, the only hope is for a military coup. In Panama, the feeble attempt made was poorly planned, ineffectively carried out, and apparently depended on U.S. military intervention by the forces stationed in Panama to guard the Panama Canal. In Iraq, a coup was never likely. Saddam Hussein had potential rivals and opponents killed (some reportedly personally) or exiled. He had total political control; not one of his advisers would have dared to disagree with him. Opposition in all probability would lead to torture and execution (he, again reportedly, enjoyed watching his victims being thrown into vats of acid).

Nor could popular discontent be translated into political action that might compel Iraq's leader to change his policy. There was no opposition leader or group through which to channel popular discontent into action. Eight years of war with Iran, in any case, had shown that the Iraqi people could live with extraordinary hardships. It also had shown that their leader left them little choice since their lot was not his main concern. A reduction in their daily caloric intake would have little effect on him. Saddam Hussein, the hand-picked elite around him, and the Republican Guard forces would have enough to eat. An embargo, in short, may inflict a great deal of pain on a civilian population, but Saddam Hussein had a high level of tolerance for his people's pain, including that inflicted by him.

Nowhere was this more visible than after the war when the embargo remained in effect. While the Iraqi people suffered from lack of food and medicine, especially the children, Saddam Hussein sought to evade the cease-fire terms that called for destroying his mass-destruction weapons. This ensured that the sanctions would not be lifted and that Iraq would not be able to sell oil to buy the goods it needed.* Thus, the Iraqi leader once and for all discredited the idea that economic sanctions alone would have dislodged him from Kuwait, even though the embargo shut off more than 90 percent of Iraq's imports and 97 percent of its oil export revenues.

As the Bush administration saw it, the key to success, then, was communicating to Saddam Hussein that if the embargo did not compel him to withdraw from Kuwait unconditionally, military force might. Economic and military power, in short, had to be perceived by the target country as part of a

---

* Once Iraq was defeated, the Bush administration, together with Britain, declared that the United States would oppose the lifting of sanctions as long as Saddam Hussein remained in power. Why Washington expected the elite around the Iraqi leader to overthrow him is unclear since the elite, like Saddam Hussein, continued to live well and many of his appointees were relatives. Only the mass of Iraqis suffered the effects of prolonged sanctions. Indeed, shortages of food and medicine became so bad that the head of the UN mission in Iraq recommended relaxation of the embargo.

But as expected, Saddam Hussein remained Saddam Hussein, continuing to lie about biological weapons research and how many chemical weapons he had and revealing only bit by bit under the threat of renewed air attacks information about secret uranium enrichment and plutonium extraction programs for nuclear weapons. In short, because of Saddam Hussein the Iraqi people faced a famine as he sought to manipulate their misery to escape the pressure to comply with the cease-fire terms. He thus rejected a plan whereby Iraq could on a one-time basis sell up to $1.6 billion in oil for six months, the proceeds of which would be disbursed by the United Nations in part to pay the reparations demanded for Iraqi destruction, the UN costs in implementing the cease-fire terms, and the costs of the food and medicine the United Nations thought Iraq would require. In his efforts to get the sanctions lifted and continue his arms efforts, Saddam Hussein specifically blocked the distribution of food and medicine to tens of thousands of Iraqis by a number of nongovernmental organizations. The strategy was clear: end the sanctions and earn money by maximizing the world's pity and blaming the United States.

But the Western powers refused to relax the sanctions. Whether this would continue if photos of starving Iraqis continue to appear on Western television sets remains to be seen. In the *New York Times*, see Patrick E. Tyler, "Bush Links End of Trading Ban to Hussein Exit," and "Iraqi Suffering Deepens as the Economy Rots," May 21 and November 10, 1991, respectively; and Paul E. Lewis, "Head of the U.N. Mission in Iraq Asks Council to Relax Sanctions," and "U.N. Finds Hussein to Blame for Widening Travail in Iraq," July 13, 1991 and February 6, 1992, respectively.

continuum; economic power was *not* an alternative to the use of force.[35] If the former worked, fine. But if it did not, harsher and more punitive measures would be employed. President Bush and the United Nations had declared that if Saddam Hussein did not pull out from Kuwait, force would be used to achieve this objective. The question was whether that possibility was really credible to Iraq's ruthless and tough-minded leader, especially in view of the growing opposition to war in the United States as it became more likely. When the United Nations declared that the Iraqi leader had until January 15, 1991, to make up his mind, most Democrats in Congress voiced increasing opposition to going to war. Claiming to support President Bush in his objectives, they argued that the embargo had not had enough time to work; a year or two might be necessary to compel Iraq's withdrawal from Kuwait. Others—including former high government officials, leading organizations claiming to represent the Christian churches, media commentators, and the prestigious *New York Times*—joined the Democrats, opposing the use of force. The Vietnam syndrome was clearly still alive. That, of course, was Saddam Hussein's principal assumption, and it was why he refused a diplomatic solution, even though any "rational" leader calculating the power arrayed against him would have accepted such a solution (indeed, most U.S., European, and Israeli experts predicted that he would do so at the last moment).

Two additional points are worth emphasizing. One is that however credible initially the added threat of war might have been to the success of economic sanctions, the longer the delay in using force, the less credible was the threat. Those who argued for longer reliance on sanctions did so on the grounds that postponement of the use of force would mean a shorter and less costly war against a weaker Iraq. In brief, the argument allegedly was not about whether to fight, only when. But if the allies waited a year, eighteen months, or longer, the threat of war, which was to pressure Saddam Hussein to give way while the sanctions were still the only punishment, would be emasculated. To put it more bluntly, many of those who pleaded "give sanctions time to work" were silently saying, "If they don't work, let's forget the whole thing." The other point is that if the aim of the embargo was not merely to compel Saddam Hussein to pull out of Kuwait but also to destroy the military capability with which he threatened all his neighbors, a retreat from Kuwait might have been only temporary, to be resumed after the United States had withdrawn its forces and Hussein had acquired nuclear arms. Even if successful, the embargo would not have destroyed Iraq's military strength or the regime, which was the actual critical problem because it sought to dominate the entire area. Indeed, as was discovered after the war, Iraq was within an estimated twelve to eighteen months of obtaining the atom bomb—and those advocating sanctions wanted to wait patiently for up to two years for them to work! Iraq was even working on a hydrogen bomb, which was a total surprise to the outside world. In short, had the war been postponed long enough, the West would have confronted a nuclear-armed Iraq.

It is also well to remember that not only the target country suffers but the embargoer as well. There is always a price to be paid. It may be the lost income for farmers or industrialists or bankers, as was the case for the U.S. embargo on the Soviet Union after Afghanistan. In the case of Iraq, the costs were also high for the United States: a steep rise in oil prices, thus boosting inflation and pushing the country's economy, already heading downward, into a recession. Despite these results, the president initially received widespread support for the embargo. But when he escalated the military pressure by increasing the 230,000 forces in Saudi Arabia and the Persian Gulf to 430,000, the criticism that he should give the embargo more time began, although the critics never answered whether they would be willing to use force if at the end of twelve or eighteen or twenty-four months it became clear that economic sanctions had failed. This was not an idle question since in fact time has shown that even after six weeks of intense aerial bombardment of Iraq, even after the coalition's invasion of Kuwait had begun, and even after Saddam Hussein had accepted a Soviet plan for withdrawal, he still did not reverse his annexation of Kuwait. He did so only after his forces were defeated. What chances, therefore, were there that after a year or two economic sanctions would have compelled Iraq to withdraw from Kuwait and give up its claim of annexation? The answer would appear to be none.

A potentially greater cost would be political: the collapse of the UN coalition. The administration feared that if U.S. forces stayed in Saudi Arabia too long, particularly past the Muslim celebration of Ramadan and the later pilgrimages to Mecca, they might undermine the conservative traditions of Saudi society and even lead to instability if Saddam Hussein were able to exploit his charge that the presence of "infidels" (the U.S. and other Western troops) defiled Muslim holy places. There were other political concerns as well. An open alliance between the United States (Israel's friend) and the Arab states was fragile at best, and, while the Soviet Union, China, and France had supported the UN resolution threatening war (China actually abstained from that vote), they remained reluctant to sanction the use of force if economic measures failed. Indeed, any one of a number of considerations could overnight break up the anti-Iraqi coalition and leave its members scurrying to Baghdad to strike the best deal they could: for example, a major Israeli-Palestinian clash; a setback to Gorbachev, such as the foreign minister's resignation or the Soviet military crackdown in Lithuania, jeopardizing U.S.-Soviet cooperation on Iraq and other issues; or a perception by the Arab states aligned with the United States that it was faltering in its task of ejecting Iraq from Kuwait, which would leave Saddam Hussein triumphant and the dominant regional power. In addition, there was the problem of maintaining the support of Turkey, Egypt, and the other states hit hard economically because they opposed Saddam Hussein. The Iraqi confrontation was also potentially costly to America's alliance systems. While France and Britain sent forces to Saudi Arabia, Germany and Japan, pleading constitutional reasons, sent no forces and, relative to their GNPs, made smaller contributions than they might have to sustaining Operations Desert Shield and Desert Storm. One liberal columnist observed that not enough notice has been taken of the fact that the victors of World War II were shedding blood and treasure on behalf of the losers, Germany and Japan, now the world's most prosperous nations, "neither of which shows much gratitude or mercy in trade relations, and both of which benefit from Mid East oil more than do the U.S., Britain and France." [36] The resentment this produced in the United States, as well as the angry reactions of these countries because they claimed they had made significant financial contributions, exacerbated tensions already created by trade conflicts—even though Germany and Japan, once the fighting started, contributed the giant share of the cost.

Economic Coercion and High Politics

Economic sanctions, like force, are political instruments.[37] Like war, they seek to achieve specific political aims: to compel the targeted state to comply with the preferred policies of the sanctioning state (Kissinger's economic linkage policy toward the Soviet Union); to deter or, if not to deter, to punish an adversary (Carter's grain embargo against Moscow); to eliminate a perceived hostile regime (Castro and the Eisenhower sugar quota or the Reagan-Bush squeeze of Panama); or to communicate disapproval toward an adversary (or all of the preceding examples). All of these apply to the U.S. and UN-imposed sanctions on Iraq.

But almost all of these publicly imposed sanctions failed to achieve their political objectives. The main reason for failure was not only that the targeted nations were usually able to avoid economic pain, but also that their leaders and populations recognized that their stake in maintaining their policies was high. Compliance was considered to be the surrender of each nation's dignity and independence to decide its own future. The Soviets learned this lesson in the late 1940s when Stalin cut off all trade and aid to Yugoslavia after his quarrel with Marshal Tito. Stalin failed in the effort to eliminate Tito, who simply shifted to American and West European markets, while the people rallied to his support. Indeed, as a leader of the Yugoslav guerrilla movement against the occupying Nazi armies during World War II, Tito had come to symbolize Yugoslav nationalism.

It is also a lesson that the Soviets taught the United States in 1975, when they rejected a commercial agreement because of American demands that they change their policy on emigration, especially for Jews. No power, and certainly not a great power, will admit publicly that it has mistreated its own citizens; none will promise to improve its behavior under pressure. Domestic affairs are considered the business of the national government and of no one else. To insist on domestic changes is an affront. The Soviets therefore turned down the agreement. (In contrast, quiet, behind-the-scenes diplomacy had gained the release of 35,000 Soviet Jews in 1973.)

In a clash between a nation's vital interests and economic benefits, high politics takes priority over low politics. *Attempts at economic coercion are gener-*

ally self-defeating when the target state believes high-politics issues are at stake. Instead, such attempts strengthen the morale of the targeted nation and stiffen its resistance to negotiations. Indeed, what is usually overlooked when sanctions are applied is that even if the leaders of the targeted state wished to comply, they cannot. They would be accused of capitulating to foreigners' demands and jeopardizing their nations' security and independence. In short, they would lose domestic support if they complied. Even in Panama, where many *Panamanians* hoped the United States would succeed, pressure did not work.

One has to ask why, given this failure rate, states indulge in applying sanctions at all. One reason is that sanctions, such as those against South Africa for its policy of apartheid, are a way of expressing displeasure with another nation's policy and defusing domestic critics. They are essentially *symbolic* sanctions. Although South African exports to the United States, its largest trading partner, declined by 10 percent (more so than with other industrial countries), they flourished with the newly industrializing Asian countries. Trade with Taiwan doubled to $1 billion in 1987 alone. Overall, South Africa, a developed country with abundant natural resources, *increased* its trade.

The largest economic impact of sanctions, resulting from the disinvestment by U.S. companies (Ford, Coca-Cola, General Motors, Mobil, Goodyear, IBM, and others), was on South Africa's capitalists who made a fortune buying the departing American corporations cheaply while the latter continued to sell their products as before. The loss of jobs was felt mainly by South Africa's black population, who also lost significant amounts of welfare spending that the purchasers of U.S. companies curtailed. And the imposition of sanctions, as noted earlier, are expensive to the party imposing them—for example, the University of California spent $600 million to divest its retirement portfolio of the stocks of companies doing business with South Africa. More broadly, the main loss may have been U.S. influence in South Africa.[38] Why then did South Africa change its apartheid policy? In part, it was the nation's political and psychological isolation. But mainly it was the belief that the domestic situation would only grow worse as opposition to apartheid increased that led the new president of that country, F. W. de Klerk, to create a new South Africa acceptable to the world and to the majority of the people in his country. In 1990, the European Community, which had been shipping goods to South Africa via its neighbors, partially lifted its sanctions. And in 1991, the United States lifted them as well. In both Europe and the United States, public opinion had swung toward encouraging South Africa and ending its outlaw status.

In Panama, an embargo was applied because little else could be done. For domestic and international reasons, Reagan felt that he could not send in U.S. forces. With military action ruled out, sanctions were seen as better than nothing; at least they avoided—or were supposed to avoid—the appearance of the United States as helpless. Carter had done the same thing in 1979 when

Iran seized the U.S. embassy in Tehran. Unable to gain the hostages' release, the president halted the purchase of Iranian oil. But because the United States purchased only a small amount of Iranian oil, this cutoff was basically symbolic. To a frustrated American public, the president's move gave the impression of action just short of the use of force, which, it was widely believed, would result in the hostages' death. The real hope of the president was that the action would limit the political damage from the incident. For a while it did, but Carter's failure to secure the hostages' freedom month after month finally hurt him in the next presidential election, contributing to his defeat by Reagan. Why then do governments—especially democratic ones— continue to use sanctions? In large part, sanctions are actually symbolic actions aimed at minimizing domestic damage and avoiding the image of impotency at home and abroad.

This was obviously not true for Iraq, where what might be called *strategic* sanctions were imposed to change the target state's external behavior which threatened the vital interests of the sanctioning states. Unlike the other case studies, this embargo posed the issue of economic coercion versus the use of force. Those who argued for giving economic sanctions time to work had a strong case. Rarely had there been such widespread international support for an embargo or a state so vulnerable as Iraq. An embargo would avoid heavy losses of life and any unexpected consequences of military action. And over time, it would help the formation of a domestic consensus. Yet a lengthy embargo depended on the survival of the anti-Iraqi coalition. That such a disparate alliance could even be organized was a tribute to President Bush's diplomacy and each member's recognition of its interests.

But time probably favored the target state. Indeed, one of Iraq's tactics was to stall for time in order to probe for weaknesses in the opposing coalition and exploit them. Saddam Hussein, after all, did not have to run for reelection, nor did he have to worry about declining ratings in the polls, opposition newspapers, and a critical legislature. President Bush did have cause for concern. Time might further erode support for sanctions. Most of the critics arguing for more time would have been as strongly opposed to going to war later as they were at the outset. In fact, they knew full well that at the end of the one year (at least) needed for the sanctions to take sufficient effect, the country would be starting the 1992 presidential campaign. Thus, waiting a year really meant delaying the use of force for over two years—until the presidential campaign was over. By that time, war was no longer really credible; no administration was likely to start its four years in office by launching a war. Saddam Hussein would emerge the victor, with all the implications that held for the future emergence of a nuclear-armed Iraq, for the stability of the Middle East-Persian Gulf area, and for the newly emerging post-cold war international order.

The issue, in fact, was never one of economic coercion versus force, as the critics suggested by their arguments; economic pressure could be successful only if backed credibly with military power. Rather than alternatives, they were part of a continuum: if sanctions did not bring about Iraq's withdrawal from Kuwait, then force would be used. The question all along was how to convey this to Saddam Hussein. For all of President Bush's skills in organizing an unprecedented alliance to oppose Saddam Hussein and in mobilizing UN support for economic sanctions and the use of force, the Iraqi leader (at least initially) seemed to refuse to believe that his adversaries would go to war against him. The critics in the United States were especially persuasive in making him think that Washington would be unable to make good on its threats; Bush was merely bluffing. As in the case of Panama, this demonstrated how difficult it is in a democracy—at least, American democracy—to credibly link economic sanctions to the possible use of force in order for sanctions to work and to avoid the use of force.

THE GREAT POWERS AND THE THIRD WORLD

Economic Aid

The unequal distribution of wealth between the First and Third worlds was the original reason for the distribution of U.S. economic aid to the developing countries during the cold war. In the 1950s and 1960s, the heyday of foreign aid, it was feared that if the gap between the rich and poor nations widened, the resulting social instability and political turmoil would give rise to revolutionary conditions. Thus, if the new nations could not transform themselves into urbanized industrial societies able to provide a decent standard of living, they might look at the example of the Soviet Union—which apparently in one generation successfully transformed itself from an agricultural society into a leading industrial state—and adopt communism as a more efficient means of modernization. Implicit in the Western promotion of economic growth, then, was the assumption that poverty would be exploited by the Soviet Union. Development assistance was to prevent this expansion of its influence. It also was assumed that such aid would nurture more open societies and democratic institutions, which in turn were expected to ensure the peaceful behavior of these nations.[39]

For the developing countries, the bipolar distribution of power in the postwar world enhanced their ability to attract the funds needed for their development. Because the superpowers were unwilling to risk total war, and because each hoped to win friends and influence people in the developing areas, foreign aid became an instrument of policy. In the nuclear age, aid was a substitute for arms. According to political scientist George Liska,

> In our times, economic activities are not an alternative [to war]; they are a substitute. They are no longer a preferable alternative to clearly feasible war and to equally despicable but apparently dispensable power politics. They are instead

a substitute for practically self-defeating major war, and they are more than ever an instrument of the again respectable politics of power.[40]

Foreign aid thus became an instrument of economic warfare in the political competition for influence.

The Soviet aid program, begun in the mid-1950s in response to the U.S. effort, was generally confined to states that were either politically vital (such as India), or perceived by the West as "troublemakers" (such as Egypt, Iraq, Algeria, and Cuba). In short, its principal purpose was to weaken Western influence in the Third World. Yet the limitations of Soviet aid stemmed from its long-range political aims, which did not coincide with the aspirations of the developing countries. Admittedly, short-range tactical Soviet goals were often compatible with national independence and nonalignment in foreign policy. One of the attractions of Soviet aid was that it strengthened the newly independent nation by reducing its otherwise exclusive dependence on its former colonial country or on the United States. But ultimate Soviet aims diverged sharply from the objectives of the new states. Most of those nations keenly remembered their long colonial subjugation; they were not about to substitute Soviet colonialism for the Western variety. Their nationalism was directed against *any* foreign control, and this posed a real dilemma for the Soviets. When the Soviets did not interfere in domestic politics, they enjoyed good relations with the recipient nations (such as India). But when they sought to pressure a government to support Soviet positions, attempted to overthrow governments, or refused to support governmental goals, they alienated friendly states (such as the Sudan, Egypt, and Somalia).

Since the principal purpose of the American aid program—which was opposite that of the Soviet program—was to stop the advance of communism, the term *economic aid* was actually something of a misnomer.[41] The giant portion of American aid in the 1950s and 1960s was military aid to support mainly the armies of allied nations around the Sino-Soviet periphery: Nationalist China, South Korea, South Vietnam, Pakistan, and Turkey. Such military assistance was rationalized as a form of economic aid, for the recipient nation could then—theoretically at least—spend less of its own resources on military forces and instead invest more of its own resources on its economic development. In 1981, Reagan's first year in office, security-related assistance represented 50 percent of total U.S. aid; in 1987, that figure stood at 62 percent, and it would have been higher had the administration's aid request been fully granted.[42]

The 1970s, moreover, had witnessed significant changes in aid policies. Both superpowers had become aware that "instant development" was an unrealistic expectation. The efforts seemed never-ending, and the disappointing results of the aid had tired and disenchanted the two principal competitors. Given the enormity of the developing countries' problems, this was hardly surprising. The total of all aid given seemed small by comparison. Both superpowers also recognized that aid did not necessarily buy allies or votes in the United Nations. The Soviet Union had become disillusioned with the more radical nationalist leaders it had once sought as partners against the West. Similarly, the United States had become disenchanted with those who had kept biting the hand that fed them. Moreover, much of the aid was wasted and went into the private bank accounts of corrupt leaders, too little filtered down to the masses. Competition for the Third World also seemed less urgent as other external and domestic commitments became more pressing, especially after the early 1970s when the Western economies were hit by high oil prices, inflation, and unemployment all at the same time. Once the rivalry resumed after 1975, the principal instrument of competition shifted even more to military aid (see Chapter 20).

The result of this situation was that American aid declined in relation to the rising gross national product. In the late 1940s, Marshall Plan aid had totaled 2 percent of GNP. By the beginning of the 1970s, nonmilitary aid had fallen to 0.29 percent of GNP, the lowest figure for all the major donor countries. And in 1986, American aid constituted 0.0018 percent of GNP! That being the first year of a congressional effort to substantially reduce government expenditures under the Gramm-Rudman-Hollings bill, foreign aid was cut, and the amount has been cut every year since. Defense, by contrast, received 6 percent of the national income (but even that figure is below the 10 percent of the 1950s). Today, of the leading seventeen economic powers, the United States remains last in terms of foreign aid given as a percentage of GNP. Small countries such as the Netherlands, the three Scandinavian countries, and Belgium have been among the leading donors—that is, until 1989 when Japan became the world's largest donor. American aid was extended to 102 countries by the late 1970s, although eight of them received 75 percent of the total. By 1989, U.S. aid went to 117 countries or 70 percent of all existing states at the time.

Most developing countries thus received "so little aid that it is too small to make the difference between war and peace, friendship and enmity, or development and underdevelopment." [43] During the 1980s, 40 percent of all aid went to Israel and Egypt. This left little for human needs programs or emergencies, such as helping the new democratic government in the Philippines recover after the gutting of its economy by the previous dictatorial regime. Moreover, during the Reagan years the emphasis in development programs was on a larger role for private enterprise: less government intervention in the economy, more private enterprise, and attractive conditions for foreign capital investment were the prescription. And given the failure of the economic planning and state-controlled industries of so many countries, as well as the successful examples of the newly industrialized countries, the Reagan prescription had wide appeal.

During the Brezhnev and Gorbachev years, Soviet economic assistance also reached a low point. The inability of the Soviet Union to provide economic development assistance on the scale expected by its Third World friends was a serious handicap in its efforts to influence the less-developed states. The

Soviets simply had too many economic problems at home to afford the constant demands for economic aid. One Cuba to support at an estimated $12–$14 million per day in the late 1980s and a Vietnam costing approximately $2 million a day were enough! Angola, Ethiopia, Nicaragua, and other pro-Soviet Marxist states, which even among the developing countries were the least successful economically, were told to rely basically on their own efforts; the Soviets would help only to the extent of their ability.[44]

Soviet aid was cut even more as the government focused on preventing the nation's economic collapse. Its failure to support client states was a major factor in Moscow's desire to settle several regional conflicts, and it was why Cuba's Castro, one of the few unreconstructed Communists left, was preparing his people for a life of even greater austerity while the Cuban community in the United States speculated on how long Castro could maintain power.

The United States had similar economic problems at the time. Confronted by the opportunity to improve its sense of security by supporting the new but economically troubled democracies in Eastern Europe, including the members of the Commonwealth of Independent States, and by an obligation to rebuild Panama's shattered economy and restore its democracy, as well as to assist the democratically elected governments in Nicaragua and El Salvador after long U.S.-supported civil wars in those countries, the government was constrained by its budget deficit. Two-thirds of the foreign aid program drawn up before the Iraqi invasion of Kuwait in 1990 still went to Israel (which has intense congressional support), Egypt, and Pakistan.[45]

Furthermore, little attention was given to Third World countries in general. In those countries where most of the world's population lives, neither the old nor the new order can be stable unless the economic and social prospects of the developing countries improve. Despite the internationally endorsed target of a commitment of 0.7 percent of the industrialized countries' GNP to foreign aid, their average is 0.32, and the U.S. contribution is now 0.15 percent of GNP. The developing countries themselves have not helped matters by their excessive spending on arms instead of on their development. Clearly, a change of priorities is required by both donors and recipients. But without the competition characterizing the cold war, the prospects of aid for the developing countries does not look promising. U.S. public opinion has turned increasingly hostile to giving foreign aid when the money is needed at home to help cure domestic problems, including ending the recession.

International 'Debt Bomb'

With the decline in both American and Soviet aid and the high cost of oil in the 1970s, the developing countries began to borrow billions of dollars of investment capital and to go deeply in debt. The result was the "debt bomb." Such private capital is available from two important sources. One source, examined below, is money loaned by banks to either business or government. The other is multinational corporate investments in enterprises ranging from traditional raw material extraction to manufacturing plants (see Chapter 16).

By 1988, about thirty developing countries had collectively run up an astronomical $1.3 trillion debt, about half of it loaned by some of the West's largest multinational banks and the rest by governments and international lending agencies such as the International Monetary Fund (IMF). Approximately $440 billion was owed by Latin American countries, and three-quarters of this amount was owed by Argentina ($54 billion), Brazil ($117 billion), Mexico ($105 billion), and Venezuela ($32 billion).[46] In the early 1980s, the expectation was that should a significant amount of this debt be repudiated, it would bankrupt many banks and create a financial crisis in Western countries. Since that time, the latter have apparently learned to live with this debt and to manage it.

The root of the debt crisis was the rise in oil prices from $3 to $34 a barrel that occurred from 1973 to 1982. The oil-producing countries earned huge amounts of "petrodollars," much of it then invested in the West or deposited in Western banks. But the developing countries were hard hit by the steep increase in their oil bills. Simultaneously, Western economic aid dropped off as the Western economies slumped. The developing countries therefore had to choose between greater belt tightening or going into debt to buy the oil so that they could continue their development and pay for their imported food. Eager banks, holding surplus petrodollars, were only too eager to lend them money. This was, of course, very profitable for the banks, which competed with one another to extend loans and did not worry very much about being repaid. The developing countries used their commodities as collateral; a few borrowers, such as Mexico and Venezuela, were oil producers and wanted the money to develop their oil resources further.

The developing countries, however, could not repay their loans because commodity prices fell sharply. This stemmed mainly from the recession (the result of the steep increase in oil prices) and affected the economies of industrial countries, whose demands for raw materials declined. If an oil producer such as Mexico could not pay off its debt in these circumstances, how could other countries pay, especially such nations as Kenya, Bangladesh, and Zaire, which depended on the export of one item such as coffee, jute, and copper? Chile, for example, dependent on copper exports, suffered a painful setback as a debtor when copper prices fell by more than 50 percent from $1.50 a pound in 1980 to 62 cents a pound by 1985. It lost $29 million for each penny drop in the copper price. For the agricultural economies of Central America, this was a disaster. They suffered several years of no growth or negative growth and increased unemployment in a region already suffering considerable domestic upheaval and international strife.

Another reason the debts of the developing countries became such an unbearable burden was the stronger U.S. dollar. When they had borrowed the money, the developing countries thought the dollars could be repaid easily. The United States was suffering from major inflation in the late 1970s, and the developing countries expected to repay their loans with cheaper dollars. But in the early 1980s, the dollar's value rose sharply relative to other currencies because of the huge Reagan budget deficits, and interest rates remained high. Inflation was gradually brought down, however.

Even to pay off the annual interest on their loans, the developing countries had to borrow more money. To prevent these countries from defaulting on the loans they could not pay back, the banks, ironically, loaned them more! The debtors had their bankers over a barrel; the bankers feared that the debtors might organize a debtor cartel and repudiate their loans. Increasingly, in fact, the debtors did rebel. But to obtain more funds, the banks or the IMF required the recipient governments to cut government spending, balance their budgets, bring down inflation with wage controls, and get their economies in order. The resulting austerity, as subsidies for social programs were cut and food prices rose, led to riots in the Dominican Republic, the invasion of supermarkets in Rio de Janeiro, and strikes throughout Latin America. Over the preceding forty years, Latin America's economy had grown, permitting limited benefits for the people in housing, health, and education. All that was wiped out as exports fell.[47] Paying the annual interest left little capital for investing in economic development, let alone in social programs. In fact, to the degree that they are paying back their loans, *the developing countries are exporting capital they need to the industrialized nations!* In 1987, Latin America paid 30 percent of its export receipts to international banks and institutions; Argentina and Venezuela paid 50 percent. The total the Latin American nations paid out over what they received from the developed countries was just over $30 billion, triple the amount in 1983. Altogether they have paid out $160 billion on the over $400 billion debt.[48] It is not surprising, therefore, that economic growth has stopped, inflation has destroyed the savings of the middle class, and everyone's living standards have declined. Foreign aid in these circumstances can do little to help.

The dilemma is obvious: if the debtor nations default on their loans, they will endanger their credit ratings. Or they can tighten their belts and receive new loans but risk domestic political explosions as living standards fall and the division between the rich and poor grows. The implications for American security interests are also obvious. Most of the Latin American debtors are democracies, but several of these democracies are new and fragile. Their political futures may be endangered and dictatorships of the left or right may return in an area in which authoritarianism has had a long tradition. It was debt or democracy for such new democracies as Argentina and Brazil.[49]

Peru in these circumstances decided to repay only 10 percent of its export earnings (and lost its creditworthiness when it defaulted on a $180 million repayment). Brazil declared it would not pay its debt with recession, unemployment, and hunger, but it finally reversed itself because the banks retaliated by reducing trade credit lines and delaying other loans. Castro advised the Latin American states not to pay their debt at all. Indeed, it is surprising that a debtor cartel has not been organized by Argentina, Brazil, and Mexico.[50]

The Latin American countries were not totally without a case. The U.S. deficit, which initially had raised the value of the dollar, was the major reason for their difficulties in repaying their loans. Each percentage increase in American interest rates added tens of millions, if not hundreds of millions, of dollars to what they owed. In 1984, a 1 percent increase added $600 million to Argentina's debt, and, in the words of its president, "jeopardized his country's social peace."[51] Even though the value of the dollar declined after 1985, the dollar has remained expensive because the Latin American currencies also have declined in value. Unlike the United States, whose debt exceeds that of Argentina, Brazil, and Mexico, the Latin American countries have not been able to follow the U.S. recipe for cutting *its* debt to its Western allies and trading partners: driving the value of the dollar down by half and in effect telling its Japanese and German creditors that the United States will repay only half of its debts.[52] Take it or leave it! The short-term solution has been *rescheduling* the Third World debt—that is, simply stretching out the time for repayment, or reducing the interest rate. But this does not suffice because what the developing countries have paid back has amounted to a huge transfer of funds from those poorer countries to the richer developed ones, exceeding by far the inflow of capital from the latter. Thus, while avoiding crises in the short run, such a solution only postpones the critical issue of eventual repayment.

In recognition of this fact, the United States in 1985 accepted the Latin American position that growth-oriented policies, not austerity programs, were more likely to enable the Latin American countries to meet their financial obligations. According to a plan proposed by then treasury secretary James Baker, economic growth would be encouraged by rewarding countries that adopted market-oriented policies with increasing support from commercial banks as well as the World Bank. But the banks, understandably, refused to extend further credit, and the Baker plan was therefore inadequately funded. The fact that in the 1980s the growth rates of the industrialized democracies were lower than during the troubled 1970s did not help either. Because banks began to recognize that they were unlikely to collect much of what they were owed anyway, large-scale debt cancellation seemed a more appropriate strategy. Moreover, the outflow of capital from developing to developed states could not continue. In 1988, the Latin debtors transferred $50 billion to Western states, $12 billion more than in 1987. This capital was needed at home if development was to be resumed. In 1988, France took the initiative by proposing a new debt relief program. It announced that it would cancel one-third of the debt of sub-Saharan African countries and urged its allies to do the same.[53] In response, a group of the wealthier countries (including France, Britain, the United States, and Japan) and multilateral organizations (including the World Bank and International Monetary Fund) pledged to help the poorer and more indebted African countries whose per capita incomes were less than $250 per year.

This three-year Special Program of Assistance (SPA-1) was renewed in SPA-2 in 1991.[54]

In 1989, the United States proposed, and the 151 members of the World Bank accepted, a debt-relief strategy to reduce the $1.3 trillion Third World debt by $70 billion. A debt cancellation of Latin American countries need not, as once expected, destroy the private banks or seriously damage the American financial system. It might instead gain new customers for U.S. goods and slash the trade deficit since it was the onset of the debt crisis and the loss of previously growing Latin American markets, which accounted for one-third of U.S. exports, that were one main cause of the trade imbalance. Mexico, for example, was the third largest export market for U.S. products. Indeed, in 1990 U.S. exports were valued at $28 billion or 550,000 jobs for the American economy. Every 1 percent growth of the Mexican economy, then, translated into a $300 million increase in U.S. exports.[55] Thus, debt reduction was good for the U.S. economy, and it was good for the young and fragile Latin American democracies. One thing is certain: if the debt crisis is not resolved and sets off further rioting, as in democratic Venezuela in 1989 when more than 300 died and thousands were wounded, Latin America's young democracies may be endangered. One need only note the 1992 military coup attempt in Venezuela and the suspension of democracy by Peru's democratically elected president to fight the Shining Path insurgency in his country. Large income disparities are not likely to create stable political systems. Whether a 20 percent reduction in the debt, as the banks have negotiated with Mexico under the United States' Brady plan (named after Bush's secretary of the treasury, Nicholas Brady), will have a sufficient impact on resolution of the debt problem, even if it is extended to other states, remains a question. Brazil's debt, the largest in Latin America, is now being negotiated.

Most observers tend to be pessimistic, however, although there is widespread agreement that debt relief needs to be extended to more countries, especially low-income ones, and the amounts forgiven increased. Certainly, *Time*'s comment seemed appropriate: "Never in history have so many nations owed so much with so little promise of repayment." [56] That was one reason the Bush administration, grateful for Egypt's leadership among Arab states in organizing opposition to Iraq, felt it could forgive its $7 billion debt. But unfortunately, in the post-cold war period, the strain on the world's finances—needed for modernizing Eastern Europe and the Commonwealth of Independent States, among other things—will make it even harder and more costly for many Third World nations to attract Western capital. Even the industrial nations need billions of dollars of capital for the upkeep of their infrastructures. The big question facing the debtor states, especially in Latin America, is whether despite this shortage of capital they can resume economic growth and reduce poverty by adopting free-market solutions as Mexico has done the last few years.[57]

THE PRODUCER CARTEL AND THE WEAK STATES

Energy Crisis

The year 1973 was marked by the Yom Kippur War in the Middle East. That same year OPEC's Arab members, who held the world's largest oil reserves, instituted an embargo against the United States and the Netherlands to protest those countries' political support of Israel. The Arab states also planned monthly production cutbacks for the other non-Communist industrial states. In addition, OPEC raised oil prices from $3 to $12 a barrel. It was this ability to control supplies and prices that made OPEC a powerful producer cartel and at the time a model for the developing countries of how to use their control over certain resources to enhance their bargaining strength and income. OPEC's impact on the Western industrial countries was devastating. Its actions caused not only minor inconveniences to consumers, who had to pay more for gasoline and other oil-based products, but also a profound upheaval in entire economies, ways of life, and standards of living. OPEC upset the economic growth plans of many states, developed and developing alike. Economic issues rose to the top of the international agenda and became intensely politicized. The "energy crisis"—high oil prices and a lack of secure supplies—was born.

In the Western industrial nations and Japan, the quadrupling of oil prices immediately affected living standards. Families could no longer buy as much because gasoline and heating oil, as well as plastics, synthetics, and other oil-based materials, became much more expensive. Food prices also rose because cultivation and distribution depended on energy. The rising price stoked Western inflation, already high, and simultaneously precipitated the worst recession since the Great Depression of the 1930s, with very high unemployment rates. This "stagflation" in turn made recovery more difficult. The economic growth rates of all industrial countries were set back. Western Europe and Japan, the United States' principal allies, were hit much harder than the United States, for they were far more dependent on OPEC oil. In fact, the large consuming nations no longer appeared to be in control of their own economies. Anti-inflationary policies could not be effective as oil prices continued to rise. By the spring of 1980, the Western countries had 18 million unemployed, and the figure was still going up. An estimated $240-$250 billion worth of industrial capacity lay idle. The 1982 unemployment figure reported for the twenty-four major industrial democracies was more than 30 million people!

The energy crisis starkly demonstrated the fragility of all Western economies. Relatively inexpensive oil had led to the neglect of vast coal deposits in Europe and the United States. From 1955 to 1972, Western Europe's use of coal had shrunk from three-quarters of total energy sources to about one-fifth, while the share of its energy from oil rose from one-fifth to three-fifths. The American experience was similar. In 1964, the United States was still the

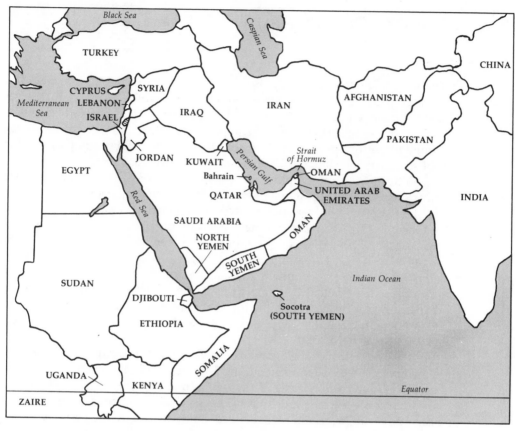

Figure 15-1 The Middle East and Northeastern Africa

world's leading oil producer; in 1965, the Middle East overtook that position. In 1970, U.S. production peaked and then started declining. By 1976, the industrial West—Western Europe, the United States, and Japan—consumed 65 percent of the world's oil production. This meant that they increasingly used oil from other nations. The Middle East and Africa, which had two-thirds of the world's oil reserves, consumed only 4 percent.

It was this oil-hungry world that OPEC faced when it broke the monopoly of Western oil companies. OPEC's power was clear from the American example. The United States became an importer in the 1970s. By 1976, it was importing 42 percent of its oil at a cost of $35 billion a year. Of its total consumption of 17.4 million barrels per day (mbd), it was importing 7.3 mbd (at 42 gallons per barrel). Almost 40 percent of this imported oil came from the Arab members of OPEC (AOPEC), four of which—Saudi Arabia, Kuwait, Iraq, and the United Arab Emirates—along with Iran, possessed more than 50 percent of the world's known reserves and produced 40 percent of its supplies (see Figure 15-1).

By the summer of 1979, the United States was importing 45 percent or 9 million barrels *each day* out of a total of 21 million barrels used *each day*. From 1973 to 1979, American oil imports had increased more than 40 percent. Despite the clear warnings of 1973-1974, these imports increased rather than decreased its dependence. In 1973, 70 percent of the oil the United States imported was from OPEC; by 1977, this figure had risen to 86 percent. The percentage of these imports from AOPEC rose from 22 to 43 percent. Then in late 1978 and early 1979, disaster struck. The Iranian cutback in oil production after the collapse of the shah stretched supplies so tightly that prices increased almost 100 percent in less than one year.[58] By December 1979, the price of oil stood at $24 a barrel, up from about $13 a barrel in January 1979. (Some countries, however, were already selling their oil for up to $40 a barrel in the tight market.) American oil costs for that one year alone rose $28 billion. By the spring of 1981, the average price had risen to $36 a barrel, an increase in just over a year of more than 100 percent. In 1982, the price stabilized at $34 a barrel, $21 higher than the price in 1973. Forecasters were unanimous that the future would be one of scarcity and persistent price increases.

Minipowers versus Great Powers

There was an irony in this situation. None of the oil-producing states could be considered a major power, not even Iran with its substantial population. Most of these states had small populations, little industry, and virtually no military muscle. All they had was oil! But with that oil they were able to influence not only the domestic affairs but also the Middle Eastern policies of the non-Communist industrial states. Japan first and then Western Europe acceded to Arab demands to show more sympathy for the Palestinian cause. Even the United States, long a major supporter of Israel, decided to play a more even-handed role, and shortly after the 1973 war then secretary of state Henry Kissinger began trying to bring about a more lasting peace in the region. The weak had come to seem omnipotent, the strong impotent. It appeared that the world had turned upside down as one by one the Western states, former rulers of these small countries and still military giants relative to OPEC's members, complied with some Arab wishes. Clearly, power relations do not always follow the rule that the nation that can produce "more bang for a buck" can achieve its demands and successfully resist the demands of others.

The highly public and dramatic use of their economic power by some OPEC members seems to contradict the earlier conclusion that the exercise of economic sanctions is counterproductive. The most powerful military states in the world passively accepted high inflation rates, a recession, the declining value of the dollar, and continual oil price increases. Could there be much doubt that OPEC's price increases were far more damaging to the West than the loss of West Berlin, the placement of Soviet missiles in Cuba, or the loss of South Vietnam? Can one disagree with political scientist Robert Tucker's conclusion that "it is the oil cartel, and not the rising military power of the

Soviet Union, that has formed the greatest threat in the 1970s and early 1980s to the structure of American interests and commitments in the world"?[59]

The key question, however, remains: How could modern countries, with larger populations and sizable armed forces, repeatedly acquiesce in the raising of oil prices, which devastated their economies? Were the oil barrels of the Arab and non-Arab OPEC members more powerful than the West's gun barrels? The very question suggests part of the answer: the West refused to use force in a situation in which a half century earlier would have resulted in a swift recourse to force.[60] OPEC claimed it had the right to determine prices for its oil and to deny that oil to Western nations through an embargo or reduced production. The West, by its acceptance of such measures, legitimated OPEC's claim. It interpreted the principle of national self-determination to mean that if another country owns resources, it can do with them what it pleases, regardless of the difficulties inflicted on itself and the rest of the world. In these circumstances, the use of force could only be considered illegitimate.

Indeed, this interpretation of the principle of national self-determination by the West led it to acquiesce in the virtual disregard by some OPEC members of their contracts. As noted oil expert Walter Levy said in 1980 at the end of a decade of rising oil prices,

> The producing countries . . . in fact do not recognize as binding supply or price arrangements even if freely concluded by them. Recently they have gone so far as to change agreed-upon prices retroactively. This, they argue, they are entitled to do under the doctrine of sovereign control by producing countries over their natural resources. . . .
>
> Because of the fear of being arbitrarily cut off from supplies, Western nations and their [oil] companies now accept within a wide range practically any economic or political terms that a producing country may impose upon them.[61]

Leverage, Cartels, Oil Gluts, and War

OPEC's strong bargaining position for the decade after 1973 reflected five conditions. First, the West was so dependent on imported oil that even sharp increases in price did not reduce demand by very much. Second, there were limited possibilities for substituting other energy sources for oil in the short run. Third, a small number of producer nations—the Arab states—controlled most international trade in this commodity. Fourth, these suppliers, united by culture and language, had common political goals, especially on the issue of Israel. And fifth, because of the small size of their populations, these suppliers were invulnerable to an embargo by the consumer nations.

But cartels tend to sow the seeds of their own destruction by driving prices up to levels that (1) cause consumers to do with less or (2) cause new producers to enter the field. Thus by the early 1980s, the conditions that had given OPEC its leverage during the 1970s began to change. First, the steepness of the price increases resulted in genuine conservation measures, such as designing more fuel-efficient cars, commercial jets, housing, and appliances.

Second, the number of non-OPEC oil sources increased: for example, Alaska, Mexico, and the North Sea (Norway and Britain). Third, the production of alternatives such as coal and natural gas began to increase. The high price of oil made coal and natural gas more profitable, resulting in expanded production. In addition, it stimulated research into such areas as oil shale, solar energy, and synthetic fuel, although the subsequent oil glut led to cutbacks in this research. Only nuclear energy did not expand much because of popular opposition in many Western countries, especially after the 1979 Three Mile Island accident (which was to be powerfully reinforced by the Soviet mishap at Chernobyl in 1986). Fourth, OPEC members were often at odds with one another. As the 1980s began, Iran and Iraq were at war, and Libya sought the overthrow of the Saudi monarchy for allegedly allying itself with the United States and Israel and betraying the Arab cause. Fifth, the global recession after 1981 led to a sharp reduction in the demand for oil.

The consequence of the decreased demand for oil was an oil glut and downward pressure on prices. OPEC's eightfold increase in prices from 1973 to 1980 had by 1982 resulted in a drop in its share of the world oil market from almost 60 percent to less than 40 percent. Production was down 22 percent from 1981 and 45 percent from 1979. The official price of $34 per barrel of oil fell to $28. The decline of oil consumption continued, and non-OPEC oil production increased. OPEC's future as a producer cartel was in jeopardy. As it was no longer able to firmly control the price of oil, its production by 1985 was down to 16 mbd from the 1979 high of 32 mbd. OPEC's members competed with one another for the largest share of the remaining oil market (while non-OPEC oil increased from 17 mbd to more than 27 mbd). The unofficial price at which members were willing to undersell one another fell further to below $20 by early 1986, dropping to the $10-$12 range. Since 1973-1974, the West had paid more than a trillion dollars to OPEC, the largest forced transfer of wealth since the Spanish conquistadors plundered gold from ancient Peru. But this economic "bleeding" ended. The United States had by 1985 cut its dependence on oil imports to less than 30 percent from the 1977 peak of 46 percent. And, more important, it had shifted the source of most of its oil imports to Western Hemisphere countries (Canada, Mexico, and Venezuela).

OPEC, trying to survive, urged its members to eliminate the oil glut by sticking to the production cuts it set for each member. But that only gave rise to internal tensions. The oil-producing states with large populations needed all the money they could earn to support their development plans (Nigeria) or pay for their wars (Iran and Iraq). Cutbacks in production and revenues tended to be resisted. OPEC's problems also were worsened by a price war with non-OPEC oil producers, especially Britain, which had become a large producer (1 mbd). OPEC's goal was to retain its share of the world oil market, which had dropped from 66 percent in 1976 to less than 30 percent in 1987. But non-OPEC, non-Communist production had increased by 30 percent, from almost 21 mbd in 1980 to 26 mbd in 1987; Soviet, Chinese, and Eastern

European production was boosted by 25 percent, from 12.5 mbd to 15.5 mbd. Oil prices were therefore expected to fall further unless the non-OPEC oil producers, also fearful of rapidly falling prices, would agree to stabilize them.[62] In 1988, OPEC met with seven non-OPEC members—Angola, China, Colombia, Egypt, Malaysia, Mexico, and Oman—who were collectively producing about half the output of OPEC's thirteen members. But no agreement was reached on how much the non-OPEC states and OPEC should cut oil production. Once the fighting between Iran and Iraq ceased and the cheap oil prices had once more raised demand, prices climbed back to $18 a barrel.

Was OPEC dead? No. Oil remains an essential fuel, and oil consumption still exceeds new discoveries by a ratio of two to one. Moreover, OPEC continues to control three-quarters of the world's known oil reserves. Any upswing of the Western economies, stimulated by cheaper oil, thus should raise the demand for OPEC oil, strengthen its bargaining position, and render the Western industrial states vulnerable again to pricing pressures and possible supply disruptions. For example, by 1987, U.S. imports had once more risen sharply from their lowest level of 1984 and had become almost as important a component of the trade deficit as imported manufactured goods. In 1988, oil imports exceeded 50 percent, surpassing the record of 46 percent set in 1977. The United States was again becoming dependent on imported oil, and forecasters predicted that oil imports would rise to 80 percent by the next century, with a corresponding rise in the trade deficit that would become permanent. Europe, although less wasteful in the use of energy, remained dependent in 1988 on importing more than 60 percent of its oil; Japan imported almost all of its oil.

Foreign policy events too affected the price and supply of oil. After Iraq's August 1990 invasion of Kuwait and the imposition of an embargo on oil exports from Iraq and Iraqi-occupied Kuwait, which removed 4 million barrels a day from the market, oil prices in the West shot up, gyrating between $21 a barrel—the price OPEC had set in response to Iraqi pressure for higher oil prices just before it invaded Kuwait—and $40 a barrel in expectation of shortages. Saudi Arabia, however, raised its daily production from 5.4 to 8.3 million barrels a day. Together with the increased production of the other OPEC members, as well as such non-OPEC countries as the Soviet Union, Britain, and Norway, the world supply of oil three months later was higher (23.5 mbd) than before the embargo (20 mbd). This steadied prices and prevented their shooting up to $60 a barrel or higher, as had been widely expected once the fighting began. Even before the conflict was over, however, oil prices fell, and they may fall even further once Iraqi and Kuwaiti oil begin to flow again. Iraq's resumption of oil exports is likely to be some time off, although Kuwait's resumption is imminent. The question is whether other OPEC members, especially Saudi Arabia, are willing to cut their quotas to keep oil prices up; if not, the price will decline.

Thus ironically, Saddam Hussein may have weakened OPEC, whose support he will need to raise oil prices so that he can pay off his debts and pay for

Iraq's imports. He has left Saudi Arabia, with a quarter of the world's oil reserves, in a more dominant position than ever. Its interests will be, as before the 1990 crisis, to maintain moderate oil prices, and access to Western markets on whose economic health its own fortunes depend and to avoid the development of non-OPEC oil supplies as well as alternative fuels. Moreover, it will want to maintain good relations with the United States, the only power that can guarantee its security.[63] Nevertheless, despite the probability of future moderate and stable oil prices, it remains worrisome that since 1985, 90 percent of the increase in the world's oil production has come from the Persian Gulf. This is especially true for the United States, the new protector of the Gulf, because its oil imports in the absence of a change in energy policy are likely to rise to between 55 and 65 percent by the end of the decade, and higher after the year 2000.[64] America's oil dependency and costs will therefore grow and its energy vulnerability will increase if opposition to oil exploration offshore and in Alaska remains strong for environmental reasons, and opposition to the use of coal because of acid rain and other reasons and nuclear energy because of safety concerns continues.

For the developing countries, OPEC appeared in the 1970s to be the example of how to use their control of resources to raise prices. The UN Conference on Trade and Development (UNCTAD), which mainly represented the developing nations possessing many of the resources that other states (especially the developed ones) imported, encouraged the formation of resource cartels during the 1970s because higher prices obviously were the way to raise Third World incomes and thereby redistribute the global wealth. Nevertheless, efforts to fix prices for tin, bauxite, potash, lead, zinc, copper, nickel, sugar, cotton, timber, and jute all failed, largely because of the availability of substitutes and adequate supplies of these commodities.* Moreover, higher prices encouraged the appearance of output from new sources in the international market. But the principal reason OPEC could be a model for the non-oil, resource-rich developing countries was OPEC's own collapse as a cartel. The OPEC countries, at least its Arab members, learned the limits of using oil as a nationalistic weapon to assert their power and maximize their wealth, and, more important, they learned the need for long-term access to markets and customers and for acting as reliable suppliers of oil at reasonable prices.

---

* One current exception to these developing country failures is rubber. Natural rubber is more heat- and tear-resistant than the synthetic rubber used for the condoms and gloves popularized by the AIDS epidemic.

ECONOMICS AND POWER

Instrument of the Wealthy

As already noted in Chapter 8, historically there is a clear correlation among economic power, military power, and the rise and fall of the great powers. Since the Industrial Revolution, it has been the economically most advanced powers—first Britain, then Germany, Japan, and the United States—who have been the most active players and exercised the principal influence. The powers who fell behind economically even when they had large populations—such as Austria, Hungary, France, and czarist Russia—saw their status and influence diminish as each in turn was defeated in battle.

Wealthy nations have been able to afford not only all types of guns but also a whole range of nonmilitary instruments. As a result, they have not had to resort to force in the pursuit of their objectives as often as the weaker states. The more economically advanced states have been able to use their economic weapons by offering or withholding foreign aid, making food available in time of need, providing their businesses with the incentives to invest private capital in other countries (trade follows the flag), exporting the advanced technology other countries seek, and opening or closing their markets to foreign products (see Chapter 16). These and other weapons are means of exercising leverage. Withholding aid may help force another nation to comply with one's demands; offering access to one's markets may achieve the same purpose. Indeed, the wealthy states do not need to resort to force as frequently as the less wealthy states.

According to Kenneth Waltz, " 'non-recourse to force' is the doctrine of the strong," which is what Karl Marx called the replacement of the cannon by capital. E. H. Carr illustrated the point long ago: "Great Britain's unchallenged naval and economic supremacy throughout the nineteenth century enabled her to establish a commanding position in China with a minimum of military force and of economic discrimination. A relatively weak power like Russia could only hope to achieve a comparable result by naked aggression and annexation." [65] That was largely true during the cold war as well.

This issue of the superior economic power of the West, as noted earlier, was also at the heart of Third World countries' complaints during the cold war that the international political and economic order was grossly unfair and dominated by the First World, which made the economic rules and received the giant's share of the economic and political benefits. They saw the international laws of supply and demand as "stacking the deck" against them. These complaints would not have surprised Friedrich List, a nineteenth-century German political economist, who, after studying the economy of Britain, the world's first industrial state to champion free trade, advised Germany against free trade:

I saw clearly that free competition between two nations which are highly civilized can only be mutually beneficial in case both of them are in a nearly equal position of industrial development, and that any nation which owing to misfortune is behind others in industry, commerce, and navigation . . . must first of all strengthen her own individual powers, in order to fit herself to enter into free competition with more advanced nations.[66]

The free market may well be a superior mechanism for allocating goods when those competing and exchanging goods are of approximately equal strength, but when one nation is clearly more advanced economically, free trade benefits that nation more because it is able to penetrate the markets of economically weaker countries. If the latter do not protect themselves with tariffs to keep cheaper foreign imports out, home industries cannot develop. Free trade is the weapon of the strong; tariffs to protect "infant industries" are the weapon of the weak.

The laws of the free market are *not* neutral. Power is the "invisible hand" determining the distribution of wealth. Among nations that are equal in economic power, economic relations may well breed interdependence, as among the European Community, the United States, and Japan. Between the economically strong and the economically weak, however, the inevitable result is the dependence of the latter. Economic weapons, then, remain "preeminently the weapons of strong powers." [67]

Increasingly it appears that this is also true among the economically strong states. Some are simply more advanced than others. Their relationship may be one of interdependence, but this relationship may be an asymmetrical or unequal one. The United States was the champion of free trade when it was the world's strongest economic power. Today, in an increasingly interdependent economy, it seeks to protect various industries from foreign competition (see Chapter 16). The strong do not usually need protection; the weak do.

Conditions for Economic Coercion

If wealth gives states positions of general influence, the actual exercise of economic coercion by any state depends on three conditions: (1) a high degree of control over the supplies of goods or services the targeted state needs; (2) the intense need of the targeted state for the economic goods or services; and (3) a calculation by the targeted state that compliance with the demands made on it is less costly than doing without those goods or services.[68] These conditions gave OPEC leverage during the 1970s, even though its members possessed few of the normal components of power. The industrial countries' lives were so dependent on imported oil that any major disruption would have played havoc with their economies. Paying higher prices was preferable to doing without. But these three conditions are frequently not present, as the examples of sanctions against Cuba and Iraq, among others, show.

Sanctions are most effective if applied collectively; individual national sanctions are rarely effective. The critical condition is the cost calculation. As noted at some length, the targeted nation may be better able to calculate these costs if these sanctions are backed up with the credible threat of the use of force. Compliance is least likely if the cost to the targeted or coerced nation is perceived to be its national independence or what is sometimes called its national honor or prestige. States prefer to suffer economic or low-politics deprivation before yielding to high-politics demands. Political scientist Richard Olson has suggested, therefore, that since many instances of failure take the form of publicly visible economic sanctions, economic coercion ought to be exerted invisibly:

> In most cases of economic coercion, the sanctions are more subtle; they are applied in areas in which the target is the solicitor: aid, investment, finance, and technology. Trade sanctions are usually highly visible.... Furthermore, trade, however unequal the terms, is a partnership in which groups in both the sender- and target-countries stand to lose when sanctions are applied. This is much less the case in the more subtle and complex areas of international technology transfers, finance, investment, and aid. Ours is a capital- and technique-scarce world, with keen competition among LDCs for what is available....
>
> First World governments, their aid agencies, international financial institutions such as the World Bank or the regional development banks, private bank consortia, and multinational corporations are, for many LDCs, integral and influential parts of the domestic economy and policy-making apparatus. Dependency is indeed vulnerability; as George Ball has asked in apparent commiseration: "How can a national government make an economic plan with any confidence if a board of directors meeting 5,000 miles away can by altering its pattern of purchasing and production affect in a major way the country's economic life?" [69]

Also according to Olson, "Relatively covert, subtle economic sanctions will ultimately be *politically* effective with only moderate, purely *economic* effects." [70] The dependency of the target permits the exercise of economic coercion without publicity and patriotic rallying around the flag in that state. Delays in delivery of spare parts, drying up of credit, decline in value of investments, reduction of multilateral and bilateral loans, and refusal to refinance debts—not publicly announced cuts in quotas or embargoes—are more effective, though less visible, means of coercion.

Visible or invisible, it is well to remember that sanctions are not cost-free, as farmers, businesspeople, and bankers in the United States and Western Europe have learned. Indeed, sanctions may involve substantial costs to the nation or nations seeking to punish or coerce another nation. A key question, therefore, is always whether imposing sanctions is worth the trouble.

Coercion versus Rewards

States have been more successful in attaining their aims by offering economic rewards than by depriving target nations of economic products and services. Rewards provide economic improvement and higher standards of living. Such rewards led to Western Europe's economic recovery after World War II and to the strengthening of NATO. They laid the foundation on which European nations have been integrating their economies and establishing the basis for possible political union and status as a superpower. They twice helped attract the Soviet Union to détente. And, although economic aid in its various forms may not have given either superpower during the cold war the degree of influence it would have liked to develop (even though many economic projects and technical-assistance programs were successful), it did help stabilize regimes (at least in the short run) and enhance the independence of some new nations, allowing them to resist seduction or pressure from the other superpower.

Admittedly, the line between rewards and coercion may be narrow. Rewards granted to bolster an alliance relationship or compliant behavior may be withheld if the recipient pursues policies that are at odds with those of the aid giver. Thus in 1991, the United States announced that it would not give Israel $10 billion in loan guarantees to house the stream of Soviet Jewish immigrants before the convocation of a Middle East peace conference in October. The U.S. position had always been that Israel should seek peace with its Arab neighbors on the basis of exchanging the lands it had conquered in the 1967 war for peace, just as it had returned the Sinai Desert for peace with Egypt. But Israel's conservative governing party had since 1977 claimed that the West Bank and Gaza Strip (claimed as well by the Palestinians as their own state) were a historical part of Israel. It therefore proceeded to plant Jewish settlements in those areas, despite repeated protests by various U.S. administrations that these settlements were not only illegal but also an obstacle to peace. But each predecessor to Bush had continued to provide Israel with considerable economic and military assistance, permitting the Israelis to avoid facing the choice between keeping what the Israelis called the liberated territories and what the Arabs called the conquered territories and negotiating a permanent peace with most Arab states. Bush decided that without an Israeli freeze on settlements (which the government was unwilling to make) the United States would not provide the loan guarantees. It believed the Israelis would use the funds to settle Soviet immigrants in these territories, among other places, thereby undermining the peace conference, which the administration had so painstakingly negotiated. In other words, to enhance U.S. leverage Washington wanted to delay the guarantees until after it saw whether the Israelis would attend the conference and whether their position would then be flexible or intransigent. For the same reason, the Israelis wanted the guarantees before the conference so it could safely ignore all later protests about its declared unwillingness to exchange land for peace. Thus, Washington was willing to reward Israel, but only after it had complied with the long-term U.S. formula for peace. Israel condemned the U.S. position as coercive.

Economics and Morality

Finally, appearances of morality are not unimportant in relations among nations and in the shaping of national reputations. Exercise of the economic weapon appears more moral than the military one, or perhaps one should say less immoral. In reality, it may be no more or less immoral. A wartime blockade, for example, may cause just as many—or more—people to starve to death as would be killed by high explosives in a series of air raids. In postwar Iraq, the breakdown of the electrical system threatened widespread cholera, and shortages of food, including milk, stemming from the continued UN economic blockade until Saddam Hussein had complied with the cease-fire terms, if not relinquished power, jeopardized the health and lives of ordinary citizens and especially those of the children. Yet it was the only way the United Nations could compel Saddam Hussein, safe in his well-furnished bunker, to comply with the cease-fire terms that he surrender his nuclear capability. In a sense, economic sanctions were crueler and less discriminating than the high-tech bombs dropped on Baghdad. That is why Carr called the popular distinction between dollars and bullets an illusion. Power is "one and indivisible," he argued.

> It uses military and economic weapons for the same ends. The strong will tend to prefer the minor and more "civilised" weapon because it will generally suffice to achieve his purposes; and as long as it will suffice, he is under no temptation to resort to the more hazardous military weapons. But economic power cannot be isolated from military power, nor military from economic. They are both integral parts of political power; and in the long run one is helpless without the other. . . . But generally speaking, there is a sense in which dollars are humaner than bullets even if the end pursued be the same.[71]

For Review

1. What are the main economic tools used by states in conflict?
2. What conditions are necessary for one state to actually undertake economic coercion of another?
3. Why is it easier to compel a state to comply on low-politics issues than on high-politics issues?
4. What roles did foreign aid play in the relationships between the superpowers and their allies, as well as between the superpowers and the developing countries?
5. What is the developing country "debt problem," and what are its domestic and international effects?
6. In what ways have such developing country producer cartels as OPEC used their control over certain resources to enhance their bargaining strength and income? Has it always worked?

Notes

1. The impact of economics on international politics and the uses of economic means for political ends were first explored in David H. Blake and Robert S. Walters, *The Politics of Global Economic Relations*, 3d ed. (Englewood Cliffs, N.J.: Prentice-Hall, 1987); Joan E. Spero, *The Politics of International Economic Relations*, 4th ed. (New York: St. Martin's Press, 1990); and C. Fred Bergsten, *The Future of the International Economic Order* (Lexington, Mass.: D. C. Heath, 1973). Also see various articles by Bergsten: "The Threat from the Third World," *Foreign Policy* (Summer 1973): 102-134; "The Responses to the Third World," *Foreign Policy* (Winter 1974-1975): 3-34; and "Coming Investment Wars?" *Foreign Affairs* (October 1974): 153-175. Finally, see C. Fred.Bergsten and Lawrence B. Krause, eds., *World Politics and International Economics* (Washington, D.C.: Brookings, 1975).

2. Theodore Ropp, *War in the Modern World*, 2d ed. (New York: Collier, 1962), 203-204.

3. Paul M. Kennedy, *The Rise and Fall of British Naval Mastery* (Malabar, Fla.: Robert E. Krieger, 1982), 306-309.

4. Williamson Murray, *The Change in the European Balance of Power* (Princeton, N.J.: Princeton University Press, 1984), 4-27.

5. See Walter C. Clemens, Jr., *The U.S.S.R. and Global Interdependence* (Washington, D.C.: American Enterprise Institute, 1978) for a skeptical interpretation of the likely impact of interdependence on the Soviet Union. Also see Elliot Hurwitz, "The Politics of Soviet Trade," *New York Times*, August 25, 1980.

6. Eric Schmitt, "Saudis Reported to Look for Loans," *New York Times*, February 13, 1991.

7. William Safire, "Friends, More Than Interests," *New York Times*, February 1991.

8. Walter S. Mossberg, "Japan and Germany Shirk Gulf Duties with Nary a Peep from the White House," *Wall Street Journal*, December 24, 1990.

9. David Wessel, "The U.S. Spent $31.5 Billion on Gulf War," *Wall Street Journal*, April 30, 1991.

10. Zbigniew Brzezinski, "America's New Geostrategy," *Foreign Affairs* (Spring 1988): 686. For the changes during Gorbachev's first four years, see Charles Gati, *The Bloc That Failed* (Bloomington, Ind.: Indiana University Press, 1990).

11. For a more detailed view, see Steven Greenhouse, "Year of Economic Tumult Looms for Eastern Europe," *New York Times*, December 31, 1990. Also see in the *Wall Street Journal*, Barry Newman, "These Days, Bulgaria Longs for Its Old Ties to the Soviet Union," April 30, 1991; and Philip Revzin, "East European Market Beckons, Then Proves Daunting to U.S. Firms," May 13, 1991. Newman emphasizes not only that all the liberated Eastern European nations were feeling the pain of their rupture with the Soviet Union, but also that the Soviet republics might have wanted to rethink their desire to break away from Moscow.

12. Clyde Haberman, "12 European Nations Formally Initiate Closer Federation," *New York Times*, December 16, 1990.

13. Clyde H. Farnsworth, "Direct Cash Aid Would Be Wasted on Soviet Economy, Study Says," *New York Times*, December 20, 1990.

14. Alan Riding, "Eastern Leaders at Summit Warn against New Divisions in Europe," *New York Times*, November 21, 1990.

15. Serge Schmemann, "Moscow to Ask Help from West on Reform Plan," *New York Times*, May 18, 1991.

16. Also from the *New York Times,* see Fox Butterfield, "Soviet and U.S. Economists Discuss a Bailout for Moscow," May 21, 1991; and Serge Schmemann, "What Role for the West in Russia's Revolution?" May 27, 1991.

17. Felicity Barringer, "Compassion and Pragmatism on Help for Moscow," *New York Times,* July 8, 1991, showed that in interviews many Americans favored a gamble to foster stability in the USSR but wondered whether the country could afford it and whether it would pay off in terms of stable U.S.-Soviet relations. Also see Robert Eisner, "Should We Aid the Soviet Union? Yes, It Helps Us Too," *New York Times,* August 27, 1991.

18. Steven Greenhouse, "Wealthy Nations Wary of Offering Quick Soviet Aid," and William E. Schmidt, "Gorbachev, in Oslo, Links World Peace to Perestroika," *New York Times,* June 6, 1991.

19. Martin Feldstein, "A Different Kind of 'Grand Bargain,' " *Wall Street Journal,* July 9, 1991.

20. Peter Gumbel, "Realism Tempers Soviet Search for Aid," *Wall Street Journal,* July 9, 1991; and Francis X. Clines, "Kremlin to Look for Investments at London Summit," and Steven Prokesch, "Caution on Helping Soviet Economy Is Emphasized by Industrial Nations," *New York Times,* July 10, 1991. Also see Clines, "Soviet Chief Vows To Be His Own Man in London," and Steven Greenhouse, "7 Offer Moscow Technical Help," *New York Times,* July 15 and 18, 1991, respectively. Private enterprise, by contrast, faced its traditional fears of capitalism after seventy years of communism. See Clines, "Fears of Capitalist Exploitation Slows Soviet-Chevron Oil Venture," *New York Times,* August 16, 1991.

21. Judy Shelton, "Should We Aid the Soviet Union? No, It Would Set Back Reform," and Peter Passell, "A Centerless Soviet Economy May Not Be So Bad, Western Experts Say," *New York Times,* August 27 and September 5, 1991, respectively. Also see Craig Forman, "Soviet Economy Holds Potential for Disaster As the Union Weakens," *Wall Street Journal,* September 3, 1991.

22. Robert Blackwill and William Hogan, "An Army of Experts-in-Residence," *New York Times,* September 11, 1991.

23. Elaine Sciolino, "Chaos Looms Over Soviets, Gates Says," *New York Times,* December 11, 1991.

24. Thomas L. Friedman, "Baker Presents Steps to Aid Transition by Soviets," *New York Times,* December 13, 1991.

25. Richard Nixon, "The Challenge We Face in Russia," *Wall Street Journal,* March 11, 1992.

26. Andrew R. Rosenthal, "Bush and Kohl Unveil Plan for 7 Nations to Contribute $24 Billion in Aid for Russia," A1, and Steven Greenhouse, "Buying Time for Yeltsin," A1, and "Excerpts from Bush's Remarks on Aid Plan: 'Today We Must Win the Peace,' " *New York Times,* April 2, 1992, A11.

27. Francis X. Clines, "Rift over Military Widens at Meeting of Ex-Soviet Lands," and Celestine Bohlen, "Russian President Moves to Create a Separate Army," *New York Times,* February 15 and March 17, 1992, respectively. Also see Laurie Hays, "As He Builds a Nation, Ukraine Chief Becomes Thorn in Yeltsin's Side," *Wall Street Journal,* March 17, 1992.

28. Steven Greenhouse, "$44 Billion Needed to Aid Ex-Soviets, I.M.F. Says," *New York Times,* April 16, 1992.

29. Sylvia Nasar, "How to Aid Russians Is Debated," *New York Times,* January 20, 1992. Also from the *New York Times,* see Leslie Gelb, "The Russian Sinkhole," March 30,

1992; Richard Portes, "Who Can Save Russia?" April 2, 1992; and Steven Green-house and Thomas L. Friedman, "Aid Package for Russia Seems to Be Far from Wrapped Up," April 9, 1992.

30. Richard Millett, "Looking beyond Noriega," *Foreign Policy* (Summer 1988): 46-64; and Steven Erlanger, "U.S. Economic Warfare Brings Disaster to Panama," *New York Times*, June 9, 1988.

31. Leigh Bruce, "Iraqi Economic Collapse Seen in Months," *International Herald Tribune*, September 20, 1990; and John F. Burns, "In Cities of Iraq, Food Abounds, Not Spare Parts," *New York Times*, October 17, 1990.

32. Tony Horwitz and Geraldine Brooks, "Wily Smugglers Keep Embargoed Supplies Flowing into Iraq," *Wall Street Journal*, December 10, 1990; and Patrick E. Tyler, "Iraqis' Food Rations Are Reduced As Trade Embargo Cuts Supplies," *New York Times*, January 2, 1991.

33. Ibid. Also see excerpts from the testimony by CIA Director William Webster on the embargo's drain of Iraq, *New York Times*, December 6, 1990.

34. Andrés Suarez, *Cuba* (Cambridge, Mass.: M.I.T. Press, 1967), 86.

35. For an argument that it was, see Gary C. Hufbauer and Kimberly A. Elliott, "Sanctions Will Bite—and Soon," *New York Times*, January 14, 1991.

36. Tom Wicker, "In the Nation," *New York Times*, January 23, 1991.

37. Richard S. Olson, "Economic Coercion in World Politics: With a Focus on North-South Relations," *World Politics* (July 1979): 472-479; and Anna P. Schreiber, "Economic Coercion as an Instrument of Foreign Policy: U.S. Economic Measures against Cuba and the Dominican Republic," *World Politics* (April 1973): 387-413. Also see Otto Wolff von Ameringen, "Commentary: Economic Sanctions as a Foreign Policy Tool?" *International Security* (Fall 1980): 159-167; James M. Lindsay, "Trade Sanctions as Political Instruments: A Re-Examination," *International Studies Quarterly* (June 1986): 153-173; and Roy Licklider, "The Power of Oil: The Arab Oil Weapon and the Netherlands, the United Kingdom, Canada, Japan and the United States," *International Studies Quarterly* (June 1988): 205-226. For the use of aid as a tool for rewards and punishment, see Charles W. Kegley and Steven W. Hook, "U.S. Foreign Aid and U.N. Voting: Did Reagan's Linkage Strategy Buy Defence or Defiance?" *International Studies Quarterly* (September 1991): 295-312.

38. Keith Bradsher, "Trade Embargoes: Do They Work?" and Thomas W. Hazlett, "Did Sanctions Matter?" *New York Times*, July 14 and 22, 1991, respectively. Also see George W. Shepherd, Jr., ed., *Effective Sanctions on South Africa* (Westport, Conn.: Praeger, 1991).

39. This assumption was never made explicit in the doctrine of foreign aid for reasons analyzed by Robert A. Packenham, "Developmental Doctrines in Foreign Aid," *World Politics*, January 1966, 194-225; and Packenham, *Liberal America and the Third World* (Princeton, N.J.: Princeton University Press, 1973).

Also see Eugene R. Black, *The Diplomacy of Economic Development* (New York: Harper & Row, 1966), 19, 23. For a general analysis of the conditions necessary for democracy to flourish, see Seymour M. Lipset, *Political Man* (Garden City, N.Y.: Doubleday, 1959), 45-67.

40. George Liska, *The New Statecraft* (Chicago: University of Chicago Press, 1960), 3.

41. For the classification of aid generally followed here, see the excellent article by Hans J. Morgenthau, "A Political Theory of Foreign Aid," *American Political Science Review* (June 1962): 301-309.

42. David R. Obey and Carol Lancaster, "Funding Foreign Aid," *Foreign Policy* (Sum-

mer 1988): 141-155.

43. Ibid., 105. On Japan's rise to number one donor, see David E. Sanger, "Japan To Be No. 1 Giver of Foreign Aid," *New York Times*, January 20, 1989.

44. Francis Fukuyamu, "Gorbachev and the Third World," *Foreign Affairs* (Spring 1986): 715-731.

45. Sen. Bob Dole, "To Help New Democracies, Cut Aid to Israel, 4 Others," *New York Times*, January 16, 1990.

46. Diana Tussie, *Latin America in the World Economy* (New York: St. Martin's Press, 1983).

47. Carlos Fuentes, "The Real Latin Threat," *New York Times*, September 15, 1985.

48. Alan Riding, "Latins Want Bush To Help on Debts," and Clyde H. Farnsworth, "Money Loss Grows for Poorer Lands, World Bank Finds," *New York Times*, November 29, 1988, and December 19, 1988, respectively. Also see Obey and Lancaster, "Funding Foreign Aid," 153.

49. Abraham F. Lowenthal, "Threat and Opportunity in the Americas," in annual issue entitled "America and the World 1985," *Foreign Affairs* (1985): 558-561.

50. *New York Times*, September 26, 1985. Also see Harold Lever and Christopher Huhre, *Debt and Danger* (Boston: Atlantic Monthly Press, 1986).

51. *New York Times*, May 11, 1984.

52. Richard Rothstein, "Give Them a Break," *New Republic*, February 1, 1988, 22.

53. Peter T. Kilborn, "U.S. to Give Poor Lands More Time to Repay Debts," *New York Times*, June 21, 1988; and Steven Greenhouse, "Fund Plans to Forgive African Debt," *New York Times*, June 9, 1988.

54. Peter Truell, "About $8 Billion Earmarked to Aid African Nations," *Wall Street Journal*, October 31, 1991.

55. Bill Richardson, "Mexico—The Answer to Bush's Domestic Troubles," *Wall Street Journal*, December 12, 1991.

56. Quoted by Robert Gilpin, *The Political Economy of International Relations* (Princeton, N.J.: Princeton University Press, 1987), 317.

57. Steven Greenhouse, "Rebuilding Troubled Regions Will Strain World's Finances," *New York Times*, March 26, 1991; Mack Senner, "The Grim Shortage of Global Capital," *New York Times*, July 28, 1991; Nathaniel C. Nash, "A Breath of Fresh Economic Air Brings Change to Latin America," *New York Times*, November 13, 1991.

58. On the collapse of the shah, see George Lenczowski, "The Arc of Crisis," *Foreign Affairs* (Spring 1979): 796-820; Richard Cottam et al., "The United States and Iran's Revolution," *Foreign Policy* (Spring 1979): 3-34; and especially Gary Sick, *All Fall Down* (New York: Random House, 1985).

59. Robert W. Tucker, "Oil and American Power," *Commentary* (September 1979): 39.

60. See Louis J. Halle, "Does War Have a Future?" *Foreign Affairs* (October 1973): 20-34; Klaus Knorr, *On the Uses of Military Power in the Nuclear Age* (Princeton, N.J.: Princeton University Press, 1966); and Knorr, "The Limits of Power," in *The Oil Crisis*, ed. Raymond Vernon (New York: Norton, 1976), 229-243.

61. Walter J. Levy, "Oil and the Decline of the West," *Foreign Affairs* (Summer 1980): 1003-1004.

62. Youssef M. Ibrahim, "Gulf War's Fallout," *New York Times*, December 17, 1987.

63. Youssef M. Ibrahim, "Saudi Oil Exports Increase Sharply, Erasing Shortages," and "Turbulence Is Expected for OPEC," *New York Times*, October 4, 1990 and December 11, 1990, respectively; James Tanner, "War May Encourage Oil Price Modera-

tion by Bolstering Saudis," *Wall Street Journal*, February 25, 1991; and Edward L. Morse, "The Oil Revolution," *Foreign Affairs* (Winter 1991/92): 36-56. Iran too appears to support this position. See Youssef M. Ibrahim, "Iran's Leaders Ask Wide Cooperation and Ties to the West," *New York Times*, May 28, 1991.

64. Theodore H. Moran, "Economics and Security," *Foreign Affairs* (Winter 1990/91): 82-85.

65. E. H. Carr, *Twenty Years' Crisis, 1919-1939* (London: Macmillan, 1951), 130.

66. Quoted in Edward Mead Earle, "Adam Smith, Alexander Hamilton, Friedrich List: The Economic Foundations of Military Power," in *Makers of Modern Strategy* (Princeton, N.J.: Princeton University Press, 1943), 140.

67. Carr, *Twenty Years' Crisis*, 131.

68. Klaus Knorr, "International Economic Leverage and Its Uses," in *Economic Issues and National Security*, ed. Knorr and Frank Trager (Lawrence, Kan.: Allen Press, 1977), 99-125; and James A. Nathan and James K. Oliver, "The Growing Importance of Economics: Can the United States Manage this Phenomenon?" in *Evolving Strategic Issues*, ed. Franklin D. Margiotta (Washington, D.C.: National Defense University Press), 73-99.

69. Olson, "Economic Coercion," 477, 481.

70. Ibid., 485.

71. Carr, *Twenty Years' Crisis*, 131, 132.

CHAPTER 16

The Multinational Corporate Revolution, Interdependence, and the Coming Trade Wars

GOING GLOBAL

Many critical decisions about the world economy are no longer made by states but by nonstate actors. Of these, the principals are the national firms that have become multinational corporations (MNCs). According to one observer, the rise of the multinational corporation represents the "central macroeconomic event of the postwar world" because it has globalized technology, production, investment, and marketing.[1] In the 1960s, American multinational corporations set the pattern for this globalization by spreading to Europe as they sought to exploit the business opportunities represented by the Common Market (more formally known as the European Economic Community—EEC), avoid the tariffs the latter would have imposed on their products had they been exported from American factories to Europe, and save on transportation costs. American corporations, given their size and ability to mass-produce goods, were in an advantageous situation to compete with European corporations, many of whom still produced mainly for the home market despite the (in the past not always successful) efforts of European states to eliminate internal barriers to trade and the free movement of capital and labor. The expectation was that a Western European-wide market would encourage the expansion or merger of European companies to become more like American mass-production corporations. They then would be able to provide European consumers with a greater number of less expensive products, as well as be able to stand up to and compete with the incoming U.S. companies.

But the growth of American MNCs and their extension to Europe, important as it was, was less fundamental than the spread of American mass-production techniques to Japan, as well as to the newly industrialized countries (NICs)—Hong Kong, Singapore, Taiwan, and South Korea—and a few other developing countries. Before the 1960s, American workers had been paid high wages because their productivity was high. The technology, training, and management that backed up these workers, who had only high school educations, had not yet been transferred or duplicated overseas. In the 1960s they were. Japan was the first to combine the high labor productivity of America with an educated labor force working for low wages. Earlier, the rising industrial states such as Britain, Germany, and the United States had become major economic powers by being innovators and focusing first on the home market. Japan chose the path of imitation and an export strategy.[2] The target markets were those of the industrial West, especially the United States, which was the world's biggest market because of its combination of a large population, affluence, and considerable consumer spending, much of it on credit (unlike in Japan or, until recently, in Europe). The Japanese deliberately concentrated on such industries as steel, shipbuilding, automobile, and consumer electronics, which in the United States were unionized, high-wage sectors, thereby giving the low-wage producer the competitive advantage.[*] Others then followed Japan's example. As the value of the Japanese yen rose against that of the dollar in the latter 1980s, thereby increasing prices for Japanese goods, countries such as South Korea and Taiwan exploited this advantage. In 1987, the year Japan produced more cars than the United States, South Korea operated the world's most modern steel mills, and Taiwan's central bank had reserves of nearly $70 billion, second only to Japan's.

To protect itself, Japan too has gone multinational, moving production to such low-wage countries as Thailand, Malaysia, the People's Republic of China, and Mexico. Fearing U.S. protection and attracted by the size of the market, Japanese corporations have been building plants in the United States: Honda in Ohio, Isuzu in Indiana, Mitsubishi in Illinois, Mazda in Michigan, Nissan in Tennessee, and Toyota in Kentucky and California. Collectively, the Japanese car producers in this country are one of the four major automobile producers. Honda manufactures more cars in the United States than in Japan and plans to export 50,000 cars back to Japan, as well as to Europe (and when the Europeans, trying to protect their car market, wanted to keep this "Japanese" car out, it was the United States that protested!). Japanese "transplants" produced 1.5 million cars in 1990. When imports for that year were added to transplant production, they equaled one-third of total U.S. production (compared to one-fifth in 1985). Other Japanese corporations with U.S. operations (such as Sony, Sharp, and Toshiba) contributed over 10 percent of America's total exports in 1990. Indeed, the exports of all foreign-owned companies added up to a quarter of American exports.[3]

---

[*] This is no longer true today. In 1990, German workers earned $14.31 an hour in pay and benefits in comparison with $17.58 for Japan and $12.63 for America. Sylvia Nasar, "Boom in Manufactured Exports Provides Hope for U.S. Economy," *New York Times*, April 21, 1991.

Going "multinational" is not, of course, confined to American and Japanese firms. Europe too has its giants such as Nestlé (Switzerland), Philips (the Netherlands), Michelin (France), and British Petroleum. After 1992, European firms are likely to become more competitive, both in Europe and in the international marketplace. In fact, the world now has three major industrial areas or poles: North America, Western Europe, and the Pacific Rim countries. The latter confront the more mature industrial economies with a new reality. America's former protégés are now full-fledged competitors increasingly producing goods they had previously imported—and at far lower prices.

Two things are striking about the new economic globalism. First, very visible to travelers are the familiar names and products encountered abroad. McDonald's restaurants are found in Tokyo, Paris, and now even in Moscow. Michelin radial tires are fitted on American cars, and Nikon cameras and Toyota cars and vans are used widely on all continents. Second, and less visible and well known, is the tendency of corporations that consumers still identify with their countries to manufacture products abroad. For example, AT&T produces so many of its products in Taiwan that it is one of that country's largest exporters; General Electric is Singapore's largest private employer; and the Whirlpool Corporation employs 43,500 people in forty-five countries, most of them non-American. As for IBM, 40 percent of its employees are foreign. Bell South operates in over thirty countries, and Bell Atlantic owns New Zealand's telephone companies.[4]

The globalization of the American car is well along. Beginning in the early 1970s, Chrysler imported small cars and trucks made by Mitsubishi, of which it owned 12 percent until the recent termination of this arrangement, and sold them under the Plymouth, Dodge, and Chrysler labels; Mitsubishi V-6 engines powered various Chrysler cars. The Ford Probe and Mazda MX-6 come off the same Japanese-managed assembly line near Detroit. While they look different, these cars are only dissimilar versions of the same car. Engines and transmissions for both cars are designed and manufactured by Mazda in Japan; seats, tires, and batteries are American-made. Probe's styling is Ford's. Ford has a 50 percent stake in Mazda's Detroit plant. Ford is also exploring collaboration with Nissan. Elsewhere, the Ford Festiva is Korean-made, and the Tracer is built in Mexico. General Motors (GM) owns 42 percent of Isuzu. The Chevrolet Spectrum is an Isuzu-made import, and the Spring is a Suzuki import (GM owns a 5 percent interest in Suzuki). GM will be a major supplier for Isuzu vehicles to be produced at Isuzu's new plant in Indiana. In a joint venture with Toyota known as the United Motor Manufacturing Company, GM also produces the Chevrolet Nova and Toyota Corolla FX-14 in a plant in California managed by Toyota. Some GM and Ford cars have more Japanese components than Japanese cars. For example, the popular Honda Accord and Mazda 626 have a higher domestic content (U.S.-made parts) than the Ford Crown Victoria. But the situation can be even more complicated. Smith Corona, once a U.S. typewriter manufacturer, is now a British corporation that produces typewriters in Singapore and Indonesia, which are then shipped to the United States.

Its Japanese competitor, Brothers Industries, has transferred its operations to Tennessee.[5]

Increasingly, unless a company is willing to "go multinational" and arrange intercorporate alliances and cooperation, its future may be in trouble, be it in manufacturing, marketing, finance, or other services. Because cars, for example, are produced all over the world, manufacturers favor tire companies that can supply them wherever they are. Thus in 1988, Pirelli of Italy and Bridgestone of Japan fought a takeover battle over Firestone Tire and Rubber Company.[6] In the emerging global tire market, a company has to be a global player to compete effectively. The United States, being such a huge market, made the fight for control of Firestone critical for both companies. Bridgestone won, joining Goodyear and Michelin as a company to be reckoned with in both the United States, where it can serve the increasing number of Japanese car plants, and Europe where Firestone had extensive operations. A German tire company, Continental, which gained access to the American market by buying Uniroyal and Japan's Sumitomo Rubber, has an 85 percent interest in Britain's Dunlop. Goodyear produces tires in Brazil for sale on the West Coast to compete with Korean tires offered to West Coast distributors at 15 percent below Goodyear prices. And both Goodyear and Michelin are seeking entry to South Korea because of its growing importance as a car maker.

A global strategy, then, is becoming imperative for companies trying to survive and prosper in an increasingly *interdependent* economy, in which each nation, to assure its national prosperity, must participate. A strong market presence in the United States, Europe, and Japan has become essential. Transnational joint ventures, mergers, licensing, production, and marketing arrangements among manufacturers that result in market entry, technological exchange, and lower production costs in the competitive global economy obviously place companies that do not establish similar links in a potentially dangerous situation. McDonnell-Douglas, trying to survive as a manufacturer of civilian aircraft as its defense orders are cut, unsuccessfully sought 40 percent Taiwanese investment capital and Asian subcontractors to help build the next-generation jumbo jet and to maximize its appeal to Asian airlines. In the words of Susan Strange, an English economist,

> As more and more enterprises have been drawn into the competitive game of world markets, because they could no longer survive by supplying just the local market, the so-called multinationals ... are no longer playing walk-on parts, auxiliaries to the real actors. They are at the centerstage, right up there with the governments.
>
> Indeed, a growing number of enterprises have begun to resemble states, and sometimes behave like them, sending diplomatic missions to other firms or to governments; making alliances with other firms or with states. ... And just as the state was never concerned simply with the pursuit of security, so the transnational company is seldom concerned simply with the pursuit of immediate profit. ... Its concern is with survival, security against takeover, or dwindling market share.[7]

As companies shift much of their production to the developing countries, blue-collar employees in the developed countries are decreasing in number (foreign companies in the United States insist on nonunion labor). Accompanying America's "deindustrialization," growth in employment—at least until the recession of 1990-1992—has come in nonmanufacturing and non-blue-collar jobs.[8] The multinationalization of production means that capital too is mobile, moving to where production costs are low. An American company has no economic reason to pay American workers a wage of about $15 an hour if Korean or Taiwanese or Mexican workers will do the same tasks for $3 an hour—thus the term *outsourcing*. For example, in the late 1980s Boeing imported almost 30 percent of the parts for its planes: tail cones from Canada, aluminum skin panels from Japan, Rolls-Royce engines from Britain, and various tail sections from Italy, Ireland, and China. Thus "sourcing" is competitively driven, but as with licensing and joint ventures, it does raise questions about what is a U.S. product and what is a foreign product. How does one decide?[9] With production moving offshore, even in the high-technology sectors such as computers and telecommunications, and companies increasingly using robots in the manufacturing process, industrial job insecurity and downward pressure on wages are the new facts of life for American labor. The castoffs often find themselves in lower-paying service jobs ("flipping hamburgers"), and to make ends meet many families now have two wage earners. But, citing the postwar stagnation of British industry, one expert has said that "a country, an industry or a company that puts the preservation of blue-collar manufacturing jobs ahead of international competitiveness ... will soon have neither production nor jobs. This attempt to preserve such blue-collar jobs is actually a prescription for unemployment."[10]

Is America Becoming Less Competitive?

The result of all this is that while American MNCs remain competitive and profitable by relocating production and becoming "de-Americanized," America's economy in America is becoming less competitive. Many companies that stayed home lost market shares; those that prepared themselves for the competition became meaner and leaner, shedding both blue- and white-collar workers, including executive personnel, in their efforts to become more efficient and effective. For a nation whose industries were once the envy of the world and whose products were widely desired abroad—"Made in the USA" was a label denoting high quality and a reasonable price—having to compete in the international marketplace has been a shock. Too long used to having the huge American market largely to itself and never having to export much to be profitable, U.S. industries have found the sudden exposure to global, and especially Japanese, competition abroad *and* at home to be a brutal experience. That Americans invented color television, the videocassette recorder, and the microwave oven, virtually all of which are now produced by the Japanese and South Koreans and are flooding the U.S. market, stands as an indictment of American industry and management. Between 1970 and

1987, for example, U.S. industry saw its proportion of the color television market shrink from 90 percent to 10 percent.[11]

Did American manufacturers learn from their early mistakes? Not if one judges by the facsimile (fax) machine. That too was a U.S. invention, but now not one fax machine offered for sale is made in the United States. Today, the Japanese view their competitors in most areas of consumer electronics as the newly industrialized Asian countries, not the United States.[12] The Reagan administration's policy of cutting taxes while greatly raising defense expenditures, thereby creating a trillion-dollar debt and gigantic trade imbalances as the value of the dollar rose sharply in the early to mid-1980s, hurting U.S. export industries and agriculture and unleashing a flood of cheaper imports, did not help either. Of the top twenty nations with which the United States traded in the late 1980s, it had a surplus with only three. America imported more from than it sold to West Germany, Italy, and Japan (which it defeated in war), as well as Canada, Mexico, and such countries as Sri Lanka, Bangladesh, and the Ivory Coast. While this situation had improved by 1991 as exports to Europe showed a $20 billion trade surplus, the fact remains that manufacturers and labor suffered a new sense of insecurity and vulnerability. Those sectors of industry and labor that were increasingly uncompetitive expressed their concerns in terms of complaints about unfair foreign competition and a search for protective legislation. Once an advocate of free trade, the United States now seeks "level playing fields" because it has acquired a healthy stake in the international economy. About 10 percent of its gross national product is exported to the rest of the world, up from about 4 percent in the 1960s. Moreover, one-third of its cropland is committed to exports. And in the 1980s approximately one-quarter of the after-tax profits of U.S. corporations came from overseas operations (this figure excludes their exports from the United States because these constitute domestic earnings).[13]

Corporations without Countries

What has brought on the "transnational organizational revolution in world politics"?[14] Three factors stand out: the development of rapid transportation and communication; the evolution of technical and organizational capabilities to operate across long distances; and the emergence of strong consumer economies. This revolution became very visible in business in particular because of the emergence of strong consumer-oriented economies in the industrialized First World and because of the evolution of such high-technology industries as electronics. Moreover, many industrial concerns found exporting to be increasingly disadvantageous. Because of the lower local labor costs in the importing country, corporations decided that they could remain competitive only if they established manufacturing facilities there. They thus are better able to sell their goods in the local market, as well as in the U.S. market, when they ship their less expensively made overseas products back home.

It is then not surprising that U.S. corporate investments in Europe after the formation of the European Economic Community (EEC) in 1958 were enor-

mous, and the companies resulting from these investments were very successful. American corporations, accustomed to coping with the different regula-
tions of various states in the United States, adapted better than many of their
European competitors to operating within what is now called the European
Community (EC). European firms, which historically have confined themselves to protected national markets, usually lagged behind U.S. corporations.
The transnational business organization operating in multiple markets shifts
its resources from one country to another as needed. Its aim is to maximize
profits, and the various national markets function as parts of a single larger
one, in which capital, technology, and other resources can be shifted at will.
American firms, thinking in continental terms, thus became more "European"
than European firms. In fact, the largest corporations in Europe are presently
American.[15] This overseas investment pattern suggests that the growth of the
MNC is a rational response to new business opportunities, as well as a
defensive move to protect overseas markets to which these firms had exported. Using the tools of modern business available in the 1960s—telexes,
telephones, and jetliners—American MNCs were able to coordinate operations and pursue a virtually global business strategy. European and Japanese
MNCs have since repeated this pattern.

The early observers of MNCs interpreted this expansion of MNCs optimis-
tically. According to them, if there were no interference with the free international movement of capital, technology, and goods, the MNCs would create a
new world of plenty for all and conflict for none. Each MNC was viewed as
an independent actor. With its managerial skills and technology, it could
stimulate economic development, eventually abolishing poverty throughout
the less-developed areas. Thus, corporate selfishness would lead to maximum
global welfare. Furthermore, in a world divided by nationalism, the MNCs
could provide the impetus for creation of a world community. George Ball, a
former undersecretary of state, argued that the MNC, which he called
"Cosmocorp," had outgrown the state; national boundaries were anachronis-
tic because they confined MNC activities.[16] Unlike traditional imperialism,
which presumably encouraged the state to open up new lands for business to
exploit, the new business corporation sought not territorial and political
control but access to different markets.

In this multinational context, the Cosmocorps' managers were the new
"globalists"—the advance men and women of "economic one-worldism,"
who viewed the globe as a single market or, in management expert Peter
Drucker's words, "a global shopping center." Dependent on foreign states for
permission to produce and sell within their frontiers, these managers regarded states, national egotism, and assertive foreign policies as contrary to
their interests. Their primary loyalty was to the corporation, rather than to the
nation, and global corporate interests took precedence over national interests.
Because MNCs needed peace—national rivalries were economically too costly
from their perspective—they would act as a major restraint on foreign adven-
tures as peace and profits became interdependent. Welfare politics would

replace power politics. The MNCs, having burst through the confining jurisdictions of national sovereignty, would bring a better life to all people.
Unable to fulfill their citizens' expectations, nation-states would then become
anachronisms, and the MNCs would likely replace them as the most visible
and potent actors on the world scene. Indeed, some claim that the managers
of IBM, General Motors, Exxon, General Electric, Coca-Cola, Xerox, and other
large MNCs make decisions daily that have a more immediate and visible
impact on consumers' lives than governments. The chief executive officers of
such companies, it has been asserted, have the organization, technology,
money, and ideology to manage the world as an integrated unit. The MNC
managers claim that they can succeed where conquerors and empires have
failed.[17]

WILL THE NATION-STATE SURVIVE?

Do MNCs threaten the viability of nation-states and the future of the state
system? It is easy to understand why states are concerned about the MNCs in
their territories. Even advanced industrial states are wary. Multinational
corporations represent high technology. Will other industrial economies become their "technological colonies"—that is, dependencies of the country
whose MNCs possess the most advanced technology and skills? A French
observer wrote, in the late 1960s,

> Electronics is not an ordinary industry; it is the base upon which the next stage of
> industrial—and cultural—development depends. In the nineteenth century the
> first industrial revolution replaced manual labor by machines. We are now living
> in the second industrial revolution, and every year we are replacing the labor of
> human brains by a new kind of machine—computers.
>
>   A country which has to buy most of its electronic equipment abroad will be in a
> condition of inferiority similar to that of nations in the last century which were
> incapable of industrializing. Despite their brilliant past, these nations remained
> outside the mainstream of civilization. If Europe continues to lag behind in
> electronics, she could cease to be included among the advanced areas of civiliza-
> tion within a single generation.[18]

By the early 1970s, just after these words were written, American MNCs
already controlled 80 percent of Europe's computer business, 90 percent of its
microcircuit industry, 50 percent of its transistor industry, and 65 percent of
its telecommunications. In addition, they controlled sizable portions of more
traditional industries such as the automobile (40 percent) and synthetic rubber (45 percent) industries. Concern that the U.S. MNCs would come to
control the technologically most advanced, most rapidly growing, and most
profitable sectors of industrial economies was understandable, even though at
the time American firms owned only 5 percent of overall European corporate

assets. Today, this European fear of falling behind the United States (and now Japan as well) continues, and it is one of the principal reasons that the countries of the European Community have decided to make another effort to unite in 1992. Now, of course, the United States shares the fear of what will happen as foreign corporations buy up more and more American industries and America becomes more dependent on foreign technology (especially in the area of electronics). Indeed, American observers are writing books voicing concerns similar to those voiced by Europeans not long ago.[19]

Another worry about MNCs is their huge sizes and assets compared with the gross national products of the host states.[20] This issue is particularly sensitive in the developing countries, which fear that MNCs will dominate their economies, "repatriating" profits and draining capital from states that need it. Additional complaints are that they fail to produce the goods needed for modernization. For example, Coca-Cola attracts money that could be spent on such necessities as food and educational materials. MNCs also are said to impose Western culture and consumer-oriented values on their host countries (the term *cultural imperialism* is often used).[21] These fears about MNCs, however, have changed significantly as the developing countries' needs for MNCs have grown because of the decline in foreign aid and the drop in commodity prices. The generally poor economic performances of many developing countries, previously committed to publicly run economies, have led their governments to reassess the value of private enterprise and capital.

But whether an MNC operates a manufacturing plant in Europe or an extractive industry in the Third World—and it is the former that has attracted most American investment capital[22]—the common fear in the host country is that the MNC will exploit its power in a way that will hurt national interests. For example, if an MNC finds the investment climate no longer suitable in one country, it can pick up its chips and move to another country, leaving behind unemployment and ill-feeling. Or, because other states seek to attract the MNC, it can play one state off against the other. During the cold war, the United States attempted on occasion to use MNCs as instruments of its foreign policy, forbidding shipment of certain products to designated countries. This restriction applied to all U.S. corporations, domestic as well as multinational. A foreign country wishing to pursue a friendlier policy toward a U.S. adversary or simply to improve its balance of payments could thus be prevented from trading these restricted products if they were manufactured by a subsidiary of an American MNC. The apprehensions of nations about the control over their own economies have been strengthened by MNC political interference. Past examples include International Telephone and Telegraph's efforts at subversion in Chile and bribes offered and subsidies paid by Lockheed and other firms to governmental and political leaders in many countries for orders or the right to sell their products. Host governments are understandably sensitive to infringements of their right to maintain control over their economies and foreign policies. Many Americans shared this fear as foreign money poured into the United States in the 1980s. America appeared up for sale—and cheaply too.

Yet states probably will survive the challenge of the new transnational business actor. The reason: they need each other, even though some conflict between the two is unavoidable. Their conflict is complementary. According to political scientist Samuel Huntington,

> It is conflict not between likes but between unlikes, each of which has its own primary set of sanctions to perform. It is, consequently, conflict which, like labor-management conflict, involves the structuring of relations and the distribution of benefits to entities which need each other even as they conflict with each other. The balance of influence may shift back and forth from one to the other, but neither can displace the other.[23]

Indeed, the MNC appears to strengthen rather than weaken the state because it needs the latter's permission for access to its territory. The multinational corporation may well be one of the leading reasons for the increasing role of the state in economic affairs and the extension of state power into the economic realm. In Europe, for example, governments intervened in the economic sphere to create domestic conditions to counterbalance the size and influence of American corporations. This will be even truer after 1992 when the European Community's expected last steps toward economic integration will stimulate mergers and more efficient and competitive European and global MNCs. In the United States, too, the government has increasingly involved itself in the economy to ensure "fair play" in international trade and U.S. competitiveness in modern technologies. Still, America's free-trade ideology has severely constrained its willingness to adopt an industrial policy. Other Western governments, especially Japan's, have been less hesitant to support specific industries in order for them to become internationally competitive.

In their relationships with MNCs, host countries are setting the terms of access to their markets and establishing the kinds of relations in which they benefit in the form of employment, taxes, balance of payments, transfer of technology, and acquired managerial skills, while simultaneously permitting the MNCs to earn enough to want to stay. Some hosts establish employment quotas for nationals, require MNCs to locate in so-called depressed areas (for which they may, however, receive tax incentives), forbid layoffs, and demand the training of whatever local workers are required (which may be subsidized). Almost all host countries set dates by which time they will own 51 percent of the company. They also may set export figures for the MNCs (although some may be reluctant to comply with these to avoid competing with their own brands in other countries). In recent years, MNCs, in return for access to markets, have increasingly complied with these kinds of demands by the host countries. The result has been greater cooperation between host states and MNCs. As one observer has noted,

> In short, sovereignty is no longer at bay in most countries. To be sure the degree of this shift in power differs from country to country, and from industry to

industry. It is virtually complete in most industrial host countries and some developing countries as well, and is well underway in many other developing countries.[24]

In turn, corporations essentially want to be left alone to do their business, although the fear remains that the large MNCs will interfere in national politics. Their interest in politics stems from their desire to gain access to a nation's market and a hospitable environment in which to make money. MNCs are very flexible. They will work with a democratic government in a democratic society and with despotic and even racist governments in other countries. In the short run, the MNCs may well reinforce the status quo in the societies in which they operate. In the long run, however, they may help undermine the status quo by making visible new technologies, ideas, social and cultural values, and ways of life that challenge, especially in the developing countries, the more traditional cultures. As relations with host nations have become closer, however, MNCs' relationships with their home nations have grown more and more distant. Labor, particularly, has become protectionist, opposing what the unions call the "export of jobs" to developing countries, especially Taiwan, South Korea, and Singapore. Political pressures have grown on the U.S. government to restrict the outflow of investment capital when the nation is suffering from high unemployment and balance-of-trade deficits (more money going out to pay for imports than coming in from exports). But basically, Western governments have supported the desires of their MNCs to be left free to pursue their profits and market shares abroad.

MEANING OF INTERDEPENDENCE

The growing interdependence of the Western industrial democracies means not only that their economies are becoming more intertwined, but also that through such close interconnections one nation can hurt another. An interesting example is the case of the Japanese firm Toshiba. During the Reagan years, Toshiba was found to be guilty of selling the Soviets the American machinery needed to make their nuclear submarine propellers quieter (before, the noisiness of Soviet submarines had allowed the U.S. Navy to keep track of them). This gross violation of U.S. security enraged Congress to the point of considering a ban on all Toshiba products for a number of years. But U.S. manufacturers, among whom AT&T, IBM, General Electric, Honeywell, Xerox, and Hewlett-Packard were the most prominent, lobbied against such legislation; they had all become too dependent on Toshiba electronic components for their products. Thus, as worrisome as this very dependence on foreign suppliers for critical components of arms (as noted in Chapter 7) had become to U.S. officials, Congress, in seeking to punish just one foreign MNC, would be hurting U.S. industries and jobs as well.

It is this intertwining of corporate and national economies that is described by the term *interdependence*. Two characteristics of interdependence are sensitivity and, more important, vulnerability.[25] If events in one nation's economy affect another nation's economy but the latter can take countermeasures to minimize the consequences, the latter's economy is sensitive but not vulnerable. But if such remedial measures are unavailable, the latter may be hurt because it is vulnerable to another nation's actions. Two or more countries are therefore interdependent when none of them can withdraw from the relationship without each being hurt by doing so. Each state's economy is hostage to the other; that is the real meaning of mutual vulnerability. "Interdependence allows states to compel each other to cooperate on economic matters, much as mutual assured destruction allows nuclear powers to compel each other to respect their security. All states are forced by the others to act as partners in the provision of material comfort for their home publics."[26] In short, all states benefit from their being interdependent.

One example is the U.S.-Japan relationship. Until recently, Japan needed protection by the United States, through which it gained secure access to a stable and expanding world market. But, above all, Japan required access to the huge American market, the largest for its exports, to maintain its economic well-being. In its turn, in the 1980s the United States depended on Japan to create jobs by building factories in this country and to buy U.S. Treasury bonds (at a time when the dollar was losing value) to help cover the enormous U.S. deficit. If Japan had not bought Treasury bonds, the high American interest rates would have risen even higher until enough foreign buyers could have been found to purchase these bonds. But this would have resulted in Americans paying billions of dollars more for housing, cars, and other items they purchased on credit. The United States also has become increasingly dependent on Japan for important new technologies, including those for some of the country's most advanced weapons systems. Each country in this economic relationship was—and remains—hostage to the other.

Yet such interdependent relationships are, as this example suggests, not necessarily symmetrical. The United States borrowed capital from Japan, giving it influence. But Japan needed access to the huge U.S. market for its exports, thus giving Japan a stake in the economic health of the United States; economic decline would affect the value of Japanese investments and the volume of its exports. Japan was, therefore, more dependent on the United States, with its huge and diverse economy, than the latter was on Japan. In brief, if two countries depend on one another economically, but one depends on the other more, that asymmetry is a source of power. But not all interstate relationships are interdependent. Basically, it is the nations of North America (Canada and the United States) and America's European allies and Japan—all developed, pluralistic, democratic societies—that have become interdependent. In fact, the degree of interdependence among them has become so great that one analyst has referred to the emergence of a new "international business civilization." [27] By contrast, the relationship between the First World and most of the Third World countries (excluding the newly industrialized and OPEC countries) remains one of inequality or dependency. The existence of interdependence among the Western states who remain allied to one another suggests that trade follows the flag. American power created this alliance system, and the corporate extensions came later. But if political action created an interdependent economic relationship in its wake, the subsequent economic conflicts among allies were to have profound effects on the cohesion of these alliances as the international "free-trade" economy, initially dominated by the United States, became increasingly divided by competitive mercantilist policies.

FREE TRADE AND THE INTERNATIONAL ECONOMY

This state of affairs came about slowly. After World War II, the American economy emerged healthy and preponderant. Those of Europe and Japan were shattered. The United States therefore took the lead in organizing alliances against the Soviet Union and in establishing an international economy in which trade would flourish, stimulating economic growth and prosperity among its allies. The General Agreement on Tariffs and Trade (GATT) was the principal organization created in 1947 to deal with the trade issue. Its basic philosophy and goal was one of free trade. Liberals had long believed that unhampered trade would result not only in maximum economic welfare for the participating states but also in more peaceful relations among states. Each state would benefit from such trade and therefore had a vested interest in continuing its trade relationship (but because war would disrupt trade and hurt a nation's prosperity, it was counterproductive). Thus, GATT was designed to create free trade among states by gradually lowering tariff barriers and stimulating trade. This emphasis on free trade was stirred not only by a belief in prosperity and peace but also by the memories of the depression years of the 1930s when each of the Western industrial states had cut imports while stimulating its exports by various means. [28] This economic nationalism had been unworkable, however. When country A had cut imports and exporting country B could not earn money by trading, how could B buy goods from A? The end result had been a decline in world trade and a deepening of the depression. Thus, it should not be surprising that after World War II the United States adhered to the belief that free trade was good economically and politically. This belief was reinforced by self-interest. With the world's most powerful economy, the United States would obviously benefit from free trade—that is, access to other nation's markets. Similarly, in the nineteenth century when Britain had been the world's first nation to industrialize, it had advocated free trade.

The effects of free trade in the postwar period were everything everyone had expected. GATT grew from twenty-three member states in 1947, mainly Western, to 108 in 1992. By cutting tariffs substantially in successive rounds of negotiations, GATT could claim much of the credit for the postwar growth of world trade and production. The explosive consumer demand after World War II sustained economic growth. According to political economists David Blake and Robert Walters, it appeared "that the lessons of the 1930s had been learned; international oversight of national foreign economic policies has been successful in promoting production and in curtailing the excesses of economic nationalism with its negative economic and political consequences."[29]

But these "good times" ended during the 1970s because of three events. One was détente. The Western alliance had, on the whole, remained cohesive after World War II, with its member states perceiving the Soviet Union as a threat. But this perception changed during the détente years. National interests, once more or less subordinate to the collective interests of the alliance, began to assert themselves more forcefully. The second event was the revival of the European and Japanese economies. American economic supremacy, which had been unnatural because it resulted largely from the destruction of European and Japanese industry, began to decline. After 1945, the United States had 50 percent of the world's gross national product; by the late 1980s, that figure was 23 percent, still substantial but a relatively steep drop. This figure represented both a genuine U.S. decline and what was earlier referred to as the rise of "the others" (Chapter 8). National economic interests therefore tended to come to the fore and cause divisive conflicts. The third event was the shock of OPEC's actions, supplemented by the later fall of Iran's shah, which led to skyrocketing oil prices and simultaneous recession and inflation among Western oil-importing states. All these occurrences reinforced the trend of emphasizing economic issues.

If foreign policy has among its purposes the protection of a nation's economic welfare, then the preoccupation with employment, inflation, economic growth, and stable oil supplies was understandable. But it also intensified intra-alliance conflicts. The decline of the United States as the economically dominant power in the West meant that the rules of the (economic) game were harder to establish and enforce. States that once had little choice but to go along now had a choice. Thus today, economic cooperation has become much more difficult as Western governments respond primarily to domestic pressures, not that of their allies and friends.[30]

MERCANTILISM AND 'EVEN PLAYING FIELDS'

Whereas free trade is aimed at global prosperity, the new mercantilism of today is concerned primarily with maximum national welfare.[31] Originally,

Table 16-1 Comparison of Free-Trade and Mercantilist Ideas about the International Economy

	Free Trade	*Mercantilist*
Actor	Multinational corporation	State
Nature of economic relations	Clashing interests and harmony	Clashing interests and conflict
Goal of economic activity	Maximization of global welfare	Maximization of national welfare
Economic-political assumption	That economics should determine politics	That politics determines economics

SOURCE: Adapted from Table 6, "Comparison of the Three Conceptions of Political Economy," in Robert Gilpin, *U.S. Power and the Multinational Corporation* (New York: Basic Books, 1975).

in fact, free-trade theory had been a reaction to the older mercantilism practiced by the states of Europe during the sixteenth, seventeenth, and eighteenth centuries. States in that era were interested in enhancing their power and wealth; increasing their power meant increasing their wealth and increasing their wealth meant increasing their power. States, therefore, encouraged exports and discouraged imports to earn the gold needed to support armies and growing civil governments. Mercantilism rejected the free-trade school's optimism that states' economic interests were basically harmonious; instead, it believed that economic interests were in conflict (see Table 16-1). Mercantilism also repudiated the notion of interdependence—the free-trade notion brought up-to-date—which claimed that nations must cooperate in finding solutions; instead, it placed its emphasis on unilateral action.

Now, the term *mercantilism* has been revived to describe policies adopted initially by the Europeans and the Japanese, but also increasingly by the United States. Today's mercantilism is based on protection of employment and production, stimulation of exports, and reduction of imports to gain and maintain a favorable trade surplus. A trade surplus for one nation, however, is balanced by another's trade deficit; all states cannot achieve surpluses simultaneously. This means that economic growth and jobs for one state result in a decline of both in another. Mercantilism, therefore, compels states to compete for the largest possible share of the world market to ensure their national welfare and economic security.

Japan's aggressive export policy (the success of which it owes to the efficiency of its industries), the inventiveness of its engineers (thanks to its educational system), and the quality production and consumer appeal of its products have already been noted. Although Japan's economy is considered to be a private-enterprise one, it has long been guided by the Ministry of International Trade and Industry (MITI), which, acting as an economic version of the famous old Prussian General Staff, selected the industries that were to grow and targeted the countries whose markets were to be penetrated. It coordinated these plans with research and investment capital. Japan's state-guided trade policy may have made Japan an economic giant, but it has made its policies suspect as well.[32] One of Reagan's secretaries of commerce, in condemning Japan's trading practices as "unfair," gave voice to the widespread fear that Japan's "export policy has as its object not participation in, but dominance of, world markets." [33] In 1991, French prime minister Edith Cresson similarly accused Japanese manufacturers of a desire to conquer the world and not playing by the rules. She was particularly concerned that if the Japanese knocked the Europeans out of the semiconductor and computer fields, it would imperil crucial industries dependent on electronics—as had happened in the United States. Having conquered the United States, Japan was now ready to take on Europe. Japan, in short, was widely perceived as waging "predatory trade" or industrial warfare to become the hegemonic power in the economic sphere. It is, in that respect, a new type of political economy. Its corporations seek not only profits, as all corporations do, but to increase their market share; for this they are willing to postpone or reduce profits for years. According to a Dutch journalist with many years of experience in Japan, the international domination in as many industrial areas as possible is part of "a single minded, politically driven and evidently unstoppable economic expansion" to make the world safe for Japan." [34]

This may not be the Europeans' aim, but to promote their exports they too have subsidized the products of their less-competitive industries, such as steel, to undersell American-made products in the United States. In no area, however, has this been more irritating to the United States than in agriculture. For years, the efficiency of U.S. agricultural production has allowed the United States to serve as the breadbasket for the rest of the world. In 1981, a banner year, American farmers exported a record 162 million metric tons of food worth $44 billion.[35] Throughout the 1970s, when dollars were flowing out at a record level to pay for oil, large agricultural sales on the international market were the main reason the trade imbalances did not become even larger. But after 1981, the volume of these exports declined, despite the continued export of U.S. grain to the Soviet Union. This resulted in part from the high value of the dollar in the early 1980s but in large part from surplus production by other countries. Western Europe, once a large importer of American food, now overproduces because of the high subsidies paid to its farmers. These surpluses are then "dumped" on the world market because, as inefficient producers, Europeans price their farm products too high to compete internationally. This policy costs European taxpayers $35 billion a year, increases food prices up to 40 percent, and devastates farmers in lower-cost exporting countries. This problem will not be easily remedied, however, for the EC is basically a bargain between French agriculture and West German industry, both looking for a wider European market (although West German farmers, while small in number, are politically powerful and benefit from this deal as well). Thus, the political forces that made the Common Market possible impede both the trading and broader political relationship between Europe and the United States.[36]

The problem is not limited to Europe. India has begun to export grain; China's agricultural production has increased greatly in recent years; and other developing countries, such as South Korea and Thailand, will soon become greater agricultural producers and exporters (many of these developing countries were food importers until recently). Competition among old and new food producers for a share of the international market is thus the prospect for the future. Indeed, 1985 American grain exports were down by about 50 percent from the 1981 level of 48 million metric tons, and this surplus grain cost the United States approximately $20 billion a year to store. The U.S. government therefore decided in 1986 to do what other countries have been doing all along—subsidize farm products for export and sell them at competitive world prices—but overproduction remains a problem. America's competitors are undoubtedly determined to preserve their market shares.

The results of the growing economic conflicts among the interdependent Western states are several. First, the U.S.-West European-Japanese alliance— the foundation of U.S. security and economic well-being, once cemented by a visible Soviet threat—is now increasingly divided by commercial and financial rivalries. During the cold war, the logic of national security necessitated cooperation against the common enemy; the growing economic rivalry was subordinated to the priority of preserving the alliance relationships. But once the external threat had disappeared, economic competition could no longer be contained by the requirements of strategic cooperation. Furthermore, as amply illustrated in Chapter 8, the United States has not held its own in this competition, particularly against Japan. Investing two to three times as much as the United States in new factories, equipment, and research, Japan is expected to overtake the United States as the number one economy by the beginning of the twenty-first century if it continues on its present course.[37]

Second, this competition has, among other things, led—and will lead—to a series of trade wars or, more accurately, "subsidy wars," as each partner subsidizes its less-efficient manufacturers or agricultural sectors so that they can export their goods by undercutting their rivals' prices. Such subsidies are part of the broader protectionist strategy demanded by domestic pressures to prevent unemployment and the closing of increasingly uncompetitive plants or inefficient farms, or to spur economic growth and employment in competitive industries. For example, Europeans heavily subsidize Airbus Industries, a consortium of several nations formed to compete against Boeing and increase their share of the global commercial jet market. Despite a recent agreement to limit such subsidies, many foreign trade experts expect such practices to continue when the EC makes its final move toward integration in 1992.[38] The

Japanese too have subsidized efficient industries by dumping their products—at prices lower than those charged domestically—on the world market to drive their competitors out of business (for example, those producing 64k chips for computers). Then, of course, prices go up. An additional danger is that Japanese companies may keep the most advanced chips for themselves to maintain or increase their competitive advantage. Such "trade wars" are thus properly named; they are the economic equivalent of military coercion.

Third, fair or unfair, this competition has led to widespread resentment and ill-feeling, charges of "uneven playing fields," and cries for "fair competition." As the world's largest and most affluent consumer market, the United States is the target of Japanese, EC, and Third World exports.[39] While much of the competition was fair and U.S. consumers obviously liked imported goods, the United States nevertheless negotiated a series of its own mercantilist measures—"voluntary" restraints—affecting steel, automobile, television set, shoe, and textile imports, to cite but a few, in response to domestic pressures (but despite these ceilings on imports, the U.S. industries declined). These protectionist moves, moreover, have been costly to the taxpayer. The protection of the car market by imposing quotas on Japanese imports in the mid-1980s cost the American car buyer an average $500 as Japanese car prices rose when demand exceeded supply and the "Big Three" U.S. auto makers, instead of underselling the Japanese, raised their prices too. Japanese profits rose and were invested in building U.S. auto plants, thereby getting around the quotas, and in designing and producing luxury cars to compete against the top-line U.S. autos. Meanwhile, the Big Three, with the pressure off to become more competitive, did not invest their extra profits in more modern plants and equipment and thus continued to lose market shares to the Japanese who now competed with them not only in lower-priced cars but in the higher-priced ones as well.[40] The lesson was plain: prohibiting or reducing imported goods reduces competition and the incentive to hold prices down, thereby stoking inflation. It protects the industries that because of their inefficiency are the least equipped to survive, but it does so at a high cost to the entire economy. It also invites retaliation against American goods, leaving everyone worse off than if all markets had remained open.

The 'Japan Problem'

While the American market, despite numerous restrictions, remains the magnet for other nations' imports, Japan is again an example of a country tenaciously guarding its industries against imports from the United States and Europe. Imports into Japan (as well as into the newly industrialized countries) have been held to an extremely low level—the lowest of any of the industrialized countries—not by imposing tariff barriers, which are lower than those of the United States, but by means of nontariff barriers: long traditional relationships between suppliers and buyers; families of firms that deal with one another exclusively or mainly; a distribution system that does not pass savings on to consumers and prefers to deal with "mom-and-pop" stores rather than large supermarkets (so that the Japanese generally pay far higher prices for their own goods than, say, Americans); a high savings rate that lowers the price for capital for research and development and investments; protection of key industries deemed vital for economic growth or national security, such as computers and satellites; and, not least, a preference for their own products.

In support of a policy of "buying Japanese," the Japanese usually claim that they are not responsible for the trade imbalance, that the fault lies elsewhere—especially in shoddily made, unreliable American products. Japan's trade surplus in 1991, the largest in the world, soared to $100 billion, or roughly the sum of all other countries' deficits, and it is still rising. The fact is that Japan's market is essentially closed to foreign products and investments. No industrial state, not even Germany, has a trade surplus with Japan. The same is true for Asia's "little Japans." Thus, while Japan, a big beneficiary of free trade, should be its strongest proponent, its policies, by creating unemployment and shrinking industries in the United States and Western Europe, weaken support for the free-trade system.

Trade barriers are only slowly being reduced after lengthy, item-by-item negotiations, amid mutual recriminations. The Japanese are forever inventive in rejecting imports on cultural grounds. Pharmaceuticals that have been extensively tested elsewhere are rejected because they have not been tested on Japanese subjects in Japanese laboratories. Foreign skis were once rejected because Japanese snow was said to be wetter than European or American snow. The Champion spark plug company, having been turned down in a bid to equip a brand of Japanese cars, once offered to supply spark plugs for free and was still not accepted! Because Japan bases its refusal to buy foreign products on allegedly cultural reasons, any criticism of such Japanese decisions becomes an attack on Japan itself, which then leads to national assertiveness.[41]

Not surprisingly, the result is that the Japanese, proud of their economic efficiency and accomplishments, have become resentful of what they call "Japan-bashing." They charge that the pressures on them to open up their markets to more American exports and the efforts to impose ceilings on Japanese exports to the United States reflect a declining and increasingly uncompetitive American economy.[42] The Japanese have a case when they point to the United States' huge federal budget deficit, which has made it the largest debtor in the world; its low savings rate; its too little investment in plant modernization and too much in leveraged buyouts during the decade of the 1980s, which led to piling up corporate debt but contributing little to U.S. competitiveness; the focus of American business on short-term results; its inadequate spending on education; and its antitrust laws that discourage corporate collaboration. Thus, even if the Japanese complied with American demands and bought all the citrus fruit, beef, medical equipment, car telephones, and other products the United States feels they should buy, the trade deficit with Japan would be reduced by only a few billion dollars. If both countries wiped out all barriers to trade, the trade deficit might grow as voluntary restraints on imports were lifted.[43] Americans are drawn to Japanese products, even when higher priced than similar American ones, because of the quality and value of Japanese production. The fundamental problem is not unfair trade but American productivity and quality. Still, the fact remains that Japanese products have access to the American market, but even comparative U.S. products, with a few exceptions, do not have similar access to the Japanese market.

The consequence is mutual resentment. This has translated into rising anti-Americanism in Japan, where disdain for the decline of the United States has become a major force. American anger is especially strong because of the perception that it is the very allies that the United States helped to recover after the war—Japan as well as Europe—that are now not only competing unfairly but also destroying the U.S. economy. The Japanese reciprocate this resentfulness, often charging that "Japan-bashing" is not inspired simply by jealousy and American anger at no longer being number one (for which the Japanese feel the Americans have no one to blame but themselves) but also by racism. They point to the outcry when the Japanese buy such symbolic American properties as Rockefeller Center and the lack of any criticism of European investments. They fail to mention, of course, that while the Japanese system manages to keep out most investments and imports from the United States and Europe, Europeans buy many U.S. products and allow U.S. investments.[44] It is a reciprocal relationship, as was evident just before the Iraqi invasion of Kuwait in 1990 when the United States, after a trade deficit of $28 billion with the EC in 1986, gained a trade surplus, while the deficit with Japan, although down, painfully persisted. Nevertheless, the Japanese continue to complain that "Japan bashing" is unfair and begrudges the Japanese the fruits of their hard work.

Europe too has restricted imports, but not to the degree of Japan. In Europe, unemployment has been high and economic growth low since the 1970s. Europeans favored détente even when the United States did not because they were seeking markets in the East to replace those lost to the Japanese and Americans. Europe's openness and fast economic growth after the war helped the development strategy and involvement in the world economy of the newly industrialized countries. But those European industries that played so large a role in Europe's rapid postwar growth have been hard hit by Japanese and NIC competition. As a result, various European nations have placed severe restraints on Japanese imports. In these circumstances, the United States has repeatedly expressed its concern that Europe, with its over 300 million people (customers), will become a protectionist bloc—"Fortress Europe"—rather than a key player in a prosperous and growing international economy.[45]

Finally, but by no means the least important, is the impact of this mercantilism on the developing countries. For example, the EC has become one of the world's largest sugar exporters, impoverishing producers in the Philippines, the Caribbean, and Central America. The developing countries were already hurt by the general slowdown of the world's economy, which led the industrial countries to resort to mercantilism. The Third World's prospects for economic growth depend on the industrial countries' demands for their natural resources and markets for their manufactured products. But the decline in commodity prices, Western tariff and nontariff barriers, and the Third World's debt problem have dimmed the hopes of the developing countries for development, exacerbating an already grave situation as incomes decline and poverty worsens.

This mercantilist challenge to the more liberal international economic order of free trade will not be easy to deal with, although the security and prosperity of the U.S.-West European-Japanese alliance depend on the outcome. Efforts to cooperate have been made, however. The Japanese, realizing that their economic strategy of maximizing exports and minimizing imports is generating adverse reactions in the United States and Western Europe, have become aware that Japan must expand its domestic market and become more of a consumer/importer society and less of a saver/exporter. Nevertheless, despite economic forecasts and Japan's stimulation of domestic demand, as well as the sharp drop of the dollar and the rise of the yen, its high exports have continued.[46] Indeed, its trade surplus was soaring in 1990, despite a drop in exports to the United States; exports to Europe and Asia more than made up the difference.[47] America's monetary strategy to make U.S. products cheaper and Japan's more expensive to correct the imbalance of trade worked only so far. Japanese companies made themselves even more efficient, cutting profit margins, even operating at a loss at times, to maintain their market shares.

More significantly, the question was whether Japan would change to a more consumer-oriented, import society. According to at least one skeptic who knows Japan well, the formal concessions the Japanese have made on certain agricultural and manufactured products will be nullified by the informal arrangements that are at the heart of the Japanese power structure. The alliance between bureaucracy and business (as well as rice farmers) and the Liberal Democratic Party (which has governed Japan without interruption since the U.S. occupation of Japan after World War II) is not very sensitive to public opinion and voter sentiment. If Japanese consumers, paying the world's highest prices for their own products, as an electorate "actually did have a mandate, the United States would have an easier task. . . . [A] majority of Japanese understand that their interests are championed by the American government pleading for structural reforms benefitting the consumer. The United States is sometimes even half-jokingly referred to as Japan's only authentic political opposition party."[48]

The Farm Subsidy Problem

The trade problem of free trade versus mercantilism is nowhere better illustrated than in agriculture. All the industrial countries recognize the growing burden of spending $100 billion a year on farm subsidies, which continue to increase while many governments are attempting to cut fiscal deficits. The United States, Europe, and Japan agree that farm supports must be cut. They are bad for budgets, bad for prices, and bad for the developing countries' economies. President Reagan proposed dealing with this problem by ending agricultural supports by the year 2000. The problem, however, is that farmers in all the developed countries are well organized and politically powerful. Japanese farmers, who are among the world's most inefficient, have even managed to pressure the government to pay them six times world prices for the rice they produce to maintain Japanese self-sufficiency. In Japan, elimination of subsidies may put those in power out of power since Japan's governing party receives large contributions from beef and rice farmers. European farmers, as noted, while relatively few in numbers, also have political clout disproportionate to their numbers. The EC, a densely populated area, would under a genuinely free-trade system be the world's largest food importer. Instead, the EC countries, as noted earlier, set their price supports so high that their farmers massively overproduced. These surpluses were then dumped on world markets through export subsidies. An accord on ending farm subsidies is therefore unlikely.

Yet the latest GATT negotiations among its 108 members, which by 1992 had dragged on for six years, were aimed at applying liberal trade rules to the farm trade. The EC proposed cutting its subsidies to its 10 million farmers, but French framers protested vigorously even a modest 30 percent cut over a ten-year period. The United States, however, together with Australia, Argentina, Brazil, and other countries—mainly seventy developing countries that sought to increase their exports of food, clothing, and textiles to the industrial world by $50 billion a year—argued for much deeper cuts: farm supports by 75 percent and export subsidies by 90 percent. Most of the nations that exported farm goods refused to sign an overall GATT agreement unless the EC was willing to make much deeper cuts. Thus, agriculture threatened the future of GATT which since 1947 had reduced tariffs by 75 percent and contributed to everyone's prosperity. Indeed, agriculture blocked GATT's aim of a further one-third reduction on manufactured products and the removal of barriers in intellectual properties, such as improved copyright and patent protection (U.S. companies are losing an estimated $60 billion a year from piracy to Brazil, India, Taiwan, South Korea, and elsewhere), as well as in such services as construction, tourism, banking, and telecommunications. In short, the failure to agree to farm rules jeopardized free-trade rules, which since World War II have helped world trade grow from $60 billion to $6 trillion, and which could increase this trade even further by an estimated $4 trillion over the next decade.[49]

The United States and Third World producers in GATT, arguing that their farms produce at lower costs than those of Europe's smaller farms, expected, of course, that big cuts in farm protection would permit their farmers to capture a larger share of the world's farm trade. The developing countries were unwilling to sign an agreement covering intellectual properties or services—essentially dropping barriers protecting their own nascent service industries—unless they received substantial concessions in farm trade and access to Western markets for their products. But the Europeans held steadfast. This conflict over agricultural subsidies and protection could not have come at a worse time. Many developing countries were trying to become efficient and competitive in the world market by moving away from state guidance and control of their economies, and Eastern Europe was abandoning its managed trade with the Soviet Union. Thus, Western Europe's blocking of food imports and dumping of surplus production in international markets at subsidized prices severely hurt developing country and Eastern European farmers and economies. With the end of the cold war, Europeans no longer had to make concessions to maintain U.S. protection against the Soviet military threat. As for the United States, it no longer needed its allies as much. Therefore, both sides were more insistent on their economic positions, jeopardizing the global trading system, hurting all participants, and enhancing the possibilities of the emergence of regional trading blocs and trade wars. The fact is that even if a last-minute compromise is reached to avoid the appearance of failure, as appears likely, the era of GATT is basically over (indeed, when Russian and Ukrainian agricultural produce reappear on the international market, the fight for market shares will intensify and threaten to drive more European and U.S. farmers off the land). The three leading economic poles cannot agree on common rules to govern their economic competition; removal of the domestic obstacles is simply too economically painful and politically risky for governments facing the angry voters who would be negatively affected by these changes.

The Death of GATT?

Governments are, as this example suggests, subject to contradictory pressures. The forces of interdependence compel them to cooperate to find collective solutions. To do that, Western leaders meet annually at an economic summit conference, demonstrating their awareness that no unilateral solutions are possible. But none can forget their voters at home. Markets may be global, but political constituencies still end at the borders of their nation-states. Even regular meetings of the G-7 countries (Britain, Canada, France, Germany, Italy, Japan, and the United States), undertaken to coordinate the economic policies of the Western industrial nations, cannot overcome deep divisions of national interests. The G-7 suffers not only from deep U.S.-Japanese differences, but also from growing European-Japanese ones, as well as U.S.-European ones as Europe nears its final thrust toward full economic integration. Agriculture is only one very visible and contentious area of conflict. Despite the fact that the United States and Europe sell each other nearly $100 billion in goods and services, the American fear is that Europe will increasingly resort to government subsidies and industrial policy to further its economic aims. In 1991 and 1992, besides the global farm talks, the key issue was interest rates. Washington wanted to lower interest rates to end the recession in the United States and avoid one in Europe. The Bush administration was especially concerned that an economic slowdown in Europe would reduce the demand for U.S. products since exports to Europe had helped offset the decline of sales in the United States, thus limiting the effects of the recession. If exports were to drop, it might be harder to shake off the U.S. recession. Moreover, lower interest rates would stimulate the European economies. But Germany, the strongest economy in Europe, was increasingly absorbed with reviving the former East German economy, which was costing far more than anticipated. German bankers felt that the billions being spent to help East Germany would overheat the economy and stoke inflation; therefore, they raised interest rates, even though the effect was to slow Europe's growth and irk its major EC partners who felt their economies were underheated. Thus, the stake was larger than that of the United States; global economic growth had slowed to only 1 percent in 1990 and was heading for zero growth in 1991. Indeed, the impact reached beyond the United States and Western Europe to the developing countries and the Eastern European countries seeking to become free-market democracies. Would the G-7 be able to stimulate economic growth, leading to greater interdependence, or would it be unable to reverse the global economic stagnation, thereby encouraging the breakdown into competing trade blocs?

Although the annual G-7 summit meetings of presidents and prime ministers at times resemble social affairs and photo opportunities more than serious cooperative efforts to align their economic and financial policies, the issues confronting them are significant, and such meetings are not necessarily wasteful as political leaders gather and talk informally, clarifying their political problems and searching for feasible compromises. In 1985, for example, their finance ministers did agree to adopt the U.S. strategy of lowering the value of the dollar to cut imports and increase U.S. exports. And in 1991, the chiefs of government invited Mikhail Gorbachev to talk to them about his plan for market reforms. They discussed as well the possibilities of Western foreign aid and of G-7 membership for the Soviet Union after decades of isolating itself from the world economy (thus perhaps making the G-7 the G-7½). In 1992, on the heels of the collapse of the Soviet Union, the G-7 finance ministers approved $24 billion in assistance to Boris Yeltsin's Russia.

The future of trade therefore appears to be "managed trade."[50] Rather than supply and demand in an unregulated market, quantifiable goals and market shares for each nation's industries will be negotiated according to the principle of reciprocity.[51] The U.S.-Japanese semiconductor agreement negotiated during the Reagan years guaranteeing U.S. companies at least 20 percent of the Japanese market is illustrative. The rationale was embodied in the 1988 U.S. trade law: the protection of American workers from foreign competition, not free trade. "Fair trade" is enshrined in the legislation, meaning that the United States will play tit-for-tat with such countries as Japan and the NICs, which now have easy access to the U.S. market. The whole point of this legislation was to boost American exports by pressuring other countries to lower their trade barriers. The United States has entered the mercantilist age in full force.

During the Bush trip to Japan in January 1992, it became clear that, despite its free-trade rhetoric, the administration sought a guaranteed market share in Japan for U.S. autos and auto parts. Equally clear, if the administration failed to gain greater access for American goods to Japan's markets, Congress would act to compel Japan to lower the never-ending huge U.S. trade deficit with Japan (three-quarters of which was in transportation) by 20 percent a year over a five-year period (although it was unclear why U.S. consumers, who felt that Japanese cars were better made, would switch to U.S. cars until their quality and reliability matched those of their competitors, many of which were made in the United States by American workers). Europeans are demanding similar "reciprocity." The EC's deficit with Japan at the beginning of 1992 was $41 billion; the Europeans did not intend to provide Japanese car producers free access to their market and watch their automobile industry suffer the same fate as the American industry. They set 16 percent as the market share for Japanese cars produced in Japan and in Europe during the 1990s, although that figure might be breached by the export of Japanese cars produced in the United States because of Washington's pressure to increase U.S. exports.

The point is that GATT and multilateral negotiations appeared to be superseded by bilateral negotiations: the United States with Japan, the EC, Canada, and Mexico; the Europeans with the Japanese; and each with the United States. As each of these three leading economic poles increasingly looked at trade issues only from its particular perspective and did not submit disputes to GATT, relying mainly on bilateral negotiations and solutions, multilateralism was robbed of its meaning. Today, this appears to be the best alternative to "level playing fields" for everyone.

But how good an alternative this really is remains to be seen. Most observers believe that the worst of all scenarios would be the emergence of three huge regional blocs. The first bloc would be the European Community, whose twelve-member core includes Britain, France, Germany, and Italy. Such nonmember Western European states as Finland, Sweden, and Austria, which in 1991 became part of the greater European economic zone, have applied for full EC membership. And the fledgling Eastern European democracies of Hungary, Czechoslovakia, and Poland will likely gain access for their products by the end of the century. The second bloc would be composed of Japan and the newly industrialized Pacific Rim countries. Japan's industries, in search of cheaper labor, are increasingly relocating in the Pacific Rim NICs, as well as in such countries as Malaysia, Thailand, Indonesia, and the Philippines, all members of ASEAN (Association of Southeast Asian Nations). This has already resulted in closer economic relations among these Asian countries, with Japan clearly in a position of preeminence. Increasingly, these countries are being pulled into Japan's orbit; the Greater Co-Prosperity Zone that Japan sought unsuccessfully by military force during the 1930s and 1940s is now being sought by economic means. Japan's Ministry of International Trade and Industry "sees its role as coordinator of a newly emerging structure of subcontractor economies in Southeast Asia—the beginnings of a yen-bloc bulwark against American and European economic power." [52] Such a bulwark not only might make Japan less dependent on exports to the United States, but also might provide the basis for Japan's overtaking the United States early in the next decade. Indeed, 1990 was the first year Japan sold more to Asia than to the United States. The third superbloc would be composed of the United States and Canada in North America. Already possessing the largest trading relationship between any two countries, the two countries have signed a free-trade agreement designed to integrate their automobile, energy, banking, transportation, and other industries. And together they are negotiating with Mexico to form a Canadian-American-Mexican free market. President Bush has made overtures to the rest of Latin America and has already signed trade and investment agreements with fourteen nations. (Interestingly, Australia and New Zealand, as well as Taiwan and Malaysia, have expressed an interest in joining in on a bilateral basis.) Indeed, given the poverty and low educational levels in Latin America, the "educational geography" of such countries as South Korea, Taiwan, and Singapore, which are more integrated with the United States than Japan, may be more important than physical geography. [53]

Such essentially protectionist blocs, with free trade only among its members and "managed trade" carefully negotiated among the three blocs, would certainly be incompatible with good relations among Europe, the United States, and Japan, let alone any alliance relationships. The postwar *Pax* Americana might then give way to a Europe dominated by Germany (developing the less-developed Eastern Europe), an Asia dominated by Japan (developing the less-developed Southeast Asia), and the Americas dominated by the United States (but probably doing little to develop the less-developed countries in its sphere). Such negotiated trade relations, as distinct from essentially free-trade arrangements, are bound to limit the potentials of world trade and all participants' prosperity, quite apart from the political friction and bad feelings they will cause. [54]

The retreat from the postwar liberal trade system that helped make the West rich will hurt all the principal players, smash the best hope for the developing countries to lift themselves out of poverty, and revive memories of the 1930s and the contribution of protectionism to the economic crash. The United States, Japan, and the EC appear increasingly to view their economic relationship in terms of a trade war. This war is the one that will really matter in the future as the industrial nations struggle for market shares and standards of living. The fact that the states that have long composed the Western alliance are poised between interdependence, on one side, and economic nationalism—that is, political and strategic independence—and potential economic warfare, on the other, testifies to the two principal and contradictory forces at work in the post-cold war international system. Trade negotiations in the 1990s look like they will become what arms control negotiations were during the cold war—a means of avoiding hostilities among states to whom the distribution of wealth is now more important than the balance of power.

For Review

1. Why are Western corporations increasingly going multinational?
2. What conditions have made this "transnational revolution" possible?
3. What is interdependence and how has it affected relations among nations?
4. Why has the free-trade regime been increasingly supplanted by mercantilism?
5. Will trade wars or cooperation be the result, and why?

Notes

1. Michael Moffitt, "Shocks, Deadlocks, and Scorched Earth: Reaganomics and the Decline of U.S. Hegemony," *World Policy Journal* (Fall 1987): 557; and Robert Reich, *The Work of Nations* (New York: Knopf, 1991).
2. Peter F. Drucker, "Japan's Choices," *Foreign Affairs* (Summer 1987): 923-924.
3. Reich, *Work of Nations*, 128-129.
4. Ibid., 120-121.
5. Robert Reich, "Dumpsters," *New Republic*, June 10, 1991, 9-10; and David E. Sanger, "Fair-Trade Case Has a Twist: Japanese Charge a U.S. Rival," *New York Times*, April 12, 1991.
6. Jonathan P. Hicks, "A Global Fight in the Tire Industry," *New York Times*, March 10, 1988.
7. Susan Strange, "The Name of the Game," in *Sea-Changes*, ed. Nicholas X. Rizopoulos (New York: Council on Foreign Relations, 1990), 241-242.
8. Peter F. Drucker, "The Changed World Economy," *Foreign Affairs* (Spring 1986): 775. Also see Louis Uchitelle, "Trade Barriers and Dollar Swings Raise Appeal of Factories Abroad," *New York Times*, March 25, 1989; and "U.S. Businesses Loosen Link to Mother Country," *New York Times*, May 21, 1989.
9. Reich, *Work of Nations*, 112-113.
10. Drucker, "The Changed World Economy," 777.
11. Martin Crutsinger, "U.S. Edge in Technology Is Slipping," *Gainesville Sun*, September 8, 1988.
12. David E. Sanger, "Japanese Electronics Thrive despite Asian Competition," *New York Times*, December 18, 1988.
13. Richard N. Cooper, "International Economic Cooperation: Is It Desirable? Is It Likely?" *Washington Quarterly* (Spring 1988): 91.
14. Samuel P. Huntington, "Transnational Organization in World Politics," *World Politics* (April 1973): 333ff. Also see Abdul Said and Lutz R. Simons, eds., *The New*

Sovereigns (Englewood Cliffs, N.J.: Prentice-Hall, 1975); and Charles P. Kindleberger, ed., *The International Corporation* (Cambridge, Mass.: M.I.T. Press, 1970).

15. Robert L. Pfaltzgraff, *The Atlantic Community* (New York: Van Nostrand Reinhold, 1969), 80, 108-110.

16. George W. Ball, "Cosmocorp: The Importance of Being Stateless," *Atlantic Community Quarterly* (Summer 1968): 168; and Reich, *Work of Nations*, 140-141.

17. Richard J. Barnet and Ronald E. Müller, *Global Reach* (New York: Simon & Schuster, 1975), 13.

18. J. J. Servan-Schreiber, *The American Challenge* (New York: Avon, 1969), 42.

19. Martin Tolchin and Susan Tolchin, *Buying into America* (New York: Times Books, 1988). See David E. Sanger, "Key Technology Might Be Sold to the Japanese," *New York Times*, November 27, 1989, detailing the possible sale of a semiconductor equipment plant, which would leave the United States almost completely dependent on Japan for the tools to make future generations of computer chips. As before, Americans pioneered this technology. Yet the Bush administration is considering cutting even the small amount of government financing of U.S. high-tech that now exists because it opposes an industrial policy (like Japan's) in the name of the free market. See John Markoff, "Cuts Are Expected for U.S. Financing in High-Tech Area," *New York Times*, November 16, 1989.

20. Robert Gilpin, *The Political Economy of International Relations* (Princeton, N.J.: Princeton University Press, 1987), 242-252, assesses the pros and cons of the impacts of MNCs on host countries.

21. A strong indictment of MNCs is found in Barnet and Müller, *Global Reach*.

22. David H. Blake and Robert S. Walters, *The Politics of Global Economic Relations*, 3d ed. (Englewood Cliffs, N.J.: Prentice-Hall, 1987), 91-94; and Joseph S. Nye, Jr., "Multinational Corporations in World Politics," *Foreign Affairs* (October 1974): 162.

23. Huntington, "Transnational Organization," 366.

24. C. Fred Bergsten, "The Coming Investment Wars?" *Foreign Affairs* (October 1974): 125ff.; and C. Fred Bergsten, Thomas Holst, and Theodore H. Moran, *American Multinationals and American Interests* (Washington, D.C.: Brookings, 1978).

25. Robert O. Keohane and Joseph S. Nye, Jr., *Power and Interdependence*, 2d ed. (Boston: Little Brown, 1988), 12-16.

26. John Mearsheimer, "Back to the Future: Instability in Europe after the Cold War," *International Security* (Summer 1990): 43.

27. Strange, "Name of the Game," 238ff. Also see Reich, *Work of Nations*, who predicts the end of national economies as we have known them.

28. Blake and Walters, *Politics of Global Economic Relations*, 11-14.

29. Ibid., 14.

30. For a more optimistic view of regime maintenance, see Robert O. Keohane, *After Hegemony* (Princeton, N.J.: Princeton University Press, 1984).

31. Kevin T. Philipps, *Staying on Top* (New York: Random House, 1985).

32. Paul Kennedy, *The Rise and Fall of the Great Powers* (New York: Random House, 1987), 463. For a detailed analysis, see Chalmers Johnson, *MITI and the Japanese Miracle* (Stanford, Calif.: Stanford University Press, 1982).

33. Quoted by Theodore H. White, "The Danger from Japan," *New York Times Magazine*, July 28, 1985, 42. Also see Clyde V. Prestowitz, Jr., *Trading Places: How We Allowed Japan to Take the Lead* (New York: Basic Books, 1988), Ch. 1, especially 13, 21-24; and James Fallows, "Containing Japan," *Atlantic Monthly*, May 1989, 40-54.

34. Karel van Wolferen, "An Economic Pearl Harbor?" *New York Times*, December 2, 1991, and "The Japan Problem Revisited," *Foreign Affairs* (Fall 1990): 48. Also see, Lester Thurow, *Head to Head* (New York: Morrow, 1992), 117-124. This book's subtitle is *The Coming Economic Battle among Japan, Europe, and America.*

35. *New York Times*, April 20, 1986.

36. Blake and Walters, *Politics of Global Economic Relations*, 29.

37. See, among others, Thurow, *Head to Head.*

38. Thurow, *Head to Head*, 181-182.

39. Moffitt, "Shocks, Deadlocks," 569; and Bernard K. Gordon, *Politics and Protectionism in the Pacific* (London: International Institute of Strategic Studies, 1988), 14-17.

40. On protectionism, see Steven Greenhouse, "Trade Curbs: Do They Do the Job?" *New York Times*, April 16, 1992.

41. For how the Japanese have responded to U.S. pressure with tokenism and culturalism, see Aurdia George, "Japan's America Problem: The Japanese Response to U.S. Pressure," *Washington Quarterly* (Summer 1991): 5-19.

42. Susan Chira, "New Pride Changes Japan's View of U.S.," *New York Times*, June 28, 1988. See, for example, the article by the chairman of the Sony Corporation: Akio Morita, "Something Basic Is Wrong in America," *New York Times*, October 1, 1989.

43. Martin E. Weinstein, "Trade Problems and U.S.-Japanese Security Cooperation," *Washington Quarterly* (Winter 1988): 22.

44. For a view that argues that, Canada aside, the best foreign markets for the United States are not in Europe but in the Asia-Pacific region (Japan and the NICs), see Bernard K. Gordon, "Who Really Buys American?" *National Interest* (Winter 1990/91): 48-56.

45. Steven Greenhouse, "The Growing Fear of Fortress Europe," *New York Times* (Business section), October 4, 1988.

46. Susan Chira, "U.S. Currency Policy Speeds Japan in Vast Economic Role," *New York Times*, November 27, 1988; and David E. Sanger, "Warning from Tokyo on Trade and Dollar," *New York Times*, January 18, 1989.

47. James Sterngold, "Japan's Rising Trade Surplus Alarms Competitors," *New York Times*, June 14, 1991.

48. van Wolferen, "The Japan Problem Revisited," 43. Also see Alan Romberg and Tadashi Yamamoto, eds., *Same Bed, Different Dreams* (New York: Council on Foreign Relations, 1990); and Edward J. Lincoln, *Japan's Unequal Trade* (Washington, D.C.: Brookings, 1990).

49. From the *New York Times*, see Steven Greenhouse, "Free-Trade Talks Imperiled by Fight on Farm Subsidies," November 13, 1990; Clyde H. Farnsworth, "Winners and Losers in Trade Talks," November 29, 1990; and Peter Passell, "Adding Up the World Trade Talks: Fail Now, Pay Later," December 16, 1990. From the *Wall Street Journal*, see Peter Truell, "Trade Talks Are Key for Many U.S. Firms, and They Are Worried," December 3, 1990; and Philip Reyzin, "EC's Farm Subsidies That Imperil Trade Have Deep Roots," May 12, 1991.

50. Robert Kuttner, *The End of Laissez-Faire* (New York: Knopf, 1991); Clyde Prestowitz, Ronald A. Morse, and Alan Tonelson, *Powernomics* (Lanham, Md.: Madison Books, 1991); and Thurow, *Head to Head*, essentially argue the same thing: the need for vigorous government intervention in the market to direct investments to certain industries and to punish America's economic enemies with a vigorous trade policy.

51. Prestowitz, *Trading Places*. Also see Jagdish Bhagivati, *Protectionism* (Cambridge,

Mass.: M.I.T. Press, 1988) for an analysis of the opposing forces of protectionism and global corporate competition.

52. van Wolferen, "The Japan Problem Revisited," 48; and David E. Sanger, "Power of the Yen Winning Asia," *New York Times*, December 5, 1991.

53. Thurow, *Head to Head*, 85.

54. Louis Uchitelle, "Blocs Seen Replacing Free Trade," *New York Times*, August 26, 1991.

CHAPTER 17

Changing the Rules of the Game: A Conclusion

Nuclear weapons and economic interdependence have affected not only the manner in which military and economic power can be used but also the effectiveness with which they can be used. What particularly stands out are the restraints placed on the exercise of these traditional instruments of statecraft. Equally striking is the effect these restraints have had on the hierarchy of states in which the strong—historically subject to few restraints—have generally dominated international politics. The great powers have been called that because of their great military and economic power, which they have used when necessary. But today it is commonly held that war is obsolete because it has become too destructive and costly, as well as antithetical to the values of democratic countries. If true, one of the principal means by which the great powers historically have assured their hegemony and simultaneously kept order in the system has been removed.

Let us now look more closely at the proposition that war has become obsolete, implying that the recent Gulf war is not the norm for the future. The impact that such a proposition, if true, may have on the state system will be revealed by analyzing more closely the different kinds of wars possible: between developed countries, between developed countries and Third World states, and between Third World states.

WARS BETWEEN DEVELOPED STATES

Among those offering often conflicting views about the stability of bipolar and multipolar systems, Kenneth Waltz made a persuasive, but not conclusive, case for bipolarity (see Chapter 6). One reason for his choice was that the two factors underlying the stability and peace of the cold war period were virtually indistinguishable. One factor encompassed the simple structural division between friend and foe, the clear definition of each superpower's vital interests and spheres of influence, and the hierarchical character of each superpower's principal alliance. The second factor was nuclear weapons. It was concluded in Chapter 6 that it might indeed be more accurate to attribute the "long peace" to both the bipolar structure of the U.S.-Soviet rivalry *and* the possession by both sides of large nuclear arsenals, which left no doubt that a nuclear war would be suicidal if fought.

The absence of *total* war between the superpowers and their allies for almost five decades testifies dramatically to the discipline and restraint the "bomb" imposed on the exercise of power by the United States and Soviet Union. Rather than eliminating the human race, nuclear weapons appear to have eliminated large-scale war among the world's most powerful states, both nuclear and nonnuclear. Those

> years of living with nuclear weapons without warfare are not only evidence that war can be avoided but are themselves part of the reason why it can be; namely, increasing experience in living with the weapons without precipitating war, increasing confidence on both sides that neither wishes to risk nuclear war, diminishing necessity to react to every untoward event as though it were a mortal challenge.[1]

After 1945, in fact, there was only one war between two great powers, the United States and Communist China, although China claimed it was not officially at war because the Chinese troops in Korea were all "volunteers" and the United States defined that conflict not as a formal war but as a "police action" carried out under UN auspices. This forty-five-year record is unprecedented. Indeed, John Kennedy's national security adviser, McGeorge Bundy, has asserted that the nonuse of nuclear weapons has become so firmly established that each ten-year period has turned out to be less dangerous than the one before it.[2]

The analysis here, however, does not assert that the old model of international politics, in which great-power wars were the norm, has been outdated and warfare has been replaced by welfare. During the cold war, force was not used in Europe, the area of primary confrontation between the two superpowers. But the fact that force was not employed did not mean that the threat of using force did not play the major role in preserving the peace. In deterring an enemy attack, force may not have been used, but that did not suggest that the possibility of its use was futile. Indeed, it was the certainty that force would be used and the very abundance of military power in Europe that in fact eliminated the likelihood that either superpower would resort to it.

Nuclear weapons had a particularly sobering effect in ensuring the post–World War II long peace. Nuclear arms not only prevented a total war between the United States and the Soviet Union, despite the scope and intensity of their rivalry, but also led them to manage their crises very carefully when they did erupt: in Berlin (1948-1949 and again repeatedly from 1958 to 1961), in Quemoy and Matsu in the Taiwan Straits (1954-1955 and 1958), and especially in Cuba during the missile crisis (1962). A crisis was defined in terms of a high expectation of violence. Vital interests were at stake, and one power challenged the status quo which the opponent resisted. If the possible use of violence underlay much of international politics, this possibility rose close to the surface during crises. In this sense, crises stood at the crossover point from peace to war, even if their occurrence suggested that the balance was being kept. As dangerous as crises were, none escalated into war, as probably would have occurred in the prenuclear period. Bipolarity ensured that when one power intruded on the adversary's sphere of influence, the adversary would be aware of this threat to its vital interests and respond to it. Simultaneously, the presence of nuclear weapons reminded both powers that the penalty for going to war might be extinction. Thus, in both deterrence and crises they resorted only to threats of force, not the use of force. That significant shift stemmed from nuclear weapons and was the reason why the period after 1945 was called the age of deterrence and crisis management. Deterrence gave rise to arms control and a sustained effort to stabilize the balance to ensure that nuclear war would never be fought. The fact that the last direct U.S.-Soviet confrontation occurred in 1962 testifies to the increasing focus of the two powers on crisis avoidance.[3]

Despite the Reagan administration's efforts to abolish the specter of nuclear war by means of a technical solution—Star Wars—it is ironic and probably closer to the truth to say that *if nuclear weapons had been eliminated, relieving fears of a nuclear holocaust, wars between the major powers might have become more likely because such hostilities would have been considerably less damaging.* There was clearly a trade-off between the destructiveness of war and the likelihood of war. Total wars were incompatible with "absolute weapons," but they were not incompatible with weapons of more limited destruction. Thus, the abolition of nuclear arms, had it been possible, would have presented a cruel dilemma: it would have removed the fear of national if not global, suicide, and it would have made it feasible once more to contemplate the use of war as an instrument of state policy whose gains might exceed its losses. It is not that the great powers have resorted to conventional warfare lightly. The destruction and loss of life in the two world wars were immense, and none of the European states wished to repeat the experience.[4] Indeed, a large-scale conventional war with contemporary weapons would have been considerably more destructive. Perhaps even in the absence of nuclear weapons war might not then have broken out. But can it be doubted that it was the fear of *extinction* that was the ultimate incentive to be cautious and guard against misperceptions and miscalculations? It was the possibility that even the slightest chance of a war would spark a nuclear conflagration that kept the peace in Europe during the cold war.

For all the horror of World War II, in which the number of casualties far exceeded that of World War I, there were winners and losers—and even the latter recovered. Therefore, if during the cold war there had been only conventional weapons, one side might have risked initiating a war because the ultimate penalty would *not* have been suicide but perhaps victory. Nor would the cost of such a conventional conflict have necessarily been high if a state had quickly achieved its goal—not necessarily total victory—with a new version of the German *Blitzkrieg*. But the scale of destruction of a nuclear war would have been incomparably greater; the difference between vast losses, from which eventual recovery would have been possible, and the certainty of nearly complete annihilation from which recovery would have been unlikely, cannot be ignored. Thus, eliminating nuclear weapons would have reduced the risks and costs of a possible war, weakening deterrence; what was unthinkable would have become thinkable. Then, it may be that one could no longer have said, "Perhaps the most striking characteristic of the postwar world is just that—that it can be called 'postwar' because the major powers have not fought each other since 1945."[5]

The conclusion is clear: By preventing war not only between the United States and the Soviet Union but also among all the great powers, nuclear weapons appeared indeed to have made war among the developed industrial states obsolete. Undoubtedly, this revolutionary change was further strengthened by the fact that at least the Western industrial states are democracies, and war among democratic nations—nations that believe in settling domestic differences peacefully by means of elections and voting, as well as negotiations and conciliation—is unknown, perhaps because their leaders believe that in foreign policy too they ought to be able to settle conflicts with other democracies by means of compromise.* The rivalries of the industrial democracies have moved from the battlefield to the economic arena, and power is increasingly measured not by conquest and glory but by capital surpluses and balances of payments. Accounts are settled in yen, Deutsche marks, and dollars, not by what Otto von Bismarck called "blood and iron." What all this means is that at the top of the state hierarchy a condition of relative pacification exists—relative because, despite nuclear weapons and the spread of democracy in recent years to some Third World states, the use of force between developed and less-developed countries has not been eliminated.

WARS BETWEEN DEVELOPED AND THIRD WORLD STATES

During the cold war, the United States and the Soviet Union used the threat of using force only against each other. This was enough to prevent war because the war in question was a nuclear war. But they could not prevent all wars, even some rather large-scale conflicts. North Korea and Communist

---

* Admittedly, as noted earlier, democracy after the French Revolution unleashed modern total war. Once at war, modern democracies have excelled at crusading.

China in the Korean War were not deterred by the possibility of war with the United States; nor was North Vietnam in the Vietnam War. And Argentina was not deterred by the British bomb in the Falkland Islands conflict. One might have thought that the North Koreans, Chinese, North Vietnamese, and Argentinians would have feared not only their adversaries' overwhelming power in the conventional sense but also the possible use of nuclear weapons by their foes if these wars had dragged on and the casualties had mounted. But they assumed that nuclear weapons would not be used, and they were right. Their adversaries did not use them, mainly for political reasons.

Nuclear weapons were weapons of deterrence among the nuclear powers only. The first atomic bomb was dropped on an Asian country, introducing the suspicion of racism since the bomb had not been dropped on the Germans (they already had surrendered, but that did not erase the suggestion that racism was involved in the 1945 attacks on Hiroshima and Nagasaki). The likelihood that such a bomb would be used again on Asian or some other Third World countries was therefore zero. As President Dwight Eisenhower exclaimed when his advisers were debating the possibility of using atomic weapons against Communist China during the Dien Bien Phu crisis of 1954, "You boys must be crazy. We can't use those awful things against Asians for the second time in less than ten years." [6] The United States, like Britain, was in this sense self-deterred. The moral and political stigmas associated with using nuclear weapons were too severe. Even so, why did the use of violence against Third World states decline when there was no danger that such a use of force would lead to a nuclear war?

Growing Capacity of the Third World to Resist

One significant factor in explaining this state of affairs has been the rise of nationalism. Ever since the French Revolution, the growth of nationalism has made it increasingly difficult to conquer *and* pacify foreign territories and populations. The conquered peoples of Europe resisted their Nazi oppressors. Today, the use of force against even a weak Third World country with a strong sense of national identity—and a foreign attack is usually a powerful stimulant to nationalism—can be quite costly. In Vietnam, by the time American forces disengaged in 1973 after eight years of fighting, the costs had far exceeded any conceivable gains. The loss of 58,000 American lives, thousands of injuries, expenditures of approximately $150 billion, and the use of overwhelming firepower in behalf of an authoritarian government were too costly in terms of the nation's self-image. The American army, which suffered from discipline, drug, and racial problems, paid the price in low morale and was saved from collapse only by the end of the war. The political turmoil and social divisions within the United States were yet another heavy price. Pacification can thus be made so costly and difficult for a foreign power that it will give up its effort, if it is not deterred from intervening in the first place. This was also true for the Soviet Union. In eight and a half years and with over 100,000 troops, it was unable to pacify Afghanistan. It too withdrew.

Increasing Great-Power Costs

In the nineteenth century, it was Western technology, in addition to the absence of nationalism and the will to resist, that helped the European colonial countries conquer much of the non-European world. In the words of the English couplet, "Whatever happens, we have got / The Maxim gun, and they have not." That huge technological advantage in combat is unlikely in the future. Nationalism, added to the lethal character of modern conventional weapons, may well deter future great-power interventions in developing countries (except in those instances where unambiguous vital interests are at stake) because of the cost in lives and materiel that the developing countries may exact. Arms themselves are becoming lighter, more portable, and more accurate. And precision-guided munitions (PGMs) are becoming inexpensive enough for even smaller countries, or guerrilla movements, if they do not receive them free from one of the great powers (as the Afghan rebels did from the United States). When a relatively inexpensive missile of a developing country presents a genuine threat to a multibillion-dollar aircraft carrier off its coast or to a multimillion-dollar aircraft in its sky, a great power will think twice about intervening. Even in brief spurts of force, such as the air attacks the United States employed in Libya in 1986, the aircraft carriers were kept well out to sea and the attacks were carried out in the evening or at night to minimize losses. In later interventions, it was not accidental that the United States used force against Libya, a third-rate power; against Grenada, "protected" only by 700 Cubans, almost all of them construction workers; and against Panama, defended by a corrupt and unprofessional military.

Nothing would be more foolish in the wake of the quick and relatively painless victory over Iraq than for the United States to think that other states will give as poor an account of themselves as Iraq. After all, the ground war was expected to lead to heavy American losses—altogether roughly 10,000 allied soldiers killed and wounded, according to the initial Pentagon estimates[7]—which is why even the chairman of the Joint Chiefs of Staff, Gen. Colin Powell, as well as his predecessor, Admiral William Crowe, vividly remembering Vietnam, reportedly counseled initially against the use of force. If in the future Third World states acquire weapons of mass destruction and the missiles to deliver them, Western powers will be even more reluctant to intervene because of the potential costs to their forces, regional allies, and even their homelands. One need but ask what would the United States have done if Iraq had exploded a nuclear weapon *before* it seized Kuwait?

Western Moral Constraints

National self-determination is a fundamental democratic principle. In fact, it was in the name of national self-determination that the colonies demanded their freedom after World War II. Thus, when a Western nation with a predominantly white population and a colonial past attempts to coerce one of the non-Western, largely nonwhite former colonies, guilt and moral repugnance are aroused in democratic societies. Examples are the opposition within

Britain and the Commonwealth countries to the Suez War in 1956 and America's domestic resistance to the Vietnam War (as well as criticism in allied countries) from 1965 to 1973.

Moreover, when the enemy is able to suggest successfully that it is fighting against political oppression and social injustice, U.S. intervention on the side of apparent repression also arouses opposition. Unlike the two world wars, which were straightforward fights between dictatorships and democracies that aroused moral support rather than revulsion, an intervention on the side of those less than 100 percent democratically pure tends to mobilize political opposition, divide the public, and provoke critical world opinion. Even shortly after Iraq's blatant and unambiguous case of aggression, op-ed newspaper articles, as well as news commentators and politicians, let alone the "peace movement," raised objections to intervening in Saudi Arabia to defend one monarchy and liberate another (Kuwait), as if the character of these regimes rather than the consequences of Saddam Hussein's aggression were the chief issue.

Constraints are applied then not only to the actual use of force against a potential adversary but also to the scope of this force. Nothing stimulated domestic protest more than the air war against North Vietnam, and the protest influenced the conduct of the war. The Johnson administration felt so vulnerable on this issue that it limited its attacks to certain kinds of targets to reduce civilian damage and loss of life. President Richard Nixon, unable to use ground forces because of domestic opposition to heavy casualties, gradually withdrew them. When he blockaded and heavily bombed North Vietnam in 1972, however, he precipitated intense protests from members of Congress, influential journalists, and the public. The Christmas bombing, which Nixon claimed would compel the Hanoi government to accept a cease-fire (as it did shortly after, although the contribution of the bombing is not known), was especially harshly criticized.

Big Western democratic nations, in short, have tended to lose long, small wars since 1945. If a country's will to keep on fighting can be eroded, its superior military capability will be neutralized. Indeed, the capability may as well not exist. British scholar Andrew Mack has said that for this reason

> the [Chinese Communist] slogan "imperialism is a paper tiger" is by no means inaccurate. It is not that the material resources of the metropolitan power are in themselves underestimated by the revolutionaries; rather, there is an acute awareness that the political constraints on their maximum deployment are as real as if those resources did not exist, and that these constraints become more rather than less powerful as the war escalates.[8]

Thus, adding up the components of power—even the conventional ones—would not have resulted in an accurate prediction of the outcome of the Vietnam War.

Public scrutiny of every aspect of war has made a tremendous difference. When the democracies use force, they cannot do so as they did a hundred years ago. The media report on every facet of the hostilities, no matter how embarrassing or politically damaging it may be to the government, and criticize and revisit the military's efforts to control their reporting. After the Argentinians seized the Falkland Islands, the British launched a successful expedition to recover them. Among other things, they sank the Argentinian cruiser *General Belgrano*, with heavy loss of life. For this act, the British government was heavily criticized at home and abroad. As one British observer noted,

> It was an important military victory for Britain, yet it turned into a political defeat because of the premium that the international community put on the appearance of avoiding escalation. Any military action which is not self-evidently for defensive purposes ... becomes an outrage. *Measures such as economic sanctions or blockades are deemed more acceptable than any military action which tends to lead to direct casualties.*[9]

In short, the Western democracies can no longer act in accordance with the idea that "all's fair in love and war."

By contrast, before the war in Afghanistan the absence of open societies and moral qualms was generally seen as beneficial to the Soviet Union, other Communist states such as Cuba, and most developing countries. It was widely believed that the costs of intervention could be more easily sustained in such countries, where public opinion did not play the strong independent role it did in the West and therefore did not exert a restraining or inhibiting influence on authoritarian government leaders. Not only did the Soviet Union intervene repeatedly in Eastern Europe, as well as in Afghanistan, but, together with Cuba, it also intervened in Angola and Ethiopia in Africa. Yet the cost of fighting the war in Afghanistan and the cost of supporting Cuban forces fighting in behalf of the Marxist regimes in Angola and Ethiopia and Vietnamese forces fighting against local insurrections in Cambodia appear to have caused Moscow to think twice about future interventions. It withdrew its forces from Afghanistan in 1989 and encouraged diplomatic settlements elsewhere.

Why the Great Powers Have Tended to Lose 'Small Wars'

Thus, the above conclusion might be revised to say that great powers—democratic *or otherwise*—tend to lose protracted, small wars more often than not. Historically, there has been a dramatic turning point. Although the weak cannot defeat the strong on the battlefield (the traditional objective of war), they have learned to try to wear them out and win the war politically on the great power's home front. In other words, it is enough not to lose. The key to the intervening power's ability to stay the course in a protracted conflict is preserving public support. Television, by bringing the pictures of war and atrocities into the West's living rooms, has accentuated this problem. Today, then, wars may be lost because political leaders miscalculate their people's willingness to fight a long war. Even nondemocratic leaders finally give up because of the drain of unending wars on their economies and people's lives.

It may now be more understandable why Saddam Hussein refused to withdraw from Kuwait, despite the massive U.S. and allied power arrayed against him. The man was ruthless and egocentric but presumably not suicidal.[10] Did he really think that he could win a war against the United States and its partners? The answer was yes. He did not believe that a country that had pulled out of Vietnam after 58,000 casualties and out of Lebanon after the loss of 241 marines had the stomach for war. And if it came to war, he did not believe that heavy losses of life would be acceptable to the American public; rather, it would spark antiwar protests. Since he was quite willing to suffer huge losses, as he had shown during the eight-year war with Iraq, he felt he could win. He might not win militarily, but if he could avoid defeat, force the Americans and their allies to use ground forces to dislodge his entrenched and presumably battle-tested forces, and then inflict heavy casualties, the American will to continue the fight would wither. He thus would win politically. The essential battle, he expected, would be fought in the United States. That country would be the primary—political—battlefield.

As for the final outcome, if his regime survived what he called "the mother of all battles" in a relatively strong position and he was able to use the money earned from oil exports to buy more conventional weapons and the components of mass-destruction weapons, he would remain a threat to the region, and the United States would not have accomplished its goal of freeing the area from the Iraqi threat of domination. Indeed, in the latter, Saddam Hussein would emerge as a more powerful threat not only to his neighbors, but, with his longer-range missiles, also to Europe. The Iraqi leader's assumption, of course, was that the war would be a long one. But the Bush administration knew that the United States had to win the war relatively quickly and, more important, with as few casualties as possible. President George Bush did not want to be a Republican Lyndon Johnson.

As it turned out, Saddam Hussein had massively miscalculated. Not only was President Bush determined to face him down, but he also skillfully mobilized U.S. public opinion to support him and pulled and held together a broad international coalition to expel Saddam Hussein from Kuwait, preferably by diplomacy but, if not, by force. If it came to war, Bush intended to neutralize Iraq as a threat to its neighbors by destroying its efforts to acquire weapons of mass destruction, as well as much of its conventional military capability and economic infrastructure. As the first post-cold war president—unencumbered with worries about Soviet or Chinese intervention—Bush could promise his generals and the public that a war with Iraq would not be another Vietnam. Unlike in Korea and Vietnam, once hostilities started limitations would not be imposed on the conduct of the war.

And Bush kept his promise. Devastated by five weeks of an air onslaught, the Iraqi army collapsed as soon as the ground war started.[11] In its long war with Iran, Iraq had not experienced anything like the round-the-clock allied air attacks with precision-guided munitions and the consequent destruction and demoralization. The war was over before Saddam Hussein knew what had hit him and his badly led, poorly fed, demoralized army. Iraq, itself, according to a UN report, had been bombed back "to a preindustrial age." [12] (But because Iraq was hardly a very industrialized country, and because in Baghdad at least Saddam managed to restore the electrical power, water, and telephone services within a few months, one has to question whether the United Nations' description was not somewhat exaggerated.)

In the United States, onlookers celebrated the end of the Vietnam syndrome. America's pride in its armed forces, as well as their skillful performance and high-technology weapons, all suggested that if in the future the country faced a similar situation, it would be less hesitant and more confident in resorting to force. Still, the more cautious will keep in mind that when force is used against Third World states that can mobilize their populations, or when the enemy turns out to be more skillful in the conduct of conventional warfare, such hostilities might last longer than forty-three days and involve more than 148 killed (35 by friendly fire) and 467 wounded (72 by allied fire).[13] Then public opinion, rallying around the flag at the outset, might again erode as the war stretches out and the casualty list mounts.

Future Interventions: Relatively Brief, Painless, and Successful

It appears that the principal prerequisites for future Western interventions are a worthy cause, the assurance of relatively few casualties, and good chances for successfully achieving one's objectives in a short period of time.[14] The operation in Grenada in 1983 was quick and relatively painless, ending with the withdrawal of U.S. troops and an election. In 1986, the United States responded with air attacks to Libya's purported involvement in a terrorist attack against U.S. service personnel in West Berlin. And in 1989 in Panama, the American forces sent in to depose Gen. Manuel Noriega were overwhelming in size, and they acted with great speed. All these operations contrasted sharply with those in Korea and Vietnam, which were lengthy, did not achieve their objectives quickly, and were expensive in lives and materiel, as well as in economic and political costs in the United States. Time and casualties were the two key variables. Short and not very costly interventions in terms of loss of life might be tolerated by the public, but not long and costly ones.

There were, of course, reasons for the U.S. successes in Grenada. As an island, it could be isolated by air and naval power. U.S. forces held overwhelming numerical and technological superiority; 8,000 troops faced only 700 Cubans, who were not professional soldiers, although it still took the United States three days to conclude its military task. British operations against the Falkland Islands were similarly successful because the site was isolated and the Argentinian troops, although larger in numbers, were not as well trained as the British.

The Persian Gulf intervention in 1987 was consistent with the United States' post-Vietnam use of force. Acting on the request by Kuwait, then ironically an ally of Saddam Hussein in his war against Iran, the United States committed itself to the protection of oil tankers belonging to Kuwait. It "reflagged" the tankers as American and then provided them with naval escorts. Several shooting incidents with Iran followed as Iran attacked some oil tankers in retaliation for Iraqi air attacks on tankers going to and from Iran. In effect, the United States, officially neutral in the war, tilted toward Iraq, the weaker party, because it did not want to see a militantly Islamic Iran win that war, become the dominant Persian Gulf power, and thereby threaten the oil kingdoms on whom the West had become so dependent. The United States, however, was very restrained in its retaliatory actions against Iran (except when it mistakenly shot down an Iranian airliner, killing almost 300 people). No escalation of the conflict occurred because both the United States and Iran wished to avoid a war, and American opinion supported this U.S. intervention because it avoided land warfare and heavy casualties. The operation was entirely a naval action.

President Bush's intervention against Iraq in Saudi Arabia was the nation's first large-scale ground commitment since Vietnam. But by concentrating initial U.S. efforts on an air war against Iraq, Bush hoped to avoid a protracted and costly ground war. The Bush administration believed that by bombing troop emplacements, supply and communication lines, command and control centers, and air defense targets and air bases, supplies to the Iraqi army in Kuwait could be cut, leaving those forces to die on the vine. The then eventual destruction of Iraq's economy, military infrastructure (especially its ability to produce chemical, biological, and nuclear weapons), and its war-making capability would lead to the collapse of the Iraqi war machine. Air power, in short, won the war before ground operations even began. To be sure, only an army can dislodge another army and occupy territory.

If the Iraqis had stored months of supplies, this softening up might have taken time, but it would have eventually succeeded.[15] A large land battle with heavy casualties would then not be necessary. Indeed, the one that finally occurred was basically a mopping-up operation. The point was *not* to play Saddam Hussein's game. According to one observer, "[a long] air siege will act like a particularly ferocious and vastly accelerated program of sanctions, enfeebling the Iraqi regime and economy."[16] Such a siege would also achieve objectives that sanctions could not achieve: the destruction of Iraqi unconventional weapons, as well as its conventional capability. Nevertheless, it is well to remember that the war against Iraq was short in part because President Bush ended the fighting after the liberation of Kuwait, in accordance with UN resolutions. Despite considerable public concern over the fate of Iraq's Kurds and Shiites, the president refused to send U.S. forces to Baghdad to depose Saddam Hussein and have the United States administer a country involved in a civil war. Memories of the 241 marines blown up in Beirut during Lebanon's civil war in 1983 suggested that a longer Iraqi civil war might be considerably costlier in terms of U.S. casualties. Why risk public disaffection after a triumph costing so few lives? Was Saddam Hussein then so wrong when he told a U.S. foreign service officer that the United States did not have the stomach to lose 10,000 soldiers in battle?

WARS BETWEEN THIRD WORLD STATES

Since World War I, the rising costs of war have led the industrial democracies—Western Europe, Japan, and, increasingly, the United States—to question the legitimacy of war or, at least, offensive war. The issues that are likely to compel them to use force are becoming more and more narrowly defined in terms of self-defense, however difficult it is in reality to distinguish between the offensive use of force and self-defense. There is a growing perception by the public that war, and even the threat of force, for coercive purposes is illegitimate. Since the ill-fated Suez invasion of 1956, European military forces have declined in their capacity to project their power beyond Western Europe. Britain had to stretch itself and remove much of its navy from NATO duties to recapture the Falkland Islands. Even then the United States had to help with intelligence and certain supplies. The British and French participation in the coalition war against Iraq was their first large-scale intervention outside of Europe since Suez.

After the Vietnam war, American vital interests were defined more and more selectively. The memory of that war haunted U.S. policy makers. When they considered interventions with ground forces in the Third World, they limited them to minor operations: Grenada, Panama, a half-hearted effort in Lebanon, and the naval intervention in the Persian Gulf. In both El Salvador and Nicaragua, congressional and U.S. public opinion were strongly opposed to intervention. Thus, the United States began increasingly to rely on covert intervention and support of proxies with U.S. military and advisers.

During the cold war, Communist states were not similarly constrained by the principle of national self-determination. Until 1989, the Soviet Union regarded self-determination as illegitimate in Eastern Europe, where it used force several times. Opposition to Soviet domination was defined as "counter-revolutionary" and "reactionary," rather than as legitimate attempts by Hungary, Czechoslovakia, and Poland to gain control of their own destinies. In the non-Western world, however, the Soviet Union used self-determination as a means of reducing or eliminating Western influence. The governments or movements that the Soviet Union supported were defined as those of national liberation, and the factions that opposed them were condemned as "reactionary" and "imperialist."

But the Soviet attitudes too changed as a result of experiences in Afghanistan and the heavy cost of supporting pro-Soviet governments in Africa and elsewhere. Thus, Vietnam withdrew its troops from Cambodia, and Cuba withdrew from Angola. Eastern Europe was no longer dominated by Moscow. And in the Third World, the U.S.-Soviet pattern was one of disengagement from Third World rivalry and confrontation.

The developing countries themselves strongly supported national self-determination, the legitimizing principle on which rested their claims to independence from colonial masters. But they interpreted it in two ways: against the West and against one another, for many of the former colonies laid claim to the people and territory of neighboring states on the basis of ethnic identification. For the developing countries, the principle of self-determination has justified intervention. For example, Vietnam invaded Cambodia in 1978. China, in turn, temporarily invaded Vietnam. Egypt intervened in Yemen in the 1960s, and Yemen and South Yemen clashed in the late 1970s. Syria sent its forces into Lebanon after the civil war there began in 1975, and their presence finally secured Syrian control in 1990. Since the early 1950s, India has seized the Portuguese colony of Goa on the Indian subcontinent, intervened in East Pakistan during the Pakistani civil war, and been instrumental in depriving Pakistan of its eastern territory and destroying it as a rival. In addition, Tanzania invaded Uganda in 1979 to overthrow its dictator, and the 1980s saw Iraq attack Iran, Somalia invade Ethiopia, Argentina seize the Falkland Islands, and Libya invade Chad. The 1990s started with Iraq's seizure of Kuwait. Rather than a decline in the use of conventional force, there has been a global shift in attitudes toward the utility of force.[17] Can it be doubted that it was the Argentinians' belief that Britain would do nothing that led them to seize the Falklands by force? In all likelihood, had not Britain's prime minister Margaret Thatcher—the "iron lady"—been in power at the time, Britain would have acquiesced in Argentina's seizure of the Falklands. Saddam Hussein made a similar miscalculation about the United States and the character of George Bush. Many of the new states, then, are behaving just as states have behaved for centuries.

This shift in the use of force since World War II has constituted a dramatic reversal. During the cold war, Europe enjoyed a peace it had not known before. Indeed, over the last 150 years the trend in Europe has been a decline in warfare, although this had been balanced by increased casualties per war, especially the two world wars in this century. During roughly the same 150-year period, Western colonialism restrained the frequency of war in Asia, Africa, and Latin America. But since 1945, 89 percent of all wars have occurred in the Third World, with the fewest in Latin America and the most in Asia. It might therefore be said that the contemporary system is characterized by the relative decline of the superpowers (with the Soviet Union dropping out of this category); relative pacification at the top of the international hierarchy; and a continuation of the "state of potential war" at the levels below the top—especially among Third World states. The fact is that nuclear powers, because their attention was focused on the awesome destructiveness of nuclear weapons, have been unwilling to initiate a war in which the risks of annihilation were great and the chances of victory slim. War, then, has essentially become the tool of Third World states. But if these states are able to obtain nuclear and chemical weapons—and it appears that the various control regimes can only at best slow down this process—can one really assume that the Third World states will replicate the deterrent pattern of the superpowers?

ECONOMIC CONSTRAINTS

Now that the Soviet-American confrontation and the need for military alliances are things of the past, the industrial powers are giving greater priority to economic objectives and are under less pressure to subordinate these to strategic goals. In addition, because of the corresponding decline in the importance of military power, economic means appear to be replacing military methods as the webs of interdependence, which first grew between the United States and its NATO allies in Europe and Asia, then spread to the newly industrialized and OPEC states and beyond. If left to develop freely, the logic of commerce would govern the world, and international business would replace international politics as a network of economic transactions spanned the world. The world would be transformed into one huge shopping mall.

While leading to fierce competition, on the one hand, the logic of commerce also results in "alliances between economic entities in any location to capitalize ventures, vertically integrate, horizontally co-develop, co-produce, or co-market goods and services," on the other hand.[18] Competitively or cooperatively, these interactions evolve across national boundaries. The market does not respect sovereign borders because they are perceived as major obstacles to the optimization of unfettered global commercial relations. The sum is a world without boundaries to separate potential customers. In the meantime, the emphasis is on cooperative relations among states in order to maximize the benefits of international trade.

The opposing logic remains that of the traditional international system with its accent on self-interest, adversarial, zero-sum ("More power, security, and wealth for me is less security, power, and wealth for you") relations among states. Not surprisingly, with a vested interest in their survival, states do not fully accept a logic that would ignore their frontiers; they are, after all, sovereign territorial entities. As still the primary players, they continue to guard their territory jealously, provide their citizens with security from foreign threats, and strive for relative advantage in the international arena. No state can ignore considerations of military security, domestic economic stability, and even national pride in preference to the potential economic gain from maximum participation in the global economy.

International politics is thus unlikely to disappear, to be replaced by international business. But it does explain the coexistence of a growing interdependence among states—gradually reducing national control over economic and financial policies as it links their destinies together—with conflict among the same states as they seek to protect their economies and their economic and fiscal autonomy by such means as thinly disguised efforts to restrict imports or subsidize exports or funding of competitive technologies. Military power is obviously irrelevant to resolving commercial and financial issues between interdependent countries, although perhaps such measures as sharply devaluating one's currency or trade wars for low-politics issues should be likened to the threat of force for the traditional high-politics issues. In any event, the tension between these two trends, and between the imperatives political leaders have learned from long socialization by an anarchical state system and its zero-sum political-military game, as well as the growing interdependence espoused by a nucleus of Western states, is reflected in the ambiguous relationship among the Western democracies. They are both fierce competitors and partners. In a sense, their economic relationship may be compared to the cold war military relationship of the United States and the Soviet Union: an adversary-partnership. The result is a constraint on their freedom and a constant tension between the mercantilist pursuit of their national interests and their common collective interests.

THE EROSION OF HIERARCHY

Earlier, the contemporary post-cold war state system was described as unipolycentric. The United States has remained the only superpower, but power has been widely diffused in the international system. Moreover, the shifting emphasis from military to economic power and the changing contextual nature of power has meant that one cannot predict accurately the outcome of any relationship between any two states. The great powers, to be sure, have hardly been impotent; they have had many means of exercising power. Their military power has allowed them to extend protection to other nations; their economic power has meant that they can offer all sorts of economic rewards; their economic vitality in this technological age, as well as the attractiveness of their cultural and social values, have made them models for others to follow; and there has always been that ancient skill diplomacy, which has permitted those adept in its uses to convert assets such as these into genuine influence on the international scene. Nevertheless, the accumulated effect of the changes in contemporary international politics analyzed above has been to erode the historical hierarchy or structure of dominance based on military power. An astute observer, noting these trends in the 1970s, commented,

> Clearly, if the inequalities that have traditionally marked state relations are to decline, the institution that has afforded the primary means for maintaining inequality must also decline. The effective challenge to inequality requires, at the

outset, that the more extreme forms of self-help—especially military force—no longer perform their time-honored functions. Provided that physical coercion of the weak by the strong has largely lost its former utility, as many now believe, nothing would appear to be of comparable moment in altering the hierarchical structure of international society. It is in the assumption that the rising material and moral costs of employing force now effectively inhibit—or very nearly so—the strong from resorting to force against the weak that we must find one of the root sources, if not *the* root source, of the challenge to inequality.

Nor is it reasonable to expect that a growing disutility of military power will have no effect on the economic power wielded by the strong. Although disparities in economic power remain in a world where military power is presumed to be increasingly at a discount, the effects of these disparities must surely be altered as well and in the same direction. . . .

. . . [R]ecent experience has shown that even against a very small state, and one with a vulnerable economy, the effectiveness of economic coercion alone may prove surprisingly limited. In part, this is so for the evident reason that economic coercion permits the weak alternatives that physical coercion does not. Then, too, the limited effectiveness of economic coercion may in some measure be attributed to the same sources that limit the effectiveness of physical coercion. While the legitimacy of the former has not been subject to the same standards as has the latter, economic coercion has been called increasingly into question. . . . This argument draws added force once it is recognized that economic coercion can only have its full effects to the extent it leaves open the option of physical coercion.[19]

Does all this mean that, despite the successful war with Iraq, there may be a growing disjunction between power and order in the contemporary international system—that is, greater disorder? Has the "natural order" been turned upside down? We will take a closer look at this question in the next chapter.

For Review

1. Why is it often said that war has become obsolete?
2. Despite the optimistic forecast that war is now obsolete, some wars are still more likely than others. Which kinds of wars are the most likely? The least likely? Analyze the reasons for this state of affairs.
3. Why did Saddam Hussein think that he could win a war against the U.S.-led coalition arraigned against him? Why was he wrong?
4. Explain why the effects of the "logic of commerce" may contradict the opposing logic of the state system.
5. What are likely to be the consequences for the hierarchy of states and international order of changes in the historical use of force by states?

Notes

1. Thomas C. Schelling, "What Went Wrong with Arms Control?" *Foreign Affairs* (Winter 1985/86): 233.

2. McGeorge Bundy, *Danger and Survival* (New York: Random House, 1988), 616. Also see Werner Levi, *The Coming End of War* (Beverly Hills, Calif.: Sage, 1981); and a critique of John E. Mueller's *Retreat from Doomsday* (New York: Basic Books, 1989), by Robert Jervis, "The Political Effects of Nuclear Weapons: A Commentary," *International Security* (Fall 1988): 80-90.

3. Alexander L. George, Philip J. Farley, and Alexander Dallin, eds., *U.S.-Soviet Security Cooperation* (New York: Oxford University Press, 1988).

4. Mueller, *Retreat from Doomsday*, 93-116. Also see Carl Kaysen, "Is War Obsolete?" *International Security* (Spring 1990): 42-64.

5. Jervis, "The Political Effects of Nuclear Weapons," 80. Also see by Jervis *The Meaning of the Nuclear Revolution* (Ithaca, N.Y.: Cornell University Press, 1989).

6. Quoted by John Lewis Gaddis, *The Long Peace* (New York: Oxford University Press, 1987), 142.

7. John H. Cushman, Jr., "Pentagon Report on Persian Gulf War: A Few Surprises and Some Silences," *New York Times*, April 11, 1992.

8. Andrew J. R. Mack, "Why Big Nations Lose Small Wars: The Politics of Asymmetric Conflict," *World Politics* (January 1975): 139-140.

9. Lawrence Freedman, "The War of the Falkland Islands, 1982," *Foreign Affairs* (Fall 1982): 209 (emphasis added).

10. See particularly the analysis of Dr. Jerrold Post, a professor of psychiatry and politics at George Washington University, who for over two decades provided psychiatric evaluations of world leaders for the U.S. government. Daniel Goldman, "The Experts Differ on Dissecting Psyches," *New York Times*, January 29, 1991.

11. For an early assessment of the air campaign by the U.S. Air Force, see Eric Schmitt and Michael R. Gordon, "Unforeseen Problems in Air War Forced Allies to Improvise Tactics," *New York Times*, March 10, 1991.

12. Paul Lewis, "U.N. Survey Calls Iraq's War Damage Near-Apocalyptic," *New York Times*, March 22, 1991.

13. Cushman, "Pentagon Report."

14. For three pre-Iraq books very critical of the U.S. armed forces' preparations for fighting in the future, see Edward N. Luttwak, *The Pentagon and the Art of War* (New York: Simon & Schuster, 1984); Arthur T. Hadley, *The Straw Giant* (New York: Random House, 1986); and Richard A. Gabriel, *Military Incompetence* (New York: Hill and Wang, 1985). Also see, Bruce Jentleson, "The Pretty Prudent Public: Post-Vietnam American Opinion on the Use of Military Force," *International Studies Quarterly* (Spring 1992): 49-73.

15. Michael R. Gordon, "U.S. Officials Conclude Air Power Is Not Enough to Defeat Hussein," *New York Times*, January 27, 1991.

16. Eliot A. Cohen, "The Unsheltering Sky," *New Republic*, January 11, 1991, 23-25. Also see R. A. Mason, "The Air War in the Gulf"; and William J. Taylor, Jr., and James Blackwell, "The Ground War in the Gulf," *Survival* (May/June, 1991): 211-229 and 230-245, respectively.

17. A similar thesis has been suggested in "Is International Coercion Waning or Rising?" by Klaus Knorr, *International Security* (Spring 1977): 92-110; and in Knorr,

"On the International Uses of Military Force in the Contemporary World," *Orbis* (Spring 1977): 5-27.

18. Edward N. Luttwak, "From Geopolitics to Geo-Economics: Logic of Conflict, Grammar of Commerce," *National Interest* (Summer 1990): 17.

19. Robert W. Tucker, "A New International Order?" *Commentary*, February 1975, 43-44.

Part Five

FROM STATE SYSTEM TO GLOBAL SYSTEM

CHAPTER 18

Preserving Peace
within the State System

Can the problem of how to preserve peace be resolved *within* the existing state system? Can the behavior of states be restrained, and can states be made more responsible? Can peace be achieved through cooperation among states in an international organization such as the United Nations, and through international legal and moral norms? For many of its advocates, the United Nations—the first approach to preserving the peace discussed in this chapter—symbolizes the expectation that war will be abolished because, ideally at least, it embodies the new spirit of internationalism that is supposed to replace national egotism. In the words of former senator and chairman of the Senate Foreign Relations Committee J. William Fulbright, the United Nations is an institution intended to protect "humanity from the destructiveness of unrestrained nationalism" and therefore to be strengthened by subordination of short-run national needs to long-run international needs.[1]

Two other approaches to preserving the peace stress the self-restraint that states would have to exercise if they obeyed international law (second approach) or behaved more morally (third approach). How realistic are these three approaches to making the state system safe for humanity? If they offer practical solutions, the abolition of the state system may not be necessary; if they do not, the case for creation of a new world order may be stronger.

UNITED NATIONS

To understand the United Nations, it is necessary to understand what it is *not*. It is not the "great peacemaker" and solver of all problems. It is not a superstate, usurping members' sovereignty and imposing its will on them.

Nor is its behavior independent of states' national interests and political considerations. UN decisions are not made according to some impartial, nonpolitical, and therefore purportedly superior standard of justice. The organization is not above politics because it cannot exist or act independently of its members' politics. Rather, it reflects the political interests, attitudes, and problems of its member states. It is only the channel through which the power and purposes of its members are expressed. The United Nations is not a substitute for power politics; it only registers the power politics of the state system. It is a mirror, not a panacea; it has no magic wand by which it can resolve all international problems. It could not transcend the past cold war or anticolonial struggles; it had to function in the world as it then existed. It could not solve any problems that its members, because of conflicting interests, were not prepared to solve. The United Nations' failures demonstrated only its members' inabilities to reach agreement. Have post-cold war conditions changed sufficiently to raise expectations about the contributions the United Nations might make to international peacekeeping and peacemaking?

First Phase: Preservation of the Wartime Grand Alliance

Because the United Nations is not a superstate but a body registering its members' political interests, attitudes, and problems, its functions can best be understood in terms of the changing conditions of the state system. After its birth in 1945, the United Nations in its first phase reflected the hope that, once victory over Germany had been won, cooperation among the great powers would continue and peace would be maintained. Primary authority for the preservation of peace and security in the United Nations was vested in the Security Council (originally composed of eleven members, six of them on two-year rotation; the total membership has since been raised to fifteen, with ten members on a two-year rotation). The real authority, however, was to be exercised by the five permanent members: the United States, Soviet Union, Britain, France, and China (at first Nationalist China and later Communist China). With the approval of at least seven members of the Security Council, including all the permanent members, the council could take enforcement action against aggression. Each permanent member of the council could veto such action, however. Any decision made was then to be obeyed by all members of the United Nations. Thus, through an oligarchical structure that reflected the global distribution of power, the great powers were able to become the masters of the United Nations. Indeed, the United States and the Soviet Union, the only two great powers remaining in 1945, were the real masters. As long as the two superpowers could maintain harmony, peace would be preserved.

The security system therefore was directed only against the smaller nations; if they disturbed the peace, they could be squashed if the great powers could agree to take punitive action. The United Nations was, in the words of one delegate to its first conference, "engaged in establishing a world in which the mice could be stamped out but in which the lions would not be restrained."[2] The purpose of the veto was to prevent one of the great powers from mobilizing the United Nations against another great power. Because a decision to punish a great power for aggression would precipitate global war, the

> insertion of the veto provision in the decision-making circuit of the Security Council reflected the clear conviction that in cases of sharp conflict among the great powers the Council ought, for safety's sake, to be incapacitated—to be rendered incapable of being used to precipitate a showdown, or to mobilize collective action against the recalcitrant power. The philosophy of the veto is that it is better to have the Security Council stalemated than to have that body used by a majority to take action so strongly opposed by a dissident great power that a world war is likely to ensue.[3]

Conflicts among great powers were to be handled *outside* the United Nations under collective self-defense arrangements, which did not require prior Security Council authorization.

Second Phase: American Instrument for Prosecuting the Cold War

As the two superpowers took opposite sides at the beginning of the cold war, the United States sought to mobilize the support of the United Nations for the containment of the Soviet Union and thus to associate its own policies with the humanitarian, peaceful, and democratic values underlying the organization. The transition from the first to the second phase was most dramatically illustrated in the Korean War. The United States felt it had no choice other than to oppose the Soviet Union, but it acted under UN auspices. Soviet absence from the Security Council on the day of the vote to intervene in Korea enabled U.S. opposition, but such an absence was not likely to occur a second time. The United States therefore introduced the "Uniting for Peace" resolution in November 1950 to transfer primary responsibility for the preservation of peace and security to the General Assembly should the Security Council be paralyzed by a veto. Constitutionally, this transfer of authority should not have been possible. The General Assembly only had the authority to debate, investigate, and make recommendations on issues of international peace and security; it could offer no recommendations affecting matters on the Security Council's agenda. By placing an issue on its agenda, then, the council supposedly could reduce the assembly to a debating society.

The Americans argued, however, that the United Nations' responsibility for the preservation of international peace and security should not be abandoned just because the Security Council was paralyzed. If the council could not fulfill its "primary responsibility" for this function, the assembly would have to assume the task. It need hardly be added that in the assembly, as it was then constituted, the United States could easily muster the two-thirds majorities needed for important resolutions from among members of the North Atlantic Treaty Organization (NATO) countries, the older British dominions, the Latin American republics, and one or two Asian states. The Soviet Union was, of course, consistently outvoted, though it was still able to use the body as a forum for its own point of view. American policies were therefore legitimated by world public opinion.

American use of the assembly to support anti-Communist policies did not last long. Just as the configuration of power underlying the original Security Council—the wartime alliance—had changed shortly after the establishment of the United Nations, so the political alignment at the outbreak of the Korean War was not destined to survive even that war, despite the Uniting for Peace resolution. The United States initially had received UN support for two reasons. First, an overwhelming number of member nations, including the nonaligned states,[4] saw in the North Korean aggression a test of the United Nations itself. If the organization failed to respond, it would follow the League of Nations into the dustbin of history. Second, the smaller powers saw in the transfer of authority on security matters to the assembly an opportunity to play a larger role than assigned to them in the original UN charter. But Communist Chinese intervention in Korea in late 1950 made American-sponsored use of the United Nations as an instrument of collective enforcement against the Communist bloc more difficult. The involvement of a major Communist power and the possibility that the American government might accede to strong domestic pressures to extend the war to China by air bombardment, naval blockade, and the landing of Nationalist Chinese forces on the mainland, dramatized the wisdom of the UN architects' original effort to prevent the involvement of that organization in military conflicts among great powers. The danger of a large war, which might even bring in the Soviet Union, was simply too great.

In addition, the twelve Arab-Asian members of the General Assembly were determined to remain nonaligned in the cold war. Their earlier support for American intervention in Korea had been motivated by their concern for the United Nations as an institution. It was essential that North Korean aggression be met, and, because the United States had the strength to take appropriate measures, the Arab-Asian members had approved of the original American reaction. But they had no desire to participate in collective measures against one side or the other, which in effect would have forced them to become allied to one of the cold war blocs through the mechanism of the UN voting procedure.

The question was how to prevent a military clash between the great powers and, simultaneously, to avoid becoming aligned in the cold war themselves. The answer was to shift the function of the United Nations from enforcement to conciliation.[5] The United Nations was to serve as an instrument of mediation in conflicts between the great powers. The original assumption that peace could be preserved by having five lions, led by the two biggest lions, act as world guardians was replaced with recognition of the imperative to keep the lions from mauling one another to death—and trampling the mice while they were at it.

Table 18-1 United Nations Membership, 1946-1992

Year	Members
1946	55
1950	60
1955	76
1960	99
1965	107
1970	127
1975	144
1985	159
1990	159
1992	178[a]

SOURCE: Successive issues of the *United Nations Yearbook* (New York: United Nations, 1946-1992).

[a] New states consist mainly of the fifteen former Soviet republics, plus three former Yugoslav republics.

Third Phase: Preventive Diplomacy

A third phase of the United Nations thus began. In the first phase, the members had been dedicated to preserving the wartime Grand Alliance; in the second, the United Nations had become an American instrument for prosecuting the cold war. The second phase had begun to fade during the Korean War. By exerting great pressure, the United States could still, in the spring of 1951, obtain the two-thirds majority needed in the General Assembly for a condemnation of Communist China. Yet already it was having to make concessions to muster these votes—the price being that it not follow the condemnation with additional military or economic measures. Instead, the United States was to place primary emphasis on the conciliatory efforts of the Arab-Asian bloc—supported by most of the NATO allies, who also were concerned about possible escalation of the conflict—to end the war.

By 1955, the United Nations had reached adolescence, and it matured quickly as the number of newly independent members, especially African, grew rapidly after that year. In 1955, six new Asian and North African states were admitted to the organization; the next year four more were added. In 1960, the number of new states admitted was seventeen, mainly from sub-Saharan Africa. By 1974, Asian, African, and Latin American states made up three-quarters of the 138 members (see Table 18-1). Both the American and the Soviet blocs previously had used the United Nations for their own cold war purposes, but the neutral bloc soon learned how to use the organization to erase the vestiges of Western colonialism as quickly as possible. The General Assembly was a particularly good forum in which to voice anticolonial sentiments and state demands for the new international economic order (the global redistribution of wealth and power between rich and poor countries).

In this third phase, the United Nations could not help becoming involved in the cold war. The Soviet Union and the United States, to be sure, did not allow the organization to interfere in *their* respective clashes. The Soviets had no intention of permitting the United Nations to intervene in Hungary or Czechoslovakia. Nor would the United States permit it to become involved in negotiations over the post-1958 Berlin crises, Cuban problems,[6] and the war in Vietnam. East-West issues were only debated; no action was taken. The superpowers handled their own direct confrontations. But, on the periphery of the cold war, the United States and the Soviet Union were constantly tempted to interfere in the conflicts arising from the end of colonialism. Such interference, by threatening the peace and involving neutrals in the cold war, was bound to lead the nonaligned nations to take protective action. The United Nations was for them more than a political platform. It was also a shelter in which they sought refuge from great-power pressure. In this third phase, they thought of the United Nations as *theirs,* and they were determined to use it to remain nonaligned.

The chief function of the United Nations thus became "preventive diplomacy"[7]—that is, the stabilization of local conflicts *before* either of the superpowers could become involved and provoke its antagonist's intervention. To describe it differently, preventive diplomacy was intended to keep American-Soviet clashes from extending beyond the cold war zone. At the same time, by containing the cold war, the small nations could safeguard their independence and control their own future to some extent. The mice were to keep the lions apart so that they could not grapple with each other and trample them. The chief means of stabilization was establishment of a "United Nations presence" in these peripheral quarrels. The organization thus functioned as a fire brigade, devoted to minimizing potential hazards. It could not douse a fire, but its presence could signal that fire was imminent or had already broken out and should be controlled quickly.

In a real sense, during the cold war the United Nations performed a crucial function in a highly combustible world. But to perform this role, it needed not only the support, or at least the acquiescence, of the superpowers but also the active support and participation of the Third World countries. Their willingness to do so stemmed from two tendencies. The first was the tendency of developing-country problems to spill over into the international arena. This occurred, for example, when each party to a conflict had friends in the superpower camps. Another example was the disintegration of a state.

The second tendency was for these kinds of developing-country problems to attract the attention of the Soviet Union and the United States, leading to possible confrontations and military conflict. The two superpowers were attracted, of course, because these problems might bring to power groups favorable to one side and thus inimical to the other, or they might result in regional expansion that would benefit one side and hurt the other. If one of the two superpowers was unwilling to tolerate what it saw to be a local or regional setback, it would intervene; if it feared that its opponent might intervene, it might even make the first move. In either instance, it risked counterintervention. The conflicts that arose on the periphery of the American-Soviet rivalry thus tended to feed the major confrontation between the two superpowers.

The UN Role as "Peace-Keeper" in Interstate Conflict and Civil War. The United States and the Soviet Union actively competed for influence in the Middle East after 1955, when the Soviets and the Egyptians concluded an arms agreement. The rivalry of the superpowers was superimposed on Arab-Israeli hostility and intra-Arab competition. Indeed, diplomatic support, economic aid, and military assistance from the two superpowers fueled the Arab-Israeli conflict through several wars. Without this competition for influence, the fundamental struggle could not have continued. Who else would have provided the Arab and Israeli armies with equipment?

With each war in the Middle East the possibility of superpower involvement became greater. In 1956, when the British, French, and Israelis captured the Suez Canal, the Soviets threatened to rain rockets on Paris, London, and Tel Aviv. The Soviets were putting on a show, and it was a good one. Hostilities had already ceased, thanks to American pressure on its allies to desist, but the Arabs, apparently believing that Soviet threats had led to the cease-fire, were grateful to the Soviets. The Soviets were primarily responsible for precipitating the 1967 Arab-Israeli war, for they had deliberately floated false rumors of an Israeli force poised to invade Syria. The Syrians, naturally, reacted immediately. What then could Egypt, at that time the acknowledged leader of the Arab world, do but mobilize its forces and send them into the desert? Moreover, the Soviet fleet made its first appearance in the Mediterranean, presumably as a symbol of Soviet commitment to the Arabs and as a warning to the United States not to interfere while the Arabs, with their enormous amounts of Soviet military equipment and training, defeated the Israelis. But Israel won again, even more quickly than in 1956. This time, however, it kept the territories it had captured. They were to be traded for genuine peace and recognition by the Arabs of Israel's right to exist. But no Arab leader would even sit down with Israeli representatives to talk.

In 1973, Egypt and Syria, frustrated by the resulting status quo, launched an attack in order to recapture the 1967 territories. Despite initial successes, their armies were finally thrown back. As Egypt's armies stood on the verge of defeat, the Soviets mobilized paratroopers and threatened unilateral intervention if American forces did not join Soviet troops to enforce the cease-fire that the two superpowers had agreed on. The United States placed its forces throughout the world on alert as a warning to the Soviet government against such an intervention, and the crisis passed as the United States pressured Israel to obey the cease-fire. But the administration of Richard Nixon also sought to avoid an Egyptian defeat and complete Israeli victory; total humiliation for one side and total victory for the other were not judged conducive to persuading the two sides to sit down together and talk about troop disengagement and a possible peace settlement. Another reason the United States sought such a settlement was the fear that another Arab-Israeli war might precipitate a direct superpower clash. A fifth conflict among the regional rivals might balloon beyond control.

A contrasting situation occurred in 1960 when the Republic of the Congo (now Zaire) became an independent state. Disorder soon prevailed, especially after the province of Katanga (now Shaba) seceded. Katanga's rich copper mines were the Congo's main source of revenue, and secession threatened the survival of the entire nation. The Congolese premier, Patrice Lumumba, therefore demanded that the United Nations crush Katangan president Möise Tshombe's mercenary army and help to restore Congolese unity. When his demand went unheeded, Lumumba appealed to the Soviet Union for help against the "colonialists." He received both Soviet diplomatic support and military supplies, and it looked as if the Soviet government was about to establish an important base in Africa. Lumumba thereupon was dismissed from office by Congolese president Joseph Kasavubu, whom the United States supported in an effort to prevent the establishment of a Soviet foothold in central Africa. The Soviets, however, refused to recognize Lumumba's successor, insisting that only the parliament had the right to dismiss Lumumba and that, as it had not done so, he was still the legitimate Congolese prime minister and must be restored to his office. The subsequent murder of Lumumba exacerbated the situation.

The national coalition government of the Congo, formed in early 1961, thus faced a major crisis from the beginning, a crisis that could only benefit the Soviet Union unless a solution was found. The government, committed to a policy of nonalignment, had national reunification as its first objective. Failure to achieve this goal would undermine its authority and lead to collapse from political and financial weakness. The transfer of power to a more radical pro-Communist government would then be a real possibility. The central government, to head off its own collapse, might even turn toward the Soviet Union, just as Lumumba had done. In either instance, there would be a Soviet-American confrontation in the Congo.

It was in such situations—in which the two superpowers were drawn into confrontations that threatened the peace of the world—that the United Nations in its third phase played its most important role. Just as the Security Council was the intended focus of authority in the first phase and the General Assembly the focus in the second phase, the secretary-general was the principal actor in the third phase. No longer merely the principal administrative officer of the organization, the secretary-general, largely through partnership with the nonaligned nations, became its leading political officer. It was Secretary-General Dag Hammarskjöld who, by establishing the precedent of a UN presence in troubled areas, first assumed the role of "custodian of brushfire peace." The most dramatic expression of this custodianship was the establishment of a "nonfighting international force" for political, not military, purposes. The size of the force, drawn primarily from states not involved in the particular dispute, and its firepower were not as significant as its political presence, which forestalled the use of Soviet or American forces.

During the Suez crisis in 1956, a UN Emergency Force (UNEF I) supervised the withdrawal of British, French, and Israeli troops from Egypt. It did not seek to *compel* withdrawal through combat. The cease-fire agreement was the prerequisite for its use, yet the mere fact that it was available made it easier to obtain British, French, and Israeli agreement to withdraw. Once withdrawal had been completed, fewer than 5,000 UN soldiers were left to guard the Israeli-Egyptian frontier and to maintain peace in that area. Symbolically, it was Egyptian president Gamal Nasser's demand that these forces be withdrawn in 1967, leaving Egypt and Israel to confront each other directly, that led to the Six-Day War. Similarly, the interposition of UN forces between Israeli and Egyptian troops after the 1973 war helped keep the peace. These forces stood between hostile troops on both the Egyptian front (UNEF II) and the Syrian front (UN Disengagement Observer Force, or UNDOF) as American secretary of state Henry Kissinger patiently negotiated disengagements of the combatants as a prelude to more comprehensive peace negotiations.

Not all peace-keeping operations have been as successful (see Table 18-2). The force sent into southern Lebanon in 1978 to cope with the Palestine Liberation Organization (PLO) attacks on northern Israel (and Israeli retaliation) was unable to deal with the PLO presence. In 1982, the Israelis invaded Lebanon to try and finish the PLO off, in the process sweeping the UN force aside. It was one thing to interpose UN soldiers between two opposing armies and prevent further violence when the superpowers had agreed that further fighting might escalate and involve them, but quite another to stop guerrillas infiltrating a border. Even the Israelis, for all their punitive retaliatory strikes before 1982, did not succeed in this—hence their invasion.

Conditions for Peace-Keeping Forces.   At least three conditions were imposed on such an international force. First, it had to be neutral and therefore exclude permanent members of the Security Council. Second, the nation in whose territory the force was to show its "presence" had to grant permission for such entry. In this way, the host nation, as a sovereign state, exercised some control over the composition of the international force and could exclude troops from nations it considered unfriendly or undesirable. It also could demand the withdrawal of these troops, as Egypt did in 1967. Even had the secretary-general not agreed to their withdrawal, he would have had no option; UNEF I was a small force and not fit for fighting. (Israel had refused to accept UN forces on its side of the frontier with Egypt; had it done so, it would have been protected against an Egyptian strike by their very presence.) UNEF II, however, was placed under the jurisdiction of the Security Council and thus differed in this respect from UNEF I, which had been created by the General Assembly. Because the presence of UN forces had to be approved every six months, they could not be terminated during that period except with the

Table 18-2 Third World UN Peace-Keeping Operations during the Cold War

Date	Location	Purpose
1948-present	India and Pakistan	To monitor cease-fire between India and Pakistan
1956-1967	Egypt	To secure cease-fire between Egyptian, Israeli, British, and French troops in Sinai Peninsula
1960-1964	The Congo	To ensure Belgian troop withdrawal and prevent civil war
1973-1979	Sinai Peninsula (Egypt)	To observe cease-fire between Israel and Egypt
1974-present	Cyprus	To prevent fighting between Greek and Turkish Cypriots (UN troops have maintained buffer between the two communities since partition in 1974.)
1974-present	Golan Heights (Israel)	To observe cease-fire between Israel and Syria
1978-present	Lebanon (southern area north of Israeli border)	To confirm Israeli withdrawal from area and restore security

unanimous consent of the five permanent Security Council members. A veto by any one of them at the semiannual meeting could have ended the mission.

The third condition was that the UN force could not intervene in any purely internal conflict and become party to the dispute. In Egypt in 1956 and again in 1973, the force was not used to impose a specific settlement on Nasser and then-president Anwar Sadat, respectively; it merely disentangled the combatants. The UN presence was not intended to deal with the causes of the two wars but with their effects. The same was true in the Congo, though with a special twist. But it was precisely the United Nations' refusal to interfere in the domestic politics of the Congo that created most of the difficulties. After the Congo had disintegrated, the head of the "national" government insisted that the UN operation in the Congo crush the secession of Katanga. In the end, the international organization could not isolate itself from the Congolese civil war. The effect of UN *non*intervention was to freeze the schism and to ensure the collapse of the Congolese government because Katanga's rich copper mines were the major source of national revenue. Although UN forces eventually did fight to crush the secession of Katanga, the third condition of domestic non-intervention remains. One need look no further than the American-organized multinational force in Beirut in 1982-1983 for contrast; when the United States became partisan in the civil war, the mission turned into a disaster.

During the cold war, the nations of the Third World, it must be noted, used this preventive diplomacy function *only* if the superpowers permitted them to do so. The assumption underlying the pacifying role of the nonaligned states was that both the United States and the Soviet Union wished to avoid escalating conflict in their desire to prevent nuclear war. This gave them a vested interest in keeping peripheral conflicts under control. They thus at least acquiesced in the establishment of a UN presence: "It cannot be done *against* the major parties; it cannot be done *by* them; it can only be done *for* them and by their leave."[8]

In conflicts not involving direct American-Soviet confrontations, especially to achieve preventive diplomacy, four kinds of UN action were possible: a pro-Western action, an impartial action, no action at all, or a pro-Soviet action. Obviously, the American preference was that order; the Soviets preferred the exact opposite. Neither extreme was really feasible, but the difficulty was that between the remaining alternatives the United States preferred impartial, neutralizing action, whereas the Soviet Union preferred inactivity. The United States feared that inactivity would lead either to a Soviet advantage or to a collapse requiring American intervention—and Soviet counterintervention. It also hoped that impartial action would accomplish pro-American results. Conversely, the Soviets hoped that inaction would produce pro-Soviet results and prevent American intervention. The Soviets feared that the course preferred by the United States might indeed yield results detrimental to Soviet interests.

Consequences of Preventive Diplomacy. By limiting the scope of marginal conflicts and seeking to stabilize tense situations, preventive diplomacy on the whole served U.S. purposes better than Soviet ends. For example, in Egypt in 1956 and 1973, UN forces helped preempt possible Soviet intervention. In the Congo in 1961, UN intervention eliminated the bridgehead the Soviets had established. The Soviet Union was therefore frustrated. From its perspective, the moving force in both crises, but especially in the Congo, had been the secretary-general, and the results demonstrated the need for a Soviet veto over his actions. The Soviets thus proposed a "troika" plan, calling for the appointment of three secretaries-general, each representing a major bloc in the world. The Soviets sought to supplement their actual veto in the Security Council and their virtual veto in the General Assembly (where they usually found enough votes among the nonaligned states to prevent a two-thirds majority vote against them) with a hidden veto at the top of the Secretariat. This veto would ensure that the United Nations could not do anything that was in any way detrimental to Soviet interests.

The nonaligned states unanimously opposed the troika plan to hamstring the secretary-general. They valued the organization as the bastion of their independence and "neutralist" positions in the cold war. Because of Soviet refusal to pay for UN peace-keeping operations and American insistence that the Soviet Union pay or it lose its voting rights in the General Assembly, the international body became deadlocked and remained so until American leaders saw that they would receive little support for stripping the Soviet Union of its voting rights in the assembly. They were then willing to recognize instead the principle that no great power had to pay for peace-keeping operations it regarded as detrimental to its interests.

It was inconceivable that the United States would have been any more likely than the Soviet Union to financially support operations that were injurious to its national interests. Indeed, when the United States abandoned its position, it declared that it too reserved the right not to pay for future peace-keeping operations of which it disapproved. Although at the time this move may have been a face-saving way out of an awkward situation, the United States went further than the Soviets and reduced its overall contribution to the United Nations in 1971 from 40 to 25 percent of the annual budget. Later, it withheld its annual contribution to compel reforms enhancing American influence in the organization and withdrew from one of the United Nations' specialized agencies to voice its displeasure about the anti-Western—especially anti-American—attitudes and emotions that appeared to characterize the United Nations in general in the fourth phase of its development.

Can the United Nations Prevent Wars? Although the United Nations' peace-keeping role prevented the continuation and escalation of fighting in which one or both of the superpowers were not participants themselves, this success should not be confused with the prevention of war. That was one lesson of the war in 1967, when Egypt exercised its sovereign right to expel UN forces. Sometimes wars do not even come under the jurisdiction of the United Nations. For example, in 1971 Pakistan brutally crushed an attempt by East Pakistan to secede and become independent. Claiming that the proposed secession was a domestic matter, the Pakistani government rejected UN intervention. India, burdened by 10 million refugees from East Pakistan and eager to eliminate its only rival on. the subcontinent, went to war with Pakistan, helped establish the state of Bangladesh, and sent the refugees back there. India too rejected UN intervention. When the Vietnamese invaded Cambodia in 1978 to overthrow the pro-Chinese Pol Pot government and impose a pro-Vietnamese government—after which Chinese forces crossed the frontier with Vietnam to teach the Vietnamese a lesson—none of these Communist states wanted a debate on aggression in Indochina. It would have been too embarrassing. Nor have all conflicts in Africa received attention in the halls of the United Nations. In 1977, Somalia actively supported, perhaps even sponsored, an uprising in the Ogaden area of Ethiopia; later the Ethiopians, with Soviet-Cuban support, moved toward Somalia's border, but no debate occurred. Nor was there debate when Idi Amin of Uganda provoked Tanzania in 1978, and, in the subsequent war, Tanzanian troops deposed him. Similarly, the Iraqi attack on Iran in 1980 was never placed on the Security Council's agenda; nor was Libya's invasion of Chad in the same year.

Civil wars, with their potential for spilling over into interstate conflict, and the barbarous treatment of people by their own governments usually are not placed on the international agenda either. While the Nigerian government was engaged in civil war against the Ibos in the secessionist state of Biafra from 1967 to 1970, approximately half a million people died, but the issue was not debated in the United Nations because many developing countries did not wish to legitimate Biafra and encourage secession in their own countries. After its victory in Cambodia, the Communist government of Pol Pot adopted a barbarous policy of genocide against its own people, yet this problem never appeared on the UN agenda. An estimated 1 million of Cambodia's 8 million people reportedly died as a result of these policies before the regime was forcibly replaced in 1979 by a Vietnamese puppet regime. These issues were not even discussed by the United Nations because that body consisted of sovereign states, which meant that each had the right to exclude any intervention aimed at protecting the rights of individual citizens. But the increasing number of wars that were *not* brought before the Security Council raised a serious question about the relevance of the United Nations on peace and security issues.

Fourth Phase: First World-Third World Confrontation

The years after 1973 were heady ones for the developing countries. The success of the Organization of Petroleum Exporting Countries (OPEC) in controlling worldwide oil prices suggested that the former colonies need no longer take a back seat to their former masters, the Western industrial democracies. The developing countries' strategies of modernization had by and large failed. Western economic aid was declining and "import substitution" had not stoked the fires of development; producer-cartels were thought to be a better strategy. With its global forum and public attention, the United Nations was the obvious place to publicize Third World grievances. In fact, the developing countries controlled the General Assembly, where in 1964 they had organized the United Nations Conference on Trade and Development (UNCTAD). By the mid-1970s, UNCTAD was 120 members strong, and the "Group of 77" had emerged as an informal working coalition to push issues of interest to the developing countries. Thus, in the General Assembly the developing countries focused the international spotlight on the relationship of the rich and poor nations, expressed their anger and resentment, blamed the West for their continued underdevelopment, and demanded a new international economic order in 1974.

Anti-Western Phase. The years of confrontation after 1973 were filled with strident rhetoric within the United Nations and within the nonaligned movement outside. The Western countries were continually criticized for past and present exploitation of the developing countries even while they were being called on for assistance. The Communist countries, which offered virtually no material help, suffered no rebuke and even enjoyed acclaim for their view that poor countries are poor because they have been exploited by the rich. The temper of the developing countries, most of which in the past had prided themselves on nonalignment, was symbolized by their 1979 meeting in Cuba.

Vietnam and North Korea, which, like Cuba, were not nonaligned at all, attended this meeting and tried to influence the assembly to support Soviet policy. Although the subsequent Soviet invasion of Afghanistan aroused the overwhelming disapproval of the nonaligned countries, later nonaligned meetings did not hesitate to criticize American policies while abstaining from mentioning Soviet policies. Even in calling for the withdrawal of Soviet forces from Afghanistan, the reference was to "foreign forces"; the nonaligned refused to mention the Soviet Union by name. The 101-nation 1986 meeting in Zimbabwe condemned the United States by name fifty-four times—including for "state terrorism" against Libya—and the Soviet Union not once.

Thus, not a double but a triple standard seemed to prevail. The Western democracies, particularly the United States, were frequently condemned by name, while the Soviet bloc, especially the Soviet Union, if criticized at all, was criticized in milder tones and often only by implication. The developing countries themselves rarely criticized one another. Because Israel was usually seen as a Western state, to attack it was to attack the West and the United States. Indeed, it was the Middle Eastern situation that first suggested the possibility that the United Nations was entering a fourth, anti-Western phase. In 1974, the General Assembly invited the head of the Palestine Liberation Organization, a nonstate actor whose acts of terrorism and hijacking it had debated only a few years earlier, to address it. It treated PLO leader Yasir Arafat as a head of government and greeted him with sustained applause while limiting the time for an Israeli reply, which was delivered to a virtually empty auditorium. Simultaneously, the Arab-African-Asian majority, supported by the Communist states, barred Israeli participation in the previously nonpolitical United Nations Educational, Scientific, and Cultural Organization (UNESCO). A year later, a coalition of African, Asian, Arab, and Communist nations enacted a General Assembly resolution equating Zionism with racism (which was repealed in 1991 by a vote of 111-25, the naysayers being mainly Islamic and remaining hard-line Communist states, as well as thirteen abstentions). In addition, the assembly ousted South Africa from its sessions because of that nation's racial practices; the Security Council, which exercises ultimate suspension power, had refused to do so. Finally, the PLO, as well as SWAPO (South West African People's Organization in Namibia), were given "permanent observer" status at the United Nations. Both even received UN funds—all in the name of national liberation and their status as future states. In 1979, in fact, Idi Amin, then president of Uganda and chairman of the Organization for African Unity (OAU)—a man who had voiced approval of the slaughter of Israeli athletes at the Munich Olympics and who had said that Adolf Hitler's only error had been not killing more Jews—charged that the United States had been colonized by Zionists and that Israel had no right to exist. Indeed, while the majority in the General Assembly recognized the rights of Palestinians, it refused to accept the same rights for Israel, over whose birth the United Nations had presided.

Concern for human rights also became very selective, especially during the 1980s. There was a "Special Rapporteur" on human rights for El Salvador but not for Nicaragua. And Israel and South Africa remained the perennial targets. Most of those attacking the policies of U.S. allies were themselves authoritarian regimes with very poor human rights records. Thus, the result was sometimes bizarre, as when, for example, Iran and Vietnam condemned Israel as a "non-peaceloving state" (because peaceloving, according to the UN Charter, is a prerequisite for membership, to declare a state the opposite means that potentially it could be expelled). Symptomatic of the United States' diminished ability to mobilize the United Nations in behalf of Western interests were the thirty vetoes it cast from 1981 to 1986 and its departure from the International Labor Organization from 1977 to 1980 and UNESCO in 1983.

An Arena for Opposition or Conflict Resolution?   In the early 1980s, former U.S. ambassador to the United Nations Jeane Kirkpatrick voiced an additional charge.[9] Not only did the developing countries frequently vent their anti-American sentiments, she said, but the United Nations, by repeatedly debating the same issue and sometimes calling for sanctions (usually against Israel and South Africa), generated "a process of conflict extension, polarization, and exacerbation." Rather than facilitating the resolution of disputes, the United Nations was debating hardened positions, embittering the contending nations. American successes, she observed, increasingly amounted to little more than blocking anti-American resolutions. U.S. policy thus added up to not much more than "damage control," such as warding off attacks on Israel.

The reason for this outcome, Kirkpatrick pointed out, was the increase in bloc voting. There was the East European bloc, the twenty-member Arab bloc, the twelve-member European Economic Community plus Japan, the forty-two-nation Islamic Conference, and the more than 100-nation nonaligned bloc (of which approximately one-third were African states and which included the above members of other developing-country groupings). The General Assembly had grown to 159 members in which every state had one vote, whether it was Communist China, with more than 1 billion people, or St. Kitts and Nevis, a microstate with a population of less than 100,000. Thus, the thirty-eight microstates with populations of fewer than 1 million had an influence in the United Nations totally disproportionate to their size, population, wealth, and financial contribution to the UN budget. At that time, the ten major industrial nations contributed 80 percent of the UN budget, while the eighty smaller countries contributed less than 1 percent; yet the latter, as members of the General Assembly, decided the budget. With this organization into blocs, the developing country-Soviet bloc coalition, for example, could easily muster anti-Western majorities in the General Assembly and most of the specialized agencies, such as UNESCO, while often ignoring other critical peace and human rights issues, especially those they did not want aired (see Table 18-3).

Table 18-3 UN Member Countries, 1945-1992

Americas		*Europe*	
1945 (Original members)			
Argentina	Guatemala	Belgium	Ukraine
Bolivia	Haiti	Byelorussia (now	United Kingdom
Brazil	Honduras	Belarus)	USSR[a]
Canada	Mexico	Czechoslovakia	Yugoslavia
Chile	Nicaragua	Denmark	
Colombia	Panama	France	
Costa Rica	Paraguay	Greece	
Cuba	Peru	Luxembourg	
Dominican Republic	United States	Netherlands	
Ecuador	Uruguay	Norway	
El Salvador	Venezuela	Poland	
		Turkey	
1945-1965			
Jamaica		Albania	
Trinidad and Tobago		Austria	
		Bulgaria	
		Finland	
		Hungary	
		Iceland	
		Ireland	
		Italy	
		Malta	
		Portugal	
		Romania	
		Spain	
		Sweden	
1965-1989			
Antigua and	St. Kitts	Germany[b]	
Barbuda	and Nevis		
Bahamas	St. Lucia		
Barbados	St. Vincent		
Belize	and the		
Dominica	Grenadines		
Grenada	Suriname		
Guyana			
1990-1992			
		Armenia	Latvia
		Azerbaijan	Lichtenstein
		Bosnia and	Lithuania
		Herzegovina	Moldova
		Croatia	Russia (replaced USSR)
		Estonia	Slovenia
		Georgia	Tajikistan
		Kazakhstan	Turkmenistan
		Kyrgyzstan	Uzbekistan

Table 18-3 Continued

Asia/Oceania		Africa	
Australia		Egypt	
China		Ethiopia	
India		Liberia	
Iran		South Africa	
Iraq			
Lebanon			
New Zealand			
Philippines			
Saudi Arabia			
Syria			
Afghanistan	Pakistan	Algeria	Mali
Burma	Singapore	Benin	Mauritania
Cambodia	Sri Lanka	Burkina Faso	Morocco
Cyprus	Thailand	Burundi	Niger
Indonesia		Cameroon	Nigeria
Israel		Central African	Rwanda
Japan		Republic	Senegal
Jordan		Chad	Sierra Leone
Kuwait		Congo	Somalia
Laos		Gabon	Sudan
Malaysia		Gambia	Tanzania
Maldives		Ghana	Togo
Mongolia		Guinea	Tunisia
Nepal		Ivory Coast	Uganda
Yemen[c]		Libya	Zaire
		Madagascar	Zambia
		Malawi	
Bahrain	Solomon Islands	Angola	Mauritius
Bangladesh	United Arab	Botswana	Mozambique
Bhutan	Emirates	Cape Verde	São Tomé and
Brunei	Vanuatu	Comoros	Principe
Fiji	Vietnam	Djibouti	Seychelles
Oman	Western Samoa	Equatorial Guinea	Swaziland
Papua New Guinea		Guinea-Bissau	Zimbabwe
Qatar		Lesotho	
North Korea		Namibia	
South Korea			
Marshall Islands			
Micronesia			

SOURCE: Department of State, *Atlas of United States Foreign Relations*, 2d ed. (Washington, D.C.: Government Printing Office, 1985), 18.

[a] In 1991, replaced by Russia.
[b] Until 1990, West and East Germany.
[c] Until 1990, North and South Yemen.

The upshot, Kirkpatrick said, had been twofold: (1) the United Nations ha become increasingly less relevant to many of the world's problems, and (2) it capacity for conflict resolution had decreased as repeated condemnations ha made it even more difficult to find a compromise solution. Moreover, rea soned debate had more and more fallen prey to ritualistic and repetitiv slogans whose aims were, directly or implicitly, to condemn the Unite States, and which only served to aggravate conflicts rather than resolve them The "all-too-familiar scenario," said Kirkpatrick,

> features one victim, many attackers, a great deal of verbal violence and a larg number of indifferent and/or intimidated onlookers.
> In these carefully staged productions, the Security Council serves as the stage the presence of the world press ensures an audience, the solidarity of the "blocs' provides a long procession of speakers to echo, elaborate and expand on the original accusations. The goal is isolation and humiliation of the victim—creation of an impression that "world opinion" is united in condemnation of the targeted nation. The enterprise more closely resembles a mugging than either a political debate or an effort at problem solving.[10]

In these circumstances, and particularly because the United Nations was widely regarded as unfriendly to American values and interests (as it had been unfriendly toward the Soviet Union during its second phase), the United States played "hard ball" with funds for its upkeep. In 1985, the U.S. Senate passed a resolution reducing the American contribution to the UN annual budget from 25 percent to 20 percent by October 1986 unless the UN voting formula of one state, one vote was changed. That resolution called for the United Nations to shift to a system in which each member state's voting strength on budget matters was proportional to its financial contribution. The four largest contributors—the United States, Japan, West Germany, and France—would then have slightly more than 50 percent of the vote and control of the budget. The current formula, it was charged, constituted "taxation without representation."

After carrying out a self-examination, the United Nations recommended in 1986 that the largest contributors have a proportional influence, to be ensured by requiring budget decisions by consensus. Thus, presumably, the larger donors could veto the budget. In 1988, the United States was $467 million in arrears and owed an additional $65 million for peace-keeping operations, reflecting its frustration with the United Nations' anti-Western bias and its wasteful, inefficient ways. But, just as the United Nations was facing the possibility of bankruptcy, President Ronald Reagan released $44 million outstanding for 1988, promised an additional $144 million for 1989, and committed the nation to paying all past debts over a number of years. But the Congress paid no heed. In 1989, it cut $123 million from the $715 million that President George Bush had requested for the UN budget; the $96 million that Bush had wanted to pay as the first installment on the over $400 million that the United States was in arrears was eliminated as well. Congress even cut $30 million from the $111 million that the country contributed for UN peace-keeping operations. In 1992, the United States remained the biggest defaulter, still owing $304 million for the regular budget and over $100 million for peace-keeping operations (altogether 102 nations had failed to pay their required contributions for a total of $1 billion). It was certainly ironic. The United Nations was on the brink of insolvency at the time that member states expected it to take on unprecedented responsibilities in the post-cold war era.[11] But Congress, as before, slashed the funds the president sought for these operations in 1992.

Fifth Phase: The Post-Cold War Role of Peace Maker

In the late 1980s, several events occurred that allowed the United Nations to once again play a prominent role in world affairs.[12] First, the Third World's confrontation with the West had come to naught. The demands for a new international economic order had failed. Given their own economic problems and the failure to solve them, as well as their need for Western assistance, including that of the multinational corporations, the developing countries moderated their tone; market solutions and private capital became more attractive.

Second, the Soviet Union, which had for over a decade aligned itself with the Third World's complaints against the West, sought a respite from more conflict to focus on its domestic problems. It thus saw the United Nations as an institution that would both help resolve some of the entanglements it had gotten itself into (and sought relief from) and manage future Third World crises in which it wished to avoid becoming involved. Mikhail Gorbachev specifically called for a more active role for the Security Council and the use of peace-keeping forces in regional conflicts. He also proposed establishing a number of "war-risk reduction centers" around the world that would watch for and monitor military activities. To show Soviet confidence in the organization, he paid Soviet back dues to the United Nations, including almost $200 million for peace-keeping operations the Soviet Union had long opposed.

Third, the United States, which had found going it alone—when, for example, it invaded Grenada, bombed Libya, and ignored the International Court of Justice (World Court) on Nicaragua—the preferred course during the time the United Nations and some of its agencies had become platforms for anti-Western propaganda, also saw renewed possibilities for strengthening the United Nations and furthering U.S.-Soviet cooperation.

Finally, the late 1980s was a period in which no country or bloc was really in charge of the international organization. The West had dominated in the early stages of its development, only to be succeeded by the developing countries. But the new primacy of the Security Council had decreased their influence in the General Assembly. U.S. interest in the organization was revived by the success of the United Nations in ending the eight-year Afghan war, from which the Soviets withdrew in 1989. In fact, it was the UN undersecretary-general for special political affairs who had patiently mediated the 1988 agreement between Pakistan, which had supported the Afghan rebels and not recognized the Communist regime as Afghanistan's legitimate government, and the latter, whose sole support was the Soviet Union. The United Nations also supervised the Soviet pullout.

But even before this occurred, some prominent Americans had called for a larger role for the Security Council and the United Nations itself in world affairs. For example, George Ball, undersecretary of state during the Kennedy and Johnson administrations, had noted that the presence of a UN peace-keeping force in Lebanon after Israel's 1982 invasion might have spared the lives of the over 200 U.S. Marines assigned to a multinational peace-keeping force (composed of several NATO countries) who were killed after that force became involved in the civil war in that country. Former Carter secretary of state Cyrus Vance and Nixon secretary of defense Elliot Richardson had pointed out that in 1987, the United Nations, not the United States, should have reflagged nonmilitary vessels in the Persian Gulf. They argued that because past UN peace-keeping operations had been "widely respected and rarely attacked, even in zones of bitter conflict," and U.S. reflagging only fueled tensions with Iran, such a move would have cooled tensions and assured commercial shipping peaceful passage.

While this advice went unheeded, the United Nations' success in Afghanistan (where forty observers oversaw the Soviet withdrawal) was followed by a role for that organization in the Persian Gulf once Iran stated in 1988 that it wanted to end the war. The subsequent cease-fire was monitored by a 412-person UN military observer group, while Iran and Iraq, with the help of UN Secretary-General Javier Pérez de Cuéllar, sought to find mutually acceptable terms to conclude their almost eight-year-long hostilities (although the fighting had ceased, the war actually ended when Saddam Hussein, facing the U.S.-led coalition, surrendered Iraq's territorial gains). Peace-keeping was suddenly back in style—and in a variety of countries. During the same period, the United Nations became involved in ending the sixteen-year war in the Western Sahara between Morocco and the Polisario guerrillas. In 1990, in Namibia (or Southwest Africa), the United Nations supervised elections after that country gained its independence. Namibia had become an independent state in 1989 after the U.S.-brokered 1988 agreement had provided for South African forces to pull out of that country in return for a Cuban troop withdrawal from Angola, its northern neighbor, where the South Africans had supported the guerrillas against Angola's Marxist government.

Later in 1990, the five permanent Security Council members, after months of wrangling, agreed to a plan for a truce that could end the thirteen-year-old civil war in Cambodia and establish a UN administration until a new government is elected. These negotiations followed the withdrawal of the Soviet-supported Vietnamese forces but were complicated by China's support of the murderous Communist Khmer Rouge faction, which, after killing over a million of its citizens, had been overthrown by the Vietnamese invasion of

Cambodia in December 1978. The other members of the Security Council wanted to avoid returning the Khmer Rouge to power. In seeking to prevent renewal of the civil war, the Cambodian peace treaty provided for a coalition government, including the Khmer Rouge, until elections could be held in 1993. In Latin America, the United Nations had in early 1990 supervised Nicaragua's first free election, which, to the surprise of the Sandinistas who had expected to manipulate the election in their favor, unseated them. The task suddenly appeared never-ending. In Cyprus, the United Nations was working with the governments of Turkey and Greece to settle the quarrel between the Turkish and Greek populations of the Eastern Mediterranean island. And even farther east, the quarrelsome former Soviet republics of Azerbaijan and Armenia have asked the United Nations to help them resolve their bloody dispute. Finally, a small peace-keeping unit of fifty observers was sent to Somalia to supervise a fragile truce between warring factions in that country's capital. From 1945 to 1988, or for forty-three years, the United Nations carried out eight peace-keeping operations. Since then, the number has risen to a dozen.

By 1992, about 10,000 UN troops were already deployed in the Sinai Peninsula between Egypt and Israel, in the Golan Heights between Syria and Israel, in Cyprus, in Southern Lebanon, and on the Indian-Pakistani frontier. United Nations involvement in the Western Sahara, Namibia, Yugoslavia, Cambodia, and elsewhere would vastly extend these peace-making and peace-keeping functions and raise costs to about $4 billion. In Yugoslavia, the cost of deploying 14,000 troops was estimated at $600 million. In Cambodia, the dispatch of 22,000 troops to disarm about 200,000 guerrillas belonging to the quarreling factions and supervise everything from cease-fires to public security, including safeguarding human rights and ensuring fair elections, would amount to $2 billion. Still, if successful, the United Nations' contributions to world peace would be vastly disproportional to the cost of these varied operations; the U.S. contribution would be a fraction of the weapons it is still producing to deal with a non-existent Soviet threat.[13] As these examples amply illustrate, peace-keeping had evolved from separating the combatants during the cold war to peace making, a much more complex task, in the post-cold war period. In the long run, given the number of possible future peace-making operations, what may be required is a permanent UN force for rapid deployment when needed.

Future of the United Nations

Improved U.S.-Soviet relations enabled the Security Council to become a more effective means of resolving long-standing regional disputes. Most earlier UN peace-keeping operations had been related to Third World conflicts, primarily the product of the decolonization process. Because these conflicts, if allowed to go on, threatened to pull in the superpowers, peace-keeping forces provided a buffer. But in Afghanistan, Angola, and Cambodia the superpowers were directly involved. There, Soviet troops or Soviet proxies—the Cuban and Vietnamese armies—had placed friendly regimes in power in the 1970s, and during the Reagan years the United States had supported the rebels. Although earlier the superpowers had kept the United Nations out of the East-West rivalry, they later found it a useful means of resolving some regional disputes that had long soured their relationship. Specifically, the United Nations had shown once more how, by acting as a third party, it could allow the contestants to save face and extract themselves from situations that had become too burdensome.

After Iraq's 1990 invasion of Kuwait, the United Nations, finally freed from the paralysis imposed on it for so long by the two superpowers, emerged more as the organization that it was intended to be at the time of its founding. Led by the United States, which had the will and capability to prevent Saddam Hussein from following up his August 2 seizure of Kuwait with an invasion of Saudi Arabia, and fully supported by the Soviet Union, as well as the other three permanent members of the Security Council (Britain, France, and China), the Security Council reacted with a series of resolutions. These resolutions condemned the invasion and demanded an unconditional Iraqi withdrawal from Kuwait; imposed trade and financial embargoes on Iraq and occupied Kuwait; declared Iraq's annexation of Kuwait null and void; approved of the right to enforce the economic embargo by allowing the United States and other nations to halt all shipping to and from Iraq (while this resolution did not explicitly authorize the use of force, the United States interpreted it as permitting force if circumstances required it); halted all air traffic to and from Iraq; declared Iraq responsible for all damage and personal injuries as a result of its occupation of Kuwait (Iraq looted virtually everything) and asked nations to prepare claims for financial compensation and submit evidence of human rights violations; and, finally, authorized the United States and its allies to expel Iraq from Kuwait if Saddam Hussein did not withdraw from Kuwait by January 15, 1991.

Fundamentally, then, during the Iraqi crisis the United States, its principal NATO allies, and the Soviet Union moved toward restoration of a global concert of powers.[14] After over four decades of cold war, it was easy to forget that the original United Nations had been organized precisely as a great-power concert. Its members—especially the Soviet Union and the United States—were to be responsible for maintaining peace in the international system. Specifically, the Security Council—occupied by the two superpowers plus Britain, France, and China, all possessing veto power and permanent membership—was before the cold war the only organ with the authority to act on the issue of peace and security; the General Assembly could only debate and make recommendations. In the Gorbachev era, the idea of great-power cooperation had been revived in both the bilateral negotiations on START and the multilateral negotiations on the conventional force reductions. While the diplomacy of arms control had focused on ending the cold war, the cooperation between the two former chief adversaries pointed toward the emerging post-cold war system. Bush's move in making the initial overture to Gorbachev after Iraq's invasion of Kuwait was a bold one because it reversed an over forty-year policy of keeping the Soviet Union out of the oil-rich Gulf so vital to Western industry. Gorbachev's response also involved a dramatic reversal of policy: abandoning a former ally.

It is not surprising that in the wake of the UN/Iraqi confrontation the great powers would focus attention on the United Nations' conflict resolution and peace-making mechanisms.[15] In a meeting of their heads of government in early 1992, the permanent members not only affirmed their expectation that the United Nations would play the central role in preserving peace and security as cold war tensions disappeared, but also declared that the secretary-general should revive "preventative diplomacy" by identifying potential trouble spots in advance and intervening before they got out of hand.[16]

Two factors will affect the future effectiveness of the United Nations on peace and security issues. One is the willingness of the United States, the principal mover behind the United Nations during Operations Desert Shield and Desert Storm, to ensure enforcement of the tough peace terms imposed on Iraq. These demanded that Iraq scrap its chemical and biological weapons; hand over all nuclear materials, destroy all components involved in building nuclear arms (as well as missiles with a range over ninety miles), and accept restrictions on future arms purchases; acknowledge the Iraqi-Kuwaiti frontier it had itself recognized from 1963 to 1990, as well as the presence of UN observers in an demilitarized zone between the two countries; and pay a portion of its oil revenues into a UN-administered fund for reparations to Kuwait and other victims of its aggression (although it might in fact be a long time before a devastated Iraq could make substantial payments into the fund). If Iraq accepted these punitive and preventive conditions, economic sanctions were to be lifted (although Washington later said that they will stay in place until Saddam Hussein is removed from power). More than that, these terms also were intended to calm the security fears of Iraq's neighbors and to discourage other regional bullies who might have expansionist appetites.

The Iraqi government accepted these terms; it could hardly do otherwise. But what would the United Nations do if the Iraqi strongman violated or obstructed UN implementation of the cease-fire agreement? Presumably he would face not only UN on-site inspectors of Iraq's war factories and the UN bureaucracy in New York but also the U.S. government. According to one observer, "Since Mr. Bush has just succeeded in turning the U.N. into a useful instrument for enhancing world order, he can't let Saddam Hussein steal his success."[17] In short, implementation of the UN cease-fire resolution, which depends on the willingness of the Bush administration to fully enforce it, will largely determine whether the United Nations will become a major instrument for developing some degree of world order. Indeed, after the war, Saddam Hussein violated the cease-fire terms repeatedly: by giving inaccurate information about Iraqi missile stocks, enriched uranium supplies, and chemical warheads; obstructing UN inspectors, even firing on them; and refusing to acknowledge the existence of a biological weapons program. Thus, the president could not walk away from this challenge without jeopardizing some of his principal objectives during the war: eliminating Iraq as a regional threat and strengthening the UN role in the post-cold war world.

Nor did he. President Bush repeatedly threatened to use air power if Iraq continued to evade UN inspection. But each time Iraq backed down at the last moment, revealing a little bit more of its vast weapons and missile program while still seeking to hide what it could. Its nuclear weapons program was far vaster and more sophisticated than anyone had suspected. It was now estimated that Iraq could have produced an atomic bomb within twelve to eighteen months had the war not intervened; hydrogen bomb research also was discovered. To ensure that Iraq would not become a nuclear power while Saddam Hussein was in power, the Security Council not only banned Iraq's nuclear, biological, and chemical weapons programs completely, but also decided to monitor the situation indefinitely to ensure that these programs had been eliminated. Together with the U.S. and British declarations that economic sanctions would not be lifted while Saddam Hussein stayed in power, the signal was clear that the reestablishment of normal relations with Iraq would not occur until Saddam Hussein was replaced. The United States and its principal allies also intervened to organize a safe haven in northern Iraq for the persecuted Kurds and warned the Iraqi strongman not to send troops or aircraft into this area. What is striking about all these arrangements is that they were made even though they substantially infringed in Iraq's sovereignty. As the Iraqi ambassador to the United Nations bitterly complained, with its ban on his country's nuclear weapons program, the United Nations had put Iraq under permanent trusteeship, contrary to the UN Charter, and that no sovereign country would or could submit to such a plan.

The second factor—and in the long run more critical to the United Nations' effectiveness—will be a restructuring of the Security Council. Its permanent members are still the five powers that won World War II. But as the Soviet Union was disintegrating and Russia acquired the formerly Soviet seat (which used to pay 10 percent of the UN budget), the European states were moving toward greater integration. Neither Germany nor Japan, the world's two economic superpowers, is represented on the Security Council, yet Germany is the fourth largest financial contributor to the United Nations, and Japan is the second (France and Britain are fifth and sixth; the former Soviet Union was third). No Third World potential power (such as India, Nigeria, or Brazil, all influential states in their particular regions) is represented as well. The Council thus no longer accurately represents the emerging power structure. If the United Nations is to play a more active global role, adjustments will be necessary, although the five permanent members are likely to resist changes that will diminish their influence. But changes are likely during this decade. Among the interesting issues is whether all the great European powers, including Germany, will be represented, or will the EC be allotted one seat? And will the potential non-European powers, possibly including Japan, be granted permanent seats but no veto power?

In a still flammable world, then, the United Nations' role is one of increasing importance. Optimism about the future, however, should be tempered with caution, for, as the Iraqi experience demonstrated, the United Nations cannot prevent or halt wars unless the participants want to stop and are looking for help and a face-saving exit. Indeed, because Saddam Hussein was unwilling to withdraw from Kuwait, the United Nations had to go to war to force him out. In Yugoslavia, after the revival of the civil war, as Bosnia declared independence, it would have taken NATO troops to quash the Serbian-controlled Yugoslav army; but NATO was reluctant to intervene. Thus, the UN peacekeepers, already present, were kept out of harm's way. Only economic sanctions were applied to what remained of Yugoslavia. Before 1989, the United Nations had been unable to convince the Soviet Union to withdraw its troops from Afghanistan, to influence Vietnam to pull out of Cambodia, to end the Iran-Iraq war, or to resolve the conflicts in Nicaragua and El Salvador. An editorial in the *New York Times* summed up the situation:

> The problem is that an assembly of nations called "sovereign," subject to no higher authority, can never be more than the sum of its members. Nations can behave inside the UN only as they behave outside, bartering interests, including their interest in peace. But the Charter notwithstanding, they insist on the right to redress grievance by force, which is what distinguishes a nation from province, county, town or individual.
>
> To yield that right, nations would need a common parliament to write laws, courts to interpret them and police to enforce them. They would have to disarm and pay taxes to a protecting authority instead. The United Nations cannot evolve into such a higher authority; it was designed to foreclose it, to let peoples relate only inter*nationally*, through the prism of their armies.
>
> That does not mean the UN is useless as mediator when any parties want to avoid war. But it does mean that anarchy—the absence of higher authority—is the desired, if undesirable condition.[18]

In short, the sovereignty of the member states will continue to limit the UN's contribution to resolving nations' security problems. Nevertheless, there can be no question that the organization helps to limit the impact of anarchy.

INTERNATIONAL LAW

In a decentralized system, international law exercises little restraint on state behavior when vital interests are at stake. On the whole, however, states generally do obey legal norms, which tend to reinforce the restraints imposed by calculations of power and prudence. But if the limited impact of international law can be attributed to the primitive nature of the state system rather than to any inherent lack of merit, the fact that in routine matters—which is the stuff of everyday behavior—international law does constrain states in their relationships with one another demonstrates once more that the international system is not one of pure anarchy but of qualified anarchy.

Sources of International Law

Not surprisingly, given the nature of the international system, the states themselves are the principal source of international law. Most international law is customary. Certain norms of conduct that have evolved over a long time have at some point become accepted as binding by the states that have followed them; new states tend to accept them automatically. Customary law, then, rests on general consent. The other principal kind of international law is treaty law. Unlike customary law, which is applicable to all states, treaty law binds only the parties that sign and ratify the treaties. As two states alone can hardly establish a general rule of conduct, treaty law usually reflects agreement by a large number of states. In 1982, for example, 117 nations, mainly Third World, voted for a new treaty governing the use and exploitation of the seas. The United States voted against the new Law of the Sea, however, as did West Germany and Britain, and forty-six other nations abstained.

Despite widespread opinion to the contrary, states usually obey international law because they need it. The rise of states as independent political units made the development of law necessary. Each sovereign state enjoyed complete jurisdiction and authority over its own territory and people, but it enjoyed neither beyond its boundaries. As states are compelled to coexist, however, they have to regulate their relations. If they are to stay in official contact, they must exchange representatives, which means that the rights and immunities of diplomats have had to be defined so that they can be protected on foreign soil. Other matters that have had to be covered include how title to territory is acquired (a matter that retains some importance because of continuing frontier disputes), ceded, and recognized. Also to be dealt with are a state's jurisdiction over its territorial waters, its air space, and aliens on its soil; conditions under which treaties come into effect and are terminated; legal methods for resolving disputes; and conduct of warfare and determination of the rights of neutrals.

The 1982 Law of the Sea, for example, covers such issues as territorial waters (twelve nautical miles from the coastline); the right of "innocent passage" through territorial waters for all ships, including military; the right of ships to pass through international straits (for example, Gibralter or Hormuz) that do not become territorial waters; a 200-mile economic zone in which coastal states have the exclusive right to fish and other marine life; a 350-mile zone for the exploitation of oil, gas, and other resources; and arrangements for the mining of seabed nodules of copper, nickel, cobalt, and zinc. The United States, as well as West Germany and other European Community countries, did not sign the treaty, largely out of fear that the organization in charge of the mining would be controlled by the developing countries. Still, coexistence requires rules.

Obedience and Disobedience of International Law

It should now be obvious why states do not normally violate international law—indeed, why it is virtually self-enforcing, except in the area of warfare. Legal norms provide a degree of order and predictability in an all too uncertain and chaotic environment. States expect to benefit from the reciprocal observance of obligations; if a particular state gains a reputation for not keeping its agreements, other states will be reluctant to sign further agreements with it, and reprisals may occur as well.

This rule is as true for Western states, among which customary international law originated, as for non-Western states. It has sometimes been held that Western-derived international law is unacceptable to the Third World and that the law must therefore be developed further to reflect the values and interests of the latter. But this view has led to confusion. On the one hand, the non-Western states are attempting to articulate their economic and political interests, shaped mainly by their desire for modernization, so that they can play a more influential role in the state system. On the other hand, they seek to express their resentment of a legal order that mirrors primarily the interests of the rich and powerful Western states. The new countries have thus accepted the prevailing law, invoking it in disputes with other states when it favors them, while seeking certain changes—for example, in the areas of foreign investments and property and the settlement of claims after expropriation and nationalization of such holdings. Yet even on the latter issue, it is suspected that as some of the newer states gain greater stakes in the international system and become exporters of capital, their views will move closer to those held by the more industrialized Western states.

Because of the anarchical nature of the state system, international law has its shortcomings, however. The international legal system, unlike a national or municipal one, exists in the absence of a supranational legislature. Customary law and treaty law are substitutes for legislated rules. The difficulties inherent in a decentralized system are clear: states may disagree about when a custom becomes a legal norm; they may differ in defining their obligations because even well-established customary law may be unclear on specific details; and there is no accepted authority to impose a uniform interpretation. Law that evolves over time is also slow to adapt to rapidly changing conditions. As a result, it may become obsolete. Treaty law may not be subject to such obsolescence, but it does not apply to nonsignatories. Few treaties are signed by even a majority of states, let alone all states. This may mean that while parties to a treaty are bound by its terms with regard to each other, their relationship to nonparties continues to be based on customary law. Treaty law, like customary law, also may suffer from a lack of specificity. Nor is there a supranational executive to impose sanctions when international law is violated as in domestic systems, although, as one noted British international legal expert, J. L. Brierly, has noted,

> The weakness of international law lies deeper than any mere question of sanctions. It is not the existence of a police force that makes a system of law strong

and respected, but the strength of the law that makes it possible for a police force to be effectively organized. The imperative character of law is felt so strongly within a highly civilized state that national law has developed a machinery of enforcement which generally works smoothly, though never so smoothly as to make breaches impossible. If the imperative character of international law were equally strongly felt, the institution of definite international sanctions would easily follow.[19]

In a sense, the term *law* is a misnomer in this context. A proper designation would be *norm*—a prescribed rule of conduct to which one *ought* to adhere. To not adhere to it may bring a bad conscience, disgrace, or even social ostracism. A law is similar, except that violation also leads to legal sanctions (fines, jail sentences, or executions). But there is no international government with a superior force that can be applied to those states that break the law. The principal shortcoming of international law, in these circumstances, is that its subjects decide when it applies! No state is indicted, tried, and punished. States normally obey international law and accept their obligations under it because it applies to everyday relations. On the whole, the routine business of coexistence makes light demands on states and does not have a major political significance. When the law is violated, it is because of issues that involve high political stakes, and the offended party usually applies its own sanctions.

International Law and the 'National Interest'

Such violations are relatively few in number but tend to be dramatic and sensational when they occur, giving rise to the impression that international law is weak. For example, during the 1950s the United States sent U-2 intelligence planes over the Soviet Union in the name of national security, even though the Soviet Union had legal jurisdiction over its own air space and had given no permission for such flights. In the 1960s, Cuba, as a sovereign state, had a perfect right to welcome the strategic missiles of the Soviet Union on its soil, and the United States had no legal right to demand their withdrawal. Yet in 1962 American security interests and the balance of power with the Soviet Union were perceived to require such withdrawal. The United States therefore blockaded Cuba, but, because a blockade is legally a *casus belli*, a reason for war, this action was called a quarantine. In these and similar instances, it would be more correct to say that international law is *restricted* in the range of its application rather than that it is weak or ineffective. This limited range of application contrasts greatly with the broad freedom of independent action that states claim for themselves.[20]

States thus ignore international law when it would restrain them from doing what they believe they must do in their interest. When Italy invaded Ethiopia in 1935, international lawyers thought that Italy had violated the League of Nations Covenant and that sanctions ought to be invoked. Yet Britain, and especially France, wished Italy to remain a friend and potential ally against the new Germany of Hitler. Sanctions would alienate Italy and make it more difficult to keep the European balance. International law is also a problem for smaller states concerned with their security. For example, surrounded in the 1950s and 1960s by states that were clearly hostile and refused to recognize its right to exist, Israel struck preemptively in 1956 and again in 1967, when it believed that its enemies were about to attack. Yet such a war is generally considered illegal.[21]

In 1979, Iran seized the U.S. embassy in Tehran, even though, according to international law, embassies are regarded as parts of the nation they represent and diplomats are legally immune to seizure and captivity. The new militant Islamic regime insisted that the United States had violated international law since World War II by interfering in Iran's domestic affairs through its support of the shah. It demanded his return for trial (and presumably execution) for what it condemned as his cruel tyranny and alleged subservience to the United States. In short, Iran claimed that the United States had violated international law and that seizure of the embassy and its personnel—labeled spies rather than diplomats—was retribution for past injustices and therefore legitimate. The United States took the case to the International Court of Justice, which found that the hostage-taking was illegal and the hostages should be freed. Iran ignored the ruling. The United States then took the matter to the UN Security Council, where the Soviet Union cast a veto. In these circumstances, the United States fell back on self-help and attempted the ill-fated hostage rescue mission. Self-help, in this instance, was the only course left to protect America's legal rights.

Disputes fall into two categories: (1) those that are amenable to settlement on a legal basis or *justiciable*, and (2) those that are political or *nonjusticiable*.[22] Political disputes are usually nonjusticiable, not because there is no law that can be invoked but because they involve vital interests. If a state is dissatisfied with the status quo—for example, the settlement imposed on it at the end of a war—it does not appeal to the law for a remedy because the law upholds the status quo. On the basis of existing law, an appeal for legal revision would be disallowed; agreements are binding. Thus, the question of revision is not judicial but political; judicial methods are of no avail. In the 1930s, for example, Germany knew that it was violating the Versailles peace treaty and that international law would support the territorial status quo. Because it rejected the status quo, Germany would not submit its claims to an international court. This kind of dispute can be resolved peacefully by negotiations and compromise but not by appeal to the law. The distinction between a legal and political problem is therefore arbitrary, reflecting a state's attitude toward the status quo. Still, it is a critical distinction, as became clear in 1984 when Nicaragua took the United States to the International Court of Justice, accusing the United States of intervening in its internal affairs by supporting counterrevolutionary actions against its government and of mining and blockading its ports. The court ruled unanimously that the United States must halt such actions and by a 14-1 vote that, Nicaragua being a sovereign state, its political independence "should be fully respected and should not be jeopardized by any military or paramilitary activities."[23]

When Nicaragua took the case to court, however, the United States announced that it would not accept the court's judgments in matters relating to Central America for a period of two years—even though a nation withdrawing from the World Court's jurisdiction was required to give six-months advance notice. The United States accused Nicaragua of misusing the court for political and propaganda purposes and of hiding efforts to export revolution to its neighbors. The latter, the United States claimed, provoked the U.S. assistance to the contras.[24] Calling the court's findings "clearly erroneous," the U.S. State Department claimed that the issues "represented political questions that are not susceptible to resolution by any court" under the UN Charter. The implication of this statement was that if the court proceeded to hear Nicaragua's arguments and evidence and ordered the United States to stop supporting the contras, the United States would defy the court, which, of course, could not compel compliance. The United States also stated a broader rule: in the future it would refuse to participate in "cases of this nature." After October 1985, the United States announced, it was formally ceasing to recognize the authority of the World Court except in nonpolitical cases.[25]

The U.S. decision to flout the court was widely criticized. The United States was supposed to stand for the law and be a law-abiding country, but it refused to participate in the court and accept its verdict. "It's like Al Capone saying he refuses to recognize the jurisdiction of the criminal court. It's the most compelling admission of guilt one can imagine," said one of the American lawyers arguing Nicaragua's case. The Reagan administration's defense was summed up by a quote from Winston Churchill, made in reference to the democracies' observance of international law during the 1930s: "It would not be right or rational," Churchill reportedly said, "that the aggressor powers should gain one set of advantages by tearing up all laws and another set by sheltering behind the innate respect for the law of their opponents."[26] Nicaragua was openly proclaiming its right—indeed, its revolutionary duty— to intervene in neighboring El Salvador to help the guerrillas there overthrow El Salvador's government. Should respect for international law prevent the United States from defending its interests?

States create the law, interpret it, and decide when to obey it. The International Court of Justice has no compulsory jurisdiction. Refusing to submit a dispute to it is the legitimate right of sovereign states. Because most states do not submit issues of vital interest to legal resolution, most international law enforces itself. And because international law would not have evolved had it not been useful to states, it is not surprising that the compliance record is high. Nevertheless, no state will normally submit a case on an important issue if it feels it may lose—and certainly not cases that involve vital interests. The United States, knowing it would probably lose the Nicaraguan case, did what might have been expected. By the same token, Nicaragua, a weak state, took the case to court to help strengthen its political and psychological position relative to the United States. The reverse was true with Iran. Iran knew the law and did not show up to argue its case; the United States, however, did—

not so much because it expected Iran to obey the court's ruling but to strengthen its political and moral case.

Interestingly, and indicative of international law's utility, in 1988 the Reagan administration proposed to Moscow that the two countries allow the World Court to arbitrate a list of disputes arising from some sixty treaties and conventions they had signed and that they agree in advance to accept the court's verdicts. Thus, the United States moved to once again accept the court's jurisdiction in areas that do not threaten national security interests. And Moscow agreed, in a radical shift from the past when it did not allow the court to settle such quarrels. But this does not change the fundamental fact that on issues vital to them, states will ignore international law. No more gruesome reminder of this fact exists than Iraq's violation of the prohibition against gas warfare. It used poison gas against Iranian troops and, after the fighting ceased, against its own Kurdish minority. But, except for the United States, the world yawned. To be sure, an international conference was called in 1988 in which Iraq participated, but it was neither condemned or punished; Iran was not even mentioned. In turn, it raised the key question of what international law means in a system so conspicuously unable and unwilling to control such a gross violation.[27]

MORALITY OF NATIONS

The anarchical nature of the state system also limits the impact of moral norms on the competition and rivalry of states. Indeed, in probably no sphere of human endeavor is there a greater gap between actual behavior and professions of moral principles and declaration of noble intentions than in international politics. A frequent definition of a diplomat is "an honest man sent abroad to lie for his country." A man or woman who slays another human being is normally called a killer; if apprehended, tried, and convicted, the killer is isolated from society in prison or, in many countries, put to death. But a person who kills other people called enemies on behalf of his or her country is hailed as a hero, presented with medals, and sometimes even immortalized in a statue or on a postage stamp. Ordinary soldiers receive veterans' benefits from a grateful country. A leader of the Italian unification movement once said, "If we did for ourselves what we are doing for Italy we should be real scoundrels."

The usual explanation for the alleged immorality of states is that their concern for their security requires them to do "whatever must be done." In a domestic system of law and order, the resulting sense of security allows individuals and groups to act with at least some degree of morality, but in the international system the absence of law and order means that all states, like the cowboys in a lawless western town, must go armed and must be prepared to shoot when their lives are endangered. According to the philosophy of

Thomas Hobbes, the war of every man against every other man in a state of nature arose not from fear of death but from fear of *violent* death at the hands of another. In the resulting state of perpetual war nothing was unjust. The idea of right and wrong, justice and injustice, simply had no place. The present state system is essentially a Hobbesian jungle; in a jungle one must behave appropriately. The "nice guy" is devoured.

In such a system it is perhaps wise to adapt and to play the game of nations, however rough that game is at times. For a national leader, being a good person and possessing moral intentions are not enough. Prime Minister Neville Chamberlain of Great Britain was such a person. More than anything, he wanted to avoid another war with Germany and to spare his people another awful bloodletting. Surely, preserving the peace was a moral goal. Peace is precious, not to be sacrificed lightly, and to be forfeited only if absolutely unavoidable. Had Chamberlain been a less noble individual, had he been more willing to take up arms and risk surrendering peace, he might have saved the peace he so treasured.

This line of thinking suggests that power and morality are antithetical. If, on the one hand, a state is concerned with security and power, it must throw off morality as so much excess baggage. But if, on the other hand, it seeks to act morally, it will suffer badly in the international struggle. This position, however, is false. Acts by individuals and groups, subnational or national, all involve moral considerations: decisions involve choices, and the choice of one course over another is influenced by moral predispositions, which are inherent in larger social values. In an international context, it is more accurate to say that *the closer relations among states move toward enmity, the more likely the states are to adopt policies normally considered immoral; the closer relations move toward friendship and the more secure the states feel, the more moral will be the conduct of their foreign policies.*[28]

Whatever the degree of morality that influences states in different situations, the source of this morality lies within the states themselves, giving rise to the following points.

Nationalism and Morality.   States identify their interests with morality. Clearly, no state is going to admit publicly that its actions are unethical. Former president Julius Nyerere of Tanzania once said on behalf of his country and the "poor nations" of the world,

> I am saying it is not right that the vast majority of the world's people should be forced into the position of beggars, without dignity. In one world, as in one state, when I am rich because you are poor, and I am poor because you are rich, the transfer of wealth from the rich to the poor is a matter of right; it is not an appropriate matter for charity.... If the rich nations go on getting richer and richer at the expense of the poor, the poor of the world must demand a change, in the same way as the proletariat in the rich countries demanded change in the past.[29]

The developing countries believe they are poor because the Western industrial states are rich. They therefore have a legitimate grievance based on the West's plunder of their resources and continued "capitalist" exploitation. The Western countries owe them reparations and help as a moral obligation and historic duty. This formulation is the essence of the claim for a new international economic order. The definition of what is moral and what is immoral is egocentric—and obviously very practical if it induces guilt feelings among the former colonial powers so that they seek to relieve those feelings by means of "alms for the poor."

Different Definitions of Morality.   States define morality differently, as President Nyerere's words illustrate, according to whether they are satisfied with their position in the state system. A status quo state, which benefits from the current distribution of power, will espouse a morality identified with the interests of the larger state system and will emphasize peace. If its interests coincide with those of most other members of the system, there is no occasion for challenges from the other members: upholding the peace will give the state a political and psychological advantage against challengers, which must threaten war or actually go to war to effect change and can therefore be denounced as aggressors and warmongers. The status quo state stresses the need for diplomacy, claiming that no problem is insuperable and that all can be settled by patient and sincere negotiations rather than by unjustified intimidation or force. The peace of a region—of the world—should be everyone's prime consideration; no injustice or wrong, however strongly felt, is worth the even greater injustice of war and the sacrifice of peace.

In contrast, a revisionist state that seeks to transform the status quo to its own advantage will attempt to avoid being morally discredited by claiming that it is underprivileged, that it is a "have-not" state, and that it seeks only equality or national self-determination. A good example occurred at the November 1976 UN General Assembly meeting when a resolution was passed linking South Africa's apartheid policy with Western governments and especially with the government of Israel. This resolution called the South African government "illegitimate," having "no right to represent the people of South Africa." It declared support for "the legitimacy of the struggle of the oppressed people of South Africa and their liberation movement, by all possible means, for the seizure of power by the people." [30] This resolution was an open call for the use of violence, justified in this instance by the morality of the goal—the end of discrimination and the equality of all people, black and white. The challenger must convince other states that the status quo demands alteration because it is no longer morally justifiable.

Here again morality can be a very practical instrument. The weak usually have few other weapons, and appeals to morality in states where public opinion is accessible to foreign persuasion can be effective. If the international system could be made to function according to moral principles, the inequality of power among states would not matter. It would even work to the advantage of the weak. Equally noteworthy, the moral issues raised publicly in international forums and those not raised reflect political circumstances and votes taken in international organizations. For example, the issue of the human rights of blacks in South Africa has been made an international issue by black African states in the United Nations, but the issue of the human rights of black Africans in some black African states whose rulers abuse the political and civil rights of their subjects has not been raised in the same forum. Black leaders do not want to raise the issue of human rights in their own states, and they have enough votes to prevent it.

Moral Restraints on National Behavior.   Although it is not surprising that states try to justify themselves, it would be a mistake to assume that "anything goes" just because officials who decide specific policies stamp them "morally approved." The domestic principles of a state can and do act as restraints on its behavior. For example, many Britons, as well as many people throughout the English-speaking world, disapproved of the British intervention at the Suez Canal in 1956 because they believed colonialism was no longer legitimate and the invasion of Egypt unjustifiable in an age of nationalism.

Similarly, in the 1960s many people in the United States—and in much of the rest of the world—found American support of the Saigon government in Vietnam illegitimate. In that "civil war" Hanoi's leaders were widely identified with the principle of national self-determination. How could the democratic United States support an autocratic regime that denied every democratic principle to which the United States professed commitment, in a war against those who were fighting for national unity and independence? In addition, the often massive use of force against a small unindustrialized country—on which the United States dropped more bombs than it had dropped on both Germany and Japan during World War II—seemed outrageous. The means used to wage the war and the destruction wrought appeared excessive to many in light of the proclaimed moral purposes of the intervention. Both the ends and the means of U.S. policy in Vietnam were widely questioned.

These two examples are part of a growing normative restraint—anchored in the values of Western democratic societies—in military confrontations between the First and Third worlds. The use of force in such conflicts, short of a clear threat to national security or prestige, is now widely regarded as illegitimate in the West. In 1974, after the Organization of Petroleum Exporting Countries quadrupled oil prices and caused a surge in Western inflation and unemployment, no Western power thought of using force. OPEC's right to set prices, even to withhold oil, was recognized.

Historian Arthur Schlesinger, Jr., once rather picturesquely remarked that a nation's foreign policy is the face that it wears to the world, and, if this policy embodies values that appear incompatible with the nation's ideals, either the policy will lose public support and have to be abandoned or the nation will have to toss its ideals overboard. A nation, like an individual, must in the final analysis be true to itself, or the "consequent moral schizophrenia is bound to convulse the homeland." [31] During the Cuban missile crisis in 1962, to cite only one example, when President John Kennedy and his advisers were debating whether to attack or blockade the island, Robert Kennedy argued strongly against attack on the grounds of American tradition. A surprise attack, which would kill thousands of Cuban civilians, seemed inconsistent with that tradition. The United States was not like Japan, and his brother, the president, was not like Tojo Hideki, who had launched the surprise attack on Pearl Harbor. There were, of course, other reasons— "practical" reasons—that helped the government decide in favor of the blockade, but morality unquestionably contributed to the decision. The moral factor was also perceived by Robert Kennedy to be politically beneficial. A surprise attack, he declared, "could not [have been] undertaken by the United States if we were to maintain our moral position at home and around the globe. Our struggle against Communism throughout the world was far more than physical survival—it had as its essence our heritage and our ideals and these we must not destroy." [32]

One of the more interesting recent moral phenomena in the United States was the rejection during the 1980s of nuclear arms by American Catholic and Methodist bishops.[33] Up to the 1980s it had been widely agreed that nuclear war was bad for one's health. This was hardly news; the threat to biological survival was the reason for the policy of deterrence. But such groups as the Physicians for Social Responsibility began to reemphasize this message as if it were new. Their stated intention was to counter what they claimed was widespread mass complacency about the dangers of the arms race and the use of nuclear weapons. It was the context within which this message was promulgated that was new. The point was not to reinforce support for deterrence but to point to its failure; the message focused on "the day after." The only solution to this terrible nuclear problem was nuclear disarmament.

But if the physicians pointed to the danger that nuclear arms posed for people's bodies—a nuclear war would be "the last epidemic"—the bishops pointed to the consequences that their possession posed for people's souls. The use of nuclear weapons was condemned as immoral, even in retaliation against an enemy's first use. Nuclear war was contrary to the churches' teachings and could not, therefore, receive their blessings. Defense of a free society was not a sufficient reason for having such weapons. Because deterrence stemmed from the possession of nuclear weapons *plus* the will to use them if the enemy struck—it was *not* just the product of the possession of these weapons—denunciation of the determination to use them, whether for moral or other reasons, meant that deterrence no longer existed. At best, it became a sheer bluff. Besides, if the use of nuclear weapons was immoral, then deterrence must have been immoral too. One could not have a morally acceptable deterrent strategy without an operational doctrine governing its use. Basically, the moral position pointed to a unilateral nuclear disarmament. Here it is useful to remember that the only time a nuclear weapon had been used was at the end of a war against a fanatical enemy who did not possess the bomb and therefore could not retaliate in kind.

The bishops' position was an interesting reflection of the growing Western view that the use of force was immoral except in strictly defensive circumstances to ward off "aggression." Deterrence had not been questioned on moral grounds until the 1980s, and the bishops' stance raised a host of questions. Was not the purpose of deterrence to prevent war? Was not prevention of a nuclear attack moral, even if this goal was achieved by producing nuclear weapons? Were not the latter the lesser evil and the prevention of nuclear war the greater moral good? (The French Catholic bishops thought so.) Could the threat of using nuclear weapons be equated morally to their actual use? In short, could one jump from the condemnation of nuclear war to the rejection of a deterrent strategy? Would not the two churches' positions also lead to policies that would, if adopted, result in the greatest of all evils, a nuclear attack or submission to a foreign, antireligious, dictatorial power? [34] Was survival the highest moral good of both churches' teachings? Or was it justice? Should a moral nuclear strategy not only have deterred nuclear war but also helped contain the expansion of a system of government that all Western states agreed was tyrannical? And had not nuclear weapons achieved *both* objectives since World War II? In short, had not the moral attacks on deterrence ignored the forty-year history of deterrence? [35]

The bishops' position was also interesting in another respect: when they proclaimed their positions as religious leaders, they tended to portray themselves as the guardians of moral principles and wisdom—which, they said, were superior to geopolitical, economic, and military considerations—and to claim that as churchpeople they had special insight and judgment. Besides the National Conference of Catholic Bishops, the National Council of Churches was especially prominent in pronouncing its views on foreign policy after Vietnam, persistently condemning the United States' anti-Communist policies more than communism and consistently finding "justice" on whichever side was hostile to the United States. During Operations Desert Shield and Desert Storm, many church leaders opposed the deployment of U.S. forces to the area and later the World Council of Churches, of which the National Council of Churches* is a member, "deplored" the U.S. decision to resort to war.[36]

Despite Saddam Hussein's aggression, the brutality of his regime, his threat to American values and interests, his quest for the very nuclear weapons that

---

* In expressing its radical views, the National Council of Churches did not limit itself to international policy. On the 500th anniversary of the arrival of Columbus, it adopted a resolution condemning such a celebration by declaring, "What some historians have termed a 'discovery' in reality was an invasion and colonization with legalized occupation, genocide, economic exploitation, and a deep level of institutional racism and moral decadence." Quoted by Richard John Neuhaus, "Just War and This War," *Wall Street Journal*, January 29, 1991.

the Catholic bishops in particular had so strongly denounced throughout the 1980s, virtual global support through the United Nations for the goal of freeing Kuwait, and the action of the Congress, the church groups remained opposed to what the president declared to be a just war. One had to wonder that if in the eyes of the leaders of these two important sectors of American Christianity Saddam Hussein did not provide the material and moral reasons for the U.S. use of force, under what circumstances would it ever be? Had the leadership of both groups become functionally pacifist? Still profoundly affected by Vietnam, they apparently had become convinced that as a racist, imperialist, militarist, and sexist society, America could not serve good ends in this world.[37]

For a contrasting view of morality and policy, one need but note that once hostilities started, American air power was limited as much as possible to military targets; large-scale destruction of civilian areas was minimized. Even after the Iraqi military reportedly moved its heavily bombarded control and communications system and some air force planes to civilian areas, the coalition air forces did not target them. In the words of the commanding officer, "We are a moral, ethical people, and therefore we're not going to do business that way. Yes, sure, it gives them an advantage, but we are not going to reduce ourselves to that level of immoral conduct just to even the score." [38]

Thus, there may exist differences within the United States about the morality of war in general and about any specific war, as well as about how that war is waged. But as Gen. Norman Schwarzkopf's comment suggests, in the final analysis a nation must be true to its sense of what is right and wrong if it is to live with itself and justify its actions. That is why most Americans, uneasy as they were about the potential cost in casualties of the war, supported the president's stand against Iraq, the embargo and, later, the use of force. Moreover, this is true not just in wartime; a moral code affects a nation's overall behavior since all foreign policy decisions involve making choices, and the policies chosen, while influenced by multiple considerations, include moral values. The problem is that while there may exist broad agreement on general moral principles, their application to specific conditions arouses controversy and differences of opinion.[39]

Morality in an Insecure World

A nation, particularly a democratic nation, thus can find itself in a dilemma, caught between its values and its security interests, at least in terms of its immediate foreign policy. It is, after all, always easier to justify short-term deviations from the nation's values if it can be maintained that in the long run the deviations protect the values. Noted earlier were the tensions inherent in any U.S. policy that calls for alliance with undemocratic states to enhance U.S. security. Similar, but more shocking to many Americans, is the tension between the democratic ethos and security that has been revealed in a number of other ways: assassination plots by the Central Intelligence Agency (CIA) against foreign leaders, especially Fidel Castro; the overthrow of a legitimately elected government in Chile; the "secret" bombing of Cambodia; and the Reagan contra war. The dilemma of making foreign policy in the face of conflicting pressures and values is finding a way to *achieve some of the principal objectives with minimum sacrifice of other equally important objectives.* In giving priority to competing objectives, how does a state balance security and welfare; security, democracy, and individual liberty; and security and peace (see Chapter 4)? The problem is *not* simply how to choose between one element and another, but how to achieve the best combination of all the elements.

There is no more dramatic or tragic illustration of this dilemma than the events leading up to the seizure of the U.S. embassy in Tehran in 1979. The shah, admittedly both dictatorial and ruthless, was also strongly pro-American. He had supported President Anwar Sadat of Egypt in his search for peace after 1973, and he had long supplied oil to Israel, even during the 1973 war. The United States in turn firmly supported the shah over the years. In 1953, for example, the CIA had restored him to power after he had been forced to flee his country. But there is not much doubt that the shah's secret police used torture, and it was always clear that the shah was quite unpopular. American interests, however, were equally clear: control of the strategic Persian Gulf and plentiful supplies of oil. In 1979, Iranian oil constituted only 4 percent of American consumption, but U.S. allies in Europe and Japan were very dependent on it.

Could there have been a greater disaster for the United States and its allies than the shah's collapse? Oil prices shot up virtually 100 percent in one year because of reductions in Iranian oil supplies and the resulting tight world market. Egypt lost a staunch friend and had to buy its oil elsewhere, as did Israel, which felt even more insecure now that Iran was also militantly anti-Israel and supported terrorist groups in Lebanon. These groups, besides establishing themselves in Beirut, where they seized Western hostages, also established a presence in southern Lebanon on Israel's northern frontier. Furthermore, the security of the Persian Gulf, which the United States had counted on the shah to guard, was now endangered by a zealous religious regime bent on fomenting an Islamic rebellion against the United States and overthrowing pro-Western Arab Muslim leaders in the oil kingdoms along the Persian Gulf. To prevent Iran's domination of the Persian Gulf during the Iran-Iraq war, the United States sent a naval armada into the Gulf when the war appeared to be going well for Iran.

It is also questionable whether the Iranians themselves were better off under this regime, which was bent on restoring traditional customs. It banned Western music, dance, and drink; tried to crush all opposition; and killed its enemies in ways all too reminiscent of the shah's own dictatorial rule. Modernization fell by the wayside, and the economy declined, creating large-scale unemployment and inflation. Was then American support for the shah "criminal"?[40] Indeed, given the subsequent actions of Iranian-supported terrorist groups against the United States in the Middle East, including twice blowing up the American embassy in Beirut and killing 241 U.S. Marines in a suicide attack, this question is all the more pertinent. Morally, a nation may not approve of some of its allies and friends, but should it therefore disassociate itself, even seek to replace those governments, regardless of the character of the governments that may follow? [41]

The later U.S. confrontation with Iraq surely poses this question even more sharply. In seeking to prevent Iranian hegemony in the Gulf, Washington aligned itself with Iraq; Saddam Hussein was viewed as a counterbalance. But after Iran, finally exhausted by its own internal revolution and the lengthy war, sued for an end to hostilities, Iraq was left in a potentially dominant position. Arming itself with modern weapons and aiming to increase its strength even further by seeking missiles and nuclear arms, it then sought to convert its potential dominance into actual hegemony when it invaded Kuwait and threatened Saudi Arabia. The collapse of the shah, in short, resulted in a great deal of regional turmoil, war and deaths, and a deepening and costly American involvement, finally culminating in the United States having to go to war in order to reestablish some semblance of a balance.

Nor did the successful prosecution of the war against Saddam Hussein end America's moral dilemma. During the hostilities, the United States had encouraged his overthrow. The Kurds and Shiites attempted to do precisely that. But after defeating the Iraqi army and compelling its withdrawal from Kuwait, President Bush decided not to send U.S. and other UN forces to Baghdad. He worried that it would draw the United States into a long and bloody civil war, leave the United States as the administrator of an occupied Iraq, and alienate the Arab members of the coalition. He also was concerned that a weakened Iraq would be fought over by Iran and Syria; in the meantime, the Kurds, seeking to unify all Kurds (even in surrounding states) in a new Kurdish state, would be precipitating enormous turmoil in the area. But having encouraged an uprising against the Iraqi strongman, how could the president in good conscience morally abandon those who responded to the U.S. call for Saddam's overthrow and stand by while he not only remained in power and violated the cease-fire terms calling for the destruction of all Iraqi mass-destruction weapons, but also sought revenge against those who had defied him and attempted to end his rule? The U.S. calls for democracy and human rights, preached during the war and reiterated so often during the collapse of the Soviet Union—indeed, made the conditions for U.S. recognition of the Soviet republics—certainly rang very hollow and hypocritical to the Iraqis who felt abandoned by the United States. [42]

Morality as an Incentive to Crusades

While morality may serve generally as a constraint on state behavior, despite the frequent dilemmas involved in moral choices, it also can "unrestrain" or unleash foreign policy. For example, an attempt to impose moral values on another state may transform a conflict of interest, perhaps resolvable through hard bargaining, into a conflict of moral philosophies, between good and evil, which tends not to be resolvable peacefully. Those who view the international arena as one in which St. George must always be slaying dragons completely misunderstand the nature of international politics. From this perspective, international politics becomes a matter of virtue and vice, in which purity is used to vanquish villainy, rather than a useful tool for analyzing the behavior of states in terms of their sense of insecurity, their legitimate interests and aspirations, the great difficulties in their coexistence, and their common and conflicting interests. And, if the struggle among states is viewed as a struggle between right and wrong, those who *know* they are right all too often become zealots and crusaders. Like a religious fanatic, a state convinced that it represents morality easily and rapidly strikes poses of absolutism and self-righteousness.

Translated into foreign policy—as postwar American foreign policy has amply demonstrated—such moralism has several undesirable results, two of which are failure to recognize other governments because of moral disapproval and unwillingness to meet with adversaries to reconcile conflicting interests. In addition, states that view themselves as moral arbiters also exhibit a crusading spirit in peace and war, which makes it difficult for their governments to distinguish between vital and secondary interests and may even entice them into disputes that involve only peripheral interests (as in the American intervention in Vietnam). Finally, a nation imbued with the crusading spirit is likely to transform war into total war to seek the unconditional surrender of the infidel. Crusaders remain oblivious to the fact that total military victory may make a postwar balance of power much more difficult to attain. Thus, moralism not only results in misunderstanding of international politics but, when applied to policy, also guides it on a course that in most instances will be detrimental to the state's own interests. Countries in which fanaticism has led to rigidity and self-righteousness are intolerant of other countries; thus coexistence with them becomes very difficult, if not impossible. Zeal and peace are mutually exclusive, for zeal gives rise to intervention in order to reshape and reform other states. Do democratic states have a moral mandate to remake other states in their own images? Indeed, can any state really expect—should it have the right to expect—to do more than influence the foreign policy behavior of another state when the latter impinges on its interests? Should foreign policy also concern itself with reforming another state domestically and make virtue a key criterion for its foreign policy?

In international politics the moral thing to do may be to avoid "the histrionics of moralism" and to restrain the tendency to self-righteousness and moralizing. It may be morally satisfying to appear noble and altruistic, but the impact of such aspirations on international politics has generally been to make national positions more rigid, render diplomacy less able to reconcile conflicting positions, and transform wars into total wars. In the words of George Kennan, "In a less than perfect world, where the ideal so obviously lies beyond human reach, it is natural that the avoidance of the worst should often be a more practical undertaking than the achievement of the best, and that some of the strongest imperatives of moral conduct should be ones of a negative rather than a positive nature"—as in the strictures of the Ten Commandments.[43]

What is the bottom line? It is that moral questions and claims may be simple to state, but they are not simple to answer. Moral judgments that seem easy at first glance often turn out not to be so clear-cut. Furthermore, what one party calls moral is not necessarily moral to another. There are no universal standards of morality or of justice. This lack of agreement in turn reflects the decentralized nature of the state system. There do not, then, appear to be solutions to the security problem in the state system.

For Review

1. What is the United Nations, and how has it evolved over time?
2. How does the contemporary United Nations contribute to the preservation of peace? What made this role possible?
3. What is international law?
4. What is international morality?
5. In what ways have international law and morality affected the behavior of states in their relations with one another?

Notes

1. J. William Fulbright, "In Thrall to Fear," *New Yorker*, January 8, 1972, 59.
2. Quoted in *Power and International Relations*, by Inis L. Claude, Jr. (New York: Random House, 1962), 59.
3. Ibid., 160; and Inis L. Claude, Jr., *Swords into Plowshares*, 4th ed. (New York: Random House, 1971), 80-86.
4. Egypt, because of its complaint that the United Nations had not supported it in the war against Israel in 1947-1948, was an exception.
5. Ernst Haas, "Types of Collective Security: An Examination of Operational Concepts," *American Political Science Review* (March 1955): 40-62, examines this transition from "permissive enforcement" to "balancing."
6. Only after the Cuban missile crisis of 1962 had already been resolved was the United Nations to be used in Cuba—and then it was to check that all Soviet missiles had been removed. But because Fidel Castro refused to submit to international inspection and the United States was certain that all the missiles had been shipped back to the Soviet Union, the United Nations remained uninvolved.
7. Andrew Boyd, *United Nations* (Baltimore: Penguin, 1963), 85ff.; Inis L. Claude, Jr., *The Changing United Nations* (New York: Random House, 1967), 23ff.; Arthur L. Burns and Nina Heathcote, *Peace-keeping by U.N. Forces* (New York: Holt, Rinehart & Winston, 1963); and Linda B. Miller, *World Order and Local Disorder* (Princeton,

N.J.: Princeton University Press, 1967). For one of the less successful ventures, see Bjorn Skogno, *UNIFIL* (Boulder, Colo.: Lynne Rienner, 1988), an analysis of international peace-keeping in Lebanon from 1978 to 1988. For an overall assessment of peace-keeping in the Middle East since 1974, see John Mackinlay, *The Peacekeepers* (Winchester, Mass.: Unwin Hyman, 1989).

8. Inis L. Claude, Jr., "Containment and Resolution of Disputes," in *The U.S. and the U.N.*, ed. Francis O. Wilcox and H. Field Haviland, Jr. (Baltimore: Johns Hopkins University Press, 1961), 101-128 (emphasis in original).

9. *New York Times*, January 30, 1982.

10. *New York Times*, March 31, 1983.

11. Paul Lewis, "U.N.'s Fund Crisis Worsens As Role in Security Rises," *New York Times*, January 27, 1992.

12. Edward C. Luck and Toby Trister Gati, "Gorbachev, the United Nations, and U.S. Policy," *Washington Quarterly* (Summer 1987): 19-35. Also see The United Nations, *The Blue Helmets*, 2d ed. (New York: United Nations Publications, 1991), which covers all UN peace-keeping operations through June 1990 (Angola, Central America, and Iran-Iraq); and Thomas Boudreau, *Sheathing the Sword: The U.N. Secretary-General and the Prevention of International Conflict* (Westport, Conn.: Greenwood Press, 1991).

13. Philip Shenon, "Cambodia, Bleak and Fearful, Yearns for U.N. Peacekeepers," *New York Times*, March 5, 1992; and Barbara Crosette, "Spending for U.N. Peacekeeping Getting a Hard Look in Congress," *New York Times*, March 6, 1992.

14. Coral Bell, "Why Russia Should Join NATO: From Containment to Concert," *National Interest* (Winter 1990/91): 39.

15. John W. Sewell, "Foreign Aid for a New World Order," *Washington Quarterly* (Summer 1991): 37.

16. Paul Lewis, "Security Council to Chart Its Future Role," *New York Times*, January 8, 1992.

17. Fred C. Ikle, "Bush vs. Saddam—The Final Round," *Wall Street Journal*, April 12, 1991.

18. *New York Times*, September 11, 1982 (emphasis in original). Also see by former UN secretary-general Kurt Waldheim, "The United Nations: The Tarnished Image," *Foreign Affairs* (Fall 1984): 93-107.

19. James L. Brierly, *The Law of Nations*, 6th ed. (New York: Oxford University Press, 1963), 73. Also see Werner Levi, *Law and Politics in the International Society* (Beverly Hills, Calif.: Sage, 1976).

20. Brierly, *Law of Nations*, 74.

21. Hedley Bull, *The Anarchical Society* (New York: Columbia University Press, 1977), 108-109, 143-144.

22. Percy E. Corbett, *Law and Society in the Relations of States* (New York: Harcourt, 1951), 77-79.

23. *New York Times*, November 15, 1984.

24. *New York Times*, January 19, 1985.

25. For a critical assessment of recent U.S. policy, see Patrick Daniel Moynihan, *On the Law of Nations* (Cambridge, Mass.: Harvard University Press, 1990).

26. Quoted by Michael A. Ledeen, "When Security Preempts the Rule of Law," *New York Times*, April 16, 1984.

27. Charles Krauthammer, "The Curse of Legalism," *New Republic*, November 6, 1989, 44.

28. Arnold Wolfers, *Discord and Collaboration* (Baltimore: Johns Hopkins University Press, 1962), 54.

29. Quoted by P. T. Bauer and B. S. Yamey, "Against the New Economic Order," *Commentary* (April 1977): 27.

30. *New York Times*, November 10, 1976.

31. Arthur M. Schlesinger, Jr., "National Interests and Moral Absolutes," in *Ethics and World Politics*, ed. Ernest W. Lefever (Baltimore: Johns Hopkins University Press, 1972), 35.

32. Robert F. Kennedy, *Thirteen Days* (New York: New American Library, 1968).

33. National Conference of Catholic Bishops, *The Challenge of Peace* (Washington, D.C.: United States Catholic Conference, 1983); and *New York Times*, December 26, 1985. For the final draft, see *New York Times*, April 27, 1986. A critical evaluation is found in James E. Dougherty, *The Bishops and Nuclear Weapons* (Hamden, Conn.: Archon Books, 1984).

34. Charles Krauthammer, "On Nuclear Morality," *Commentary*, October 1983, 48-52. Also see Robert W. Tucker, *The Nuclear Debate* (New York: Holmes & Meier, 1985); and Joseph S. Nye, Jr., *Nuclear Ethics* (New York: Free Press, 1986).

35. On the morality of alternative means of preserving mutual security in the post-cold war world, see Charles W. Kegley, Jr. and Kenneth L. Schwab, eds., *After the Cold War* (Boulder, Colo.: Westview Press, 1991).

36. Paul Starr, "No Vietnam," *New Republic*, February 18, 1991. While Starr, a self-acclaimed liberal, examines why so many liberals opposed the war or only supported it lukewarmly, much of his critique is applicable to the churches with their post-Vietnam liberal view toward the use of force. Also see Robert P. Beschel, Jr. and Peter D. Feaver, "The Churches and the War," *National Interest* (Spring 1991): 69-75.

37. For a trenchant analysis, see George Weigel, "The Churches and War in the Gulf," *First Things* (A Monthly Journal of Religion and Public Life) (March 1991): 37-43.

38. R. W. Apple, Jr., "Commander Claims Gains in Breaking Iraqi Army's Will," *New York Times*, February 5, 1991. Also see Robert W. Tucker, "Justice and the War," *National Interest* (Fall 1991): 108-112.

39. On the dilemmas facing the Catholic bishops and the National Council of Churches, see Peter Steinfels, "How Do You Tell a Victorious War from a Just One?" *New York Times*, March 17, 1991.

40. If so, most of the world's leaders can be called "criminal," for few have not supported regimes that have jailed domestic opponents and violated human rights. Indeed, many rule their own countries in this manner.

41. For two critical views of U.S. policy toward the shah, see Richard W. Cottam, *Iran and the United States* (Pittsburgh: University of Pittsburgh Press, 1988); and James A. Bill, *The Eagle and the Lion* (New Haven, Conn.: Yale University Press, 1988).

42. Tony Horwitz, "After Heeding Calls to Turn on Saddam, Shiites Feel Betrayed," *Wall Street Journal*, December 26, 1991.

43. George F. Kennan, "Morality and Foreign Policy," *Foreign Affairs* (Winter 1985/86): 212.

C H A P T E R   19

Peace through Transformation of the State System

FROM MICROPOLITICS TO MACROPOLITICS: FROM DOOM TO SALVATION

International organizations, international law, and morality may mitigate the basic anarchical character of the state system, but they do not fundamentally change state behavior. Having no ultimate protector, states generally have little choice but to assume the worst, and because they act on these worst assumptions, they stimulate their neighbors and other potential adversaries to do likewise. The latter's behavior then confirms the original assumptions and outlook of the former.

According to the proponents of a world government, if the security dilemma is inescapably built into the state system, then perhaps the only way to elude it is to devise methods of overcoming the decentralized nature of the international system. They assert that the atomic bomb precipitated the urgent need to build a world state and reproduce internationally the law and order and peaceful change found within the more advanced domestic systems (see Chapter 5). The reason is all too obvious: deterrence could not last forever. Sooner or later, if the cold war lasted, there would be a nuclear war. It would destroy not only the United States and Soviet Union but also most of humanity. Deterrence and arms control might delay its eruption, but nuclear war could not be avoided forever. Moreover, this was not just a matter for the United States and the Soviet Union to decide; the entire world had a stake in the prevention of nuclear war. It was therefore necessary to transcend the state system. Only by overcoming its decentralized nature could peace be ensured.

With the cold war over, low-politics issues are being cited as the urgent reasons for changing the structure of the state system.[1] In a global economy, national solutions for managing national economies no longer suffice; interdependence requires transnational management. The population growth rate, as noted in Chapter 10, clearly has worldwide implications. It destabilizes national societies when they are unable to fulfill popular expectations (leading to massive legal and illegal migration to the developed world, among other things); places greater pressure on global resources; leads to widespread deforestation to provide firewood and to make more room for people and farms; and even affects the world's atmosphere (the greenhouse effect). Birthrates are not therefore a solely national problem, to be solved at the national level; they are a global problem to be solved at the global level, requiring a global authority.

It is environmental problems, however, that have most dramatically pointed to the inadequacy of national solutions. For example, in the summer of 1988 medical wastes washed up on the Atlantic beaches of New England, New York, and New Jersey. It was as if the earth were saying, "Enough is enough; no more pollution." Four environmental issues stand out. The first is the greenhouse effect or the warming of the planet's atmosphere. This occurs when waste gases—chiefly carbon dioxide (mainly from cars, factories, and power dams in the industrial world and from the burning of the forests in the developing countries) and chlorofluorocarbons (CFCs, the industrial chemicals that carry chlorine up to the ozone layer), as well as nitrogen oxides, pollutants spewed out of automobile exhausts—escape into space, trapping heat from the earth's surface. While the experts disagree on how much warming has occurred, how much will occur in the future, and how rapidly and disastrous the effects of this phenomenon will be, the dangers that loom are scary: the melting of the North Pole ice; the rise of the oceans, flooding land areas (Florida may disappear or become submerged); and the onset of drought in once-fertile farmlands. The second issue is the depletion of the ozone layer over Antartica (and potentially the Arctic), as well as a higher-than-expected depletion over the United States. Because this layer screens out the sun's ultraviolet rays, its thinning results in higher rates of skin cancer and other damage to humans, crops, and forests. The industrial nations agreed in 1990 to stop producing CFCs by the end of the century and the developing countries by 2010. Thus, concentrations in the atmosphere will continue to grow for another decade or more before they start to wane and the protective ozone shield begins to recover (although it may regain full strength only after another century).[2]

The third environmental issue is the spreading acid rain and other atmospheric pollution that threaten the survival of forests and lakes. And the fourth is toxic and solid-waste disposal, symbolized in 1988 by the barge from New York City that after five months at sea was unable to dump its cargo of garbage. In fact, America and the industrial countries of Europe are trying to turn West Africa into a huge dumping ground. Thus, the earth's natural life-support systems all seem to be suffering catastrophic decline. Some environmentalists have even warned that the human use of water, air, land, forests, and other systems is pushing these systems over the "thresholds" beyond which they cannot absorb use without permanent change and damage. Indeed, in early 1992 the World Watch Institute reported that the world had no more than forty years to reverse the environmental deterioration, although up to that point no single major trend in environmental degradation had yet been turned around.*

Thus, it is not surprising that environmental problems are increasingly showing up on the international political agenda. One example was the Earth Summit held in Rio de Janeiro in June 1992 on the theme of "sustainable development." [3] European governments have been very concerned about the disappearing ozone layer and warming of the earth. They, as well as Japan, have urged capping emissions of carbon dioxide, the principal gas trapping heat in the atmosphere, at 1990 levels. But the United States, the world's foremost emitter of carbon dioxide, has resisted, claiming that such a step would be too costly. Moreover, the developing countries, whose primary interest is development and that rely heavily on fossil fuels, argue that if the West wants them to develop in an environmentally safe way, it will have to pay them. Nevertheless, the Rio Earth Summit legitimated the environment as a new global political issue. As Donald Marquis's typewriting cockroach expressed the urgency of this issue:

> It wont be long now it wont be long
> man is making deserts of the earth
> it wont be long now
> before man will have used it up
> so that nothing but ants
> and centipedes and scorpions
> can find a living on it. [4]

Other observers argue that the vast disparity in wealth between rich and poor nations, as well as the widespread poverty in developing countries, also require a fundamental change in the attitude and structure of the contemporary state system. People also have a right to self-determination and self-government and to social and political justice within their societies (the "inalienable rights" of freedom, self-expression, and human dignity). To ensure peace and build a more harmonious "spaceship earth," it is therefore incumbent to build a more decent and humane world without poverty and social injustice.

Thus, high- and low-politics issues appear to demand a shift from the state system to a global one—from an emphasis on national interests to the common interests of humankind, from power politics to planetary politics. Nuclear bombs, overpopulation, ecology, and political and social needs impel

---

* The United States is the world's most serious offender as a throwaway society: 16 billion disposable diapers, 1.6 billion pens, 2 billion razors and blades, 220 million tires, plus enough aluminum to rebuild the country's commercial airfleet every three months. "Planet of the Year," *Time*, January 2, 1989, 45.

national leaders to change habits and ways of thinking inherited from an earlier, prenuclear age. In a period when the problems facing the world are increasingly transnational, traditional ways of looking at the world can only result in disaster for all humankind. It is a matter of either doom or salvation.

It is claimed, in other words, that *the presently accepted concepts of state behavior are outdated.* Reflecting the experiences of the historical state system, current thinking has not yet caught up with the "necessities" of a rapidly changing world. Thus, international politics can no longer afford to focus on the states in the system, their objectives, and their interactions. The focus must be enlarged from the individual nation-state—the "micropolitics" examined up to this point—to world politics or "macropolitics." According to political scientist Richard Sterling, this requires posing questions central to global concerns: What is the *international* interest? Which policies and institutions appear to benefit all people, and which appear to benefit some but not others? Which are likely to disadvantage them all? One also must ask what any given nation-state contributes to the international interest and judge the value of any particular national interest in terms of the answer to that question.[5]

But hoping that national leaders will adjust to the era of world politics by asking themselves what is in the international interest and guiding themselves by it will not suffice. It is one thing to declare that states can no longer think in narrow, parochial, nationalistic terms and to demand that they think in more enlightened global terms. But how is that to be achieved in an essentially anarchical system? The logical answer is that the structural constraints must be overcome. The present system must be replaced by a world government. Governments preserve peace and maintain law and order on the domestic scene. If a government can be created that would supersede the governments of sovereign nations, it can, like national governments in their own spheres, ensure global peace and find solutions to the world's low-politics problems.

WORLD GOVERNMENT THROUGH FEDERALISM: THE AMERICAN EXAMPLE

It is often argued, by analogy, that under the American Articles of Confederation the states retained their sovereignty and continued their quarrels. But, under the Constitution, the states were reduced in status to nonsovereign members of a new federal system in which the federal government, to ensure domestic tranquillity, could apply national law directly to individuals. Can it not be argued then, as advocates of world government do, that the American Constitutional Convention was the "great rehearsal"[6] for a global convention that will transfer the sovereignty of all nations to a world government, created to ensure global peace through establishment of the rule of law? Such partisans seem to believe that wherever a legal order is established—that is, wherever a government applies law directly to its citizens—government functions as a peace-keeping institution. What leads them to this conclusion? Inis Claude has suggested that one factor is the attractiveness of certain terms and the images that they produce in people's minds—terms such as *government* and *law and order:*

> A clue may perhaps be found in the intimate association between the idea of world government and the fashionable theme of world rule of law. Law is a key word in the vocabulary of world government. One reacts against anarchy—disorder, insecurity, violence, injustice visited by the strong upon the weak. In contrast, one postulates law—the symbol of the happy opposites to those distasteful and dangerous evils. Law suggests properly constituted authority and effectively implemented control: it symbolizes the supreme will of the community, the will to maintain justice and public order. This abstract concept is all too readily transformed, by worshipful contemplation, from one of the devices by which societies seek to order internal relationships, into a symbolic key to the good society. As this transformation takes place, law becomes a magic word for those who advocate world government and those who share with them the ideological bond of dedication to the rule of law—not necessarily in the sense that they expect it to produce magical effects upon the world, but at least in the sense that it works its magic upon them. Most significantly, it leads them to forget about politics, to play down the role of the political process in the management of human affairs, and to imagine that somehow law, in all its purity, can displace the soiled devices of politics. Inexorably, the emphasis upon law which is characteristic of advocates of world government carries with it a tendency to focus upon the relationship of individuals to government: thinking in legal terms, one visualizes the individual apprehended by the police and brought before the judge.[7]

Apart from the seductive quality of certain terms and the favorable images they create, the key argument of proponents of world government is that peace depends primarily on the creation of a government that, because of its superior power, is able to enforce the law on individuals. This argument, however, shows that these proponents misunderstand the function of government and exaggerate the coercion necessary to maintain law and order. Admittedly, government power does play a role in preserving peace. A peaceful society is—at least to a degree—a policeful society. At the same time, however, as evident in the earlier analysis (Chapter 5), this power is not the principal factor in achieving peace, particularly in democratic societies. There have simply been too many civil wars, coups d'état, revolutions, and secessions to justify as much trust as world federalists place in the establishment of government as a solution for the disorder inherent in the international system. If a national government can fail to produce law and order and keep a nation united, then how confident can one be that world government is the answer to anarchy and war?

The fact is that domestic peace stems from the political negotiations and compromises struck among conflicting organized interests with a common political culture. It is not the application of law to individual violators and their imprisonment for disobeying the law that are primarily responsible for domestic peace. Neither is it the policeman swinging a club or the judge hearing a case and sentencing citizens who broke the law. Most citizens obey laws not out of fear but out of habit, respect, and recognition of their legitimacy. Peace then is essentially the product of constant political adjustment and accommodation, accomplished through the efforts of the much-maligned politicians. When groups and classes have what they consider to be genuine grievances and unfulfilled aspirations for which they are seeking—but are unable to find—redress, then disorder, rioting, and civil war are likely. Applying a law that sanctifies the status quo becomes an incitement to conflict, not a solution. Thus, the issue is not what the law is but what it should be. The analogy of catching the individual lawbreaker and applying sanctions is hardly appropriate; indeed, it is irrelevant.

The example of American nation building—from confederation to federation—in fact offers evidence that it is a mistake to believe that the mere creation of government is the answer to conflict. Those who argue for world government consistently underrate the difficulties encountered in forming the United States of America. They want to show that if the will to organize a world government is present, it can be done. This falsifies history. More than will is required; a common political culture or sense of community is necessary. Such a sense of community is apparent in the Preamble to the U.S. Constitution, which declares that the Founders' purpose was to establish a "more perfect union." There was already a union, formed during the long colonial period and tested in the war for independence; it had only to be made "more perfect." By 1787, Americans already shared a language, a common cultural tradition, and a democratic heritage.

> The thirteen colonies formed a moral and political community under the British Crown, they tested it and became fully aware of it in their common struggle against Britain and they retained that community after they had won their independence. . . . The community of the American people antedated the American state, as a world community must antedate a world state.[8]

The final test of this union came during the Civil War, in which the issues of slavery and the country's values had to be settled before the United States could become a durable political community. And it is precisely the absence of an equivalent sense of global community or political culture that makes it impossible to establish a world government—along with, it should be added, a historical amnesia in which the civil wars and political disorders of the West have been forgotten and the past romanticized, especially that of the United States and Britain. One need but look at the dramatic examples of national unraveling (the former Soviet Union) and ethnic assertion (the civil war in Yugoslavia) to realize how difficult even building a nation and maintaining its unity can be.

SUPRANATIONAL COMMUNITY BUILDING THROUGH FUNCTIONALISM

If the establishment of a democratic world government by means of federation is hardly likely to occur in the near future, is there then another way to overcome the divisiveness of present-day nationalism and establish at the international level the sense of community that is the basis of government? Several political scientists have studied this issue empirically. How have political units in the past been integrated into larger political organizations, the authority of which then superseded their own? How relevant are these historical examples to the contemporary problem of integrating nation-states into a supranational political community?

Eliminating the 'Security Dilemma'

Three of the terms just used—*integrating, supranational,* and *political community*—are noteworthy. Karl Deutsch and several associates who analyzed various instances of the integration of political units in the preindustrial era have defined *integration* as "the attainment, within a territory, of a 'sense of community' and of institutions and practices strong enough and widespread enough to assure, for a 'long' time, dependable expectations of 'peaceful change' among its population."[9] Closely related is the term *supranational,* which refers to the formation of a community and institutions above those of the integrating states. This community would have the authority to make on behalf of the states political decisions that would require their obedience (as the American federal government has authority superior to that of the individual states). *Supranational,* then, is not to be confused with the term *international.* An international or intergovernmental organization is an organization composed of states. Its decisions are reached through negotiation and compromise among the states, not imposed from above. Finally, according to political scientist Amitai Etzioni, a *political community* is

> a community that possesses three kinds of integration: (a) it has an effective control over the use of the means of violence (though it may "delegate" some of this control to member-units); (b) it has a center of decision-making that is able to affect significantly the allocation of resources and rewards throughout the community; and (c) it is the dominant focus of political identification for the large majority of politically aware citizens.[10]

Among states, the threat of violence remains a key element in the resolution of differences, but the chief characteristic of a supranational organization is the absence of intimidation and war. The anarchical model of the state system, with its frequent focus on threat and counterthreat, force and counterforce, is no longer applicable. Deutsch and his colleagues have called such an enlarged supranational organization a "security community."[11] Historically, they distinguish between two kinds of such communities: the *pluralistic* security community, composed of states that retain their national autonomy while forming specific and subordinate agencies of cooperation on particular matters (such as those formed by the United States and Canada or by Norway, Denmark, and Sweden), and the *amalgamated* security community, in which states surrender autonomy to a new set of central political institutions (as did the separate provinces of Italy and of Germany at the time these countries were unified and born in the nineteenth century). Deutsch found that pluralistic security communities are easier to achieve and more durable; amalgamated security communities are more difficult to establish and more likely to fail.

The main point of studying this building process was to discover how states have learned to redefine their national interest in terms of peacefully cooperating with one another and to overcome their historic patterns of regarding each other as potential adversaries.[12] More specifically, study has focused on the transformation of Franco-German hostility into Franco-German friendship; after three wars in seventy years, this was a fundamental change in attitude. This transformation occurred within the context of the post-World War II creation of the European Economic Community (ECC)—now called the European Community (EC)—none of whose members expects any longer to go to war against any other member.

The movement toward a united Europe that has followed World War II has been the principal experiment undertaken by industrialized states in supranation building. Interested in the conditions essential to produce a successful amalgamated security community, Deutsch and his colleagues found, not surprisingly, that some of the conditions present in preindustrial amalgamations were also present in the experiment that began in 1950 with the formation of the European Coal and Steel Community (ECSC) and produced eight years later the European Common Market (see Figure 19-1). The European experiment is the sole modern example of nation-states seeking to integrate themselves into a larger political unit by shedding sovereignty and nationalism. If successful, the European Community could be the first of several regional building blocs on which a globally integrated world order could be based.

Conditions for Supranation Building

One condition for building a United States of Europe was a compatibility of values and expectations among the amalgamating states. The six original EC members, sometimes called the Inner Six, certainly had such a compatibility. All were pluralistic societies (although Germany and Italy recently had been fascist states), and each had representative political institutions. In the larger countries—West Germany, France, and Italy—as well as in smaller Belgium, the governing Christian Democrats shared a European outlook and held similar views on social welfare, the free market, and other issues.

A second condition was the belief by the political elites of the integrating countries that their way of life was distinctive. To them, the iron curtain was more than an ordinary political division; it separated the "West" from the "East," thus forming two distinct geographical and cultural entities. Christian

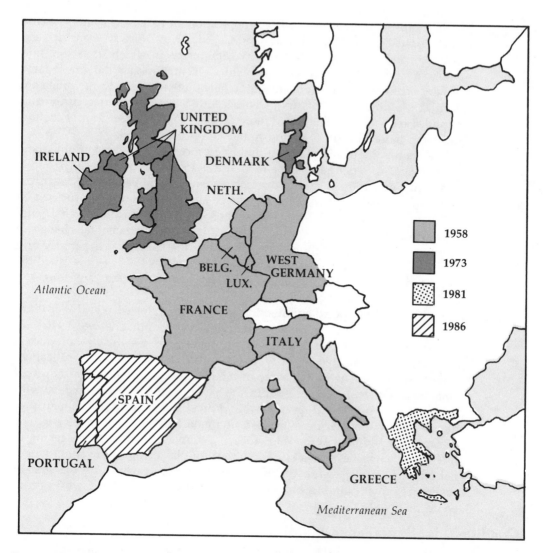

Figure 19-1 Evolution of the European Community, 1958-1986

Democrats were particularly disposed to think of the East-West conflict in terms of the historic struggle between Christendom and the "barbarian" invaders from the East, such as the Mongols and the Turks. Russia, usually regarded as non-European, now fitted this role. For the Christian Democrats, the defense of "civilization" once again required Western countries to subordinate their own differences and unite in the struggle against the Communist Soviet Union.

A third condition of particular significance in amalgamation was the expectation of mutual economic benefit. For the Inner Six, this benefit was to be realized in two ways: (1) through the mutual elimination of trade barriers, import quotas, and other restrictions; and (2) through establishment of a common tariff to protect this market. European industry would then enjoy an enormous potential market, and efficient enterprises would presumably expand and modernize to take advantage of this enlarged market. By the same token, inefficient enterprises unable to compete—and unwilling to make the effort—would be closed. Business in general would profit from European integration. Labor would acquire a similar stake in the new Europe as production rose and the levels of employment and real wages followed. To be sure, workers in less efficient industries would lose their jobs, and they might have to move to other areas in search of new employment. But in general the EC would produce more jobs. Consumers also would benefit from the expanding economy. As they saw national economic barriers tumbling and industry converting to techniques of mass production—large-scale production at reasonable cost and with sufficient wages to enable consumers to buy in quantity—they too would recognize the advantages of the EC.

These conditions, then, are among those necessary for the existence of a supranational community. Others include superior economic growth, high political and administrative capabilities in the participating units, unbroken links of social communication, broadening of the political elite, mobility of individuals, and multiple avenues of communication and transaction.[13]

Process of Supranation Building

But how about the *process* of integration? How does it occur? Functionalists think they know. David Mitrany, the founder of this school of thinking, assumed that the *vertical* divisions between states, which produce conflict and war, can be overcome by tying the various functional areas of the economies of different countries together *horizontally* to resolve their common social, economic, and humanitarian needs.[14] He regarded these needs as essentially nonpolitical and noncontroversial, for they involve such values as welfare and social justice rather than national security and prestige. As each area of need is tackled, a transfer of state authority to supranational institutions occurs; as more needs are satisfied, more and more authority is transferred to supranational institutions. Thus, sovereignty is whittled away until at some point nations find themselves brought very close together in this ever-expanding web of activity. They then have a greater stake in maintaining peace and transferring national authority to new supranational organs. As political scientist Frederick Schuman aptly phrased it, integration of the various functional areas could bring "peace by pieces."[15] Mitrany called it a "working peace system," distinct from peace safeguarded by the balance of power. In Mitrany's words, "the problem of our time is not how to keep nations peacefully apart but how to bring them actively together."[16]

Ernst Haas was the first to study this process of integration in great detail after the start of the movement toward a more unified Europe. Like Mitrany and Jean Monnet, the French master planner of the New Europe, Haas found the driving force behind integration to be economic self-interest. There had to be something in it for everyone. Haas also emphasized, as did the French government when it launched the ECSC, the importance of step-by-step economic integration. In 1950, Foreign Minister Robert Schuman of France proposed that the Inner Six pool their coal and steel industries in the ECSC. The choice of coal and steel, the backbone of industry, was deliberate, for it would tie together German and French heavy industry to such an extent that it would become impossible to separate them. Germany would never again be able to use its coal and steel industries for nationalistic and militaristic purposes.

Economic Spillover.　Because the coal and steel sector forms the basis of the entire industrial structure, Haas has suggested that it was chosen for its economic "spillover." The ECSC would exert pressure on the unintegrated sectors of the economy, and, as the benefits of pooling heavy industry became obvious, these other sectors would follow suit. The ECSC was thus the first stage in an attempt to create a wider market. It was expected that this approach would be extended gradually to other functional areas of the economy such as agriculture, transportation, and electricity, with the eventual creation of a federal European state enjoying a huge market and a highly developed mass-production system. Once integration had been set in motion, it would pick up momentum on its own.

The first economic spillover occurred in 1958, when the Inner Six established the European Economic Community, then known as the Common Market. Their aim was the formation of an economic union. All tariffs, quotas, and other restrictions hampering trade among themselves would be completely eliminated; in turn, they would establish a common tariff to reduce imports and to keep as much of the market for themselves as possible. Furthermore, they would gradually abolish restrictions on the movement of labor, capital, and services within the community. Finally, the Inner Six established a third community, Euratom, for the generation of industrial energy. Together, the ECSC, EEC, and Euratom would constitute a European community or EC.

Political Spillover.　Apart from economic spillover, the most important effect Haas stressed was political spillover. To be more than just a customs union, the Common Market had to have a uniform set of rules to govern the economic and social policies of its member countries.[17] For example, if one nation were to adopt a deflationary policy, its industries would be able to undersell those of its partners and capture their markets. Clearly, this kind of development had to be prevented. Or, if a nation, after abolishing its tariffs for a specific industry, then subsidized that industry's production or imposed an internal tax on competitive foreign goods, it would gain an obvious advantage for its own industry. Such discrimination by a single government had to be forbidden. Uniform rules could not be established, however, to simply prevent deviant behavior; affirmative action also was required. Because prices reflect production costs, which in turn partly reflect national regulation of wages, hours, working conditions, and social welfare programs, the industries of a nation with lower standards have an advantage over competitors in neighboring states. A single set of standards in such areas as minimum wages, maximum hours, and welfare programs was therefore necessary. In addition, as workers would be able to move from one country to another in search of employment and better jobs, there had to be a single social security program for all six nations. This increasing need to harmonize the social and economic policies of the Inner Six would demand a single governmental center for policy formulation in Europe. Common policies would require common institutions with supranational authority.

In real terms, such supranational authority, one observer has noted, "starts to come into play when a state agrees . . . to carry out decisions to which it is itself opposed. Most obviously, such a situation arises when it has agreed to be outvoted if necessary by other states—either by a simple or by some weighted or qualified majority." [18] Common institutions with supranational authority extending beyond trade and tariff matters play a central role in furthering the larger political community:

> If economic integration merely implied the removal of barriers to trade and fails to be accompanied by new centrally made fiscal, labor, welfare, and investment measures, the relation to political integration is not established. If, however, the integration of a specific section (e.g., coal and steel), or of economics generally (e.g., the "General Common Market") goes hand in hand with the gradual extension of the scope of central decision-making to take in economic pursuits not initially "federated," the relation to the growth of political community is clear. [19]

The development of a political community is demonstrated most readily by interest group activity. In a developed supranational economy, those whose interests are affected by the decision-making institutions, adversely or otherwise, will organize to lobby at the supranational level to influence particular decisions—just as in the United States, where various interest groups lobby at the state and federal levels. [20] In an open, pluralistic society, interest groups and political parties (as aggregates of interest groups) normally act at whatever level of government important political policies are decided. This pattern was indeed the aim of the EC's founders; interaction between decision-making institutions and the multitude of interest groups was considered of vital importance to the political integration of the Inner Six. [21]

Social Spillover. In the long run, however, the self-interests of various groups will not suffice. A truly federal Europe must have popular support as well. Eventually, the political spillover leads to social spillover or the transfer of national loyalty to the supranational community:

> As the process of integration proceeds, it is assumed that values will undergo changes, that interests will be redefined in terms of a regional rather than a

purely national orientation and that the erstwhile set of separate national group values will gradually be superseded by a new and geographically larger set of beliefs. . . .

As the beliefs and aspirations of groups undergo change due to the necessity of working in a transnational institutional framework, mergers in values and doctrines are expected to come about, uniting groups across former frontiers. The overlapping of these group aspirations is finally thought to result in an accepted body of "national" doctrine, in effect heralding the advent of a new nationalism. Implied in this development, of course, is a proportional diminution of loyalty to and expectations from the former separate national governments. Shifts in the focus of loyalty need not necessarily imply the immediate repudiation of the national state or government. Multiple loyalties have been empirically demonstrated to exist.[22]

Based on the logic of the integration of economic, political, and social functions, the EC was designed to develop into a United States of Europe through three stages: a *customs union,* an *economic union,* and a *political and social union.*

Limits of Functional Logic

Three fundamental assumptions underlay this logic: (1) that economic and social, or low-politics, problems could be separated from political and security, or high-politics, issues; (2) that the ever-widening vested interests and habits of cooperation formed in the low-politics area would spill over into high politics; and (3) that there would be a massive shift of loyalty from the nation to the new supranational community as citizens—producers, laborers, farmers, and consumers—came to recognize the economic benefits of the new and larger community.

Inseparability of Economics and Politics. The ups and downs of the European unification movement reflect the validity of these assumptions. It should not have come as too great a surprise to discover that in practice, even if not in theory, social and economic affairs are not neatly separable from political considerations. The modern industrial welfare state testifies to this. Virtually no social or economic issue—whether it be farmers' subsidies, corporate survival, women's rights, or abortion—stands outside the realm of political controversy and action. This is just as true in international politics. Years ago, Inis Claude asked,

> Is it in fact possible to segregate a group of problems and subject them to treatment in an international workshop where the nations shed their conflicts at the door and busy themselves only with the cooperative tools of mutual interests? Does not this assumption fly in the face of the evidence that a trend toward the politicization of all issues is operative in the twentieth century?[23]

States have remained jealous guardians of their sovereignty, national identities, and military strength. France and the other five countries of the Inner Six may have pooled their coal- and steel-producing facilities to increase their standards of living, but it was quite another story when it came to coordinating their foreign and defense policies with each other and later EC member countries. Indeed, the original impetus for the formation of a united Europe was political, not economic. The French sought to insure themselves against any future danger from German rearmament and aggressive policies, as well as to gain equality of status and influence with the "Anglo-Saxons" in the Western alliance. More broadly, France viewed the ECSC as the initial step toward a French-led United States of Europe. Europe was not to be merely a region of butchers and candlestick makers, as implied by the later term *Common Market*, but a world power ranking with the United States and the Soviet Union. Otherwise, how could Europe stand on its own feet and play a role again in world affairs? A divided, weak Europe would remain subordinate and subservient to the United States.

Success, an Obstacle to Political Unity.   Nor did the economic spillover have quite the results it promised to have. Economically, of course, the EC has been successful. Its twelve members with over 300 million consumers constitute the largest market in the world. As a single unit, the EC possesses great bargaining strength on economic issues, and it has been responsible for tariff reductions among all the industrial countries and easier access to one another's markets. Trade among the six founding members has grown even faster, and this growth probably has been a major factor in the industrialization of France and northern Italy.

Ironically, by the 1980s the economic success of the EC was proving to be one of the greatest obstacles to further political spillover. As the national wealth of EC members rose, the urgency for further integration declined. The functional analysts had emphasized that fulfillment of some needs would result in growing support for the integration of other sectors of the economy and further development of new supranational attitudes. But contrary to these expectations, economic gains through the customs union seem to have led to protection of the status quo and reduced support for further integration.[24] The citizens and interest groups who gained the most economically from the European unification movement attributed those benefits largely to their own governments. Thus once more, the confidence in nation-states, supposedly lost as a result of defeat in World War II and the postwar economic collapse, was enhanced.

Even more ironically, the post-1973 recession, which lasted into the 1980s, also strengthened the concern with national interests. Member states tried to protect industries and jobs by keeping out imports from other EC states. This policy, in turn, made EC decisions more difficult to reach as governments, facing voter wrath, were less able to make the necessary compromises. France and Italy, for example, waged a "wine war" when French growers tried to keep out cheaper Italian wine. In fact, because farmers possessed power disproportionate to their numbers, the EC was swimming in lakes of wine and building mountains of butter, dumping surplus food on the international market, competing with U.S. farmers, and undermining the competition of the poorer nations of Asia and Latin America. The increasing national resistance to free trade was accompanied by growing government support for troubled industries.

At a time when cooperation was not always present in the low-politics arena, one could not be too optimistic about its transfer to the high-politics arena. Admittedly, in the 1980s there were some indications of new life in the European unification movement. Greece joined the EC in 1981, and Spain and Portugal joined in 1986. Like Greece, which had been admitted after it shed its right-wing regime, Spain and Portugal were rather fragile democracies. The rationale for their admission was obviously the extension and stabilization of democracy in these countries, making democracy more secure throughout Europe. All three, however, were less developed industrially than the other EC nations, and the larger number of members made efforts to integrate more difficult. Therefore, although the EC countries were prosperous and at peace, the United States of Europe remained a distant objective. The automatic spillover from the economic to the political arena had not been automatic enough. More than forty years after the launching of the ECSC and more than thirty years after the EC began its life, nationalism and the nation-state were alive and well in Western Europe. National loyalties remained.

Future of the European Community.   The functionalists' belief in "the victory of economics over politics," in short, may have been exaggerated, as was the emphasis on the domestic conditions for integration. The neglect of external conditions as a motivation for integration was particularly ironic given the bipolar environment that stimulated the drive for a United States of Europe. Indeed, just as the Soviet threat had spurred the movement, so the disappearance of the perceived Soviet threat slowed its momentum. As the defeated and discouraged Continental states recovered from the devastation and economic collapse after World War II, and as the unique circumstances in which integration was launched changed, the larger vision apparently dimmed.

In 1984, a special committee of the EC, convened to address the problem of declining confidence in the EC, stated that Europe was in a state of crisis and counseled that "Europe must recover faith in its own greatness and launch itself on new ventures—the setting up of a political entity." [25] But the committee was very cautious in offering recommendations. The fact was that the nations of Europe no longer thought of themselves as partners in the great enterprise of "building Europe." Each concentrated on how to get the best deal for itself. The focus was on trading off oranges and lemons, Riesling and Chianti. With their minds still on the grocery list, it was not surprising that the EC countries attached thirty footnotes listing their reservations to twenty-three pages of the committee's report.[26] Britain, Denmark, and West Germany expressed reservations about the committee's insistence on moving toward greater integration. Ireland, a neutral, objected to defense aspects of the plan. But without a common foreign and defense policy, a European political community was meaningless.

Nevertheless, the European movement picked up new momentum because of two external influences on the community. One influence was the slow growth of the European nations' economies and the continuing high unemployment rate as Japan and, to a lesser extent, the United States continued to increase the technology gap in such critical areas as computers and semiconductors. Spurred by the facts, the twelve EC members set 1992 as the date for the final elimination of all the internal nontariff barriers to trade that replaced the abolished tariffs. After 1992, trade (goods and services), capital, and labor will be able to move anywhere within the EC. This, as noted earlier, required "harmonization" of social and economic policy throughout the community to prevent favoritism or protection for selected industries. The goal was to reinvigorate the EC, create a truly common market as originally envisaged, and transform Europe into an economic superpower as companies expand beyond their national frontiers. With the world's largest domestic market of about 336 million people at the end of 1992, European industries would merge and organize on a European-wide basis and become more competitive at home with the United States and Japan, as well as in the international market, thereby accelerating European economic growth. In short, European integration is now viewed as a prerequisite for competing in the global economy. If everything goes according to plan, after 1992 Europe will gain exceptional leverage in world trade and world affairs.[27]

The other external influence on the EC is Europe's defense and how much longer Europeans, forty-seven years after World War II, feel they will be able to count on the United States. The 1980s saw increasing disharmony in the alliance even before the cold war ended as (1) Europe became economically more competitive, often underselling American agriculture; (2) Europeans and Americans differed on what policies to pursue toward Moscow; (3) the United States spent more on Europe's defense as a percentage of gross national product than the Europeans; (4) pacifism and neutralism became very visible in European protest movements against the deployment of U.S. intermediate-range missiles to counter those of the Soviet Union; (5) Asia, the Persian Gulf, and Central America increased in importance; (6) the huge U.S. deficit required large cost cuts; and (7) the ability of the United States to sustain its growing commitments declined. Thus, if not a disengagement, an increasing devolution of Europe's defense to the Europeans seemed inevitable. This trend was accentuated by improved East-West relations, the erosion of the image of the Soviet Union as an enemy, the internal "de-Communization" of the states of Eastern Europe, and the collapse of the Warsaw Treaty Organization (WTO).

Although NATO, unlike WTO, has not been dismantled and is searching for a new rationale to justify its existence, the Europeans have initiated some tentative moves toward closer defense arrangements. But the Persian Gulf demonstrated the fragility of the moves toward a united Europe. After the Iraqi invasion of Kuwait, Europeans were unable to react collectively and firmly, even though Europe was more dependent on Gulf oil than the United

States. Britain, for example, immediately sent 43,000 troops, reviving its "special relationship" with the United States, which had faded in recent years as the American-West German relationship grew stronger with the receding cold war. Germany, however, with one of the largest armies in Europe, invoked constitutional restrictions on the "out-of-the-area" use of German forces and demonstrated a strong streak of pacifism, even though Germany itself was not threatened and the war was sanctioned by the UN.* The French, while sending 16,000 troops, declared initially that they could be used only to get the Iraqis out of Kuwait, not in Iraq proper (later, they changed their minds). Other European states made token contributions. How could a Europe unite on common policies when British and French soldiers were fighting in a war from which Germany stood aloof? The European efforts also threatened to strike a blow to American-European relations after the war. A week after the fighting started a *Wall Street Journal*/NBC poll showed a rising resentment against Japan and Germany in the United States.[28] From the U.S. perspective, Americans supplied most of the soldiers and did most of the dying, whereas their two richest allies made only verbal commitments to assist financially. Adding insult to injury, the sums appeared paltry relative to the GNPs of those countries, and then both nations were slow in delivering that aid.

Thus, the Europeans, who at the end of the cold war had felt confident that they constituted an economic superpower, demonstrated that they were as dependent as ever on U.S. political leadership and military power. Saddam Hussein had once more shown that military power remained important and that economic power, hailed as the new measure of influence, could not stop Iraqi aggression. Therefore, on the one hand, the Persian Gulf crisis tended to suggest that a United States of Europe was an elusive mirage and that Europe was rather impotent. Divided instead of united, its last-minute peace efforts rebuffed rather contemptuously by Saddam Hussein, Europe was essentially irrelevant from the time he invaded Kuwait in August 1990 to the outbreak of war in January 1991—and the world took notice. In the words of Luxembourg's foreign minister, the crisis had shown "the political insignificance of Europe." His Belgian colleague was even more specific: "Europe is an economic giant, a political dwarf, and a military worm." [29]

This impression of a "toothless Europe" was reinforced shortly afterward by the EC's fumbling effort to avoid a civil war in Yugoslavia after Croatia and Slovenia declared their independence.[30] Despite twelve EC-arranged cease-fires, they all failed, prompting UN political intervention and UN peace-keeping forces. This time the peace held until Bosnia seceded and the Serbian-led army intervened on behalf of the large Serbian minority. In the

---

* While Germany sent only eighteen fighters to Turkey, the German government even debated whether they were to be sent into action if Turkey were attacked by Iraq, although Germany was obligated by its NATO commitment to defend fellow member Turkey. Presumably, that is why the aircraft were sent in the first place.

face of European passivity, after leaving this European issue to the Europeans, the United States asserted its leadership, leading to UN economic sanctions, but no military action. But precisely because these crises exposed the EC, with its twelve nations and 336 million people, as an economic giant with a weak and divided political voice and no common military power, they may yet stimulate the EC to start coordinating its foreign and defense policies. In short, economic competition and security considerations may provide another impetus for European integration.

The ethnic and nationalistic quarrels erupting in Eastern Europe and the disintegration of the Soviet Union cannot be separated from the security and prosperity of Western Europe. Instability in the East is bound to affect the entire European body politic. EC assistance to the former Soviet Union ranges from loans to help the shift to a free-market economy to emergency food shipments. The additional cost of making Eastern European industry viable and competitive has been estimated at billions more (although no such capital amounts are being invested). Indeed, in order to improve their chances, Poland, Hungary, and Czechoslovakia are already taking the steps needed to apply for EC membership. The EC is critical to the future hopes of people who, having freed themselves from communism, fear that the change to market economies may result in only poverty and unemployment. They need access to the European Community for their goods if their transition to democracy and a free market is to have a chance.

The eagerness to join the EC also infected the seven members of the European Free Trade Association (EFTA). This organization is composed mainly of neutral countries (Austria, Lichtenstein, Sweden, Finland, and Switzerland, as well as two NATO members, Iceland and Norway), which, besides not having aligned themselves with NATO during the cold war, did not share the EC's stated purpose of political and economic integration. But with the prospects of a larger trading bloc, they wanted to join with the EC in one huge common market. In late 1991, the EC and EFTA agreed to form the world's largest trading bloc of nineteen nations and 380 million people. EFTA members became nonvoting members of the EC.[31] (See Figure 19-2.)

Indeed, Austria, Sweden, and Finland should be full EC members in the near future. And with the three Baltic republics having reestablished their nationhood, other republics such as Ukraine having declared their independence from Moscow, Yugoslavia's Croatia, Slovenia, Bosnia, and Macedonia having become independent of Belgrade, and Czechoslovakia's possible division into two separate states, all potential applicants to the EC, the whole definition of Europe may change.[32] Within a dozen years, the EC may include twenty-four states, perhaps more.

In the meantime, the EC is caught between "widening" the community by inviting in the new democracies in the East and "deepening" the community by speeding up the integration of the present twelve members. Most states favor the latter, largely because of nervousness about a reunited Germany and their determination to ensure that it is tightly knit into the EC fabric and

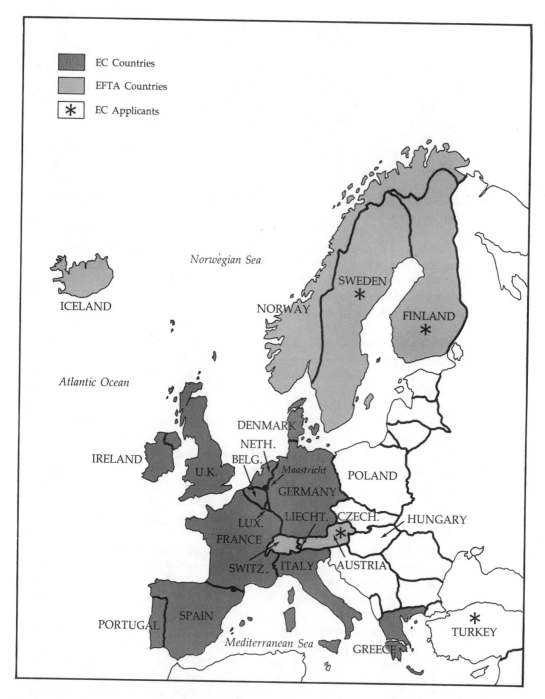

Figure 19-2 Building Blocs of a New Europe

unable to dominate a looser European arrangement; European unity is also the best guarantee that no European state will ever make war on its neighbors again. Indeed, it was Germany, whose reunification in 1990 had made its neighbors nervous, that became the chief spokesperson for a federal Europe, precisely because its leaders remembered that a nationalist Germany had repeatedly disrupted Europe's peace. The question was whether in "deepening" the EC, its member states were willing to give up more of their sovereignty and, if so, how much. The French and Germans, for example, proposed enlarging a joint military brigade as a step toward the creation of a European army. They also suggested common foreign policies toward Eastern Europe and the Soviet Union, the United States, the Middle East, and such issues as arms control, nuclear nonproliferation, and UN peace-keeping operations. Certainly, real economic unity cannot be reached without political unity, and a politically united Europe would be meaningless without common defense and foreign policies.

Proposals, however, are one thing; collective action is another. In December 1991 in Maastricht, the Netherlands, the EC took a major step toward a stronger European federation, even though because of British concerns about sovereignty the ultimate goal was called an "ever closer union." Specifically, the EC committed itself to greater political and economic unity, including establishment of common foreign and defense policies whenever possible by a majority vote and establishment of a common currency, the ECU (European Currency Unit), before the end of the century. Eleven of the twelve EC members (all but Britain) also agreed to work together in "social affairs" by strengthening workers' rights, working conditions, and social security. If fully implemented, the Maastricht agreements will revolutionize the nature of the nations composing the EC and transfer significant powers to the community. Thus, in view of the EC's interest in ensuring the success of the former Soviet satellites' transformation to democracy and free enterprise, and the EFTA members' interest in joining, the issue of whether the EC should be "deepened" through the integration of the existing members or "widened" by inclusion of new states was settled by doing both at the same time.[33] The big question, of course, is what will happen in the wake of the 1992 Danish electorate's narrow defeat of the Maastricht agreements? Will it spur other countries to preserve their symbols of national sovereignty, such as the deutsche mark and the pound? Will Europe be only a common market, a considerable achievement in itself, or will Denmark's action be only a temporary halt on the way to a more politically united Europe?

One thing, however, is certain. This Europe of 380 million, whether it is only a common market or political union, will become an economic giant. With oil and natural gas from Russia, it could be self-sufficient in energy. And with its well-educated and essentially prosperous population (as well as cheap labor in Eastern Europe), this emerging Europe, controlling access to the world's largest market, is likely to influence profoundly, if not write, the post-GATT rules of managed trade between trade blocs.[34]

INTERDEPENDENCE AND A MORE HARMONIOUS WORLD

All this being said, the transformation of the state system to a global system is not likely to occur soon. A world government cannot be established by a new constitutional convention, nor—even if the European experiment of transcending the nation-state manages to succeed over the next decade or two—can a world state be built on regional building blocs ("peace by pieces") in the foreseeable future. The process is simply too time-consuming, and the conditions for supranational integration are clearly not present in the nonindustrialized and nondemocratic areas of the world. Speed has been an important ingredient in this process, however, because during the cold war the constant fear of a nuclear war and catastrophe made transformation of the state system a matter of great urgency. Forty years of avoiding that ultimate disaster was no guarantee, it was argued, that it could be successfully deterred another four decades.

It was in this context that interdependence first appeared and seemingly offered a promising solution in the post-Vietnam late 1970s as the cold war resumed after détente I. *Interdependence was to be a sort of halfway house between the anarchy of the contemporary state system and the promise of a world-state in the future.*[35] Believers in the promise of interdependence expected the state system to continue but with the fangs of national interest drawn. Even before a world government came into existence, they expected some of its benefits—greater cooperation, less emphasis on violent resolution of conflict, more emphasis on joint, peacefully negotiated solutions—to be evident. States may remain the principal actors and a world-state only the ultimate objective, but interdependence increasingly would bind all states together, catch them in its web, and make their individual security, especially their economic fortunes, dependent on one another. Whatever the problems confronting a single state, solutions would no longer be national solutions achieved by sacrifices made by other states. Instead, they would be reached collectively and benefit all. The maxim of the historic state system, "Your gain is my loss," would be replaced by the maxim "We shall all lose or gain together" in the new interdependent state system—that is, the emphasis of the "new politics" would shift from conflict to cooperation. Interdependence was seen as a replacement for an increasingly outdated power-politics approach and analysis of international politics. The actual evolution of economic interdependence demonstrated, however, as it did for the earlier functionalist version, the limits of the changes that could be expected in the character of international politics. But it was the assumptions underlying the theory of interdependence that led to all the optimistic conclusions.

The first assumption was the priority of low-politics goals. The switch from high-politics foreign policy goals to low-politics goals stemmed from modernization. As traditional societies became industrialized, modernization resulted in better standards of living, first in Europe in the nineteenth century, later in North America, and now in the rest of the world. For most of the world's citizens, low-politics issues have become more important than high-politics issues. In democratic countries, where the "revolution of rising expectations" began, electoral pressures ensured governmental attention and commitment to improving people's lives. But all governments today must be increasingly responsive to low-politics issues. Their success is judged by the level of social services provided and the rate of growth of the gross national product. Management of the economy—even a free-enterprise economy—by government is politically necessary to ensure high employment, rapid economic growth, economic stability, and an equitable distribution of income. Governmental incompetence in economic management is not easily forgotten or forgiven at election time in democracies, and in Eastern Europe it led to the fall of the Communist regimes, while in the Soviet Union itself the party lost its legitimacy.

A second assumption underlying independence was that states are no longer self-sufficient. The days of autarky, when the great powers at least had or controlled the resources they needed and were in charge of their own economic destinies, are gone. No longer able to satisfy their people's demands for greater prosperity, governments increasingly have had to enter into the international economy. To fail to do so would be too costly politically because economic growth would be slow. Governments thus are drawn further and further into interdependence, even if they do not want to be. Foreign policy becomes thoroughly enmeshed with such issues as trade, aid, development, monetary stability, exchange rates, and debt problems, and the division between foreign and domestic policy becomes blurred, if not nonexistent.

The third assumption followed logically: low politics involves cooperation; high politics involves conflict. Nations that have become interdependent on bread-and-butter issues have no choice but to cooperate if they wish to promote their own prosperity. On security issues, states still operate as separate political units. A single nation's gain in power and security is usually still seen by a potential adversary as a loss of power and security for itself and as something to be opposed. But a gain in prosperity for the same nation depends on gains in prosperity for other nations as well. In the new socioeconomic game, states gain or lose together. An interdependent world is a world of exchange and sharing; war would disrupt this mutually beneficial relationship.

The fourth assumption concerned the irrelevance of force to low-politics issues. Interdependent states must cooperate over a long period; the use or threat of force is counterproductive in a game of coordination. Coercion or violence may pay off on a single issue, but, given the need for long-term collaboration, the resulting anger and resentment may lead to some sort of economic retaliation. If another nation possesses a much-needed commodity, it is hardly helpless, even if it is inferior militarily. The gains from force would therefore be few, if any, and the costs probably quite high. In brief, the very meaning of power has changed. Given the uselessness of force, the need for cooperative behavior if common problems are to be solved, and the complexity of such issues as population control, increased food production, development of alternative energy sources, monetary stability, and economic growth, power has become a matter of technical expertise and persuasive skills so that states can find collective solutions.[36]

The final assumption underlying interdependence was the equality of states. In a world of many states, many issues, many games played simultaneously, and the nonuse of force, the historical hierarchy has eroded. All states are essentially equal on welfare issues. The dominance of the superpowers and traditional power politics have disappeared. Security is basically a given, and the primary objective of states is welfare.

The envisioned interdependent world, then, was one in which states still exist but not the kinds of states studied here so far. Interdependence will have "tamed" them, drawing in the "sharp teeth of sovereignty." It also will have dissolved selfish national interests and bonds of national loyalty.[37] Economic and technological forces will bind states together, and national frontiers will become increasingly irrelevant, for economic cooperation will cross borders. Interdependence may not engender world government, but it will make the nation-state and power politics irrelevant in a world without frontiers. Nations will no longer be able to solve their own problems adequately and serve their people's desires for better lives. Such global problems as insufficient natural resources and energy, overpopulation, poverty, and shortages of food, as well as the potential revolutionary situations created by the division between rich and poor nations, will be solvable only at the global level. National solutions will no longer be possible.

This view, prevalent in the 1970s and 1980s, described an international system that differs radically from the one described earlier. While the structure of the state system remains, the power hierarchy has been replaced by a new egalitarianism. Force is no longer thinkable, and the key values of national security, prestige, and power have been replaced by economic welfare, consumerism, social justice, and environmental concerns. If there is one word that sums up the distinction, it is *cooperation*.

This cooperation was institutionalized in *regimes*, a set of rules or decision-making procedures used to resolve disputes about and encourage cooperation on a particular issue.[38] In a world in which population growth, pollution, poverty, and nuclear proliferation had transnational consequences, and in which social and economic forces, whether oil prices or the "debt bomb," affected many if not all nations, international regimes became the new focus of studies. Regime members were not only individual states but also international governmental and nongovernmental organizations. Regimes spanned everything from such high-politics issues as U.S.-Soviet arms control and nuclear diffusion to the more usual low-politics issues such as international trade, monetary systems, management of the seas, population, and health. These were all areas in which states found it beneficial to have a set of rules to guide them and inform them about the multilateral problem-solving procedures. Indeed, short of world government, regimes became the prototype of a

Table 19-1 Distinctions between Power Politics and Interdependence

	Power Politics	*Interdependence*
Issues	High politics: security, balance of power, spheres of influence	Low politics: natural resources, energy, food and population, environment
Actors	States (primarily in the First and Second Worlds)	States (primarily in the First and Third Worlds), multinational corporations
State relationships	Conflicting national interests	Interdependence, common interests, and transnational cooperation
Rule	Conflict: "Your gain is my loss" (balance of power)	Cooperation: "We shall all lose or gain together" (community building)
Management	Bilateral	Multilateral
Role of power	Coercion	Rewards
Role of force	High	Low, if not obsolete
Organization	Hierarchical (bipolar or multipolar)	More nearly egalitarian
Future	Basic continuity	Radical change

more ordered, peaceful, and cooperative world—and in the long run, perhaps, a transition toward a world government. Table 19-1 sums up the basic distinctions between the old security game and the new socioeconomic game, which was perceived to have taken its place.

INTERDEPENDENCE AND AMERICAN NORMS

The fundamental assumption underlying both supranational integration and interdependence was that *technological, economic, and social forces operating transnationally will inevitably drive all nations toward greater cooperation.* With a faith in the determinism of economic forces reminiscent of Marxism, proponents of this view were ready to abandon the troublesome world of politics. Perhaps their emphasis on economic necessities should not have been surprising. Americans are especially prone to see economics as the universal palliative for the human condition. The basic assumption of laissez-faire capitalism is that people are motivated economically; the laws of supply and demand will thus transform individual economic selfishness into social benefits, "the greatest good for the greatest number." The role of the government is to stay out of the market. The best government is the one that governs least because political interference with economic laws will upset the results those laws are said to produce.

Not surprisingly, when the logic of the free market is projected internationally, it is possible to conclude that a peaceful international society will be created by free trade. People all over the world will gain a vested interest in peace if they carry on their economic relations. War and trade are supposedly incompatible. War impoverishes and destroys, creating ill will among nations, whereas commerce benefits all participating states. Moreover, war is economically unprofitable, whereas commerce is nationally and individually profitable and creates a common interest in the preservation of peace. Free trade and peace, then, are one and the same cause. This version of the argument for interdependence was already quite popular at the time the United States was born.

> This feeling that one civilization now encompassed the whole world was reinforced by the astounding growth of economic interdependence. The [national political] barriers that existed seemed artificial and ephemeral in comparison with the fine net by which the merchants tied the individuals of the different nations together like "threads of silk." ... [T]he merchants—whether they are English, Dutch, Russian, or Chinese—do not serve a single nation; they serve everyone and are citizens of the whole world. Commerce was believed to bind the nations together and to create not only a community of interests but also a distribution of labor among them—a new comprehensive principle placing the isolated sovereign nations in a higher political unit. In the eighteenth century, writers were likely to say that the various nations belonged to "one society"; it was stated that all states together formed "a family of nations," and the whole globe a "general and unbreakable confederation." [39]

Implicit in this view was the notion that economics was good and politics bad—economics binds people together; politics drives them apart. This version of interdependence largely reflected an attempt to escape from power politics into a calmer, more decent and humane world.[40] For many disillusioned supporters of U.S. cold war policies, the Vietnam War intensified this urge to escape from the wicked world of power politics. Having previously supported a policy that they believed was a crusade in defense of democracy against totalitarianism, they now sought both forgiveness for past errors and a new way to achieve the same goal of a more just and peaceful world. Economics (good and healing), not power (bad and divisive), would achieve this objective. But more than just a reaction to Vietnam, interdependence also represented a deeply felt utopian streak—usually left implicit—in American thinking on international politics. The state system, conflict, and war remained unacceptable. If the United States could no longer abstain from power politics by isolating itself or abolish power politics by democratizing its wicked practitioners, then it would dissolve the nature of international politics in the *bonhomie* of interdependence.

Interdependence, then, according to some of its more original and enthusiastic proponents, was a plea for establishing a world beyond the contemporary nation-state; for changing international behavior and building a better and more cooperative world order; for subordinating power politics to welfare politics and national interests to planetary interests; and for recognizing before it is too late that humanity shares a common destiny. *Advocacy of interdependence thus became a prescription for a strategy of placing constraints on the national egotism and assertiveness of states by catching them in a "web of interdependence" in which they become so deeply enmeshed that they are unable to extricate themselves without suffering great harm, thereby compelling them to cooperate for the "good of humanity."* An argument based on a description of the facts of interdependence, whether in security or in economics, thus shifts almost imperceptibly to advocacy of a course of policy intended to abolish conflict in the state system in favor of a focus on the welfare of all people.

Yet, as British economist Susan Strange has pointed out, the state system is basically characterized

> not by discipline and authority, but by the absence of government, by the precariousness of peace and order, by the dispersion not the concentration of authority, by the weakness of law, and by the large number of unresolved conflicts over what should be done, how it should be done, and who should do it.
>
> Above all, a single, recognized focus of power over time is the one attribute that the international system conspicuously lacks.[41]

That the term *regime* is used so often to describe cooperation between states in these circumstances suggests the special meaning with which the term has been vested: the collective management by the "international community" *in the absence of world government* of what is now commonly called the transnational or global agenda (population, food, resources, ocean management, and so forth). Regimes composed of agreements—treaties plus associated international machinery—are viewed as an essential ingredient of a spreading "global political process" or expanding "politics of global problem solving."[42] According to Strange,

> All these international arrangements dignified by the label *regimes* are only too easily upset when either the balance of bargaining power or the perception of national interests (or both together) change among those states who negotiated them. In general, moreover, *all the areas in which regimes in a national context exercise the central attributes of political discipline are precisely those in which corresponding international arrangements that might conceivably be dignified with the title are conspicuous by their absence.*[43]

Strange then succinctly concludes that regime theory "gives the false impression . . . that international regimes are indeed advancing against the forces of disorder and anarchy."[44]

In fact, presently two opposing forces are at work. On the one hand, there is the trend toward greater economic interdependence, which is most visible in the 1992 final push toward a common market in Western Europe, the association of the EFTA with the EC, and the interest of the countries of Eastern Europe and potentially some of the Soviet republics in the EC. Also visible are the North American market between the United States and Canada (a market shortly expected to include Mexico and perhaps later all of Latin

America), the U.S.-Japanese economic relationship, as well as the growing ties between Japan and other Asian countries. Yet nationalism remains alive and well in the relationships among the industrial democracies which are at the core of this more interdependent world. Among EC members, it remains a question whether they are ready to accept a common currency and can move beyond economic ties to common foreign and defense policies. Simultaneously, among the Western states, one of the great dangers, as noted earlier, is the possibility of trade wars among the larger trading blocs.

On the other hand, and dramatized since the collapse of the Soviet empire, is the breakup of nations: Yugoslavia, the Soviet Union, and potentially Czechoslovakia. But this phenomenon is not confined to Eastern Europe and the Balkans or the developing countries. The Quebeçois in Canada have not given up their vision of independence, nor, for example, have the Scots in Britain. Which is the greater force, the trend toward economic union or that toward political self-determination? Will the spread of democracy and the free market, if they last, favor the former? Or will the end of bipolarity and the expansion of democracy to former authoritarian states, whether in Eastern Europe or Africa, strengthen the latter?

For Review

1. If anarchy is the basic cause of conflict, how can states overcome their differences in order to create a world-state?
2. Why is the American experience of building a federal system not a model for the world today?
3. How was functionalism supposed to overcome national differences and contribute toward building a greater "security community"?
4. What were the original expectations about interdependence and why?
5. What common assumption underlies both supranational integration and interdependence?

Notes

1. For example, Dennis Pirages, *Global Ecopolitics* (North Scituate, Mass.: Duxbury Press, 1978); and Pirages, *Global Technopolitics* (Pacific Grove, Calif.: Brooks/Cole, 1980). A popular summary is *Time's* January 2, 1989, issue, "Planet of the Year: Endangered Earth." Also see Lester R. Brown et al., *State of the World 1988* (New York: Norton, 1988); and Mel Gurtov, *Global Politics in the Human Interest* (Boulder, Colo.: Lynne Rienner, 1988).
2. William K. Stevens, "Ozone Layer Thinner, But Forces Are in Place for Slow Improvement," *New York Times*, April 9, 1991. One of the more interesting aspects

of environmental concern is the attention paid to cow gas as a contributory factor to global warming. See the full-page advertisement, "The Goal: A 50% Reduction of Beef Consumption by 2002," *New York Times,* April 14, 1992.

3. An apt summary of this continuing degradation of the planet was written by William K. Stevens, "Humanity Confronts its Handiwork: An Altered Planet," *New York Times,* May 5, 1992.

4. Don Marquis, *the lives and times of archy and mehitabel* (New York: Doubleday, Doran, 1941), 266.

5. Richard W. Sterling, *Macropolitics* (New York: Knopf, 1974), 5-6. Also see Jonathan Schell, *The Fate of the Earth* (New York: Avon Books, 1982), 218-231.

6. Emery Reves, *The Anatomy of Peace* (New York: Harper & Row, 1945), 253-270. Also see Carl Van Doren, *The Great Rehearsal* (New York: Viking, 1948), for a discussion of American constitutional nation building as an example for the world.

7. Inis L. Claude, Jr., *Power and International Relations* (New York: Random House, 1962), 260-261.

8. Hans J. Morgenthau, *Politics among Nations,* 4th ed. (New York: Knopf, 1967), 498, 499. Also see Crane Brinton, *From Many One* (Cambridge, Mass.: Harvard University Press, 1948).

9. Karl Deutsch et al., *Political Community and the North Atlantic Area* (Princeton, N.J.: Princeton University Press, 1957), 5.

10. Amitai Etzioni, *Political Unification* (New York: Holt, Rinehart & Winston, 1965), 4.

11. Deutsch et al., *Political Community,* 3-21.

12. On the process of "learning" and of defining national interests (and how these definitions change), see Joseph S. Nye, Jr., "Neorealism and Neoliberalism," *World Politics* (January 1988): 235-251; and for a case study, see Nye, "Nuclear Learning and U.S.-Soviet Security Regimes," *International Organization* (Summer 1987): 371-402.

13. Deutsch et al., *Political Community,* 46-58.

14. David Mitrany, *A Working Peace System* (London: National Peace Council, 1946).

15. Quoted by Inis L. Claude, Jr., *Swords into Plowshares* (New York: Random House, 1956), 376.

16. Mitrany, *Working Peace System,* 7.

17. Two of the better early discussions of the expected harmonizing of national policies are Michael Shanks and John Lambert, *The Common Market Today—and Tomorrow* (New York: Holt, Rinehart & Winston, 1962), 56-105; and U. W. Kitzinger, *The Politics and Economics of European Integration* (New York: Holt, Rinehart & Winston, 1963), 21-59. Also see Emile Benoit, *Europe at Sixes and Sevens* (New York: Columbia University Press, 1961).

18. Kitzinger, *Politics and Economics of European Integration,* 60-61.

19. Ernst B. Haas, *The Uniting of Europe* (Stanford, Calif.: Stanford University Press, 1958), 12-13.

20. On the institutions of the contemporary EC, see Alberta B. Sbragia, ed., *Euro-Politics* (Washington, D.C.: Brookings, 1990).

21. Haas, *Uniting of Europe,* xiii.

22. Ibid., 13-14. Also see Ron Inglehart, "An End to European Integration?" *American Political Science Review* (March 1967): 91-105; and Inglehart, "The Silent Revolution in Europe: Intergenerational Change in Post-Industrial Societies," *American Political Science Review* (December 1971): 991-1017.

23. Claude, *Swords into Plowshares,* 385.

24. This result is explained by the concept of "equilibrium": see Leon N. Lindberg and Stuart A. Scheingold, *Europe's Would-Be Polity* (Englewood Cliffs, N.J.: Prentice-Hall, 1970). Also see Joseph S. Nye, Jr., *Peace in Parts* (Boston: Little, Brown, 1972).

25. *New York Times,* December 4, 1984.

26. *New York Times,* December 9, 1984.

27. Steven Greenhouse, "As Europe Unites, Outsiders Line Up to Join the Club," *New York Times,* September 4, 1988.

28. "42 Percent of the Voters Said They Lost Respect for Japan While Only 10 Percent Said They Gained Respect. By 23 to 17 Percent, They Have Lost Respect for Germany," *Wall Street Journal,* January 25, 1991.

29. Both quotes are from Craig R. Whitney, "Gulf Fighting Shatters Europeans' 'Fragile Unity,'" *New York Times,* January 25, 1991.

30. In the *New York Times,* see Alan Riding, "A Toothless Europe?" July 4, 1991; and Josef Joffe, "History Repeats, Europe Forgets," August 28, 1991. Also see David Brooks, "A European Superstate? Forget It," *Wall Street Journal,* August 12, 1991.

31. Alan Riding, "Europeans in Accord to Create Vastly Expanded Trading Bloc," *New York Times,* October 23, 1991; Helmut Schmidt, "Birth of a Multination, Maybe," *New York Times,* December 8, 1991; and Mark M. Nelson and Martin duBois, "Pact Expands Europe's Common Market," *Wall Street Journal,* October 23, 1991.

32. Writing in the *New York Times* are Steven Greenhouse, "Ukrainians See a Split as the Law of Nature," December 28, 1990; Greenhouse, "Now Is the Time to Invest in the Soviets," September 1, 1991; and John Tagliabue, "Slovaks Want an Open Marriage," December 28, 1990.

33. Gregory F. Treverton, ed., *The Shape of the New Europe* (New York: Council on Foreign Relations, 1991), 2. And in the *New York Times,* see Alan Riding, "Paris and Germans Propose Creation of European Army," October 17, 1991; Zbigniew Brzezinski, "Conflicted on Europe," November 10, 1991; and Stephen Kinzer, "Germany Now Leading Campaign to Strengthen the European Community," December 2, 1991.

34. Lester Thurow, *Head to Head: The Coming Economic Battle Among Japan, Europe, and America* (New York: Morrow, 1992), 75-85. For a negative assessment of the EC's future, see Walter Goldstein, "EC: Euro-Stalling," *Foreign Policy* (Winter 1991-1992): 129-147.

35. For some of the basic books and articles on the nature of interdependence and the role of power, see Seyom Brown, *New Forces in World Politics* (Washington, D.C.: Brookings, 1974); Brown, *New Forces, Old Forces, and the Future of World Politics* (Glenview, Ill.: Scott, Foresman, 1988); Robert O. Keohane and Joseph S. Nye, *Power and Interdependence,* 2d ed. (Boston: Little, Brown, 1977); Andrew M. Scott, *The Dynamics of Interdependence* (Chapel Hill: University of North Carolina Press, 1982); and Stanley Hoffmann, "Choices," *Foreign Policy* (Fall 1973): 3-42. More popular treatments can be found in Lester R. Brown, *World without Borders* (New York: Vintage, 1973); and Pirages, *Global Ecopolitics.* Excellent critiques may be found in Karl J. Holsti, "A New International Politics? Diplomacy in Complex Interdependence," *International Organization* (Spring 1978): 513-531; and Stanley J. Michalck, Jr., "Theoretical Perspective for Understanding International Interdependence," *World Politics* (October 1979): 136-150.

36. James N. Rosenau, "Capabilities and Control in an Interdependent World," *International Security* (Fall 1976): 44.

37. For a critique of the theory of interdependence as applied to relations between the

First and Third worlds, see Robert W. Tucker, *The Inequality of Nations* (New York: Basic Books, 1977). For a suggestion that the United States make world order, rather than the balance of power, the focus of its policy, see Stanley Hoffmann, *Primacy of World Order* (New York: McGraw-Hill, 1978).

38. Keohane and Nye, *Power and Interdependence*; and the Spring 1982 issue of *International Organization*, which was completely devoted to regimes.

39. Felix Gilbert, *To the Farewell Address* (Princeton, N.J.: Princeton University Press, 1961), 57.

40. For the contrasting and conflicting views on whether or not interdependence is utopian, see Ray Maghoori and Bennett Ramsberg, eds., *Globalism vs. Realism* (Boulder, Colo.: Westview Press, 1982).

41. Susan Strange, "Cave! Hic Dragones: A Critique of Regime Analysis," *International Organization* (Spring 1982): 487.

42. Frederic S. Pearson and J. Martin Rochester, *International Relations* (Reading, Mass.: Addison-Wesley, 1984), Part IV, 395.

43. Strange, "Cave! Hic Dragones," 487 (emphasis added).

44. Ibid., 491. For an interesting critique of integration and regime theory, see Yale H. Ferguson and Richard W. Mansbach, *The Elusive Quest* (Columbia: University of South Carolina Press, 1988), 198-211.

CHAPTER 20

Violence in a 'Unipolycentric' World

The state system remains fundamentally intact. For all the enormous events and changes witnessed by the post-World War II system—decolonization and the birth of many new states, the conflict between rich and poor nations, the nuclear revolution, the global American-Soviet rivalry, growing economic interdependence, and the move toward an integrated Western Europe—the continuities of international politics persist. Even the new environmental issues and calls for "global solutions to global problems" do not mean that observers of ancient conflicts would not quickly recognize the fundamental character of the contemporary "game." [1]

In a world of nation-states, national solutions retain priority over global solutions; indeed, they are a prerequisite for a broader international effort. Fertility, for example, has not been very amenable to agreement among states. The problem of rapidly growing populations is still primarily a national responsibility. What can foreign governments do in the absence of a domestic will to manage this issue? Similarly, emergency food shipments or worldwide food reserves to cope with famine and malnutrition are no substitute for national policies emphasizing agricultural development. These problems, however, require greater national commitments and shifts of internal priorities and resources than most developing countries have been willing to make in the past. For many, painful and difficult structural reforms in land-owning patterns also will be necessary. "Global welfare cannot be properly managed abroad until it has been tolerably managed at home. Without a prior exercise of domestic political authority, the global welfare crisis will not admit to efficient interstate control." [2] States remain the most effective means for resolving nations' internal problems. Like charity, global welfare management must begin at home.

The fact is that the structure of the state system remains decentralized. Given its anarchical character and its emphasis on self-help to protect national security and independence, nations remain trapped by the security dilemma as each nation's effort to enhance its own security turns into a prime cause for insecurity. Even the shift from international anarchy to a security community in Western Europe stemmed fundamentally from America's security guarantee. By protecting Western Europe against the Soviet Union, the United States also protected the European states against one another and laid the foundation for cooperation among them. Moreover, in extending its deterrence to its North Atlantic Treaty Organization (NATO) allies and by making a long-term commitment to their individual and collective security, the United States removed the self-help imperative. Specifically, the American security guarantee removed the principal cause of conflict among the European states: the search for a national defense policy in which all states in an anarchical system trapped by the "security dilemma" must engage. In the absence of a U.S. protective shield, would West Germany, France, Italy, and Britain have moved toward European integration in response to the Soviet threat? During the alliance-building period of the 1950s,

> neither the Soviet challenge nor the destruction of the European balance during World War II were powerful enough to prompt the West Europeans to transcend their history.... By promising to protect Western Europe against others *and against itself*, the United States swept aside the rules of the self-help game that had governed and regularly brought grief to Europe in centuries past.[3]

Indeed, as the postwar European status quo dissolves, the key question hanging over post-Maastricht Europe is whether the states of Western Europe will once more fall to quarreling with one another, or will their final push toward a larger European Community survive? Equally important, will a reunited Germany be tightly integrated into Western Europe, or will it play East off against West, destabilizing Europe and once more arousing fears of German hegemony, as it did from 1871 to 1945?

The socioeconomic game is also played within the larger framework of the security game. But instead of economic interdependence generating a new kind of international order that weakens the traditional reliance on forcible means of conflict resolution, age-old security problems are likely to continue conditioning the character of interdependence. The United States' postwar security policy and its alliance with Europe established the conditions for the high degree of interdependence that exists today not only within the European Community (EC) but also between its members and the United States. Multiple public and private links in trade, investment, production, and finance bind these highly industrialized states together.

As for Japan, it is often said to be the model of the new "trading state" that will gradually replace the historic territorial-military state because of, first, the increasing priority of low-politics objectives and the ability of industrial economies to satisfy the popular demand for economic prosperity, and, second, the decreasing needs of states to conquer territory as a means of enhancing their wealth and power. In a "trading world," these economic gains could be realized by domestic development; external expansion and war would no longer be necessary. Thus, Japan is the wave of the future because it has demonstrated that the benefits of peaceful economic development and trading with other nations are considerably greater than those arising from military competition and territorial aggrandizement. Japan today is not a "smaller edition" of the United States—that is, a great power once it has converted its economic and financial capabilities into military power and defined a political role for itself. "It is not the American model that Japan will ultimately follow. Rather, it is the Japanese model that America may ultimately follow."[4]

Japan too has been largely able to ignore high-politics considerations since World War II. Instead, it has concentrated on its economic development and an export strategy. This is not because Japan has had no security problem, but rather because the United States has extended deterrence to that country. In nearby Korea, American troops fought a war to keep hostile power distant. Without the U.S. protection of South Korea and the U.S.-Japan security treaty, Japan would have had a security problem, just as the European states did. Instead of devoting less than 1 percent of its gross national product to military spending for most of the postwar period (only in the 1980s did it exceed that level by a small amount), Japan might have had to devote the 3-4 percent common among NATO allies.

If the immediate future is unlikely to witness a transformation of the state system, it will, however, witness three significant changes in the characteristics of the system: (1) more awareness of the global ecological disasters facing humankind, requiring the cooperation of all states;* (2) the greater prominence of economic and financial issues in international politics; and (3) a new strategic environment. The first change was cited briefly in Chapter 19. Certainly, the time for "political ecology"—governmental action, especially by the Western industrial states—appears at hand, as symbolized by the Earth Summit held in Rio de Janeiro in 1992 and attended by 178 countries. The second change has already received much attention in this text. The last change, however, is the focus of this final chapter because this book is concerned mainly with the issue of war and peace.

NEW STRATEGIC ENVIRONMENT: PROLIFERATION OF NUCLEAR ARMS

Hovering over the entire state system has been the threat of the proliferation of nuclear weapons (Table 20-1).[5] During the cold war, there were five

---

* For example, the twelve EC states have committed themselves to holding emissions of the gases that warm the atmosphere to 1990 levels by the year 2000, although Washington has refused to commit itself to that goal for fear that restricting the fuels such as oil and coal that emit carbon dioxide—the main contributor to the greenhouse effect—would be too costly.

Table 20-1 Proliferation of Nuclear Weapons in the Post-Cold War World

Probable	Threshold	Future
India	North Korea	Argentina
Israel		Brazil
Pakistan		Iraq
South Africa		Libya
		South Korea
		Taiwan

SOURCE: Based on Patrick M. Cronin and Jonathan T. Dworken, rapporteurs, *Weapons Proliferation and U.S. National Security* (Alexandria, Va.: Center for Naval Analyses, 1990), 3.

nuclear powers: the United States, Soviet Union, Britain, France, and China, all of whom symbolically occupied the permanent seats in the UN Security Council. There were also four *de facto* nuclear states—Israel,[6] Pakistan,[7] South Africa, and India. India has exploded a "peaceful" bomb, but it also has disclaimed possessing nuclear arms even though it is known to have developed a stockpile of nuclear weapons.[8] And several other states may acquire the bomb soon, including North Korea, which began a program in 1987 and could have a nuclear bomb by the mid-1990s.[9] Libya, which has sought to buy appropriate technologies from various countries; and, until the 1991 war, Iraq (which, by the terms of peace, is not supposed to seek nuclear and other weapons of mass destruction). Why did these and other states, several of them protected during the cold war by the United States with its vastly superior nuclear capability, seek their own nuclear weapons? Why do other states continue to want to acquire a nuclear arsenal?

Why Seek 'the Bomb' ?

Do potential nuclear states not know that a few bombs or missiles are neither an effective deterrent nor a credible retaliatory force? Are they unaware that the extremely high cost of the special delivery system needed for these weapons adds enormously to the cost of obtaining a minimal nuclear strike force? The United States was able to afford five stages of nuclear force development—from subsonic bombers to supersonic bombers to stationary missiles (powered by liquid and solid fuels) to mobile missiles with single warheads to those with multiple warheads. But Britain could not. Perhaps the costs could be reduced if national deterrents could be based on missiles from the start and if the rate of technological change in delivery systems could be slowed or stabilized by agreement among the major powers. The costs, nevertheless, would remain immense. But, more important, the costs of such weapons far outweigh their potential benefits because they are not usable without staking one's very existence on them and they are not accompanied by the influence one might expect. Why seek such dangerous and expensive power?

National Security.   One answer is that, despite the costs and the sacrifice of other needs, national security considerations remain foremost. During the cold war, allies of the United States became increasingly concerned about the credibility of American defense commitments that were made in a period when the United States had an atomic monopoly and vast strategic superiority but that would have had to be carried out in an era of strategic parity. The United States could have easily honored its pledge of protection when it was essentially immune from destruction, but could it have afforded to do so when keeping its word might have spelled its own destruction? First Britain and then France acquired nuclear capabilities because they were uncertain, in view of the growing number of Soviet intercontinental ballistic missiles (ICBMs), that the United States would always and in all circumstances come unhesitatingly to their defense.

And what would West Germany, South Korea, and Israel have done if they had felt unprotected? West Germany and South Korea were U.S. allies (West Germany was forbidden to produce and deploy nuclear arms in the treaty admitting it to NATO), yet if they had felt isolated or vulnerable to external pressures from a hostile state, would not they have been tempted to seek nuclear arms? Indeed, even now the concern remains that a reunified Germany might some day seek nuclear weapons, even though it has legally forsworn to do so. And if North Korea, increasingly isolated politically and failing economically, acquires such arms in the future, can South Korea, despite the nonaggression act signed by the two Koreas in 1991, be far behind?[10] And if both Koreas go nuclear, can Japan, a neighbor of a nuclear China, afford to remain nonnuclear? Similarly, will Iran, a resurgent power in the Persian Gulf, abstain from the search for nuclear arms with a potential nuclear power, Iraq, to the west and nuclear competition to the east between Pakistan and India? Finally, can it be doubted that had it not been for American diplomatic support and extensive military assistance, Israel might already have declared itself a nuclear power?[11] A state such as Israel, often isolated politically and pressured by friends to settle conflicts with its neighbors, is a particularly good candidate for trying to enhance its security by acquiring a nuclear arsenal. Indeed, most estimates suggest that Israel has as many as 200 warheads, and one source has suggested that it may be as high as 300.[12] Another candidate is Taiwan; the United States dropped its security treaty with the Nationalist Chinese government when it recognized the Beijing government in 1979.

It is notable that quests for the bomb often appear to come in pairs. For example, both the United States and the Soviet Union exploded their first bombs during the 1940s. As the Sino-Soviet split grew, China exploded its bomb in 1964, and India's rivalry and past border conflicts with China undoubtedly were as influential in leading to India's 1974 detonation as its bitter quarrel with Pakistan, which then sought its own bomb to counter India's.

Prestige.   "Nukes," then, became status symbols. Just as a great power once demonstrated its primacy by acquiring colonies and a strong navy, so after World War II it had to acquire nuclear weapons. For nations that were .once great powers and that continued to harbor the great-power syndrome and for nations determined to become great powers, nuclear weapons were symbols of strength. In their view, not to possess such weapons was to retreat from greatness and to abandon power and international respect—and therefore self-respect. In the nuclear age, was a nation not impotent if it did not own such arms? Could a nation still claim the authority to make its own decisions on vital issues if it was dependent on another power's nuclear protection? National pride and self-recognition were powerful incentives to the development of national nuclear deterrents.

For Great Britain, nukes became a desperate matter of keeping the *great* in its name, despite its rapid decline in power after 1945. These weapons also fitted its image of itself as the United States' junior partner. For France, defeated during World War II, then suffering the loss of Indochina in 1954, humiliation at Suez in 1956, the loss of the war in Algeria in 1962, and enduring a status in Europe second to Britain and later to West Germany as well, the nuclear bomb became a means of regaining international respect and self-respect. China, carved up during the nineteenth century by the European powers, including Russia, regarded the bomb as a symbol of great-power status and national dignity, as well as a weapon for protection against first the United States and then the Soviet Union. It was indeed difficult not to associate such status and influence with possession of nuclear weapons because the United States, Soviet Union, Britain, France, and China were also all permanent members of the UN Security Council. The bomb seemed to be the admission fee to a rather exclusive club that discriminated against nonnuclear states. As a proponent of India's nuclear weapons program voiced it, "Nuclear weapons are the international currency of power." [13]

India, China's rival and a competitor for leadership in Asia, was the first nation to break the nuclear membership barrier. Brazil, rich in uranium, has sought to establish itself as the number-one power in Latin America. Indeed, Brazil and Argentina, both governed until recently by the military, were jealous rivals. After its defeat by Britain in the Falkland Islands, a humiliated Argentina had an even stronger reason to seek nuclear arms. But Brazil and Argentina's new democratic civilian leaders dampened this rivalry, at least momentarily. For mutual reassurance, the two countries negotiated an agreement over the five-year period 1985-1990, which provided for a system of mutual inspection with the help of the International Atomic Energy Agency (IAEA). In 1990, Brazil's civilian government uncovered a fifteen-year-old secret military bomb project that they halted. Brazilian physicists concluded that the military was only one to two years away from having the materials for a Hiroshima-type bomb. Brazil's new president declared at the time that his country would not conduct nuclear explosions, even for peaceful purposes (as India had claimed for its explosion). [14] The Argentine military government, before it quit in 1983, announced that it had the technology to enrich uranium. But the 1990 agreement between Brazil and Argentina in fact renounced the manufacture of nuclear weapons, although neither country declared that it would sign the Treaty on the Nonproliferation of Nuclear Weapons (NPT), described later in this chapter.[15] Other states, however, are continuing to develop nuclear weapons. The only question is how many will seek them. This, as noted earlier, may be largely a matter of regional ambitions and rivalries: status symbols will become more important to developing states seeking regional and international roles. Israel's bombs may be unannounced, but even if Iraq does not resume the quest for its bomb, perhaps Syria will; the Israeli nuclear arsenal will provide the justification, if not the stimulus, for an Arab bomb. And Iran, potentially the strongest Gulf power, and Algeria may be seeking the bomb as well to realize its potential power.

Domestic Politics.   A final reason states seek nuclear arms is related to domestic politics. In fact, such considerations may reinforce the other two reasons. A nation beset by economic and social problems and low morale may—if it possesses the technological capability—seek the bomb to boost morale, restore national confidence, divert attention from domestic problems, and, of course, mobilize popular support for the government. Great powers traditionally have held military parades to stimulate patriotic feelings. In the same way, Charles de Gaulle in France and Indira Gandhi in India benefited politically from national pride in their first countries' nuclear explosions. Although such a benefit may be only temporary because it does not alter the domestic conditions that may underlie political unpopularity, that possibility does not lessen the incentive to join the nuclear club. Can a nation be truly sovereign, asked de Gaulle, if it cannot take care of its own defense, if it must depend on a foreign state for its security? Leaders of other countries, including developing states, may ask the same question.

Likely Results of Diffusion

Today, 496 civilian nuclear reactors are in operation or under construction in thirty-two nations to produce energy to meet legitimate economic and industrial needs. This does not mean that these states will necessarily seek nuclear weapons. The decision to do so will involve *political* decisions and will depend on each nation's political circumstances and objectives. There is no technological momentum that automatically requires nuclear reactors to be followed by nuclear bombs. Several European states, as well as Japan and Canada, have both the reactors and the requisite nuclear skills but have decided not to build bombs.

Nor would diffusion have equal impacts throughout the world. A Japanese decision to go nuclear would have profound effects, a Swedish decision little. A small Indian nuclear force may frighten Pakistan, but it is not likely to intimidate China. An Israeli nuclear force may overwhelm Israel's neighbors, but it would not be effective against Russia. Indeed, one nuclear explosion does not turn a country into a nuclear power. A militarily significant force requires a credible delivery system and, for many countries, a much larger investment of economic and technological resources than that needed for conventional military forces.[16]

Nonetheless, in a system of nearly 170 nations, the diffusion of nuclear weapons to perhaps twenty or thirty nations will raise considerably the statistical odds of nuclear conflict. It may be unfair to think of non-Western nuclear states as juvenile delinquents of some sort, but such thoughts are generated by the instability of some governments and the fanaticism of some leaders, which raise the specter of irresponsible behavior. Imagine what might have happened had Fidel Castro been in charge of Soviet missiles in 1962—when reportedly he repeatedly urged Moscow to attack the United States—or what Muammar al-Qaddafi might do with a few nuclear bombs. But, even if all leaders were stable, wise, and careful in their calculations, would they be able to avoid accidents or miscalculations in every single confrontation that might occur? Will some states that have acquired a few bombs, especially if they have regional or even extraregional ambitions, not feel compelled to exploit this advantage and attack potential adversaries before the latter acquire their bombs? Will even the major powers be safe? The relatively tiny forces that most potential nuclear states might muster do not appear to threaten the major powers. Yet could not some of them perhaps "rip off an arm," to use de Gaulle's vivid term for what he thought his small French force could do to the Soviet Union? Would they not gain leverage even with a capability of destroying one or two of the major powers' cities?

The Special Case of the Disintegrating Soviet Union

The disintegration of the Soviet Union added new and unexpected twists to the state of nuclear affairs. About 80 percent of Soviet strategic weapons were in Russia; the others were in Ukraine, Belarus, and Kazakhstan, all of which declared they wished to become nuclear-free zones. Russia initially offered to take all the strategic nuclear weapons located in these republics. Later, after the Soviet Union was replaced by the Commonwealth of Independent States (CIS), Russia's president, Boris Yeltsin, declared that Russia (with 1,035 ICBMs and 59 nuclear submarines) would be the only nuclear power; the other three republics in which they were based would eliminate their weapons within the START arms control agreement and the subsequent reduction of tactical nuclear arms pledged by George Bush and Mikhail Gorbachev.

But the danger was that this disavowal of nuclear weapons might change for several reasons. One was these republics' strong sense of nationalism, especially Ukraine's. Indeed, while Ukraine reaffirmed its determination to eliminate its 176 ICBMs by the end of 1994, it was not long before it announced that it would halt the transfer of its tactical nuclear arms to Russia where they were to be sent for dismantling—although later it again pledged itself to transfer them by July 1, 1992.[17] A second reason things might change is that during the negotiations among the republics about their relationships within the new CIS, these strategic weapons—and perhaps the tactical nuclear arms—might become part of the leverage used by the non-Russian republics. All of them have grounds for concern about a possible threat from Russia, the largest and most powerful of the republics even without nuclear arms. Historically the Russians have dominated the czarist and Soviet empires. Thus, the non-Russian republics may not find it that appealing to eliminate their nuclear weapons. Kazakhstan, in fact, with 104 ICBMs, announced that it would not allow Russia to be the only nuclear state in the association; if Russia kept nuclear weapons, it would keep those left after the previously agreed-on arms control measures had been carried out. A third reason for a possible change of heart by Ukraine, Belarus, and Kazakhstan is that there may be some appeal in becoming "instant nuclear powers" and enhancing their sense of national prestige and independence. Ukraine, on declaring its independence, became the world's third largest nuclear power with 3,000 nuclear warheads, including 176 ICBMs with 1,240 warheads; Kazakhstan would be the fourth largest.[18]

Another and potentially very dangerous consequence of the Soviet Union's disintegration and reduction of its military-industrial complex is that thousands of unemployed scientists and technicians trained in building nuclear weapons might try to sell their knowledge for hard currencies to such countries as Iraq, North Korea, Libya, or Iran, just as Soviet industries are already selling their missile engines, space stations, and other parts of their space program. There were an estimated 900,000 military and civilian personnel in the nuclear weapons community. Of these, about 2,000 have a knowledge of nuclear weapons design and 3,000-5,000 have worked in uranium enrichment and plutonium production. One example of a group selling its expertise is the International Chetek Corporation, which is selling "peaceful nuclear explosives" for such commercial applications as the incineration of toxic wastes and breeder reactors. "As glasnost mutates into an unbridled high-tech sell-off . . . what is on sale is not Manhattan Project surplus, but systems explicitly made for fighting World War III that never was." [19] What then are the implications of this "Have bomb, will travel" attitude for nuclear proliferation? Will the Saddam Husseins be able to buy what they need in their nuclear quests—both nuclear experts and perhaps even some tactical nuclear weapons? To resolve this problem, the United States and other Western states offered a plan that would establish a scientific institute to keep the thousands of Soviet nuclear scientists and other military scientists occupied at home. And Yeltsin proposed a plan for joint U.S.-Russian cooperation on a global antimissile shield to protect countries against accidental or unauthorized missile launchings. These plans for the employment of Soviet nuclear scientists indicate the widespread fear that the breakup of the Soviet scientific complex could lead to a rapid diffusion of nuclear weapons among Third World states.[20]

Strategies to Slow Proliferation

Technological Strategy.   One possible way to halt or slow nuclear proliferation is use of a technological strategy. The United States now refuses to export plutonium reprocessing and uranium enrichment facilities. To set an example for other nations, President Jimmy Carter announced in 1977 that within its own boundaries the United States would not use plutonium as a commercial reactor fuel. Congress, in fact, has approved a law banning economic or military aid to any country that sells or receives such facilities not subjected to adequate safeguards.[21] West Germany and France have sold nuclear fuel cycles in the past, though both have declared that they will not export reprocessing plants in the future.[22] The pressure to sell remains, however, because the nuclear business is profitable. But there are other reasons besides profit. For example, France and especially Italy provided nuclear assistance to Iraq until its war with Iran in 1980. Italy, which imported one-third of its oil from Iraq during the 1970s, was seeking to ensure long-term access to Iraqi oil.[23]

The basic approach, however, has been multilateral. In 1975, the United States, Soviet Union, Britain, West Germany, France, Japan, and Canada met to devise a series of principles for regulating their nuclear exports. The seven original members of this Suppliers' Club (which later expanded to include Belgium, the Netherlands, Sweden, Italy, Switzerland, East Germany, Poland, and Czechoslovakia) agreed that recipients of nuclear technology must apply internationally accepted safeguards drawn up by the International Atomic Energy Agency and that they must give assurances that they will not use these imports for making nuclear explosives, even for such peaceful purposes as excavation.[24] President Carter was particularly insistent on tighter safeguards and controls. He proposed that the IAEA inspect "all nuclear materials and equipment" of countries receiving nuclear fuel from the United States for their reactors so that closer supervision could be exercised over their nuclear energy programs. (India has been a major exception.)[25] The Reagan administration's attitude toward nuclear proliferation, however, was not as strict. Pakistan's efforts to acquire a bomb, for example, were less of a concern than its help against the Soviets in Afghanistan.

But the IAEA is grossly understaffed; in 1990, it had only 197 inspectors to cover the 934 facilities under safeguard.[26] It can report violations but cannot apply sanctions. Indeed, it is questionable whether the agency is capable of detecting all diversions of nuclear weapons. The implementation of safeguards to ensure against the diversion of nuclear materials requires the cooperation of the nations possessing the nuclear reactors. Iran, for example, has forbidden any IAEA inspection of its nuclear facilities since the 1979 revolution. North Korea has not permitted IAEA inspection either, although in December 1991 it declared that it would allow IAEA inspection of all its nuclear facilities in the future. But even worse, inspectors have no authority to search for secret sites. After the discovery in 1991 of Iraq's extensive violation of its pledge not to acquire nuclear weapons under the nonproliferation treaty, the IAEA director asked governments to give him any evidence they had on countries violating the treaty. He would then order special inspections of suspected sites, even if that country had not declared them to be nuclear sites or had placed them under IAEA safeguards. Yet, despite the worry that other countries might be cheating, IAEA inspectors would have no automatic right of entry. Special inspections could be ordered only by the UN Security Council and in countries that had signed the nonproliferation treaty. Even if it detects diversion, the IAEA is powerless to act. The technological strategy, in fact, may be deficient *even if* all members of the Suppliers' Club cooperate (an uncertainty at best given the profits involved), for the club may find itself outflanked by the club of "nuclear outcasts," composed of such insecure states as Israel and South Africa. These states can help one another while evading international restrictions. In return for uranium from South Africa, Israel reportedly has shared its nuclear expertise. Other potential suppliers are Argentina, Brazil, India, and China.

Thus, it may be too late to turn back the technological clock. In 1980, the nuclear experts from sixty-six countries who had participated in the International Nuclear Fuel Cycle Evaluation concluded after two years of study that the U.S. strategy for curbing the diffusion of nuclear weapons by banning the manufacture and use of plutonium was too late. A country could not be stopped from building a bomb by outlawing plutonium-based technology; too much scientific knowledge and technology to develop nuclear weapons are available—indeed, they may have outstripped international control mechanisms.

Legal Strategy.   In addition to a technological strategy, there is a legal one. For example, the almost 142 current signatories of the Treaty on the Nonproliferation of Nuclear Weapons, which expires in 1995, agreed that if they are already nuclear powers, they will not provide nuclear weapons to other countries; if they are not nuclear powers, they will not try to manufacture nuclear devices. They also will accept IAEA-administered safeguards for their peaceful nuclear activities. The aim was to ensure that nuclear materials are not diverted into weapons making. The legal strategy for halting proliferation involves gaining maximum adherence to the treaty. All former Warsaw Pact countries were treaty signatories, reflecting Soviet concern about nuclear diffusion. The weakness of this approach is that any country can terminate its adherence to the treaty with only ninety days' notice. Furthermore, Argentina, Brazil, China, France, India, Israel, and Pakistan, all believed to possess advanced nuclear technology, have not yet signed the pact. Both China and France have announced that they will sign the NPT, but China made no commitment to halt its current export of nuclear technologies, allegedly for civilian purposes, which could be adapted to nuclear weapons programs—for example, the sales of missile parts to Pakistan—and, as noted earlier Brazil and Argentina agreed only to inspect one another under IAEA supervision.

Thus, the number of holdouts is shrinking. In 1992, Ukraine, Kazakhstan, and Belarus all pledged to sign the NPT.

It is worth emphasizing in this context that IAEA serves only as a monitoring agency for verifying national accounting systems for nuclear materials. It is also an agency very dependent on the good will of the nations whose facilities it is inspecting. The problem is not only the few nations resisting NPT—India, Pakistan, and Israel—but also some of the signatory nations. A nation bent on cheating can certainly do so, as Iraq did. After the Gulf war, its initial admission—under threat of a possible U.S. military attack—that it had been running three secret programs to enrich uranium, followed by a later admission that its scientists had secretly extracted a small amount of plutonium from spent fuel (usable as an explosive in an atomic bomb), alarmingly demonstrated that it was possible to violate the NPT pledge not to produce nuclear arms while opening nuclear sites to IAEA inspections. North Korea is another suspected NPT signatory.[27]

What was particularly troubling about the Iraqi effort to produce enriched uranium and plutonium was that while part of the effort relied on advanced methods and imported equipment, part of it—to America's great shock—relied on the now old-fashioned technology used by the United States fifty years earlier in making the two atomic bombs that were dropped on Japan; Iraq reproduced this technology. Not only does this make a nonnuclear state's acquisition of a bomb easier, especially if it already has an ostensibly peaceful nuclear program, but it also raises the question of how future efforts can be prevented even if current production facilities are destroyed (as may happen in the case of Iraq).[28] Moreover, who else is circumventing the NPT by using long-ago declassified blueprints? [29]

Political Strategy. Finally, there is a political strategy, based on ensuring the security of nonnuclear states. The choices surrounding the proliferation of nuclear arms remain fundamentally political, rather than technical, and they are agonizing because conflicting values and consequences are at stake.[30] A number of policy options are available. One is to protect the security interests of potential nuclear states by supplying them with conventional arms or giving them a sense of security through an alliance relationship with the United States (although providing conventional weapons may risk starting a local conventional arms race). A second option is for potential rival states to try to settle some of their differences and perhaps even cooperate on specific nuclear programs. In recent years, the civilian governments of Argentina and Brazil ended their nuclear weapons programs. India and Pakistan negotiated an agreement not to attack one another's nuclear facilities, but theirs is a long and bitter rivalry. The Nationalists on Taiwan and the Chinese Communists on the mainland are also seeking to improve their relationship. In the Middle East, progress in the peace talks between Israel and the Arab states would help relieve regional insecurities, but the prospects for a resolution of Israeli-

Arab-Palestinian differences remain clouded, thus casting a pall over President Bush's call for the destruction of all weapons of mass destruction in the Middle East. A third option is pressure, which the United States applied to South Korea and Taiwan; it forced Taiwan to shut down its largest civilian reactor. In 1988, the United States urged the Saudis to sign the nonproliferation treaty as evidence that they had no intention of acquiring nuclear warheads for the medium-range missiles they had purchased from China. Americans were concerned that this might spark a new Middle East arms race. The Saudis signed. In 1991, concern over North Korea's possible acquisition of the bomb in the near future led the United States to seek Soviet, Chinese, and Japanese help—pressuring North Korea to halt its suspected nuclear weapons program. Japan later withheld recognition and economic aid for North Korea.

Thus, with the present state system, its anarchical nature, and the security problem that it poses for all member states, "there are no simple solutions that are feasible, no feasible solutions that are simple, and no solutions at all that are applicable across the board." [31] Or, as two physicists and one political scientist wrote,

> In the final analysis, it would be illusory to think that nuclear weapons proliferation could be severely limited by imposing controls on the sale of nuclear power facilities. The fundamental problem remains: minimizing the motivation nations have to acquire nuclear weapons altogether. This involves issues far beyond the realm of a nation's interests and involvement in the development of nuclear power to generate electricity. [32]

The fact is, however, that during the cold war preventing nuclear proliferation was not an absolute for either superpower. Strategic interests often took priority. Because the United States needed the help of Pakistan to assist the anti-Soviet guerrillas in Afghanistan, as noted, it tended to close its eyes to Pakistan's active quest for a bomb. Or profits took precedence. West Germany's government, for example, chose to ignore the involvement of West German companies in nuclear transactions with India, Pakistan, Iraq, and Brazil. Only in the latter case did the Carter administration successfully vigorously voice its objection. But by and large, West Germany was too invaluable an ally in NATO, and Washington exercised little pressure on its government. Whether the end of the cold war and the Iraqi example will provide the great powers with a greater collective incentive to give greater priority to nonproliferation and less to the kinds of strategic and commercial interests that they had heeded earlier remains to be seen. [33]

Proliferation and the Military Option: Preventive War?

The important psychological barrier posed by the nonproliferation treaty is not a foolproof one. Future proliferation is most likely to occur in the developing world. Among the industrial democracies, only Germany and Japan are potential nuclear states. Protected by the United States during the cold war, neither needed to pursue nuclear weapons. Moreover, the victors of

World War II were determined to prevent German acquisition of nuclear arms, and West Germany forswore such acquisition. It did so again after reunification. Japan too was not eager to obtain nuclear weapons. Indeed, since Japan had been the first nation on which two bombs had been dropped (at the end of World War II), it suffered from what has been called a "nuclear allergy." But in the post-cold war period, no longer needing American protection, both states have regained more freedom of maneuver and more voice in how they want to conduct their foreign policies. Like other great powers throughout time, and more recently Britain and France, Germany and Japan may pursue nuclear arms at some point in the future. Both powers have the right almost fifty years after their defeat to expect that their former enemies and postwar allies will accept them as they would other great powers.

Yet the threat of nuclear diffusion does not really come from these two countries. As noted in Chapter 6, Germany, Europe's dominant economic power, is most likely to pursue its goals in Eastern Europe by economic means. German influence and prestige will grow as it helps the states to its east with capital investment and trade. No longer enduring a threat to its security from the former Soviet Union (which needs Germany economically), and enjoying prosperity at home, and despite finding integration of the former East Germany into the national economy somewhat painful, Germany has no need to pursue its goals by military means, including nuclear weapons. In fact, to do so would create a coalition against it. For Japan, the logic is similar. It is achieving economically the kind of influence throughout Asia that it sought unsuccessfully militarily during World War II. Because its security is not threatened, Japan does not need to build up its military power, let alone develop nuclear weapons. Quite apart from strong Japanese domestic resistance to a powerful military, the rest of Asia would react politically too. Japan did extremely well as a "trading state" during the cold war; it has no reason to change its course now. Thus, nuclear proliferation is unlikely to occur in the developed world.

One hopeful sign in this respect is the nonproliferation treaty. It has become a politically powerful symbolic norm. Whether nations acquire nuclear weapons depends on their leaders' calculations of the gains and costs. If the strong international approval of the nuclear nonproliferation treaty is any evidence, their leaders must take into account the increasing international disapproval of states with nuclear ambitions. Thus, security, prestige, and domestic motivations for seeking nuclear weapons must be balanced not just against financial costs and military advantage, but also against the widespread belief among nonnuclear states that states wanting such weapons are a threat to peace. The widespread global support for the nonproliferation treaty has raised the political price for acquiring nuclear arms, thereby perhaps lowering the incentive to do so, at least for some nations. It also maintains the pressure on the nonsignatories. Nevertheless, in the final analysis, as the states that have already acquired nuclear weapons have shown, the decision to have—or not to have—the bomb is very much a national decision, at best only marginally influenced by external pressures to forgo it.

All this being said, the real issue is not so much whether nuclear proliferation can be halted but whether a world with multiple nuclear states is manageable. Today, it is possible to pursue the requisite technologies *covertly*, leaving the world guessing about a state's nuclear status. Iraq, Pakistan, and Israel are examples of this situation. And if the most that can probably be expected is the slowing of proliferation, can the nations acquiring nuclear weapons be stopped from using them?

The critical question is whether the deterrence that restrained the superpowers can be replicated among the new nuclear states at the regional level. This seems dubious. It is unrealistic to assume that all future nuclear state governments will be stable and unsusceptible to civil wars, strong ideological passions, territorial designs, or "crazy" leaders; that they will be able to resist any temptation to preempt when either their missiles/bombers or their adversary's nuclear delivery systems are vulnerable to a first strike; and that accidental war or unauthorized use can be prevented. Indeed, rather than increasing a nation's security, the acquisition of nuclear weapons may result in the opposite.

This was demonstrated in 1981 when Israel, fearing that Iraq might produce nuclear bombs to be dropped on Israel once a French-built reactor was constructed, attacked preventively.[34] Iraq had led the Rejectionist Front against Israel after Egypt and Israel had made peace. Even though Iraq had signed the NPT, Israeli leaders had good reasons for suspecting that Iraq sought to acquire nuclear weapons,[35] and that its leader was ruthless enough to use them on Israel's few cities. At the time of the Israeli bombing, there was great outrage at the United Nations and even in Washington, which was seeking to improve its relationship with Iraq, the foe of Iran. How dare Israel interpret its national security interests so broadly that it, a nonsignatory of NPT, could attack a signatory state with which Israel was not at war and which had declared that it had no intention of building a nuclear weapon.

In retrospect, Israel's preventive attack made good sense. In its war with Iran, Iraq used chemical warfare in 1984 when its forces were on the defensive against larger Iranian forces engaged in an effective "offensive to end all offensives." The Iraqis apparently felt that their choice was between offending world public opinion and being overrun by the Iranians.[36] Had Iraq possessed nuclear weapons at the time, was it not equally likely that Saddam Hussein would have used them in the circumstances he faced? Indeed, considering that nuclear weapons are far more destructive than chemical ones, why, after he had failed to achieve a quick victory and the Iranians had launched a successful counteroffensive, should Saddam Hussein have endured a long war with heavy casualties and skyrocketed his debt to other Arab states when a few bombs dropped on Iranian forces or cities or both would have won a speedy victory?

In any event, the key question is whether the Israeli bombing of the Iraqi reactor was merely a deviant case. No other country has used such a preventive strategy against a potential adversary who might be seeking a nuclear capability. The United States did not do so against the Soviet Union, which did not do so against China (although reportedly it sounded Washington out about a joint attack and was rebuffed), which in turn did not do so against India, which has not preempted against Pakistan. Not even Israel has attempted a repeat performance, although its policy remains that of preventing hostile Arab states from introducing nuclear weapons. Israel considers this an issue of survival. Unlike the superpowers who believed that nuclear weapons deterred nuclear weapons, Israel does not believe—and did not in 1981—that its possession of nuclear weapons would deter an Iraq or other hostile states. Admittedly, Israel has never declared itself to be a nuclear state, but if the Israelis felt that they had to make that absolutely clear, leaving no doubt in the minds of their potential enemies, they could do so. Perhaps if Iraq had not invaded Kuwait and precipitated a war Israel might have been tempted to attack Iraq again before it gained nuclear weapons—estimated before that war to be anytime from 1993-1995. Before the Gulf war, the Iraqi leader, in trying to discourage just such a preventive strike, announced that he would "scorch half of Israel" if it attacked Iraq. Presumably, he hoped Israel would not dare risk a repeat performance of its 1981 attack.

The broader question raised by the Israeli attack, however, remains. How will states, especially the great powers, deal with the growing threat of the diffusion of ever more dangerous and potent military technologies, be they nuclear, chemical, biological, or the missiles to deliver them (the last three are covered later in this chapter)? Perhaps, as President Bush has suggested, the Western powers will exercise more stringent control over exports of nuclear technology than in the past to prevent their industries from helping the nuclear ambitions of the developing states. Specifically, Bush has proposed a freeze and eventual ban on missiles, a ban on poison gas weapons, and an end to the production of material for use in nuclear arms.[37] But will the Iraqi crisis of 1990 really be such a decisive turning point in the history of nuclear proliferation? Perhaps in some circumstances, arms control measures and confidence-building steps might be tried. But regional problems such as those in the Middle East-Persian Gulf area seem less subject to the techniques used by the superpowers during the cold war. Even in moments of great tension, the superpowers did not go to war. And over the entire four decades of their "adversary-partnership" relationship, they talked to one another.

By contrast, the states of the Middle East-Persian Gulf area have a history of warfare, and some key countries do not even talk to one another. Can one be sure that ambitious regional regimes that have devoted considerable resources over many years to the quest for weapons of mass destruction can be deterred as the United States and the Soviet Union deterred one another? Can ruthless rulers (such as Saddam Hussein), who seem to place little value on human life or freedom, or fanatical leaders (such as the late Ayatollah Khomeini of Iran), who talk of seeking martyrdom, really be deterred from seeking their objectives by the likelihood that their countries will suffer catastrophic damage if they miscalculate? Will they indeed believe that they may be committing suicide? Would they find it credible that the United States or another Western state with a sizable nuclear arsenal would stop them once they possess the capability to destroy American bases overseas or a British or French city or two—and some day, perhaps, an American city or two? Thus, when a Libya is suspected of having built chemical warfare facilities, as in 1987-1988 when the Reagan administration was said to be considering a strike to destroy them but did not, or an Iran is about to acquire nuclear or biological warfare capabilities, will the United States, Britain, France, and others just stand by passively? Will they just hope that the Qaddafis and Saddam Husseins will somehow be deterred from threatening to use or using these weapons to achieve their purposes? Should not the Israeli option of preventive war be considered seriously by the great powers? Indeed, can it be avoided? Once a regional state has nuclear weapons, will it not be too late for preemption? Even if the great powers possess an overwhelmingly superior arsenal, the prospect that the adversary might hit a couple of cities may well self-deter them. The brutal truth about the post-cold war world is that relatively small and less-developed countries, such as Iraq, may from one day to the next emerge as threats not only to states in their region but also far beyond.

It may perhaps be said that the United States is not the world's policeman, especially in the post-cold war period. But if the most powerful nation militarily in the world fails to act, who will? Whether it is the kind of aggression expressed in Kuwait, which probably would have been unopposed had Washington not acted, or the dangers that will likely follow the acquisition of some of the most lethal weapons by such states as Iraq under the present leadership, the consequences for the world may be disastrous if the United States fails to lead—if necessary alone but preferably with other great powers, perhaps acting through the United Nations. In a unipolycentric world, only the United States can preserve a minimum of order.

To put it more starkly: until now nuclear weapons have been considered a means of deterrence or inhibiting war and of imposing restraints on conflicts. The question today then is whether their acquisition by some states would not provoke a war against those countries. For example, if Iraq had withdrawn from Kuwait and Saddam Hussein had been left in power with time to further develop his military power and to renew his aggression when he had acquired more lethal weapons, what would have been the point? He had to be defeated, neutralized as a military threat to the region, and deprived of his arsenal, especially his potential for weapons of mass destruction. The U.S.-led war against Iraq should therefore be classified as a preventive war.

This fact was reinforced by Iraq's violations of the cease-fire terms calling for the destruction of its stocks of mass-destruction weapons, including its enriched uranium and nuclear facilities, which even the United States believed it had largely destroyed during the war. But after the war an Iraqi defector revealed the existence of several nuclear sites previously unknown to U.S. intelligence and the fact that Iraq had twice the amount of enriched uranium previously believed, enough for possibly two Nagasaki-size bombs. What was particularly shocking about this was not only the failure of Western intelligence agencies and Iraq's ability to evade the NPT, which it had signed, but also the revelation that Iraq could probably have put the bomb together within twelve to eighteen months instead of the three to five years estimated before the war. Indeed, with German components for a previously unknown uranium enrichment complex,[38] it might have produced four to five bombs a year in addition to any that might have been produced by other methods. Not only had the United States underestimated the size and sophistication of Iraq's nuclear weapons program and overstated the damage inflicted during the air war, but also it appeared that Iraq had even been working on a hydrogen bomb, as well as a missile to carry nuclear warheads. The defector's information also raised questions about whether chemical and biological plants and storage areas may have escaped detection and destruction during the war. When the UN inspectors charged with the task of destroying Iraq's nuclear facilities showed up, they were refused admission.

Having gone to war basically to destroy Saddam Hussein's potential to threaten or wage war with mass-destruction weapons, the allies could not then let him hang onto this capability. Thus, they made repeated threats of air strikes against suspected nuclear, as well as biological and chemical, sites whenever Iraq sought to block the UN inspectors. But since the Iraqis clearly have been dispersing and hiding their uranium and other nuclear materials, and some of their nuclear facilities have been concealed and hardened, bombing suspected sites is no more a guarantee of destroying Iraq's nuclear capability than the bombing during the war. Saddam Hussein may yet be able to build a bomb.[39] Without question, he has taught the world the folly of relying too much on "inspectors" to "safeguard" against nuclear proliferation. Other Third World dictators now know they can build a bomb with minimum risk of detection. If war and subsequent UN inspections cannot halt Iraq from building a bomb, how can other states be stopped short of military action?

But in the words of the British foreign secretary, speaking for the Western allies in the recent war, "We are going to make sure, one way or another, that Iraq does not become . . . a nuclear power."[40] In first going to war, and then considering new air attacks to prevent Iraq from becoming a nuclear power, the United States and its allies had in fact adopted the Israeli solution. In the new post-cold war world, it may become not only necessary to deter but also, if required, to disarm states that are likely to acquire and then threaten to use nuclear and other mass-destruction weapons.

PROLIFERATION OF MISSILE TECHNOLOGY AND CHEMICAL-BIOLOGICAL WARFARE CAPABILITIES

The danger stemming from potential nuclear proliferators is increased even more by the growing proliferation of missile technology. Missiles armed with conventional explosives (such as the SCUDs during the Gulf war) are usually inefficient. But if they are inaccurate as well (as were the SCUDs) they are militarily ineffective.* Bombers, by comparison, are much more efficient and effective because they can carry large bomb loads and, unless shot down, they can be used on multiple missions. Missiles carry relatively small warheads and are not reusable. But armed with mass-destruction capabilities, a missile can be extremely efficient and effective. Its enormously destructive warhead does not even have to be very accurate to destroy its target—although today most Western missiles are quite accurate (as is the later-generation SCUD)—and its great speed gives it a far greater ability to penetrate and survive any defenses than a bomber. It is this mating of what is rapidly becoming a "conventional" delivery system with unconventional warheads that accentuates the danger of regional states acquiring the knowledge and capability to build an atomic bomb.[41]

This is not to say that missiles with conventional explosives are not feared. During the Iran-Iraq war, the latter used missiles with conventional explosives to attack Iranian cities and demoralize their inhabitants. China has exported missiles not only to Saudi Arabia but also to Iran, where in 1987 they threatened U.S. warships in the Persian Gulf. It also has supplied much of the technology for Brazil's missiles. In fact, since the superpowers, of whom the Soviet Union had been the principal supplier of missiles, eliminated their short- and intermediate-range missiles, China has had a near monopoly on ballistic missiles with a range of 300-3,000 miles.[42] Besides these states, surface-to-surface missiles of varying ranges, payloads, and accuracy are now found in the arsenals of Afghanistan, Algeria, Egypt, India, Iran, Israel, Korea (North and South), Libya, Syria, Taiwan, and Yemen. In several instances, countries have successfully modified the foreign-supplied missiles, especially extending their range. Indeed, in late 1989 Iraq tested a forty-eight-ton, three-stage, twenty-five-meter-long missile that allegedly had a range of about 2,000 kilometers—far enough to hit targets in Europe. Israel is developing a missile based on its satellite launch vehicle that could have a range of 5,200-7,200 kilometers, sufficient to hit all targets in the Middle East as well as Moscow. Israel already has a missile in the 1,300-kilometer range, and India has one with a range of 2,500 kilometers. As one Indian official reportedly said, "As long as China can reach New Delhi with its ICBMs, India will remain in a weak position. . . . Can any self-respecting country accept that?"[43]

This spread of ballistic missiles is a Third World phenomenon (see Table 20-2). Twenty developing states in the Middle East, South and East Asia, Latin America, and southern Africa either possess or are trying to acquire missiles. What is most disturbing is that the area of greatest concentration is the North Africa-Middle East-Persian Gulf region. No less committed are the countries of South and East Asia.

---

* Politically, however, they can be damaging. In January 1991, after Iraqi-launched SCUDs began to rain down on Israel, considerable U.S. skill was required to restrain Israel from responding in kind or from breaking up the anti-Iraqi coalition.

Table 20-2 Proliferation of Ballistic Missiles in the Post-Cold War
World

IRBM	*MRBM*	*SRBM*
Brazil[a]	Argentina[a]	Afghanistan
India[a]	Brazil[a]	Argentina[a]
Iraq[a]	Egypt[a]	Brazil[a]
Israel	Iran[a]	Egypt
Saudi Arabia	Iraq	India[a]
South Africa[a]	Israel	Indonesia[a]
	Libya[a]	Iraq[b]
	North Korea[a]	Israel
	Pakistan[a]	Libya
	Taiwan[a]	North Korea
		Pakistan[a]
		South Korea
		Syria
		Taiwan
		Yemen

SOURCE: Based on Patrick M. Cronin and Jonathan T. Dworken, rapporteurs, *Weapons Proliferation and U.S. National Security* (Alexandria, Va.: Center for Naval Analyses, 1990), 8.

NOTE: Missile ranges are: intermediate-range ballistic missile (IRBM), 1,000 kilometers; medium-range ballistic missile (MRBM), 300-1,000 kilometers; and short-range ballistic missile
(SRBM), 100-300 kilometers (not covered by the Missile Technology Control Regime organized
in 1987). Under the terms of the Persian Gulf war cease-fire, Iraq is supposed to destroy all
missiles with a range of more than 144 kilometers or ninety miles.

[a] Under development, although Argentina has announced that it is ending its missile development.

In 1987, after four years of negotiations, the United States, Canada, Britain,
France, Italy, West Germany, and Japan organized the Missile Technology
Control Regime (MTCR) to limit the export of all technology that might assist
other countries in building missiles.[44] The fear, of course, was the mating of
nuclear warheads and missile technology as more nations mastered the latter.
To the degree that nuclear materials and technological diffusion could not be
prevented, only slowed down, control of the means of delivering warheads
was a second line of defense. Otherwise, acquisition of missiles from China,
for example, could create "instant" nuclear powers.

But a policy to limit the export of missile technology may be too late since
the signatories did not include the Soviet Union or China. The Soviet Union
(in early 1990, before its breakup, however, had declared it would adhere to
the MTCR's export guidelines).[45] While China too vowed to observe the
MTCR's guidelines, Washington specifically warned that country against
further sales to the Middle East.[46] North Korea too, has been an active post-
Gulf salesman of an upgraded SCUD missile with a larger, longer-range, more
accurate warhead (able to carry a chemical warhead) to Syria, Libya, Egypt,
and Iran.[47] Indeed, even among the signatories of the MTCR questions have

Table 20-3 Proliferation of Chemical Weapons in the Post-Cold War World

Known	*Probable*	*Reported*
Iraq[a]	Iran	Afghanistan
	Israel	Burma
	Libya	China
	Syria	Egypt
		Ethiopia
		North Korea
		South Korea
		Taiwan
		Thailand
		Vietnam

SOURCE: Based on Patrick M. Cronin and Jonathan T. Dworken, rapporteurs, *Weapons Proliferation and U.S. National Security* (Alexandria, Va.: Center for Naval Analyses, 1990), 6.

[a] Under the terms of the Persian Gulf war cease-fire, Iraq is supposed to surrender its stocks of chemical weapons and not produce or seek other such weapons.

been raised about whether Germany and France, together with Belgium, Denmark, Sweden, and Switzerland, are willing to abstain from lucrative sales that will help such countries as Brazil build a rocket motor capable of launching long-range missiles, which then can be sold to such states as Iraq and Libya, its best arms clients, who seek these missiles.[48] But quite apart from the question of whether the MTCR will be undermined by some of its members and the fact that Third World nations (except for China) have not yet placed nuclear warheads on their missiles, it must not be overlooked that these missiles can carry chemical warheads.

The gases used in such warheads can be easily manufactured or bought in the international market. Iraq used chemical warfare regularly in its eight-year war against Iran; in fact, Iraq was the first nation to do so on such a scale since World War I. By the time U.S. forces were sent in 1990 to defend Saudi Arabia, Iraq's chemical weapons program was probably the largest in the Third World.[49] Iraq admitted that it possessed 18,000 shells, bombs, and missiles filled with poison gas and paralyzing nerve agents. After the war, however, this admission turned out to be on the low side. Among other countries, Egypt, Iran, Israel, Libya, North Korea, Syria, Taiwan, and Vietnam are all believed to have active programs as well (see Table 20-3). Altogether, according to the U.S. Central Intelligence Agency, twenty nations are seeking to develop or already possess chemical weapons. Chemical agents may not be as destructive as nuclear weapons against a protected and forewarned population, but the shock effect and the horror of such weapons are nevertheless very great. What was therefore particularly disturbing was the lack of any global condemnation of Iraq when it first used lethal gas, even though, for its signers, chemical warfare was outlawed by the 1925 Geneva Protocol. Given this lack of protest and condemnation, why should any country fear violating a possible future ban on global production? Clearly, that is what the Soviet Union and the United States expected when they agreed in 1990 to reduce their chemical stockpiles by 98 percent over a number of years and immediately stop production of chemical arms even without waiting for the global production ban to take effect; a year later, the United States declared that it would destroy all its supplies.

Even more horrible is the possible use of biological weapons in the future. Because just tiny amounts of bacterial agents can cause widespread infection, they are potentially much deadlier than chemical weapons. The CIA has estimated that at least ten nations are trying to produce such biological weapons. Any state with a pharmaceutical industry can produce biological warfare agents. Again, Iraq, one of the 111 signers of the Biological Weapons Convention in 1972, reportedly had a biological warfare facility. Thus, as a preventive measure U.S. and British forces opposing Iraqi forces in 1990-1991 received germ warfare shots.[50] Syria also is said to have a biological research facility.

DIFFUSION OF CONVENTIONAL ARMS

The possible spread of nuclear and other mass-destruction arms is still largely in the future, although missiles are being found more widely. The spread of conventional arms, however, is a reality. The arms trade has been growing rapidly, symptomatic of the diffusion of power in the state system from the Western industrial states to the developing countries. During the 1970s, it also reflected the need of the Western states to earn money to pay for oil, as well as the continuing competition of the superpowers for influence in the Third World. Arms became not only big business (for the Soviets as well as the West) but also a key instrument of contemporary diplomacy. Both the United States and the Soviet Union used arms sales to gain influence and compete for the allegiance of certain developing countries. Sales also have become, in a sense, a substitute for the traditional means of seeking these goals, such as alliances and the deployment of forces in other countries for their protection.

> Arms sales ... have become a key instrument of diplomacy for the weapons suppliers, in some cases the best one available to them. There has been a decline in the traditional instruments of reassurance and diplomacy, such as formal alliances, the stationing of forces abroad, and the threat of direct intervention. At a time when the major powers are less likely to intervene with their own armed forces, they are more prone to shore up friendly states through the provision of arms or to play out their own competition through the arming of their proxies. *A contributing factor has been the reduction of other instruments of diplomacy, such as developmental aid. Both the United States and the Soviet Union now give less in economic than in military assistance.*[51]

Size of Arms Sales

Several features about these arms sales are worth noting. The first is their sheer magnitude. Arms sales totaled more than $20 billion in 1980 (in constant 1977 dollars). The United States and the Soviet Union were the largest suppliers; in 1978 each sold about 40 percent of the total. French and British sales quadrupled during the 1970s. In fact, by the end of the decade arms sales accounted for more than half of their trade surpluses.[52] For the Soviet Union, arms sales became a major means of earning dollars with which to buy Western technology and food. From 1979 to 1983, the United States and the Soviet Union were responsible for 57 percent of the world's total arms exports. American exports of $40 billion were 28 percent less than Soviet exports of $56 billion; the Soviets accounted for one-third of all arms exported during this period. During the closing years of the 1970s, and most of the 1980s, the Soviet Union exported more tanks, self-propelled guns, surface-to-air missiles, and supersonic aircraft to the Third World than did the United States.[53]

Even after the cold war, both the Soviet Union and the United States retained strategic interests in various regions, and each still had a sizable arms industry seeking profitable ventures with countries that could afford to pay the price. For the Soviets, their excess weapons remained a source of badly needed hard currency; for the United States, arms continued to be a means of providing security for friends, making up for dwindling foreign aid funds, and keeping the military production lines open. Indeed, given the reductions in conventional forces expected by the end of the cold war, both superpowers were expected to sell more arms, which otherwise would have been destroyed, particularly to Third World states. U.S. arms sales were $7 billion in 1986 and 1987, $12 billion in 1988, and $11 billion in 1989.[54] In 1989, the Soviet Union and United States accounted for $23 billion of total world sales of $32 billion[55]—and the U.S. total was expected to climb steeply as it withdrew its forces in 1992 from Saudi Arabia after the war with Iraq and sought to strengthen local regimes so that they could more effectively guard regional security. It was ironic that, as the Soviet Union vanished, the latest versions of Soviet jet fighters and tanks were reportedly available for sale to Third World states by former Soviet republics desperate for cash.

Expansion of the Arms Market and Suppliers

A second important feature of arms sales is the expansion of the arms market. Earlier arms transfers went from the superpowers to their NATO and Warsaw Pact allies. In the 1970s, members of OPEC with large trade surpluses, such as Saudi Arabia and Iran under the shah, bought arms from the United States and other Western states. Iraq and Libya bought their arms from the Soviet Union and the Eastern bloc nations. Israel and Syria too received large arms shipments from the United States and the Soviet Union, respectively. By 1979, about 35 percent of all arms shipped to the Third World went to the Middle

East. In 1983, the Middle East received 42 percent of the world's arms imports. During the remainder of the decade, the Middle East countries received more than half of the world's arms trade. From 1987 to 1990, the United States sold $30.7 billion in arms to the Middle East; the Soviet total was $17.5 billion. For the first time since 1983, Washington surpassed Moscow as the region's largest supplier, in part because of the successful performance of U.S.-made weapons in the Iran-Iraq war.

Other developing countries in Africa, Asia, and Latin America also increased their arms purchases during the 1980s. India, for example, signed a $1.6 billion arms deal with Moscow; Ethiopia, a very poor country, bought more than $1 billion in arms from the Soviet Union. All in all, more than three-quarters of the global arms trade went to the Third World—$128 billion in arms from 1977 to 1981. By 1986, the developing countries were importing $180 billion in arms, a 40 percent increase in five years.

Indeed, from 1985 to 1990 Third World countries bought $301.7 billion in arms, 30 percent of which went to Saudi Arabia and Iraq. The year 1990 was one of the highest in terms of the total value of arms transfer agreements ($41.2 billion). The U.S. total reached $18.5 billion, and the Soviet total declined from $12.7 to $12.1 billion from 1989 to 1990.[56] Simultaneously, the developing countries expanded their own arms production and sales dramatically. China has become the third largest exporter of arms to the Third World not only producing missiles but also cornering the market as a supplier of less-sophisticated but reliable conventional weapons—often improved clones of Soviet weapons of the late 1950s and mid-1960s—at cut-rate prices.[57]

Reportedly, China is also building nuclear reactors in Algeria and perhaps in Iran. It gave Pakistan copies of its plans for its untested warheads. Brazil, the fifth largest arms provider, produces such varied arms as light tanks, armored cars and personnel carriers, trainer aircraft, and missiles of all kinds. It has exported its weapons to forty countries, concentrating on the Middle East where it found the Iran-Iraq war especially profitable.[58] Argentina, Israel, India, and even the city-state of Singapore also have become arms manufacturers, supplying a wide range of such weapons as tanks, artillery, aircraft, submarines, and small arms and ammunition.

Thus, the great powers have increasingly lost control over arms distribution as the number of suppliers multiplied.[59] If the East Asian economic powers, especially Japan and South Korea, ever decide to sell more than Toyotas and Samsung TVs and VCRs, they would undoubtedly quickly assume a competitive position, thus diversifying the sources of arms suppliers even more.[60]

The numbers of weapons involved are truly impressive. Egypt, India, Israel, Iraq (until its 1991 defeat), and Syria each have more battle tanks than Britain or France; indeed, in 1990 Iraq had more than Germany when it launched World War II. Israel and Iraq have more armored personnel carriers and India has more combat aircraft than all the NATO powers except the United States. India has the world's third largest army and seventh largest navy.[61] Iraq, more heavily armed than highly industrialized Belgium, had a war machine in 1990 (including chemical weapons and missiles) that was stamped "Made in the West." In the words of a Middle East analyst, "This is a Frankenstein monster that the West has created." [62] During the early days of the war with Iran, Iraq became the world's largest purchaser of arms, although later it sought the technology to develop its own arms industry to free itself from dependence on foreign suppliers.[63] Ironically, then, the West went to war to destroy a military machine that it had helped Saddam Hussein purchase.[64] Thanks to Saddam Hussein and his run-in with Iran in the 1980s, the arms trade was very profitable for Western governments and companies, particularly German firms, which supplied both Libya and Iraq with the means for chemical warfare. German firms, as well as Swiss ones, supplied nuclear-processing equipment, and the Germans also played a role in giving Saddam Hussein's SCUD missiles greater range, including the ability to hit Israel.* Without West Germany, Iraq would not have been as powerful a threat to its neighbors as it was; even after the war began, German firms reportedly continued to break the embargo. But private companies in other Western countries also were not above making a profit, including U.S. firms.[65]

'Conventional' Weapons

A third feature of arms sales is the character of the weapons themselves. In many instances, these weapons can hardly be described as conventional. If the adjective *conventional* means *nonnuclear*, it is accurate; if it means just *ordinary* arms—that is, surplus arms or obsolete arms—it is not always accurate. The arms sales of the 1970s, for example, often included some of the most modern and sophisticated weapons found in the arsenals of Western suppliers and the Soviet Union. Thus, the United States sold F-15 and F-16 fighters, the Abrams main battle tank, and AWACS surveillance planes. The Soviet Union sold MIG-29 fighters, T-72 tanks, and SU-24 bombers (some of those sold to Libya had refueling nozzles), and it "loaned" seventeen submarines to India. Britain and France too sold top-of-the-line military equipment. Before the Iranian revolution in 1979, the British were selling to the shah most of their best battle tanks because he could afford more of them than Britain could for its own forces in Germany. Thus the weapons some regional states acquired were impressive not only in quantity but also in quality.

In truth, many so-called conventional weapons have become anything but conventional. A good number are precision-guided munitions or missiles (PGMs), which operate surface to air, surface to surface, and air to surface. Unlike the older generations of arms, which needed many rounds to hit the target, these new weapons usually require only one or two shots. They are

---

* Given Germany's slaughter of 6 million Jews in World War II, many by gas in concentration camps, some observers found it more than ironic that Germany would help Iraq produce components for chemical weapons and increase the range of SCUD missiles. William Safire charged Germany, in fact, with creating an "Auschwitz in the Sand" in his column "Friends, More than Interests," *New York Times,* February 6, 1991.

guided to their targets by laser beams or heat (infrared) rays. Also referred to as "smart bombs," they are becoming commonplace despite their technological sophistication. By modern standards, many of these weapons are reasonably priced, light, and ignitable by a small team. But such highly accurate and not-too-expensive weapons can inflict some very costly damage. For example, a $100,000 surface-to-air missile can shoot down a $35 million fighter, or a surface-to-surface missile costing a few hundred thousand dollars can hit a $2 billion aircraft carrier. When this occurs, the costs are prohibitive, even for a major power, and will probably deter it from efforts to coerce smaller countries. During the fighting in the Falkland Islands, for example, $200,000 French Exocet missiles fired from French-built fighters piloted by Argentinians hit and destroyed a couple of British ships—one of which was a $50 million destroyer—from twenty miles away.

PGMs have generally been thought to favor the defense and to make any military engagement costly because they destroy so much war materiel very quickly. Thus, the diffusion of modern arms cannot be regarded lightly because they are "conventional." In the 1973 Arab-Israeli war, the highly trained Israeli army and air force suffered enormous losses initially and were driven back by Egyptian and Syrian forces equipped by the Soviet Union with electronic warfare capability. Israel had none at the start of hostilities but later received the means for electronic countermeasures from the United States and reversed the early defeats. Nevertheless, the 1973 war was a dramatic turning point in modern warfare. The 1991 Persian Gulf conflict, of course, demonstrated just how effective PGMs are used as offensive weapons. They were utilized initially to destroy Iraq's command and control centers, then supply and communications lines to its forces in Kuwait, and finally with pinpoint accuracy, against many of Iraq's best tanks and much of its powerful artillery in that country.

Given the increasing prominence of regional rivalries, this diffusion of modern weapons may tempt states to use force to resolve their differences or attain their ambitions. Examples include the war between India and Pakistan in 1971; Argentina's 1982 invasion of the Falkland Islands and the subsequent war with Britain; the eight-year-long Iran-Iraq war in the 1980s; and Iraq's invasion of Kuwait and threat to Saudi Arabia in 1990 (India and Pakistan also almost came to blows over Kashmir in 1990). To the degree that this diffusion includes PGMs, the United States and other Western states may be more hesitant to intervene in the future despite the successful intervention against Iraq.

Indeed, to summarize, the diffusion of even so-called conventional arms will, like the spread of nuclear weapons, have profound effects on the new strategic environment. First, the great powers—despite a strong motivation to preempt against some nuclear proliferation—must think twice about intervening against lesser states (the Iraqi experience may be unique). Not only can these states mobilize popular resistance, but, if they possess sufficient numbers of PGMs, they can potentially destroy—at a relatively low cost to themselves but at a prohibitive cost to the great powers—the latter's expensive military equipment. This further raises the great powers' costs of war and may strengthen their tendency to self-deterrence, except in the most extreme cases. Great powers used to be the primary actors because they had sizable populations, advanced economies, and large military forces. Today, regional states with few of these attributes—but with strategic aspirations and involvement in regional rivalries—can threaten their neighbors and even the great powers because they may possess modern weapons. Thus, such states can play significant roles internationally.

Second, many of these regional powers, few of which have the populations and resources of say a China, India, or Brazil, are politically unstable, ambitious, and even reckless. Their acquisition of missiles—in addition to all the other modern arms—is therefore particularly dangerous. Once they also possess nuclear, chemical, or biological warheads, they may be particularly tempted to use them for purposes of political intimidation to change the status quo.[66]

Third, and most dangerous of all, increasingly regionally ambitious states with growing military capabilities will be able to project their military power greater distances from their borders. This poses a potential threat not only to neighboring states, one of which may be an ally or friend of a major power, but also to other forces (for example, U.S.) operating in the area.[67] Even more worrisome is the proliferation of longer-range missiles because it will expose the territories of the major powers to potential attack, including the republics of the former Soviet Union, the states of Western Europe, and eventually the United States. In short, in the future regional states possessing a real set of perceived grievances or the goal of regional hegemony, as well as intermediate-range missiles—and perhaps someday intercontinental-range missiles—with chemical or nuclear warheads may be able to menace world peace as never before. This capability of an increasing number of developing countries to penetrate Western air spaces is a new strategic reality. It will profoundly affect the security of these states and the relationship between the industrialized countries and the Third World and will constrain Western options. At a minimum, regional states can raise the price of Western intervention. Col. Muammar al-Qaddafi has said that had he possessed long-range missiles at the time of the U.S. air strike against Libya, he would have targeted New York City.[68] Is it then any wonder that President Bush has proposed the elimination of missiles from the Middle East!

Required, of course, are far more stringent controls on the transfer of modern weapons by the major powers acting in concert or else these weapons may be used against U.S. and other Western forces. For example, French Exocet missiles were used by the Argentinians against British forces in the Falkland Islands, and Kuwait's U.S.-supplied Hawk antiaircraft missiles, captured by Iraq, and French- and German-built missiles may have been used against American, French, and British pilots in the Persian Gulf war. After that conflict, President Bush called on the major arms suppliers to curb the sale of those conventional weapons they agree most threaten the military stability of the Middle East, and France proposed that the five permanent members of the UN Security Council, who account for 80 percent of all arms sales, limit the sale of arms worldwide. Later, the United States, Soviet Union, China, France, and Britain began to discuss how they could restrain arms sales to this volatile area.[69] But given the lucrative nature of the arms business for both government and private industry (especially at a time of declining defense budgets), the interests particular great-power governments may have in strengthening specific countries, and the availability of alternative arms suppliers in the Third World, this is unlikely to happen.[70] Indeed, the United States, which does not want to station ground troops in the Persian Gulf area, is not about to stop sending conventional weapons to friends and allies in the area. Israel, Egypt, Saudi Arabia, Kuwait and the other Gulf states, and possibly Turkey all want new and better weapons. Since 1991, U.S. arms sales alone have mushroomed to $8.5 billion. At best, the proliferation of weapons, especially missiles armed with chemical or other mass-destruction warheads, may be slowed down. In any case, an additional weapon available to such smaller states, as well as nongovernmental organizations with their own set of grievances, is terrorism itself.

TERRORISM AS WARFARE

Concern about the diffusion of nuclear and conventional arms is matched by that about the widespread use of terrorism. Terrorism stems from the number of "just" causes and people determined to achieve their objectives, even at the cost of their own lives, in the contemporary world. And in a world of multiplying ethnic and religious divisions such causes seem to be increasing. As long as there are "just" causes, there will be groups who resort to terrorism because they believe that there are no legitimate ways to redress their grievances and realize their aspirations. Stemming from the Latin *terrere*, meaning "to frighten," terrorism seeks to achieve its goals by frightening those who appear to be standing in its way.[71]

Categories of Nonstate Terrorists

Nonstate terrorists in the post-World War II period fell into three categories. The first was the national liberation group or the so-called state-in-waiting. Most such groups resorted primarily to guerrilla warfare. Examples were plentiful: the Communists in China; the Vietminh and Viet Cong in Vietnam; Castro's rebels in Cuba; the Sandinistas in Nicaragua; the former Patriotic Front, which sought majority rule in white-dominated Rhodesia and is now the government of Zimbabwe; the Afghan resistance to the Soviet Union; the Southwest African People's Organization, which in 1989 achieved power in a Namibia finally freed from South African control; and the Polisario, which wanted to establish its own state in the western Sahara independent from Morocco. But some national liberation movements resorted mainly to terror—for example, the Palestine Liberation Organization (PLO), which sought a Palestinian state (although in late 1988 it forswore the use of terror in words, if not in action); the Irish Republican Army, which wanted a united Ireland; and several Puerto Rican groups, which were working toward an independent Puerto Rico.

The second category of nonstate terrorist was the revolutionary group, many of which existed in Western societies. Such groups proclaimed their goals as the overthrow of capitalism because it was unjust domestically and aggressive internationally. They included the Japanese Red Army, the Italian Red Brigade, the German Red Army Faction, and the French Direct Action. After late 1984, some of these groups and others cooperated in attacks on NATO targets ranging from U.S. airbases to European arms manufacturers and bankers. Many of these terrorist groups had international links and did not limit themselves to actions only in their own countries. Since the cold war, the Italian and French groups broke up, and the German group gave up.

The third category was ethnic or religious groups seeking either redress for past injuries or greater autonomy within a state, if not independence. Examples are the Basques in Spain; the Armenians, who have carried on their campaign against Turkey in both the United States and Europe; and the Sikhs in India, who assassinated both its prime minister and, later, one of its moderate leaders. Sikhs are also suspected of blowing up an Air India 727 over the Atlantic Ocean in 1985 and of attempting to do the same with another plane. In the latter incident, the bomb went off after the passengers had deplaned in Tokyo.

Terrorism as Television Theater

To carry out their missions, terrorists resort to various means: assassination, seizure of embassies, hijacking of airplanes (even one ocean liner), kidnapping, and bombing. Although these acts are criminal in character, terrorist groups' political aims make such terrorism a form of political violence. Fundamentally, terrorism is a weapon of the weak; the terrorists would lose a straight test of strength with the forces of "law and order." Terrorism—like guerrilla warfare—is consistent with Carl von Clausewitz's definition of war as the continuation of politics by other means.

As weak as they may be, terrorists wage their "war" by attracting publicity for their cause through their acts. Whether it is the seizure of an airliner or ship, the kidnapping of government officials or nongovernmental personnel, including tourists, or the murder of one or more individuals, these dramatic acts are viewed by millions on television and are covered by all the media. Television coverage especially provides an incentive for the performance of such acts. It offers a world stage on which the terrorists play and draw global attention, and the jet airplane allows them to strike quickly anywhere in the world and then fly to safety.

Terrorism is public theater in which there are no innocent bystanders. For the terrorists, everyone is a player; there are no distinctions between soldiers with rifles and tourists carrying Michelin guides. The audience may condemn terrorist acts as senseless and brutal and decry these acts all the more when the victims are educators, clergy, and tourists. But these actions, while brutal, are not senseless or random; rather, they are the actions of fanatical—not demented—advocates of a cause who know what they want and are often willing to kill themselves and others for this cause.

If terrorists believe, rightly or wrongly, that a particular country—for example, the United States—is the cause of their grievances or blocks them from achieving their goal, they will consider *all* Americans guilty. Therefore, attacks on U.S. embassies or the seizure of diplomats or just "plain Americans" publicize their anti-Americanism. They are also intended to exact a cost, show the impotence of the United States because it cannot prevent such attacks, and undermine the legitimacy of the pro-American governments. Terrorists want people to feel helpless and defenseless and to lose faith in the government's ability to protect them. In the name of their cause, the ends justify all means.

State Terrorism and Undeclared Wars

A new phenomenon appeared in the 1980s—terrorism by states.[72] The smaller states, with their relatively weak military forces, or their relative dependence on external supplies of arms, found terrorism an attractive alternative to war. Terrorism expert Brian Jenkins has called terrorism a form of "surrogate warfare." He also has said,

> Finding modern conventional war an increasingly unattractive mode of conflict, some nations may try to exploit the demonstrated possibilities and greater potential of terrorist groups, and employ them as a means of *surrogate warfare against another nation.* A government could subsidize an existing terrorist group or create its own band of terrorists to disrupt, cause alarm, and create political and economic instability in another country. It requires only a small investment, certainly far less than what it costs to wage a conventional war, it is debilitating to the enemy, and it is deniable. . . .
>
> We are likely to see more examples of war being waged by groups that do not openly represent the government of a recognized state: revolutionaries, political extremists, lunatics, or criminals professing political aims, those we call terrorists, perhaps the surrogate soldiers of another state. Increasingly, there will be *war without declaration, war without authorization or even admission by any national government, war without invasions by armies as we now know them, war without front lines, war waged without regard to national borders or neutral countries, war without civilians, war without innocent bystanders.*[73]

Terror, then, shrinks the power differential between the United States and such countries as Iran, Syria, and Libya. Terrorists can do things governments cannot; moreover, the beauty is that governments that use terrorists as proxies can disavow them. Thus, through its support of radical Shiite Muslim groups such as the Islamic Jihad (Holy War) or Hezbullah (Party of God), Iran can seek to gain revenge for past U.S. support of the shah and to weaken, indeed eliminate, U.S. power from the Middle East-West Asia areas. Syria, an ally of Iran against Iraq, also helped Iran organize the Shiite terrorist network and used such groups to undermine American support for Lebanon's former pro-Western and pro-Israeli Christian-dominated government.* Or the Hezbullah can threaten to kill the American hostages it has seized (ninety-two in Lebanon from 1984 to 1991) if the United States takes some action Iran does not like, such as sending warships into the Persian Gulf. Iran can officially repudiate such a threat, but obviously it also would benefit from U.S. restraint stemming from successful intimidation. For example, Iran benefited when President Ronald Reagan tried to swap American hostages for the arms the Iranians needed in the war against Iraq.

To the radical Shiite groups, the United States, the West's leading country, represents a secular civilization that has achieved great political, economic, and military power. It is also democratic, liberal, culturally preeminent, and dynamic, and it is spreading its influence to the Islamic world, which is weak, poor, and less developed. The 1979 seizure of the U.S. embassy in Tehran, and, during the 1980s, the bombing of the embassy in Kuwait (4 killed), the two bombings of the embassy in Lebanon (63 and 14 killed), the suicide bombing of the U.S. Marine compound in Beirut (241 killed), the attempt to blow up the U.S. embassy in Rome (foiled by the Italian police), and the kidnappings in Beirut of American citizens (only one of whom worked for the U.S. government and he was murdered) all testify to the fact that these Muslim radicals saw themselves as waging an undeclared war against the United States. This anti-American pattern was practiced especially by those who followed the Ayatollah Ruhollah Khomeini. As the graffiti on a Beirut wall said, "We are all Khomeini." [74] To them, the United States was the "Great Satan," the devil to be exorcised. (None of this is intended to suggest that other Western states and friends were not targets; French and Israeli soldiers in Lebanon also were attacked.) Simultaneously, the Iranians wanted not only to revive but also to spread Islamic—and especially Shiite—civilization. This anger against the United States and its alleged creation Israel did not end with the release of the last U.S. hostage in December 1991. The condemnation of the United States as the world's Satan continued. With the collapse of communism, Washington was accused of trying to use the Middle East peace conference (which met for the first time in November 1991) to dominate the entire region. The "war" against America would therefore go on.

---

*Because the United States intervened militarily in Lebanon's civil war, Syria supported the Sunni and Shiite Muslims and Druze factions, all pro-Arab. The 1983 attack on the American marine barracks with 12,000 tons of gas-enhanced explosives was organized in Syrian-controlled territory in Lebanon. It was either agreed to by the Syrians or, more likely, assisted by them, for this attack took careful planning and was carried out with military precision. Only an organization skilled with explosives could have assembled the bomb.

Many reasons are usually given for terrorist acts, such as U.S. support of Israel, revenge of a victim of retaliation (Israel's usual reason), and, not unexpectedly in a world of terrorists, the release of comrades who were captured and jailed. There are literally thousands of reasons for terrorist acts; if it were not one, it would be another. On December 21, 1988, Pan Am flight 103 with 259 persons aboard, including 189 Americans, most going home for the holidays, blew up over Scotland. According to ABC and Frontline public television investigations, this was an act of pure vengeance, instigated by Iran's former interior minister, for the mistaken shooting down earlier that year of an Air Iran airbus carrying 290 passengers by the U.S.S. *Vincennes'*. The act was carried out by the Popular Front for the Liberation of Palestine-General Command, an extremist anti-American group committed to the destruction of Israel. But Libya was involved. U.S. government investigators believe that the Popular Front, based in Damascus, Syria, paid agents of Libya's leader, Colonel Qaddafi, to carry out the bombing after discovering that their operations in West Germany had been penetrated by the German police. The timing device incorporated into the bomb was of Libyan origin.[75]

Indeed, in 1991 the U.S. government indicted two Libyan intelligence agents. Declaring that it had no evidence linking Iran or Syria to the bombing, Washington held Libya's Colonel Qaddafi responsible in this clear case of state terrorism. Presumably, Qaddafi was seeking revenge for the 1986 attack on his country that tried to kill him and did kill a daughter. Whether the denial of Iranian and Syrian complicity was the result of insufficient evidence for an indictment against these two countries, or the result of downplaying their involvement because of changing U.S. relations with them—as Syria, a hard-line Arab state, joined the Middle Eastern peace process and Iran was becoming more moderate—remains unknown.

Terrorism Iraqi Style

After the United States organized opposition to his invasion of Kuwait in 1990, Saddam Hussein threatened repeatedly that if war came terrorists would attack American targets in the Middle East, Europe, and perhaps even in the United States. Such groups as the Popular Front for the Liberation of Palestine, responsible for the 1988 Pan-Am bombing, were now headquartered in Baghdad. While in fact no acts of terrorism occurred, the threats and the widespread expectation that they would occur reduced international and U.S. airline bookings drastically. Instead, in what became known as environmental terrorism, Saddam Hussein released millions of barrels of oil into the Persian Gulf. The effects were devastating on everything from marine life to bird life to the ecosystem. And to make matters even worse, in an act of spiteful pyromania he set 732 of Kuwait's oil wells on fire before retreating from that country. The fires consumed 5 million barrels of oil a day—three times Kuwait's prewar production—cost $90 million a day, covered thousands of hectares, threatened subsurface water, and spewed 50,000 tons of sulfur dioxide (a prime cause of acid rain) and 100,000 tons of soot into the air daily, with incalculable consequences for the environment of Kuwait. The effects beyond that country are not yet completely clear. While some authorities fear effects similar to those of a nuclear winter because the 30-odd million tons of smoke the burning wells were expected to emit in a year have been realized, no one really knows for sure because pollution on such a scale has never been experienced and the damage is expected to extend as far as 1,000 kilometers from Kuwait.[76] It took until November 1991 to put out the fires, long enough but far shorter than originally expected.

If these acts can be called terrorist attacks, as they were, they were certainly novel, far-reaching in their effects, and uniquely difficult because the nations of the world did not really know how to cope with them. Scientists, therefore, have proposed that environmental terrorism as an instrument of war be outlawed. After the war, there was a lot of talk about trying Saddam Hussein as a war criminal for these acts, as well as for his pillaging of Kuwait for everything from chairs and telephones to rare art (and then burning down the museums). This pillaging was deliberate, part of his campaign to erase Kuwait's history. But no trial was held.

In another act of terrorism, at the outset of the crisis Saddam seized all foreigners as hostages. Although he initially freed small numbers of hostages in response to the pilgrimages and pleas of various Western (including Japanese) politicians, his ultimate goal was to divide the alliance against him. The most blatant example was his release of all French and German hostages to encourage the preference of those countries for a diplomatic solution and to pressure Washington to put off military action. Worse, however, was Saddam Hussein's manipulation of American and British men (he initially held their wives as well, only to release them and divide families). They were placed at the strategic sites that, in the event of war, would be immediate targets, such as airfields and chemical, biological, and nuclear facilities. From time to time, however, he let a few Americans go to encourage opposition to the president's policy.

The hostages were obviously intended to deter an attack *and* allow Iraq to keep Kuwait, the fruit of its aggression. When President Bush sent over another 250,000 forces in November 1990 to reinforce his message that Iraq's choice was to either get out of Kuwait peacefully or be forced out, the Iraqi leader announced he would start releasing all hostages in batches over a three-month period starting at Christmas. That would cover the very best time for an attack: U.S. forces were supposed to be in place by mid-January when the weather would be cool; by March the weather would again be very hot and Muslims would be keeping Ramadan, a holy observance, followed shortly by the visit of pilgrims from all over the Muslim world to Mecca in Saudi Arabia. Not only was that not a good time to be at war with Iraq, but also it would be better to have already defeated Iraq and be withdrawing all "infidel" troops lest Saddam Hussein effectively exploit the issue of infidels at the holy sites to undermine the legitimacy of the Saudi regime and the support of the Arab states aligned with the United States.

Ironically, after this shrewd offer Saddam Hussein changed his mind once more. He let all the hostages go before Christmas, stating that his military was now ready for war and no longer needed the hostages to deter an attack, but that the release was a reward to the antiwar forces in the United States. He specifically cited Senate Democrats, who had been advising the president "to give sanctions more time." Clearly, Saddam was still trying to manipulate the hostages, partly to cleanse his own tarnished image and partly to restrain Washington.

Once the war started, Iraq's principal act of terrorism, besides its "eco-terrorism," was the launching of Soviet-made SCUD missiles against cities in Saudi Arabia and Tel Aviv in Israel. He wanted to involve Israel in the war in an effort to transform it into an Arab-Israeli conflict. The Arab governments aligned against him would then be forced to quit, if not change sides. Because these missiles were inaccurate and incapable of hitting military targets, their use against civilian city dwellers was widely referred to as "SCUD-terrorism."

Reprisals against Terrorists

In 1984, Secretary of State George Shultz expressed the anger and frustration of most Americans when he said that the United States must not allow itself to become "the Hamlet of nations, worrying endlessly over whether and how to respond" to terrorist attacks. After the assault on the marine barracks in 1983, the United States, despite talk of retaliation, did not act. By contrast, the Israelis and French, who also had been attacked, did strike back.

The dilemma is obvious. On the one hand, if the victims of terrorism react passively, terrorists are incited to further attacks to demonstrate their strength and the target's impotence. Only by exacting a heavy price from the perpetrators can a nation discourage such attacks. On the other hand, punishment depends on knowing who and where the members of a terrorist group are and then having the right means with which to retaliate. Even if one has that information, such as the whereabouts of the Iranian-controlled radical fundamentalist Muslims, how does one punish an enemy who deliberately surrounds itself with innocent civilians? Should this be allowed to discourage retaliation? A country such as the United States is restricted—and should be—by its standards of morality. The problem of retaliation is especially problematic when terrorists operate from another state's territory. For example, Lebanon was too weak to expel the PLO; indeed, continual Israeli air attacks and an invasion to drive the PLO out left Lebanon in shambles. Its former pro-Western government then collapsed; the civil war intensified among all its religious and ethnic factions; Syria gained dominant influence; and millions of formerly friendly Lebanese, especially the Shiites living in southern Lebanon on Israel's border, grew to detest Israel. This proved fertile ground for pro-Iranian terrorist groups.

In the case of state-sponsored terrorism, is the alternative to strike at the source? Did the United States really want to retaliate against an Iran, a major country, strategically located, which someday must play its role in the regional balance and help contain Iraq (as Iraq will have to play its role helping to balance Iran)? Did it particularly want to act just at a time when (upon the death of Khomeini) a more moderate, pro-Western leader had become leader? His help would be needed to gain the hostages' release, and his leadership was being contested by Khomeini's militant followers who remained opposed to any reconciliation with the United States. Or should it act militarily against Syria, which was suspected of being involved in two of the worst terrorist acts: the 1983 attack against U.S. Marines in Lebanon and the 1988 bombing of Pan Am flight 103? Syrian leader Hafez-al-Assad also sheltered one of the best-known terrorists, Abu Nidal, and was thought to be involved in an attempt to blow up an Israeli airliner in Britain, an issue over which London broke diplomatic relations with Syria. Like Saddam Hussein, he was also ruthless at home, eliminating opposition, once destroying the entire town of Hama with his artillery. Syria was no pushover like Libya. In an attack on Syrian positions in Lebanon in 1983, the United States lost two planes. Syria was well armed with Soviet weapons. In addition, American and Syrian interests have not always been in conflict. Syria's control over Beirut improved in 1990 after its troops defeated the Christian militia resisting the government; this was expected to lead it to help free the U.S. hostages. And, in the same year, Syria, a state with militantly anti-Israeli and anti-American credentials, aligned itself with the United States and sent troops to Saudi Arabia. This step was politically important, although many American observers were concerned that this tactical relationship might be as expedient as the earlier relationship with Iraq against Iran.[77]

Retaliation, then, is not as easy as it appears. Each act reverberates, sometimes in ways that cannot be controlled. Repercussions may range from violating one's own moral standards, to endangering relations with friendly states, to, during the cold war, perhaps driving an unfriendly state into Soviet arms with even more damaging consequences. There are no easy solutions, and each case must be decided on its own merit. Not surprisingly, there is no agreement among states about what to do. For one party, a terrorist may be a freedom fighter; for another, inaction is at least unprovocative. Why act and buy trouble? When the United States struck Libya in 1986 for its sponsorship of terrorism, most U.S. allies refused to allow American bombers from England to fly over their territories. Because the British government gave its permission to use bombers based in Britain, it was widely condemned by the British public. America's moderate Arab friends also protested.

There are only three broad prescriptions on how to deal with terrorists: the incorrect way, the correct way, and the best, but most unlikely, way. An example of the incorrect way was the 1986 Reagan arms-for-hostages deal with Iran. The president had taken a tough public position that the United States would never deal with hostage takers because to reward terrorists would only encourage them to undertake further acts of terrorism, a position he had successfully pursued in several cases. He neglected to do so, however, in the case of the hostages seized by pro-Iranian groups in Beirut. Moved by their plight and the constant public pleas from the hostages' families, the president unsuccessfully sought their release by bartering with Iran.

The correct way was demonstrated in 1988 when hijackers seized a Kuwaiti airliner to demand the release of fifteen terrorists jailed in that country—the same terrorists whose freedom was part of the price during the Iran affair. The Kuwaitis refused to capitulate even though the terrorists killed two Kuwaitis, dumped their bodies on the tarmac, and threatened to kill themselves and all their passengers. The hijackers finally released the latter in return for their own freedom.

The best but most unlikely prescription for dealing with terrorists is for the victim states to cooperate with all the economic and diplomatic means at their disposal against the states that sponsor or harbor terrorist groups. Only once, in 1992, did the United Nations act against a terrorist state, and that action did not come until terrorism has seemingly run its course and the United States, Britain, and France agreed to act through the Security Council. After decades of terrorism in the air without punishment for the states that harbor, if not sponsor, suspects, the three Western powers, acting through the United Nations, held Libya accountable for its involvement in the explosion of Pan Am 103 (259 deaths) and of a French airliner in 1989 over Niger in Africa (171 deaths). They demanded the surrender of the two agents accused of blowing up the U.S. plane. When Colonel Qaddafi refused to comply, the United Nations followed up by severing international air links to Libya, reducing Libyan embassy personnel, and imposing an embargo on sales of aircraft and spare parts, as well as on all arms. These were essentially symbolic sanctions, though indicative of more painful future sanctions—such as an embargo on oil sales—if Libya refused to hand over the two accused agents. And if these measures failed, there were such steps as blockading harbors and attacking military and economic targets (oil storage and loading facilities, for example) to inflict severe economic damage. But whether military action would be used in the face of general Arab opposition by governments reluctant to align themselves again with the West against another Arab state remains to be seen.

Has Terrorism Run Its Course?

On December 4, 1991, the last U.S. hostage of the more than thirty Westerners abducted in Lebanon was released by his captors. No military action against Iran or pro-Iranian terrorist groups had preceded the release. What then are the lessons to be drawn from the use of retaliatory tactics? One lesson is clear: when hostages are taken, they should not be overvalued. Obviously, their seizure is news, and the media, especially television, usually dramatize the plight by interviews with family and loved ones. But if a government reacts to the publicity given to the terrorists' cruelty and the pressure to "do something" to gain the hostages' release, more seizures and a higher price for the hostages may be the result. The hostage-takers believe they have seized valuable human assets. This can end only in concessions without any assurance that any released hostages will not be balanced by new seizures, as happened after the initial Reagan arms-for-hostages deal. But President Bush, Reagan's vice president, refused to deal with the hostage-takers or to pay a ransom. As in the initial phases of the U.S. confrontation with Saddam Hussein, he played down the hostage issue. At the same time though, he offered Iran and Syria incentives to end the hostage crisis. He could do this because the entire international political context had changed.

This is the second and more fundamental lesson: the release of hostages—and perhaps terrorist acts as a whole—requires a political change so that the hostages not only are no longer valuable but may indeed block any desired improvement of relations between the states that sponsored the terrorism and the nations whose hostages were taken. The end of the cold war and the U.S. victory over Iraq radically altered the situation for the two states sponsoring terrorism. Syria, which had long received Soviet diplomatic support and military assistance, was now seeking to improve its relationship with the United States, the one superpower left after the Soviet collapse (a position vividly dramatized by the swift and effective use of American military power against Saddam Hussein). Iran, where the ayatollah was succeeded by the more pragmatic Hashemi Rafsanjani, also now sought to establish more normal relations with the West. Its economy was in shambles and the United States had established its dominant influence in the Persian Gulf area, where Iran had previously sought to expand its power. At least for the moment, economic reconstruction appeared to take priority over religious fanaticism, as did strengthening its regional influence once more after Iraq's defeat. Thus, the hostages had become a liability and the hostage situation ended. In these circumstances, the UN secretary-general was able to negotiate the hostages' release.

Whether the new post-cold war situation will discourage terrorism is still unknown. The sources of terrorism in the Middle East, America's substantial great influence (heightened by recent events), and the Arab-Israeli conflict are still present. Thus, much depends on the future. Will the Middle East peace process be able to successfully mediate this conflict, thereby eliminating one source of terrorism? Will the fervor of Islamic fundamentalism, which appears to be spreading, revive or fade? For example, reportedly Sudan recently became the new home for terrorist groups from Libya and Lebanon, and the post-1989 Islamic Sudanese military government appears bent on exporting its revolution to such secular neighbors as Egypt, Libya, and six African nations, including Ethiopia with its large and impoverished Muslim population.[78]

But conditions in other areas also have changed. National liberation groups have become inactive. For example, the PLO, having supported Iraq during the war, found itself largely on the sidelines during the regional peace negotiations. Marxist-Leninist revolutionary organizations withered with the collapse of communism in Eastern Europe. And in 1992 the German Red Army Faction announced the end of its twenty-year campaign of violence against "imperialism and monopoly capitalism." A principal source of training, weapons, and money had vanished.

Still, in 1992 the State Department continued to list six countries that were known to support terrorism: Cuba, North Korea, Iraq, Iran, Libya, and Syria. Iran remains on the list despite some recent signs of moderation. Seeking to exploit the U.S. defeat of Iraq to regain its influence over regional politics and OPEC oil policy, Iran has become a fervent opponent of the Middle East peace process. In early 1992, the Hezbullah assassinated an Israeli diplomat in Ankara, Turkey, and struck at the Israeli embassy in Buenos Aires, destroying it, killing twenty people, and injuring 200 more, mainly Argentinians.

Ethnic hatred and conflicts, which have come to the forefront in the post-cold war world, may well remain a cause of terrorism. The Kurdish Workers Party, for example, trying to exploit sympathy for the Kurds of Iraq, has resorted to terrorism to carve an independent Kurdistan from part of Turkey.

Has Terrorism Paid Off?

On the surface, the answer to this question appears to be positive. Iran gained some of the weapons it wanted. Syria managed to coerce the withdrawal of the U.S. Marines from Lebanon, which it sought to dominate. Libya put itself on the map by its support of terrorist activities. But it is hard to measure the impact of terrorism on government policies. Did governments not pursue certain policies or change policies to ward off terrorist activities? When the United States attacked Libya, Europeans were upset. Most terrorist activity outside the Middle East occurred in Western Europe. They were certainly not eager to encourage any additional acts.

On balance, however, terrorism has not paid off. The states sponsoring terrorism made the State Department's annual list and, in general, earned themselves the unenviable reputation as "outlaw" states. If it did not lead to a disruption of diplomatic relations, it did leave them somewhat battered. And they paid a material price, whether it was the refusal of Western business to help Iran reconstruct and improve its oil fields or military attacks on Libya, in which its leader became one of the targets. The sudden Iranian eagerness to rid itself of the Western hostage problem, which had endured since 1984, testifies to the need of a leading terrorist state to rid itself of the moral stain with which it was marked and improve its political and economic relationship with the states that had been the target of terrorism. But that is unlikely to happen, at least with the United States, until Iran calls off the Hezbullah's campaign against Israel. And, as noted, Libya has discovered for the first time that the United States and Western Europe will resort to economic sanctions; even another use of force is possible.

Still, certain conditions may favor the continuation of terrorism. These conditions include: the political fragmentation of states or unstable regimes in all areas, including Eastern Europe, and of groups holding grievances against the established order; commercial jets that provide both hostages and the means to transport them and their captors; states that remain sympathetic to terrorists and provide them with training, money, and sanctuary; and the mass media, especially television, that provide instant coverage and publicity for the terrorists' demands and causes. International terrorism also benefits from the trend toward smaller, lighter, more portable, more accurate, and cheaper weapons. Today, a small number of people can inflict the same kind of damage that earlier could have been inflicted only by large military units. These arms can be acquired relatively easily by terrorists. What is especially frightening is that one day some fanatical group, perhaps a separatist or secessionist group, might steal or divert nuclear materials, sabotage a nuclear reactor, or threaten to blow up a city.[79] A fear almost as great is the use of chemical weapons, perhaps supplied by such a state as Libya or Iraq to a terrorist group. Even biological weapons may someday be used. And this fear will grow if the terrorists have missiles.

Finally, terrorists presumably have a vested interest in continued terrorism. On the one hand, terrorists genuinely hate their enemies, whom they see as the embodiment of evil. This makes it extremely difficult for their enemies to meet their stated grievances. On the other hand, within their own communities, those who wear the mantle of terrorism possess status and prestige and by their acts gain money for themselves and their organizations. Reportedly, besides its regular financial support of the Hezbullah in Lebanon, Iran paid $1 million for each hostage released after August 1991. Terrorism, in short, was a profitable business and may yet resume.[80]

A FEW FINAL WORDS

The cold war years of nuclear bipolarity constituted a system of restraint. Bipolarity meant that the superpowers needed to watch mainly each other. It also guaranteed that, wherever feasible, action by one state led the adversary to react, thereby ensuring that the central military balance and regional balances outside of Eastern Europe and Latin America were kept. The nuclear arsenals of the principal rivals also made it imperative that they discipline their use of power. Both recognized, as President Reagan used to put it, that nuclear war cannot be won and therefore must not be fought. Deterrence was thus a successful policy.

But nuclear polycentrism is potentially a catastrophe. It is unlikely to reproduce the restraint and caution of the U.S.-Soviet balance and stabilize regional balances. Many Third World states suffer from unstable governments, civil wars, secessionist drives, and irredentist aims, and the proliferation of mass-destruction weapons may not be symmetrical. The party already possessing a nuclear capability, rather than being deterred by the new embryonic nuclear weapons of the adversary, may be tempted to wipe out the latter's new arms while it is still vulnerable to attack and its force small. As noted earlier, the Israeli raid on the Iraqi reactor in 1981 may have set a precedent. In addition, and perhaps even more important, conflicts such as those between Israel and its neighbors, India and Pakistan, and the two

Koreas have a long history of violence and an intensity that was lacking most of the time in the cold war superpower contests.

The future obviously remains unknown, but certain trends appear clear from the analysis. One is that the post-cold war international system is likely to be unstable. Another is that the United States will remain the dominant power. Despite its relative economic decline, it is still the principal player in the military (nuclear and conventional), diplomatic, ideological and cultural, and even economic games. But power in the international system is more diffused than ever before. The increased proliferation of advanced military technology to rising regional powers is symptomatic of the shift from bipolarity to "unipolycentrism." As noted earlier, the strong no longer dominate and the weak no longer submit. If anything, the international hierarchy often appears to be topsy-turvy. Moreover, while military power remains important, as demonstrated in 1991 when a small country of 17 million people precipitated a major crisis and held the world at bay for five months, and only America could mobilize an effective reaction, it is likely to play a less critical role than during the cold war. Economic power will play a more significant roll than earlier.[81] As the increasing emphasis in recent years on economic growth and competitiveness in the global market testifies, the changing character of the key issues and of power is widely recognized.

Thus, while the cold war may have ended, the world remains a dangerous place. Conflicts—to be sure lesser ones, but conflicts that could escalate—will take its place. A partial list includes the national and ethnic splintering of the Soviet Union, Yugoslavia, and perhaps other Eastern European countries; regional conflicts outside of Europe, such as those among the Arab states; the rise of Islamic fundamentalism as a potent and intolerant movement; proliferation of nuclear, chemical, and biological weapons and missile technology; the possible economic collapse of Eastern Europe, including the Commonwealth of Independent States; and, more broadly, the global trading system's breakup into regional blocs, increasing economic rivalries, and "managed trade."

Indeed, it needs to be reemphasized that not much comfort should be drawn from the current conventional wisdom that economics will replace politics and substitute harmony and welfare for conflict and war. Economic exchanges among nations may be of mutual benefit, but they also are likely to result in rivalries, protectionism, and national profit-seeking at the cost of other nations. The free-trade GATT system that led to the increasing prosperity of the Western industrial nations was the result of American predominance among the Western allies and the U.S. belief in free trade at a time its economy was preeminent. Indeed, the belief that interdependence will weaken nationalism and the nation-state, thus eliminating anarchy and the basis of "power politics," appears contradictory to the nationalist passions fragmenting so many nations.

All these political and economic problems not only affect the United States but also cannot be resolved without it. There will be no rest for the United

States in the post-cold war system.[82] Isolationism, however attractive it is now that the Soviet threat has largely disappeared, is impossible. Great powers' interests have always transcended that of just physical security which, given its nuclear arsenal, is easy for the United States to maintain. Only the United States has the kind of power to organize opposition to a Saddam Hussein, or, earlier, to bring Egypt and Israel to sign a peace treaty, or, perhaps in the future, to end the Palestinian-Israeli and Arab-Israeli conflicts. America may have lost its dominant position in the international economy, but without the United States, because of its size, the international economy cannot be managed. Neither Germany nor Japan, for all their economic achievements and influence, are yet willing to accept that role. Whether international politics is analyzed in terms of traditional "power politics" with its focus on "high politics," or in terms of the newer school of interdependence with its focus on "low politics," the United States remains at the center of this unstable world.[83]

For Review

1. Can the proliferation of nuclear weapons be halted or slowed by means short of war? What are the best options?
2. What kind of case can be made for the use of preventive war to stop such proliferation? Is all proliferation equally dangerous?
3. What are likely to be some of the effects on international politics of the spread of missiles, which may carry nuclear, biological, or chemical warheads, to more and more states?
4. In what ways are the consequences of the diffusion of mass-destruction weapons similar to or different from the consequences of the diffusion of high-tech conventional weapons?
5. What has been terrorism's role in the contemporary world? Is it likely to decline or increase?
6. Based on the trends suggested in this chapter, and indeed in the preceding four chapters, how would you characterize the emerging post-cold war system?

Notes

1. Robert Gilpin, *War and Change in World Politics* (New York: Cambridge University Press, 1983), 7; and Michael Howard, *The Causes of Wars,* 2d ed. (Cambridge, Mass.: Harvard University Press, 1983), 16-21.
2. Robert L. Paarlberg, "Domesticating Global Management," *Foreign Affairs* (April 1976): 571.

3. Josef Joffe, "Europe's American Pacifier," *Foreign Policy* (Spring 1984): 72 (emphasis added).

4. Richard Rosecrance, *Rise of the Trading State* (New York: Basic Books, 1986), xi.

5. See Leonard Beaton and John Maddox, *The Spread of Nuclear Weapons* (New York: Holt, Rinehart & Winston, 1962); Beaton, *Must the Bomb Spread?* (Baltimore: Penguin, 1966); Raymond Aron, "Spread of Nuclear Weapons," *Atlantic Monthly,* January 1965, 44-50; George H. Quester, *The Politics of Nuclear Proliferation* (Baltimore: Johns Hopkins University Press, 1973); Quester, "Can Proliferation Now Be Stopped?" *Foreign Affairs* (October 1974): 77-97; Lincoln Bloomfield, "Nuclear Spread and World Order," *Foreign Affairs* (July 1975): 743-755; Daniel Yergin, "Terrifying Prospect: Atomic Bombs Everywhere," *Atlantic Monthly,* April 1977, 47-65; Richard K. Betts, "Paranoids, Pygmies, Pariahs and Nonproliferation," *Foreign Policy* (Spring 1977): 157-183; Lewis A. Dunn, "Half Past India's Bang," *Foreign Policy* (Fall 1979): 71-88; Dunn, *Controlling the Bomb* (New Haven, Conn.: Yale University Press, 1982); Dunn and William H. Overholt, "The Next Phase in Nuclear Proliferation Research," *Orbis* (Summer 1976): 497-524; Ernest W. Lefever, *Nuclear Arms in the Third World* (Washington, D.C.: Brookings, 1979); Jed C. Snyder and Samuel F. Wells, Jr., *Limiting Nuclear Proliferation* (Cambridge, Mass.: Ballinger, 1985); Leonard S. Spector, *Going Nuclear* (Cambridge, Mass.: Ballinger, 1987); Spector, *The Undeclared Bomb* (Cambridge, Mass.: Ballinger, 1988); and with Jacqueline R. Smith, *Nuclear Ambitions* (Boulder, Colo.: Westview Press, 1990); McGeorge Bundy, *Disaster and Survival* (New York: Random House, 1988), 463-516, 525-535; and Mitchell Reiss, *Without the Bomb* (New York: Columbia University Press, 1989).

6. On Israel's acquisition and strategy, see Shai Feldman, *Israeli Nuclear Deterrence* (New York: Columbia University Press, 1982); and Shlomo Aronson, *The Politics and Strategy of Nuclear Weapons in the Middle East* (Albany: State University of New York Press, 1992); and on the broader nuclear arms race in the Middle East, see Frank Barnaby, *The Invisible Bomb* (London: I. B. Tauris, 1989).

7. Paul Lewis, "Pakistan Tells of Its A-bomb Capacity," *New York Times,* February 8, 1992.

8. Edward A. Gargan, "Diplomats Are Edgy as India Stubbornly Builds Its Nuclear Arsenal," *New York Times,* January 21, 1992; and Barbara Crosette, "India Is Pressed on Atom Project," *New York Times,* February 12, 1992.

9. Leonard S. Spector, "The North Korean Nuclear Threat," *Wall Street Journal,* April 19, 1991; and Andrew Mack, "North Korea and the Bomb," *Foreign Policy* (Summer 1991): 87-104.

10. Elaine Sciolino, "C.I.A. Chief Doubts North Korean Vow on Nuclear Arms," *New York Times,* February 26, 1992; and David E. Sanger, "2 Koreas Agree to A-Inspection by June," *New York Times,* March 15, 1992.

11. For an analysis looking into the future, see Robert E. Harkavy, "After the Gulf War: The Future of Israeli Nuclear Strategy," *Washington Quarterly* (Summer 1991): 161-179.

12. Seymour M. Hersh, *The Samson Option* (New York: Random House, 1991).

13. Quoted by Tina Rosenberg, "Nuking The Nukes," *New Republic,* January 28, 1991, 21. For nuclear proliferation in South Asia, see Beahma Chellanny, "South Asia's Passage to Nuclear Power," *International Security* (Summer 1991): 43-72.

14. James Brooks, "Brazil Uncovers Plan by Military to Build Atom Bomb and Stops It," *New York Times,* October 9, 1990.

15. Shirley Christian, "Argentina and Brazil Renounce Atomic Weapons," *New York*

Times, November 29, 1990.

16. Lefever, *Nuclear Arms in the Third World,* 9-11.

17. David Binder, "4 New Republics Provide Details on Dismantling Ex-Soviet Arsenal," *New York Times,* February 2, 1992; and Eric Schmitt, "U.S. Gains Pledge on Ex-Soviet Arms," *New York Times,* April 1, 1992.

18. Reportedly, three of Kazakhstan's tactical nuclear weapons are missing and could turn up in Iran. Philip J. Hilts, "Tally of Ex-Soviets' A-Arms Stirs Worry," *New York Times,* March 16, 1992.

19. Tom Clancy and Russell Seitz, "Five Minutes Past Midnight," *National Interest* (Winter 1991-1992): 9; and Elaine Sciolino, "U.S. Report Warns of Risk in Spread of Nuclear Skills," *New York Times,* January 1, 1992.

20. From the *New York Times,* see William J. Broad, "A Soviet Company Offers Nuclear Blasts for Sale to Anyone with the Cash," November 7, 1991; William C. Potter, "Russia's Nuclear Entrepreneurs," November 7, 1991; Barbara Crosette, "U.S. Weighs Aid for Russian Nuclear Scientists," and Thomas L. Friedman, "U.S. to Offer Plan to Keep Scientists at Work in Russia," January 25, 1992; Friedman, "Ex-Soviet Atom Scientists Ask Baker for West's Help," February 15, 1992; and Friedman, "Baker and Yeltsin Agree on U.S. Aid in Scrapping Arms," February 18, 1992.

21. In 1979, it appeared that the United States might be relaxing its opposition to the use of plutonium by its principal allies (*New York Times,* October 25, 1979). Also see Michael Brenner, "Carter's Bungled Promise," *Foreign Policy* (Fall 1979): 89ff.

22. On West Germany's plan, see Norman Gall, "Atoms for Brazil, Dangers for All," *Foreign Policy* (Summer 1976): 155-201; and Steven J. Baker, "Monopoly or Cartel?" *Foreign Policy* (Summer 1976): 202-220. On how the United States helped France develop its nuclear capability, see Richard H. Ullman, "The Covert French Connection," *Foreign Policy* (Summer 1989): 3-33.

23. *New York Times,* March 18, 1980.

24. *New York Times,* February 24, 1976.

25. *New York Times,* April 28, 1977.

26. Rosenberg, "Nuking the Nukes," 22.

27. From the *New York Times,* see Paul Lewis, "Iraq Now Admits a Secret Program to Enrich Uranium," July 9, 1991; Jerry Gray, "Baghdad Reveals It Had Plutonium of Weapons Grade," August 6, 1991; and Sheryl Wu Dunn, "China Backs Pact on Nuclear Spread," August 11, 1991.

28. Elaine Sciolino, "U.S. Doubts Iraq's Accounting of Nuclear Material," *New York Times,* July 9, 1991.

29. William J. Broad, "Iraqi Atom Effort Exposes Weakness in World Controls," and Gary Milhollin and Gerald White, "Stop the Nuclear Threat at the Source," *New York Times,* July 15 and August 10, 1991, respectively.

30. Betts, "Paranoids, Pygmies"; and Lefever, *Nuclear Arms in the Third World.*

31. Betts, "Paranoids, Pygmies," 178.

32. Ted Greenwood, George W. Rathjens, and Jack Ruina, *Nuclear Power and Weapons Proliferation* (London: International Institute for Strategic Studies, 1977), 32. Also see Lewis A. Dunn, "Building on Success: The NPT at Fifteen," *Survival* (May/June 1986): 221-233.

33. John Simpson and Darryl Howlett, "Nuclear Non-proliferation: The Way Forward," *Survival* (November/December 1991): 483-499; and Lewis A. Dunn, *Containing Nuclear Proliferation,* Adelphi Papers, 263, Winter 1991 (Published by Brassey's

for the International Institute for Strategic Studies).

34. Shai Feldman, "The Bombing of Osirag—Revisited," *International Security* (Fall 1982): 114-142.
35. Ibid., 115.
36. Thomas L. McNaugher, "Ballistic Missiles and Chemical Weapons: The Legacy of the Iran-Iraq War," *Security* (Fall 1990): 17.
37. Andrew Rosenthal, "Bush Unveils Plans for Arms Control in the Middle East," *New York Times*, May 30, 1991.
38. Paul Lewis, "Iraq Admits Buying German Materials to Make A-Bomb," and "Inspectors Uncover New Data on Iraqis' Nuclear Program," *New York Times*, January 15 and 20, 1991, respectively.
39. Gary Milhollin, "Building Saddam Hussein's Bomb," *New York Times Magazine*, March 8, 1992, 30ff.
40. R. W. Apple, Jr., "Leaders Express Support for Gorbachev," *New York Times*, July 17, 1991, as well as the paper's editorial "Iraq's Nuclear Menace" on July 11, 1991. Also see Patrick E. Tyler, "Saudis Pressing U.S. for Help in Ouster of Iraq's Leader," *New York Times*, January 19, 1992. The Saudis wanted the United States to organize a large covert program to topple the Iraqi leader by arming the Kurdish and Shiite opposition.
41. Steve Fetter, "Ballistic Missiles and Weapons of Mass Destruction: What Is the Threat? What Should Be Done?" *International Security* (Summer 1991): 5-42.
42. James L. Tyson, "U.S. Tries Again to Staunch China Arms Flow," *Christian Science Monitor*, August 4, 1988.
43. Quoted by Geoffrey Kemp, "Regional Security, Arms Control and the End of the Cold War," *Washington Quarterly* (Autumn 1990): 41.
44. Frederic J. Hollinger, "The Missile Technology Control Regime: A Major New Arms Control Achievement," in Arms Control and Disarmament Agency, *Arms Control Update* (Washington, D.C.: Government Printing Office, 1988), 25-27.
45. See William C. Potter and Adam Stulberg, "The Soviet Union and the Spread of Ballistic Missiles," *Survival* (November/December): 1990, 543-557, for Soviet declarations and practices in this area.
46. Keith Bradsher, "Baker Warns China against Selling New Missiles," *New York Times*, June 13, 1991.
47. Steve Emerson, "The Postwar SCUD Boom," *Wall Street Journal*, July 10, 1991.
48. Gary Milhollin and Gerard White, "The Brazilian Bomb," *New Republic*, August 13, 1990, 10-11.
49. Michael Eisenstadt, *The Sword of the Arabs* (Washington, D.C.: Washington Institute Press, 1990). Also see W. Seth Carus, *Chemical Weapons in the Middle East* (Washington, D.C.: Washington Institute for Near East Policy, 1988).
50. Malcolm W. Browne, "Germ Warfare Regarded as a Hard Enemy to Fight," and Michael R. Gordon, "Gulf G.I.'s to Get Germ Warfare Shots," *New York Times*, December 28, 1990.
51. Andrew J. Pierre, "Arms Sales: The New Diplomacy," *Foreign Affairs* (Winter 1981/82): 269 (emphasis added). Also see Pierre, *The Global Politics of Arms Sales* (Princeton, N.J.: Princeton University Press, 1981).
52. Richard W. Stevenson, "No Longer the Only Game in Town," *New York Times* (Business section), December 4, 1988. On France, see Edward A. Kolodziej, ed., *Making and Marketing Arms* (Princeton, N.J.: Princeton University Press, 1987).
53. Arms Control and Disarmament Agency, *World Military Expenditures and Arms*

Transfers, 1984 (Washington, D.C.: Government Printing Office, 1985), 18.

54. Robert Pear, "Prospects of Arms Pacts Spurring Weapons Sales," *New York Times,* March 25, 1990.

55. Tom Wicker, "Arming the New Order," *New York Times,* March 21, 1991.

56. Leslie H. Gelb, "Arms Sales Heavy," and Robert Pear, "U.S. Ranked No. 1 in Weapons Sales," *New York Times,* March 24 and August 11, 1991, respectively.

57. Stephanie G. Neuman, "The Arms Market: Who's on Top?" *Orbis* (Fall 1989): 509-531, for further details on global trends in arms sales.

58. Ethan B. Kapstein, "The Brazilian Defense Industry and the International System," *Political Science Quarterly* (Winter 1990-91): 587.

59. Stephanie G. Neuman, "Arms, Aid and the Superpowers," *Foreign Affairs* (Summer 1988): 1044-1066, for the view that military aid was a potent tool for the superpowers in enhancing their control over the developing countries.

60. Kemp, "Regional Security," 44.

61. Ibid., 37-38.

62. Glenn Frankel, "Iraq's War Machine: Made in the West," *International Herald Tribune,* September 18, 1990.

63. Ibid.

64. Kenneth R. Timmerman, *The Death Lobby* (New York: Houghton Mifflin, 1992). Also see "Iraq's Bomb, Chip by Chip," for the companies and dollar amounts of each transaction. This list was compiled by Gary Milhollin and Diane Edensword, *New York Times,* April 24, 1992.

65. For a partial listing, see Jill Abramson and Edward T. Pound, "If Crisis Eases, Iraq Would Still Pose a Threat for Which the U.S. Must Shoulder Some Blame," *Wall Street Journal,* December 7, 1990. Especially disturbing were reports of U.S. firms helping Iraq acquire a capability for biological warfare. See Eric Nadler and Robert Windrem, "Deadly Contagion," *New Republic,* February 4, 1991, 18-20.

66. Steve Fetter, "Ballistic Missiles and Weapons of Mass Destruction," *International Security* (Summer 1991): 5-42. Also Martin S. Navias, "Ballistic Missile Proliferation," *Survival* (May/June 1989): 225-239.

67. To combat the transfer of missile technology, the Bush administration in 1992 considered boarding North Korean ships headed for Iran loaded with SCUD missiles allegedly for Syria and Iran, although it was unclear whether these missiles could be legally seized. Patrick E. Tyler, "U.S. Weighs Boarding Korean Arms Ships," *New York Times,* March 6, 1992.

68. Quoted by Thomas G. Mahnken, "The Arrow and the Shield: U.S. Responses to Ballistic Missile Proliferation," *Washington Quarterly* (Winter 1991): 193.

69. Alan Riding, "Talks Begin on Arms Sales to 3d World," *New York Times,* July 9, 1991.

70. Walter S. Mossberg and Rick Wartzman, "Back to the Race: Mideast Arms Outlays Seem Unlikely to Face Any Tough New Curbs," *Wall Street Journal,* March 4, 1991; and Patrick E. Tyler, "Cheney Wants No Limit on Arms for Gulf Allies," as well as Michael Wines, "Third World Seeks Advanced Arms," *New York Times,* March 20 and 26, 1991, respectively. Also see Janne E. Nolan, "Controlling the Global Arms Market," *Washington Quarterly* (Summer 1991): 125-138; and Nolan, *Trappings of Power* (Washington, D.C.: Brookings, 1991).

71. Walter Laqueur, *Terrorism* (Boston: Little, Brown, 1977). Also see Claire Sterling, *The Terror Network* (New York: Holt, Rinehart & Winston, 1981); Yonah Alexander, *International Terrorism,* rev. ed. (New York: Praeger, 1981); Benjamin Netanyahu,

Terrorism (New York: Farrar, Straus, Giroux, 1986); and Donna M. Schlagheck, *International Terrorism* (Lexington, Mass.: Lexington Books, 1988).

72. Ronald Reagan, "The New Network of Terrorist States," and Robert B. Oakley, "Terrorism: Overview and Developments," Current Policy Nos. 721 and 744, respectively (Washington, D.C.: Department of State, 1985).

73. Brian M. Jenkins, "High Technology Terrorism and Surrogate War: The Impact of New Technology on Low-Level Violence," in *The Other Arms Race*, ed. Geoffrey Kemp, Robert L. Pfaltzgraff, Jr., and Uri Ra'anan (Lexington, Mass.: Lexington Books, 1975), 102 (emphasis added).

74. Daniel Pipes, "Undeclared War," *New Republic*, January 7 and 14, 1985. Also see Pipes, "Fundamentalist Muslims," *Foreign Affairs* (Summer 1986): 939-959. For the "inside story of America's war against terrorism," see David C. Martin and John Walcott, *Best Laid Plans* (New York: Harper & Row, 1988).

75. Michael Wines, "U.S. Inquiry Links Libyan Operatives to Pan Am Blast," *New York Times*, October 10, 1990; and Robert H. Kupperman and Tamara Kupperman, "The Politics of Pan Am 103," *New York Times*, November 16, 1991. For a different interpretation, see "Why Did They Die?" *Time*, April 27, 1992.

76. Tom Wicker, "Smoke Over Kuwait," and "Kuwait Still Burns," *New York Times*, April 4 and July 18, 1991, respectively; and Ken Wells, "The Battles Are Over, But Gulf Environment Still Fights for Its Life," *Wall Street Journal*, October 15, 1991.

77. A. M. Rosenthal, "Our Ally, the Killer," and Rachel Ehrenfeld, "With Friends Like Syria," *New York Times*, October 2 and 28, 1990, respectively.

78. Jane Perlez, "Sudan Is Seen as Safe Base for Mideast Terror Groups," *New York Times*, January 26, 1992.

79. Thomas C. Schelling, "Thinking about Nuclear Terrorism," *International Security* (Spring 1982): 61.

80. Conor Cruise O'Brien, "Thinking about Terrorism," *Atlantic Monthly*, June 1986, 62-66; and Eric Schmitt, "U.S. Says Iran Paid Captors $1 Million for Each Release," *New York Times*, January 20, 1992.

81. David E. Sanger, "Tokyo in the New Epoch: Heady Future, with Fear," *New York Times*, May 5, 1992.

82. Josef Joffe, "Entangled Forever," *National Interest* (Fall 1990): 39-40; and Owen Harries, "Of Unstable Disposition," *National Interest* (Winter 1990/91): 102-106.

83. Charles Krauthammer, "The Lonely Superpower," *New Republic*, July 29, 1991, 23-27.

Glossary

actor Individuals or organizations, including nation-states, that play a role in and influence international politics.

ABM Antiballistic missile, designed to "knock down" incoming missiles or their warheads (nuclear bombs) before designated targets are struck.

alliances Agreements among states to support each other militarily in case of attack or to enhance their mutual interests. Alliances supplement national power and clarify spheres of interest. (Examples: North Atlantic Treaty Organization and Warsaw Pact.)

anticolonialism Rejection of the former "father" or "mother" country by a Third World state.

appeasement In contemporary usage, a term of shame meaning one-sided concessions to an adversary. Before the Munich Conference of 1938, the term was respectable because it referred to the settlement of legitimate grievances and the consequent avoidance of war.

arms control Process of securing agreements that restrict the numbers, types, and performance characteristics of strategic weapons. In the U.S.-Soviet context of the cold war, the process was aimed at stabilizing mutual deterrence and avoiding nuclear war by eliminating the incentive to strike first at the other side.

arms race Arms acquisitions by a nation or alliance, through increases in the production of weapons or technological breakthroughs, to compete with its adversaries. During the cold war, arms races often were characterized by an action-reaction pattern among nations that were either trying to stay ahead of, or at least not fall behind, their adversaries.

balance of power Relationship in which nations strive to achieve security through establishment of an approximate power equilibrium in the state system, thus reducing the probability of warfare or domination. In short, power checks power.

balance of trade Difference between the value of a nation's exports and the value of its imports. The balance will be either a surplus or a deficit.

behavioral approach School of thought that developed in reaction to idealism and realism. Behaviorism claimed to have no *a priori* assumptions about state behavior and emphasized the need for empirical research. How to study, especially by means of value-free quantitative methods, often appeared to be its preoccupation rather than the key substantive issues in the "real world."

bilateral Between two states.

bipolar system International system dominated by *two* superpowers or coalitions. This system is characterized by a high degree of insecurity, clear distinctions between friend and foe, sensitivity to power shifts, arms races, and cohesiveness of each coalition.

boycott Economic weapon used by one nation or nations to pressure another nation by cutting off its imports.

bureaucratic politics See ***governmental politics model.***

capitalism Economic system based on the private ownership of property, a free market based on the laws of supply and demand, a general absence of governmental interference, and the pursuit of individual profit.

cartel An agreement by the producers of commodities (for example, oil) to control production and pricing.

Carter Doctrine U.S. guarantee of protection extended to the Persian Gulf oil kingdoms after the 1979 Soviet invasion of Afghanistan.

cold war Relationship characterized by conflict and competition, often accompanied by tension and hostility, that evolved between the United States (the West) and the Soviet Union (Communist bloc) after World War II.

COMECON Council for Mutual Economic Assistance, founded in 1949 by the Soviet Union as a means of integrating the economies of the East European states and asserting Soviet control over them. Mongolia, Cuba, and Vietnam were allowed to join later. Dissolved in 1991.

Common Market See ***EEC.***

Commonwealth of Independent States The loose association of eleven of the former Soviet republics, of which Russia, the successor state to the Soviet Union, is the largest.

communism Revolutionary ideology and political movement that seek the destruction of capitalism and its replacement by a collectivist society in which private ownership of property is no longer necessary. Subsequently, both social and economic classes and the state will cease to exist.

containment Post-World War II American foreign policy aimed at blocking Soviet expansion through countervailing American economic and military power. It was expected that the Soviet leadership would eventually mellow, abandon its expansionist drive, and accept the international status quo.

conventional weapons Nonnuclear weapons.

counterforce strategy Strategic weapons targeted at the adversary's military capabilities such as bomber bases, ICBM silos, and air defense installations.

countervalue (countercity) strategy Strategic weapons targeted at the adversary's population centers and industries, targets that it presumably values and does not want to lose.

crises Intense, relatively brief superpower confrontations that became substitutes for war in the nuclear era. Crises involved threats to vital national interests, an increased perception of the possible use of force, and each party's reputation for power.

cruise missile Nuclear missile, resembling a pilotless aircraft, that operates entirely within the earth's atmosphere and is launched from the air or sea.

crusade Policy characterized by an unshakable missionary zeal to eliminate evil from the world. It tends to be transformed into a total war to utterly destroy the adversary.

CSCE Conference on Security and Cooperation in Europe, composed of the members of NATO, including the United States and Canada, the members of the now-defunct Warsaw Pact (including most of the former Soviet republics), as well as neutral nations. It is expected to play a major role in the resolution of conflicts among the European states in the post-cold war period.

Cuban missile crisis Thirteen tense days in October 1962 when the United States and the Soviet Union clashed over the issue of Soviet missiles emplaced in Cuba. The crisis ended with Soviet leader Nikita Khrushchev's promise to remove the missiles in exchange for President John Kennedy's pledge not to invade Cuba.

decision-making approach Level of analysis that focuses primarily on the specific policy makers and bureaucracy officially responsible for the conduct and implementation of foreign policy.

delivery vehicles or launchers ICBMs (land-based intercontinental ballistic missiles), SLBMs (sea-launched ballistic missiles), and intercontinental bombers, all capable of delivering nuclear warheads or bombs.

dependency Analytical perspective that views the state system and international economy as divided between the *core* First World (industrial capitalist states), which is rich because it dominates the global economy, and the *peripheral* Third World, which is poor because it is exploited.

détente In general, a relaxation of previously tenser relations between two or more countries. During the cold war, détente meant in the United States that U.S.-Soviet global conflict and competition could be moderated and restrained by cooperation in such areas as arms control, trade, and technology.

deterrence (nuclear) In the bipolar nuclear context of the cold war, the assumption that total war was synonymous with mutual destruction because both superpowers possessed effective second-strike capabilities. The resulting standoff, if it was perceived as credible by rational policy makers on both sides, prevented the outbreak of war.

developing country Less-developed countries of the international system, usually categorized as belonging to the Third World. Economic backwardness or ineffective, weak political institutions are typical of these states.

diplomacy International negotiations or bargaining to settle conflicts among states over such issues as territorial divisions, arms ratios, and trade imbalances.

disarmament Agreement to reduce (or abolish) existing military forces or weapons.

divide-and-rule Balance-of-power technique in which nation A attempts to exploit existing differences among nation B and its allies to gain an advantage.

domino theory Belief that if one country falls to the enemy, that country's neighboring nations will also fall, upsetting the balance of power.

East Term formerly referring to the Communist states of Eastern Europe as well as the Soviet Union.

East-West conflict Another term for cold war or the American-Soviet conflict and competition for influence in the world.

EC European Community, composed of the European Coal and Steel Community, European Economic Community, and European Atomic Energy Community (Euratom).

EEC European Economic Community (also known earlier as the Common Market), founded in 1958 to create unified national economic policies (such as a uniform external tariff wall and mobile labor and capital) among its original members (Belgium, France, Italy, Luxembourg, the Netherlands, and West Germany). The original members were joined by Britain, Denmark, and Ireland in 1973, Greece in 1981, and Portugal and Spain in 1986, for a total membership of twelve states.

embargo Economic weapon used by one nation to prevent its goods from being sold to the targeted nation.

first strike See ***counterforce strategy.***

First World Advanced urban-industrial economies and political democracies of Western Europe, North America (Canada and the United States), and Japan.

foreign policy Nation's efforts to realize its objectives or national interests in the state system.

free trade International movement of goods unhampered by tariff and nontariff restrictions.

functionalism Theory that envisions economic and social cooperation among nations in various fields and eventually a new international political community.

games nations play   Games analogy used in this book to refer to the need for states in the international system to pursue a strategy—a set of moves to be made in a competitive and conflictual situation—to advance their interests.

GATT   General Agreement on Tariffs and Trade, organized in 1947 by the Western industrialized states. GATT, which now has over 100 members, has become the key global arena for negotiating tariff and other reductions to stimulate trade.

GDP   Gross domestic product or the sum market value of all consumer and capital goods and services produced in a year, excluding foreign earnings. This index, long used in Europe, has been used in the United States since late 1991, replacing GNP, in calculating economic power rankings among nations.

General Assembly   Body of the United Nations in which all its members are represented. Intended originally to be an advisory organ to the Security Council, its influence has grown with the addition of many Third World nations, which now constitute the majority.

glasnost   Term referring to Mikhail Gorbachev's efforts in the Soviet Union to allow more openness or freedom to express viewpoints different from officially sanctioned ones and to reexamine Soviet history.

GNP   Gross national product or the sum market value of all consumer and capital goods and services produced in a year. This indicator or index was used widely until late 1991 in calculating economic power rankings among nations. See **GDP**.

governmental politics model   Pluralistic decision-making approach that stresses the bargaining among the executive/legislative branches, nongovernmental interest groups, and executive agencies participating in the making of foreign policy.

great power   See **pole.**

greenhouse effect   General warming of the planet, resulting in rising sea levels, shifting agricultural zones, and other problems, caused by a buildup of gases, especially carbon dioxide, that trap heat in the earth's atmosphere.

Group of 7 (G-7)   Seven Western industrial, free-market nations (United States, Canada, Britain, France, Germany, Italy, and Japan), whose political leaders and economic ministers meet regularly to discuss and iron out differences in economic policy.

Group of 77 (G-77)   Founded in 1976 by seventy-seven developing countries and with a present membership of 125, a group that has been called the "poor nations' trade-union" in North-South negotiations.

groupthink   Term coined by Irving L. Janis to indicate the tendency of the members of a decision-making group to conform to the group's apparent views rather than ask awkward questions. Policy is therefore made on the basis of insufficient information and the failure to consider all available options.

guerrilla warfare   See **revolutionary warfare.**

guns versus butter   Competition between objectives, which many states confront— that is, security (military-defense) needs compete for priority with welfare needs (such as schools, hospitals, education, and housing).

hegemony   Superiority or dominance of one state over other states.

high politics   Term used to describe security and prestige issues, which usually involve military power.

human rights policy   Moral and political commitment to individual freedoms and opposition to governments that flagrantly violate these principles.

ICBM   Land-based intercontinental ballistic missile, which can be launched at targets 6,000 miles away. (Example: U.S. Minuteman III.)

idealist approach   School of thinking that focuses on how nations *ought* to behave to eliminate international conflict and create greater international cooperation and peace.

ideology   Comprehensive set of beliefs that critically describes and explains contemporary reality while prescribing a better state of affairs in the future.

IGOs Intergovernmental organizations, which may be classified as global (United Nations) or regional (Organization of American States, League of Arab States). Political, military, social, and economic functions also can distinguish IGOs (North Atlantic Treaty Organization and World Health Organization).

imports Products shipped to a nation from another nation.

incrementalism Tendency of policy makers to move forward step by step on a specific course of policy while concentrating on momentary, short-run aims rather than on comprehensive, long-range planning.

intangible components of power Components that do not lend themselves to accurate calculation or quantification such as a state's national morale, quality of leadership, or the effectiveness of its political system.

integration Creation within a territory of a "sense of community" and of legitimate institutions and practices, leading to an expectation of "peaceful change" among its population.

intentions versus capabilities A state's goals or objectives versus its power to achieve them.

interdependence Argument that the nations of the world have become *mutually sensitive* and *vulnerable* through an interrelationship of socioeconomic and technological issues and that their future behavior will be oriented toward long-term collaboration rather than toward conflict over security issues.

international system See *state system.*

intervention State or alliance involving itself either overtly or covertly in the affairs of another state to influence policy and events.

irredentism Desire of state A to annex territory of state B, which contains people who possess linguistic, racial, or ethnic backgrounds similar to those of state A's citizenry.

isolationism In general, noninvolvement of a state in the affairs of the international system, although the degree of disinterest can vary considerably.

kiloton weapon Nuclear weapon, the yield of which is measured in thousands of tons of TNT. A 10-kiloton weapon is equal to the explosive power of 10,000 tons of TNT.

Kto, kovo? In the parlance of the leaders of the former Soviet Union, "Who will destroy whom?" Signified the belief in the irreconcilable struggle between capitalism and communism.

levels of analysis As used in this book, the levels of the state system (balance of power), the nation-state (its internal nature), and decision making (leadership elites), which are analyzed to explain and describe how and why nations play the games they do.

limited war Armed conflict fought for limited political objectives and with definite restrictions on the use of force.

low politics Term used to describe welfare or socioeconomic issues.

macropolitics View that the *international interest* of humankind should be given priority over the traditional national interests of states in an increasingly interdependent world.

MAD Mutual assured destruction, a doctrine that was at the heart of strategic deterrence and was aimed at preventing all-out war between the United States and the Soviet Union. Because both sides would have been destroyed regardless of who struck first, nuclear war was prevented.

Marshall Plan Massive program of American economic aid ($15 billion) aimed at rebuilding war-torn Western Europe from 1948 to 1952.

Marxism Doctrine developed during the nineteenth century by Karl Marx and Friedrich Engels, which explained historical developments as a series of economic class struggles. Capitalism would eventually be overthrown by a proletarian (workers) revolution against the bourgeoisie (propertied, exploiting class), ushering in a classless, nonpropertied, nonexploitive utopia.

mass-destruction weapons   Nuclear, chemical, and biological weapons.

megaton weapon   Nuclear weapon whose yield is explosively equivalent to 1 million tons of TNT. For example, a 5-megaton missile warhead would equal the explosive power of 5 million tons of TNT.

mercantilism   Political philosophy that proposes the use of economic means to increase the prosperity and power of one's own state at the cost of other states.

microstates   States with populations of less than 1 million (such as Grenada or the Seychelles), which are often unable to defend or economically sustain themselves.

MIRV   Multiple independently targeted reentry vehicle or a single ballistic missile that carries a cluster of warheads with each warhead capable of hitting a separate target.

misperception   Belief that wars occur because decision makers have good-and-evil or black-and-white images of the world that filter out any incoming information that conflicts with their preconceived cognitive maps. But for these maps, international harmony and peace would prevail.

MNCs   Multinational corporations or business enterprises that conduct their operations across international boundaries and in multiple markets, in effect creating a global shopping center. American MNCs include Exxon, Pepsi-Cola, and General Motors.

modernization   Long, complex, and often painful transformation of a state from an agrarian, politically fragmented entity to an urban-industrialized, politically unified society. Modernization involves fundamental changes in the population's values and expectations.

MTCR   (Missile Technology Control Regime) Organized by the principal Western states to limit the export of technologies that might help other countries, principally Third World states, to build missiles.

multilateral   Between more than two states.

multipolar system   System that has at least four approximately equal powers. In contrast to simple and rigid bipolarity, multipolarity is complex and flexible. Frequent alliance realignments and lowered sensitivities to changes in the balance of power are characteristic of this international structure.

nation-state or nation   See **sovereign state**.

national interests   Ordering of priorities in accordance with national goals. Varies considerably with changing governments that tend to define these interests differently.

national morale   Intangible component of power that refers to a population's patriotism, national loyalty, and willingness to sacrifice during times of war or international tension.

national style   Each state's own approach to foreign policy based on its historical experience, political and social values, economic status, and cultural perspective.

NATO   North Atlantic Treaty Organization, the alliance between the United States and Western Europe, established in 1949.

neocolonial   Pejorative term used to describe the status of developing countries that, while politically independent, are said to be still economically controlled and exploited by the developed Western capitalist states.

neutralization   Balance-of-power technique or hands-off policy toward a strategically important country lying between two major powers.

NGO   Nongovernmental organization, such as a multinational corporation; national liberation, terrorist, religious, and humanitarian organizations; and other groups such as the Catholic church and the Red Cross.

NICs   Newly industrialized countries, a term used to describe the Pacific Rim nations (Hong Kong, Singapore, South Korea, and Taiwan), as well as other developing states such as Malaysia and Brazil.

NIEO New international economic order. This is the more equitable distribution of the world's wealth demanded by the developing countries since the 1970s because the present order favors the rich Western industrial nations, which allegedly exploited them in the past and continue to do so.

nonalignment Policy of not aligning formally (particularly evident in the Third World) with either the Communist or free-world alliances, mainly during the bipolar cold war period.

nontariff barriers Informal barriers to free trade designed to make the importation of foreign products very difficult.

North Term usually referring to the Western democratic industrialized states (including Japan).

nuclear proliferation Acquisition of nuclear capabilities by a significant number of middle- and lower-rank states.

nuclear nonproliferation treaty In an effort to prevent the spread of nuclear weapons, the 1968 treaty forbids the transfer of nuclear weapons, technology, or material to nonnuclear states. The latter, if they are signatories, are obligated to forgo the acquisition of nuclear weapons.

nuclear winter Scenario devised in 1983 by scientists in which the smoke and soot created by a full-scale superpower nuclear war would block out the sunlight for months, if not years, causing extensive freezing of the earth's surface and extermination of most of its plant and animal (including human) life.

OPEC Organization of Petroleum Exporting Countries (Algeria, Ecuador, Gabon, Indonesia, Iran, Iraq, Kuwait, Libya, Nigeria, Qatar, Saudi Arabia, United Arab Emirates, and Venezuela), a producer cartel whose purpose is collectively to fix the levels of production and the price of crude oil on the world market.

peace Complex, multifaceted concept, which, in its most general sense, refers to the absence of major warfare in the international system.

peaceful coexistence Soviet term, which, while acknowledging the dangers of nuclear war, asserted that the Communist-capitalist struggle could be channeled into nonmilitary areas of competition.

peace-keeping forces Nonfighting UN forces inserted between Third World belligerents to provide a buffer zone and halt fighting. First used during the cold war to prevent intervention by the two superpowers in Third World regional conflicts, thereby transforming them into a global conflagration.

perestroika Term referring to Soviet leader Mikhail Gorbachev's efforts to restructure the Soviet economic and political system.

petrodollars Money paid by the industrialized states to OPEC for oil.

PGMs Precision-guided munitions, more often known as smart bombs, which can hit their intended targets with great accuracy.

pole Major actor or state in the international system often referred to as a great power.

political community Community that effectively controls the means of violence, possesses a set of political institutions that peacefully allocates resources, and has a population that shares a common political identification.

political idealism See ***idealist approach.***

polycentrism State system with many assertive state actors other than the great powers.

population explosion Term reflecting concern that the rapid increase in the world's population, stemming from the high birthrates in the Third World, will overwhelm the earth's resources.

power (among states) Capacity of one state to influence others in accordance with its own objectives—that is, to change the behavior of the others or prevent them from taking a particular action.

power politics Term frequently used pejoratively to condemn international politics for its concern with power, conflict, and war. Its standard definition, originating in Europe, is a state's use of military or economic coercion to increase its own power or interests.

preemptive strike   Defensive attack to forestall what is believed to be an imminent first strike by the opponent. Differs from preventive strike, which is motivated by the offensive aim of eliminating the enemy and is independent of a perception that it is about to strike.

prestige   Nation's reputation for power among other states, determining the degree of respect that it is accorded.

preventive diplomacy   UN peace-keeping function in which multinational forces are injected into a conflict. During the cold war, the motivation was to prevent the possible intervention of the superpowers and escalation of the conflict.

preventive strike   A first strike by one state on another perceived as hostile and seeking ultimately to eliminate the other.

proxy wars   Use of surrogates by the superpowers during the cold war to advance their interests when they wanted to avoid a direct confrontation with its danger of nuclear war.

quota   Numerical limit on imports.

rapprochement   Reconciliation of two nations that were adversaries.

rational actor model   Decision-making approach that stresses a clear definition of policy goals and an examination of the alternative means of attaining those goals.

Reagan Doctrine   American support of guerrilla forces trying to overthrow the governments of countries in which the Soviet Union had directly or through proxies established Marxist regimes in the 1970s.

realist approach   School of thinking that focuses on the conflicts and rivalries among nations in an anarchical system. Balance of power plays a central role in this analysis, and war remains a continuing characteristic of international politics, to be avoided or limited through prudent management. War cannot be erased, however.

revisionist state   State that is dissatisfied with the contemporary distribution of power in the system and tries to change it in its favor.

revolutionary state   State whose leadership condemns the existing order as oppressive and exploitive and seeks to liberate humankind, bringing it freedom, justice, and peace. (Examples: late eighteenth-century France and the twentieth-century Soviet Union.)

revolutionary warfare (guerrilla warfare)   Lengthy conflicts fought by insurgents (or self-proclaimed liberators) whose primary goal is to capture state power as a means of transforming the nation's sociopolitical structure and economy.

SALT   Strategic Arms Limitation Talks, negotiations between the United States and the Soviet Union, which began in 1969. The 1972 SALT I consisted of two agreements: a limit on ABMs and a five-year freeze on ICBMs and SLBMs. The 1979 SALT II agreement, not ratified by the United States, set ceilings on offensive missiles and bombers.

SCUD missile   Soviet missile used by the Iraqis against Saudi Arabia and non-belligerent Israel during the Gulf War in 1991.

SDI   Strategic Defense Initiative, a proposal for a primarily space-based defense to destroy incoming missiles and protect America's population. More frequently called Star Wars because its technological feasibility is still very questionable, SDI may become operational at some future date as a limited defense of ICBMs, thus strengthening deterrence rather than replacing it as envisioned in 1983 by President Reagan.

search and destroy   Primary U.S. ground strategy in the Vietnam War in which American forces in helicopters searched for Communist guerrillas in the countryside to destroy them.

second-strike capability Ability, after absorbing a nuclear first strike from the enemy, to deliver a retaliatory blow with sufficient remaining force (missiles and bombers) to destroy the enemy.

Second World Term formerly used to refer to the Soviet Union and the Communist states of Eastern Europe.

Security Council Primary organ in the United Nations responsible for the preservation of peace and security. The fifteen-member council can take enforcement action against international aggression, provided one of the five permanent members—United States, Russia, Britain, France, and China—does not veto it.

security dilemma In an anarchical state system, follows from a state's attempt to ensure its security by increasing its power. As its potential adversary does the same, the first state's sense of insecurity recurs, leading it to increase its power once more, and so on.

security policy Basic policy of a noncrisis nature. (Examples: defense spending, foreign aid, and arms control policy.)

Sino-Soviet split Conflict between Communist China (People's Republic of China) and the Soviet Union over ideological interpretations, leadership of the international Communist movement, disputed territories, and major policy issues.

SLBM Submarine-launched (long-range) ballistic missile. (Examples: U.S. Poseidon and Trident.)

South Term encompassing the developing countries.

sovereign state Primary political actor in the international system. Each of the almost 170 states in this system is characterized by a territorial base, jurisdiction over its internal and external affairs, and, to varying degrees, a concept of self-identity (nationalism) and unity.

sphere of influence Geographic areas under the influence or domination of a great power. (Example: Central America for the United States.)

stable deterrence American-Soviet strategic nuclear balance in which the deterrent forces of both sides were invulnerable to the opponent's first strike.

stable state system International system characterized by minimal violence and the peaceful settlement of national differences.

stagflation Simultaneous occurrence of recession and inflation.

stalemate Form of conflict resolution in which victory for either side is rejected as a result of *mutual* battlefield exhaustion, reluctance to invest further resources, or unwillingness to escalate because of the risks involved.

START Strategic Arms Reduction Treaty, the Reagan administration's term for the SALT negotiations. START's purpose was to emphasize strategic arms *reductions* rather than the arms limitations or ceilings on the numbers of weapons each side could have allegedly emphasized in the SALT bargaining.

state-centric Analysis focusing on the behavior of nation-states as the principal actors in international politics.

state system Regular and observable interactions of political actors (primarily nations) within a basically anarchical global context.

status quo state State that is satisfied with the current distribution of power in the system (or at least not sufficiently dissatisfied that it seeks to change it).

strategic balance During the cold war, the nuclear balance of power between the two superpowers. *Parity* was another term often used to describe this balance.

superpowers Nations that possess an extraordinary amount of power (military, economic, diplomatic), allowing them to pursue an independent role in global affairs, or states whose actions have a substantial effect on the policies of other political actors throughout the entire state system. Term generally referred to the United States and Soviet Union in the period after World War II.

supranational actor Best exemplified by the European Community (EC), in which twelve sovereign states have transferred a degree of their sovereign authority on economic issues to a superior decision-making body. (See *EC.*)

tacit negotiations　Informal, indirect bargaining among states as opposed to traditional, face-to-face diplomacy.

tangible components of power　Usually, components that can be measured or quantified such as a nation's population, size, military strength, and economic productivity.

tariff　Tax imposed on imports.

terrorism　Use of political violence by nonstate actors (although some are state-supported) to intimidate their enemies and gain publicity for their causes.

Third World　Non-Western, largely economically underdeveloped countries.

totalitarianism　Political system that attempts to control every aspect of a citizen's life.

total war　War in which the political objectives of complete victory over the enemy are matched by the full mobilization of a nation's military, economic, and social resources. (Example: World War II.)

transnational actor　Nongovernmental organization characterized by having its headquarters in one country but conducting its centrally directed operations in two or more countries. (Example: multinational corporation.)

triad　Strategic deterrent composed of bombers, submarines, and ICBMs.

Truman Doctrine　The 1947 presidential pronouncement that "it must be the policy of the United States to support free peoples who are resisting subjugation by armed minorities or outside pressures." Originally directed at Greece and Turkey, the doctrine actually marked the beginning of the containment era and the U.S. role in preserving the balance of power in a bipolar world.

UNCTAD　United Nations Conference on Trade and Development, usually equated with a Third World coalition strategy focusing on North-South economic issues.

unilateral　One-sided.

unipolarity　Situation in which a single state dominates and organizes the international system.

unipolycentric　Post-cold war state system in which the United States remains militarily the lone superpower, but power is widely diffused so that many actors besides the traditional great powers assert their interests.

United Nations　International organization with virtually global membership, founded after World War II as a successor to the defunct League of Nations to preserve international peace.

Uniting for Peace resolution　U.S.-sponsored UN resolution passed in November 1950. It transferred the authority to preserve peace from the Security Council to the General Assembly so that support for American anti-Communist policies in Korea would not be blocked by Soviet vetoes.

unstable deterrence　During the cold war, U.S.-Soviet nuclear balance in which one or both of the deterrent forces became vulnerable, thereby tempting the other side to strike preemptively, especially during a crisis.

unstable state system　International system prone to the outbreak of major wars.

utopianism　See *idealist approach.*

war　Hostilities between states that are conducted by armed force.

warhead　Part of a missile that contains the explosive material.

Warsaw Treaty Organization　Soviet alliance with the states of Eastern Europe organized in 1955. Also known as the Warsaw Pact. Dissolved in 1991.

West　Same as *North.*

world government　Idealistic concept of a supreme global authority that would make wars among states impossible.

yield　Explosive force of a warhead.

zero-sum　What one nation gains (for example, security), another loses. International politics is often said to be a zero-sum game, underlining its conflictual character.

Select Bibliography
of Books

International Politics and the State System

Aron, Raymond. *Peace and War.* Garden City, N.Y.: Doubleday, 1966. Paperback ed. Melbourne, Fla.: Krieger, 1981.

Bull, Hedley. *The Anarchical Society.** New York: Columbia University Press, 1977.

Carr, Edward H. *Twenty Years' Crisis, 1919-1939.** New York: Macmillan, 1951.

Claude, Inis L., Jr. *Power and International Relations.* New York: Random House, 1962.

Dougherty, James E., and Robert L. Pfaltzgraff. *Contending Theories of International Relations.** 3d ed. New York: Harper & Row, 1990.

Duchacek, Ivo D. *Territorial Dimension of Politics.* Boulder, Colo.: Westview Press, 1986.

Ferguson, Yale H., and Richard W. Mansbach. *The Elusive Quest.* Columbia: University of South Carolina Press, 1988.

_____. *The State, Conceptual Chaos, and the Future of International Relations Theory.* Boulder, Colo.: Lynne Rienner, 1989.

Fromkin, David. *The Independence of Nations.** New York: Praeger, 1981.

Gilpin, Robert. *War and Change in World Politics.* New York: Cambridge University Press, 1983.

Herz, John H. *Political Realism and Political Idealism.* Chicago: University of Chicago Press, 1951.

Kennedy, Paul M. *The Rise and Fall of British Naval Mastery.* Atlantic Highlands, N.J.: Humanities, 1986.

_____. *The Rise and Fall of the Great Powers.* New York: Random House, 1987.

Keohane, Robert O., ed. *Neorealism and Its Critics.* New York: Columbia University Press, 1986.

Knorr, Klaus, and James N. Rosenau, eds. *Contending Approaches to International Politics.** Princeton, N.J.: Princeton University Press, 1969.

Krasner, Stephen D. *Defending the National Interest.** Princeton, N.J.: Princeton University Press, 1978.

Note: *See chapter notes for additional books and articles.*
* Indicates paperback.

Mandelbaum, Michael. *The Fate of Nations.* New York: Cambridge University Press, 1988.

Morgan, Patrick M. *Theories and Approaches to International Politics.** 4th ed. New Brunswick, N.J.: Transaction Books, 1986.

Morgenthau, Hans J. *Politics among Nations.* 6th ed. Kenneth W. Thompson. New York: Knopf, 1985.

Niebuhr, Reinhold. *Moral Man and Immoral Society.* New York: Scribner's, 1952.

Rosenau, James N. *Turbulence in World Politics.* Princeton: Princeton University Press, 1990.

Small, Melvin, and J. David Singer. *Resort to Arms.* Beverly Hills, Calif.: Sage Publications, 1982.

Smith, Michael Joseph. *Realist Thought from Weber to Kissinger.* Baton Rouge: Louisiana State University Press, 1987.

Waltz, Kenneth N. *Man, the State, and War.** New York: Columbia University Press, 1959.

———. *Theory of International Politics.** Reading, Mass.: Addison-Wesley, 1979.

Wight, Martin. *Power Politics.* ed. Hedley Bull and Carsten Holbraad. New York: Holmes & Meier, 1978.

Wolfers, Arnold. *Discord and Collaboration.** Baltimore: Johns Hopkins University Press, 1962.

Peace and War

Aron, Raymond. *Peace and War.* Garden City, N.Y.: Doubleday, 1966. Paperback ed. Melbourne, Fla.: Krieger, 1981.

Beer, Francis A. *Peace against War.** San Francisco: W. H. Freeman, 1981.

Blainey, Geoffrey. *The Causes of War.** 3d ed. New York: Free Press, 1988.

Bueno de Mesquita, Bruce. *The War Trap.* New Haven, Conn.: Yale University Press, 1981.

Clausewitz, Carl von. *On War.* Edited and translated by Michael Howard and Peter Paret. Princeton, N.J.: Princeton University Press, 1976.

Harvard Nuclear Study Group. *Living with Nuclear Weapons.** New York: Bantam Books, 1983.

Howard, Michael. *The Causes of War.** Cambridge, Mass.: Harvard University Press, 1983.

Levy, Jack. *War in the Modern Great Power System, 1495-1975.* Lexington: University of Kentucky Press, 1983.

Midlansky, Manus. *The Onset of War.* Winchester, Mass.: Unwin Hyman, 1988.

Preston, Richard A., and Sydney F. Wise. *Men in Arms.* New York: Holt, Rinehart & Winston, 1979.

Ropp, Theodore. *War in the Modern World.* 2d ed. New York: Collier, 1962.

Walt, Stephen M. *The Origin of Alliances.** Ithaca, N.Y.: Cornell University Press, 1990.

Wright, Quincy. *A Study of War.* Abridged ed. Chicago: University of Chicago Press, 1964. Paperback ed. 1983.

American Foreign Policy

Almond, Gabriel A. *The American People and Foreign Policy.** New York: Holt, Rinehart & Winston, 1960.

Beschloss, Michael R. *Kennedy and Khrushchev, 1960-1963.** New York: Harper Collins, 1991.

Blechman, Barry M., and Stephen S. Kaplan. *Force without War.* Washington, D.C.: Brookings, 1978.

Bowker, Mike, and Phil Williams. *Superpower Détente.* Newbury Park, Calif.: Sage Publications, 1988.

Brzezinski, Zbigniew. *Game Plan.* Boston: Atlantic Monthly Press, 1986.

Gaddis, John L. *The Long Peace.* New York: Oxford University Press, 1987.

_____. *Russia, the Soviet Union, and the United States.* New York: Random House, 1978.

_____. *Strategies of Containment.** New York: Oxford University Press, 1982.

Gati, Charles, ed. *Caging the Bear.** New York: Bobbs-Merrill, 1973.

George, Alexander L., ed. *Managing U.S.-Soviet Rivalry.** Boulder, Colo.: Westview Press, 1983.

Gilbert, Felix. *To the Farewell Address.** Princeton, N.J.: Princeton University Press, 1961.

Haass, Richard N. *Conflicts Unending.* New Haven, Conn.: Yale University Press, 1990.

Halle, Louis J. *The Cold War as History.* New York: Harper & Row, 1967. Paperback ed. 1971.

Hanreider, Wolfram F. *Germany, America, Europe.* New Haven, Conn.: Yale University Press, 1989.

Hyland, William G. *The Cold War Is Over.* New York: Times Books, 1990.

Jones, Joseph M. *The Fifteen Weeks.** New York: Viking, 1955. Paperback ed. New York: Harcourt, Brace, 1965.

Kennan, George F. *American Diplomacy 1900-1950.** Chicago: University of Chicago Press, 1951. Enlarged ed. 1985.

Larson, Deborah. *Origins of Containment.* Princeton, N.J.: Princeton University Press, 1985.

Mandelbaum, Michael, and Strobe Talbott. *Reagan and Gorbachev.** New York: Vintage Books, 1987.

Morgenthau, Hans J. *In Defense of the National Interest.* New York: Knopf, 1951. Paperback ed. Lanham, Md.: University Press of America, 1983.

_____. *A New Foreign Policy for the United States.** New York: Holt, Rinehart & Winston, 1969.

Mueller, John E. *War, Presidents, and Public Opinion.* New York: Wiley, 1973. Paperback ed. Lanham, Md.: University Press of America, 1985.

Nye, Joseph S. *Bound to Lead.* New York: Basic Books, 1990.

Orme, John David. *Political Instability and American Foreign Policy.* New York: St. Martin's Press, 1989.

Osgood, Robert E. *Ideals and Self-Interest in America's Foreign Relations.** Chicago: University of Chicago Press, 1953.

Pastor, Robert. *Condemned to Repetition.* Princeton, N.J.: Princeton University Press, 1987.

Rizopoulos, Nicholas. *Sea Change.** New York: Council on Foreign Relations, 1990.

Schraeder, Peter J., ed. *Intervention in the 1980s.* Boulder, Colo.: Lynne Rienner, 1989.

Smith, Gaddis. *American Diplomacy during the Second World War, 1941-1945.* New York: Wiley, 1966. Paperback ed. New York: Random House, 1985.

Spanier, John. *American Foreign Policy since World War II.** 12th rev. ed. Washington, D.C.: CQ Press, 1992.

Thomas, Hugh. *Armed Truce.* New York: Atheneum, 1987.

Tsou, Tang. *America's Failure in China.** Chicago: University of Chicago Press, 1963.

Tucker, Robert W. *The Purposes of American Power.** New York: Praeger, 1981.

_____. *The Radical Left and American Foreign Policy.** Baltimore: Johns Hopkins University Press, 1971.

Weintraub, Sidney, ed. *Economic Coercion and U.S. Foreign Policy.* Boulder, Colo.: Westview Press, 1982.

Memoirs and Biographies of American Statesmen and Administrations

Acheson, Dean. *Present at the Creation.** New York: Norton, 1969.

Ambrose, Stephen E. *Eisenhower*. Vols. I and II. New York: Simon & Schuster, 1983 and 1984, respectively.

_____. *Nixon*. Vols. I and II. New York: Simon & Schuster, 1987 and 1989, respectively.

Brzezinski, Zbigniew. *Power and Principle*. New York: Farrar, Straus, Giroux, 1983.

Byrnes, James F. *Speaking Frankly*. New York: Harper & Brothers, 1947.

Carter, Jimmy. *Keeping Faith*. New York: Bantam, 1982.

Cleva, Gregory P. *Henry Kissinger and the American Approach to Foreign Policy*. Lewisburg, Pa.: Bucknell University Press, 1989.

Cohen, Warren I. *Dean Rusk*. Towota, N.J.: Cooper Square, 1980.

Eisenhower, David. *Eisenhower at War: 1943-1945*. New York: Random House, 1986.

Eisenhower, Dwight D. *White House Years: Mandate for Change*.* Garden City, N.Y.: Doubleday, 1963.

_____. *White House Years: Waging Peace*. Garden City, N.Y.: Doubleday, 1965.

Gerson, Louis L. *John Foster Dulles*. New York: Cooper Square, 1967.

Haig, Alexander M., Jr. *Caveat*. New York: Macmillan, 1984.

Hoopes, Townsend. *The Devil and John Foster Dulles*. Boston: Little, Brown, 1973.

Immerman, Richard H., ed. *John Foster Dulles and the Diplomacy of the Cold War*. Princeton, N.J.: Princeton University Press, 1990.

Kissinger, Henry. *The White House Years*. Boston: Little, Brown, 1979.

_____. *Years of Upheaval*. Boston: Little, Brown, 1982.

Nixon, Richard. *RN*.* New York: Grosset & Dunlap, 1978.

_____. *Seize the Moment*. New York: Simon & Schuster, 1992.

Reagan, Ronald. *An American Life*. New York: Simon & Schuster, 1990.

Rusk, Dean, with Richard Rusk and Daniel S. Papp. *As I Saw It*. New York: W. W. Norton, 1990.

Schulzinger, Robert D. *Henry Kissinger*. New York: Columbia University Press, 1989.

Truman, Harry S. *Memoirs*.* 2 vols. Garden City, N.Y.: Doubleday, 1958.

Soviet Foreign and Military Policy

Adomeit, Hannes. *Soviet Risk Taking and Crisis Behavior*. Winchester, Mass.: Unwin Hyman, 1982.

Berman, Robert P., and John C. Baker. *Soviet Strategic Forces*.* Washington, D.C.: Brookings, 1982.

Bialer, Seweryn. *The Soviet Paradox*. New York: Knopf, 1986.

_____. *The Domestic Context of Soviet Foreign Policy*. Boulder, Colo.: Westview Press, 1981.

Bialer, Seweryn, and Michael Mandelbaum, eds. *Gorbachev's Russia and American Foreign Policy*. Boulder, Colo.: Westview Press, 1988.

Brzezinski, Zbigniew K. *The Grand Failure*. New York: Scribner's, 1989.

_____. *Ideology and Power in Soviet Politics*.* Rev. ed. New York: Holt, Rinehart & Winston, 1967.

Dallin, David J. *Soviet Foreign Policy after Stalin*. Philadelphia: Lippincott, 1961.

Deibel, T. L., ed. *Containing the Soviet Union*. McLean, Va.: Pergamon-Brassey, 1987.

Dinerstein, Herbert S. *War and the Soviet Union*.* Rev. ed. New York: Holt, Rinehart & Winston, 1962.

Doder, Dusko, and Louise Branson. *Gorbachev*. New York: Penguin, 1991.

Donaldson, Robert H., ed. *The Soviet Union in the Third World*. Boulder, Colo.: Westview Press, 1980.

Douglas, Joseph D., Jr., and Amoretta M. Hoeber. *Soviet Strategy for Nuclear War*.* Stanford, Calif.: Hoover Press, 1979.

Garthoff, Raymond L. *Détente and Confrontation*.* Washington, D.C.: Brookings, 1985.

_____. *Soviet Strategy in the Nuclear Age*.* Rev. ed. New York: Holt, Rinehart & Winston, 1962.

Gati, Charles. *The Bloc That Failed*. Bloomington: University of Indiana Press, 1990.

Hammond, Thomas T. *Red Flag over Afghanistan.** Boulder, Colo.: Westview Press, 1984.

Haslam, Jonathan. *The Soviet Union and the Politics of Nuclear Weapons in the Nuclear Age, 1969-77.* Ithaca, N.Y.: Cornell University Press, 1990.

Holloway, David. *The Soviet Union and the Arms Race.** 2d ed. New Haven, Conn.: Yale University Press, 1984.

Horelick, Arnold L., and Myron Rush. *Strategic Power and Soviet Foreign Policy.* Chicago: University of Chicago Press, 1966.

Kaiser, Robert G. *Why Gorbachev Happened.* New York: Simon & Schuster, 1991.

Kaplan, Stephen S. *Diplomacy of Power.** Washington, D.C.: Brookings, 1981.

Kennan, George F. *Russia and the West under Lenin and Stalin.* Boston: Little, Brown, 1961. Paperback ed. New York: New American Library, 1961.

Korbonski, Andrzej, and Francis Fukuyama, eds. *The Soviet Union and the Third World.* Ithaca, N.Y.: Cornell University Press, 1987.

Leites, Nathan. *The Operational Code of the Politburo.* New York: McGraw-Hill, 1951.

_____. *A Study of Bolshevism.* New York: Free Press, 1953.

Lynch, Allen. *The Soviet Study of International Relations.* New York: Cambridge University Press, 1987.

Mackintosh, J. M. *Strategy and Tactics of Soviet Foreign Policy.* London: Oxford University Press, 1962.

Nahaylo, Bohdan, and Victor Swoboda. *Soviet Disunion.* New York: Free Press, 1990.

Nogee, Joseph L., and Robert H. Donaldson. *Soviet Foreign Policy since World War II.** 4th ed. New York: Macmillan, 1992.

Papp, Daniel S. *Soviet Policies toward the Developing World during the 1980s.* Maxwell Air Force Base, Ala.: Air University Press, 1986.

Pipes, Richard. *Survival Is Not Enough.** Rev. ed. New York: Simon & Schuster, 1986.

Rubinstein, Alvin Z. *Moscow's Third World Strategy.* Princeton, N.J.: Princeton University Press, 1988.

Saivetz, Carol R., and Sylvia Woodby. *Soviet-Third World Relations.* Boulder, Colo.: Westview Press, 1985.

Scott, Harriet F., and William F. Scott. *The Armed Forces of the USSR.* Boulder, Colo.: Westview Press, 1978.

Sherr, Alan B. *The Other Side of Arms Control.* Winchester, Mass.: Unwin Hyman, 1988.

Smith, Hedrick. *The New Russians.* New York: Random House, 1990.

Taubman, William. *Stalin's American Policy.* New York: Norton, 1982.

Ulam, Adam B. *Dangerous Relations.** New York: Oxford University Press, 1983.

_____. *Expansion and Coexistence.** 2d ed. New York: Holt, Rinehart & Winston, 1974.

Valkenier, Elizabeth K. *The Soviet Union and the Third World.* New York: Praeger, 1985.

Von Laue, Theodore H. *Why Lenin, Why Stalin?** Philadelphia: Lippincott, 1964.

Wolfe, Thomas W. *Soviet Power and Europe, 1945-1970.** Baltimore: Johns Hopkins University Press, 1970.

_____. *Soviet Strategy at the Crossroads.* Cambridge, Mass.: Harvard University Press, 1964.

Zimmerman, William. *Soviet Perspectives on International Relations, 1956-1967.* Princeton, N.J.: Princeton University Press, 1969.

Developing Countries and Modernization

Berger, Peter L. *The Capitalist Revolution.** New York: Basic Books, 1986.

Berliner, Joseph S. *Soviet Economic Aid.* New York: Holt, Rinehart & Winston, 1958.

Black, C. E. *The Dynamics of Modernization.** New York: Harper & Row, 1966.

Black, Eugene R. *The Diplomacy of Economic Development.** New York: Atheneum, 1963.

Brandt Commission. *North-South.* Cambridge, Mass.: M.I.T. Press, 1980.

Crabb, Cecil V., Jr. *The Elephants and the Grass.** New York: Holt, Rinehart & Winston, 1965.

Ehrlich, Paul R. *The Population Bomb.* * New York: Ballantine, 1968.

Emerson, Rupert. *From Empire to Nation.* Cambridge, Mass.: Harvard University Press, 1960.

Faaland, J., and J. R. Parkinson. *The Political Economy of Development.* New York: St. Martin's Press, 1986.

Gupte, Pranay. *The Crowded Earth.* New York: Norton, 1984.

Hansen, Roger D. *Beyond the North-South Stalemate.* New York: McGraw-Hill (for the Council on Foreign Relations/1980s Project), 1979.

Heilbroner, Robert L. *The Great Ascent.* New York: Harper & Row, 1963.

Higgins, Benjamin, and Jean Downing Higgins. *Economic Development of a Small Planet.* New York: Norton, 1979.

Huntington, Samuel P. *Political Order in Changing Societies.* New Haven, Conn.: Yale University Press, 1968. Paperback ed. 1969.

Janowitz, Morris. *The Military in the Political Development of New Nations.* * Chicago: University of Chicago Press, 1964.

Johnson, John J., ed. *The Role of the Military in Underdeveloped Countries.* Princeton, N.J.: Princeton University Press, 1962.

Krasner, Stephen D. *Structural Conflict.* Berkeley: University of California Press, 1985.

Lewis, W. Arthur. *The Evolution of the International Economic Order.* * Princeton, N.J.: Princeton University Press, 1978.

Martin, Laurence W., ed. *Neutralism and Nonalignment.* * New York: Holt, Rinehart & Winston, 1962.

Meken, Jane, ed. *World Population and U.S. Policy.* New York: Norton, 1986.

Millikan, Max F., and Donald L. M. Blackmer, eds. *The Emerging Nations.* * Boston: Little, Brown, 1961.

Moran, Theodore H. *Multinational Corporations and the Politics of Dependence.* * Princeton, N.J.: Princeton University Press, 1974.

Mortimer, Robert A. *The Third World Coalition in International Politics.* 2d ed. Boulder, Colo.: Westview Press, 1984.

Myrdal, Gunnar. *The Challenge of World Poverty.* New York: Pantheon, 1970.

_____. *Rich Lands and Poor.* New York: Harper & Row, 1957.

Nordlinger, Eric A. *Soldiers in Politics.* * Englewood Cliffs, N.J.: Prentice-Hall, 1977.

Nossiter, Bernard D. *The Global Struggle for More.* New York: Harper & Row, 1987.

Organski, A. F. K. *The Stages of Political Development.* New York: Knopf, 1965.

Rostow, W. W. *Stages of Economic Growth.* * New York: Cambridge University Press, 1960.

Rothstein, Robert L. *Global Bargaining.* Princeton, N.J.: Princeton University Press, 1979.

_____. *The Third World and U.S. Foreign Policy.* Boulder, Colo.: Westview Press, 1981.

_____. *The Weak in the World of the Strong.* New York: Columbia University Press, 1977.

Salas, Rafael. *Reflections on Population.* 2d ed. New York: Pergamon Press, 1985.

Singer, Hans, and Javed A. Ansari. *Rich and Poor Countries.* 4th ed. London: Unwin Hyman, 1988.

Staley, Eugene. *The Future of Underdeveloped Countries.* * Rev. ed. New York: Holt, Rinehart & Winston, 1961.

Tapinos, Georges, and Phyllis T. Piotrow. *Six Billion People.* New York: McGraw-Hill (for the Council on Foreign Relations/1980s Project), 1978.

Tibi, Bassam. *Islam and the Cultural Accommodation of Social Change,* trans. Clare Krojzel. Boulder, Colo.: Westview Press, 1990.

Tinbergen, Jan. *Reshaping the International Order.* New York: Dutton, 1976.

Tucker, Robert W. *The Inequality of Nations.* New York: Basic Books, 1977. Paperback ed. 1979.

Ward, Barbara. *The Rich Nations and the Poor Nations.* * New York: Norton, 1962.

Wattenberg, Ben J. *The Birth Dearth.* New York: Pharos Books, 1987.

Wriggins, W. Howard, and Gunnar Adler-Karlsson. *Reducing Global Inequities.* New York: McGraw-Hill (for the Council on Foreign Relations/1980s Project), 1978.

Wright, Robin. *Sacred Rage.* New York: Linden Press, 1985.

Foreign Policy Decision Making

Abel, Elie. *The Missile Crisis.* Philadelphia: Lippincott, 1966.

Allison, Graham T. *Essence of Decision.* Glenview, Ill.: Scott, Foresman, 1971.

Barnet, Richard J. *The Roots of War.** Baltimore: Penguin, 1973.

Betts, Richard K. *Soldiers, Statesmen, and Cold War Crises.* Cambridge, Mass.: Harvard University Press, 1978.

Blight, James, and David A. Welch. *On the Brink.* New York: Hill and Wang, 1989.

Builder, Carl H. *The Masks of War.* Baltimore: Johns Hopkins University Press, 1989.

Caldwell, Dan. *The Dynamics of Domestic Politics and Arms Control.* Columbia: University of South Carolina Press, 1991.

Destler, I. M. *Making Foreign Economic Policy.* Washington, D.C.: Brookings, 1980.

Gelb, Leslie H., and Richard K. Betts. *The Irony of Vietnam.** Washington, D.C.: Brookings, 1979.

George, Alexander L. *Presidential Decisionmaking in Foreign Policy.** Boulder, Colo.: Westview Press, 1980.

Graber, Doris. *Public Opinion, the President, and Foreign Policy.** New York: Holt, Rinehart & Winston, 1968.

Halperin, Morton H. *Bureaucratic Politics and Foreign Policy.** Washington, D.C.: Brookings, 1974.

Head, Richard G., Frisco W. Short, and Robert C. McFarlane. *Crisis Resolution.* Boulder, Colo.: Westview Press, 1978.

Hilsman, Roger. *The Politics of Policy Making in Defense and Foreign Affairs.** New York: Harper & Row, 1971. Reissued. Englewood Cliffs, N.J.: Prentice-Hall, 1987.

Janis, Irving L. *Victims of Groupthink.** 2d ed. Boston: Houghton Mifflin, 1982.

Kennedy, Robert F. *Thirteen Days.** New York: Norton, 1967.

Levering, Ralph B. *The Public and American Foreign Policy, 1918-1978.* New York: Morrow, 1978.

Purvis, Hoyt, and Steven J. Baker, eds. *Legislating Foreign Policy.* Boulder, Colo.: Westview Press, 1984.

Rourke, John T. *Congress and the Presidency in U.S. Foreign Policymaking.* Boulder, Colo.: Westview Press, 1983.

Shoemaker, Christopher C. *The NSC Staff.* Boulder, Colo.: Westview Press, 1991.

Spanier, John, and Eric M. Uslaner. *American Foreign Policy Making and the Democratic Dilemmas.** 5th ed. Pacific Grove, Calif.: Brooks/Cole, 1989.

Spanier, John, and Joseph L. Nogee, eds. *Congress, the Presidency and American Foreign Policy.** Elmsford, N.Y.: Pergamon Press, 1981.

Talbott, Strobe. *The Master of the Game.* New York: Knopf, 1988.

Wittkopf, Eugene R. *Faces of Internationalism.* Durham, N.C.: Duke University Press, 1990.

Perception and Psychology

Blight, James G. *The Shattered Crystal Ball.* Savage, Md.: Rowman & Littlefield, 1990.

De Rivera, Joseph H. *The Psychological Dimension of Foreign Policy.* Columbus, Ohio: Merrill, 1968.

Holsti, Ole R., and James N. Rosenau. *American Leadership in World Affairs.* Boston: Allen & Unwin, 1984.

Jervis, Robert. *Perception and Misperception in International Politics.** Princeton, N.J.: Princeton University Press, 1976.

Jervis, Robert, Richard Ned Lebow, and Janice Gross Stein. *Psychology and Deterrence.* Baltimore: Johns Hopkins University Press, 1985.

Kelman, Herbert C., ed. *International Behavior.* New York: Holt, Rinehart & Winston,

1965.

Klineberg, Otto. *The Human Dimension in International Relations.** New York: Holt, Rinehart & Winston, 1964.

Lebow, Richard Ned. *Between War and Peace.** Baltimore: Johns Hopkins University Press, 1984.

Stoessinger, John G. *Nations in Darkness.** 4th ed. New York: Random House, 1986.

———. *Why Nations Go to War.* 5th ed. New York: St. Martin's Press, 1989.

White, Ralph K. *Nobody Wanted War.** Garden City, N.Y.: Doubleday, 1968.

Deterrence and Arms Control

Allison, Graham T., Albert Carnesale, and Joseph S. Nye, Jr., eds. *Hawks, Doves, and Owls.** New York: Norton, 1985.

Berkowitz, Bruce D. *Calculated Risks.* New York: Simon & Schuster, 1987.

Boffey, Philip J., et al. *Claiming the Heavens.* New York: Times Books, 1988.

Brodie, Bernard. *Strategy in the Missile Age.** Princeton, N.J.: Princeton University Press, 1959.

Bull, Hedley. *The Control of the Arms Race.** 2d ed. New York: Holt, Rinehart & Winston, 1965.

Bundy, McGeorge. *Danger and Survival.* New York: Random House, 1989.

Carnesale, Albert, and Richard N. Haass, eds. *Superpower Arms Control.* Cambridge, Mass.: Ballinger, 1987.

Collins, John M. *American and Soviet Military Trends since the Cuban Missile Crisis.** Washington, D.C.: Georgetown University, Center for Strategic and International Studies, 1978.

Freedman, Lawrence. *The Evolution of Nuclear Strategy.* New York: St. Martin's Press, 1981.

George, Alexander L., et al. *The Limits of Coercive Diplomacy.** Boston: Little, Brown, 1971.

George, Alexander L., and Richard Smoke. *Deterrence in American Foreign Policy.** New York: Columbia University Press, 1974.

George, Alexander L., Philip J. Farley, and Alexander Dallin, eds. *U.S.-Soviet Security Cooperation.* New York: Oxford University Press, 1988.

Glazer, Charles L. *Analyzing Strategic Nuclear Policy.* Princeton, N.J.: Princeton University Press, 1991.

Herken, Gregg. *Counsels of War.* Enlarged ed. New York: Oxford University Press, 1987.

International Institute for Strategic Studies. *The Military Balance.** Published annually.

Jervis, Robert. *The Illogic of American Nuclear Strategy.* Ithaca, N.Y.: Cornell University Press, 1989. Paperback ed. 1985.

———. *The Meaning of the Nuclear Revolution.* Ithaca, N.Y.: Cornell University Press, 1989.

Jervis, Robert, et al. *Psychology and Deterrence.** Baltimore: Johns Hopkins University Press, 1989.

Kahan, Jerome H. *Security in the Nuclear Age.** Washington, D.C.: Brookings, 1975.

Katz, Arthur M. *Life After Nuclear War.** Cambridge, Mass.: Ballinger, 1981.

Krepon, Michael. *Strategic Stalemate.* New York: St. Martin's Press, 1985. Paperback ed. 1986.

Levine, Robert A. *Arms Debate.* Cambridge, Mass.: Harvard University Press, 1963.

Mandelbaum, Michael. *The Nuclear Revolution.* Cambridge, Mass.: Cambridge University Press, 1981.

Martin, Laurence, ed. *Strategic Thought in the Nuclear Age.* Baltimore: Johns Hopkins University Press, 1980.

McNamara, Robert. *Blundering into Disaster.* New York: Pantheon, 1986.

Morgan, Patrick M. *Deterrence.** 2d ed. Beverly Hills, Calif.: Sage Publications, 1983.

Mueller, John E. *Retreat from Doomsday.* New York: Basic Books, 1989.

Nacht, Michael. *The Age of Vulnerability.** Washington, D.C.: Brookings, 1985.

Newhouse, John. *Cold Dawn.* New York: Holt, Rinehart & Winston, 1973.

Office of Technology Assessment. *The Effects of Nuclear War.** Washington, D.C.: Government Printing Office, 1980.

Payne, Keith B. *Nuclear Deterrence in U.S.-Soviet Relations.* Boulder, Colo.: Westview Press, 1982.

———. *Strategic Defense.** Lanham, Md.: University Press of America, 1986.

Quester, George H. *The Future of Nuclear Deterrence.* Lexington, Mass.: Lexington Books, 1986.

Ranger, Robin. *Arms and Politics 1958-1978.* Boulder, Colo.: Westview Press, 1979.

Schell, Jonathan. *The Fate of the Earth.* New York: Knopf, 1982.

Schelling, Thomas C. *Strategy of Conflict.* Cambridge, Mass.: Harvard University Press, 1960.

Schelling, Thomas C., and Morton H. Halperin. *Strategy and Arms Control.** 2d ed. Elmsford, N.Y.: Pergamon-Brassey, 1985.

Scoville, Herbert, Jr. *The MX.* Cambridge, Mass.: M.I.T. Press, 1981.

Smoke, Richard. *National Security and the Nuclear Dilemma.* 2d ed. New York: Random House, 1987.

Talbott, Strobe. *Endgame.** New York: Harper & Row, 1979.

———. *The Master of the Game.* New York: Knopf, 1988.

Tucker, Robert W. *The Nuclear Debate.** New York: Holmes & Meier, 1985.

Wolfe, Thomas W. *The SALT Experience.* Cambridge, Mass.: Ballinger, 1979.

Limited War (Conventional and Revolutionary)

Blaufarb, Douglas S. *The Counterinsurgency Era.* New York: Free Press, 1977.

Blechman, Barry M., and Stephen S. Kaplan. *Force without War.* Washington, D.C.: Brookings, 1978.

Gabriel, Richard A. *Military Incompetence.* New York: Hill and Wang, 1985.

Galula, David. *Counterinsurgency Warfare.* New York: Holt, Rinehart & Winston, 1964.

Greene, T. N., ed. *The Guerrilla—and How to Fight Him.** New York: Holt, Rinehart & Winston, 1962.

Hadley, Arthur. *The Straw Giant.* New York: Random House, 1986.

Kissinger, Henry A. *Nuclear Weapons and Foreign Policy.** New York: Harper & Row, 1957. Abridged ed. New York: Norton, 1969.

Lebow, Richard Ned. *Between Peace and War.* Baltimore: Johns Hopkins University Press, 1981. Paperback ed. 1984.

———. *Nuclear Crisis Management.* Ithaca, N.Y.: Cornell University Press, 1987.

Mao Tse-tung on Guerrilla Warfare. Translated and with an Introduction by Samuel B. Griffith. New York: Holt, Rinehart & Winston, 1961.

Osgood, Robert E. *Limited War.* Chicago: University of Chicago Press, 1957.

———. *Limited War Revisited.* Boulder, Colo.: Westview Press, 1979.

Paret, Peter, and John W. Shy. *Guerrillas in the 1960's.** Rev. ed. New York: Holt, Rinehart & Winston, 1962.

Smoke, Richard. *War: Controlling Escalation.* Cambridge, Mass.: Harvard University Press, 1978.

Snyder, Glenn H., and Paul Diesing. *Conflict among Nations.** Princeton, N.J.: Princeton University Press, 1977.

Spanier, John W. *The Truman-MacArthur Controversy and the Korean War.** Cambridge, Mass.: Harvard University Press, 1959. Rev. paperback ed. New York: Norton, 1965.

Thayer, Charles W. *Guerrilla.** New York: Harper & Row, 1963.

Vietnam War

Berman, Larry. *Planning a Tragedy.** New York: Norton, 1982.

_____. *Lyndon Johnson's War.* New York: Norton, 1989.

Fall, Bernard B. *Viet-Nam Witness, 1953-66.* New York: Holt, Rinehart & Winston, 1966.

Herring, George C. *America's Longest War.** New York: Wiley, 1979. 2d ed. Philadelphia: Temple University Press, 1986.

Hoopes, Townsend. *The Limits of Intervention.** New York: McKay, 1969.

Karnow, Stanley. *Vietnam.* New York: Viking, 1983.

Krepinevich, Andrew F. *The Army and Vietnam.** Baltimore: Johns Hopkins University Press, 1986.

Lewy, Guenter. *America in Vietnam.** New York: Oxford University Press, 1978.

Lomperis, Timothy J. *The War Everyone Lost—And Won.** Baton Rouge: Louisiana State University Press, 1984. Paperback ed. Washington, D.C.: CQ Press, 1987.

Oberdorfer, Don. *Tet.* Garden City, N.Y.: Doubleday, 1971.

Palmer, Bruce, Jr. *The Twenty-Five-Year War.* Paperback ed. New York: Simon & Schuster, 1985.

*The Pentagon Papers.** Chicago: Quadrangle, 1971.

Pike, Douglas. *Viet Cong.** Cambridge, Mass.: M.I.T. Press, 1966.

Rotter, Andrew J. *The Path to Vietnam.* Ithaca, N.Y.: Cornell University Press, 1987.

Sheehan, Neil. *A Bright Shining Light.** New York: Random House, 1988.

Summers, Harry G., Jr. *On Strategy.** New York: Dell, 1984.

Thompson, Sir Robert. *No Exit from Vietnam.* New York: McKay, 1969.

Persian Gulf

Cohen, Roger, and Claudio Gatti. *In the Eye of the Storm.* New York: Farrar, Straus, Giroux, 1991.

Miller, Judith, and Laurie Mylroie. *Saddam Hussein and the Crisis in the Gulf.* New York: Times Books, 1990.

Sciolino, Elaine. *The Outlaw State.* New York: Wiley, 1991.

Woodward, Bob. *The Commanders.* New York: Simon & Schuster, 1991.

Nuclear and Nonnuclear Proliferation

Dunn, Lewis A. *Controlling the Bomb.** New Haven, Conn.: Yale University Press, 1982.

Greenwood, Ted, Harold A. Feiveson, and Theodore B. Taylor. *Nuclear Proliferation.** New York: McGraw-Hill (for the Council on Foreign Relations/1980s Project), 1977.

Lefever, Ernest W. *Nuclear Arms in the Third World.** Washington, D.C.: Brookings, 1979.

Nolan, Janne E. *Trappings of Power.* Washington, D.C.: Brookings, 1991.

Pierre, Andrew J. *The Global Politics of Arms Sales.** Princeton, N.J.: Princeton University Press, 1981.

Spector, Leonard S. *Going Nuclear.* Cambridge, Mass.: Ballinger, 1987.

_____. *The Undeclared Bomb.* Cambridge, Mass.: Ballinger, 1988.

Spector, Leonard S., and Jacqueline R. Smith. *Nuclear Ambitions.* Boulder, Colo.: Westview Press, 1990.

Economics and Trade

Bhagwati, Jagdish N. *Protectionism.* Cambridge, Mass.: M.I.T. Press, 1988.

Blake, David H., and Robert S. Walters. *The Politics of Global Economic Relations.** 4th ed. Englewood Cliffs, N.J.: Prentice-Hall, 1992.

Dertouzos, Michael L., et al. *Made in America.* Cambridge, Mass.: M.I.T. Press, 1989.

Flamm, Kenneth. *Mismanaged Trade.* Washington, D.C.: Brookings, 1990.

Gilpin, Robert. *The Political Economy of International Relations.* Princeton, N.J.: Princeton

University Press, 1987.

Hofheinz, Roy, Jr., and Kent E. Calder. *The East Asia Edge.** New York: Basic Books, 1983.

Kuttner, Robert. *The End of Laissez-Faire.* New York: Knopf, 1991.

Lincoln, Edward J. *Japan's Unequal Trade.* Washington, D.C.: Brookings, 1990.

Phillips, Kevin T. *Staying on Top.* New York: Random House, 1985.

Prestowitz, Clyde V., Jr. *Trading Places.* New York: Basic Books, 1988.

Prestowitz, Clyde V., Ronald A. Morse, and Alan Tonelson. *Powernomics.* Lanham, Md.: Madison Books, 1991.

Spero, Joan E. *The Politics of International Economic Relations.** 4th ed. New York: St. Martin's Press, 1990.

Thurow, Lester. *Head to Head.* New York: Morrow, 1992.

Tolchin, Martin, and Susan Tolchin. *Buying into America.* New York: Times Books, 1988.

United Nations

Bailey, Sidney D. *The United Nations.** New York: Holt, Rinehart & Winston, 1963.

Bloomfield, Lincoln P., et al. *International Military Forces.* Boston: Little, Brown, 1964.

Boyd, Andrew. *United Nations.** Baltimore: Penguin, 1963.

Burns, Arthur Lee, and Nina Heathcote. *Peace-keeping by U.N. Forces.* New York: Holt, Rinehart & Winston, 1963.

Calvocoressi, Peter. *World Order and New States.* New York: Holt, Rinehart & Winston, 1962.

Claude, Inis L., Jr. *The Changing United Nations.** New York: Random House, 1967.

_____. *Swords into Plowshares.* 4th ed. New York: Random House, 1971.

Dallin, Alexander. *The Soviet Union at the United Nations.** New York: Holt, Rinehart & Winston, 1962.

Franck, Thomas M. *Nation against Nation.* New York: Oxford University Press, 1985.

Goodrich, Leland M. *The United Nations in a Changing World.* New York: Columbia University Press, 1976.

Haas, Ernst B. *Why We Still Need the United Nations.* Berkeley: Institute of International Studies, University of California, Berkeley, 1986.

Nye, Joseph S., Jr. *Peace in Parts.* Boston: Little, Brown, 1971. Paperback ed. Lanham, Md.: University Press of America, 1987.

Roberts, Adam, and Benedict Kinsgbury. *United Nations, Divided World.* Oxford, England: Clarendon Press, 1988.

Skjelsbaek, Kjell, and Anthony McDermott. *The Multinational Force in Beirut, 1982-1984.* Gainesville: University Press of Florida, 1991.

Stoessinger, John G. *The United Nations and the Superpowers.** 4th ed. New York: Random House, 1977.

United Nations. *The Blue Helmets,* 2d ed. New York: United Nations Publications, 1991.

International Law

Bozeman, Adda B. *The Future of Law in a Multicultural World.* Princeton, N.J.: Princeton University Press, 1971.

Brierly, James L. *The Law of Nations.* 6th ed. New York: Oxford University Press, 1963.

Corbett, Percy E. *Law and Society in the Relation of States.* New York: Harcourt, 1951.

Deutsch, Karl W., and Stanley Hoffman, eds. *The Relevance of International Law.* Garden City, N.Y.: Doubleday, 1971.

Henkin, Louis. *How Nations Behave.** New York: Holt, Rinehart & Winston, 1968.

Kaplan, Morton A., and Nicholas DeB. Katzenbach. *The Political Foundations of International Law.* New York: Wiley, 1961.

Moynihan, Daniel Patrick. *On the Law of Nations.* Cambridge, Mass.: Harvard University Press, 1990.

International Morality

Butterfield, Herbert. *International Conflict in the Twentieth Century: A Christian View.* New York: Harper & Row, 1960.

Davidson, Donald L. *Nuclear War and the American Churches.* Boulder, Colo.: Westview Press, 1983.

Dougherty, James E. *The Bishops and Nuclear Weapons.* Hamden, Conn.: Archon Books, 1984.

Herz, John H. *Political Realism and Political Idealism.* Chicago: University of Chicago Press, 1951.

Johnson, James Turner. *Just War Tradition and the Restraint of War.* Princeton, N.J.: Princeton University Press, 1981.

Lefever, Ernest W., ed. *Ethics and World Politics.** Baltimore: Johns Hopkins University Press, 1972.

National Conference of Catholic Bishops. *The Challenge of Peace.* Washington, D.C.: United States Catholic Conference, 1983.

Niebuhr, Reinhold. *The Children of Light and the Children of Darkness.* New York: Scribner's, 1944.

————. *The Irony of American History.** New York: Scribner's, 1952.

————. *Moral Man and Immoral Society.** New York: Scribner's, 1952.

Nye, Joseph S., Jr. *Nuclear Ethics.* New York: Free Press, 1986.

Thompson, Kenneth W. *Political Realism and the Crisis of World Politics.* Princeton, N.J.: Princeton University Press, 1960.

Wolfers, Arnold, and Laurence W. Martin, eds. *The Anglo-American Tradition in Foreign Affairs.* Northford, Conn.: Elliot's Books, 1956.

Functionalism and Community Building

Deutsch, Karl, et al. *Political Community and the North Atlantic Area.* Princeton, N.J.: Princeton University Press, 1957.

Etzioni, Amitai. *Political Unification.** New York: Holt, Rinehart & Winston, 1965.

Haas, Ernst B. *The Uniting of Europe.* Rev. ed. Stanford, Calif.: Stanford University Press, 1968.

Kerr, Anthony J. *The Common Market and How It Works.* Oxford, England: Pergamon Press, 1983.

Lindberg, Leon N., and Stuart A. Scheingold. *Europe's Would-Be Polity.** Englewood Cliffs, N.J.: Prentice-Hall, 1970.

Shragia, Alberta B., ed. *Euro-Politics.* Washington, D.C.: Brookings, 1990.

Transnationalism, World Order, and Socioeconomic Issues

Barnet, Richard J., and Ronald E. Müller. *Global Reach.** New York: Simon & Schuster, 1975.

Bergsten, C. Fred, Thomas Holst, and Theodore H. Moran. *American Multinationals and American Interests.** Washington, D.C.: Brookings, 1978.

Brown, Lester R. *In the Human Interest.** New York: Norton, 1974.

————. *State of the World 1988.* New York: Norton, 1988.

————. *World without Borders.** New York: Vintage, 1973.

Brown, Seyom. *New Forces, Old Forces, and the Future of World Politics.* Glenview, Ill.: Scott, Foresman, 1988.

Gilpin, Robert. *U.S. Power and the Multinational Corporation.* New York: Basic Books, 1975.

Hanson, Eric. *The Catholic Church in World Politics.* Princeton, N.J.: Princeton University Press, 1987.

————. *The Catholic Church.* Princeton, N.J.: Princeton University Press, 1990.

Hopkins, Raymond F., Robert L. Paarlberg, and Mitchel B. Wallerstein. *Food in the Global Arena.* New York: Holt, Rinehart & Winston, 1982.

Johansen, Robert. *The National Interest and the Human Interest.** Princeton, N.J.: Princeton University Press, 1980.

Keohane, Robert O. *After Hegemony.* Princeton, N.J.: Princeton University Press, 1984.

Keohane, Robert O., and Joseph S. Nye, Jr. *Power and Interdependence.** 2d ed. Glenview, Ill.: Scott, Foresman, 1989.

_____, eds. *Transnational Relations and World Politics.* Cambridge, Mass.: Harvard University Press, 1972.

Kim, Samuel S. *The Quest for a Just World Order.* Boulder, Colo.: Westview Press, 1983.

Kindleberger, Charles P., ed. *The International Corporation.* Cambridge, Mass.: M.I.T. Press, 1970.

Laqueur, Walter. *Terrorism.* Boston: Little, Brown, 1977.

Maghoori, Ray, and Bennett Ramberg, eds. *Globalism vs. Realism.** Boulder, Colo.: Westview Press, 1982.

Mansbach, Richard W., Yale H. Ferguson, and Donald E. Lampert. *The Web of World Politics.** Englewood Cliffs, N.J.: Prentice-Hall, 1976.

Mendlovitz, Saul H., ed. *On the Creation of a Just World Order.* New York: Free Press, 1975. Paperback ed. 1977.

Miller, Lynn H. *Global Order.* Boulder, Colo.: Westview Press, 1985.

Pirages, Dennis. *Global Ecopolitics.** North Scituate, Mass.: Duxbury, 1978.

_____. *Global Technopolitics.** Pacific Grove, Calif.: Brooks/Cole, 1989.

Reich, Robert. *The Work of Nations.* New York: Knopf, 1991.

Rosecrance, Richard. *The Rise of the Trading State.* New York: Basic Books, 1986.

Said, Abdul, and Lutz R. Simons, eds. *The New Sovereigns.** Englewood Cliffs, N.J.: Prentice-Hall, 1975.

Scott, Andrew M. *The Dynamics of Interdependence.* Chapel Hill: University of North Carolina Press, 1982.

Sorous, Marvin S. *Beyond Sovereignty.* Columbia: University of South Carolina Press, 1986.

Sterling, Claire. *The Terror Network.* New York: Holt, Rinehart & Winston, 1981. Paperback ed. New York: Berkley Publishing, 1984.

Taylor, Philip. *Nonstate Actors in International Politics.* Boulder, Colo.: Westview Press, 1982.

Vernon, Raymond. *Sovereignty at Bay.* New York: Basic Books, 1971.

_____, ed. *The Oil Crisis.** New York: Norton, 1976.

Willetts, Peter, ed. *Pressure Groups in the Global System.* New York: St. Martin's Press, 1982.

World Commission on Environment and Development. *Our Common Future.* New York: Oxford University Press, 1987.

Index